Strategic
Management

3rd edition

Strategic

Management

An **Analytical** Introduction

George **Luffman**
*University of Bradford
Management Centre*

Edward **Lea**
University of Huddersfield

Stuart **Sanderson**
*University of Bradford
Management Centre*

and Brian **Kenny**
University of Huddersfield

B BLACKWELL
Business

This edition published 1996
Reprinted 1996, 1997

Blackwell Publishers Ltd
108 Cowley Road
Oxford OX4 1JF, UK

Blackwell Publishers Inc
350 Main Street
Malden, Massachusetts 02148, USA

British Library Cataloguing in Publication Data
A CIP catalogue record for this book is available from the British Library

Library of Congress Cataloging in Publication Data
A CIP catalogue record for this book is available from the Library of Congress

ISBN: 0–631–20103–3 (Hbk) — ISBN: 0–631–20104–1 (Pbk)

Typeset in 10 on 12pt Palatino
by Photoprint, Torquay, Devon
Printed and bound in Great Britain by Hartnolls Ltd, Bodmin, Cornwall

This book is printed on acid-free paper

Contents

Preface

This book is a thoroughly updated version of the authors' previous books; *Business Policy: An Analytical Introduction* and *Cases in Business Policy*. The textbook and casebook have now been combined to facilitate use by the student and to reduce the overall cost. The text has been revised where necessary and six new chapters have been included. The new chapters expand on issues covered briefly in the previous books but which now merit greater coverage. The cases are all new and all finish in the 1990s which will help to increase the commitment of students. The book is the result of over 20 years' experience of each of the authors in teaching, research and consulting in strategic management.

Traditionally, business policy teaching has focused on the needs of the post-graduate student, where maturity, previous academic achievement and often previous work experience have provided a sound basis for the assimilation of advanced, participative learning techniques such as those provided by the business-case method. Whatever the nature of the business problems presented, such students are often able to draw upon some particular aspects of their background in relating to the task of problem analysis, strategic evaluation and determination of corrective courses of action. However, in recent years the subject has been included on many undergraduate courses, and the business community has become more concerned to understand the changing environment within which it operates.

The large increases in the number of undergraduates, especially in the last few years, and the increase in the staff student ratio have made it more difficult for lecturers to update courses continually to the extent that they would wish. In that respect this combined text and cases book is now accompanied by a student *Workbook* which provides exercises for completion by the students. This facilitates an understanding of models and techniques which are fundamental to policy analysis so that when cases are studied student time is not spent on explanation of techniques.

Business policy education relies heavily on the integrative approach which requires an application of interdisciplinary business skills and, ideally, should be introduced in the final stages of the study programme. However, it is often the case that the advanced specialist disciplines must, by practical necessity, be taught concurrently, and in spite of attempts to schedule case studies in a progressive manner, there will invariably be instances in the preliminary stages where the students' lack of appropriate conceptual knowledge and analytical techniques may seriously inhibit, if not totally nullify, the learning process. In this respect, we have selected and structured the contents with a view to alleviating this often inherent drawback and, thus, the text should be considered as an introduction to business policy. It does not itemize all appropriate research as this may tend to confuse the student who is new to the subject.

Finally, we would point out that there is no substitute for a wider reading incorporating the many excellent books and articles on business policy and corporate strategy to which we make reference from time to time in the text. We are also aware of the dangers of attempting to place case analysis into a rigid conceptual framework. The student is advised to treat on its merits each case with which he or she is confronted, and to regard the specific situational analysis as the key determinant.

In summary, therefore, we believe that this text will prove of value to students of business policy and/or corporate strategy on both postgraduate and undergraduate courses in the business studies area in general. In addition, it can prove a useful introduction to the subject for diploma students in management or in the many accounting and other professional courses in which there is a growing requirement for students to acquire a much broader appreciation of business practice. The book will also be of practical value to businessmen and women who are looking for a more systematic approach to their strategic decision-making process.

We would like to thank our colleagues Bryan Lowes, Peter Buckley and Chris Pass for their contributions to chapters 9, 13, and 17 respectively. Thanks are also due to Tim Goodfellow and his colleagues for their contribution to the final text. Finally, we would like to acknowledge those companies, students and researchers who have provided the inputs which have made this book possible.

An Introduction to Corporate Strategy

CONTENTS

PART 1

The Corporate Strategy Framework

1 Introduction to Strategy

1.1 INTRODUCTION

It is difficult to believe that some of the big successful companies of today are not going to be around in 20 or 30 years' time. However, a brief review of the past few decades is clear evidence that current success is no 'predictor' of future success. Household names and blue-chip companies over the past 20 or 30 years have disappeared completely or been subsumed by other companies. Coloroll, Horizon, Rover, Thomas Tilling, Imperial Tobacco and Polly Peck were once leading companies, now fallen altogether or much reduced in status. Dunlop and BTR provide a fascinating contrast. In the mid-1960s both were in the tyre business, with Dunlop being a large and successful company, and BTR small and relatively unprofitable. Dunlop continued in the tyre business and, after years of low profitability, was taken over by BTR who stopped tyre manufacturing, diversified and became one of the largest and most successful UK companies.

The problems facing companies are mainly the result of the increase in the rate of change in the environment in which they operate and a failure to adapt to such changes. Even for banks and building societies, where change has taken place slowly, changes over the past few years have been of such significance that a wholly different approach to the management of the businesses is required.

A further problem, which is compounded by the rate of change, is the size and cost of investment required in some businesses, for instance chemicals. As plant size, and consequently cost, increases, the length of time over which the company can expect returns may also increase. However, changes in fashion, technology or other aspects of the business may result in the plant becoming redundant earlier than expected. This increases the risk involved in investing in new plant. Also, the number of products and range of markets now covered by large multinational firms increases the complexity of forecasting future trends.

The rate of change, the size of investment and the extension of product market scope are mainly responsible for creating a relatively new problem in the business environment, namely: are existing products sold to our existing customers going to be sufficient to enable us to continue in business? In the period up to the Second

World War, change took place more slowly and business was on a much smaller scale, so that while there were business failures, the future was more easily identifiable.

1.2   THE STRATEGY CONCEPT

In order to explore the problems which result in success or failure for a company, it is necessary to begin by defining some terms. To students of business policy the wealth of terms used in texts on general management theory may, at first sight, seem confusing. 'Business policy', 'corporate strategy', 'corporate planning' and 'strategic management' seem to be used interchangeably, while the various component terms relating to strategy formulation are not always clearly defined.

Although the term 'business policy' remains in popular usage in academic circles, this title by definition fails to indicate the scope and level of activity covered by the subject area. A definition which takes in the full scope of management tasks at both corporate and functional levels is that of the 'strategy concept'. This has been defined as 'the pattern of objectives, purposes or goals and major policies and plans for achieving these goals, stated in such a way as to define what business the company is in or is to be in and the kind of company it is or is to be'.[1] The more recent term 'strategic management' has been defined as 'that set of decisions and actions which lead to the development of an effective strategy or strategies to help achieve corporate objectives'.[2]

Strategic decisions are thus those decisions that are concerned with the entire environment in which the firm operates, the whole of the resources and people who constitute the company and the interface between the two. Failure to match appropriately the firm's output to the environment can have devastating consequences.

In order to understand this relationship more clearly, a descriptive model of the firm is outlined in figure 1.1. As can be seen, the environment of the firm, although seemingly complex, particularly if a dynamic view is taken, can be broken down into a number of sub-environments. A possible danger is to treat each in isolation, as environmental change is often a complex of several sub-environments interacting with each other. However, for the the sake of analysis, they may be viewed separately. As will be stressed later, a firm rarely has the resources to scan and understand the total environment; rather, the firm has to decide on a hierarchy of what affects it most to what affects it least. This view will change over time, but the essence of strategic planning is to anticipate change, although any firm may not know the full extent of that change. For example, many oil companies may have known that the price of oil would eventually rise, but the problem was that none of them knew when or by exactly how much. This had led some critics to say that, as the environment is complex and the rate of change increasing, it is better to react than attempt to forecast and anticipate. While this option may be open for some companies, the problem is that any reaction may well mean that the company is too late and the strategic opportunity has gone.

In the centre of figure 1.1, within the firm, the chief executive and senior managers determine the management style and culture within which strategic decisions will be made. They are also responsible for determining corporate objectives and strategies appropriate to the resources and skills of the company in relation to the current and, more significantly, the expected future environment in which they will be operating.

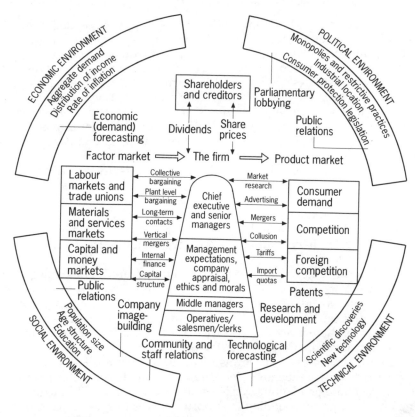

FIGURE 1.1   The firm: a descriptive model
Source: B. Lowes and J. R. Sparkes *Modern Managerial Economics* (Heinemann, London 1974). Reprinted with permission.

The model as shown has one significant deficiency: it does not encompass the dimension of time. Time and timing are critical issues in business policy analysis. Failure to identify the rate of change of key environmental variables can have a significant impact on the performance of a company. Likewise, the introduction of a new product 'too early' or 'too late' can have a similarly damaging impact.

1.3   FEATURES OF STRATEGIC DECISIONS

Strategic decisions are concerned with the whole business, not with a division of the business or one of the functional areas. However, many of the approaches and analytical tools outlined in this book are appropriate for use by divisions of companies when seeking to determine their long-term future within the context of the company in which they operate.

Much of the time of operating managers is concerned with activities in the short or medium term, whereas corporate decisions are concerned with the long term. It is important, therefore, in a large, multidivisional business to ensure that for some of their time these managers are required to review the long-term prospects of their businesses so that major opportunities and threats are identified at an early stage.

It follows from the long-term and holistic nature of strategic decisions that they are almost always unique. That is, given that the environment changes and that the firm changes, the particular circumstances which surround a specific company at a point in time are different from those it faced five years ago or even last year, and because no two companies are identical in terms of management style, products, markets and resources, it is unlikely that experience from other companies will be of direct benefit. There are often similarities over time and between companies which provide the basis for analysis and comparison, but the differences are such and the regularity of strategic decisions so spread that, in comparison with other decisions, much greater uncertainty surrounds the outcome.

Strategic decisions are the point from which all other decisions and activities in the company emanate. They therefore provide direction and thus motivation: most people prefer to know the purpose and objectives of organizations to which they belong. It should be noted that 'to do nothing' is a strategic decision. To ignore information from the environment which might afford significant opportunities or threats is a decision 'to do nothing', even though the matter may not have been discussed at a board meeting or by senior managers.

It is the key role of strategic decision-making in the organization to integrate various activities within the company and to allocate resources. As part of the reason for a given set of resources and activities being combined to create a company is to gain maximum benefit from their interaction, it is important that all parts are working to the same ends, that there is no unnecessary conflict. Thus, integration and allocation become key outcomes of strategic decisions.

A final controversy remains in terms of decision-making. Is the actual strategy pursued by a company deliberate? Does the company do what it set out to do as a result of careful strategic planning, or is some part of the actual outcome the result of leaning on the way, or responding to opportunities as they arise? There is no doubt that companies grasp opportunities as they arise. They do so within a set of strategic parameters which are already decided such as the technology they possess, the manufacturing system employed and whole sets of managerial skills. The concept of learning is an important aspect of strategic management and will be returned to throughout subsequent chapters but it is via on-the-job, less formalized learning and the consequent emergent strategies that companies improve performance and enter

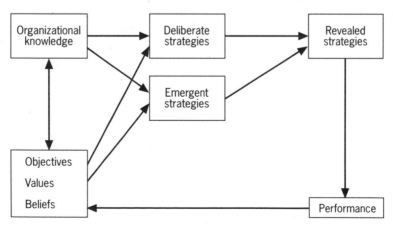

FIGURE 1.2   Strategic Decision Making Process

into new ventures in addition to the more formal stategic planning processes. As Mintzberg puts it 'strategies can form as well as be formulated'[3]. The relationship between the various aspects of strategic decision making are shown in figure 1.2.

1.4 STRATEGY AND COMPETENCE

It is perhaps a commonplace to say that that organizations should do those strategic things at which they are good. There is no doubt that superior performance is rooted in higher levels of competence. The task of senior management is to develop those appropriate competences and skills which are needed for longterm survival in the industry. Often the appropriate skills are defined by the nature and dynamic of the marketplace but occasionally some competitors rewrite the competency map leaving others stranded. An example would be British Airways and their customer relations programme. Hamel and Prahalad[4] would contend that it is the recognition and subsequent leverage and stretching of resources and competencies which lie at the heart of strategy. The ability of Marks and Spencer to lever their buying power and expertise gives them a significant strategic advantage. Similarly, their ability to stretch their competence in database management into financial services allowed them to enter the apparently unrelated business of personal financial services. This concept is more fully developed in chapter 11.

Hamel and Prahalad would futher contend that the most successful companies are those who can not only articulate the future but know how to get there. This implies a total future orientation on the part of senior management. They argue that the past, in an age of increasing discontinuity, may not be a guide to the future; hence the notion of strategy as forgetting. Similarly those companies that put more emphasis on re-invention rather than re-engineering will be more successful. Size may be no guarantee of future success, rather it will be those organizations who can develop new ways of satisfying new customers, and thus outcompeting rivals, who will succeed. Many Japanese car manufacturers were significantly smaller than American or European competitors when they entered the market but have subsequently outgrown them. The computer industry has witnessed spectacular growth through small new entrants whose strategy was based upon new competences developed for a new generation of users.

All of this requires a willingness to change. Many organizations are unwilling to accept the perceived risk of change while currently successful. Perhaps the first task of senior management is to configure the organization such that innovation and change are the norm.

1.5 THE TASK OF STRATEGIC ANALYSIS

It should be emphasized that a highly formalized system of planning is no guarantee of success but, equally, leaving things to chance constitutes the best possible guarantee of failure. The key to success is not so much in the adoption of a formal approach to strategy formulation per se, but rather in the quality and consistency of the implementation and in the organization's ability to adapt to an ever-changing business environment.

When students first begin a course in business policy they frequently express the view that they are not sure what it is they are supposed to do. Previously, their courses have been those of an information-giving nature, and it was understood that they should remember as much as they could and in addition 'read around' the subject to expand their understanding. Strategic management as a course does not respond to this treatment. There is little to remember but much to apply. The student is required to adapt the normal learning patterns to the educational purpose of a business policy course. Generally, strategic management is the educational course using material which business firms would title corporate strategy, but which in its educational setting aims to integrate features of the overall educational programme such as finance, marketing and organization behaviour. Understanding the inter-relationships between such activities enables the student to consider the corporate strategy of a business organization.

Therefore, the task of the student is to:

1   Understand the position of the company with respect to its internal strenghs and weaknesses, and the opportunities and threats which emerge from an analysis of its external environment.
2   Bring to bear other knowledge (such as that gained from economics or finance) relevant to the strategic steps the company could take.
3   Evaluate the feasibility of strategic options.
4   Select from among the options and persuasively argue why the company should follow the selected path.

It is necessary to point out here that the role of the student is not to remember and learn facts about the firm, but to understand the current position of the company and the strategic moves available to such firms in such situations and then to be able to evaluate those moves.

Educationally, the purpose is a thorough understanding of strategy and its implications, for example, setting objectives, formulating strategy, implementing strategy and considering the feasibility of such steps and the level of risks associated with them. This is done in such a way that at the end the student can understand the process of strategic thinking in a company, the constraints upon that process (for instance, the environment and the company itself) and the problems of implementation and achievement.

It is also important to add that the text is not about how to undertake 'corporate planning', which is a management process involving much greater application of techniques. Argenti, Jones and others provide adequate coverage of this topic.[5]

NOTES

1   Edmund P. Learned, C. Roland Christensen, Kenneth Andrews and William D. Guth, *Business Policy: Text and Cases* (Richard D. Irwin Inc., Homewood, III., 1965).
2   W. F. Glueck, *Business Policy and Strategic Management* (McGrawHill, New York, 1980).
3   *Henry Mintzberg, Mintzberg on Management – Inside our Strange World of Organizations* (Free Press, New York, 1989).
4   Gary Hamel and O. K. Prahalad, *Competing for the Future* (Harvard Business School Press, 1994).
5   See John Argenti, *Systematic Corporate Planning* (Wiley, New York, 1974); Harry Jones, *Preparing Company Plans: a Workbook for Effective Corporate Planning* (2nd edn, Gower, Aldershot, 1983).

Strategic Managers – The Strategic Planning Model –
Corporate Planning

2.1 STRATEGIC MANAGERS

In chapter 1 the nature and extent of strategic decisions were examined. It is now
appropriate to consider who has the responsibility for making these decisions and
how that responsibility is discharged in practice. As strategic decisions are concerned with the direction of the whole of the company in the long term, they are
clearly the responsibility of the chief executive and the board of directors.

Functions of the Board

The board of directors is appointed or elected by the shareholders to manage the
assets in the interests of the shareholders by:

- ensuring the long-term success of the company through attention to its mission,
  objectives, strategies and policies;
- disseminating information to appropriate stakeholders;
- reviewing and publishing at regular intervals the financial performance of the
  company;
- employing appropriate senior personnel to achieve these tasks;
- reviewing periodically the structure of the organization to ensure implementation of the plan.

A key question is to what extent a board of directors actually has any power? It
has been suggested that boards are best described as decision-taking, rather than
decision-making, institutions. In many cases there is no doubt that senior management engage in manipulative strategies with the aim of getting proposals through
the board by giving only generalized estimates of costs involved and minimum
expectations of outcomes. The key resides in the power of the senior management
to control information. Provided no contrary information is placed before the board,
it is often difficult to object to proposals. These tactics require effort at pre-board
meetings to prepare the cases and often summaries of board papers so that the
board can digest them at one sitting.

Membership of the Board

First of all there is the chairman. It appears that the chairman may be an executive
or non-executive chairman. In the latter case the chairman would only be employed

part time in the company and there would also be a chief executive officer (CEO) whose title may be CEO or managing director. Thomas Risk (chairman of the Royal Bank of Scotland), when it was proposed that he be non-executive chairman of the newly formed Guinness after the takeover of Distillers, said 'in company law there is only a chairman'. That is, executive and non-executive have nothing to do with it. So, is the non-executive chairman merely a figurehead who only presides at meetings or someone who does not assume direct responsibility for managing any specific part of the company but who nevertheless retains overall responsibility for the results?

In the industrialized West there are basically three types of board:

1   In Britain there is a unitary (or single) board which is mostly comprised of executive directors.
2   In the USA the board is unitary but mostly non-executive.
3   West Germany has a two-tier board system in which there is a wholly non-executive supervisory board and a wholly executive management board with no members in common.

There are a number of objections which can be made about the British system where executive directors:

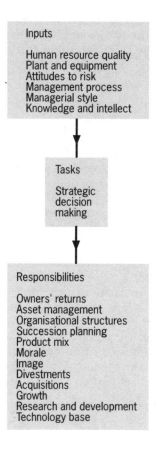

FIGURE 2.1   Functions of a Director

- may be excessively preoccupied with their own day-to-day problems and may give priority to their own responsibilities;
- may spend an inordinate time using the board to negotiate resources for their own area of responsibility;
- cannot be expected to make judgements on their own performance;
- are not likely to sack themselves should the need arise.

In this sense a fully executive board is constitutionally incapable of performing many of the tasks it is responsible for and is probably no more than a management committee.

There are arguments against the two-tier system. A letter to *The Financial Times* on 17 April 1989 from Mr Ralph Instone read as follows:

> Sir, If we are to have two-tier boards, as proposed by Mr Edgar Palamountain (letters, April 22), it will be necessary to define the matters on which the non-executive directors must pronounce.
>
> Is their opinion to be required only in the case of resisted bids, management buy outs, and other changes where a conflict of interest may arise? If so, it would be far simpler for the City Panel to require the circulation of a reasoned opinion from non-executive directors in all such operations above a certain size. But consistency would require a similar opinion in the case of all acquisitions and other transactions needing share-holders' approval.
>
> The trouble with this approach is that non-executive directors can only second guess the views of management and its advisers, presumably on the basis of the same evidence which had already satisfied the management. Does anyone suppose that a non-executive committee of the Blue Arrow board, for example, would have pronounced against the acquisition of Manpower?
>
> The improvement of managerial judgement and performance will not be secured by a division of functions between executive and non-executive directors; still less by changes in the law.

Non-executive Directors

1   What is their role?

- They should bring independence and objectivity to the board. Subordinate managers will always find it difficult to speak openly in front of their immediate superiors.
- They can provide specialist advice or skills, for example a knowledge of government procurement.
- They can form special committees, for example a compensation committee.

2   What proportion should be non-executive?

- More than is currently the case at the present time; for example William Morrison (0) and M&S (4)

3   What qualities and qualifications should they have?

- Credibility is important and so is the time to commit themselves to the company, for example two days per month at least.

4   How are they appointed?   It has usually been the case that they are appointed by the chairman and ratified at the annual general meeting (AGM). Increasingly, boards are setting up nomination committees made up of non-executive directors to give advice to the chairman. This prevents the constant appointment of friends. However, it does not help the situation where there are no non-executive directors in the first place.

Sir Owen Green, chairman of BTR, has said that non-executive directors with no particular experience of a company do not have enough information to make a real contribution. According to Allen Shephard, chairman of Grand Metropolitan, non-executive directors do not need a detailed knowledge of the business. Their role is to ask the right questions rather than to know all the answers. Their most valuable contribution has to do with strategy: does what the executives say about the future sound belivable? For Ian McLaurin, chairman of Tesco, an important role for the non-executive is in telling the chief executive when it is time to step down.

Separation of Powers

There is a great deal of debate surrounding the abuse of power by self-governing institutions, such as private limited companies. The effects of corporate decision-making in terms of the wider public interest and the subsequent failure of either the market or regulations to curb excesses has led to pressures to widen the scope of company law. Part of this general movement to regulate the governance of companies was the 1992 Cadbury Report, which dealt with financial aspects of the boards, and recommended that the roles of chairman and chief executive should be split and that there should be a significant group of 'outsiders' on boards of directors. The Cadbury Report resulted in a code of practice which was designed to allow companies to set up systems and add structures to ensure compliance with their own rules and procedures.

Extracts from Code of Best Practice
1   Board of directors
    - meet regularly
    - clear division of responsibilities
    - should include non-executive directors
    - agreed procedures
2   Non-executive directors
    - bring independent judgement to board
    - should be independent of company's business
    - fixed term
    - formal process of selection
3   Executive directors
    - contracts less than three years
    - full disclosure of pay
    - pay subject to a remuneration committee
4   Reporting and controls
    - board's assessment to be fair and balanced
    - relationship with auditors
    - audit committee including three non-executives
    - director's responsibilities to be explained

The code came into effect on 1 July 1993, and latest surveys into compliance to the code show that larger companies have moved towards the code more quickly than smaller ones by splitting the role of the chairman and chief executive officer and by having more independents on the board.

The Cadbury Report and other such initiatives in the USA are evidence of an ongoing debate surrounding the regulation of companies. Executive pay has become a fiercely debated topic, particularly the arguments surrounding the linking of pay with corporate performance.

What this means in terms of strategic decision-making is that companies have to have strong regard to their policies and procedures for corporate governance. Thus many of the processes for strategy creation will have to become more transparent in terms of adherence to agreed rules and protocols.

Responsibility and Accountability

Under UK law a director of a company is both individually and jointly with the other directors accountable for the company's viability and success, that is for its satisfactory performance. Whereas a manager shares responsibility, each director's responsibility is for the whole company. So the director is accountable to the company (which is a legal body), and the directors also have a fiduciary responsibility to the shareholders of the company, that is acting on their behalf.

Strictly speaking, the shareholders of a company own neither the company nor its assets; they own shares and these convey certain rights upon them. Similarly, directors are not servants of the shareholders. Their responsibility is to the company. Nevertheless, the authority of the board stems from the powers entrusted to it by the shareholders, in return for which the board undertakes to protect the interests of the shareholders.

If shareholders disagree with the decision of the board they cannot change the decision. They can, however, remove the directors at the next AGM. For example, if the directors propose a certain dividend payment the shareholders cannot increase it.

Company law has prescribed the extent to which a director is accountable for his actions. In 1986, the Insolvency Act extended these responsibilities by making a director liable for a 'wrongful act' which is a stage further than a fraudulent act and which can lead to claims against a director. This has led to directors seeking a legal indemnity clause in their contracts when they resign and to directors taking out insurance policies against any damages awarded.

Where a board makes a decision with which a director disagrees (especially if it involves an illegal act), then the director cannot escape responsibility by voting against the proposal or by having his or her opposition noted in the minutes. If he or she cannot prevent the decision and does not agree with it, then the only recourse is to resign.

Companies legislation says that it is unlawful for a company to make any payment to a director by way of compensation for loss of office, or as a consideration for his or her retirement, without particulars of the proposed payment, including the amount, being disclosed to and approved by the shareholders. However, this does not apply to any bona fide payment by way of damages for breach of contract or by way of pension in respect of past services.

A board of directors has statutory requirements with respect to a wide variety of issues such as financial management and reporting, health and safety, product quality and reliability, pollution emission levels and so on. The extent of liability is constantly being tested in the courts and is consequently changing regularly.

The directors' discharge of both their statutory obligations and their management of shareholders' funds has been the subject of much research. In one survey of executives it was found that in only 25 per cent of businesses did the board have any significant impact on the strategic success of their organizations. Nethertheless, by whoever or however the strategy is formulated, if the result is poor the board of directors will be held responsible.

2.2   THE STRATEGIC PLANNING MODEL

We saw in chapter 1 that few organizations operate in circumstances where the rate of change is so slow that there is no need to consider the future on the basis that what is currently being produced and sold is likely to provide a formula for success in the long term. It follows, therefore, that some evaluation process is necessary. Thus, whatever the size of the company, it needs to develop a strategic perspective. This might be achieved through a formal planning system, especially if the company is large with many markets and products to evaluate and/or where the rate of change is rapid. A strategic perspective could be achieved through the skill and experience of one person, although the evidence of the success of this mode of decision-making over the long term is not good. Indeed, the major factor evident in corporate collapse is 'the one man band' (see chapter 15).

In the short term, results based on the intuition and knowledge of one person can often be spectacular (for example, George Davies and Next), but it is often difficult to sustain such success over the long term and, whether or not it is successful, the resignation, retirement or death of these individuals often leaves a large vacuum as there has rarely been any attention focused on management development and succession.

The model outlined in this book has been described as the rational analytical model and is that most widely taught in business schools and used by departments charged with the responsibility for developing a strategic perspective often labelled strategic or corporate planning. Most practitioners have their own modifications but few vary from the basic model which follows any problem-solving situation:

- awareness of the problem;
- exploration of the problem;
- deciding what to do;
- taking action to implement the decision;
- examination and feedback of results.

A comprehensive picture of the process as it applies to strategic decisions is outlined in figure 2.2.

The simplified model contains the major features of the process and represents the structure of this book. Each chapter in parts 2–6 is preceded by this diagram with an indicator identifying the section of the model to which the chapter refers. It is hoped that this will enable readers to understand the comprehensive nature of the process. Thus, part 2, 'External Analysis', is concerned with providing models to help in analysing the environment in which the firm is operating. This provides the opportunities (O) and threats (T) facing the company. Part 3 provides a framework for an appraisal of the company's resources and capabilities, its strengths (S) and weaknesses (W). The combination of internal and external analysis is often termed SWOT analysis, following the initials outlined above.

The next action in the strategic process is to identify strategic alternatives, the focus of part 4. Once the alternative futures had been identified, the next step is to choose between these alternatives – Part 5 is 'Strategic Choice' Part 6, 'Implementing Strategies', is concerned with the job of implementing the chosen strategy.

Whether the strategic thinking is done on the back of an envelope by one person, or through a formal planning process, these are the necessary steps in the thought process.

2.3 CORPORATE PLANNING

The means by which the strategic decision-making process is pursued is outlined in the subsequent chapters of the book but some preliminary comments are appropriate with respect to two matters: the inter-relationship of planning at different levels of the business, and the planning cycle and organization.

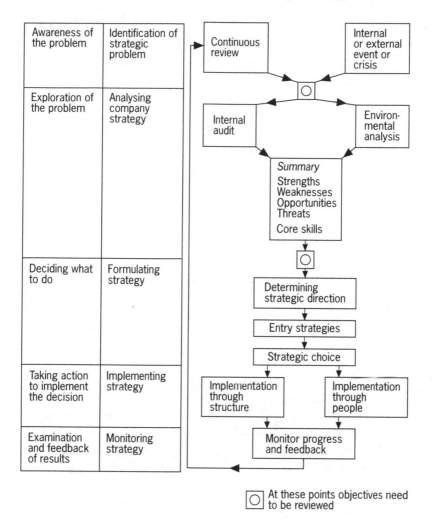

FIGURE 2.2 The strategic decision-making process

Hofer and Schendel have differentiated between three major levels of organizational strategy.[1] These are at the corporate, business and functional levels respectively (see figure 2.3). The category of 'corporate strategy' occupies the highest level of strategic decision-making and, in comparative terms, would relate to the multidivisional organization or the firm with a wide range of business interests. Such decisions might include high-level financial policy, acquisition and divestment, diversification and organizational structure.

At the 'business' level the respective decision-makers are more concerned with the immediate industry/product-market issues and the harnessing together of the individual functional units in the most efficient manner. New product development and market segmentation will play a primary role in decision-making, along with the major policy areas across the spectrum of production, R&D, personnel and finance.

Functional strategy, as is suggested by its title, relates to a single functional operation and the activities involved therein. Decisions at this level within the organization are often described as 'tactical', but it should be noted that such decisions ought always to be guided and constrained by some overall strategic consideration. For example,

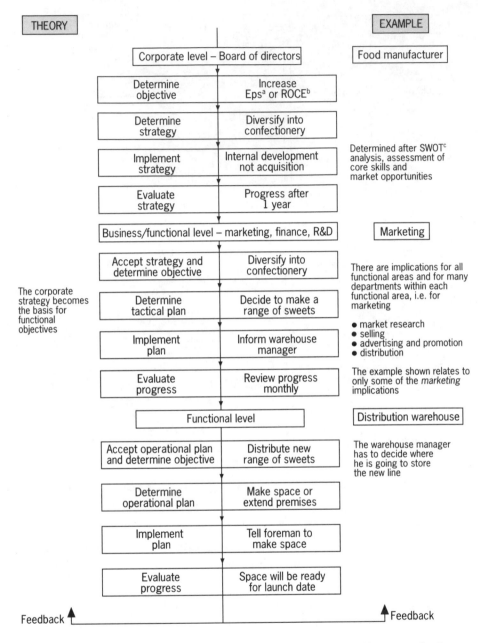

FIGURE 2.3 Strategic implications at different levels

product diversification decisions will need to be considered within the overall framework of business strategy, although what products are actually decided upon will be at the discretion of the marketing specialist, given that the investment is approved (finance) and that the appropriate production facilities (manufacturing) and manpower (personnel) are or will be available.

It is important that the implications of strategic decisions made by the board of directors are identified and implemented at all levels in the firm. At the operational level, there are actions which need to be taken if the objective from which the policy stems is to be realized. Even at this level, failure to have a fully integrated plan could have serious consequences.

Accepting this hierarchical nature of strategy, it will be appreciated that objectives and policies can be established for the three tiers of managerial responsibility discussed. Formal goals and objectives provide the means by which the organization's performance can be evaluated and, if necessary, adjusted in the face of environmental change. Similarly, the process allows for the allocation of resources in a more formalized manner and in keeping with planning effectiveness, monitoring and control.

Although this book is not focused on the nuts and bolts of the corporate planning process in businesses, an outline of a few of the issues is considered relevant. A significant issue is the determination of the planning cycle. That is, the process and times by which information will be available, so that decisions have been made before the start of the planning period. Organization for planning is also important: who should be involved, to what degree and how will the various actions of the different participants in the process be coordinated? How much information is needed and who is going to produce it are other key issues, as is the regularity with which the strategic plan should be updated.

Perhaps the most important point to emphasize is that *planning must be a dialogue* between directors and subordinates or head office and divisions. Too much 'top-down' or 'bottom-up' planning is liable to render the process ineffective. *Meaningful dialogue with realistic, not over-optimistic or over-pessimistic, plans is the only recipe for successful planning.*

NOTES

1   Charles W. Hofer and Dan Schendel, *Strategy Formulation: Analytical Concepts* (West Publishing Co. St Paul, Minnesota, 1978).

3 Values, Culture and Power

3.1 INTRODUCTION

An understandable misperception of many people approaching strategic management for the first time is that a strategic planning system is in itself sufficient to ensure that the right questions are posed, a correct analysis is performed and suitable strategies are developed. In reality, such a view ignores the basic fact that the systems themselves do none of these tasks – they are performed by people. Thus, realistically, organizations make strategic responses to a changing environment through people, either individually or collectively. It would compound the perception further if the people part of the strategic equation were seen as the complicating factor; rather, it should be regarded as the reality of the situation. The purpose of this chapter, therefore, is to provide an initial insight into important aspects of these individual and collective behavioural dimensions of the strategic process.

3.2 VALUES AND CULTURE

Many readers will probably be familiar with workplace phrases such as 'the way we do things here', 'it's not the sort of business we want to get into', 'we are different here' and so on. Such statements are often manifestations of the values and culture held by the organization and as such are powerful determinants of how an organization behaves. Further, on a macro level, there has been much debate in terms of national cultures and their effect on industrial prosperity.

Culture is a major determinant of managerial perceptions, which in turn affects recruitment, resource allocation and management, and organizational design – indeed, all aspects of an organization. Utilizing the McKinsey Seven-S framework, the relationship is shown in figure 3.1.

Shared values have been termed superordinate goals (incremental) but essentially are sets of values and aspirations which underpin objective statements and as such are fundamental to and deep seated within the organization. Whether formally expressed or not, they are omnipresent and often drive the other six 'S's in the framework.

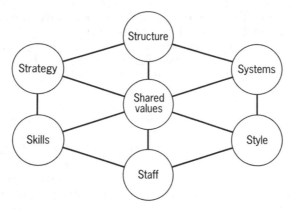

FIGURE 3.1 The McKinsey Seven-S framework
Source: R. H. Waterman, T. J. Peters and J. R. Phillips 'Structure is not Organization', *Business Horizons*, June 1980, pp. 14–26. Reprinted with permission.

3.3   CULTURE AND STRATEGY FORMULATION

Several researchers have identified typologies of culture and their effect upon strategic decision-making. Mintzberg and others have identified entrepreneurial, adaptive and planning organizations.[1] Entrepreneurial organizations tend to be characterized by growth, the search for new opportunities, with power held by the chief executive. Such organizations often exhibit dramatic change.

Organizations without clear explicit objectives tend to exhibit adaptive strategies which are often a function of conflicting goals held by senior managers. In this way they react to environmental change and decisions tend to be incremental and based upon the power conflicts in the organization, resulting in fragmented strategic decisions. Planning organizations are characterized by coordinated anticipatory decision-making which results in a number of scenarios about the future with differing strategies. This tends to promote the value to the organization of analysis and analysts.

Clearly, there is a relationship between the environment in which the organization finds itself and the strategic culture of the organization. Environments which are developing are perhaps more conducive to the entrepreneurial organization. Volatile environments may suit the adaptive mode, whereas stable environments may be conducive to the planning mode. However, much care should be taken with the above as multi-product, multi-market organizations may face different types of environment and thus many modes may be apparent in any organization.

Other researchers have attempted to classify organizations in relation to their behaviour, stemming from their culture and strategic responses over time. For example, Miles and Snow identified four typologies.[2]

1   defenders: tend to be conservative, well-tried ideas, low risk;
2   prospecters: immature, higher risk, seek market opportunities;
3   analysers: strong on monitoring strategy, formal structures;
4   reacters: find it difficult to adapt, crisis management.

In this way it can be seen that, faced with a similar problem, different organizations will respond differently. For example, faced with a decline in turnover, the defender will seek to cut costs to restore margins, 'batten down the hatches'; the prospector will look for new markets and opportunities; the analyser will spend time looking for reasons before changing, but may well have anticipated the change; the reactor will do something about it when it begins to hurt.

Research by Grinyer and Spender has shown that a manifestation of culture in many organizations' strategic decision-making is the creation of 'recipes'.[3] These tend to be strongly held beliefs and ideas about what works. As such, they are responses to changing environment which are perceived to have worked well in the past and are thus embedded in the organization. They are frequently not questioned, as to do so often results in an attack on the superordinate goals held by an organization which are manifest in the values of senior managers who attained their position via such recipes. Like many cultural aspects of an organization, they create a perceptive framework which focuses senior managers' views of the environment and the organization and can act as a constraint on strategic action. Johnson[4] has further developed the area with the creation of a 'cultural web' which defines what he terms the 'dominant paradigm' (see figure 3.2). Thus any strategic response by an organization is a function of the paradigm. The paradigm is a perceptual filter through which managers view the world. When faced with unsatisfactory performance the paradigm is invariably the last element in the strategic equation to be questioned, with managers more willing to reformulate firstly objectives and secondly strategy. Recreating the dominant paradigm involves major cultural change. Paradigm shifts often occur as a result of a large upheaval in senior management following such events as a successful takeover, the defence of a hostile bid, the appointment of a new CEO, or recurrent poor performance.

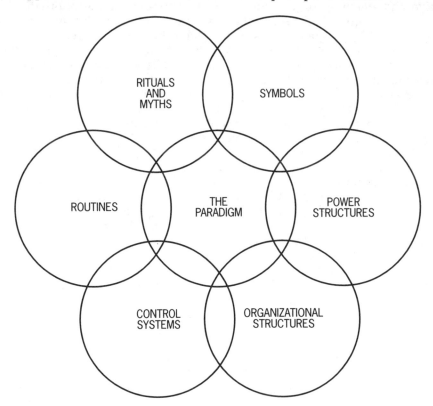

FIGURE 3.2   The Cultural web of an organization
Source: 'Rethinking Incrementalism', Gerry Johnson, *Strategic Management Journal* (Jan–Feb 1988).

3.4   STRATEGIC PERFORMANCE AND CULTURE

Given the nature of the relationship between culture and strategy, several enquirers have attempted to discover what relationships exist between performance and culture. Deal and Kennedy, researching American companies, found that successful companies (above-average long-term performance) were those who believed in something which permeated the whole organization.[5] They further argue that in addition to endemic beliefs, employees ought to be rewarded for behaviour which complies with such belief. In essence, the major aspects of culture which appear to contribute towards success are seen to be a close relationship between critical success factors and values, which are well communicated such that they become institutionalized as rituals in the organization. They are often implanted by visionary managers who set the culture. Strong cultures can assist in prioritizing problems and providing a framework for what is expected of people.

Other insights into the relationship between culture and performance are provided by Peters and Waterman in their book *In Search of Excellence*[6] While the book has suffered some academic criticism and some of the then excellent companies in their sample would no longer qualify, the book and subsequent work by the authors have provided interesting notions about success and culture. Peters and Waterman indentified eight characteristics of excellence as follows:

- a bias for action;
- close to the customer;
- autonomy and entrepreneurship
- productivity through people;
- hands-on value driven;
- stick to the knitting;
- simple form lean staff;
- simultaneous loose-tight properties.

Peters and Waterman's work has been a catalyst for a number of books in the area, for example *The Winning Streak* by Goldsmith and Clutterbuck,[7] but care must be taken in using the findings for there is a danger that the findings are themselves used as a recipe for success. If business was that simple, then everybody would be doing it. This raises the issue of, first, what are successful cultures and, secondly, whether or not successful cultures can be transplanted or initiated to improve corporate performance. The limiting factors on such a proposition stem often from difficulties in defining culture, the receptivity of organizations to new cultures and the time it takes to implement cultural change. It is perhaps easier to change culture when something serious has happened to a company; for example, a loss or an unwelcome takeover bid. These may be described as short, sharp shocks. However, the more incremental methods of cultural change, which inevitably occur and indeed have to occur, often take longer, for any organization is a function of its history, and cultural change has to take place, first, by a recognition that what is currently in place is inappropriate and, secondly, by defining what should take its place.

3.5   CULTURE AND ORGANIZATION

Organizational effectiveness is a fundamental concept in strategic planning. Aspects of organizational design are dealt with in chapter 20; at this point it suffices to discuss the relationship between organizations and culture.

Handy has provided a framework for explaining this relationship by defining four types of culture found in organizations: power, role, task and person.[8]

1 Power: These tend to be organizations with strong central authority with few rules. Typically entrepreneurial, high risk, run by powerful individuals.
2 Role: Less personality run, more bureaucratic, well-defined roles, system and procedures, more risk averse.
3 Task: Problem-solving dominates, relies heavily on expertise and teamwork, personality less important. Often results in a matrix.
4 Person: Based on serving the needs of individual members. Evident in professional organizations such as lawyers. Can be found in other three typologies. Often difficult to manage individuals as individuals may not be responsible to personal or expert power.

As can be seen from the above, Handy's typologies have a lot to do with power in organizations which can be a manifestation of the structure, the effect of coalitions or the personality of the entrepreneur.

3.6 POWER

Power is essentially the ability to engage in action and as such is important in attempting to effect strategic change. Power has both internal and external implications. The discussion of external power is left to further chapters; the emphasis in this chapter will be confined to its internal aspects.

Any discussion of power in organizations has to take account of further concepts of authority and control. Power has a contextual or relationship circumstance. For example, authority is the final power vested in specific roles or positions in an organization; often it is delegated from the top and thus the amount of authority a manager has may well depend on how much the chief executive is willing to delegate. Clearly, there may be advantages in a marriage of power and authority within an organization and many systems such as rewards are geared to such a union, but often they can be divorced from each other, particularly in terms of informal power relationships. Informal power can occur because of expertise or specialization, historical evidence of being right, clear use of internal politics or a host of other reasons. Strategically, the problem is that if power groups become dominant, then they could affect or halt necessary strategic change. It is often useful to revisit major decisions to examine the extent of the power which influenced such decisions. A continuing problem in many organizations is that powerful people control those systems whereby others gain power, and thus people get to the top because they adhere to the values of the dominant power group, thus negating the alternative view or indeed a better approach.

3.7 MANAGEMENT SUMMARY AND CHECKLIST

In this chapter an attempt has been made to introduce the reader to important behavioural dimensions of the strategic process. In essence, the proposition is that organizations do not respond to environmental change; it is people who do. Thus the effects of culture, values, power and authority have a large effect on strategy formulation and success. Discovering values in an organization is not easy for the consultant or analyst; a number of questions have to be posed, answers analysed and behaviour observed to come to a view. It is, however, for the senior manager an important aspect of the role, for culture and values do change and often have to change, thus they have to be managed, which in turn means they have to be understood in a strategic setting.

Values and culture

1   What 'cultural' statements are made by senior executives?
2   To what extent have major decisions been influenced by the culture?
3   Would you classify the company as a defender or a prospecter?
4   What are attitudes to risk – why?
5   Would you classify the company as entrepreneurial, adaptive or planning – why?
6   What do you think the dominant values are – where did they come from?
7   What evidence is there for Peters and Waterman's characteristics of excellence?
8   How would you define the organization's culture in terms of Charles Handy's classification?
9   Has the company a strong strategic recipe?

Power

1   Who has the power in the organization?
2   What are the bases of such power?
3   In reviewing decisions taken in the organization, who made them?
4   What are the attitudes of middle managers to senior managers?
5   If you have an alternative view of the company and its strategy, how easy do you think it would be to get people to listen to you?

NOTES

1   H. Mintzberg, 'Strategy Making in Three Modes', *California Management Review* 16, no. 2 (1973), pp. 44–53.
2   R. E. Miles and C. C. Snow, *Organization Strategy, Structure and Process* (McGraw-Hill, New York, 1978).
3   P. H. Grinyer and J-C. Spender, 'Recipes, Crises and Adaptation in Mature Business', *International Studies of Management and Organization*, 19, no. 3 (1979) p. 113.
4   G. Johnson, 'Rethinking Incrementalism', *Strategic Management Journal* (Jan–Feb 1988).
5   T. Deal and A. Kennedy, *Corporate Cultures, the Rites and Rituals of Corporate Life* (Addison Wesley, London, 1982).
6   T. J. Peters and R. H. Waterman Jr, *In Search of Excellence: Lessons from America's Best Run Companies* (Harper & Row, New York, 1982).
7   W. Goldsmith and D. Clutterbuck, *The Winning Streak* (Weidenfeld and Nicolson, London, 1984).
8   C. Handy, *Understanding Organizations* (Penguin, Harmondsworth, 1976).

4 Mission and Objectives

4.1 INTRODUCTION

According to an old saying, 'If you don't know where you are going, you cannot get lost.' This is perhaps of comfort to some managers but the proposition developed in previous chapters is that strategic planning is a conscious process of decision-making about the future, which involves the creation of purposeful strategies. It may be possible to think about the future without objectives, but the deployment of meaningful strategies necessitates some ends (objectives) against which means (strategies) are developed.

There has been much debate regarding the nature of objectives, for example, long versus short term, financial versus non-financial, the distinction between strategy and objectives, as well as how and who is responsible for setting them.

It is perhaps useful to distinguish between types of objectives – those concerned with broad aims and purposes and those that are quantifiable and measurable, both in the long and short run. The former tend to pose questions about what the organization is and wants to be, while the latter set specific targets for evaluation and act as control mechanisms on how well the organization is achieving its broad purpose.

4.2 MISSION

Missions tend to be about broad purposes. They often contain elements of long-term strategy as well as desired outcomes. What they often reflect are the basic values and philosophy of the organization as perceived by the senior managers who write them.

Practices regarding their dissemination appear to differ; some are actively published to the environment, some seem to be confined within the company and communicated to all personnel, some targeted to senior staff. In large companies with major strategic business units, there may be different mission statements for each subsidiary. The underlying rationale for developing and disseminating mission statements is that they act as visionary and motivating statements but also legitimize the organization in terms of what the dominant values are, why it exists, what types of businesses it will be in and what its subsequent behaviour will be.

Mission statements have been criticized for being so vaguely written that they could be applicable to any organization, also they have been termed 'motherhood' statements with commentators saying 'Well you would say that, wouldn't you?'. If mission statements are too specific then it may be difficult to gain commitment from the managers. They appear to be effective when the successful behaviour of an organization both reflects and emanates the mission statement.

4.3   EXAMPLES OF MISSION STATEMENTS

Allied Domecq

We aim to grow shareholder returns by working together across the world in our chosen sector of drinks, food and hospitality. We will enjoy providing the best quality as measured by brand performance and our customers' perceptions of the value we offer.

The BBC

The BBC's purpose is to serve the public. It has an obligation not only to make programmes of quality and excellence, but also to offer the licence-payer value for money and to be fully accountable for its performance.

4.4   OBJECTIVES

The debate surrounding objectives has been joined by many with differing views. Economic theory states that the firm should attempt to maximize profits. The proposition provides a useful starting point, but it has been criticized from a number of viewpoints, leading to reformulations of the goals of the firm by people such as Baumol, who proposed the goal of sales maximization and various others suggesting growth models. Rather than extend this debate, what is of interest here is where do objectives come from, what is their purpose and what is their nature?

4.5   SOURCES

All organization have to take into account the demands of the environment when setting objectives. The needs of the environment are complex and can result in conflicting objectives for an organization. The needs of the environment and the organization can perhaps be encapsulated by viewing such demands as pressures from stakeholders.

An organization's stakeholders	Needs and interests
Shareholders or owners	Income flows, capital appreciation
Suppliers	Continued success of the company
Customers	Quality products at preferred prices
Employees	Salaries, wages, employment
Government	Taxes, contribution to GNP
Society	Environmental issues, consumer concerns, pollution

The above represents certain key stakeholders and some of their aspirations. Against these one has to set the values and aspirations of senior managers whose personal 'stake' will affect objective setting, remembering that such managers may be shareholders.

Additionally, the interests of the various stakeholders can appear to pull organizations in differing ways. A method of dealing with this conflict may be to deal with each; sequentially, this is difficult, if not dangerous. Prioritizing objectives into some form of hierarchy may assist, particularly in terms of strategic decision-taking, but for most organizations there will often be an overriding goal of profitability. In a real sense the aspirations of all stakeholders cannot be met unless the company is profitable. Clearly, a distinction has to be made for not-for-profit organizations, and these are dealt with separately below.

Profitability is arguably different from the economists' initial notions of profit maximization for companies in a real world of imperfect information. It is somewhat doubtful if people maximize their behaviour, preferring to satisfy, that is attain satisfactory performance. Additionally, there is a continuing debate as to whether organizations can have objectives separately from the objectives of senior people within them.

4.6   OBJECTIVES AND STRATEGY

Many organizations will state their objectives in terms such as 'a certain percentage market share', 'good-quality products', 'a happy and well-rewarded workforce' and so on. The question arises as to whether these are objectives or strategies. It is easy, for example, in a price-sensitive market, to increase market share by dropping prices, but profits may disappear. There is, too, the danger that a function of a company might read its own agenda into market-share growth and set off doing things to the detriment of the organization. Such statements on their own are probably means to an end rather than the end in themselves. When stated along with profitability targets they act as constraints on the achievement of financial objectives.

4.7   THE NATURE OF OBJECTIVES

A prime purpose of objectives is to set targets or benchmarks against which performance can be measured. Thus to be of worth to an organization, objectives should be:

- measurable;
- achievable;
- realistic;
- explicit;
- internally consistent with each other;
- communicable to others.
- time bounded

In many organizations there will be a hierarchy of objectives, as below

MISSION
↓
STRATEGIC OBJECTIVES – SENIOR MANAGERS
↓
TACTICAL OBJECTIVES – MIDDLE MANAGERS
↓
OPERATIONAL OBJECTIVES – SUPERVISORS AND JUNIOR MANAGERS

They ideally 'fit' together in that senior managers' decisions create the domain within which middle managers set their objectives. Each level has however, specific concerns, and the role of senior managers is to articulate objectives which create consensus among stakeholders, whereas the role of middle managers is often concerned with implementing strategy and setting functional objectives.

4.8   NOT-FOR-PROFIT ORGANIZATIONS

A major problem for not-for-profit organizations is the apparent lack of a single discipline against which to set objectives, as for example profit. Like companies, they have a multiplicity of objectives but they are often difficult to reconcile. Thus, such organizations can end up with objectives which appear to be qualitative rather than quantitative, conflicting, complex and difficult to measure. Further, stakeholders may exert an important influence on the objectives.

Thus performance is difficult to measure. Just what constitutes a good not-for-profit organization is often a matter of debate. For example, what constitutes a good museum, art gallery, school or hospital? The satisfaction of the stakeholders, while attractive, may be difficult to achieve, for often such stakeholders are difficult to define and their needs are conflicting. A temptation is to deal with them sequentially or prioritize according to the strength of their needs. Often, surrogate measures are used, such as number of visitors, patients or examination pass rates, but these are often conditional on other external parameters.

Perhaps the answer is to measure what you can, but to be confident that the correct measure is being used in terms of stakeholders. This probably necessitates a greater knowledge of stakeholder aspirations. Not for profit organization can take different forms. Building societies have what is known as 'mutual status' with their own legal framework. They are owned by the depositors and the borrowers. As more societies move to plc status, the original corporate aims of mutuality are changed, making owners into shareholders who will expect a dividend and capital growth, wheras before they only received interest.

4.9   MANAGEMENT SUMMARY AND CHECKLIST

Objectives are essentially a matter for any organization in terms of the levels or rates of performance they describe. However, in the case of companies, it is difficult to escape those financial objectives by which the market measures their performance. The visibility of a company's financial performance is now a major strategic concern for senior managers who have to spend time 'talking to the City'.

The process by which organizations set objectives is also a senior management concern as it affects motivation, morale and the ownership of targets by managers. The process tends to be iterative in that organizations will discuss objectives in terms of company competencies and the external environment, which are the subject of subsequent chapters.

1   Does the organization have a set of explicit objectives?
2   To what extent are the stated objectives achievable?
3   How do the stated objectives fit with past behaviour?
4   Do the objectives fit the stated strategy?
5   In what terms are the objectives stated: long term, short term, financial, non-financial?
6   Do the objectives give any indication of the organization's attitudes to profits in the long and short term?
7   Are the objectives and mission the result of dominant stakeholder opinion?
8   To what extent are the mission and objectives the result of the power of a senior manager or a dominant coalition?
9   Does the mission statement have any operational meaning?

PART 2

External Analysis

5 Environmental Analysis

Introduction – The Environment of the Firm – Strategic
Posture – Environmental Forecasting – Management Summary
and Checklist

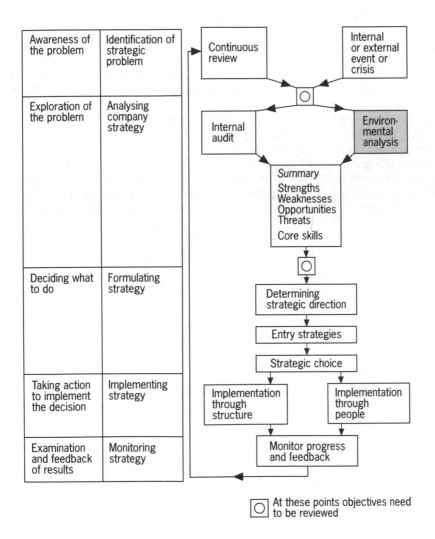

FIGURE 5.1 The strategic decision-making process

5.1 INTRODUCTION

Environmental change is one of the major influences upon the performance of business (and other) organizations, and at the same time largely beyond the control of the management of the organization. It is no accident that managers refer to a 'turbulent environment' within which they have to manage.

For some companies the environment is more turbulent than for others, as some (such as tobacco companies) may find themselves in a situation where everything appears hostile; for instance, a product in long-term decline due to health factors, government actions on taxation and advertising, and increasing social disapproval.

It is important, therefore, to have some way of screening the environment surrounding a company, the changes operating within it and the consequential opportunities and threats posed to that company. To the extent that these are in the future, then it can be considered a form of forecasting. However, it is often the case that it is sufficient to gather together and analyse the trends already apparent within that environment.

A framework is presented in figure 5.2 which can be used to prepare an overview of the factors influencing the company at the time, the changes currently under way (trends) and the potential implications of these. As the industry within which the organization finds itself is considered important, then part of this framework (industry structure) is examined in more detail in chapter 7 as it is usually of critical importance to the company.

Figure 5.2 differs from the model of the organization and its environment shown in chapter 1 in that it makes the distinction between those environments in which a company has some discretion and those where it has little. A company can do little about the general state of politics, economics and so on, but it does have some discretion over who it buys from and sells to. At the same time, however, any company must realize that the nature and dynamics of the discretionary environment is a function of the wider or given environment. It should be remembered

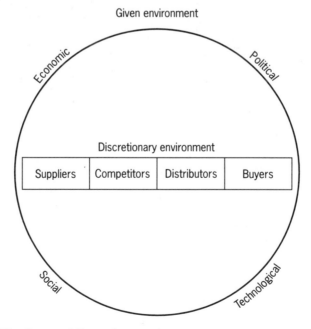

FIGURE 5.2 The firm and its environments

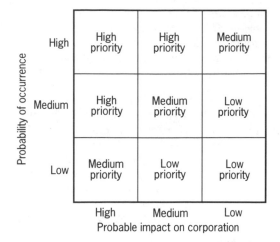

FIGURE 5.3 Issues priority matrix
Source: L. L. Lederman, 'Foresight Activities in the USA: Time for a Reassessment,' *Journal of Long Range Planning* (June 1984), p. 46, Pergamon Journals Ltd. Reprinted with permission.

that, although for planning purposes the given environment cannot be directly influenced, companies and organizations can alter their sensitivities to this environment via their strategic decision-making; for example, by choice of country to manufacture in and types of technology to use. However, once these choices are made, the new environment acts as a 'given' in the planning process.

For the organization, the task of environmental scanning is twofold: first, to isolate these environmental variables to which the organization is sensitive and, secondly, to collect data in order to understand the trends in these selected variables. There is not, unfortunately, an easy way of accomplishing the first task. It is essentially a matter of 'learning' by examining the effects of the environment upon the attainment of objectives. Essentially, it is a process of prioritizing environmental variables in terms of the likelihood of certain things happening and their consequent effect upon the organization. This is shown diagrammatically in figure 5.3.

5.2 THE ENVIRONMENT OF THE FIRM

The Economic Environment

Economic forces affect organizations in every part of their activities as they are a major influence on the various exchange processes. For example, the price of resources, both physical and human, the nature of demand and the perceptions and confidence of businessmen are all influenced by the economic environment. More specifically, a firm has to diagnose the relationship between itself and key economic variables such as:

- inflation and the effect on costs and prices;
- economic policy towards the cost of money and foreign exchange rates;
- taxation, both direct on profits and indirect on employees and goods sold;
- the stage of the trade cycle and the effect on corporate performance;
- the economic mood of the country affecting investment and risk taking.

While all firms are affected by the economic state of the world and the economic policies of government, they will not all be affected in the same manner or to the same degree. Thus, the economic environment presents both threats and opportunities. For example, a period of recession may provide a company with a reason to produce lower price goods or to move overseas. Inflationary pressures on raw material costs may force a firm to seek cheaper imports or improved manufacturing methods. Higher disposable income may provide opportunities for new segments in the marketplace.

An understanding of the nature and dynamic of the economy and its effects upon a company is a key element in strategic planning. Often the planning process begins with a view of key economic indicators such as Gross Domestic Product (GDP) and inflation. For the manager, the problems are: what to look at, where to get it and how reliable are the data. There are a plethora of economic data available, published by the government, banks, specialist agencies, newspaper and magazines. All companies are affected by movements in macroeconomic variables but the extent of the sensitivity is learned through experience. As an example, sources of key economic indicators affecting primary demand are shown below.

United Kingdom National Accounts (The CSO Blue Book) (annual)	National GDP
Accounts (The CSO Blue Book) (annual)	Sector GDP
British Business Magazine (weekly)	Total consumer expenditure and by commodity Producer prices, import penetration, exports, International comparisons
Family Expenditure Survey (annual)	Income and expenditure by households
Employment Gazette (monthly)	Employment, retail price index
Key Population and Vital Satistics (annual)	UK population and growth rates National and regional data
Bank of England Quarterly Bulletin (annual abstract)	Exchange rates International comparisons Longer runs of data on most economic variables

For many companies what is published is useful, particularly as a basis for forecasting, but it is historical data often published long after the event. For planning purposes, companies need a view of what will happen to the economy. For some companies, this means reading in the financial press the latest forecasts of, say, the Treasury model or the London Business School model of the UK economy. For others, there is a need to build their own models, particularly sector models, part of the rationale for model-building being the potential source of competitive advantage by having better and more comprehensive views of the economic environment affecting the company and its industry. More particularly, models show the relationships between variables, which for planning purposes is perhaps as useful as the results.

The Social Environment

Generally, the pace of change in the social environment which affects such factors as population size and structure and social values and expectations is slow but inexorable. Some social change is rapid, for example fashions and fads, but others take years, for example women moving into higher-paid occupations. The firm is affected not only in terms of the acceptability of its product offerings but also by such factors as attitudes to work, work practices and expectation of life-style. Social change as it affects a firm is often a complex of a number of seemingly differing phenomena. For example, the desire for one-stop shopping relies upon changes in work patterns and subsequent attitudes to leisure activities at the weekend, together with the acceptance of mass advertising by companies. Similarly, the change in the age structure of the population has created opportunities and threats for makers of baby products and suppliers of products and services aimed at the retired. The effects of social change are not confined to producers of consumer goods and services. The debate on energy supply is much affected by society's attitudes to nuclear energy.

The Technological Environment

The pace of technological change in some industries has now become so rapid that product and process life-cycles have become much shorter. This is particularly true in the new-technology-based industries of electronic engineering, robotics and computing. While some industries may feel somewhat immune from such changes, technological developments in related industries can have a large effect. For example, changes in the technology of materials in the packaging industry have had a serious effect on the canning industry.

Technological developments potentially offer to firms the ability to purchase in greater quantity, with enhanced quality, and supplant labour with capital. Indeed, such is the impact of technology in some industries that the economic rationale of the industry is changed for all time, as in the use of robotics in mass car production.

The Political Environment

Government at both national and local level can affect companies not only on a day-to-day basis through laws, policies and its authority, but also at a strategic level by creating opportunities and threats. Specifically, such threats and opportunities arise because the government

- can determine the structure of an industry through monopoly and restrictive trade practices legislation;
- is a large supplier of fiscal and trade benefits through regional development programmes and industrial regeneration policies;
- is a large customer through defence contracts, civil works, education, health, and so on;
- can protect industries from overseas competition through competition legislation; and
- can affect the mood of enterprise by privatization or nationalization.

All firms are affected by the political environment but some owe their existence to government by being defence contractors, educational equipment suppliers, hospital suppliers, etc. Such firms in a sense exist at the whim of government policy, which changes, often radically, after each election.

The Factor Market

The factor market comprises those imports of raw materials, labour and capital which are endemic to business. The relationship between a firm and its suppliers is discussed in more detail in chapter 7, but for the purposes of environmental analysis there are two aspects which are important in analysing the factor market. First, an important aspect of factor inputs is their availability. Difficulties in sourcing materials can lead firms to integrate backwards, thus internalizing their material supplies market. The availability of labour can pose severe problems for industry: hence some companies are forced into creating education programmes for new employees. Secondly, the price of factor inputs is important and often closely allied with availability. Price fluctuations make financial planning most difficult and may lead to serious attempts to substitute materials or suppliers. Some companies are sensitive to factor prices; for example, up to 80 per cent of turnover may be represented by raw material costs. Whatever the nature of the factor input, price fluctuation can have a serious effect on competitiveness.

The Product Market

The competitive environment is of such importance that it is considered in detail in chapters 6 and 7.

5.3   STRATEGIC POSTURE

The key managerial task is to ensure that the relationship between the firm and its environment is one by which the firm can attain its objectives. One of the major causes of corporate decline is that created by a mismatch between the firm and its environment. Thus, there is a strategic imperative not only to understand the nature of the environment and its dynamic but also to be aware of those environmental variables to which the firm is most sensitive. This is not an easy task in that there is no simple technique which will establish such a relationship; it is rather a matter of experience or organizational learning. However, due to cost constraints, few firms can monitor everything in their environment and thus there is a need to focus on the most sensitive environmental variables. The dangers of a strategic mismatch are obvious and can arise from any part of the environment via such factors as technological obsolescence, the gradual disappearance of a market segment served due to economic or social change, changes in legislation, raw material shortage and competition. Thus there is a need to take a forward view of the environment.

5.4   ENVIRONMENTAL FORECASTING

In many respects, taking a current view of the environment, although rewarding, misses the essence of strategy in that it is about the future, and thus a forward view is more important to strategic decision-making. How to forecast and the techniques to use depend upon the nature of the company. Single-product companies serving single-market segments will have a less complicated task than, say, multi-product, multidivisional multi-market firms. Further, the larger the firm, the more resources it may be able to devote to forecasting and increasing the sophistication of the techniques employed. Generally, most companies begin the process via informal, often verbal, methods. These would include talking to key people in the environment and to business analysts, reading the business press and 'talking to the City'. Those methods are fairly simple and cheap but they fall short of defining a relationship between the dynamics of the environment and the success of the firm. If a firm wishes to establish these relationships in a more scientific manner, then a number of techniques of varying degrees of sophistication are available. At the most simple level, single variable extrapolation is perhaps the most common. As with many forecasting techniques, it assumes the past is a guide to the future, and in the case of a product life-cycle it must be remembered that the firm's actions can alter its shape.

For many companies who can isolate a key environmental variable, this may be rewarding. If a company's sales are closely correlated to a single environmental variable such as personal disposable income, then forecasts can be made simply on the basis of linear regression analysis. For many companies, however, a single environmental variable is insufficient, and thus multiple regression techniques may have to be utilized. At this stage of sophistication, further techniques such as factor analysis and input-output modelling are possible and useful. As was mentioned above, many of the techniques rely on the assumption that the past is a guide to the future; while this may be true for many relationships, any change in the relationship renders the method less useful and strategically dangerous. Techniques have been developed to attempt to forecast without relying heavily on past data. In essence, the techniques are subjective in nature but their use can be significant, particularly where there is little past data or the forecast horizon is well into the future. Such methods would fall into the category of expert opinion, which may be structured (as in the case of delphi techniques) or unstructured (as in the case of scenario generation). Delphi is particularly useful in the field of technological forecasting where the opinion of researchers in the field may be sought about the likelihood of a technological change.

Scenarios are useful in answering 'what if' questions without the use of simulation models. Thus a firm could postulate differing future environments with the use of expert opinion, and then look at the likely future impact on the firm in terms of when strategic decisions would have to made to react to such environments. Scenario generation has been particularly successful in taking very long-term views of the environment, particularly in the field of technology.

In essence, there are two approaches to scenario building. One method is to postulate the future on the basis of change which the organization cannot affect (unconditional) and the other is to take a view of the future when the company itself contemplates changes in its strategy (conditional). Thus, for example, a company could look at scenarios if it envisaged change in major aspects of, say, its own product-market strategy. This is rather akin to the notion of the company creating its own environment as a result of its own decisions. In practice, companies often have to develop multiple scenarios based on different assumptions and covering different aspects of the environment. Thus, for example, major oil companies develop political risk scenarios, environmental ones, worldwide economic/energy ones, all of which provide views of the future which affect current decision-making, particularly with regard to the generation of contingencies as part of the planning process.

A common question in the field of strategic environmental forecasting is how far ahead one should look. Much depends upon the reaction time to environmental change, which in turn may be influenced by the production technology the firm is using. For example, it takes considerably longer to create capacity for steel manufacture than, say, to produce a piece of new software. If a company wishes to respond strategically to a perceived future change in the environment, then decisions about such a change in strategy may have to be taken some time in advance. This can be shown by gap analysis techniques as shown in figure 5.4.

The line F_1 is a desired strategic parameter, for example profitability market share, whereas F_2 is what will happen if there is no change in strategy, so by Year 2 a gap is beginning to emerge. The major problem is thus how long it takes for current decisions to begin to fill the gap. Clearly, in the example of an integrated steel plant, two years is too short a time period, for the capacity may not be on line in two years if it is to be built from a greenfield site. Thus, forecasts will have to have a time horizon which can encompass design, construction and commissioning of plant. The other strategic options would be to buy the plant from someone else or to subcontract.

Forecasting for strategic decision-making probably does not have the precision requirements of other forms of forecasting, particularly as the time horizon lengthens, but unlike short-term forecasting the outcome of such forecasts can result in larger resource commitments as part of a strategy. Thus there is an inevitable trade-off between risk and accuracy, which is partly accomplished by firms having

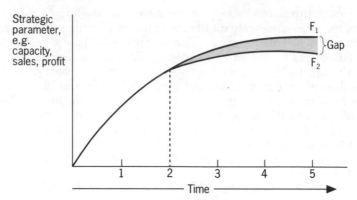

FIGURE 5.4   Gap analysis

experience in monitoring the environment continually as part of the strategy creation process.

5.5   MANAGEMENT SUMMARY AND CHECKLIST

Outlined below are some examples of the kind of issues that would need to be examined in the various environments.

Economic Environment

What effect are the following economic variables likely to have on the operation of the business?
- rate of economic growth;
- level of unemployment;
- level of prices and rate of price changes;
- balance of payments position.

What effect are the following policies and issues likely to have on the business?
- monetary policy;
- fiscal policy;
- specific balance of payments regulators such as tariffs, quotas, exchange rate changes, and so on;
- specific prices and/or incomes legislation;
- measures to reduce unemployment.

In addition, further information may be necessary if expansion is to take place in an economy in which the company has no previous experience:
- size of Gross Domestic Product (GDP) and GDP per head;
- income distribution.

Social Environment

What is the likely impact on the business of changes taking place with respect to the following social issues?
- health and welfare;
- recreational needs, such as sports, arts;
- education;
- living conditions – housing, amenities, pollution;

- working conditions;
- social changes – discrimination, equality, population trends.

Technological Environment

What impact are developments in the technological environment going to have on the business?

- transportation technology;
- energy use and costs;
- biological sciences;
- materials sciences;
- mechanization and robotization;
- computerization.

Political Environment

Whatimpactaredevelopmentsinthepoliticalenvironmentgoingtohaveonthebusiness?

- Socioeconomic system: ownership, control, regulation and deregulation;
- Competition policy: legislation on monopolies, restrictive practice and advertising;
- Government: public sector organizations, employer, purchaser, and guardian of individual, local and national interests.

Factor Inputs

Labour markets and trade unions

- Is there a continuous supply of the necessary labour skills, both manual and technical?
- Are there problems with trade unions with respect to demarcation and working practices?
- Is the business unionized or becoming more unionized – what are the implications?

Materials and services

- Are there problems in obtaining supplies of raw materials? Problems with foreign sources of supply?
- Does the price fluctuate wildly?
- Is the industry becoming more vertically integrated, which would affect supply?

Capital and money markets

- Are there problems of raising money for the businesses we are in or into which we seek to enter?
- Where is the best country to raise capital?
- What is the likely future for interest rates?

Product markets   A detailed approach to analysing markets appears in chapters 6 and 7.

Customers

- Who are our customers and potential customers?
- How big are our customers?
- How important are our top ten customers to our business?

Competitors

- Who are our competitors and potential competitors?
- How big are our competitors and are they part of a large group?
- Is competition increasing from buyers or suppliers?

6 Customer and Competitor Analysis

Introduction – Competitor Identification – Competitor
Analysis – Buyer Behaviour – Management Summary
and Checklist

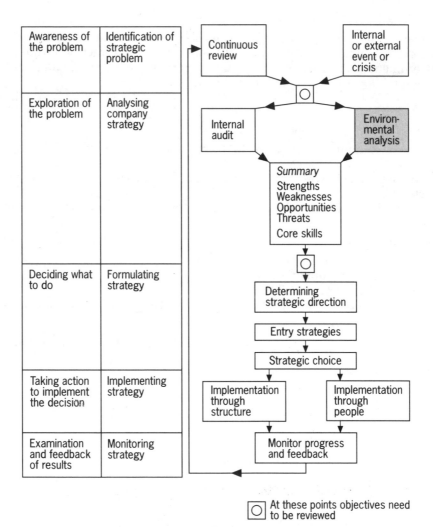

FIGURE 6.1   The strategic decision-making process

6.1   INTRODUCTION

Although companies regularly affirm that customers and competitors have the biggest influence on their profitability, not all undertake any systematic analysis of their activities. Consequently information about them is anecdotal and rarely documented.

In this chapter it is intended to look at the micro aspects of customers and competitors prior to a consideration of the interaction of the aggregates of these two groups in chapter 7. It is not intended that this will be as exhaustive a coverage as may be found in many marketing texts, but rather a consideration of the essential issues which confront the practising strategist. This chapter is therefore concerned with these two key features used in analysing where a company is at present and where it will or may or could be in the future.

Many companies are reactive, that is they respond to the actions of customers and competitors. Some companies move through this phase to become proactive, that is they seek to identify customer needs and develop an appropriate response. A new approach to above average profitability is 'in creating tomorrow's competitive advantages faster than competitors mimic the ones you possess today'.[1] This cannot be achieved without systematic analysis.

6.2.   COMPETITOR IDENTIFICATION

Detailed competitor analysis should result in a number of benefits to the company. Firstly, such analysis will confirm the nature of competition in the marketplace. Secondly, it will enable the company to make comparisons with all the other competitors on a range of different performance criteria. Thirdly, analysis will provide intelligence concerning the successes and failures of competitive activity. Fourthly, as a result of the other benefits, companies ought to be able to determine a strategy which is more likely to produce greater profitability.

A problem which is soon encountered in any analysis of competition is the question of how competition is defined. It is important when starting the analysis to ensure that all the *actual* as opposed to only the *most obvious* competitors are evaluated. It is possible, for instance, that, if the market is international but comparison is only made on a national level, the firm may come to the wrong conclusions.

Firms are on a continuous scale from direct competitors, to indirect competitors, to firms that pose little or no threat. Therefore, the analyst has to use judgement in deciding which competitors should be included in the analysis.

Another complication for the analyst is the concept of market segments. Should these be considered part of one market or do they constitute a separate market? Segments can be defined by customer size, type, needs or buying criteria or by mixtures of such variables. Further consideration of segments appears in section 6.5.

6.3   COMPETITOR ANALYSIS

Once the number of competitors has been decided it is necessary to consider the criteria which will be used to compare them. The variables which are important will be different in different markets and so table 6.1 is an example rather than a definitive framework. Consequently, each criterion will be allocated a weighting so that the evaluation is focused on the key issues. In order to make comparisons each competitive criterion is assigned a measure, this may be qualitative or quantitive.

The resulting analysis may be useful in itself for determining strategic moves or it will provide data for use in the five forces or other models to be considered later.

Most firms view competitors with hostility. However Porter[2] suggests that there can be strategic benefits to competitors. Competitors can:

- increase competitive advantage;
- improve the current industry structure;

TABLE 6.1 Competitor analysis

Factor	Measure	Weight	Company Position	Competitor 1.	Competitor 2.
A Strategy					
1 Parent company activity					
2 Retaliatory action likely					
3 Current strategy					
4 Industry assumptions					
B Management					
5 Age structure					
6 Training					
7 Leadership qualities					
C Finance					
8 Profitability					
9 Gearing					
10 Cash flow					
11 Value added					
D Marketing					
12 Advertising					
13 Selling					
14 Market research					
15 New product development					
E Customer service					
16 Faulty machines					
17 Time to breakdown					
F Organization					
18 Clarity of goals					
19 Communication					
20 Information technology					
G Personnel					
21 Staff turnover					
22 Pay rates					
H Operations					
23 Plant flexibility					
24 Plant age					
25 Experience curve effects					
26 Manufacturing cost					
I Design					
27 Number of new products					
28 Quality of staff					
J Raw materials					
29 Price paid					
30 Faults					

- aid market development;
- deter entry.

He argues therefore that there are good and bad competitors.

6.4   CUSTOMER ANALYSIS

Much research and many marketing texts are focused on final consumers. While all products and services are ultimately provided to meet a consumer need, there are many intermediate products whose market characteristics cannot be fully explained by the consumer models. It is important therefore to develop a framework which is appropriate for all types of customer.

The characteristics which lead to the bargaining power of customers are outlined in chapter 7.4. Using these characteristics as a basis for the detailed analysis of customers, table 6.2. provides the questions necessary to complete the five forces model in the next chapter.

TABLE 6.2 Customer analysis

Factor	Measure	Weight	Company Position	Customer 1.	Customer 2.
1 Proportion of customers' product accounted for by our product					
2 Customer profile					
3 Could/might customers integrate backwards?					
4 Do customers perceive differences between competitive products?					
5 Can customers switch easily to an alternative?					
6 What position are customers' products on the product life-cycle?					
7 What are the prospects for customers' customers?					

As in table 6.1., the criteria are identified together with an assessment of their importance in a given market and a measurement for comparison purposes. Clearly, for some of the criteria it may be relevant to use more than one measurement.

6.5   BUYER BEHAVIOUR

A fundamental consideration in market analysis concerns itself with the nature of demand. It is perhaps too comforting to presume that buyers will buy. Increasingly, companies are interested in questions such as when, how, why and how often? An intimate knowledge of buyer behaviour is properly the preserve of the marketing function, but it has important consequences for corporate strategy. Any firm's product offering represents its views of the market and thus is a tangible message to the environment, including such aspects as image and status. Thus a company has to consider the strategic implications of market analysis.

Few, if any, markets are composed of buyers with homogeneous needs, and it is the differences between needs which create opportunities for market segmentation

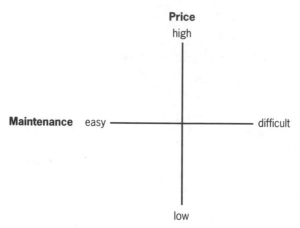

FIGURE 6.2 Product space map

and subsequent product positioning strategies. Buyers' needs are a complex of demographic, social, economic and psychological variables. When sufficient buyers of a particular type constitute a viable subset of the market, firms can consider developing specific strategies for that segment. To be viable the segment must be profitable, identifiable and capable of being communicated with. Any shortfall within these criteria renders segmentation difficult.

Basically, a firm has three options. First, it can deem differences to be unimportant and follow a policy of mass marketing where the product is undifferentiated. Secondly, recognizing differing segments, it can produce differentiated products and strategies designed to suit the needs of each segment. Finally, it can choose to concentrate on one segment only. The choice depends upon capability and the risk/return trade-off. What is important is that the strategy of the company has been 'fine-tuned' to take account of differing segments.

A further dimension is the notion of product positioning. Again, this depends on a full knowledge of buyer behaviour in that firms have to think about those product features which allow them to be successfully placed in a market. For example, suppose a company wishes to market a new hand tool and it knows that there are two important purchase considerations: price and maintenance. Thus, a product space map of the market would appear as in figure 6.2.

What is of strategic importance is where to place the product. Consideration will include the position of competing companies' products and of the company's own existing products, the perceptions of buyers to a different or similar position, the profit potential and the nature of the company's image.

As can be seen in segmentation and positioning, an understanding of buyer behaviour is important to strategy. Many firms have simply 'run out' of a market by failing to understand this important aspect of market analysis.

6.6 MANAGEMENT SUMMARY AND CHECKLIST

As these two factors are critical to the success of the firm, it is surprising that often only lip service is paid to detailed and systematic analysis of competitors and customers This chapter has given reasons why this is unsatisfactory and has provided an outline for undertaking the task. In order not to repeat this outline, the summary below concentrates on a few of the key issues.

- Is the firm conducting a regular, detailed analysis of competitors and customers?
- Do such analyses consist of both the current and likely moves by these actors?
- In customer analysis, is sufficient attention paid to changes to the customer, their purchasing behaviour and what they will be purchasing in the future?

NOTES

1 Gary Hamel and C. K. Prahalad, *Competing for the Future* (Harvard Business School Press, 1994).
2 M. E. Porter *Competitive Advantage*, ch. 6 (Free Press, New York, 1985).

Introduction – Analysis of Industries and Markets – Rivalry between Established Competitors – Bargaining Power of Buyers – Bargaining Power of Suppliers – New Entrants – Substitute Products – The Product Life Cycle – Economies of Scale – The Learning Curve – Management Summary and Checklist

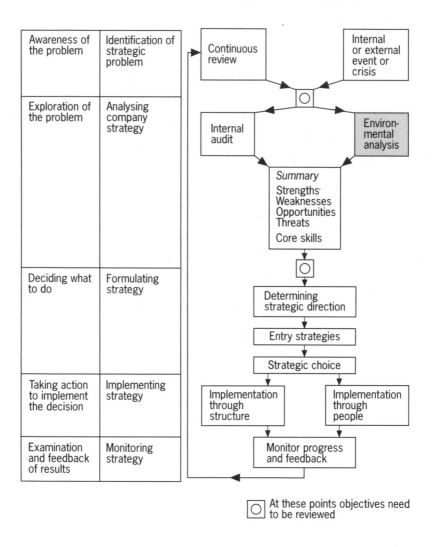

FIGURE 7.1 The strategic decision-making process

7.1   INTRODUCTION

Although forming part of environmental analysis, the competitive environment is singled out for a number of reasons. Firstly, it is seen by many in business as the most important environment with which they have to deal.[1] Secondly, many firms spend a significant proportion of their resources in the competitive environment, chiefly in the area of marketing. Thirdly, it is the most proximate environment in that its effects on the organization are continuous and direct; thus organizations are dealing with it daily.

Industries differ widely in the nature and extent of competition. What is needed is a framework for analysing the relationship between the many variables affecting competition and their overall impact on profitability. Many useful insights into the competitive process have been provided by economists, strategists and others. However, a major problem in the analysis of competition is the definition of an industry. This was discussed in section 6.2.

7.2   ANALYSIS OF INDUSTRIES AND MARKETS

A model of some of the variables and their sources were shown in figure 1.1, but this diagram is illustrative rather than analytical.

The Five Forces Model

The 'five forces' model developed by Michael Porter[2] of the Harvard Business School is powerful in its ability to describe many market situations, and also, it is widely used. However, it does have some limitations which will be discussed later. The model is based on some well established work in the field of industrial economics. What Porter has done is to develop a framework which facilitates the prediction of likely outcomes, particularly profitability, from given characteristics of a market.

The basic model will be outlined here and it will be developed further in the sections as shown below. The five forces are:

- the rivalry amongst existing sellers (see section 7.3 below);
- the power of the buyers of the company's products (see section 7.4 below);
- the power of suppliers to the company (see section 7.5 below);
- the potential entry of new competitors (see section 7.6 below;
- the extent of the threat posed by substitute products (see section 7.7 below).

In addition to the five forces, change can emanate from the traditional PEST (political, economic, social, technological) areas before impacting on any of the five forces. While such changes may ultimately feed into the variables in the model, it is possible that they may not, and in any case, it is often important to spot significant changes before they have a direct impact on the firm. For instance, if you are a clothes manufacturer or a house builder, changes in the birth rate may have no immediate effect on your business but eventually they will result in increased or decreased demand. Early identification of trends permits the company to have greater discretion over its future.

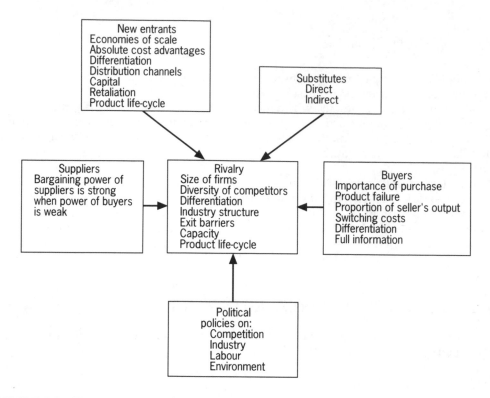

FIGURE 7.2   The determinants of competition

It is also noticeable that government legislation is often the culmination of what started as a small change in one of the other environments and gathered momentum before the government decided to act.

The key area, therefore, is the political environment. This can have an immediate effect on the industry in four main areas;

- competition policy – monopolies, fair trading, safety;
- industrial policy – government support in bankruptcy, R&D, finance;
- labour policy – working hours, minimum wage, safety.
- environment policy – pollution, conservation.

There may be other political issues specific to a particular industry. These and issues from the other environments are covered in chapter 5 but the four mentioned here often have an immediate and direct effect on the competitive process.

Problems of Market Definition

Some of the problems of market definition were discussed in section 6.2. but a further comment is necessary at this point in the five forces model. The issue of which firms should be considered as 'rivals' is not always clear cut and, although there is no easy resolution of the problem, it is important to consider some of the key parameters.

The question is one of market definition – what are the boundaries of the market? For instance, are Mars bars in the chocolate bar, chocolate, confectionery, snack food or food market? The nearer to the product, in this case chocolate bars, the closer will be the substitutes, some may be so close as to be actual competitors in terms of competition for the consumer £ spent. Also, what is the geographical scope of the market – local, regional, national, several nations (for example the European Union) or global?

Economists use the concept of cross-elasticity of demand as a measure of substitutability to resolve this issue. This is very helpful conceptually but much more difficult to use in practice because of the considerable difficulties in calculating cross-elasticities. Although there is no complete solution to the problem of precise market definition, a realization of the different shortcomings will enable the strategist to use the model appropriately and draw conclusions with additional care.

Generic Strategies

The five forces model helps the understanding of the nature and extent of the competitive forces in an industry and will in some cases provide insights which will enable managements to develop an appropriate strategy. However Porter developed a prescriptive model which provided a set of generic strategies to follow depending on the position of the company's product on a matrix. The answers to two questions provide the axes for the matrix.

- Does the firm seek to gain advantage by being low cost or differentiated?
- Does the firm seek to serve a number of segments or to focus on a few?

The strategies to be followed according to the answers to the two questions are shown on figure 7.3. In addition to the four strategies shown, there is a fifth strategy which describes the position of firms who are not clear about the balance and thrust of their strategy and are thus 'stuck in the middle'. The other strategies are outlined below.

Cost leadership, or becoming lowest cost producer, emphasizes the need for both tight cost control and the continuous search for cost reductions. It also assumes a set of customers who perceive the benefit of low prices delivered through the low cost base.

Differentiation requires strong marketing and often R&D as well as distinctive requirements from people. Further the product has to be perceived by customers as offering something unique to them and for which they are prepared to pay a premium.

Focus strategies are not aimed across all or a significant part of the industry but rather at a segment or segments within the industry where they may tailor their

	Strategic advantage	
	Low cost	Differential
Multi-segment	Cost leadership	Differentiation
Fewer single segments	Low cost focus	Differentiation focus

(Strategic target)

FIGURE 7.3 Generic competitive strategies
Source: Adapted from M.E. Porter, *Competitive Strategy* (Free Press, Glencoe, 1980) with permission.

offering, maybe to the exclusion of others. They do not usually have any competitive advantage in terms of the industry as a whole.

Problems in Using the Model

Although this model is a powerful tool for analysing industries and determining strategy the analyst should be aware that there are a number of problems experienced when it is used. The first major problem is to do with industry definition. Where do the boundaries of the industry lie? This has been discussed previously.

The second problem is the static nature of the model. Is the model based on where the industry is now or where it will be tomorrow? And if 'tomorrow', can all the actions and counteractions of all the participants be assessed? Yet, if only 'today's' model is used this takes no account of any changes which are going to happen in the future.

The third problem concerns the low cost-differentiation axis. Many consumer products do not fall absolutely into one category or the other and, while most industrial products are arguably bought on price, many other factors can affect a purchase. So the distinction between the two may be unclear.

7.3   RIVALRY BETWEEN ESTABISHED COMPETITORS

Although competition varies significantly between industries, rivalry between sellers is usually the greatest of the five forces. Competition can be based on price, product features, service, advertising or warranties. In all but monopoly situations there are constant changes taking place in these competitive forces as companies seek to gain an advantage and increase profitability. As we shall see later, while some moves will achieve this objective, others are doomed to failure. The issues affecting rivalry (see figure 7.2) are discussed below.

Relative size of firms and ownership – firms which are bigger than others, or are part of a large parent company, are better able to cope with fluctuations in demand and could sustain a price war longer than smaller companies.

Diversity of competitors – where competitors do things differently in terms of the product, production, distribution, selling and so on, the firms in the industry avoid the fierce competition engendered by having to focus mainly on price.

Differentiated product – in an industry in which there are differentiated products, competition is likely to be focused on non-price variables.

Industry structure and concentration – where there are few firms, prices tend to be set at similar levels, and as it is not in the interest of profitability for these to be changed, they often remain stable for long periods. However as the number of suppliers in an industry increases, this situation is more difficult to maintain and so price becomes increasingly important.

Exit barriers – if it is difficult to exit the industry because, for instance, there is expensive plant which has no alternative use and for which there is no market, the companies may continue in the industry at low levels of profitability.

Capacity level – in an industry in which there is excess capacity there is a tendency to reduce prices to increase sales and thereby fill the plant. Unfortunately this is usually met by an all round price reduction resulting in no increase in sales and correspondingly lower profits.

Position on the product life cycle – see section 7.8. below.

7.4   BARGAINING POWER OF BUYERS

Many factors lead to buyers having considerable power in a market. It is likely that in most markets this force is next in importance to 'rivalry' and in some industries equal to, or more important than it. Retailers, particularly food retailers, have immense purchasing power, as do many industrial buyers.

If the following features exist then the bargaining power of the buyer will usually tend to be increased.

Importance to the buyer – if the product is a large cost item to the buyer.

Product failure – if failure to perform the function for which it was purchased is not critical

Proportion of seller's output – where the purchase accounts for a large proportion of the seller's output.

Switching costs – if the cost or convenience of moving to another supplier is small.

Differentiated product – if the product is not differentiated.

Backward integration – if the buyer has the potential to integrate backwards.

Full information – where the buyer has full information on the alternative potential purchases.

7.5   BARGAINING POWER OF SUPPLIERS

It is likely that while suppliers may pose a threat to profitability in some industries, this force is not as influential in most market situations as the other four forces. As the factors relevant to suppliers are the opposite to those of the buyers which are discussed above, they will not be repeated here.

7.6   NEW ENTRANTS

If for some reason an industry is attractive to a company it may choose to enter. It could achieve this either by starting to provide the product or service itself, or by collaborating with another company in doing so. A final means of entry would be provided by the acquisition of a firm already in the industry. There could be a variety of reasons for entry, such as a growing market, a product complementary to the existing range or exceptional profitability in the industry.

New entrants differ from substitutes in that the new firm would be offering substantially the same product as existing companies. The ease with which firms can enter an industry are controlled by the barriers to entry. Entry will be easier where some or all of the following conditions are met.

Economies of scale – if there are few or no economies (see also section 7.9. below);

Absolute cost advantages – if there are no advantages from such factors as experience curve effects or ownership of a source of raw materials.

Product differentiation – where products are not differentiated and brand loyalty is low.

Distribution channels – if access to channels is open.

Capital – where capital requirements are low.

Retaliation – where the effects of retaliation are likely to be small.

Product life-cycle – at an early stage in the cycle.

7.7   SUBSTITUTE PRODUCTS

Competition from substitutes can emerge suddenly as a result of a technological breakthrough from a totally unrelated industry. Although this may be an infrequent source of new competition, changes in the prices of raw materials or consumer tastes, for example, could cause a substitute to emerge on a more frequently occuring basis from companies not currently considered competitors.

A further problem is associated with the previously mentioned market definition issue. What may seem a totally different product may actually be competing as a substitute. For instance, a foreign holiday may be competing for the £ in the pocket with replacing the car or redecorating the bedroom. While these alternatives are not technically competitive, it may be that appropriate advertising could influence the decision and so they cannot altogether be ignored.

7.8   THE PRODUCT LIFE-CYCLE

A useful starting point in market analysis may be to take a view of the nature of growth in the total market or any segment under analysis. The concept of the product life-cycle is useful in this context, although its use as a strategic planning tool may be limited, as its shape may be altered by the action of the company and thus it may become more of a self-fulfilling prophecy.

An important note of caution when using the concept of the product life-cycle for an individual product and the cycle for the market within which that product competes. Both are useful for strategic analysis, but here emphasis is placed on the market life-cycle where the strategic implications of each stage will be discussed (see figure 7.4).

Introduction or Development

In this stage, market growth is slight and there will probably be little differentiated demand. However, from a firm's point of view a great deal of expense may have been incurred in R&D, and in product and process design. In addition, marketing costs will be high, due to market research, test marketing, promotion and setting up distribution channels. It is thus highly unlikely that profits are made in this stage. The major strategic decision will have been made before this stage begins, namely, to develop and launch the product. Any firm at this stage will have predicted or hoped for the next stage in the pre-launch analysis. Certainly product performance in the marketplace will have to be closely monitored for if the market does not grow, major decisions will have to be made regarding withdrawal from the marketplace with the attendant costs and loss of goodwill.

Growth

This stage is characterized by rapid growth in sales and profits. Profits accrue due to the increase in output. Larger market share may result in price leverage and lower costs due to scale and experience effects. At this stage it is cheaper for firms to increase their market shares as the market grows. Further, some marginal firms may have been shaken out of the market. Product lines will have settled down to serve distinct segments and such standardization should lead to lower production costs.

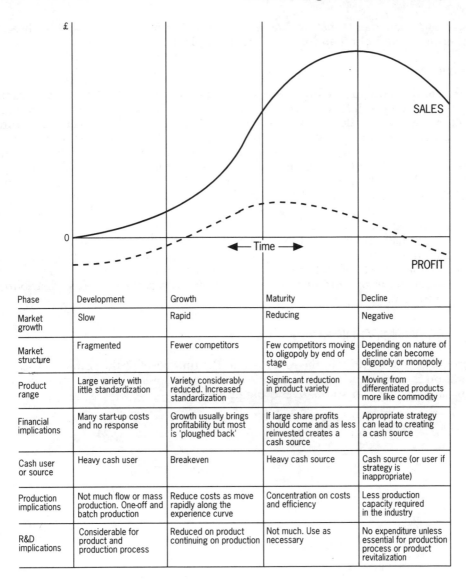

The following table appears within the figure:

Phase	Development	Growth	Maturity	Decline
Market growth	Slow	Rapid	Reducing	Negative
Market structure	Fragmented	Fewer competitors	Few competitors moving to oligopoly by end of stage	Depending on nature of decline can become oligopoly or monopoly
Product range	Large variety with little standardization	Variety considerably reduced. Increased standardization	Significant reduction in product variety	Moving from differentiated products more like commodity
Financial implications	Many start-up costs and no response	Growth usually brings profitability but most is 'ploughed back'	If large share profits should come and as less reinvested creates a cash source	Appropriate strategy can lead to creating a cash source
Cash user or source	Heavy cash user	Breakeven	Heavy cash source	Cash source (or user if strategy is inappropriate)
Production implications	Not much flow or mass production. One-off and batch production	Reduce costs as move rapidly along the experience curve	Concentration on costs and efficiency	Less production capacity required in the industry
R&D implications	Considerable for product and production process	Reduced on product continuing on production	Not much. Use as necessary	No expenditure unless essential for production process or product revitalization

FIGURE 7.4   Life-cycle effects on strategy

Maturity or Saturation

This is perhaps the most common stage for all markets. It is in this stage that competition becomes most intense as firms strive to maintain market share. Thus marketing and finance become key functional areas within corporate strategy. Further, it is in this stage that market segments emerge in greater numbers. Attempts to grow market share at this stage are expensive as, given little market growth, aggressive strategies of gaining share from competitors are expensive and lead to retaliatory moves. Any growth at this stage will depend upon growth in such variables as GNP, population and so on and thus forecasting may be easier. As this stage is normally the longest lasting, the greatest profit will be made. Thus firms will not wish to incur large expenditure on R&D and product and process design of a fundamental nature. Rather, such expenditure will normally be directed to product modification and improvements in plant capacity and quality.

Decline

As the market growth rate declines it does not necessarily follow that firms should quit. It may be possible for a firm to stay in the market to gain a large share of a declining market but this strategy has a finite limit, that is 100 per cent of nothing. Above all, great financial care has to be exercised during this stage. It may be possible to strip cost out of the product in order to maintain profitability by cutting back on promotion or on volume, or by variety reduction. Similarly, the product could be 'niched' by production for a smaller subset of the market where a large market share can be obtained. The product could be taken to new overseas markets. Any end game strategy at this stage depends upon the rate of decline in the market and the consequent effect on revenue and the consequent decision on withdrawal. Many firms have pulled out too quickly when careful financial decisions would have maintained product profitability. A further aspect of the problems of this stage concerns the launch of new products which will replace existing ones. This is particularly important for such aspects as after-sales service, stocks, distribution and production.

7.9   ECONOMIES OF SCALE

Economies of scale refer to the reduction in the unit costs of the firm as its scale of operation is increased. These economies arise from spreading costs such as R&D, plant, advertising and so on, over a bigger volume.

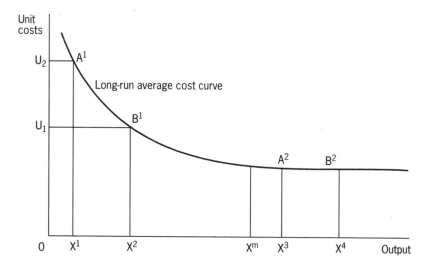

FIGURE 7.5   Unit Costs and Economies of Scale

Figure 7.5 represents a long-run average cost curve with two firms, A and B, operating at different levels. It is assumed that no diseconomies of scale are evident in this market and that producing a quantity greater than X^m will not reduce costs further. At position B^1, company B is operating at a distinct cost advantage (U2–U1) over company A at point A^1. However, if firms were able to operate at a different point, although the difference in output (X4–X3) is the same as it was at point A^1 and B^1 (X2–X1), there is no difference in costs. Also, further increases in output will yield no cost advantage.

From this analysis the output level X^m is known as the minimum efficient scale of production (MES). This level will vary between industries and, over time, the minimum is likely in most industries to increase. This becomes significant when the MES for a product is greater than total national demand. For instance a volume UK aircraft manufacturer could not operate at the MES unless sales were at least at a regional (EU) level.

7.10   THE LEARNING CURVE

The learning curve, or experience curve, represents the relationship between costs and output. Unlike economies of scale, costs fall because the firm learns to produce more efficiently as a result of its accumulated experience. Typically, costs of manufacturing can fall by between 20 and 30 per cent each time output doubles. The effect is not automatic, as companies have to realize the potential for cost saving. Thus, a firm on an 80 per cent experience curve should expect a 20 per cent drop in costs each time output doubles. Cost savings arise out of a better use of labour, materials and capital. A firm may consciously attempt to gain experience through research and investment.

7.11   MANAGEMENT SUMMARY AND CHECKLIST

Market and competitive analysis is a useful and integral part of strategic analysis involving the whole of the organization. A thorough understanding of the market is essential to corporate strategy. In a sense, a firm's product or service offering represents how well a market is understood by a company and as such is 'voted on' immediately by customers. This attempt to understand the structure and dynamic of a market should form part of the strategic process by asking key questions as summarized below:

1   What is the degree of concentration in the market? To calculate concentration it is necessary to know:
  (a) the number of competitors;
  (b) the market share of each competitor.
2   What size is each competitor? Are they part of a large group of companies?
3   How closely substitutable are competitors' products?
4   Are there any entry barriers?
5   Are there any exit barriers?
6   What is the bargaining power and influence of our customers? Could they integrate backwards?
7   What is the bargaining power and influence of our suppliers? Could they integrate forwards?
8   Are companies currently not making the product or supplying the service likely to enter the market?
9   Are technological or other changes likely to generate a substitute product?
10   Where is the product on the product life-cycle?

11   What changes are taking place in the competitive environment and what are the implications of these changes?
12   What is the impact of economies of scale on our industry?
13   Where is our company? Are our competitors on the learning curve?

NOTES

1   W. F. Glueck and L. P. Jauch, *Business Policy and Strategic Management* (4th edn, McGraw-Hill, New York, 1984), p. 134, for examples of surveys of the views of strategists. concerning the importance of different external environments.
2   M. E. Porter, *Competitive Strategy* (Free Press, Glencoe, 1980).

FURTHER READING

B. Lowes, C. Pass, S. Sanderson, *Companies and Markets*, (Blackwell Oxford 1994).

PART 3

Analysing Resources and Capabilities

8 Internal Audit

Introduction – Strengths and Weaknesses – Analysis –
Objectives – Strategy – Structure – Finance – Marketing –
Production – Research and Development – Human Resource
Management – Systems and Procedures – Matching the
Internal and External Environments – Management Summary
and Checklist

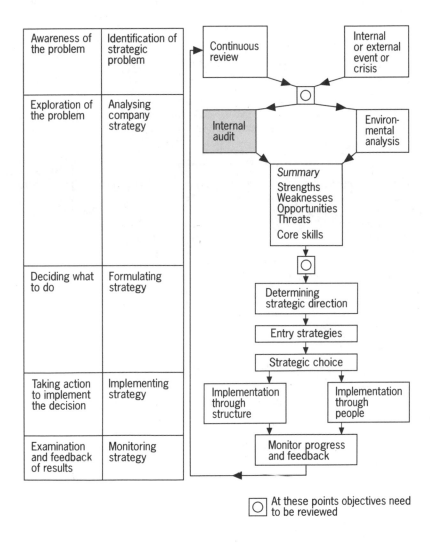

FIGURE 8.1 The strategic decision-making process

8.1   INTRODUCTION

The major task of strategic analysis is concerned with an organization taking a view of itself in order to assess its current strategic position. Put more simply, the organization is attempting to ascertain, through analysis, its strengths and weaknesses. Such an analysis is by no means simple, for it involves the firm taking a dispassionate view of itself, and given the nature of most organizations, objectivity is often difficult to achieve. Further, it must be remembered that any corporate strength can only be defined in terms of strategic importance – it is no good being good at something unless it contributes to the well-being of the organization. However, where a firm has a strength which is crucially important to its effectiveness, then it can assume the ownership of a highly prized asset and the firm can be

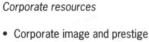

Corporate resources

- Corporate image and prestige
- Company size (overcoming entry barriers)
- Government influences
- Flexible and adaptable structure
- Effective research and development
- Effective management information systems

Factors of production and operation

- Benefits of vertical integration
- Materials availability and costs
- Production and process skills
- Experience curve effects
- Flexibility of production equipment
- Processing of by-products
- Buildings and land

Factors of markets and marketing

- Image and prestige
- Benefits of vertical integration
- Efficient distribution and location
- Promotional strength (advertising, public relations, merchandising)
- Sales and after-sales service
- Patent protections
- Marketing research

Factors of finance

- Flexible capital structure
- Total financial strength

Factors of personnel

- Skills and experience of management
- Skills and experience of labour force
- Labour costs
- Trade union relations

FIGURE 8.2   Core skills and key resources
Source: G. A. Luffman and R. Reed. *The Strategy and Performance of British Industry 1970–80* (Macmillan, London, 1984). Reprinted with permission

said to have a distinctive competence in that area. A list of possible distinctive competences is shown in figure 8.2. The analysis has one further use in that, once a firm has taken a view of its internal strengths and weaknesses, not only does it have the results of a strategic audit but such data give the firm ideas for future strategy by matching its strengths to future environmental opportunities. Further, the company can begin to do something about its weaknesses.

8.2   STRENGTHS AND WEAKNESSES

The proposition assumed above that a firm should play to its strengths while improving upon its weaknesses presupposes that a firm knows its current position. How then does a firm know what it does well and what it does badly? Any corporate competence is composed of two parts: those things which a firm can do efficiently and those which it can do effectively. They are not mutually exclusive, nor should a firm attempt one at the expense of the other. It is, however, in terms of strategy that the distinction is important. The distinction can perhaps best be seen in terms of advertising. Any campaign can be efficient in terms of cost per thousand, opportunities to see and so on, but its effectiveness depends upon creativity in design, copy and so on. In some instances effectiveness can compensate for lack of efficiency and vice versa. For example, a small producer who cannot gain the same production economies as a larger competitor can market a distinctive product to a particular segment, and thus his or her marketing effectiveness compensates as long as that marketing strategy can be maintained. Conversely, in a price-sensitive market, production efficiencies which result in lower prices may compensate for poor marketing. Thus any analysts asking themselves what the firm's corporate strengths and weaknesses are ought to carry out such analysis with the key variables of efficiency and effectiveness uppermost in their minds.

8.3   ANALYSIS

An important prerequisite in corporate appraisal is what to look at. In one sense the answer is everything, but a useful checklist is composed of the key features of the organization, normally defined by function. Such a list is shown below:

- objectives
- strategy
- structure
- finance
- marketing
- production
- research and development
- human resource management
- systems and procedures

Some of the above can assume crucial importance as a result of the nature of the business, and others appear to be important because they deal with the whole organization. Examples of the latter case are objectives, strategy and finance. Thus they are afforded separate treatment elsewhere in this book (see chapter 4 for objectives, part 4 for strategy and chapter 9 for finance). However, as all of the ingredients of a strategic internal audit are examined at the same time, those which are treated in greater depth elsewhere are included in this chapter for reasons of completeness.

8.4   OBJECTIVES

The impact of objectives in an internal strategic audit are twofold. First, the results of internal appraisal will provide a significant input into objective setting. Thus the firm will create objectives based upon its views of its distinctive competences or strengths. Secondly, objectives will provide guidelines against which to measure the performance of many internal factors within a company. Thus it should be possible to isolate those key internal factors which enhance or detract from a firm's ability to achieve its stated objectives.

As can be seen, objectives are reference points for corporate performance and as such they need to be clearly identifiable. To be of most use, objectives should be measurable, achievable, realistic and communicable. Vague statements about growth and profitability suffer from imprecision, which when performance needs to be assessed, renders meaningful analysis difficult.

The need for reasonable objectives means that commonly they are set in terms of economic performance. This in turn entails some statement about profitability. While it may be argued that profit is itself a means to an end, it is a sufficiently well-accepted measure of performance towards which all firms are striving that it can be recognized as a primary objective. A major problem with objectives arises in organizations which are not for profit, such as museums, art galleries, charities and so on. Here the problem is to determine a useful parameter against which to measure organizational performance.

A common problem is to distinguish between strategy and objectives. Often statements from senior managers about their company contain a mixture of both. For example, statements such as increase turnover, grow overseas, divest, improve product quality, spend more on research, may well be objectives for parts of the organization but generally they are means to some greater objective such as company profitability.

From a strategic viewpoint, objectives will translate themselves into lower-order objectives for functions or departments within the organization as is shown in figures 8.3 and 2.3. Thus there has to be an internal consistency between corporate and operational objectives. For example, if a firm has decided that an objective of a rate of return on capital employed of 20 per cent is desirable, then this ratio can be decomposed into its component parts, or (in the example) if an average margin of 10 per cent is further desired

$$20\% = 10\% \times 2$$

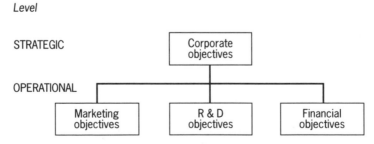

FIGURE 8.3   Relationship between corporate and operational objectives

which means that given the two objectives of return on capital employed (ROCE) and margin, a capital turnover ratio of 2 is required. To be internally consistent, the organization has to be capable of such a performance. Thus to achieve consistency, objectives may well be the result of an iterative process which will achieve such consistency.

8.5   STRATEGY

Strategy is a word which has been most widely used in the military sphere. However, now the word is used extensively in business and, as in the military context, may be defined as 'the means of achieving a given objective'. A strategy is concerned with integrating company activities and allocating scarce resources, so that the present objective can be met. In the process of planning a strategy, it is important to appreciate that decisions are not taken in a vacuum, but that any action taken by the business firm is likely to be met by a reaction from those affected: competitors, customers, labour force or suppliers. It is critical, therefore, that the effects of such reactions should be evaluated before taking decisions. Such an evaluation may lead to the abandonment of the project, to a contingency plan, or to making plans which minimize the effects of possible reactions.

The conceptual view of strategy and the relationship of strategy and objectives have been outlined above. It remains, therefore, to discuss the meaning of strategy in operational terms.

Strategy is concerned with: (a) products and technology; (b) markets and customers. A company can only stay in business by satisfying customers. Thus, for given financial objectives, a company must decide what markets and customers it is going to supply, what products will be made to satisfy those customers, and with which technological process it will manufacture the products.

It must be remembered that often a firm's strategic options are severely limited. It is rare for a company to market products to a set of customers in a totally different manner from its competitors. Thus, often a company is not just interested in the effectiveness of a given strategy; it is also concerned about its efficiency. As strategy is a most important aspect of business policy, it is discussed in greater detail in parts 4 and 5.

8.6   STRUCTURE

Any strategy has to be deployed through an organization, and thus an important aspect of strategic appraisal concerns itself with the appropriateness of organizational design.

Figure 8.4 illustrates a simplified form of a functional organization where the individual functional managers of the firm are responsible to the chief executive. The ultimate responsibility for the direction and control of the company will lie with the board of directors, and the functional managers may or may not be members of this board. (If they are they will be directors of the company.)

Figure 8.5 illustrates a simplified form of a divisional structure in which the main feature is that each division or subunit of the company operates in semi-autonomous fashion, separated from the other units. This type of organization would more easily fit a diversified company with interests in, say, pottery manufacture in one division and textile fabrics in another. There may often be little relationship between these divisions and hence little purpose in having, for example, a marketing

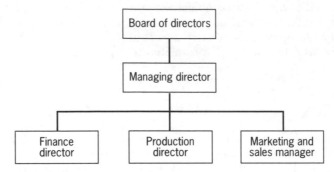

FIGURE 8.4   Functional organization structure

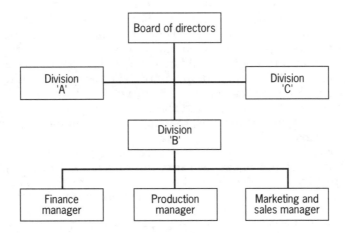

FIGURE 8.5   Divisional organization structure

director responsible for overall marketing activity. In the divisionalized structure we could expect differing performances from the divisions, and consequently they may justify the allocation of different targets by the board according to their particular product and environment. In general, the board will have overall financial control and will seek to reinvest where it feels it can make the best return on investments. Thus we may see profits flowing out of one division to be invested in another, with appropriate decisions being made at board rather than divisional level, although production and marketing decisions can be taken at divisional level by the individual managers involved.

The multidivisional diversified company is already one of the most important forms of organization, not least because it allows marketing and production autonomy at divisional level while retaining financial control at the centre. Nevertheless, it does not follow that all organizations should be shaped this way. For the small company and the company engaged in a limited product/market area, the functional organization can still be effective.

However, following strategy formulation, we do need to address ourselves to the question of whether the existing organization structure is appropriate to the implementation and monitoring of the strategic plan. We need, therefore, to ask the following questions before deciding:

1   What is going on at the moment in the company with respect to product flows? For instance, is the company vertically (or horizontally) integrated in any way?

Are these internal transactions (for example, product flows between units may require counterbalancing resource flows) appropriate in relation to the markets dealt with?

2   Does the present organizational structure facilitate these flows around and out of the company?

3   If the company has been subdivided in any way (functional or divisional), are these subdivisions congruent with the measures of performance and rewards desired by the company?

A simple illustration covering the latter point would be the case of a marketing manager whose performance (and subsequent rewards) is judged by sales returns, distribution in stockists and so on. If, however, he or she was in conflict with the production manager whose performance was measured in part by minimizing of stock-holding costs (resulting in lost orders and possible customers), then the 'organization' would not be congruent with respect to performance measures. Thus, either the organization should be changed or the performance measures allocated to the participants varied in order to achieve improvements.

Matrix Organizations

Matrix structures are arrived at in some organizations normally because there are two operations which require significant amounts of management. Thus, for example, line management might constitute one area of management and staff management another. Similarly, product or market management may be an important area, and functional management is also important (see, for example, figure 8.6). A further example can be seen in R&D management (figure 8.7). Its use as an organizational structure is independent of the scale of operations, and it possesses

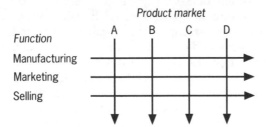

FIGURE 8.6   Product market management matrix

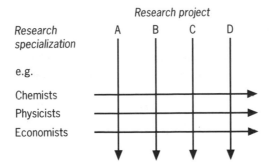

FIGURE 8.7   R&D management matrix

some distinct advantages. It balances competing managerial priorities and thus can improve decision-making. Any one manager in the matrix has to co-ordinate his or her activities, thus improving contact within the organization. However, the drawbacks of such a structure are that individual managers may have difficulties in reconciling competing claims on their efforts with consequent demotivation. Responsibility is often hard to pinpoint and subsequent protracted discussion may slow down decision-making.

8.7 FINANCE

As a corporate function, finance has many aspects which are concerned with strategy, as shown below:

- the acquisition of funds;
- the use of such funds, including project appraisal;
- the provision of information to outsiders, including the preparation of final accounts;
- the provision of internal information – the management accounting function;
- the provision of information from outside the company.

Thus, although not a line function, it is possible to take a view of its strengths and weaknesses like any other department of a business. Essentially, its function consists of two parts: first, those activities concerned with the funding of the company; and, secondly, those concerned with monitoring the use of those funds. This latter function will spread across the whole organization and will be chiefly concerned with monitoring and control systems.

Funding and investment decisions are fundamental to corporate strategy. The amount and mixture of long- and short-term debt can have serious implications for corporate performance. For example, the mixture of capital has implications in terms of future repayments and dividends. Thus a firm which borrows loan capital will have to be certain that the returns from such investment can cover at least future interest payments, and the price of the loans will be important. In this respect loan capital may be available from many sources at differing prices; thus part of the finance function responsibility is knowledge of the market for funds.

Capital investment decisions are closely linked both to strategy and to funding decisions. The appraisal techniques and models available to screen such decisions fall in part under the remit of the finance function. Thus part of the efficacy of the finance function can be gauged by its knowledge of capital investment appraisal techniques and their limitations.

The role of the finance function as a data source and information provider is important to the control of strategy. An important part of any strategy is to create and schedule control systems which will monitor its performance. Thus decisions regarding the frequency and amount of information should be taken as part of corporate strategy formulation. The quality of such information is the responsibility of the finance function. Financial information is often of two types, that which constantly flows to monitor the performance of strategy, and that which is needed less frequently but often in greater depth, for example in financial appraisal of a potential takeover victim, new product proposal, new market, divestment and so on. Imperfections in the speed of preparation and quality of such information can result in poor strategic decision-making.

The analysis of company performance is often found to be a problem for non-accountant students and analysts, and as such is considered in detail in chapter 9.

8.8   MARKETING

In a corporate context, marketing has two important functions. First, any strategic analysis could investigate the market orientation of the total enterprise. In this sense marketing is more than the function of the marketing department as it involves every function, realizing that customer satisfaction is a total responsibility. Secondly, marketing is a function within a company primarily concerned with demand management. Marketing at this functional level is responsible for positioning the company's product offering in the marketplace. This involves researching the market and focusing the market response into a particular market segment. The other major task, to assemble the company's marketing strategy, is often referred to as the marketing mix. The marketing mix is that combination of product policy, promotional policy, pricing policy and distribution which is assembled to meet the needs of the market segment and which will give the company a competitive advantage.

The amount of resource devoted to marketing will depend upon the nature of the market. For example, firms in highly competitive markets which have many buyers with diverse needs (such as fast-moving consumer goods) will devote more resources to marketing than, say, a company with few customers with special needs and limited competition. Whatever the amount devoted to marketing, the function is important in that it is the link between the firm and its customers and its strategy has a high visibility in the environment.

Competition provides a useful basis for companies in assessing the strengths and weaknesses of the marketing function. Comparisons can be made with other companies for it is rare to find competing companies conducting their marketing in such differing ways as to render comparison difficult. External comparison is not the sole method of assessment for, as with other functions, the relationship of marketing with other functions is important. For example, what demand does marketing place on production in terms of product quality and quantity? How good is market planning in terms of giving reliable forecasts for other functions in the organization?

8.9   PRODUCTION

Production is normally defined as that process which transforms tangible raw materials into saleable products or services, with the result that many of the techniques and concepts of production can be applied to the production of services. Further, the methods of strategic appraisal are common to both products and services.

Any strategic appraisal of the production process will concern itself with the efficiency and effectiveness of plant, equipment and production labour, which in turn necessitates an analysis of manufacturing costs, capacity, location and those systems inherent in production such as maintenance, quality control, stock control and production scheduling.

A significant strategic advantage is provided by the ability of a company to lower production costs for a given quality compared with competitors and to react quickly

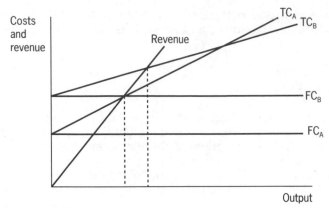

FIGURE 8.8   Product cost structures
Note: FC, fixed costs; TC, total costs

to changes in demand through good production scheduling or by having flexible plant. Such abilities depend upon the competence of production staff to purchase the right plant and machinery and to appreciate the importance of cost consciousness. The impact and nature of production costs has an important strategic aspect. For example, consider two companies with differing cost structures, where company A has a low ratio of fixed to total costs, company B has a high ratio of fixed to total costs. These are shown in figure 8.8.

The analysis is simplified by having a common sales curve. As can be seen, company B has a higher break-even point, but once past break-even its profits rise at a faster rate than those of company A whose break-even is lower. Thus company B is volume sensitive in that any fall in volume will have a greater impact on B than on A. The consequence for production is that heavy investment in plant will increase fixed costs, particularly where such investment replaces labour, and thus volumes need to be high to compensate. This phenomenon is particularly prevalent in service industries such as banks and insurance companies which have a high ratio of fixed to variable costs. However, if a company can gain a high sales volume then the additional plant can lead to economies of scale or cost saving through the experience curve effect. Similarly, large outputs often mean that the firm can afford better technology and specialist personnel.

8.10   RESEARCH AND DEVELOPMENT

Research and development includes a wide range of activities from fundamental research to product improvement. Generally, expenditure in this area is designed to promote new product development, product improvement and manufacturing process improvement.

The decision to devote resources to R&D is in itself a strategic one, based on a corporate desire to improve products and processes internally rather than buying the research needed or to be an innovator and leader rather than a follower and imitator. The risks associated with R&D expenditure stem from its ability to deliver new products or cost savings in production. The risks associated with not spending or with under-spending are a loss of technological expertise, lack of new product and process ideas, and an over-reliance on new ideas being commercially available.

A key strategic decision is how much to spend on R&D and, within the broad spectrum afforded by the area, where to spend scarce resources. Although certain technologically based industries tend to spend a significant proportion of their turnovers on R&D, it does not necessarily follow that all firms in such an industry will adopt an offensive R&D policy; some may prefer to imitate quickly, thus avoiding high research costs. However, in the imitating company there must be some technological competence to assess the research.

A further approach to the uncertainty problem with R&D expenditure is to give the R&D function a clear market orientation in such a way that projects will be assessed and controlled in relation to their potential marketing payoff. This approach should, however, not detract from the fundamental strategic analysis of R&D which essentially assesses the technological competence of the function.

8.11   HUMAN RESOURCE MANAGEMENT

The major role of the human function in terms of corporate strategy is to ensure that the quality of personnel is consistent with the jobs defined. Thus human resource management – for the task is more than the function of the personnel department – involves the recruitment, development and appraisal of personnel, together with the creation of reward and welfare systems.

When well managed, a company will have high morale, good relationships among different levels, high job satisfaction resulting in low labour turnover and absenteeism. The ability to measure some of these factors is somewhat limited, but there are obvious signals when things go wrong such as measuring absenteeism, labour turnover and industrial disputes.

In addition to the above factors, any appraisal of the human assets should investigate teamwork: how well do certain groups, such as the board, senior managers, project teams, work as a team? This is particularly important for certain key strategic tasks such as policy creation, new product development, corporate planning and strategic appraisal.

Increasingly, as markets become more hostile and firms are looking for product and process innovations to secure strategic advantage, many firms are attempting to release an entrepreneurial spirit in the organization. This is difficult in a more bureaucratic structure, but many companies are attempting to create a corporate culture which fosters entrepreneurship with all the associated attitudes to risk taking. Clearly, the ability to foster such attitudes to innovation depends upon the culture of the company which is the responsibility of senior management. Culture change is neither easy nor quick, but its impact is pervasive, affecting many aspects of human relations and management in an organization.

8.12   SYSTEMS AND PROCEDURES

Often firms neglect the various systems in a company as part of the strategic appraisal, but in one sense the whole exercise is part of a corporate planning system. There are others such as information systems, communication systems, budget systems, which are company wide and not necessarily dependent on any one function. Their efficiency and effectiveness can have an important effect upon the viability of the organization and are compounded, often, with size. The bigger the firm, the more complex such systems become. The advent of new technology has improved the ability of companies to handle the necessary data, but the systems

TABLE 8.1 Stage process audit criteria

Criteria	Stage 1: Initiation	Stage II: Contagion	Stage III: Control	Stage IV: Integration
Data processing (DP) organization				
Objective	Get first application on the computer	Broaden use of computer technology	Gain control of DP activities	Integrate DP into business
Staffing emphasis	Technical computer experts	User-oriented system analysis and programmers	Middle management	Balance of technical and management specializations
Structure	Embedded in low-functional area	Growth and multiple DP units created	Consolidation of DP activites into central organizational unit	Layering and 'fitting' DP organization structure
Reporting level	To functional manager	To higher level functional manager	To senior management officer	VP level reporting to corporate top management
User awareness				
Senior management	Clerical staff reduction syndrome	Broader applications in operational areas	Crisis of expenditure growth Panic about penetration in business operations	Acceptance as a major business function Involvement in providing direction
User attitude	'Hands-off' Anxiety over implications	Superficially enthusiastic Insufficient involvement in applications design	Frustration from suddenly being held accountable for DP expenditures	Acceptance of accountability Involvement in application, budgeting, design, maintenance
Communication with DP	Informal Lack of understanding	Oversell and unrealistic objectives and schedules Schism develops	Formal lines of communication Formal commitments Cumbersome	Acceptance and informed communication Application development partnership
Training	General orientation on 'what is a computer'	Little user interest	Increase in user interest to accountability	User seeks out training on application development and control

Planning and control

Objective	Hold spending at initial commitment	Facilitate wider functional uses of computer	Formalize control and contain DP expenditures	Tailor planning and control to DP activities
Planning	Oriented towards computer implementation	Oriented towards application development	Oriented towards gaining central control	Established formal planning activity
Management control	Focus on computer operations budget	Lax to facilitate applications development activity growth	Proliferation of formal controls	Balanced formal and informal controls
Project management	DP manager responsibility	Programmer's responsibility	Formalized system	Formalized system tailored to project
			DP department responsibility	DP and user/management joint responsibility
Project approval and priority setting	DP manager responsibility	Malfunctional managers First in, first out	Steering committee	Steering committee Formal plan influence
DP standards	Low awareness of importance	Inattention	Importance recognized	Established standards activity
			Activity aggressively implemented	Published policy manuals
Objective	Prove value of computer technology in organization	Apply computer technology to multifunctional areas	Moratorium on new applications	Exploit opportunities for integrative systems
			Consolidate and gain control of existing application	Cost-effective application of advanced technology
Application justification	Cost savings	Informal user/manager approval	Hard cost savings	Benefit/cost analysis
			Short-term payout	Senior management approval

Source: Reprinted by permission of the *Harvard Business Review.* A table from 'Controlling the Costs of Data Services' by Richard L. Nolan (July/August 1977). Copyright © 1977 by the President and Fellows of Harvard College (all rights reserved).

have to be designed and be capable of adaptation with changes in corporate strategy. Two major aspects are of importance; first, does the firm have a particular system and, secondly, how good is it? As has been mentioned, one would expect that as firms grow, then certain types of system would be incorporated or, if in existence, made more sophisticated (see table 8.1).

Thus it would be unusual for a large firm not to have a corporate planning system. How good it is depends ultimately upon user needs, in that the systems must fulfil the needs of decision-makers. Thus the question of what information goes to whom and what is done about it needs to be asked. Further, such systems have their own objectives which should not be incongruent with those of the organization. For example, a financial system designed to prevent fraud may involve a bureaucracy which slows down decision-making; thus a firm has to make the necessary trade-off between the elimination of fraud and more rapid and responsive decision-making.

Often such systems are difficult to adapt without penalty, but they are an important part of the company and thus need to be appraised regularly.

8.13   MATCHING THE INTERNAL AND EXTERNAL ENVIRONMENTS

The preceding chapters have shown what has to be taken into account when analysing an organization and its environment. In a sense the analysis is akin to a strategic audit but, unlike a financial audit, it not only concentrates on what is but also on what might be. The task is to assemble the analysis into a meaningful shape in order to plan future strategies. Emphasis has been placed on the determination of corporate strengths and weaknesses and environmental threats and opportunities. These may be shown diagrammatically in figure 8.9.

Any strategy should build on strengths towards opportunities while avoiding threats and correcting weaknesses. This is the important link between analysis and strategy selection and, although it may appear simple, its efficiency depends upon the quality of analysis. The listing of strengths and weaknesses by an organization, while often not an easy task, often results in a picture which is not totally revealing. The danger is that what may be listed turns out to be a collection of symptoms rather than causes for an organization's material health. For example, declining sales is not a problem but a symptom of perhaps something rather more deep seated, which strengths and weaknesses analysis fails to reveal. The key question is why has an organization ended up with a particular set of strengths and weaknesses? Such a simple question affords deeper analysis looking for causality. This often results in a much shorter list of core skills or, in competitive terms, answers the question: what are our differential strategic advantages?

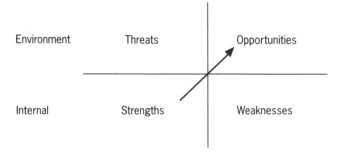

FIGURE 8.9   Summary of internal and external analysis

This further process is important, for once an organization understands its competitive differential advantages or core skills then such knowledge is powerful in guiding its future actions. Further, it allows the company to compare itself with critical success factors for the industry. All companies have to answer the question: how do we compete? In many industries there are critical factors which all competitive companies have to be competent at to be credible, but superior performance in one or more of them places that organization in a superior position with consequent effects upon profitability.

8.14   MANAGEMENT SUMMARY AND CHECKLIST

For the business analyst or the student with the case study, a checklist will be useful. The checklist can be made more effective by weighting the degree of relative strength or weakness by use of a semantic or numerical scale which allows statistical manipulation or profiling. The checklist below is illustrative rather than exhaustive and refers to the relevant sections in the chapter.

Objectives

- Are the objectives clear, explicit, measurable, achievable, realistic and capable of communication within the organization?
- Are there operational objectives which are consistent with overall strategic objectives?
- Will the objectives satisfy owners and stakeholders?

Strategy

- Is the strategy consistent with objectives and the resource capabilities of the organization?
- Does it build directly on strengths?
- Does the strategy realize synergy within the company?
- Is the strategy appropriate for the company's environment?

Structure

- Is the organizational structure consistent with the declared strategy?

Finance

- Has the company sufficient financial resources to fund its strategy?
- Is the mix of funding flexible?
- How low is the cost of capital?
- Can the company raise new capital?
- How effective is financial planning and control?

Marketing

- How efficient and effective are the component parts of the mix?
- How strong (in terms of market share) is the company in the markets served?
- How effective is product development?
- How good is the company at market research and at identifying trends and gaps in the market?

- What is the relationship between turnover and profits?
- What is the relationship between profits and the customer base?

Technology

- How does the company compare in terms of production cost?
- How does the company compare in terms of production quality?
- How up to date is the production technology?
- How effective are the production systems for maintenance, quality control, production scheduling, stock control?
- How easily can new products be assimilated into production?
- How near to full capacity utilization is the company?
- How flexible is the plant?
- Are we producing in the right location?
- Is purchasing taking advantage of bulk discounts?
- Is there a major sourcing problem with scarce raw materials?

Research and development

- How technologically competent are the staff?
- How good are the laboratories and equipment?
- How market orientated is R&D?
- How much is spent on R&D?

Personnel

- Is the recruitment policy developing the number and quality of people required to implement strategy?
- Is the training policy developing the necessary new skills and improving existing competence?
- Is the management development programme providing the quality of management necessary to implement the corporate strategy?

Systems and procedures

- Are the systems and procedures providing the means by which strategy can be implemented?

From the foregoing it can be seen that strategic internal analysis is a large task. For many companies it is an annual process; thus it has its own learning curve. Further, it must be remembered that many internal features of a company do not require much lengthy analysis; they are often very obvious. Such features as competitive strength, cost structure and profitability are often obvious. Similarly, it is possible to purchase details of competitors' performance as well as sector analysis which gives a useful set of data with which to compare oneself. However, the task remains that of the company. Evidence suggests that such an analysis often explodes many myths within organizations, forcing, as it does, management to take as objective a view as possible. The analysis is, however, of little value unless it is placed against the nature of the current and future environment facing the company, and this is discussed in part 4.

9 Financial Appraisal

Introduction – The Nature of Financial Statements – The Balance Sheet – Profit and Loss Account – Shareholder Ratios – Share Valuation and Strategy – Cash Flow – Management Summary and Checklist

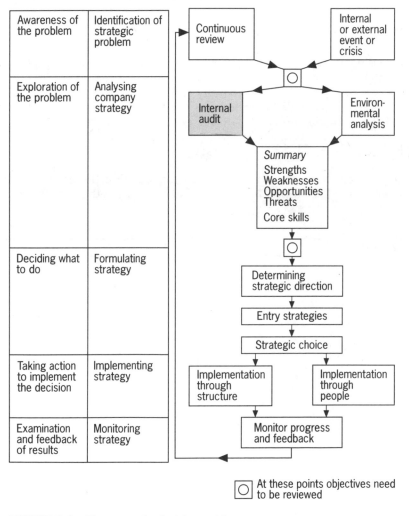

FIGURE 9.1 The strategic decision-making process

9.1   INTRODUCTION

The relationship between strategic performance and financial analysis is most important. The analysis of an organization's performance through its reported financial statements is fundamental to an understanding of strategic management. Such analysis has two components:

1   It provides important evidence of total organizational effectiveness, particularly when measured against previous performance or that of similar organizations.

2   The efficiency and effectiveness of the finance function can be assessed in terms of the acquisition and management of financial resources.

Such analysis is not confined to strategic management, as many bodies external to the organization are interested in performance, for example, banks, stock markets, trade unions, competitors, suppliers and investment analysts. Specifically, such analysis is concerned with an assessment of the financial health of the organization and is designed to provide answers to key strategic questions. Additionally the analyst is interested in the degree of risk associated with the organization as well as its returns to owners.

9.2   THE NATURE OF FINANCIAL STATEMENTS

Before proceding to an explanation of the use of financial management in strategic management, it is perhaps appropriate to explore the nature of the principle financial statements used in such analysis. Generally, the most appropriate statements are the profit and loss accounts and the balance sheets. While other statements may be important, these two often provide sufficient data for the analysis of performance.

9.3   THE BALANCE SHEET

The balance sheet of a company is a device for showing the economic state of a company in a standard form. It is *a snapshot in time* of the state of the system

TABLE 9.1 Balance sheet

Balance sheet as at . . .		
Fixed assets		
Land and buildings		800
Plant and machinery		800
Vehicles		200
Fixtures and fittings		100
Intangibles (goodwill)		100
Investments		100
		2,100
Current assets		
Stocks	300	
Debtors	300	
Cash	100	
	700	
Less current liabilities		
Bank overdraft	20	
Trade creditors	200	
Tax payable	200	
Proposed dividend	20	
Short-term loans	100	
	540	
Net current assets		160
Net assets (Total assets less current liabilities)		2,260

Financed by:	
Creditors due after one year	100
Long term loans (secured or unsecured)	800
Provisions for liabilities	100
	1,000
Capital and reserves	
Preference share capital	100
Ordinary share capital	900
Reserves – retained profit	260
	1,260
Capital employed	2,260

described in figure 9.2. It shows the *sources* of finance used by a company and the *assets* which have been acquired.

By itself the balance does not, as is often widely believed, explain how successfully the company has fared over the year – this is the role of the profit and loss account – but, rather, gives a 'true and fair view' of the company's financial position at *the moment in time* when the balance sheet is prepared.

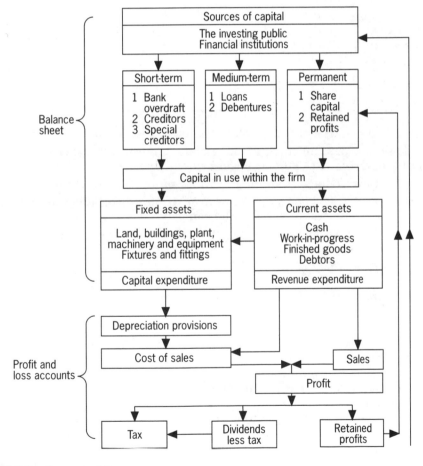

FIGURE 9.2   Sources of finance
Source G. Ray, J. Smith, 'Handy Developments Ltd', in *Text and Cases in Management Accounting (Gower).* Reprinted with permission.

9.4   THE PROFIT AND LOSS ACCOUNT

The purpose of a profit and loss (P&L) account (see table 9.2) is twofold. First, it is to measure the size of the profit, often termed earnings, for the trading period and, secondly it is to indicate those factors which have caused profits to rise or fall. In addition to the annual P&L which has to be produced for shareholders, P&L accounts are produced monthly and quarterly for management information purposes.

The P&L account calculates the gross profit or margin which shows how much has been earned (gross) from the primary revenue-generating activities of the business to cover the business expenses and leave an acceptable profit.

TABLE 9.2 Proforma profit and loss account

Profit and Loss Account for year ended ...

	£	£
Sales revenue	5,400	
Deduct cost of sales (prime cost)	4,000	
Gross profit/earnings		1,400
Deduct indirect expenses	1,000	
Profit before interest and taxation		400
Interest payable	80	
Corporation tax	90	
Net profit after tax		230
Deduct declared dividend	20	
Retained profit for the year		210

Gross profit = Sales revenue – Cost of sales

The profit and loss account charges selling and administrative expenses against the gross profit, to arrive at profit (earnings) before interest and tax.

Profit before interest and tax = Gross profit – Indirect expenses

Net profit after interest charges and tax is available for distribution to shareholders or for retention in general reserves in the company.

Retained earnings = Net profit before tax – Tax – Dividends

9.5   RATIO ANALYSIS

Five major areas may be defined as being of particular importance to strategic appraisal:

	Accountancy terms
1 Is the business profitable?	Profitability
2 Is the trading position satisfactory?	Trading
3 Is the business solvent?	Liquidity
4 Is the business properly funded and using those funds wisely?	Gearing
5 Are shareholders earning satisfactory returns?	Shareholder ratios

These questions can give rise to a host of relevant ratios derived from the financial statements. Which to use depends upon the question to be answered but generally there are some standard ratios to be calculated for each of the areas. Which ratio to use and its particular formulation is not critical, as long as the same version is used each time to ensure consistency.

Profitability

Three ratios are of interest:

1 How well have the owners of the company fared?
2 How productive have the company's investments in assets been with respect to profit?
3 How productive have the net assets been?

The relationship between the three ratios is shown in figure 9.3. For the purpose of consistency, profit before interest and tax (PBIT) is used throughout and is defined as sales minus (cost of sales plus indirect cost) or net profit (earnings) before interest and taxation. The actual meanings of the ratios are discussed below.

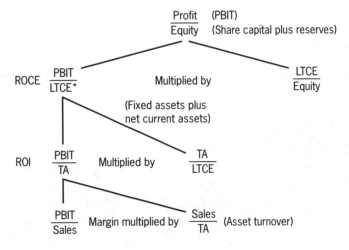

FIGURE 9.3   Relationship between ratios

Returns to owners $\dfrac{PBT}{Equity}$	Shows how well the legal owners of the company are faring. If analysis requires the amount of PBT which could be distributed to owners, then PBT becomes net earnings, i.e. profit after deducting tax and interest payments (PAIT). This latter ratio is the more commonly used.
Return on capital employed (ROCE) $\dfrac{PBIT}{LTCE}$	Shows the total profits which the invested capital has produced
Return on investment $\dfrac{PBIT}{TA}$	Shows the profit created by the firm's investment in both fixed and current assets

The rate of return on total assets can be broken down to show how profitability is made up:

$$\text{ROI} = \underset{\text{(Margin)}}{\frac{\text{PBIT}}{\text{TA}}} = \underset{\text{(Margin)}}{\frac{\text{PBIT}}{\text{Sales}}} \quad \times \quad \underset{\text{(Asset turnover)}}{\frac{\text{Sales}}{\text{TA}}}$$

The rate of return on capital employed can similarly be broken down as shown below:

$$\text{ROCE} = \underset{}{\frac{\text{PBIT}}{\text{LTCE}}} = \underset{\text{(Margin)}}{\frac{\text{PBIT}}{\text{Sales}}} \quad \times \quad \underset{\text{(Capital turnover)}}{\frac{\text{Sales}}{\text{LTCE}}}$$

Thus it is possible to see whether profit arises due to margin or turnover and which is the most important. In some industries, like food retailing, margins are traditionally low and thus turnover becomes a vital producer of profits.

The sources of data for calculating the appropriate ratios are shown in figure 9.4.

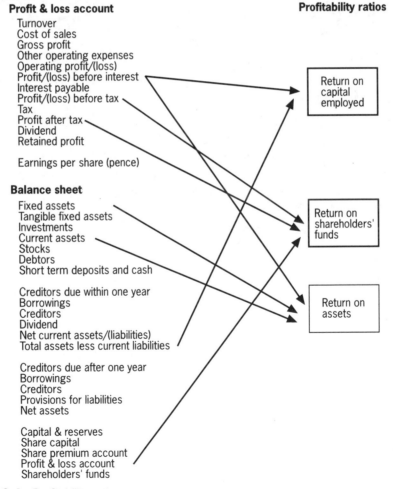

FIGURE 9.4   Profitability ratios

Trading Position

When examining a firm's trading position, analysis is designed to show what sort of returns are being made for a given sales level or investment in assets. Put another way, analysis should show the productivity of sales and assets and the relationships between them. Standard ratios which can be calculated in this area of analysis include:

$\dfrac{\text{Sales}}{\text{Capital}}$ — The number of times capital is represented in sales. Generally, if there have been no great distortions in either of the figures, the higher the ratio the better.

$\dfrac{\text{PBIT}}{\text{Sales}}$ — Operating profit to sales. Margin viewed over time shows one of the principal means of earning profit. Clearly, the higher the better, but any fall in margin would lead the analyst further to enquire ask why. Is margin being given up to maintain market share? Are costs out of control? etc.

$\dfrac{\text{Sales}}{\text{Fixed assets}}$ — How productive are the assets? Provided there are no distortions in either figure, the higher the ratio, the more productive the assets.

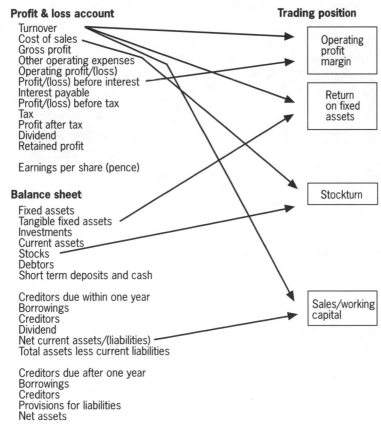

FIGURE 9.5 Trading ratios

$$\frac{\text{Sales}}{\text{Working capital}}$$ A similar ratio to the above in that it shows the productivity of net current assets.

$$\frac{\text{Sales}}{\text{Stockturn}}$$ How many times in a year is stock being turned over?

The sources of data for the calculation for the above is shown in figure 9.5.

Liquidity Position

Like many ratios, liquidity ratios have to be viewed in terms of the nature of the business. Many industries typically run on low liquidity margins. Further, a great deal depends upon when the final accounts are presented, and firms with seasonal earnings will exhibit quite differing degrees of liquidity throughout the year.

Current ratio $$\frac{\text{Current assets}}{\text{Current liabilities}}$$ Essentially poses the question 'Can the business pay its way in the near future, that is, if the stock is sold and debtors realized?'

Liquidity ratio $$\frac{\text{Liquid assets (current assets less stock)}}{\text{Current liabilities}}$$ 'Can the business pay its way immediately?'
'Acid test'

Technically, if the liquidity ratio is less than 1:1 the business is insolvent, but great care should be taken in making such statements as liquidity standards vary from industry to industry. The sources of data for the calculations of the above ratios is shown in in figure 9.6.

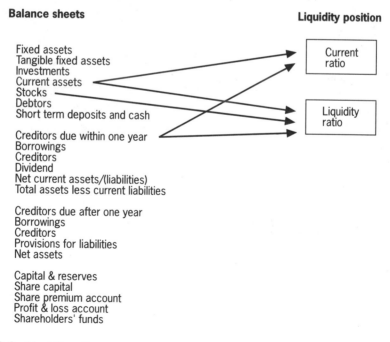

FIGURE 9.6   Liquidity ratios

Gearing

The two major sources of long-term funding for any business are loan capital and issued share capital. How a firm finances itself is a strategic decision, the results of which can have serious implications for the health of a company. The relationship between the two sources of finance is termed 'gearing' and is expressed as:

$$\frac{\text{Long-term loans}}{\text{Capital employed (loans + shareholders' funds)}}$$

	Company X	Company Y
No. of £1 issued shared	1,000	500
Long-term debt (10% interest)	–	500
	1,000	1,000

Thus company Y is 50% geared.

If the profit and loss accounts for the two companies are examined, then the picture in table 9.3 emerges.

TABLE 9.3 The effect of gearing

	Year 1		Year 2	
	Company X £	Company Y £	Company X £	Company Y £
Sales	1000	1000	1000	1000
PBIT	200	200	50	50
Interest payable	–	50	–	50
Profit remaining	200	150	50	–
Tax (50%)	100	75	25	–
Profit after interest and taxation	100	75	25	–
Earning per share	10p	15p	2.5p	–

The effect of gearing is that profit which could be distributed or ploughed back disappears to debt holders through interest payments and thus the ability of a firm to pay its interest becomes important. The impact of debt charges can be assessed by calculating a firm's interest cover expressed as:

$$\frac{\text{Profit before tax and interest}}{\text{Interest payable}}$$

Secondly, however, the earnings per share in the geared company are better than those in the ungeared company in year 1 because the geared company pays less tax. In year 2 the effect of gearing is to wipe out profit. Thus any firm has to recognize the long-term consequences of gearing in terms of the ability to pay the interest and the effect on profitability.

Earlier it was shown that the effect of gearing could be seen when arriving at profitability ratios. For example, returns to owners would be affected by gearing. Similarly, the composition of debt is important. As has been shown, firms can finance themselves by a mixture of long- and short-term debt; the relationship shown in table 9.1.

The sources of information for seeing calculations are shown in figure 9.7.

The constraints on the extent to which a company can grow can be determined by its ability to raise finance. Finance is raised from only two general sources: in the form of loans from banks, for example, and from the shareholders in the form of equity. All financing is at heart a variation of one of these. For example retained earnings are a form of equity in that they belong to the shareholders and are not distributed to them. In that sense they are equity. Similarly deferred tax owing to the government is a 'loan' from the government due to be paid at a future date just like a bank loan.

The key to raising finance from either of these two general sources of equity or loans is the past performance of the company. Bankers are happy to lend to successful companies and shareholders are happy to subscribe to rights issues or to retention of earnings when this is reflected in a rising share price. Hence there will be a maximum sustainable growth rate which will be determined by the rate of return by capital employed plus the dividend payout ratio of the firm. The maximum sustainable is determined by two variables, the determinants of ROCE and the payout ratio, as is shown below:

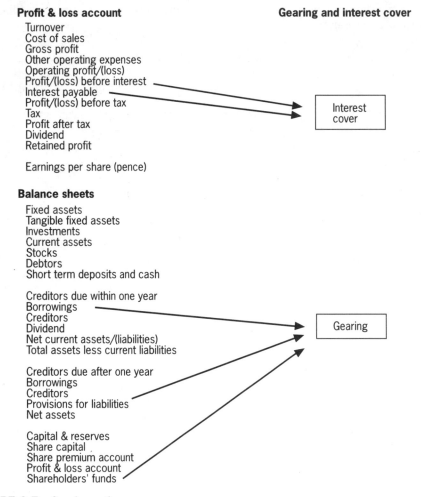

FIGURE 9.7   Gearing ratios

$$\text{Growth rate} = \frac{\text{Debt}}{\text{Equity}} (r-i) \, p + rp$$

where

r = return on capital employed
i = rate of interest
p = proportion of earnings retained

A simplified example is as follows:

	£mm
Sales	840
Profit before interest and tax	84
Interest paid	12
Profit before tax	76
Tax paid	26
Profit after tax	50
Dividends paid	25
Retained earnings	25
Debt	126
Equity	200

$$\text{Return on capital employed} = \frac{84}{326} = 0.257$$

$$\% \text{ Earnings retained} = \frac{25}{50} = 0.5$$

$$\text{Rate of interest} = \frac{12}{126}$$

$$G = \frac{126}{200} \, (0.257 - \frac{12}{126}) \frac{25}{50} + 0.257 \, (0.5)$$
$$= 0.18$$

The company therefore has a maximum sustainable growth rate capability of 18 per cent for the next year without recourse to further financing. If the company desired or planned for a higher growth rate than 18 per cent then it would need to take action on the component parts of the equation.

Debtors and Cash Flow

The ability of a company to collect the revenue is an important aspect of financial management and may be expressed as

$$\frac{\text{Debtors}}{\text{Sales}} \times 365, \text{ i.e. the number of days taken to collect debts.}$$

If the period is lengthening, this may indicate poor credit control or possibly the fact that the company is giving extended credit to gain sales. As with many ratios, much may depend upon the normal terms of trade in that industry.

While some of the ratios may be difficult to calculate from the data presented in final accounts, the information will be available within the company, thus allowing the internal analyst the opportunity to see the relationships between the ratios.

9.6   SHAREHOLDER RATIOS

A number of ratios are of interest, but what they all have in common is an attempt to demonstrate how well shareholders are faring in terms of earnings and assets in relation to their investment.

Earnings per share

This shows how much of the profit after tax has been earned per share. Although this represents earnings it will of course not all be distributed as dividend.

Dividend cover

This shows how many times the proposed dividend is covered by earnings. The higher the number the less is being paid out to shareholders as dividend. Clearly a low cover means that less is being retained in the business for future growth. Many companies attempt to have a long-term dividend policy, but clearly this is affected by the volatility of earnings and the aspirations of shareholders in terms of capital growth verses income from dividends.

Dividend per share

This shows how much dividend is being distributed per share to shareholders.

Net assets per share

This ratio shows what the assets of the company less the short-term debts are worth per share. Clearly the net asset figure will be a reflection, in part, of the company's depression and revaluation of assets policy. It could be seen as the value of the company ignoring any valuation for goodwill. The sources of data for the calculation of the above ratios are shown in figure 9.8.

Comparison

Any calculation of appropriate ratios for one year really does not tell the analyst a great deal. To provide a better basis of analysis, a comparative view should be taken, either with previous years or with similar organizations. However, to attempt analysis through time creates a difficulty due to the impact of inflation. Any financial appraisal should adjust for inflation in order to create a viable basis of comparison. How to adjust is relatively straightforward as is shown below in 9.7 'Adjusting for inflation'.

Several indices of inflation are available, perhaps the most useful being the RPI index of retail prices. This is published monthly in the *Employment Gazette* by the Department of Trade and Industry. However, for some industries this may be inappropriate, in which case *Price Indices for Current Cost Accounting* published by HMSO in the Business Monitor series may be utilized. This shows current indices for a variety of goods and services.

Comparative analysis with other companies can be difficult, as no two firms are exactly alike. However, it is possible to gather data via annual accounts to make comparisons, or, alternatively, data is commercially available from Inter-Firm

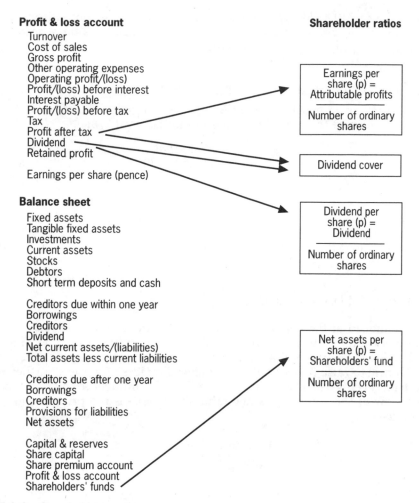

Profit & loss account

Turnover
Cost of sales
Gross profit
Other operating expenses
Operating profit/(loss)
Profit/(loss) before interest
Interest payable
Profit/(loss) before tax
Tax
Profit after tax
Dividend
Retained profit

Earnings per share (pence)

Balance sheet

Fixed assets
Tangible fixed assets
Investments
Current assets
Stocks
Debtors
Short term deposits and cash

Creditors due within one year
Borrowings
Creditors
Dividend
Net current assets/(liabilities)
Total assets less current liabilities

Creditors due after one year
Borrowings
Creditors
Provisions for liabilities
Net assets

Capital & reserves
Share capital
Share premium account
Profit & loss account
Shareholders' funds

Shareholder ratios

$$\text{Earnings per share (p)} = \frac{\text{Attributable profits}}{\text{Number of ordinary shares}}$$

Dividend cover

$$\text{Dividend per share (p)} = \frac{\text{Dividend}}{\text{Number of ordinary shares}}$$

$$\text{Net assets per share (p)} = \frac{\text{Shareholders' fund}}{\text{Number of ordinary shares}}$$

FIGURE 9.8   Shareholder – ratios

Comparisons, Extel and Datastream. Much of this information is now accessible by computer terminal. The purpose of such a cross-sectional analysis is to point up where there are differences in performance as measured by ratios and then to begin the necessary investigations into these differences.

9.7   ADJUSTING FOR INFLATION

If sales and profits are considered for two years, 1980 and 1990, it can be seen that there has been an *actual* increase in both figures

	Sales (£m)	Profit (£m)
1980	1,000	100
1990	2,000	125

However, if inflation is taken into account, a different picture emerges. The rate of inflation over the period can be taken into consideration by taking from the index of inflation figures (see above for source) the numbers for these years. They are: 1980 = 70.7, and 1990 = 125.7. Thus £70.7 in 1980 would buy the same amount of goods as £125.7 in 1990. Hence, it is necessary, if meaningful comparisons are to be made, to adjust the figures to take account of the fall in the value of money.

1980 £s must be multiplied by 125.7/70.7 = 1.778

or

1990 £s must be multiplied by 70.7/125.7 = 0.562

If the figures are adjusted to 1990 £s, the 1990 figures (£2,000m, and £125m) remain the same and the 1980 figures are multiplied by 1.778.

	Sales £m	Profits £m
1980 figures at 1990 prices	1,000*1.778 = 1778	100*1.778 = 178
1990 figures at 1990 prices	2000	125

(figures are rounded)

Thus what looked like a doubling of sales (£1,000m in 1980, £2,000 in 1990) is in real terms only [((2,000–1778)/1778)*100 = 12.5%] a 12.5% increase, and a 25% increase in profits (£100 in 1980, £125 in 1990) is in real terms [((125–178)/178)*100 –29.8%] a 29.8% *fall* in profits.

9.8   SHARE VALUATION AND STRATEGY

As was mentioned at the beginning of the chapter, the performance of a company is a matter of interest to many parties. Thus the performance of a company as reflected in its share price is a visible commentary by the Stock Exchange. The ability of a firm to raise finance will be influenced by its share price. Further, certain key strategic events such as takeovers are heavily influenced by the Stock Exchange's view of the company. A key ratio in this area is the price/earnings ratio expressed as

$$\frac{\text{CURRENT share price}}{\text{LAST REPORTED earnings per share}}$$

As can be seen, this will alter daily depending on the company's share price. Of itself, the price/earnings (p/e) ratio is not a particularly useful piece of information, except that it shows the market's assessment of the company. Generally, a firm with a high p/e ratio is indicative of the fact that the market expects more from the company.

The p/c ratio indicates how many years it would take to get back the purchase price at the current rate of earnings, assuming all earnings were paid out. This assumes zero growth in earnings. However, in the case of a takeover, the p/e ratio assumes a more important role. Supposing Company A is bidding for Company B and the following information is available:

	Company A	Company B
Issued shares (000s)	1000	500
Earnings last year (£000)	100	50
then Earnings per share (EPS) (in pence)	10	10
Price of shares (in pence)	100	100
p/e ratio	10	10

The market value of Company B is £½m, namely price of shares (£1) multiplied by number of shares (500,000); thus Company A in a share offer will have to offer Company B shareholders either £500,000 cash or 500,000 of its own shares, i.e.

$$\frac{\text{Value of Company}}{\text{Share price}} \text{ or } \frac{£500,000}{100p}$$

If, however, the share price of A is 200p with a p/e ratio of 20, then only half the number of its own shares would have to be offered, i.e.

$$\frac{£500,000 \text{ (B)}}{200p \quad \text{(A)}} = 250,000$$

The obvious attraction of having to offer only half the number of shares, by having a p/e which is higher than the 'stock market average', places a premium on boosting and maintaining a high share price.

While the role of the p/e in takeovers is important, it is not the only factor to be considered in such strategies. For a fuller list of the issues involved, see chapter 16.

9.9   CASH FLOW

Cash flow is as important to a company as its profitability. This is because cash represents the 'life blood' of the company, allowing it to continue trading and also because lack of internal funding may necessitate the company having to raise money from outside, with the consequent effects on performance of interest repayment. Further, a profitable company can have a cash problem due to its success. For example, investment in new machinery may require new finance, increasing stocks may have to be financed from outside, and proposed takeovers may have a high liquidity content. Thus, for many companies, cash management is of equal importance to profitability.

Cash flows can present a number of problems to an organization. If demand is seasonal then cash flows will be seasonal, which means that often production takes place with little inflow of revenue; similarly, in the longer term, cyclical movements in demand may affect cash flow. From a strategic point of view these phenomena ought to be recognized and built into the forecasting process, so that cash shortfalls are seen in advance. The credit control system, while not increasing the size of the cash flow, should be designed to ensure that the speed of collection is such that it meets the firm's liquidity needs.

Although cash management in a strategic sense is concerned with future flows and amounts, a useful historical technique which may be used to assist in prediction is sources and uses of funds analysis. Basically, the analysis focuses on how the firm was financed and the uses which were made of such funds. Thus a source of funds would be any decrease in assets or an increase in a liability, while a use of funds would be represented by an increase in assets or a decrease in liabilities. This is shown in an expanded form below.

Sources

- increases in retained earnings;
- increases in borrowings;
- increases in issued capital;
- reductions in cash;
- reductions in stocks;
- reductions in debtors;
- sales of investments;
- sales of equipment, plant, land and buildings.

Uses

- increases in assets;
- increases in stocks;
- increases in debtors;
- reduction in creditors.

Thus it is possible to see where the funds came from and where they went. Most published accounts now include such a statement, making it possible to analyse funds flows in an evaluative manner.

9.10   MANAGEMENT SUMMARY AND CHECKLIST

The remit of financial analysis should be sets of ratios and statements which allow the company to take a comparative view of its health. As such, the process and its outcome are an integral part of strategic appraisal.

A useful method of summarizing the financial analysis of a company is shown below.

Ratio or area of interest	Our company	Similar company or industrial sector	Comment
Profitability			
ROCE			
ROI			
Trading			
Sales/Capital employed			
PBIT/Sales			
Sales/FA			
Sales/WC			
Sales/Stocks			
Liquidity			
Current ratio			
Acid test			
Gearing			
Loans/CE			
Dividend cover			
Debtor days			
Shareholder ratios			
EPS growth			
Dividend cover			
Dividend per share growth			
Net assets per share growth			

Introduction – Value Chain Analysis – Benchmarking – Profit Impact of Market Strategy – Cost and Strategy – The Balanced Score Card – Management Summary and Checklist

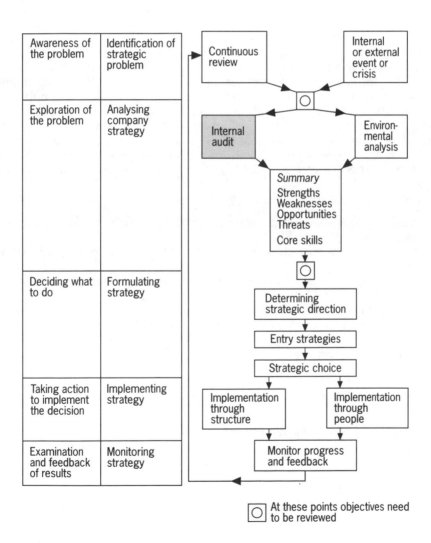

FIGURE 10.1 The strategic decision-making process

10.1 INTRODUCTION

Chapter 9 dealt exclusively with the financial aspects of strategic analysis. This chapter looks at other methods for exploring performance and for making comparisons with other organizations including competitors. As with all forms of internal appraisal the ultimate goal of such analysis is to create strategies on known capabilities and further to be able to discover sources of potential competitive advantage from the resource base of the organization. Much attention is now focused on understanding where an organization derives its value added and in turn where competitors derive their advantage. This has given an increased impetus to analyse performance by benchmarking against others and to understand more fully the behaviour of costs associated with strategies in particular markets.

10.2 VALUE CHAIN ANALYSIS

In the never-ending search for competitive advantage organizations attempt to discover, by analysis, where they have a potential source of such advantage, which through renewal they can deploy against the competition. For example, a firm which wishes to outperform its competitors through differentiating itself through quality will have to perform its value chain activities better than the opposition, a policy based on cost leadership will necessitate a reduction in the costs associated with the value adding process or a reduction in the amount of resource used.

Value chain analysis proposes a systems view of the organization composed of stages in a transformation process with inputs and outputs to each of the distinct stages. Porter[1] proposes such a model based on what he terms primary and support activities.

Primary activities include:

- Inbound logistics – all those activities concerned with receiving and storing externally sourced materials.
- Operations – the manufacture of products and services. Inputs transformed to outputs.
- Outbound logistics – all those activities associated with getting finished goods to buyers.
- Marketing and sales – Essentially an information activity informing buyers and consumers about products and services as well as their prices.
- Service – All those activities associated with maintaining product performance after the product has been sold.

Additionally Porter proposed a series of support activities which essentially are management systems and procedures supporting the primary activities. These include:

- Procurement – Managing the information flows surrounding the acquisition of resources.
- Human resource management – those activities concerned with sourcing, developing, motivating and rewarding the workforce.
- Technology development – managing the knowledge base of the organization.
- Infrastructure – Managing support systems and functions such as finance, planning, quality control and general senior management.

Porter states that these activities, in addition to supporting the primary ones, can themselves be a source of competitive advantage.

Diagrammatically the system and its associated activities can be seen in figure 10.2. Value chain analysis can be broken down into a number of sequential steps.

1   Break down the organization into its key activities. This is accomplished by itemizing each of the activities performed under the various major headings in the model.
2   Once the activities have been identified then the potential for adding value via cost advantage or differentiation can be assessed. Similarly any disadvantage can be exposed. (Companies add value to bought-in materials and services which is represented as turnover.)
3   Strategies can benefit from one-off transitory advantages but generally any organization seeks to base its strategy on a sustainable comparative advantage. Many advantages do not of themselves remain in an advantageous position. They need to be capable of renewal, hence a major source of competitive advantage is the ability of an organization to renew and thus sustain its advantage against competitors.

Such a process is not without analytical problems. Some parts of the organization may be difficult to break down, the required information may not be available, some process may be linked and any advantage is the result of such linkages. Over-disaggregation may result in units of analysis which cannot provide advantage, under-disaggregation may not reveal the sources of potential competitive advantage.

The analysis of the value chain has allowed companies to respond more quickly than competitors. In turn this led companies to understand better the notion of quality and responsiveness.

Total quality management has emerged as a powerful approach to understanding the needs of the buyer and the appropriate responses required within the organization to deliver a level of quality which results in buyer satisfaction. Competitive

Primary activities

Inbound logistics	Operations	Outbound logistics	Marketing & sales	Service
Warehousing Materials handling Inventory control Scheduling	Manufacturing Packaging Assembly Maintenance	Warehousing Shipping Order processing Scheduling	Pricing Distribution channel management promotion	After sales service Training

Supported by

Procurement	Human resource development	Technology development	Infrastructure
Purchasing physical resources	Recruiting Rewarding Developing Firing	Equipping Learning	Organizational design Staff functions

FIGURE 10.2   Generic value chain

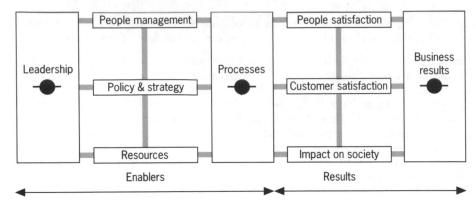

FIGURE 10.3 The European total quality award model
Source: European Foundation for total quality management, Brussels 1994.

pressures have forced companies to think of delighting buyers rather than simply satisfying them. This general process has been institutionalized in the USA by the creation of the Malcolm Baldrige Award for companies who have excelled internationally. This is now mirrored in Europe by the establishment of the EFQM (European Foundation for Quality Management) which has similar attributes. The general EFQM model is shown in figure 10.3.

In addition to the total quality management approach some companies have realized that speed of learning and implementation can be a source of competitive advantage. This has led some authors to think of time-based competition. Stalk and Hout[2] have shown a direct relationship between responsiveness of companies and profitability. For many companies speed of response is a customer-valued attribute. The response requires companies to take a holistic view of the value chain, but perhaps more importantly to prioritize responsiveness as a strategic imperative. This necessitates strong managerial action in eliminating waste, downtime and non-value-adding activities.

10.3   BENCHMARKING

Of prime importance is an organization's ability to compare itself to others. As was pointed out in chapter 9 cross-sectional analysis of financial ratios is an important step in strategic analysis. Bench marking involves the creation of a continuous process of measuring an organization's products and services, procedures and processes against successful competitors and leading companies in other industries. From bench marking companies can discover best practice and how to implement it. In some companies it is now a normal procedure to match yourself against 'best in class' as a method of improving performance. This may involve measurement against many different organizations in order to fully cover all the functions.

Clearly in order to be able to benchmark successfully any company must have a knowledge of own and competitor's strengths and weaknesses, which in turn requires the establishment of a competitive intelligence system. For many larger organizations the ability to compare different divisions allows for a form of internal benchmarking. Competitive benchmarking is a now common process of comparing and understanding competitive activity. For many organizations functional benchmarking can be accomplished without commercial pressures as best in class may be in a totally unrelated industry. This has given rise to benchmarking clubs where non-competing firms regularly exchange information.

10.4 PROFIT IMPACT OF MARKET STRATEGY

For some time managers intuitively knew that scale and market share had an effect on costs of production and marketing. The Strategic Planning Institute[3] has built up a large database of over 3,000 companies containing over 100 variables per company. It has identified key drivers of profitability including:

- relative market share (your market share in relation to the market leader);
- relative product quality;
- investment intensity (investment as a proportion of value added);
- market growth rates;
- capacity utilization;
- operating effectiveness (actual to expected employee productivity).

These and other variables allow managers to see the effect of strategic decision making. The PIMS results allow companies to measure themselves against the 'par' findings (a report showing what profitability should be given the company's input data to the model).

The findings are not without problems, some of which are discussed below.

- Are larger firms the result of innate efficiency or the ability to buy share?
- Can the PIMS variables be significantly altered in the short run?
- If certain industries are profitable why don't more enter?

Despite the criticisms the PIMS data is useful to managers as a reference point to the chosen strategy. Fundamentally share and scale effect both costs and market power, aspects of which are discussed below.

10.5 COST AND STRATEGY

An important influence on strategic choice is the behaviour of cost in an organization. This in turn is influenced by the firm's cost structure and its scale of operations. Strategic cost analysis allows the firm to identify the sources of cost advantage and their potential for building strategies based upon them. It further results in appropriate data for further reducing costs to improve the competitive position of the firm. The effect of scale is twofold, Increases in scale have automatic effects due to the fact that certain costs do not rise at the same rate as output. Fixed costs fall at a faster rate than the rate of increase in variable cost, such that in the long run there will be an output at which costs are minimised, which in turn will be the minimum efficient scale for the plant.

Secondly, increased experience due to increases in output of standard product allows the firm to 'learn' how to do things better. This latter effect is not automatic, it has to be acted upon in a conscious manner. Cost reductions due to learning have been estimated at up to 20–30 per cent when output doubles. A full list of potential sources of cost advantage and thus a useful framework for analysis has been proposed by Grant[4] (see figure 10.4).

Recent emphasis by such commentators as Peters and Waterman on the management and motivation of staff have shown that productivity gains can be accomplished as much by the proper management of staff as by efforts to increase scale and efficiency. Finally it should be noted that zealous efforts to reduce cost can result in a form of corporate anorexia which leaves little spare resource for growth and the resultant low prices may not be appreciated by customers.

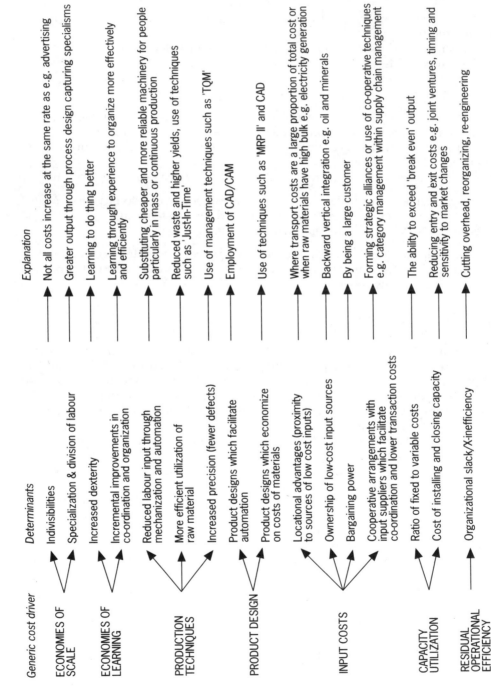

FIGURE 10.4 Sources of cost advantage

Adapted from Grant: *Contemporary Strategy Analysis*, 2nd edition, Blackwell, 1995. [5]

Market power can be the result of increasing share. Market power results in companies becoming less prone to the competitive process and can convey conditions of market leadership whereby the company can set the 'rules' for market conduct. Notwithstanding competition policy it would pay a company to increase share in low margin, low differentiation markets in order to gain power. High market share allows a company to set prices and the pace of competitive behaviour, such companies also have the ability to react strongly to attempts to lessen their market power.

10.6   THE BALANCED SCORE CARD

An approach to an overall method of tracking performance was proposed by Kaplan and Norton via what they call 'the balanced score card'. The score card is designed to be comprehensive and includes a number of generic measures such as:-

i   financial e.g. ROCE, ROI, eps, cash flow
ii   internal measures e.g. cost, productivity, yield.
iii customer e.g. sales, delivery time, relationships with customers.
iv   innovation and learning e.g. speed of new product development, learning time, technological advantage (see figure 10.5).

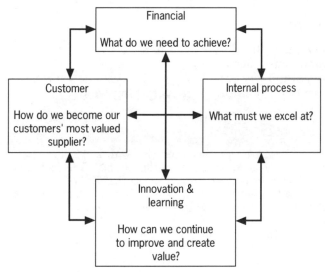

FIGURE 10.5   The balanced scorecard

10.7   MANAGEMENT SUMMARY AND CHECKLIST

Value Chain analysis

Steps

1   Describe the value chain for the production of product or service. Identify the primary and support functions.
2   Look for the linkages between the activities. These consist of the relationships between one activity and the cost of another. Advantage arises from finding more efficient or effective linkages.
3   Look for synergies between activities.

Benchmarking

1 A process for comparing yourself against either competitors or 'best in class'.
2 Benchmarking can be of total organizations or specific functions.

PIMS

1 Key questions
   How do we compare with the industry norms?
   How do our strategic variables which effect strategic performance compare?
   Is it possible to construct a strategy which is different from industry norms?
2 What are the effects of scale on strategic choices?

Costs and strategy

1 What are the effects of scale and experience on cost?
2 What other management techniques can assist in bringing costs down?
   Production techniques
   Design
   buying more effectively
   Managing people more effectively

Balanced scorecard

1 How financially successful do we need to be?
2 How do we retain customer loyalty?
3 What have we got to be good at?
4 How can we contiuously improve in everything we do?

NOTES

1 M. E. Porter *Competitive Advantage* (Free Press, New York 1985).
2 George Stalk Jnr and Thomas M. Hout, *Competing Against Time: How Time-Based Competition is Reshaping Global Markets* (Free Press, New York, 1990).
3 Robert D. Buzzell and Bradley T. Gale, *The PIMS Principles* (Free Press, New York 1987).
4 Robert M. Grant, *Contemporary Strategy Analysis – Concepts, Techniques, Applications* (Blackwell, Oxford 1991).
5 Robert S. Kaplan and David Norton, 'The Balanced Score Card – Measures that Drive Performance' *Harvard Business Review* Jan–Feb pp. 17–79 1992.

Introduction – Sources of Competitive Advantage –
Matching Competitive Advantage with Market Needs – The
Sustainability of Competitive Advantage – Strategy as Stretch
and Leverage – Management Summary and Checklist

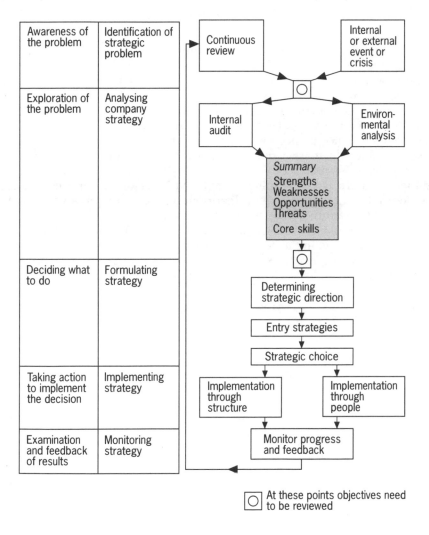

FIGURE 11.1　The strategic decision-making process

11.1 INTRODUCTION

The critical success factors required to be successful in a given industry and the competitive advantages of the firm are opposite sides of the same coin. If the company can so organize itself that it offers exactly those features which are essential to the customers in the industry then it will be achieving its profitability targets.

The analysis of the resources and capabilities of a company (see part 3) must be undertaken after the external analysis (see part 2), as it is difficult to determine whether a particular feature is a strength or weakness unless it is evaluated against the market which it is seeking to supply. In such an assessment it is possible to determine both the importance of a given feature and how good the company is at satisfying that aspect of the customer's requirement.

Coverage of the detailed sources of competitive advantage are shown on figure 11.2 and expanded upon in the three previous chapters. In this chapter it is intended to provide an overview of competitive advantage.

11.2 SOURCES OF COMPETITIVE ADVANTAGE

Competitive advantages can arise from any of three sources: core competences, tangible assets, and intangible assets.

A core competence is an individual skill, for instance financial control, or an integrated combination of skills such as the ability to successfully integrate an acquired company into the acquiring firm. Other examples could be the ability to bring new products to market more quickly than competitors, or to organize the firm to be lowest cost producer.

Tangible assets are land, buildings, plant, machinery and vehicles and may be found either in the manufacturing or distribution parts of the organization. An R & D facility would be another type of tangible asset.

Competences and tangible assets are the more obvious sources for differential advantage but often it is the intangible assets that are as, or more, important. They are often the result of a core competence, for instance, research and development skills may result in a patent, and specific manufacturing skills may lead to the firm becoming

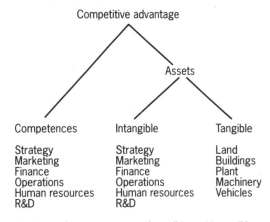

Combinations of competences and tangible and intangible assets

FIGURE 11.2 Sources of competitive advantage

lowest cost producer, which is an intangible asset. Some examples of intangible assets are shown below.

- *Supplier* – contracts, licences, special access to inputs.
- *Company* – reputation, networks.
- *Product* – patents, trademarks and copyright.
- *Marketing* – information, databases.
- *Operations* – proprietary processes, adaptable workforce, economies of scale, lowest cost producer.
- *Customers* – contracts, licences, loyalty.

Competitive advantage is usually the result of combinations of factors rather than arising from one single source.

11.3   MATCHING COMPETITIVE ADVANTAGE WITH MARKET NEEDS

Any feature of a supplier's product or service is only a competitive advantage if it meets customers' needs in sufficient volume as to enable the supplier to make a profit. The aggregated profile of customer needs, the market, is represented as M on figure 11.3.

However, although a market is a collection of customers who have similar needs, it is evident that, while there will be a great similarity in requirements, there will also be some differences. These may be real or perceived, although any perceived difference

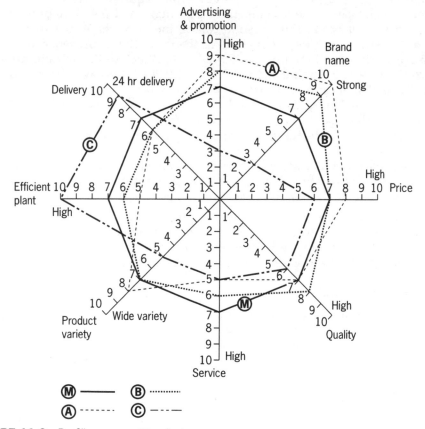

FIGURE 11.3 Profiling competitive features

is, to the buyer, real. Thus, even suppliers who are operating in the most competitive markets, in this example through branding, can do things differently. The two companies competing through branding are represented by companies A and B.

However, if a manufacturer decides to compete by supplying an own-label version for retailers then that firm would be competing on a completely different basis and its profile would be correspondingly different, represented by C on figure 11.3.

This type of profiling may help both to improve the competitive position of the firm and highlight potential areas for expansion.

11.4. THE SUSTAINABILITY OF COMPETITIVE ADVANTAGE

As the environment in which firms operate is constantly changing, so that which is a competitive advantage today may not be tomorrow. The analyst is therefore concerned with three questions:

1 What is the effect of changes in the environment on our key competitive advantages?
2 What competitive advantages are going to be needed in order to succeed in the future?
3 Is there any way that key competitive advantages can be embedded and protected?

The underlying issue in the first question is, how quickly will changes in the environment significantly erode competitive advantage and therefore profitability? The data for the answer to this question can be found in chapters 5 to 10 which cover a full internal and external analysis of the firm. The data needed to answer question 2 is again to be found in chapters 5 to 10. Which of the existing skills are being eroded or are becoming redundant? What new skills will be required to successfully implement future plans? How can they be acquired?

Hamel and Prahalad,[1] Hamel and Heene[2] and Kay[3] have made significant contributions to the discussion of competitive advantage, and in particular to the issues of developing, embedding and sustaining competitive advantage which is the focus of question 3.

There are some obvious ways by which competitive advantage can be sustained, such as patents and strong brand names. Others may be more difficult to identify precisely but may be equally effective. For instance, Hanson has developed skills in;

- identifying bid prospects which have untapped potential;
- paying a price which does not reflect the full potential;
- integrating the firm into the Hanson way of doing business; or
- at an appropriate time divesting parts of the firm for a greater price than that paid for them;
- developing the confidence of City financiers and the stock market.

None of these skills are unique and are apparently easily copied, but in combination and in their execution by the senior managers who run the firm they have provided the company with a competitive advantage which few have been able to emulate over a period of more than 20 years. This does not mean they will continue to be appropriate for the future, as is evidenced by another company – Lonrho – which had a successful recipe that lasted for 20 years, but which has now fallen from its previous heights.

These recipes, when broken into their constituent parts, often reveal ordinary skills and resources which could be individually replicated but which together represent formidable competition. These skills, which are usually the most important factor in developing competitive advantage, are built up over time and, from experience and training.

Although it is obvious, from outside the firm and with hindsight, that even recipes which have enjoyed long-term success do not go on forever, it is not always appreciated inside the company. Thus the 'perceptions' of top management concerning the future of the market are *vitally* important. Too many companies are governed by thoughts such as 'why change things that are going so well?' and 'we've done it like this for 20 years and it's always worked so far.' Indeed, poor top management perceptions concerning the future of their industry is the key reason why companies get into financial difficulties (see chapter 15). The sad thing is that they usually have access to the data but cannot, or will not, view it objectively. This is sometimes because the conclusions create a kind of petrifying fear, or often because of an over-sentimental attachment to products, customers or employees.

Learning to forget the past is overstating the case, but it is important to convince those who determine strategy to believe that the future will not be the same as the past and therefore some things will have to change. The mix of competences and resources needs to be reviewed with a completely open mind.

11.5 STRATEGY AS STRETCH AND LEVERAGE

Hamel and Prahalad[1] have contributed to the understanding of competitiveness through the concepts of 'stretch' and 'leverage'. Although it may seem that the big and powerful companies will be able to control the future of their industries, the history of business shows that this is not so. Of the top 1,000 companies in 1970 only some 140 remained as independent operating units by 1990. How do British Airways, Bodyshop, Waterstones bookshops and Amstrad succeed when they have far less power and a much lower resource base than their bigger rivals, respectively, Pan Am, Boots, W. H. Smith and IBM? Stretch is perhaps best defined as 'doing the impossible' or where 'ambition outpaces resources'. It requires a *total* commitment to achieve the desired goal which is communicated to and accepted by the whole workforce. Stretch is reaching out into new territory and discovering new things. Without a vision, the necessary commitment and the desire to embrace a different future, firms become ossified and provide a chink in their armour which will provide the opening for some much smaller competitor, who has these attributes, to enter.

Leverage is concerned with 'lean everything'. It is about getting the most out of resources. However, it is focused on using the resources to better effect rather than on reducing resources in terms of downsizing or delayering. Leverage can be achieved in five ways. Firstly, by focusing resources on key objectives. Secondly, by accumulating resources more effectively. (The firm is a vast reservoir of knowledge about operational processes, customers and competitors which needs to be mined for information which will improve the competitive position.) The third means of levering is to blend and balance resources to provide better results. The fourth is to conserve resources by constant use which would be reflected in learning curve analysis (see chapter 7.10) and by ensuring as far as possible that the firm does not present opportunities for competitors to attack. Finally, leverage can be effected by reducing the time between expenditure on the resources and the revenues flowing from them.

Some of the ways of exploiting stretch and leverage can be found in chapter 18.

As a conclusion to this analysis of competitive advantage, it may be helpful to redefine the firm and explain some of the resulting implications. Rather than define the firm as an organization which provides goods and services, it is better to think of it as 'a learning organization which is seeking to get to the future first'.

The first result of this definition will be that senior managers must spend a considerable proportion of their time in designing the future of their company. Given their other responsibilities, they will need to adopt some system by which data is available for them to do this. In previous times this is what corporate planning was intended to do, but in many firms it became too bureaucratic or was organizationally not sufficiently near the board. Even the title was unfortunate in that what is required is not planning but rather strategic thinking, not only on where the firm should be in the future, but what long-term competitive advantages can be embedded in the firm and the means by which this could be done.

Finally, is the firm continually learning systematically from its own successes and failures and those of others, or is such information held by various personnel in a rather vague and unco-ordinated way? In the final analysis it is the interpretation of this data which will determine who gets to the future first.

11.6   MANAGEMENT SUMMARY AND CHECKLIST

1   Sources of competitive Advantage

- core competences;
- tangible assets;
- intangible assets.

2   Matching Competitive Advantage with Market Needs

Profiling competitors against the critical success factors in the market should help to improve both the competitive position of the firm and highlight potential areas for expansion.

3   The Sustainability of Competitive Advantage

As the environment in which firms operate is constantly changing, they need to evaluate the appropriateness of their competitive advantages against their future plans continually.

The key that leads to success is to develop a combination of skills which, while capable of being replicated individually, are together capable of withstanding the test of time.

Learning not to regard past success as an everlasting recipe for the future is very important. Executives from successful companies often find it difficult to accept that the environment in which they operate has changed and that the recipe will definitely need to be reviewed and may need changing.

4   Strategy as Stretch and Leverage

As firms grow there can be a tendency to become bureaucratic, complacent and to lose their entrepreneurial flair. Stretch focuses mostly on entrepreneurship and the reaching out to new and greater goals and also to the communication and adoption of the vision throughout the workforce.

Leverage is more concerned with the use of resources but focuses more on exploiting them rather than reducing them through downsizing and delayering.

NOTES

1   Gary Hamel and C. K. Prahalad, *Competing for the Future*, (Harvard Business School Press, 1994).
2   Gary Hamel and Aime Heene (eds), *Competence Based Competition*, (John Wiley and Sons, 1994).
3   John Kay, *Foundations of Corporate Success*, (Oxford University Press 1993).

PART 4

Identifying Strategic Alternatives

12 Strategic Direction

Introduction – No Change Strategy – Vertical Integration – Diversification – Strategy Based on Other Criteria – Management Summary and Checklist

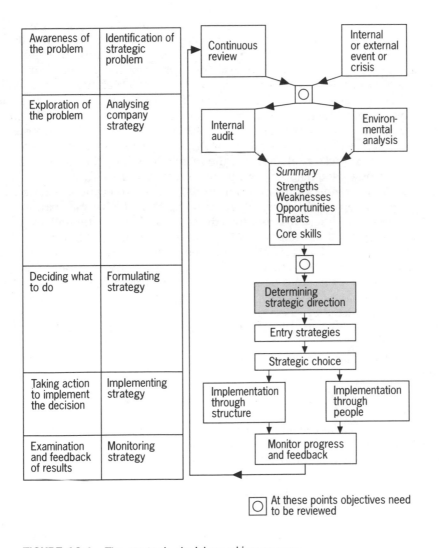

FIGURE 12.1 The strategic decision-making process

12.1   INTRODUCTION

The internal and external analysis has provided answers to the question 'Where is this company *now*?' The next stage is to determine what action the business needs to take to secure the desired long-term profitability goals. This is known as formulating strategy. There are several steps in the process of formulating strategy. Initially, it is important to decide on which products and markets offer the best means of achieving long-term company objectives. This is the concern of this chapter.

All the issues concerned in the question 'Where does this company go from here?' are outlined in this chapter. However, some issues are of such importance that they are discussed in separate chapters. The complexity of the factors relating to geographical expansion has promoted a substantial body of research. As such, chapter 13 'Global Strategies' provides some insight into the complex decisions concerning geographical expansion.

In most company portfolios there are products which are past the growth stage in the product life-cycle. The process of managing products which are in a declining market is important, and strategies for this process are outlined in chapter 14. If companies fail to adopt appropriate strategies for declining products or for other reasons, they may experience a significant decline in profitability or even collapse. In such cases, there is often a fine dividing line between collapse and recovery. Chapter 15 evaluates the factors leading to collapse and the features of the situation which will or will not make recovery possible. Thus part 4 is concerned with identifying a range of possible strategic alternatives and part 5 is concerned with the choice between these strategies and the means by which they will be executed, for instance through acquisition, divestment or internal growth.

There has been a tendency in corporate strategy texts either to focus on growth or to assume growth as an objective. However, in spite of this preoccupation, growth is rarely defined and reasons for growth as an objective are not always fully discussed. The implicit assumption is that growth means an increase in sales and profitability. However, the correlation between increases in sales and increases in profitability is negligible. In other words, increases in return on capital employed can be achieved by companies irrespective of their growth in sales.[1]

All companies have continually to review their product market offering as the environment in which they operate is constantly changing. Thus, alterations to their portfolio may result in growth, stability or a reduction in size as measured by sales or capital employed.

There are five basic directions that a company can explore when planning its future strategy:

- No change: manufacture or supply the same product or service to the same customers.
- Backward vertical integration: to manufacture or supply a product or service which is currently purchased from another company.
- Forward vertical integration: to manufacture or supply a product or service which is currently produced by a customer.
- Product extension: the development of the product offering from the existing product, through variants, to a completely new product offering.
- Market extension: the development of the markets served from the existing markets through entry to new segments, to sales to a completely different market.

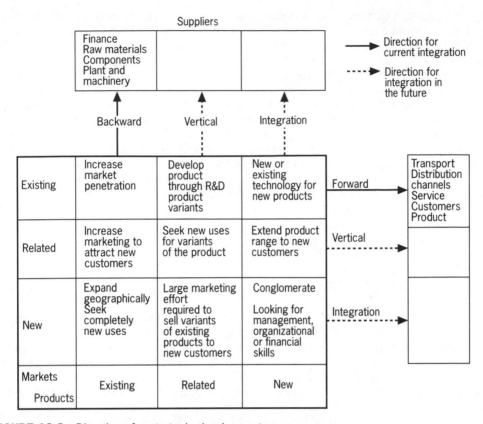

FIGURE 12.2   Directions for strategic development

The interaction of product and market extension leads to a variety of more specific directions, as can be seen in figure 12.2.

12.2 NO CHANGE STRATEGY

There are several reasons why a company may pursue a strategy of no change in the short or medium term, although almost all companies will need to change in the longer run.

The first reason for a strategy of no change with respect to markets or products could be that maintaining or increasing market share at the early stages of the product life-cycle is the best use of available resources and that diversification will not enhance earnings. Secondly, that risks associated with diversification are not commensurate with the expected returns; and, thirdly, cash or other resources are not available.

12.3 VERTICAL INTEGRATION

The reasons why companies pursue strategies of vertical integration are complex. A basic classification of such reasons is defensive/offensive. Defensive reasons are to ensure the supply or quality of some essential raw material or component (backward integration) or to ensure an outlet for the product (forward integration). For instance, many holiday tour operators purchased aeroplanes in order to guarantee availability and quality of that part of the 'package' holiday. In the past, breweries purchased public houses to guarantee an outlet for their beer.

While defensive reasons for vertical integration are pursued by the company for self-protection purposes, there is little research to explain either the reasons for or the success of vertical integration. It is suggested that it is a high-risk strategy, in that a wholly vertically integrated company is more vulnerable than a horizontally diversified company as an interruption to one part of the process affects the total entity. There is some agreement that vertical integration does not take place at the early stages of the life-cycle and that, where it has done so, profitability has been depressed. Likewise, when the product is in decline vertical disintegration is a means of exiting from the industry gradually.

Most firms are a mixture of vertical and horizontal integration, with few of the sub-units being sole suppliers of any one other sub-unit within the firm. For instance, a carton-manufacturing company may sell cartons to several businesses within its own limited company and also sell to firms outside its own parent. More detailed explanation of linkages, their advantages and disadvantages can be found elsewhere.[2]

12.4 DIVERSIFICATION

There is no generally agreed definition of diversification as a strategy. In this section diversification will be used to describe extensions to the current portfolio on both the product and market dimensions. It is important to note that, while many of the frameworks (figure 12.2 for example) used to describe and analyse the product-market portfolio suggest one or two discrete categories, relatedness to existing products or markets is on a continuum from very closely related to no relationship at all.

An outline of the impact of alterations to the product-market portfolio is given in figure 12.2. Only existing products/existing markets would not be regarded as diversification, although existing products or markets to related products or markets would not constitute a significant change from current activity. It is supposed that the further a company moves from its existing product-market portfolio and the resultant core skills and key resources, the greater the possibility of failure. Unfortunately, the research evidence on diversification and performance is somewhat contradictory and, therefore, the expectation remains unsubstantiated.

It is important to note that *acquisition and diversification are not synonymous*. Acquisition may not lead to diversification (for instance, merging with a competitor) and diversification may be achieved through development within the company. Thus the reasons outlined below for prompting companies to seek products and markets outside their existing business relate to diversification and not acquisition, although some may be relevant to both. Acquisitions are discussed in chapter 16.

The first reason for pursuing a policy of diversification is that the current products and markets are incapable of meeting growth or profitability objectives. The emergence of a gap between objectives and expected results can be caused by the raising of objectives by an aggressive management or a shortfall in revenue and profit or a combination of the two. A closely associated reason is when a hitherto unforeseen opportunity occurs to increase profitability. Similarly, development through the firm's R&D department may lead to a diversification opportunity; there is the example of the Doulton pottery group diversifying into damp proofing of houses.

Some other motivations for diversification are:

- the advent of spare cash;
- the spreading of risk;
- the need to obtain some specific skills or resources which will significantly improve the performance of the existing business.

1 *Product line extension* is the addition to the portfolio of new products, some of which will be in a related technology and others in a completely new technology. As many manufacturing companies often have significant distinctive technical knowledge and skills, they tend to stay in a given or closely related technology and expand into new or related markets. Less frequently, companies add a new product and a new technology to existing or related customers. This is usually effected through an acquisition; an example is the Lloyds Bank acquisition of Cheltenham and Gloucester Building Society.

2 *Marker extension* is the extension of the range of markets served by existing related or new products or services; for example, Allied Carpets move into curtains and furniture. Additionally, market extension can take the form of geographical expansion on a national basis, as in the case of Sainsbury's gradual move from the south of England through the midlands to the north. Also, the expansion can take place across national frontiers through exporting, licensing, joint ventures or complete manufacture and marketing facilities. It is at this point that the literature on international business becomes relevant, and international business issues are reviewed more fully in chapter 13. However, some primary motivations for such expansion can be seen from the results of a research study seeking to determine 'why companies expand overseas'.[3] The reasons most frequently given were defensive:

- to overcome tariff barriers;
- to overcome transport costs and delays;
- because of difficulties with agents and licences.

Aggressive strategies based on increasing profitability, lowering costs and so on were significantly less important than defensive strategies as a reason for expanding overseas. However, for many products, economies of scale and learning and experience-curve effects result in a domestic market of insufficient size to offer lowest long-term costs.

3 *New Product/New Market Extension – Conglomerate Diversification* is a very specific form of diversification. By definition, it is a move into a product-market area in which the company has no or few core skills either in marketing or technology. Possibly for this reason and the performance of several giant US conglomerates in the late 1960s, there is a suspicion, albeit not as strongly felt as in the 1970s, that they do not have a defensible corporate strategy. In terms of the efficient market hypothesis they ought to have low specific risk and consequently a low return. The low risk results from the portfolio effect of a large number of disparate businesses. However, some recent UK evidence[4] suggests that the returns are high and the risk low. The results, while in need of further corroborative evidence, would seem to indicate that the scepticism concerning conglomerate performance many need to be reviewed. As conglomerates have no marketing or technology links, the rationale for their existence must lie in other functional areas of the business such as financial and organizational skills.

12.5　STRATEGY BASED ON OTHER CRITERIA

While most of the strategic changes made by companies are related to existing products or markets, some changes are based on other criteria, particularly financial. If a company is pursuing a corporate strategy based solely on financial criteria, it is likely that this will lead to conglomerate diversification; that is, it will be manufacturing a range of products and operating in a group of markets which have little or no relationsip with each other.

Companies which have a strong finance function are able to use these skills to improve company performance. This is usually achieved by means of takeovers which are the result of a process of continually scanning the business environment for victims that satisfy specific characteristics. Companies which have under-utilized financial resources are an obvious target. This could result from unused borrowing capacity or accumulated tax losses which could offset taxes on current profits under certain circumstances.

Another financially orientated criterion is the ability to make greater use of existing resources or, put another way, to increase profitability. Most conglomerates are examples of this skill. This may be achieved by eliminating low profitability activities or by the introduction of better financial or other management skills. The increased utilization of assets could come from the exploitation of some physical assets, such as property or mineral deposits on land owned by the company.

The wisdom of such widespread diversification which often results from financially orientated strategies has been questioned, particularly because of the activities of a few very large conglomerates in the late 1960s. As the focus of the corporate strategy is not products or markets, it is sometimes argued that there are no skills to ensure long-term profitability and as such financial strategies are opportunistic. Indeed, the increasing activity of corporate raiders and the advent of junk bonds has led to the situation in which a legal entity is brought into being with the sole purpose of purchasing and dismembering some giant company in the usually realized expectation that the parts are worth more separately than they are as a whole.

There is some evidence to suggest that the conglomerate strategy out-performs other strategies in times of depression but is outperformed by more focused strategies when trade is buoyant. Reed is an example of a company which has moved away from a very diverse portfolio. In the early 1980s it might have been described as paper based conglomerate but in recent years has become significantly more focused on a few products on an international basis.

12.6　MANAGEMENT SUMMARY AND CHECKLIST

Businesses which are seeking to diversify need to approach the problem systematically. The first step is to determine in which direction this should be in terms of products or markets.

1　No change strategy

Companies at an early stage in the product life cycle can grow by developing their existing product to existing customers.

2　Vertical integration

This policy is pursued when a company wishes to control the sources of supply for some product or service which is used in manufacture of the current product range. Alternatively, the firm may wish to secure the outlet for a product.

3 Diversification

Diversification can take place on two dimensions, products or markets. Each dimension is on a scale from existing to new products or markets. If the product direction was both new products and new markets, this is referred to as conglomerate diversification.

4 Policy based on other criteria

If the company has differentiable skills outside marketing and technology, such as financial skills, it may choose to use these as a basis for diversification.

NOTES

1 G. A. Luffman and R. Reed, *Strategy and Performance in British Industry 1970–1980* (Macmillan, London 1984).
2 M. E. Porter, *Competitive Strategy and Competitive Advantage* (Free Press, Glencoe, 1980 and 1985); J. Kreiken in W. Glueck, *Business Policy and Strategic Management* (3rd edn, McGraw-Hill, New York, 1980), pp. 256–63; K. R. Harrigan, *Strategies for Vertical Integration* (Lexington Books, Lexington, Mass., 1983).
3 M. Z. Brooke, and H. Lee, *The Strategy of Multinational Enterprise* (2nd edn, Pitman, London, 1978).
4 Luffman and Reed, *Strategy and Performance in British Industry 1970–1980*.

13 Global Strategies

Introduction – A Simple Model of the International Economy
– The Internationalization of the Firm – Foreign Marketing
Servicing Policies – Management in Multinational Firms –
The Relationship with the Environment – Conclusion –
Management Summary and Checklist

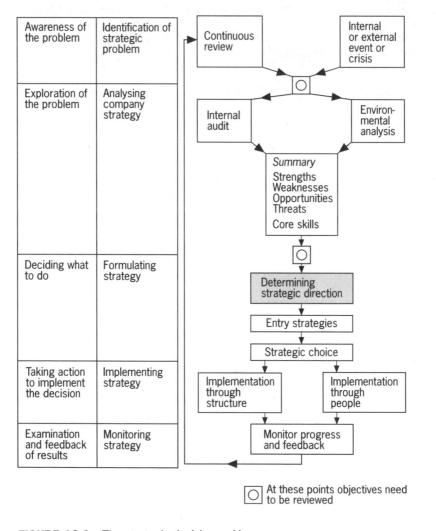

FIGURE 13.1 The strategic decision-making process

13.1   INTRODUCTION

The simplest definition of a multinational firm is one which owns outputs of goods or services in more than one country. Such a firm adds value by producing in more than one national economy. The addition of value may involve increasing the quantity of goods, enhancing their quality or improving their distribution, both spatially and temporally. Such a firm therefore faces decisions on at least some elements of the 'marketing mix': price, product, promotion and distribution.

Multinational firms most usually control assets abroad through the medium of foreign direct investment. The act of foreign direct investment involves bringing income-generating assets under the control of a foreign corporation through purchase or through the creation of new assets. There are other methods of controlling foreign assets such as control through key inputs (normally technology), through management or other key workers (in, for instance, management contracts) or through joint ownership even if exercised by a minority stake. The element of control distinguishes direct foreign investment from portfolio foreign investment, which is usually carried out by individuals, not firms.

The control of assets and operations abroad, often on a vast scale, poses a number of problems in the economic management of the multinational firm.

13.2   A SIMPLE MODEL OF THE INTERNATIONAL ECONOMY

Figure 13.2 shows a highly simplified picture of the world economy. It attempts to show different degrees of integration across various types of market. The suggestion is that financial markets are substantially integrated so that the world financial market can, for many purposes, be regarded as a single market. The market for goods and services is differentiated on a regional basis with 'single markets' either existing or emerging, for example the European Union (EU), NAFTA and so on. Such markets are increasingly uniform in regulation, standards, codes of practice (for example anti-trust) and business behaviour and so they offer the possibility of economies of scale across the market, but are substantially differentiated by these factors (and possibly by a common external tariff) from other regional markets. Labour markets, however, remain primarily national. Governments wish to regulate their own labour market and to differentiate it (protect it) from neighbouring labour markets. Many of the current difficulties in governmental regulatory policy arise from the difficulty of attempting to pursue independent labour market policies in the presence of regional goods and services markets and an international market for capital.

In contrast, multinational enterprises are perfectly placed to exploit the differences in international integration of markets. The presence of an international capital market enables capital costs to be driven to a minimum. The existence of regional goods and services markets enables firms to exploit economies of scale across several economies. Differential labour markets enable costs to be reduced by locating the labour-intensive stages of production in cheap labour economies. Horizontal integration is served by regional goods and services markets, vertical integration by differentiated labour markets and the spatial distribution of supplies of key raw materials.

This configuration of markets, and increasing steps towards globalization at many different levels, propel firms to re-evaluate their strategic position. Even firms which regard themselves as purely national in operation need to pay increasing

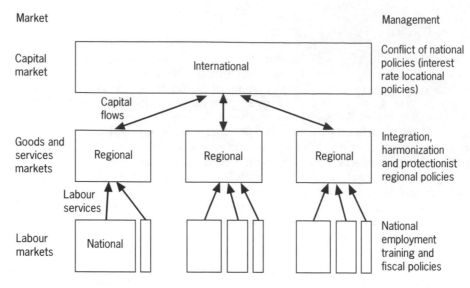

FIGURE 13.2 Internationalization of firms – conflict of markets

attention to international competition and the growing integration of markets across national boundaries.

13.3 THE INTERNATIONALIZATION OF THE FIRM

The Motives

Three main classes of motives for foreign direct investment can be identified:

- market orientated investments;
- cost-reducing investment;
- vertical foreign investment aimed at reducing the cost of raw materials or other key inputs.

Very rarely is a foreign investment decision taken for a sole overriding purpose. More often the motive is mixed, often even unclear.

There are a number of secondary or supporting motives which may come into the calculation. These can include:

- the investment climate of the host country (its tax regime, political stability, cultural closeness to the investor, provision of infrastructure);
- the firm's response to an external approach, perhaps by the host government, the firm's local agent or distributor, or from a customer, supplier or even a competitor;
- factors related to the source country, such as difficulties of supplying the market by other means, or as a response to a foreign investment by a competitor in the firm's home market.

The foreign investment decision is rarely taken for a single reason and rarely is it taken at a single moment of time. Rather it is the result of cumulative pressures and opportunities impinging on the firm. The process of foreign investment is akin to the building of a commitment in the firm.

The Process of Internationalization

The first foreign investment decision will be very different from subsequent investments. Initially, a national firm is likely to be very risk-averse as regards foreign involvement which is often seen as a leap into the unknown. Consequently, inexperienced foreign investors often require a strong stimulus even to begin to consider internationalization. Such stimuli can be internal to the firm, such as an executive with an interest in foreign expansion, or external, such as an opportunity presented by the firm's agent. Such a stimulus will usually initiate a search for information, both general indicators on the host country and then on-the-spot investigation. Careful consideration is then made by key decision-makers before the decision to go ahead (or not) is made. In observing this management process, it may never be obvious at what point 'the investment decision' is taken. Far too frequently among inexperienced investors there is insufficient assessment and investigation, often leading to disastrous outcomes.[1] One particular error is the failure to specify clear performance targets for the new subsidiary.

The Route

It is unusual for a firm to go immediately to a foreign direct investment in a country without passing through a number of intermediate stages as illustrated by figure 13.3. From home activities only, such intermediate stages may be direct exporting, foreign agency representation and a foreign sales subsidiary before embarking on a full production subsidiary. It has been found that there is a direct positive correlation between the number of stages in the route and the ultimate success of the foreign subsidiary. This is because of the learning effects permitted at each stage of the longer

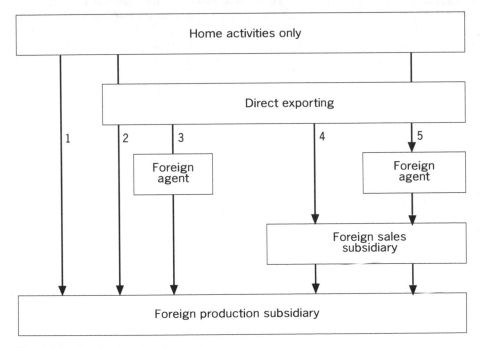

FIGURE 13.3   Routes to a foreign production subsidiary
Source: Reproduced from Peter J. Buckley, Gerald D. Newbould and Jane Thurwell, *Foreign Direct Investment by Smaller UK Firms* (2nd edn, Macmillan, London, 1988), p. 45. Reprinted with permission.

route and because the intermediate stages allow the firm to withdraw before too much damage occurs. The full route (numbered 5 in figure 13.3) allows for learning about the requirements of the foreign market in the exporting phase; the methods of doing business in the host country and how to deal with local people directly at the agency stage; the laws, taxes, how to control operations directly, selling, stockholding and promotion at the sales subsidiary stage; all in advance of having to cope with production problems abroad at the final stage. Foreign licensing or some other contractual arrangement may, of course, also be included as replacements or supplements for some of the above intermediate stages.

The Timing of the Move Abroad

The timing of a firm's move abroad is a very difficult management decision because it involves so much uncertainty and it is also very difficult to model adequately. The 'product cycle' approach to foreign direct investment suggests that the switch to foreign investment should occur according to the following cost-based formulation:

Investment abroad when $MPC_X + TC > ACP_A$
where MPC_X is marginal cost of production for export
　　　　TC is transport cost
　　　　ACP_A is average cost of production abroad.[2]

The argument here is that marginal costings are appropriate for exports because domestic production would be undertaken anyway, while the foreign unit must bear the full average costs of production.

　A fuller model of the switch to foreign investment is given by Buckley and Casson.[3] Essentially, two types of cost, fixed and variable, attach to the different forms of foreign market servicing: licensing, exporting and foreign direct investment. As the market grows, the variable cost declines and so the switch occurs from low fixed to low variable cost modes, typically from exporting to direct investment (see figure 13.4). This model is complicated when set-up costs are also included.

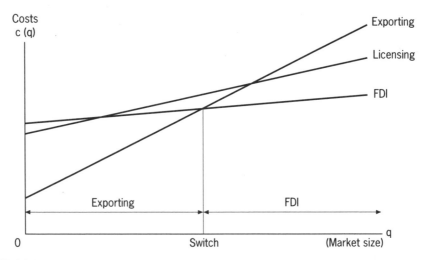

FIGURE 13.4　The timing of a foreign direct investment (FDI)
Note: In this example, licensing is never the preferred alternative.
Source: Reproduced from Peter J. Buckley and Mark Casson, *The Economic Theory of the Multinational Enterprise* (Macmillan, London, 1985), p. 105, with permission.

Key variables in the timing of the move abroad are therefore the costs of servicing the foreign market, demand conditions in that market and host market growth.

A major complicating factor in the move abroad is the action of competitors. This type of reaction among large firms has been analysed as a major influence on a foreign direct investment. Among the largest multinational firms entry into particular host country markets is often grouped in time. The important influences on this are:

- industry structure: the more concentrated the industry, the more leader-follower behaviour occurs;
- industry stability: rivalistic investment behaviour is directly connected with the break-up of industry stability under pressure from new entrants;
- the smaller the number of options open to the firm, the more likely they are to engage in oligopolistic reaction.

Interestingly, low-technology firms are defensively more active than high-technology ones.

13.4   FOREIGN MARKET SERVICING POLICIES

General

Foreign market servicing policies are the set of decisions which determine which production and service facilities serve particular markets and by what channels these are linked. There are three main modes of foreign market servicing: exporting, licensing (and other contractual arrangements) and foreign direct investment. Exporting can be differentiated from the other two methods because the bulk of value-adding activity takes place at home, while licensing can be differentiated because it is a market arrangement, not subject to complete internal control.

In practice, market servicing policy is highly complex. The methods are inter-related, that is location abroad of some activities will have knock-on effects across markets and products. Co-ordination of a foreign market servicing strategy is a major task. This is complicated by the fact that the optimum market servicing stance must alter as circumstances change, and a willingness to be flexible is vital.

Similar considerations apply to the sourcing network for inputs as an international procurement policy can be a major source of savings. Again, flexibility and monitoring of foreign operations are crucial.

Exporting

As figure 13.3 shows, exporting is often the primary means of penetrating a foreign market. It is regarded as a cheap and low-risk method of foreign selling, but the fixed costs of a low volume of export sales can be prohibitive despite the fact that there are tax advantages to be gained in many countries. The main problems of exporting are the costs of product adaptation and the difficulties caused by barriers to trade.

Research on exporting suggests that several elements are important in export success:

- the need for export sales specialists within the firm;
- the need to concentrate on the firm's most important foreign markets rather than amass haphazard unco-ordinated foreign sales;
- the importance of selection, training and control of foreign intermediaries and effecting feedback from the foreign market.

Proper representation in the foreign market is vital, and the need to protect export markets by defensive investment in sales or production subsidiaries leads to a deepening involvement and further internationalization.

Licensing and Other Contractual Arrangements Abroad

On the face of it, foreign licensing appears to represent an ideal situation, combining the technological and possible management skills of the multinational firm with the local knowledge of the host country partner. The relatively small use of licensing, which represents only 7 per cent of the UK's total foreign sales,[4] is a result of the management difficulties of effecting the firm-to-firm transfer of technology and skills which imposes heavy costs, as compared to the internalization of such resources in the multinational firm's subsidiaries.[5] The problems involved in licensing include the following:

1   Identifying the advantage to be transferred which is related to the degree of embodiment of the technology. If the technology is embodied in a machine or a brand name then transfer is easy. Often, however, the skills of multinational firms are diffuse and involve heavy transfer costs.
2   Licensing technology involves heavy policing costs, for the licensor needs to ensure that the licensee does not use technology 'in ways which have not been paid for'.
3   The licensor runs the risk of creating a competitor.
4   There exists a 'buyer uncertainty problem' (the buyer does not know what he or she is acquiring until it has been obtained, and once it has been acquired he or she will not wish to pay for it) which inhibits the market for licences or at least increases the cost by requiring insurance clauses in contracts.
5   There may be no local firm which can profitably absorb the knowledge, particularly in less-developed countries.

However, there are a number of situations where licensing may be appropriate. First, it may pay multinationals in highly concentrated industries not to compete directly through subsidiaries in the same market, but to cross-license their products to each other (for instance, in the pharmaceutical industry). Secondly, licensing may be the best form of market servicing in the presence of barriers to the other methods. Government policy may prevent exporting and may insist on local host control. Small firms may find it difficult to raise the capital and management of a direct investment but require a local presence. Finally, licensing is often a way to exploit small, residual markets at low cost.

Direct Investment

Direct investment has been considered above. Three situations occur where management chooses direct foreign investment. First, firms move abroad by investment when the market growth or profit potential is favourable relative to other forms of market servicing. Secondly, firms produce abroad where their competitive strength is greater than indigenous firms. Thirdly, multinational firms are better seekers of the most profitable and fastest growing activities than are host country firms. One form of direct investment worthy of further investigation is cost-reducing offshore production.

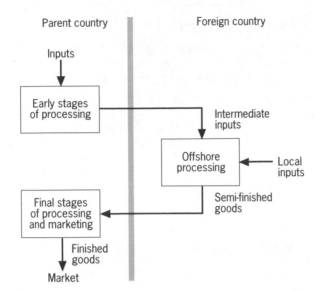

FIGURE 13.5   Schematic representation of a typical offshore production process

Offshore Production

Offshore production is the situation where one stage in an integrated production process is located abroad in order to reduce costs. The offshore plant (or foreign feeder plant) is usually located in a cheap labour country and the final output is sold in an advanced country, usually in the multinational firm's home market. A typical offshore process is shown in figure 13.5.

In the electronics industry the most popular countries for offshore investment are Singapore, Malaysia, Hong Kong, Taiwan and South Korea; for servicing the US market, Latin America is popular, particularly Mexico; and for the European textiles market, North Africa.

The decision process leading to the establishment of an offshore plant is usually prompted by a threat to the home market from a low-cost producer. The threatened firm either has to reduce costs or phase out the product. Frequently offshore establishment is the optimum way to cut the costs. Successful establishment offshore is dependent on several characteristics of the product:

- large inputs of relatively unskilled labour;
- a high value to low weight ratio in order to keep transport costs down;
- low tariffs in the reimporting country;
- a standardized product and process.

Initial problems of offshore plants, such as inadequate throughput and difficulties of management at a distance, together with the inherent risks, have receded as managements have learned to cope, and offshore production is a rapidly increasing component of international investment.

13.5   FOREIGN INVESTMENT ENTRY STRATEGY

The management decisions involved in setting up a subsidiary in a foreign country have two important dimensions: the buy or build decision and the ownership decision.

Greenfield Ventures versus Takeovers

A priori, there are strong arguments either to build a new foreign plant from scratch on a greenfield site or to acquire an existing firm or part of a firm. The proponents of greenfield entry support their case by reference to the following arguments:

1 Greenfield ventures can be a cheaper form of entry because the scale of involvement can be precisely controlled and the facility can be expanded exactly in line with achieved market penetration. This argument is likely to be particularly strong for smaller firms who face difficulty in raising the capital necessary for a takeover.
2 Building a new plant means that there is no risk of inheriting problems.
3 The most modern techniques of production and management can be installed.
4 There is likely to be a welcome from the host government for greenfield ventures which are seen as increasing activity.
5 The choice of location is open to the entrant and a least-cost site, including possible regional grants, can be chosen.
6 Where no suitable takeover victim can be found, greenfield entry can be a second best solution.

There are counter arguments in favour of entry by takeover:

1 Takeovers permit rapid market entry and allow a quicker return on capital and learning procedures. In cases of strong competition, the pre-emption of a rival firm's move may dictate takeover entry.
2 Cultural, legal and management problems, particularly in the difficult start-up period, can be avoided by assimilating a going concern.
3 The major advantage of a takeover is often the purchase of crucial assets. Such assets may, in different circumstances, be products, management skills, brand names, technology and distribution networks.
4 Takeovers do not disturb the competitive framework in the host country, and they avoid competition retaliation.

There are, however, several potential drawbacks to the takeover mode of entry. The entrant is faced with the task of evaluating the worth of the assets to be acquired. This involves a costly and difficult assessment of the synergy between these new assets and the firm's existing operations. Secondly, there may be severe problems of integrating a previously independent unit into a larger entity; and, thirdly, the search for the ideal victim often involves heavy costs.

Almost every entry decision involves giving a different weighting to the above factors. Of particular importance in determining the outcome are the specific skills of the entrant and the environmental circumstances in the host country.

Ownership Strategy

The arguments for 100 per cent equity ownership of a foreign subsidiary rely heavily on the fact that control by the parent is total and that there can be no conflict over potentially contentious issues of company policy such as dividend payments, exports, the distribution of new investment and internal transfer prices. In cases where the parent firm can supply all the necessary inputs for a subsidiary, these costs of interference need not be borne. Further information, both technical and competitive, is not leaked to outsiders who may not fully share the goals of the parent firm. Finally, some types of strategy are incompatible with joint ventures, notably those based on rapid and sustained innovation, on rationalization and on control of key inputs.

The arguments for joint ventures are more circumstantial and depend on finding a joint venture partner with complementary resources. The argument that unique resources are contributed by the local partner is usually the most important reason for joint ventures. These resources may be local knowledge, contacts or marketing expertise. Secondly, the entrant company's outlay is reduced and the risk of loss correspondingly diminished. This reduction of risk is an important reason why joint ventures, which can be easily reversed, may be a good way of effecting initial entry. Finally, in many countries some element of local shareholding is made a condition of entry.

The success of the decision to enter a joint venture will, of course, depend on the choice of partner. There are many cases on record where a good agent or distributor has become a poor joint venture partner. It is clearly difficult to appraise a prospective partner in advance, but on such an appraisal may depend the success of the foreign venture.

13.6   MANAGEMENT IN MULTINATIONAL FIRMS

Management in multinational firms is essentially a response to the same issues facing national firms: how to make a profit; how to control operations; how and in which direction to grow; how to respond to a changing environment and so on; but it is complicated by operating in more than one country and by differing national business frameworks. Consequently, each functional area of the firm – financing, marketing, production, R&D – must be organized so as to respond to global operations.

Organization

Organizationally, the multinational firm must respond to global challenges in a way which allows the maximum control of policy by top decision-makers with maximum flexibility of response to changing circumstances. This means the creation of an efficient communications network within the firm. Reporting relationships between managers is therefore vital. Channels of reporting relationships internationally can run along functional lines, where the heads of divisions (finance, marketing, production) have worldwide responsibilities, along product group lines, or the firm can be organized geographically (Middle East division and so on). The organizational problem then becomes the effective coordination of these major divisions across the other specialisms, for example in a product division structure to co-ordinate the sales of different product groups. Some multinational firms have thus adopted multiple reporting channels (sometimes referred to as matrix structures). Here the danger is that the organizational procedures may become disorientated.

An alternative response to global organization, particularly utilized by smaller multinationals, is the international division structure, where all non-domestic activities of the firm are grouped together and reporting is directly between the chief executive of the company and the chief executive of the international division. Such a structure is useful in giving impetus to an internationalization drive, but does not allow the firm to benefit fully from synergy between national and international operations and often leaves foreign activities dependent on the domestic product division.

Personnel problems in multinational firms can be severe. Expatriate executives are far more expensive than when employed at home and pose problems in promotion, pensions, emoluments and reintegration at home. Recruitment of local executives can be difficult and risky but may be forced on the company by indigenization plans, by which local governments demand that a fixed proportion of executives must be host country nationals. Cultural differences among executives often require careful handling by top management. A training programme which matches these personnel needs is a vital component of a multinational's operations.

Planning

It has become commonplace that structure should follow strategy, and the setting of strategy at the highest levels – the management plan – is a vital weapon in the economic management of multinationals. Three elements are of major importance:

- control of operations;
- decision-making by the people best equipped to judge the impact of the decision;
- the communication of information to facilitate good decisions.

The management plan should thus incorporate well-defined targets which can be measured. Multiple targets which are comprehensible to decision-makers should include a time-scale for their achievement and an action programme to tackle key problems and take advantage of opportunities. Such provisions prevent the plan being vague and give clear guidance to managers.

The key issue of developing responsibility to the managers of foreign subsidiaries while retaining control of policy in headquarters is an issue which troubles all multinational firms, however organized. It is essential that group support be given to the manager on the spot who must actually make operational decisions.

Financial Planning

Multinational operation complicates financial management by posing extra problems, but it also opens new opportunities. The possibilities for exchange loss or gain increase with multinationalization. Exchange loss is the risk of loss to a firm exposed to devaluation in the value of a currency which the firm is contracted to receive in the future or from an appreciation in the value of a currency which the firm is contracted to deliver in the future. Exporters and importers are so exposed, but multinationals are more vulnerable because of their larger trading across exchanges and because their net assets will be differentially affected in different currency areas. Consequently, a hedging policy designed to minimize these effects is necessary for a risk-averse multinational. Of course, a more aggressive policy of attempting to play the foreign exchange market is a possible alternative, but no such scheme has yet been perfected and many multi-national firms have lost money in the attempt.

The differential cost of money worldwide enables multinational firms to reduce the costs of raising capital, and the use of internal indebtedness (for example a subsidiary borrowing from the parent firm) allows flexibility in its utilization. However, each subsidiary of the firm must adapt to local financial practices and institutions. The reconciliation of local subsidiaries into an overall consolidated balance sheet can be a difficult and expensive task.

Financial planning in the multinational firm must face the issue of taxation. A spectrum of policies is possible from an outright policy of attempting to reduce taxation payments wherever possible to ensuring simply that the same profits are not taxed twice. A large amount of information on tax regimes and double taxation agreements between countries is necessary in international taxation planning and a great deal of uncertainty prevails because of the impact of changes in any of the variables affecting taxation.

The problem of withdrawing funds from abroad is a unique financial problem faced by multinational firms. A variety of channels is available including dividends (usually taxed at source and as income to the parent), royalties and management fees to the parent (often tax-deductible in the host country), repayment of loans and interest on intra-company debt, and transfer pricing on intermediate goods and services.

The problem of transfer pricing is the most controversial issue that multinational firms face. The manipulation of internal prices of goods and services to move funds around the world can achieve several objectives. Included among these are the following:

- to maximize post-tax profits;
- artificially to affect declared profit levels;
- to transfer funds in the face of changes in currency parities;
- to avoid government restrictions;
- to impose control on foreign subsidiaries.

However, such artificial prices affect the incomes of the countries between which the transaction occurs and multinationals are therefore distrusted by governments who believe that they cannot control their own economies in the presence of multinational firms. Despite the existence of constraints by customs and revenue authorities, exchange control authorities and specialist transfer price checking firms employed by some countries, suspicion remains. The practice also has drawbacks from the firm's point of view. A loss of efficiency can occur from the operation of non-market prices. A costly control system may be necessary and mistakes in transfer pricing may be expensive. The practice will continue, however, while potential gains in tax avoidance and profit potential remain.

The existence of different tax and trading regimes internationally poses the problem of evaluating the performance of foreign subsidiaries. While it is generally agreed that the same standards of performance (return on sales, performance relative to a budget) are required from individual foreign subsidiaries, allowance must be made for the impact of local conditions and possibly the impact of transfer pricing on individual subsidiaries. Evaluation of performance at a distance remains a grey area in many multinational firms.

Marketing

International marketing involves an important decision on worldwide standardization versus adaptation of the products to individual market needs. In general, adaptation will yield revenue advantages. It is, however, dangerous to make generalizations, particularly in equating market with country. India, for instance, though a very poor country on the usual indicators, has a proportionately small but, in absolute terms, large industrial sector. Most Third World countries have a minority of high income earners whose consumption patterns approximate to those of advanced countries. Consequently, multinationals are often able to segment national markets profitably.

Studies of international marketing point to the importance of non-price factors in selling. Quality, variety, reliability and meeting delivery dates are frequently adduced to lead to success in penetrating foreign markets. Information needs are correspondingly greater in foreign markets and careful pre-entry market research remains an important contributor to success.

Research and Development

Economic theories of the multinational firm stress the relationship between research intensity and multinationality of the firm. The supply of technological advances internally exploited and marketed within the structure of the firm gives an explanation for the growth of integrated multinational firms.[6] The management of R&D is vital for internationalization, and exploiting the advances of internal research provides a motor for the growth of the firm. The information flows between R&D and the other main functions are extremely important. Figure 13.6 illustrates the twoway communication necessary for management to integrate fully the fruits of research into the management process. It is often argued that the most successfully managed multinationals are those whose managements understand the implications of current research.

Global Decision-making

The management of multinational firms requires a careful monitoring of the international environment. Responsiveness to local conditions is perhaps the most important attribute of successful management practice. This section has shown the crucial importance of communication within the firm not only between countries, but between departments and divisions.

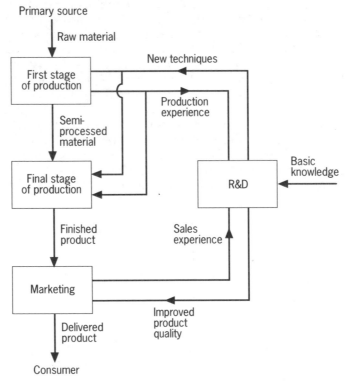

FIGURE 13.6 The integration of R&D into the management of the firm

Note: Successive stages of production are linked by flows of semi-processed materials. Production and marketing are linked by a flow of finished goods ready for distribution. They are linked to R&D by two-way flows of information and expertise.

Source: Reproduced from Peter J. Buckley and Mark Casson, *The Future of the Multinational Enterprise* (2nd edn, Macmillan, London, 1991), p. 34. Reprinted with permission.

13.7 THE RELATIONSHIP WITH THE ENVIRONMENT

Multinational firms operate in more than one economic environment and therefore have to adapt to local conditions, markets and jurisdictions. Further, they must co-ordinate activities which operate on very different bases because of different local influences.

The Host Country Environment

Understanding and adapting to foreign conditions remains a difficult problem even for the most experienced multinational firm. Different ways of conducting business and changing regulatory regimes impose learning and adaptation costs. The assessment of such costs in advance of entry can be problematic. In particular, multinationals are faced with the assessment of political risk, which is usually discounted in the home environment. Political risks arise from discontinuities in the business environment which are difficult to predict. War, revolution, nationaliza-tion, expropriation, devaluation and the imposition of controls are obvious manifes-tations. Collection of information is necessary to evaluate foreign projects and a variety of screening models exists. Prior contact with the market is an important source of knowledge of host country conditions.

In many host countries, notably those of the Third World, multinationals are regarded with suspicion and they are often made the scapegoat for many internal problems of economic management. Concern on the part of host countries is expressed with regard to the impact of multinationals on the balance of payments, their effect on the host country's economic structure, their technological impact and their alleged inflexibility towards national planning. Indeed, it is frequently the case that foreign investors are more responsive to government policy than are local firms, and the alacrity with which multinationals respond to regional incentives is an example of this. However, the vague threat posed to national sovereignty and the achievement of national goals dictates that the management of multinationals must be sensitive to local aspirations and must avoid at all costs political inter-ference or standards of behaviour below those of their best local competitor.

The Source Country

The relationship between the multinational firm and its source country can also be fraught with difficulty. The most serious accusation thrown at multinationals is that they create unemployment by 'exporting jobs'. The growth of offshore production in particular has heightened the tension. In defence, multinationals put the view that foreign investment increases job provision in the home country by providing an outlet for intermediate and capital goods in the foreign unit and preserving jobs which would otherwise disappear in the face of low-cost foreign competition. Studies of the balance between job preservation and job loss conducted in the USA have been inconclusive, as have investigations of the impact of outward direct investment on the balance of payments.

International Organizations

Because of the difficulty of controlling multinational firms at the national level, demands have grown that they should be internationally (or supranationally) regulated. To effect this a number of codes of conduct and other regulatory provisions now impinge on the management of multinational firms.

Clearly, managements in multinationals must be aware of these codes and adopt policies which do not conflict with them for the sake of public relations, if nothing else. The impact of international regulation is likely to increase and therefore to impose management costs on multinationals much more heavily in future.

13.8   CONCLUSION

The management of multinational organizations has additional dimensions not faced by the national firm. Adaptation to differing local conditions, extra information requirements, control problems, organizational problems and problems of liaising with external decision-makers are all exacerbated by international operations. However, with these problems come opportunities for growth, stability, diversification and cost reduction, leading to higher profitability. The principles of sound management do not differ between national and international firms, but the extra dimensions of the latter pose interesting challenges. The increasing interdependency in world markets means that even purely nationally orientated firms cannot ignore international competition and international opportunities.

13.9   MANAGEMENT SUMMARY AND CHECKLIST

1   What is the objective of investing abroad? Is it cost reduction, more effective servicing of demand or control of key supplies?
2   Have all the other means of servicing a foreign market been considered and evaluated? Is a form of licensing, exporting or foreign investment the most appropriate means of reaching the target market? Have other markets been assessed?
3   Has the most efficient supply (sourcing) network been established for all the units of the company, at home and abroad?
4   Has the entry into the foreign market been evaluated correctly? Is a greenfield site or takeover entry most appropriate? If acquisition is preferred, are all the potential acquisition targets fully evaluated? Is the ownership strategy matched to the objectives and to the resources available?
5   Are foreign units organized in such a way that reporting and control is flexible and efficient? Are decision-making units by function, area and product co-ordinated? Are local managers clear about their responsibilities?
6   Are conditions in the (actual and potential) host countries fully monitored and reported back to the key decision-makers?
7   Does the firm operate on a truly international basis, scanning opportunities, appraising and re-appraising its global spread and fully co-ordinating its activities on a worldwide basis?

NOTES

1   Peter J. Buckley, Gerald D. Newbould and Jane Thurwell, *Foreign Direct Investment by Smaller UK Firms* (2nd edn, Macmillan, London, 1988).
2   Raymond Vernon, 'International Investment and International Trade in the Product Cycle', *Quaterly Journal of Economics*, 80 (1966), pp.196–207.
3   Peter J. Buckley and Mark Casson, *The Economic Theory of the Multinational Enterprise* (Macmillan, London, 1985).
4   Peter J. Buckley and Kate Prescott, 'The Structure of British Industry's Sales in Foreign Markets', *Managerial and Decision Economics*, 10 (1989), pp.189–208.
5   Buckley and Casson, *The Economic Theory of the Multinational Enterprise*; Peter J. Buckley and Mark Casson, *The Future of the Multinational Enterprise* (2nd edn, Macmillan, London, 1990).
6   Buckley and Casson, *The Future of the Multinational Enterprise*.

FURTHER READING

For a thorough treatment of the management policies of multinational firms see: Michael Z. Brooke and Peter J. Buckley (eds) *Handbook of International Trade* (Macmillan, London, 1988).

Introduction – What is a Declining Industry? – Reasons for Product Decline – Factors Leading to Success or Failure – Strategies for Mature and Declining Industries – Management Summary and Checklist

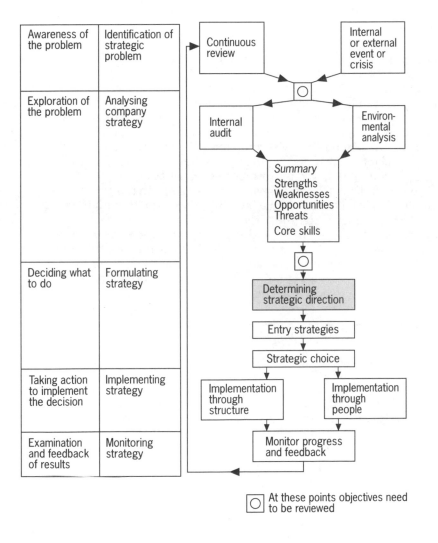

FIGURE 14.1 The strategic decision-making process

14.1   INTRODUCTION

In retrospect, examples of and reasons for the decline in the demand for products are easily identifiable. The demand for blacksmiths' services was overtaken by the advent of the internal combustion engine, chimney sweeps experienced a decline in the demand for their services with the widespread adoption of central heating as the primary means for home heating and, more recently, the Swiss watch industry has suffered a decline resulting from changes in electronic engineering.

Until the oil crises in the middle and late 1970s the increasing rate of growth of GNP and world trade had resulted in increases in demand for many products which had continued for an unprecedented period of time. These crises and the consequent reduction in economic activity, together with the increasing rate of technological change, resulted in more products facing a period of long-term decline. Long-term decline is not a new phenomenon in the industrial environment and the concept of product life-cycle provides the theoretical explanation of this observed reality. However, little attention had previously been focused on this part of the cycle. A simple view was that a product in a declining market was undesirable, so that such products should be eliminated from the portfolio as soon as possible and, furthermore, entry to such markets or products was a strategy to be avoided.

It is against this background that Harrigan, building on Porter's model, undertook some research on products in declining industries and subsequently developed a conceptual framework which sought to outline strategies which would be profitable for companies with products in such industries.[1] Also, it is argued from the BCG matrix (chapter 19) that companies need a balanced portfolio of businesses. It follows, therefore, that developing appropriate strategies for declining products is of major importance to the performance of most businesses.

It is often difficult for senior managers to accept that a product is in the decline phase. They may have been in the industry or associated with the product for many years. Also acceptance of the situation might indicate the need for substantial change to be introduced: new products, new customers, new processes and so on. Managers may have a tendency to ignore these factors and refuse to face the facts such that profitability can be seriously affected and even the existence of the firm threatened. The strategies required to cope with seriously *underperforming* companies are discussed in chapter 15.

14.2   WHAT IS A DECLINING INDUSTRY?

It will be useful to discuss two situations which are often confused with a declining industry. Figure 14.2 helps to illustrate the point.

Although the product life-cycle is usually drawn as a continuous smooth line, the reality is that sales fluctuate in the short term due to cyclical or other short-run influences. The first illusion which is sometimes believed is that any reduction sales is a product in a declining industry. It is apparent that, although sales are declining between points A and B, this is a temporary decline in what in the long term is a growing industry. Likewise, the second illusion which is too often accepted is that a temporary increase, as for instance between D and E, is evidence that the industry is now in a new growth phase. Of course, it may be, but in figure 14.2 this is only a short-term reprieve in what is clearly a long-term decline. An industry is in decline after it has reached point C on the diagram.

From this point in the cycle onwards there must be, by definition, excess capacity, that is, demand at a lower point than maximum output. Economic theory suggests

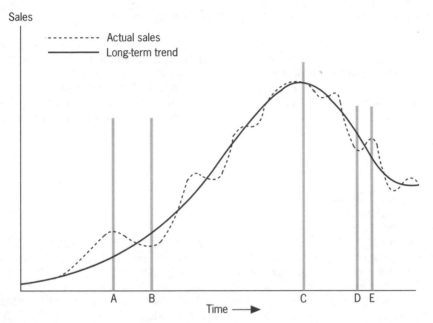

Sales

- - - - - - - - - Actual sales
———————— Long-term trend

A   B   C   D E

Time ——▶

FIGURE 14.2   The product life-cycle

that certain features of industry behaviour will result from this excess capacity such as price wars which are initially designed to increase sales in order to maintain full plant utilization. Also, companies leave the industry as the marginal producer is no longer able to operate profitably. However, there are other options and whether or not these are possible are discussed at a later point in the chapter.

14.3   REASONS FOR PRODUCT DECLINE

Causes of declining profitability are also mentioned in chapter 15, 'Corporate Collapse and Turnround'. As that chapter is concerned with underperformance whatever the state of demand, the discussion focuses on issues *within* the company. As the focus of this chapter is declining industry demand it is appropriate to focus on the *external* factors which have led to decline. The major factors are:

- technological change: to products or processes;
- social changes: cultural or fashion;
- saturation: buyers have sufficient quantities of the product.

There may be other factors, such as a new law or economic policy, but these are often preceded by one of the above factors. Also, changes may be a combination of two or all three factors. The demise of the corner shop and the growth in the number of supermarkets results from a wide range of social and technological changes.

A new technical process or source, such as natural gas, can cause the decline of a product, manufactured gas. There is a growing need for fuel but it is being provided by a different process. The introduction of powerful computer systems has reduced the demand for cash registers. A new technology has produced a product which has changed and subsumed the task of the register to meet a much wider range of customer needs. Changes in fashion in the men's clothing market have seen a significant decline in the demand for suits, and social changes such as a fall in the birthrate will cause a substantial decline in the baby products market.

Most companies operate successfully within given geographical areas and excursions into new territory are often met with fierce resistance. Thus, given this geographical limitation many markets reach saturation, that is they reach a peak when demand has been fully satisfied and there then follows a fall until, at a lower point, sales level out to satisfy the replacement market. Televisions, refrigerators and other household goods fall into this category in the UK. Of course, if the population were rising rapidly this trend might be different.

14.4   FACTORS LEADING TO SUCCESS OR FAILURE

The models used by strategists for choosing between alternative courses of action (chapter 19) are based on an external and an internal dimension or dimensions and the model described in this chapter elaborates on a particular aspect of those models. As with the multinational firm (chapter 13) and corporate collapse and turnaround (chapter 15), the specific insights into these critical areas are considered in part 4 so that the resulting analysis can be carried through the process into part 5 which can then focus solely on how the choice is made for the standard case. It is necessary, therefore, to outline the key external and internal features before suggesting the possible options which may be appropriate for a given set of circumstances.

Environmental Factors

Environmental factors can be classified under two headings:

• demand characteristics; and
• supply characteristics.

Demand characteristics are those factors which relate to the customers for the product. Outlined below are some of the key issues.

Nature of decline   The nature of the fall in demand for the industry's product is most often the key demand factor. If demand is falling slowly, this is preferable to rapid decline. Indeed, in the latter case it could be at such a rate as to render further analysis unneccessary. As well as the rate of decline, the pattern of decline is significant: steady decline being preferable to volatile decline. Also it is important in making such estimates of future demand to understand the reasons for the decline.

Industry structure   The number and size of competitors and their relative market share will enable some preliminary assessment of the nature of competition in the industry. A few large buyers are likely to lead to increased pressure on the industry unless there is some countervailing power such as a patent, few alternatives or expensive costs in switching among suppliers.

Price stability   The nature of decline and industry structure will be key factors in determining whether price stability will be maintained in the market. Falling or unstable prices are an unfavourable industry characteristic.

Product differentiation   In general, when a product reaches the decline stage of the life-cycle it is or is becoming commodity-like with no perceived differences between the product of competing companies. This is an unfavourable characteristic but not always a bar to operating successfully in the industry. However, differentiation between products does provide more opportunities.

Segments   There can be a number of segments within an industry. Each segment may contain commodity-like or differentiated products. The existence of different segments is a positive factor, in that it is likely that there will be among them pockets of demand which are not declining as rapidly as others.

The second class of external characteristics are those that relate to the companies that manufacture or *supply* the product or service which comprises the industry. Before outlining specific issues, it is necessary to discuss the general problems associated with exit and entry barriers. Either singly or in combination, several of the factors outlined below can constitute barriers. Exit barriers are circumstances, such as assets significantly overvalued in the accounts, which would create major problems should the company decide to stop operating in that business. Likewise, although entry is not often appropriate at this stage of the cycle, barriers to entry will enable those currently in the industry to manage the decline phase in an orderly manner without threat from outside interference.

Level of excess capacity   To some extent the levels of excess capacity are linked to the rate of decline but they are also a function of the increases in productivity in the industry and the rate at which firms leave the industry. High levels of excess capacity are usually extremely unfavourable, but individual firms may not be as affected as others if operating in particular segments.

Vertical integration   If firms in the supplying industry are vertically integrated there will be a greater reluctance to leave the industry. Vertical integration is therefore an unattractive industry feature.

Exit strategies   There may be reasons which make it more difficult or uneconomic to leave one industry rather than another. It will be more difficult where the assets have no alternative use, or were recently acquired and are therefore not fully depreciated. It is also difficult where the assets are a large component of total costs or are unlikely to sell for a reasonable price.

Company ownership   Where ownership is with a large corporation decisions are likely to be made on a more rational and dispassionate basis, so that a business not reaching or likely to reach a given rate of return on capital is likely to be closed or divested. However, in the one-product or single-owner company survival at any cost may result in a continuation in business until, in some cases, bankruptcy occurs. An industry therefore comprising single-product or single-owner businesses is not attractive.

Asset characteristics   Companies whose assets are in the account at significantly greater value than are realizable in resale terms whether as a divestment or after closure are going to be reluctant to leave the industry. This also applies, in industries where company assets have no alternative use. Thus an industry is unattractive in which this is the situation for several of the companies.

Company Strengths and Weaknesses

The general approach to determining company strengths and weaknesses has been outlined in chapters 8 and 9 and many factors relevant to declining demand may emerge from such an analysis. However, four factors are worthy of particular note.

Management attitudes   The perceptions the management have of the features of the industry and their reactions to them will be critical in determining the way in which the decline phase proceeds. As mentioned previously, managements often have long attachments to products and markets which mean that they experienced the products while in their growth phase. Failure to perceive, acknowledge and adapt to the changed circumstances can have serious consequences. Although this factor has been included in the internal dimension of the analysis, the collective perceptions and actions of all firms in the industry are very important and give the process a potential dynamic which makes it very difficult to predict the outcome. However, early and appropriate action is likely to bring greater success to the company.

Market share   A business which has a large market share is in a more favourable position than one with a low market share. This applies to the whole industry or individual segments.

Cost position in the industry   A feature of declining industries is the inevitability that at some point the highest-cost producer will have to exit. Also, if prices are squeezed, then the higher-cost producers' profitability will decline. Accordingly, those who are lower-cost producers have a competitive advantage.

Patents   At this stage of the cycle it is possible that patents which have protected products from competition may be near expiry date. If this is so then the impact of the loss of protection needs to be carefully evaluated. The more severe the likely competitive impact the less attractive to companies in the industry.

Before discussing the possible strategies, a number of points need to be made as a summary of the preceding analysis and as an introduction to the model. The factors mentioned above are those which are found to be the most significant in determining future strategy. On occasion, factors not mentioned here may be of critical importance and it is the skill and experience of the analyst that will enable those factors to be identified and included in the analyses. Also, it has to be borne in mind constantly that this analysis is concerned with declining demand.

Thus, the model outlined below may also be appropriate where demand has reached an equilibrium but is *definitely not appropriate for other points on the product life-cycle*. Finally, these are general rules to which there will be exceptions. Thus, again, the analyst needs acute sensitivity to identify when a general rule is not applicable.

14.5   STRATEGIES FOR MATURE AND DECLINING INDUSTRIES

From the two dimensions outlined in the previous section (14.4), environmental factors and company strengths and weaknesses, it is possible to contruct a simple model (figure 14.3) with one on each axis. Although the model has apparently four discrete cells, it should be noted that each axis is in reality continuous so that the divisions are to facilitate analysis. It can be seen that the strongest position is the top left-hand corner of the diagram: considerable strengths in an industry with a large number of favourable traits. It follows, therefore, that the bottom right-hand corner is the worst possible situation. Thus, as the product is positioned in this diagram so the strategy most likely to succeed is indicated. The bands for the four strategies are drawn diagonally across the diagram to complement the favourable (top left) to unfavourable (bottom right) axis:

- Maintain position: maintain facilities by holding or increasing market share by acquisition.

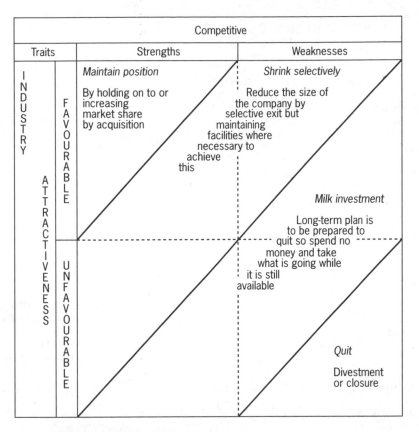

FIGURE 14.3   Strategies for declining industries

- Shrink selectively: reduce the size of the company by selective exit but maintaining facilities where necessary to achieve this.
- Milk investment: long-term plan is to be prepared to quit so spend no money and take what is going while it is still available.
- Quit: divestment or closure.

There is a danger that models explained in two-dimensional planes may be intepreted as static, whereas the reality is of a constant state of change as companies merge, close down or make new competitive moves. Thus, it is essential for the strategist to seek to identify likely competitive moves before settling for a particular policy. It is also necessary to evaluate the inherent risks in the chosen strategy.

14.6   MANAGEMENT SUMMARY AND CHECKLIST

Reasons for decline in demand

- technological change;
- social change;
- market saturation.

2   Factors leading to success or failure

Environmental Factors:

Demand characteristics	*Favourable*	*Unfavourable*
Nature of the decline	Slow speed	Rapid
	Steady	Volatile
Industry structure	Supplier power	Buyer power
Price stability	Stable	Fluctuating/falling
Product differentiation	Differentiated	Commodity-like
Segments	Some segments	No segments

Supply Characteristics		
Level of excess capacity	Low	High
Vertical integration	Significant	Non-existent
Industry structure	Few suppliers	Many suppliers
Company ownership	Part of large corporation	Dominated by owners
Asset characteristics	Undervalued	Overvalued
	Alternative uses	No alternative uses

Company strengths and weaknesses:	*Strength*	*Weakness*
Management attitudes	Knowledge of situation	Misperception or failure to acknowledge situation
Market share	High	Low
Cost position in industry	Low	High
Patent	Some time before expiry	None/nearly expired

3   Strategies for declining industries

- maintain position;
- shrink selectively;
- milk investment;
- quit.

NOTES

1   M. E. Porter, *Competitive Strategy and Competitive Advantage* (Free Press, Glencoe, 1980 and 1985); K. R. Harrigan, *Strategies for Declining Businesses* (Lexington Books, Lexington, Mass., 1980).

FURTHER READING

1 Charles Baden-Fuller and John M. Stopford, *The Mature Business* (Routledge 1992).

Introduction – Symptoms of Decline – Causes of Decline –
Feasibility of Recovery – Strategies for Recovery – Management
Summary and Checklist

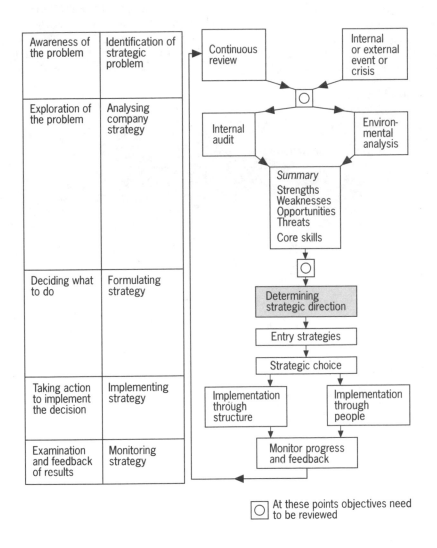

FIGURE 15.1 The strategic decision-making process

15.1 INTRODUCTION

Chapter 12 provided a means of determining the future direction of a business. However, it is possible that as a result of falling profitability, strategy is so constrained that policies adopted are focused on offsetting the threats and/or eliminating the weaknesses which have led to the falling profitability. This is a situation which will arise in most companies from time to time, and research is now beginning to supply helpful insights into the processes of decline and recovery or, in some cases, collapse. This chapter will therefore be concerned with the symptoms and causes of decline, the feasibility of recovery and the strategic policies required for recovery where recovery is possible.

15.2 SYMPTOMS OF DECLINE

What is 'decline'? As with many other aspects of corporate strategy, there is, as yet, no definitive answer to this question. Basically, a company in decline is one in which there is some doubt concerning the survival of the company. As a fundamental reason for the collapse of most companies is their inability to produce sufficient profit, a simple definition of decline is falling profitability, measured by

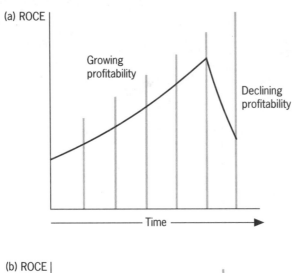

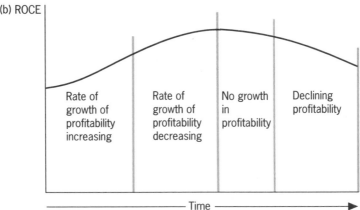

FIGURE 15.2 Patterns in declining profitability

falling returns on capital employed or earnings per share. Another dimension of decline is the time span over which decline has occurred. While accurate prediction is rarely possible, declining profitability does not usually occur without some previous indications. For example, in figure 15.2, the first example would be occasioned by some exceptional event, for instance an acquisition which 'went wrong'. The second example indicates the more likely pattern, that is that a period of declining profitability is preceded by a period of no growth and a period when the rate of growth is decreasing. Accurate prediction is difficult because the time scale over which decline takes place may vary considerably. Also, it is often difficult to decide whether a reduction in the rate of growth is a temporary and insignificant occurrence or evidence of a more fundamental problem.

Symptoms and causes are in some cases closely connected, but the objective of this section is to provide some indicators which will help to identify potential crises. As with human illness, not all symptoms may be apparent in all cases, so with corporate illness all the symptoms of decline may not be in evidence in all companies experiencing declining profitability. Symptoms of decline are generally evident in the finance and marketing figures. The most obvious financial indications are a reduction in dividends, increasing debt and decreasing liquidity. Significant research efforts here have been devoted to the prediction of decline and collapse through the use of financial models.[1] However, while these may give some general indication of the health of a business, their ability to predict bankruptcy with any overall degree of accuracy is extremely doubtful, both on the basis of the methodology used[2] and also on the results obtained. In marketing terms, declining profitability may arise where there is no real increase in sales or where market share is falling.

15.3   CAUSES OF DECLINE

It could be argued that there is only one cause of declining profitability – bad management. If management were adequately tracking the success of its products and the changes which are likely to take place in their markets and were taking appropriate action, then profits would not decline. However, as such success would require omniscience (and given that few are prophets) even the most systematic managers will make mistakes. This section will therefore discuss those aspects of the interface between the business and its environment which result in declining profitability. The answers can be separated into those which are internal and those which are external to the firm (see table 15.1).

Poor Management

All problems start at the top, and so poor management is the key to declining profitability. Those responsible for the operations of the company are making wrong

TABLE 15.1 Causes of declining profitability

Internal factors	External factors
Poor management	Declining demand for the product
Weaknesses in the finance function	Changes in the industry structure
Weaknesses in the marketing function	General economic, social or political factors
Weaknesses in the production/ operations function	
Mistaken acquisition	
Problems with a 'big' project	

decisions with respect either to the strategic decisions which are being made or to the personnel being employed to implement those decisions. The role and style of the chief executive (CEO) are critical. A major feature of corporate collapse is the autocratic style of leadership of the CEO. This is often evident when the role of chairman and chief executive are not separated and the board is not genuinely participating in the strategic decision-making process. While some flamboyant entrepreneurs succeed for a period of time, their style often leads to major problems and sometimes to bankruptcy. Recent examples include Goodman (Intasun) and Azil Nadir (Polly Peck). Poor management can also result from an unbalanced board of directors; for example, too many accountants or engineers. Another reason can be lack of depth; that is, insufficient senior management resources either in terms of quantity or quality.

Finance

Poor financial control is often a cause of falling profitability. This can result from poor budgetary control, an inadequate costing system or an inability to monitor and control cash. Other weaknesses in the finance function can arise from faulty valuation of assets and creative accounting. A major reason for the demise of many small companies is overtrading, which may arise in several forms. The most frequently occurring is when the profit from increased turnover is insufficient to finance the money borrowed in order to expand.

Marketing

An inadequate marketing function will occur in those firms which fail fully to understand and operationalize the concept of marketing. Marketing is often an inappropriate term for the activity concerned. It is regularly used for selling, advertising or distribution. The evidence of real marketing activity in an organization stems from a marketing plan which guides the whole of the company/customer relationship and will be heavily dependent on marketing research information and the generation of new product-market offerings. Companies in decline have usually failed to embrace the marketing concept in these terms.

Production/Operations

A feature of the production function found in companies with declining profitability is a high cost structure relative to other manufacturers in the same industry. This might result from inefficient production methods or from poor labour relations leading to strikes.

Acquisition Policy

For some companies, an acquisition which has failed to generate the expected returns has been a major cause of corporate decline. The benefits expected from acquisition and the reasons why these are not always forthcoming are discussed in detail in chapter 16.

Big Projects

The 'big project' is another reason which sometimes causes declining profitability or collapse. By definition, the 'big project' represents an activity that is large in terms of company resources and which is likely significantly to affect profitability one way or another. The 'project' might be a large acquisition, a major capital investment in a new process or product, a major marketing campaign or substantial expenditure on research and development.

Declining Industry Sales

The most significant factor in the external environment is a fall in the demand for the product manufactured by the company: declining industry sales. It is important to identify whether this is part of a temporary economic recession or whether it is the beginning of a long-term trend. Also, the rate of decline and the reasons for decline are key factors when considering what action should be taken to restore profitability.

Industry Structure

Changes to the industry structure may also cause profitability to decline. For example if, in an industry where there are three major firms, two of them merge, then the third company may be put at a considerable disadvantage. The concentration and nature of competition in an industry will be key determinants of profitability

Other Environmental Factors

There are changes taking place in the economic, social, political and technological environments which will influence company performance. Occasionally some feature of these environments (discussed in detail in chapter 5) has a major impact on a specific industry or company. For instance, changes to commodity prices can have a significant effect on heavy users of a particular commodity. Likewise, changes in the exchange rate or some change in fashion or technology may have a devastating impact on profitability.

15.4   FEASIBILITY OF RECOVERY

The causes of decline are a synthesis of research on corporate collapse, turnaround and managing in a declining industry. A key question for companies with falling profitability is: is recovery possible? There are several features of such situations which enable the analyst to make some assessment concerning the feasibility of recovery.

It has been suggested by Argenti that corporate collapse is the end of a gradual period of decline during which profitability begins to fall and an increasing number of the causes for decline are evident or growing in significance.[3] The concept of declining profitability and the likelihood of recovery are illustrated in figure 15.3.

The objective of all companies which are in decline is to achieve a long-term recovery. However, as profitability falls, it will become increasingly difficult to achieve this objective because the extent of the mismatch between the products of the company and the markets served widens. Once crisis level is reached, short-term solutions are often necessary, for instance, selling assets to raise cash, which may have detrimental long-term effects. 'Mere survival' and 'sustainable recovery' are ends of a continuous scale of post-crisis profitability rather than two discrete groups into which recovery companies can be categorized.

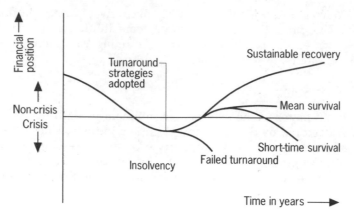

FIGURE 15.3 Types of recovery situation
Source: Stuart Slatter, *Corporate Recovery* (Penguin, Harmondsworth, 1984). Reprinted with permission.

Harrigan suggests that there are two key dimensions for determining the strategy and assessing performance in a declining industry:

* favourable or unfavourable industry characteristics;
* relative strengths and weaknesses of the business.[4]

These would be evaluated by a detailed analysis of the causes for decline. Slatter used a similar classification, as shown in figure 15.4.[5]

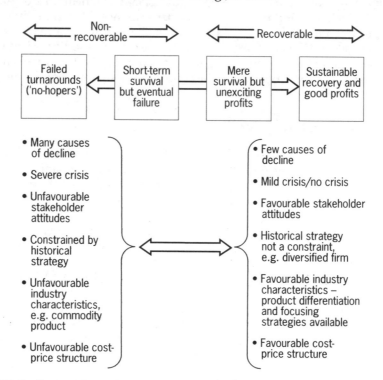

FIGURE 15.4 Factors determining the feasibility of recovery
Source: Stuart Slatter, *Corporate Recovery* (Penguin, Harmondsworth, 1984). Reprinted with permission.

15.5   STRATEGIES FOR RECOVERY

Action which may be taken to restore the ailing firm to profitability can be considered in five groups:

- organizational changes;
- finance and financial strategies;
- cost-reduction strategies;
- asset-reduction strategies;
- revenue-generating strategies.

Organizational Changes

In many turnaround situations, a key feature of the recovery is the appointment of a new chief executive (CEO) or other changes in the senior management of the company. In some cases the new CEO may be a company director who is a person with skills that can effect a return to profitability. As well as making appropriate strategic decisions, such new appointments need to change the working environment within the company. This can be achieved by attention to the ability and motivation of senior staff. Early decisions should be made on which staff, if any, need to be replaced and incentives need to be introduced in order to achieve given objectives. Also, a new chief executive may need to change the morale of the workforce. If the business has been in decline for some time and if this has now reached crisis level, morale is likely to be low. The new CEO needs to convince both management and workforce that, with appropriate new strategies, the crisis can be overcome.

It may be necessary to institute some fundamental organizational changes, perhaps with respect to different business units (such as the grouping of several units into one division). Many UK companies have an 'overseas' division, which is market orientated, in a structure which is basically product or technology based and in which the overseas companies manufacture the same products as their UK counterparts. Unless there are exceptionally good reasons this is likely to be less efficient.

The internal operations of companies may need to be altered to offset conflicts and weaknesses, and it is likely that relationships between operating divisions and head office will need to be clarified in terms of authority and control procedures.

Finance and Financial Strategies

The introduction of financial controls is usually one of the first steps taken in a turnaround situation because in many cases poor financial control has been a contributory cause of the decline in profitability. Also, it is often necessary to restructure the debt. This involves an agreement between the ailing firm and its creditors, usually the banks, to reschedule and sometimes convert interest and other principal payments into other negotiable financial instruments. Examples are the conversion of short-term into long-term debt or the conversion of loans into convertible preference shares or equity.

Cost-reduction Strategies

In severe crisis situations, cost-reduction strategies are often implemented at an early stage, as many will have an almost immediate effect. The management needs to examine which are the key areas of cost and to attend to those in the first instance. In many companies the key cost element is labour; that is, wages and salaries. An immediate effect can be achieved by banning overtime and stopping new recruitment. In the longer term it may be necessary to reduce the size of the labour force. This can be achieved through natural wastage, early retirement, voluntary redundancy or, if necessary, compulsory redundancy. The severity of the crisis will determine the speed with which the shedding of labour will need to be effected.

In some businesses the materials used in production can constitute a major cost factor. This is evident where a high-cost raw material is used, for instance, gold, or where a very large volume of a raw material is used, such as in the generation of electricity. A reduction in these costs may be achieved through seeking new sources of supply or by a redesign of the product which would seek to reduce the volume of material. It might also be possible to use an alternative material.

Cost reductions may be achieved in divisions and departments. Regular targets are those activities which do not have much impact on turnover in the short term. Depending on the nature of the business, these would include market research, public relations, advertising, education and training, and research and development. It may be necessary in the short term to reduce the size of these functions but their absence in the longer term is likely to lead to yet another crisis.

The final area for cost reductions is general overheads. This would include staff functions such as computing and head office staff. Also, the fringe benefits offered by the company could be reduced. This would include company cars, free or subsidized meals, sports and recreation facilities, pensions and holidays. At a more mundane level, heating, lighting, stationery and typing facilities can also be scrutinized.

Asset-reduction Strategies

The impact of asset-reduction strategies is not often apparent in the short term. The policy likely to have the biggest impact in this category is the divestment of a division or complete operating unit to another company as an operating business. In many crisis situations, loss-making subsidiaries are sold and this has the immediate effect of stemming the outflow of funds and of raising revenue. However, the disadvantages are that the subsidiaries are unlikely to be sold at anything more than asset value and, considering the losses, perhaps at considerably less than asset value.

Selling a successful division has the merit of securing a higher price and thus increasing the current cash flow, but in the longer term the associated profits will be lost and the sold company might have provided a basis for long-term recovery.

An alternative asset-reduction strategy is a rationalization of existing facilities, closing one plant and transferring the manufacture of the products of that company to another business in the group. The unused facilities can then be sold in parts. The sale of specific assets, including land or buildings, can be effected without complete closure of a plant and offers another means of reducing assets and obtaining cash.

Another means of reducing assets is to sell some or all of the assets to a finance company and lease them back. This would only be possible if the assets were not being used as collateral for some form of borrowing.

The foregoing discussion is primarily concerned with fixed assets, but working capital offers another area for consideration. A reduction in stocks and work-in-progress will reduce the asset base and release cash. Reducing debtors and increasing the length of time to pay creditors also reduces assets and releases cash, but creditors are unlikely to allow this to continue if the crisis in the company is apparent to those outside. In some cases, the creditors may be 'locked-in' because to insist on payment may push the company into liquidation, which would probably result in only a small percentage of the debt being repaid.

Revenue-generating Strategies

Revenue-generating strategies are usually those which take the longest time to have a significant impact on profitability, because most frequently this is the part of the business which is the crux of the problem and will be most difficult to turn around and also because expenditure is often required before extra income is generated.

Some immediate effects may result from a sharp impetus to the selling function, which could be achieved through increasing incentives to salesmen or small alterations to the product. However a longer-term marketing strategy may have no discernible effect in the short term, as the process requires time for information-gathering, decision-making, the manufacture of new or modified products, and the preparation and implementation of a sales campaign.

15.6   MANAGEMENT SUMMARY AND CHECKLIST

1   Symptoms of decline

- Financial: falling profitability, falling dividends, increased debt, decreasing liquidity.
- Marketing: falling sales.

2   Causes of decline

- Poor management: autocratic CEO with weak top management.
- Finance: poor financial control.
- Marketing: no operationalization of the marketing (as opposed to selling) concept.
- Production/operations: high cost structure.
- Acquisition policy: no comprehensive strategy to the process of acquisition.
- Big projects: failure of a project which constituted a large proportion of the firm.
- Declining industry sales: failure to acknowledge decline or adapt to the situation.
- Industry structure changes: changes which put the business at a significant disadvantage.
- Other environmental variables: technological, social, political, economic.

3   Feasibility of recovery determined by:

- Favourable or unfavourable industry characteristics.
- Relative strengths and weaknesses of the business.

4   Strategies for recovery

- Organizational changes.
- Finance and financial strategies.
- Cost reduction.
- Asset reduction.
- Revenue generation.

Please note: Not all symptoms and causes of decline are evident in all cases and sometimes some of these features may exist although the firm may not experience declining profitability. Similarly, feasibility of recovery and strategies for recovery may not be in evidence in all cases.

NOTES

1   E. I. Altman, *Corporate Bankruptcy in America* (Heath, 1971). W. H. Beaver, 'Financial Ratios as Predictors of Failure', *Journal of Accounting Research*, Supplement to Vol. 4 (1966) pp.71–111. R. Taffler and H. Tisshaw, 'Going Going Gone – 4 Factors which Predict', *Accountancy* (March 1977).
2   R. A. Eisenbeis, 'Pitfalls in the Application of Discriminant Analysis in Business Finance and Economics', *Journal of Finance*, 32, no. 3 (1977), pp. 875–900.
3   J. Argenti, *Corporate Collapse – The Causes and Symptoms* (McGrawHill, New York, 1976).
4   K. Harrigan, *Strategies for Declining Businesses* (Lexington Books, Lexington, Mass., 1980).
5   Stuart Slatter, *Corporate Recovery* (Penguin, Harmondsworth, 1984).

FURTHER READING

A fuller understanding of the issues in this chapter can be obtained by reference to the following books:

J. Argenti, *Corporate Collapse – The Causes and Symptoms* (McGraw-Hill, New York, 1976).

D. B. Bibeault, *Corporate Turnaround: How Managers Turn Losers into Winners* (McGraw-Hill, New York, 1984).

Peter H. Grinyer, David G. Mayes and Peter McKiernan, *Sharpbenders: The Secrets or Unleashing Corporate Potential* (Blackwell, Oxford, 1988).

K. Harrigan, *Strategies for Declining Businesses* (Lexington Books, Lexington, Mass., 1988).

S. Slatter, *Corporate Recovery* (Penguin, Harmondsworth, 1984).

C. BadenFuller and J. M. Stopford, *The Mature Business* (Routledge 1992).

P. N. Khandwalla, *Innovative Corporate Turnrounds* (Sage 1992).

PART 5

Strategic Choice

16 Acquisition and Divestment

Introduction – Acquisition – Divestment: Reasons and Methods – Divestment: Management Buy-outs – Management Summary and Checklist

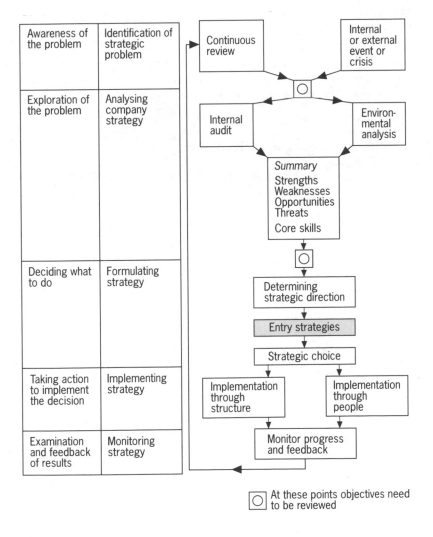

FIGURE 16.1 The strategic decision-making process

16.1   INTRODUCTION

The process for determining possible future options for the company was outlined in part 4. That process was concerned principally with the ends not the means. The means, the decision to make (internal development) or buy (acquisition) or indeed to sell (divestment), are the focus of this chapter. An investigation of the means by which the ends might be achieved is an essential precursor to chapter 19 which draws the process to a conclusion by an evaluation of the available options and the choice of a given strategy. It is certain that not all desired options can be attained, the principal obstacles being time or cost or both.

As the means are a critical factor in determining whether a desired option can be achieved, it will be useful to examine some general barriers to entry and exit. There exists a large range of entry barriers but perhaps the four most significant are:

- economics of scale;
- a patent or technological information or know-how;
- the existence of significant brand names;
- the non-availability of distribution outlets.

Some aspects of the entry barriers may also result in substantial exit barriers. In particular, the following four factors have been found to be the most frequent reasons for the reluctance of companies to exit from an industry:

- non-differentiable assets;
- capital-intensive industry;
- age and level of depreciation of the assets;
- poor realizable price.
  Additionally, loss leaders or a loss-making product which is an essential part of a range may create exit problems.

16.2   ACQUISITION

There are basically three ways of entering new markets or offering new products: acquisition, internal development or co-operative ventures. Co-operative ventures (joint ventures, minority interest, licensing, franchising, selling agents), which are discussed in the next chapter, are a hybrid of the other two entry strategies in that, rather than complete self-sufficiency or total acquisition, there is a sharing of the process which starts at product development and ends with sales to customers. It follows, therefore, that the advantages and disadvantages of internal development and acquisation are also applicable to joint ventures. A summary of the reasons for adopting these alternative entry strategies is outlined in table 16.1. Of the factors listed, timing and cost are usually the critical variables.

The strategy of acquisition is the penetration of a new market or the extension of the product range through the purchase of a firm in that business, thus instantly acquiring the requisite skills and resources, although they may not currently be operating to satisfactory performance standards. At this point it may be useful to examine whether there is any significant difference between a 'merger' and a 'takeover'. There appears to be a growing tendency to use the former term rather than the latter, possibly because it seems less hostile, yet the fact is that in many instances it is a takeover which is taking place between a 'bidding firm' and a 'victim'. There does not seem to be a consensus of definition, and as far as the City is concerned they are considered to be equally applicable.

TABLE 16.1 Internal development versus acquisition

Internal development	Acquisition
is pursued when	is pursued when
• the product is in the early stages of the product life-cycle (PLC)	• the product is in the maturity of decline stages of the PLC
• the new products or markets are close to the existing portfolio	• the company has little knowledge of the products or markets it wishes to develop
• there is sufficient time to develop internally	• earliest entry is desirable
• there are no suitable acquisitions	• there are few internal development skills within the company
• there is no production capacity in the industry	• there is production capacity in the industry
• costs need to be spread over time	• costs do not need to be spread over time

The overall cost of development will be a consideration, but may be cheaper by either means according to the specific factors apparent in the particular project under consideration

The issues surrounding mergers will be discussed in sections relating to the time sequence of an acquisition: before, during and after.

Before the Bid

It will be useful to start with the key question: why do companies seek to merge? The question is all the more pertinent as research substantially supports the view that merger is usually both more risky and more expensive than internal growth.

The motives for merging are usefully summarized in figure 16.2 and are divided into defensive and offensive reasons. It should be emphasized that this is only a summary and that each item is capable of considerable expansion. For instance 'gains in financial strength' could emerge as a result of tax advantages, gearing changes, better utilization of assets (turnaround situations) and so on. Also the diagram does not indicate the importance and effect of timing, not only with respect to the date on which the bid is made, but also in that assets and skills can be acquired more quickly than is likely through internal development.

The next question is: how do companies merge? What is the process which needs to be followed in order to maximize the likelihood of success? There are basically five steps:

1 Have clear objectives for the merger   The reasons for the merger need to be made explicit in terms of the financial and product market portfolio effects on the acquiring company. These objectives will result from the internal and external (SWOT) analysis and the projected future financial aims and objectives of the business as a whole. It should be appreciated at this early stage that no target company is likely to satisfy the specific criteria in every respect, and that it is possible that a choice will have to be made from a range of possible companies, each offering satisfaction with respect to different criteria. For example, a company satisfying most of the criteria may be well managed and successful and therefore more expensive than a company satisfying fewer criteria but at a lower price.

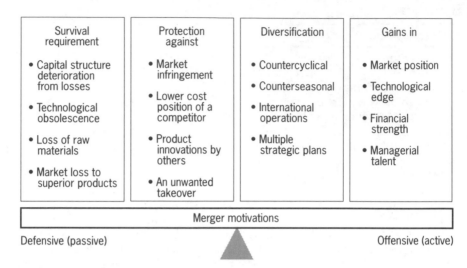

Survival requirement	Protection against	Diversification	Gains in
• Capital structure deterioration from losses • Technological obsolescence • Loss of raw materials • Market loss to superior products	• Market infringement • Lower cost position of a competitor • Product innovations by others • An unwanted takeover	• Countercyclical • Counterseasonal • International operations • Multiple strategic plans	• Market position • Technological edge • Financial strength • Managerial talent

Merger motivations

Defensive (passive)   Offensive (active)

Figure 16.2   Motivations to merge
Source: F.T. Hanera, *Business Policy Planning and Strategy* (Winthrop, Cambridge, Mass., 1976). Reprinted with permission.

2   *Be satisfied that major objectives are achievable*   It follows that, as there is rarely an 'ideal' target, it is important to focus on the key features of the objectives to ensure that they will be satisfied. The basic financial return will need to be achieved and this will be a function of the price paid and the future cash flows received after acquisition. If the expected future cash flows need to be greater than those at present, the means for increasing the flows and the time period over which they can be expected must be carefully analysed. Most acquisitions have some product-market portfolio aims and, if these will only be met in part, the implications should be considered and ways of completing the fulfilment of the aims need to be outlined. Unless the firm is to be closed and the assets sold, some evaluation has to be made of the target company management and its ability to meet the desired aims and objectives which are being planned by the acquirer.

3   *Prepare strategy to include top price and offer package*   A strategy is a complete game plan and contains contingency plans – if the target companies react in *this* way, then we, the acquiring company, will take *that* action. It is not possible to outline a comprehensive plan including all contingencies in an introductory text, but it is intended to outline the key features which should enable the reader to devise a game plan appropriate to any given situation. In general, valuation of a company is made on the basis of its assets and the ability of those assets to generate earnings. There are firms where the net assets per share comfortably exceed the market price of the share because its earnings are not at a satisfactory level. In cases where this situation is known to those outside the company, there could be several bidders who believe that they can use the assets more profitably.

Invariably the question will be: what premium over the existing share price should be bid? In such situations the experience of the merchant banks becomes invaluable and often both sides take on advisers. In the case of Fitch Lovell the shares had underperformed the food sector by 18 per cent in the year before acquisition. The bid by Booker valued Fitch at approximately 300p; this was a 40 per cent premium on the share price before the bid was announced. The price offered was 14 times current earnings against an average market p/e of 10–12, thus

Booker were expecting to be able to make better use of the assets than the existing management team.

The purchase price offered is made up of:

(a) cash per share; (b) X shares of the acquirer for every Y shares of the target; (c) a combination of (a) and (b). In the case of publicly quoted companies, we have generally available financial information such as share price, EPS, p/e ratio, and so on. Also, when a bid is made, the usual form is for the proposed 'victim' to forecast its future earnings and other performance factors (especially if in the second half of its year) and/or revalue its assets (that is, update valuations of its property holdings, and so on).

However, of crucial importance is the comparison of the p/e ratios. If that of the bidding firm is lower than that of the 'victim', then by purchasing via shares it would dilute its earnings per share (not desirable), and it is, therefore, pressed into paying cash. Thus we can see the importance to quoted companies of maintaining a high p/e ratio; first, defensively in keeping predators away and, secondly, to be used offensively if bidding for a firm with a lower p/e ratio. The effect of the p/e ratio is discussed in more detail in chapter 9.

4   *Purchase plan*   The following outline maps out one possible route by which a company may be acquired. It may be regarded as 'typical' or 'idealized' and is based upon procedures and rules for the London Stock Exchange.

Step 1   The would-be buyer collects information on its target. Normally this is done in secret – which often means there is a heavy reliance on published data. A maximum and an initial offer price are thereby fixed for the target. Where possible, information regarding the identity of the target's principal shareholders should also be gathered.

Step 2   The next step is optional. A stake may be acquired in the target company – it can be used as a springboard from which to launch a full bid. As long as the size of the stake does not exceed 3 per cent of the target company's issued share capital, the purchase can be kept secret (Sections 24–7 Companies Act 1985).

Step 3   If the bidding company acquires more than 15 per cent of the shares of the target company it is compelled offer for all the shares.

Step 4   When all is prepared (offer document, finance and so on), the buyer approaches the board of the target company and asks it to approve the bid. In order to help assure the success of the bid, it is normal for the buyer to offer a significant premium over and above the current trading price of the target's shares, in cash, buyer's shares or a mixture of the two.

Step 5   If the directors of the target company approve the bid they will then send the offer out to their shareholders asking for their acceptance.

Step 6   Initially, the bid is conditional. More than 50 per cent of the target company's shares must be offered to the bidder by the shareholders, or the would-be buyer can withdraw. Once this threshold has been exceeded the offer is declared unconditional – thereafter shareholders of the target who have agreed to sell their shares may not then withdraw.

Step 8   Various time limits have been fixed by which the various phases of the bid must be completed. Normally the offer must be open for acceptance by the target company's shareholders for at least 21 days after the offer was posted.

Step 8   If the buyer gains acceptance for 90 per cent of the target's shares within four months of making its offer, it can arrange a compulsory purchase of the remainder (Section 209 Companies Act 1948).

This very simple outline assumes that the Department of Trade and Industry, the Bank of England and the target's board of directors all approve the bid.

Step 9   If there are insufficient acceptances after 60 days the offer lapses.

5 Responsibility for the purchase   It is important to be able to identify who is responsible for the final decision to acquire another company. This has the advantage of ensuring that the bid is the focus of at least one person, and does not allow the decision to be the outcome of a committee from which no one may take the individual responsibility for seeking to ensure its success. This person may be the chief executive, the chief of corporate planning or (more likely in a multi-divisional company) a divisional managing director. The responsible person needs to be afforded all necessary resources, which would be part of the plan successfully to facilitate implementation.

In concluding the pre-bid stage it is important to note some ways in which a company can deter likely predators.

- Enhance share price through good shareholder relations, public relations, contact with the financial press.
- Make long-term contracts with directors and suppliers.
- Avoid financial attractions such as spare debt capacity, excessive cash and use sale and leaseback to avoid asset strippers.

During the Bid

The 'purchase plan' was outlined previously and the comments which describe the strategy as a complete game plan are again relevant, particularly in view of the various defensive tactics which the victim might pursue, such as:

1 Revaluation of assets and profits forecast   Some companies do not revalue assets regularly and thus a bid may be made on a wholly unrealistic valuation. During the BTR bid for Dunlop it was shown that the offer price was considerably below a price based on a revaluation of the assets. Likewise, it is possible to provide a profit forecast which indicates a considerable improvement on current performance. However, this defence is subject to the Takeover Code rules which ensure as far as possible that the figures are realistic both for revaluation and for revising the profits forecast.

2 Rubbishing the bid   Almost all companies use this technique. This defence is often used in conjunction with a revaluation and rejects the bid in the most sarcastic terms, concentrating on future earnings, lack of synergy and industrial logic, or by taking the offensive and attacking the competence of the bidding company and its management.

3 Publicity campaigns   A recent defence used to influence shareholders has been an extended publicity campaign highlighting strengths and pinpointing opposition weaknesses. Several campaigns are considered to have cost considerably in excess of £1 million.

4 White Knights   In order to escape the unwanted attentions of a would-be buyer, the target company can submit to another 'more sympathetic' company, a White Knight. This strategy is pursued when the target company management accept, at least implicitly, that their own stewardship has led to the current situation. It may not be considered a defence in that the company does lose its identity; however, it is a tactic that a bidder may have to deal with.
Laporte rescued Evode from a bid by Wassall.

5 New share issue   The City Code has now effectively stopped the use of this tactic in the UK but it could be possible elsewhere in the world.

6 Monopolies and Mergers Commission   As a defence tactic the victim would need to persuade the MMC that the merger was against 'the public interest', possibly by creating a company with such a large market share as to create a monopoly and thereby reduce consumer choice and increase prices. This tactic, if successful, can be an absolute defence or, even if unsuccessful, it can gain time for the target company to adopt other defensive measures. Lonrho and House of Fraser is a good example.

7   *Going private*   Management buy-outs are becoming increasingly common, but their use as a defence technique is very unusual. It is possible that this is seen as management acting in their own interest. However, research in the USA (where the practice is more common) indicated that shareholders received an average 56 per cent above the market price.[1] The UK example is Haden (a lift and air-conditioning contractor) rebuffing the unwanted attentions of Trafalgar House (May 1985).

8   *Friendly third parties*   The target company persuades a third party to become a shareholder. By doing this the third party 'mops up' shares on the market which might otherwise be sold or pledged to the unwanted bidder. Also, it acts as a blocking stake in that it may, with the directors' shareholding, constitute more than the 50 per cent of the shares required by the bidder to gain control. It also helps to maintain the target company share price.

9   *Selling the crown jewels*   Disposing of major assets (the crown jewels) during a takeover is now extremely difficult as the City Code forbids it. However, in the USA it is still possible.

10   *Acquire new assets*   This strategy seeks to increase the size or improve the profitability in order to reduce the attractiveness of the victim. While Waddington were being pursued by BPCC, they acquired the Business Forms division of Vickers which made them larger, stronger and improved the balance between divisions.

11   *Porcupine defences*   These are a range of strategies, currently used in the USA but not in the UK, whereby the victim makes adjustments to the equivalent of the memorandum and articles of association.

12   *Golden parachute*   This technique is the payment of bonuses to management in the event of a successful bid. This again is used in the the USA but not presently in the UK.

After the Bid

The post-acquisition phase is often the most crucial, and consequently management needs to re-focus attention on the reasons for the takeover and to take appropriate action to ensure that the expected benefits materialize. Some of the major problems experienced are outlined below.

1   *Management problems*   Integrating the acquired company into the acquiring firm has to be achieved through people. New systems, plans and strategies can only be implemented if the necessary skills are available in the acquired business. The simplistic view that all management can be removed and replaced by hiring a more competent group of staff is usually unrealistic. It is immediately obvious that this will take time and assumes that the needed characteristics are evident and that those with such characteristics will want to join the firm.

Morale and damaging internal political conflicts (see chapter 20) can affect the size of and rate at which expected benefits are realized. If morale is low, care needs to be taken to ensure it does not fall even further, and this can be done by making major decisions quickly in order that the fears of change can be set aside.

If part of the reason for the acquisition was to obtain the services of key members of the management team of the acquired company, then early discussions may be necessary to ensure that they do not leave.

These issues may seem trivial or appear to have obvious solutions, but it is often the case that the success or failure of a merger results from the way in which these problems are resolved.

2   *Competition*   It is possible that the takeover will change the competitive environment in the market (see chapter 7) and that such changes may provoke a reaction from other firms in the same business. Changes in the competitive environment may significantly affect the original objectives and expected benefits of the merger. If the changes were likely to have an adverse effect, management might choose to ignore the situation as they were committed to the original objectives. This is not a wise course of action. In some cases, renewed effort and some changes to plan may bring results, but if the evidence is that the merger cannot now bring the desired benefits, it may be better to abort the project at minimum cost. The fear of failure and bad publicity cause some managements to pursue a course which, because of a reluctance to admit a mistake, leads to even bigger problems.

3   *Finance*   Management problems and changes in the competitive environment are not the only reasons why many of the strategic advantages are often illusory. Unless it is an *agreed* bid and the acquirer can investigate the business from inside, there are many unknown factors. If the benefits are significantly less than anticipated, it is important to accept the situation and adopt appropriate rectification measures. For instance, any over payment should be funded to reserves and actually written off or provision made for it to be written off.

16.3   DIVESTMENT: REASONS AND METHODS

During the past two decades the business strategy of many firms has been focused on growth by diversification and by acquisition. It follows that the product-market portfolios of many large companies contain businesses which are small and peripheral to the main activities of the firm as a whole.

With the accent on growth, little attention has been paid to the subject of divestment: the exit from businesses no longer wanted in the portfolio. However, the latter part of the 1980s and early 1990s has seen many companies exit from businesses for a variety of reasons and in several different ways.

The period of growth was fuelled by the desire to grow big and thus, it was hoped, to enable the company to control a larger part of its operating environment than if it was small. It is also noteworthy that directors' salaries were related to the size of company turnover and not profit. However, the advent of corporate raiders in the US and Hanson and BTR in the UK have made diversified companies address the fundamental question of synergy. Do two businesses joined together into one corporation add up to more than the sum of the parts? If so, all is well and good. If not, then let them be put asunder.

There are several reasons both offensive and defensive which might cause a company to consider divestment. Such divestments have been of small, non-core parts of the organization, but occasionally as with BBA it has been a major activity of the firm.

Outlined below are some offensive and defensive reasons for divestment.

Offensive reasons
- in re-focusing the total business, this part is no longer required, even though it may meet profitability standards;

- to raise cash;
- to improve ROI;
- family company with no future family succession.

Defensive reasons

- does not and cannot be made to meet profitability standards;
- avoid acquisition (BAT is an example which sold businesses in order to avoid the unwanted attention of a predator);
- sell this part of the business in order to avoid bankruptcy;
- avoid risk: future prospects or expansion are at a level of risk which the company does not wish to embrace;
- management control of such a diverse business has become too difficult.

The process of divestment can pose some very difficult problems. It is possible that the business for disposal may be highly profitable and attractive to several buyers. However, the opposite is more often the case and as such the price obtained for such assets may be well below that paid for them as a result of a contested takeover in the past. Wright and Coyne suggest six different ways of exiting from a business.[2] In fact, not all of the divestment options involve complete loss of ownership and/or control:

- franchising;
- contracting out;
- sell-off;
- management/leveraged buy-out;
- spin-off or demerger;
- asset swap/strategic trade.

For some types of business franchising may afford the best divestment opportunity, particularly where local service or small-scale manufacturing facilities would be desirable. Contracting out is similar to franchising, but differs in that having sold the business the vendor requires the business to supply a quantity of the goods or services at a price usually for a specified time period. This gives the business guaranteed sales and the parent an assured source of supply.

The most widely described form of divestment is the sell-off. In this way the parent sells the business to another business and severs all connection. Another form of divestment is the leveraged or management buy-out which, given its recent rise as a form of exit, is afforded a separate section (16.4). With large corporate predators around demergers are beginning to appear as a form of divestment; Courtaulds, for example, has created two companies: one for its textile business and one for its chemical business. Finally, an occasional means of divestment is the asset swap. In this case little money transfers hands but a 'match' has to be found before this means of exit can be pursued.

16.4   DIVESTMENT: MANAGEMENT BUY-OUTS

A separate section on management buy-buts (MBOs) has been included for two reasons. First, they provide a new and increasingly used means for divestment. Secondly, unlike the other forms of divestment outlined by Wright and Coyne, the parties involved are different in terms of number and by nature. In an MBO there are at least three major interested parties as compared to two for other divestment situations. There are the vendors, the buyers and the venture capital providers. The vendors' role is not significantly different from other situations. However, the buyer is a group of managers who are usually going to put, what will be for them, a substantial equity stake into the new business. Other means of divestment are not usually of any major consequence to capital providers. In some cases the buyer may use internal funds and where capital is required there is a proven track record which reduces the need for detailed in-depth analysis. Also, divestments are often relatively small in terms of buyer and seller total assets. In order to explore the role of MBOs in the divestment process factors which need to be considered by each of the parties are outlined below.

Vendors

From the vendors' viewpoint the MBO often offers a more rapid and flexible approach to exit. It is not necessary to search for a buyer and all involved are conversant with the facts of the company, its value and associated risks.

It is often more satisfactory from a public relations viewpoint to sell to the managers and it certainly pre-empts the problem of 'walking' managers; that is, managers who decide to leave the company once the vendors' intention to divest becomes known. In some cases the knowledge, skills and expertise of the managers is such that were they to leave the value of the company would be substantially diminished. It also avoids the bad publicity and associated costs should closure be the only alternative.

It is more likely that, if desired, the vendor will be able to maintain a stake in the business as the buy-out team are usually looking for capital suppliers so that, provided it is a minority stake, this will usually be acceptable to both vendor and buyer. The vendor is also more likely to accept a discount on independent valuation of the company, either for personal reasons, or for financial reasons such as walking managers.

MBO Team

The MBO team may be motivated by the prospect of continued employment, enhanced job satisfaction or increased financial reward. These may all be viewed as positive attractions: however, there is considerably increased financial risk as the team members borrow money and use their own property as security.

A major advantage for the team as compared to other buyers is that they are in a much better position to determine the expected future cash flows of the business. They may be able to see opportunities in the new situation which are not available to them in the current organization with its policies, procedures and structures. The buy-out team may be in a stronger bargaining position if their knowledge of the business is such that their resignations would cause the value of the firm to fall. This issue, together with the fact that the managers have a bid, may well dissuade would-be purchasers from coming forward.

At this early stage of MBOs as a form of divestment, research is limited in volume and conclusions need to be carefully drawn as the long-term results are not yet in existence. With this caveat some results should be noted. MBOs are less likely to fail over their first two years than new start-ups. Many MBOs are followed by redundancies but also by subsequent net recruitment in real jobs and several experience cash-flow problems. This latter point is not unexpected in view of the highly geared nature of the capital structure of many of these new businesses. A further finding is that relationships with employees, customers and suppliers all improve subsequent to the formation of the new company.

Venture Capital Suppliers

Potentially successful MBOs are much sought after by capital suppliers as the failure rate over the first two years is 1 in 8 compared with over 50 per cent for new start-ups. In comparison with new start-ups, MBOs offer a history of operating, an existing management team and an ability to predict with more certainty the likely future potential of the business.

The venture capitalist is primarily concerned with the financial package. The balance between the various forms of debt and equity needs to be organized such that it does not imperil the financial viability of the company. On the other hand, the risk and return have to be balanced in order that the capital provider will be prepared to invest. It is not the purpose of this chapter to discuss valuation but this is also clearly a key issue in determining the attractiveness of the investment.

16.5   MANAGEMENT SUMMARY AND CHECKLIST

The future shape and direction of the company will be significantly determined by the ability to enter and exit from businesses at a time and cost which are attractive in relation to the objectives. There are many entry and exit barriers and some of those most regularly influencing decisions are:

Entry barriers

- economies of scale;
- a patent or technological information or know-how;
- existence of significant brand names;
- non-availability of distribution outlets.

Exit barriers

- non-differentiable assets;
- capital-intensive industry;
- age and level of depreciation of the assets;
- poor realizable price.

There are three key means of entry:

- *internal development* using existing company resources;
- *acquisition* of a firm currently operating in the new business area;
- *co-operative strategies* involving co-operation with other companies.

1 Advantages of internal development and acquisition

See table 16.1

2   Considerations before the bid

- have clear objectives;
- be satisfied major objectives are achievable;
- prepare a strategy to include top price and offer package;
- prepare a purchase plan.

3   Considerations during the bid

In the plan, the bidding company must be prepared for the following defensive tactics:

- revaluation of assets and profits forecast;
- rubbishing the bid;
- publicity campaign;

- White Knights;
- new share issue;
- Monopolies and Mergers Commission;
- going private;
- friendly third parties;
- selling the crown jewels;
- acquire new assets;
- porcupine defences;
- golden parachute.

4   Considerations after the bid has been completed

This phase of the acquisition process is often the most crucial in determining whether the takeover will be successful or not. Key areas for attention are:

- management problems: need to focus on and strive for original objectives
- competition: reactions of competitors
- financial problems: financial data and control systems and funding.

5   Reasons for divestment

Offensive reasons

- in re-focusing the total business, this part is no longer required, even though it may meet profitability standards;
- to raise cash;
- to improve ROI;
- family company with no future family succession.

Defensive reasons

- does not and cannot be made to meet profitability standards;
- avoid acquisition;
- sell this part of the business in order to avoid bankruptcy;
- avoid risk: future prospects or expansion are at a level of risk which the company does not wish to embrace;
- management control of such a diverse business has become too difficult.

6   Methods of divesting

- franchising;
- contracting-out;
- sell-off;
- management/leveraged buy-out;
- spin-off or demerger;
- asset swap/strategic trade.

7   Key actors in a management buy-out (MBO)

- vendor;
- MBO team;
- venture capital supplier.

NOTES

1 M. C. Jensen, 'Takeovers, Folklore and Science', *Harvard Business Review*, 62 (Nov–Dec 1984), pp. 109–20.
2 M. Wright and J. Coyne 'Management Buy-outs in Britain – A Monograph', *Long Range Planning*, 20, no. 4, pp. 38–49.

17 Strategic Alliances

Introduction – Reasons for Strategic Alliances – Types of Co-operative Agreement – Forming Alliances – Structure and Management – Problems of Strategic Alliances – Management Summary and Checklist

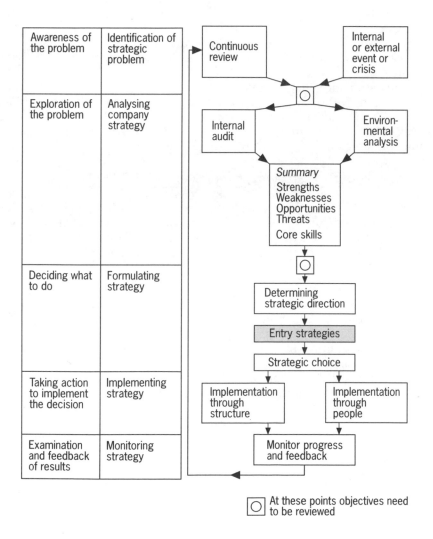

FIGURE 17.1 The strategic decision-making process

17.1   INTRODUCTION

'Do-it-yourself' (internal development) and the purchase of a company (acquisition) are two ways of entering a market and were discussed fully in chapter 16. However, these two means of entering a new market are at either end of a continuum with a whole variety of collaborative opportunities in between. This chapter will describe some of the major forms of co-operative strategies, why and how they are formed, together with some principles for management of the venture and some commonly occurring problems.

Strategic alliances are a type of business partnership in which the firms concerned, each of which retains its own corporate identity, provides its partner(s) with particular skills, competences and resources for their mutual benefit. Strategic alliances are undertaken for a number of reasons; to improve the firm's cost effectiveness, to secure access to new products and markets and, by 'mixing and matching' skills and resources to obtain the benefits of synergy and enhanced competitiveness.

Strategic alliances can take a number of forms including informal arrangements between the parties or formal contractual agreements specifying mutual obligations and responsibilities.

Alternatively, strategic alliances may be based on an equity investment with as depicted in figure 17.2 (i) firm A taking a 20 per cent stake in firm B; or (ii) a cross-shareholding in which firms A and B have a 20 per cent stake in each other; or (iii) the establishment of a separate joint venture, firm Z, in which Firms A and B each contribute an agreed amount of equity, say 50 per cent.

17.2   REASONS FOR STRATEGIC ALLIANCES

There has been a rapid increase of collaborative ventures in recent years which, in many cases, has been caused by changes in technology. These changes have often necessitated not merely an incremental increase in expenditure, but a stepped change. The more detailed reasons for the increase in strategic alliances are outlined below.

Internal Reasons

Risk.   Pooling resources and sharing risks enables partners to undertake projects beyond the capabilities of each firm separately. A new car which is expected to sell on a global scale can cost up to £2 billion to develop. Costs and risks on this scale can put a severe strain on the company's resources and put in question the very survival of the firm. Thus, the major growth in alliances has been in the higher technology markets such as pharmaceuticals, computers, telecommunications, aerospace and automobiles. Another reason for the increased risk is the shortening of

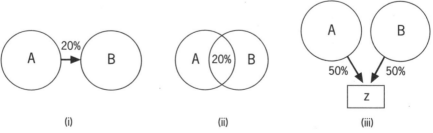

(i)   (ii)   (iii)

FIGURE 17.2   Equity arrangements

product life-cycles which means that the large R&D and production costs have to be amortized over a much shorter period.

Technological Development.   In the example of the car, not only does the large expenditure increase risk, it may be that the firm is not able to raise the required volume of capital. Also, as projects become more complex few companies can control all of the elements internally. Alliances enable the company to have quick access to technological, production and product know-how. 'Going it alone' may take a long time and acquisition may not be possible or may not give all the benefits that can be obtained through a well conceived alliance. In fast changing industries speed can be a critical factor in remaining competitive globally.

Production.   As for R&D, a major benefit of an alliance can be in the sharing of capital outlay when a large investment is needed for a new product. Again, benefits can arise from the exchange of knowledge and skills.

Economies of scale.   Specialization in some cases, and shared production in others, can enable firms to achieve the volumes necessary to take advantage of economies of scale – in procurement through bulk buying discounts, through cost savings in research and product development and in production. Also, economies can be achieved through distribution and the wider and deeper international marketing of joint products.

External Reasons

Shaping the competitive environment.   The importance of the structure and behaviour of the market were discussed in detail in chapter 7. As some features of the market led to greater profitability and some to less, an alliance may afford the opportunity to enhance the characteristics of the market to the benefit of both parties to the alliance.

Trade barriers.   The increasing 'regionalization' of international trade with the formation of various trade blocs, such as the European Union and the North Atlantic Trade Agreement has encouraged the establishment of alliances between 'outsiders' and 'insiders' in order that firms from non-member countries can secure market access. This is very important for companies which need to operate on a global scale.

17.3   TYPES OF CO-OPERATIVE AGREEMENT

There are a very large number of forms of co-operative agreement. Urban and Vendemini[1] have provided a useful classification system which will be used extensively in this section. The basis of the model is to consider what co-operative possibilities there are at each stage in the business process.

Research Contract.   One firm pays another firm to undertake research on its behalf. This can help a firm access new ideas and economize on in-house research work.

Joint research programme.   Participants collaborate in specified research work. Such collaborations can reduce costs, achieve critical mass and cross-fertilize each other's technologies.

Joint purchasing agreement.   Firms combine their purchasing power in order to achieve better procurement terms.

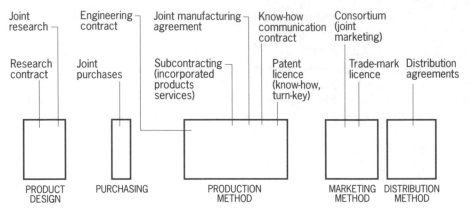

FIGURE 17.3   Forms of Co-operation agreement
Source: Urban and Vendemini (1992)

Subcontracting agreement.   One firm contracts another firm to provide part of the production and/or service process on its behalf. This can save the need to install in-house capacity and access skills and competences of the contracted firm.

Engineering contract.   A firm contracts another firm to provide particular services covering the installation or start-up of various types of industrial plant and equipment. Again, this allows a firm access to superior know-how and expertise of specialists.

Joint manufacturing agreement.   A group of two or more firms agree to participate in the manufacture of one or more specified products, either using a common unit of production or with each firm specializing in a particular production task. This can reduce production costs by enabling economies of scale to be achieved and also by undertaking a costly manufacturing process which neither of the firms could undertake alone.

Patent licence.   One firm assigns the rights to a patented technology, product and so on, to another firm for the payment of royalties. Such licences may include clauses which require that licencees who in turn make improvements to the original technology or product will make this available to the licensor. This aspect may be underscored by a cross-licencing agreement whereby each party shares the technical advances.

Trademark licence.   The trademark holder permits another firm to use the trademark in return for a fee. In some cases the trademark licence is the main element around which a more extensive co-operation is built as, for example, in franchising.

Agreement for the communication of expertise.   A so-called 'know-how' agreement in which the holder of the rights to a process passes on his or her expertise to some other firm which assists it to manufacture a product or produce a service. Again, as with licences and trademarks, there is co-operation access to a wider pool of technology and so on, than can be achieved solely from in-house efforts.

Consortium agreement.   Firms undertake joint marketing of their products. This can be particularly effective in penetrating foreign markets in the case of first time entrants who can ally with established local or foreign firms in the target market.

Distribution contract.   One firm undertakes the physical distribution of another firm's product and/or makes available itself, or contracts retailers to provide, points of sale. Such distribution arrangements can provide wider market coverage, and in the case of foreign market distributors can use their local knowledge and contacts to enhance sales potential.

17.4   FORMING ALLIANCES

Strategic alliances, as outlined in the previous section, can offer partners many potential advantages. Turning potential into performance, however, is not always a straightforward affair. Selecting the right partner is critical and the subsequent management of the venture, which will be discussed later, is just as important. There are three steps which will help to minimize the the potential dangers. These are set out here and discussed in more detail below.

1   Set objectives which state clearly how the company will benefit from the collaboration.
2   Identify potential partners and evaluate the advantages and disadvantages of each.
3   Negotiate an agreement which meets the critical success factors.

Alliance Planning

A long-termist approach rather than a 'quick fix' is preferable. Companies which have been successful with alliances have tried from the start to look where they were going and how they might get there over a 10- or 15-year time period. Effective planning of the strategic development of the business over the longerterm requires clarity about a company's strategic aspirations, that is, the long-term needs to be articulated and clearly understood. This level of aspiration, when compared with what a company can expect to achieve by going it alone, helps define what an alliance is expected to contribute to the company's successful achievement of its objectives.

As indicated above, a company's needs and objectives are critical in determining what an alliance might contribute to meeting these needs and objectives. The range of viable alliance options is directly related to specific needs, which are in turn linked to the objectives of the firm. In establishing needs and objectives, understanding the company's core resources, competencies and skills is necessary. The firm's present internalized resources, competencies and skills may be sufficient to realize its objectives.

On the other hand, the firm may need new resources, competencies and skills and these may be embraced by forming strategic alliances. The more specific the needs of the firm, the clearer is the reason for entering an alliance and in identifying which alliance partners to choose. For example, the alliance between the US concern Toys 'R' Us and McDonald's in Japan may seem odd, but Toys 'R' Us needed McDonald's expertise in site selection, logistics, recruiting and dealing with Japanese legislation; Sandoz improved its sales force management by 'borrowing' a sales manager from its joint venture partner, Sankyo, in return for the cross-licensing of two products. In most cases, by concentrating on filling a 'specific gap' rather than meeting a blanket instance that 'we need a partner', the companies have been able to create successful alliances

Partner Selection

In forming alliances, a key step is to seek and evaluate the most appropriate partners. Those which have relevant and complementary technologies, skills, resources and access to markets will form an initial list for review. Selection requires a detailed look not only at the 'strategic fit' factors but also at the potential partner's objectives and the sincerity of its intentions. A vital ingredient is a clear identity of interest between alliance partners.

Many alliances have been designed for the firm to acquire the skills it seeks. It is advisable not to be too dependent on the partner but to use the alliance as a learning exercise. In this case, both partners must learn in order for the alliance to work. This is why partners with complementary skills usually make better partners, as there is a reduced threat of any of the collaborating firms becoming direct competitors in end products or markets. In addition, firms bringing complementary skills to the alliance may find the venture provides opportunities to mix technologies from different existing competencies and skills to create entirely new skills.

As well as the evaluation of all the technical features such as skills, competences and resources, it is also important to look at two behavioural issues. Are the cultures of the two firms compatible and are the key personnel committed to the new project? These two aspects of the proposed venture could break the project even if the technical features were an ideal fit.

Negotiating the Agreement

In structuring the strategic alliance, it is vital to agree all necessary terms, including technology/know-how transfer, management structure and control systems, and a divorce settlement. This is not a sign of bad faith. If the ownership changes, or the management team alters or the objectives become outdated, there needs to be a way out

Unlike many other negotiating situations where the negotiator would want to feel that they had reached a conclusion in which the other party got a worse deal, it is important to ensure that the other party in a joint venture is also satisfied with the outcome. Any unspoken dissatisfaction over any major issue is likely to cause resentment and a less than wholehearted commitment to the project. Eventually this issue will surface, by which time resources will have been committed and exit becomes more difficult.

17.5   STRUCTURE AND MANAGEMENT

In joint ventures, key issues are the structure of the board and who should have control. It has been found in practice that where the management of the venture is dominated by one partner or is independent of both partners, the chances of success are much greater than if both partners are involved in day-to-day management. This is because it slows down decision making and stifles initiative.

At the outset of the project objectives should be clearly defined and sufficient resources allocated to their achievement. Personnel should remain in the project over a long time period in order to gain maximum knowledge of the 'other' processes.

Accountability and responsibility need to be determined, including the detail of regular reporting which will extend beyond normal accounting data. From time to time it will be necessary to review the objectives of the project and the appropriateness of the agreement.

17.6   PROBLEMS OF STRATEGIC ALLIANCES

Firstly, a strategic alliance is not usually the most favoured means for reaching objectives of the firm as the project is not fully under the control of of that firm, when compared to internal development, or, despite the difficulties, an acquisition. The alliance may fail to provide the desired results through a failure of one party to commit the necessary time or resources to the project. Also, the co-ordination costs may be much greater than expected. If this was a single firm project neither of these factors would be an issue.

It is possible that, over time, the objectives of the company may alter due to changes in the management or the environment. These changes could cause some uncertainty concerning the outcome.

The original plan for the alliance would be based on certain assumptions which, in the rapidly changing environment, might not turn out to be valid. If major assumptions are no longer valid, then some readjustment may be necessary either to the objectives or to the operations.

Management can be a major cause of problems. Management needs to be committed to the project, not people who have been allocated to the project against their wishes. Also, as it is unlikely that everything will be just as laid out in the plan, can the management adapt to new situations as they meet them? This ability to adapt requires short lines of communication, so that decisions do not have to be approved by two or more boards.

Finally the management of the partner relationship is a potential source of problems. Apart from the obvious possible conflicts there is the issue of whether adjustments to objectives will be viewed similarly by each party. Also, when new inputs of time and resources are required, it will be easier to raise these when the partnership is informed and operating harmoniously.

17.7   MANAGEMENT SUMMARY AND CHECKLIST

As a result of the increased rate of change of technology and the shortening of product life-cycles the cost of developing new products, together with the associated risks, are two of the major reasons for the rapid rise in strategic alliances in recent years.

1   Reasons for strategic Alliances
    Internal
        risk
        technological development
        production
        economies of scale
    External
        shaping the competitive environment
        trade barriers
2. Types of Co-operative Agreement
        research contract
        joint research programme
        joint purchasing agreement
        subcontracting agreement
        engineering contract
        joint manufacturing agreement
        patent licence
        trademark licence
        agreement for communication of expertise
        consortium agreement
        distribution contract
3. Forming Alliances
        alliance planning   partner selection
        negotiating the agreement

4. Structure and Management
    decision on composition of board of directors
    clearly stated objectives for the project
    accountability and responsibility
5. Problems of Strategic Alliances
    not as easy to manage as when firm is sole owner of project
    changing objectives
    changes in the environment
    quality of project management
    management of partner relationships

NOTES

1 S. Urban and S. Vendemini, *European Strategic Alliances* (Blackwell: Oxford, 1992).

FURTHER READING

Y. L. Doz and C. K. Prahalad, '*Collaborate with your competitors and win*', *Harvard Business Review* (Jan–Feb 1989).
K. R. Harrigan, *Strategies for Joint Ventures* (Lexington, 1985).
P. Lorange and P. Roos, '*Strategies for Global Competition*', *Long Range planning* Vol. 25, No. 6.
K. Ohmae, '*The Global Logic of Strategic Alliances*', *Harvard Business Review* (March–April 1989).
M. E. Porter and M. Fuller, '*Coalitions in Global Strategy*', in Porter (ed.) '*Competition in Global Industries*', (Harvard Business School Press, 1986).

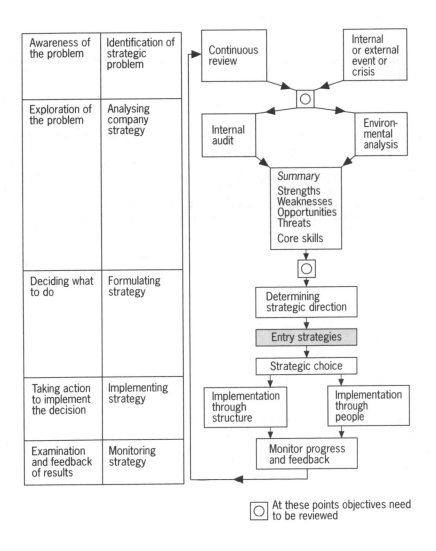

FIGURE 18.1 The strategic decision-making process

18.1 INTRODUCTION

Business strategy is a relatively new area for study and research. Strategy is a term borrowed from the military and is concerned with the how battles should be fought and how wars can be won. In business it is not very different, being concerned with how to compete and how to win. In considering the relevence of military strategy, *The Art of War* by Sun Tzu,[1] although written around 500 BC, still provides valuable insights for the business strategist today. This chapter approaches strategy from this viewpoint. It differs from other strategic models in that it is concerned with the dynamics of the marketplace, the thrust and counter-thrust of competitive action and reaction.

The detail required to operationalize this model is taken from the concepts and ideas which can be found elsewhere in this book. In particular, critical success factors and competitive advantage.

The numbers on figure 18.2 represent a market with 5 being the major segment, 2, 4, 6 and 8 being smaller segments and 1, 3, 7 and 9 being very small segments. It can be seen that A is the dominant company supplying the major segment 5, and all the secondary segments 2, 4, 6 and 8. Company B competes in the major segment, 5, three of the four secondary segments and two of the small segments. Company C operates in two small and one medium sized segment, and company D operates in one minor segment, 7. In this example it will be assumed that profitability is

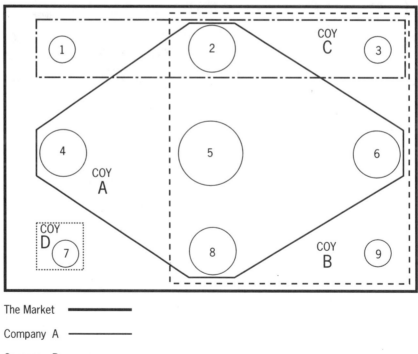

The Market ▬▬▬▬

Company A ——————

Company B – – – – – –

Company C —·—·—·—

Company D ·······················

FIGURE 18.2 Companies and market segments

positively correlated with size – the bigger the segment the more profitable it will be. There is therefore good reason to seek to supply the larger segments. The fundamental question is how can company E enter segment 5 successfully?

18.2   ATTACKING STRATEGIES

It can be seen from figure 18.3 that there are a number of strategies which can be pursued depending on the nature of the market and the competitiveness of the companies which comprise that market. Outlined below are details of nine strategies.

Frontal

In this strategy the new entrant seeks a head-on confrontation with the existing competition for segment 5 For this to succeed the competitive position of companies A and B would have to be sufficiently weak relative to the critical success factors for that segment of the industry. There are only a few situations where a frontal attack is likely to succeed over the longer term.

Firstly, if a new entrant has a significantly distinctive competitive advantage, it may be able to enter the market successfully. Japanese firms have increased their share of the western European car market on the basis of quality, whereas Lada and Skoda, while cheaper, have not been able to do so.

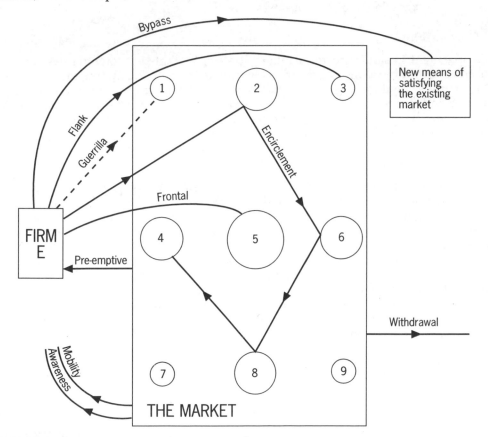

FIGURE 18.3   Attacking and defending strategies

Secondly, it may be possible to enter the market if the major competitor(s) is (are) failing to supply the needs of the market, or, referring to the previous discussion (chapter 7.6), where the barriers to entry have weakened. This is the reverse side of the first means of entry, that is, because a firm has identified a new distinctive competitive advantage, this will have reduced the effectiveness of the barriers to entry. Thus the failure of European car manufacturers to identify the customer's need for improved quality enabled the Japanese firms to enter at the weakest barrier.

Long-term contracts, government and other regulations, patents and market dominance are factors which can create inflexibility and complacency and permit a head-on confrontation to succeed.

Flanking

A flanking movement would not initially attempt to make serious inroads into the main segment of the market, but would rather start in a segment less critical to the major firms in the industry. Alternatively, a company might operate on a small scale. The diference between this strategy and the head-on confrontation is that, in the flanking strategy, the entrant wishing to compete in the major segment gains experience of marketing, operations and so on before the main confrontation begins. Asda operate a few shops in the discount sector of the food retailing business, so that, should they decide that that was where their future lay, they would already have some knowledge of that business.

Encirclement

Encirclement is similar to the flanking strategy in that the potential new entrant needs to avoid head-on confrontation but, unlike the flanking option, there is a need to occupy several of the outer segments before attacking the core of the industry. Whole industries in the UK such as typewriters, computers, and earthmoving equipment have disappeared, or are reduced to operating in small segments, as a result of geographical encirclement, usually by US firms.

Bypass

The bypass strategy occurs when a technological or marketing development completely overtakes the existing industry. For instance direct insurance, with no need for agents, brokers or sales staff, has gained significant market share as traditional insurance companies have attempted to copy the idea. The benefits arising from from marketing examples such as this are difficult to sustain over the long term as they are often easily copied. Thus, the benefits will arise from being first in the field. Technological examples are much more dramatic. The production of digital watches by electronic companies decimated the Swiss watch industry. Similarly, the introduction of word processors had a dramatic effect on the traditional typewriter industry. The problem for these two industries was that, with no knowledge of electronics, they were not able to respond quickly to their new competitors.

Guerrilla

A guerrilla strategy is concerned with winning small battles and so weakening the opposition that a major offensive becomes a possibility. The computer market is a good example. IBM had been the dominant force in the industry for over two decades, but Apple, Dec, Hewlett Packard and others won small battles here and there until IBM misread the future market, allowing others to take a significant position in the industry. This strategy is adopted where the major competitor(s) is (are) very strong, or where the entrant is small and unable to devote sufficient funds to mount a more direct attack.

At the beginning of the discussion it was assumed that the largest segment of the market was the most profitable. However, while most markets start out like this, over time the effects of the product life-cycle often cause the product to become commodity-like with profits declining. In these circumstances there are often residual pockets of demand, for instance, segments other than 5 on figure 18.2., which may be profitable. Chemicals and package holidays fall into this category. Both have fairly unattractive cores but many smaller profitable niches. Although it would seem that companies could move easily from the centre to a smaller segment, rarely are their production facilities or their marketing skills appropriate for these segments. Also, the combined size of the segments may not match the size of the core business.

The discussion so far has focused on how a new firm could enter the market. However it can be seen that these strategies can also be used by companies already in the market who wish to increase their market share.

18.3   DEFENSIVE STRATEGIES

In a chapter concerned with competitive strategies it is necessary to consider not only how to enter the market and increase market share, but also how those already in the market can defend their position. Outlined below are some defensive strategies.

Awareness

In examining the possible attacking strategies it is apparent that most of the opportunities arose because the defender failed to identify or act on a significant change taking place in their environment. Companies must adopt both an attitude and a systematic approach to their future. Phrases and concepts such as 'the learning organization', 'forgetting the past' and 'inventing the future' ought to be the basis for the culture of the company. Sadly for many firms, they are so focused on the present and what has led to current success that they spend only a derisory amount of time on thinking about the future.

Mobility

Mobility is related to awareness as, once the future has been reviewed, action needs to be taken. The opposite of mobility is 'static defence' which seeks to build on existing defences in spite of an environment which is changing.

Pre-emptive

A pre-emptive strategy could be actual or threatened, either taking action or threatening to do so. This strategy assumes that the awareness strategy has worked and a potential threat has been identified. This being so, a possible reaction would be to make a pre-emptive strike, say lowering prices, to put off the threat. Some of the newly-privatized companies have been returning money to customers in order to avert the threat of a takeover.

Withdrawal

In some circumstances, withdrawing or reducing commitment to a market may be the best option available, although many companies are reluctant to do so, not only for economic reasons, but also for other reasons. These could include an emotional attachment to the business by the senior management who have been there for many years, fear of how to exit the industry, what to do next and so on. These may seem poor reasons but they are often powerful influences when decision time comes.

BTR is a classic example of a company that took the difficult decision to exit from its core business, tyres, in the mid 1950s and is today a most successful FTSE top 100 company. Ironically, in 1985, it took over Dunlop, the company which in the mid 1960s was the fifth largest UK manufacturing company whose major product was tyres.

18.4   MANAGEMENT SUMMARY AND CHECKLIST

Business strategy is a relatively new area for study and research. As strategy is a term borrowed from the military, much can be gained from a review of military strategy. What has been discussed in this chapter is the thrust and counter-thrust of competitive activity. Outlined below are those strategies which were appropriate for attacking a market which would be new for the company, and defences which might repel such an attack.

Perhaps the most important value of this model is the emphasis it places on the dynamic nature of competition. Therefore, it is essential when using it to plot action and counteraction.

1   Attacking Strategies

- Frontal – head-on confrontation.
- Flanking – begin by supplying a segment.
- Encirclement – supply a number of different segments.
- Bypass – completely bypass the existing suppliers usually through a technological breakthrough.
- Guerrilla – spasmodic attacks on different parts of the offering of the key firms.

Defensive Strategies

- Awareness – the identification of the actual as opposed to the imagined or hoped-for situation.
- Mobility – to be constantly prepared to move from one position to another.
- Pre-emptive – to take or to threaten action to offset the expected move.
- Withdrawal – to take the often hard decision to withdraw.

NOTES

1   James Clavell (ed), *The Art of War, Sun Tzu* (Hodder and Stoughton London, 1993).

Introduction – Critical Criteria – Strategic Fit – Deciding among
Strategic Options – Management Summary and Checklist

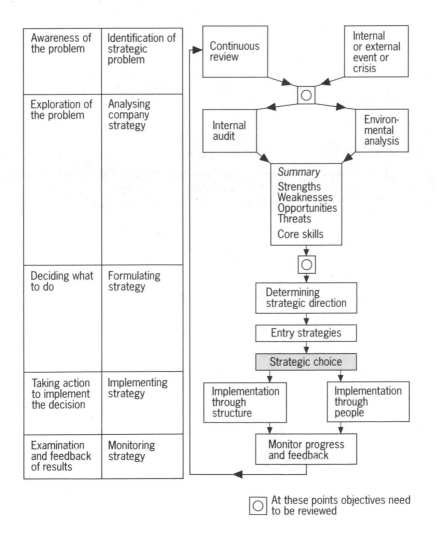

FIGURE 19.1   The strategic decision-making process

19.1   INTRODUCTION

The part of the strategic decision-making process outlined in part 4 will produce a range of strategies which may provide a means for meeting the long-term financial goals of the company. It is the purpose of this chapter to outline the means by which each of these possibilities may be evaluated in detail. In this evaluation there are three key stages (figure 19.2).

First, an assessment against key criteria. These criteria are of such fundamental importance that the failure of a potential project to satisfy any one of them immediately removes it from the list of possible future options. Secondly, the detailed evaluation of all projects which have satisfied the critical criteria. Finally, the actual choice of options. At this stage it is necessary to assess the likely opposition to a given strategic move and to consider the impact of timing on such a move.

19.2   CRITICAL CRITERIA

Criteria which are critical to strategic choices concerning the future will vary from company to company and over time, and will emerge from different parts of the strategy analysis. What follows is a brief description of the way in which critical criteria arise, together with some examples. It is not intended to be a comprehensive checklist.

Financial Objectives

The financial objectives of the company provide the first, and arguably the most important, set of critical criteria. The company will set ROCE and EPS targets and will have DCF and Payback standards which will work towards the overall targets.

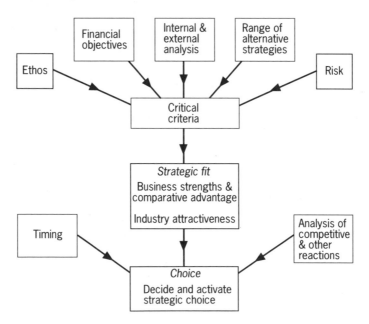

FIGURE 19.2   Process of strategic choice

Thus, a project which does not meet the minimum standard would be rejected unless there was some highly significant mitigating circumstance.

Internal and External Analysis

The internal and external analysis would have provided an outline of the major strengths and weaknesses of the company and the key threats and opportunities in the environment in which it operates. Thus if a key weakness was that the company was too vertically integrated, or too dependent on the UK economy, then a project for the future would have to avoid increasing the vertical integration and to have substantial potential in overseas markets.

Range of Alternative Strategies

The range of alternative strategies is the result of the process described in the previous two chapters. The outcome is a list of different products or markets which the company might enter and an outline of the possible means of entry.

However, some companies have blocks on certain strategies and so some future avenues will have remained unexamined. For some years BBA had a policy of operating in 'Sunset' (declining) industries. Hanson has a policy of avoiding high-tech industries. So company policy can be constrained by critical criteria in the area of strategic alternatives, and hence no future options will be considered which contravene these rules.

Ethos

The word ethos is used here to convey ethical, cultural and organizational standards which may not be considered elsewhere. In ethical terms the firm might decide not to do business with certain political regimes (Iraq, Serbia) or not to manufacture products which are harmful or cause a health hazard (smoking). A company may decide not to do business in countries in which the culture is significantly different from the culture of the country of origin of the firm. Organizationally, there may be policies with respect to pay, training, redundancy and unionization, which would be difficult to implement in the target market and therefore the project would be rejected.

Risk

All companies have an implicit or explicit risk profile, that is, there are limits to the expected amount of risk that the top management of a company are prepared to accept. In many companies the project which provides a very high return but is associated with a very high degree of risk would be rejected in favour of a project with a lower return at lower risk. In the risk scenario the company is concerned with the extent of the shortfall from the expected result and the probability of each shortfall estimate occurring. In this regard, the use of sensitivity analysis in order to make reasoned estimates of risk is essential.

19.3   STRATEGIC FIT

There are a large number of techniques available to aid the process of selecting from alternative courses of action. A comprehensive review of these options is provided by Hofer and Schendel[1] but it is intended here to concentrate on a limited range of those more widely used. It should also be noted that, as all are based on specific assumptions, the reader is encouraged to use them as a general guide to which there will be exceptions. A more comprehensive critique of the techniques is available from a series of articles in *The Financial Times* (beginning 12 November 1981) and elsewhere.[2]

Boston Consulting Group (BCG) Growth Share Matrix

The BCG framework is based on two variables, the rate of growth of the market and the relative market share (see figure 19.3). Some of the major assumptions on which the matrix is based are that:

- the market can be defined;
- profitability and market share are positively related;
- there are no barriers to entry or exit in the market concerned;
- the stage of industry maturity can be defined;
- the market is still in the positive growth stage;
- two dimensions are sufficient to describe the competitive situation.

It may seem, given these assumptions, that there is unlikely to be any market which satisfies all these criteria. However, conceptually the model helps an understanding of many markets, identifies the likely direction of cash flows, and provides a basis for a more balanced product-market portfolio.

To use the matrix, a firm would determine the values of each dimension for each of its products and when placed in the matrix this would provide an overview of the company portfolio. It would indicate whether the parts of the business were concentrated in one area. The theory suggests that portfolios should be reasonably balanced among stars, cash cows and question marks and that this is the desired direction for continued success and profitability. A company may develop a product in a high-growth market which initially has a low market share (question mark). The company should plan to increase the market share and thus move the product

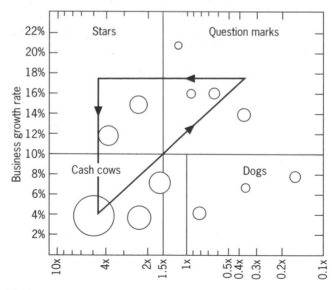

FIGURE 19.3 BCG growth share matrix
Note: Relative market share is the ratio of the firm's size to that of its largest competitor.
Source: B. Hedley, 'Strategy and the "Business Portfolio", *Long Range Planning* (February 1977), p. 12. Pergamon Journals Ltd. Reprinted by permission.

into the star category. While the product remains a star it is unlikely to release cash as, given that the market is still growing rapidly, the cash generated and maybe more, will be required for new plant to satisfy the increases in demand. As the market growth rate slows down, less cash is required for reinvestment and thus the product automatically becomes a cash cow, the cash being released rather than used for reinvestment. As the growth slows even further, the theory enables revitalization to the question mark stage and so the cycle begins again. Dogs are low market-share products in a declining industry, and so the firm should exit from these businesses unless there is a special reason for not doing so.

If there are too many stars, a cash crisis may result, if too many cash cows, future profitability may be in jeopardy, and too many question marks may affect current profitability.

Again, it needs to be stressed that the model needs to be used as a general tool for analysis, to which there will be exceptions.

Boston Consulting Group (BCG) – Strategic Environment Matrix

The later model developed by the Boston Consulting Group uses as its axes the sources and size of competitive advantage. The first dimension, the diversity of sources of competitive advantage, is concerned with the opportunities to differentiate the product or service or to be able to gain advantage in any other way.

The second dimension, the size of competitive advantage, depends on costs, particularly where there are significant economies of scale and the ability to spread large fixed costs over substantial sales volume. The size of any advantage also depends on the extent of any differential advantage. On this basis four categories can be established as shown in figure 19.4.

Fragmented businesses   These are businesses where there are many ways in which the product can be differentiated but none of these lead to a significant advantage. Examples are housebuilding and portable radios.

Specialized businesses   These are businesses where there are many sources of advantage and potentially large advantages to be realized. Examples are pharmaceuticals and luxury cars.

Stalemate   These are businesses where there are few sources of advantage and the size of any advantage is small. Bulk chemicals, basic steel and paper pulp would be examples of this category.

Volume businesses   These businesses have few opportunities to differentiate their product but where this is possible there are big advantages. These are products where large volumes lead to significant economies of scale but where the complexity of product attributes desired by the customer offer substantial competitive advantage. Examples are jet engines and food retailing.

	Size of advantage	
	Small	Large
No. of approaches to achieve advantage — Many	Fragmented	Specialization
No. of approaches to achieve advantage — Few	Stalemate	Volume

FIGURE 19.4   The new BGG matrix
Source: Boston Consulting Group 1982. Reprinted with permission.

General Electric (GE) Business Screen

The GE matrix has two dimensions, industry attractiveness and competitive position. However, on inspection, these two variables are capable of including all the factors which are likely to affect the profitability of a company. Thus, while the BCG is criticized for over-simplification, the GE matrix may be regarded as over-complicated. As with the BCG, it is important to accept that the model is useful conceptually and will enable more appropriate strategies to be adopted than if no framework were used to evaluate the portfolio of the firm.

A version of the matrix is shown in figure 19.5 and, after some explanation of the model in general, the means of determining industry attractiveness and competitive position will be discussed.

The top left-hand sector of the matrix (high industry attractiveness, strong competitive position) is the most desirable segment and the lower right-hand segment (low industry attractiveness, weak competitive position) is the least desirable. However, companies can operate in most segments successfully provided they adopt an appropriate strategy and timing schedule. The number of factors incorporated in the two dimensions means that successful operation in any one

		Business strengths		
		Strong	Average	Weak
Industry attractiveness	High	• Grow • Seek dominance • Maximize investment	• Evaluate potential for leadership via segmentation • Identify weaknesses • Build strengths	• Specialize • Seek niches • Consider acquisitions
	Medium	• Identify growth segments • Invest strongly • Maintain position elsewhere	• Identify growth segments • Specialize • Invest selectively	• Specialize • Seek niches • Consider exit
	Low	• Maintain overall position • Seek cash flow • Invest at maintenance level	• Prune lines • Minimize investment • Position to divest	• Trust leader's statesmanship • Attack on competitor's cash generators • Time exit and divest

FIGURE 19.5   Strategic moves within the GE matrix
Source: C. W. Hofer and M. J. Davoust, Successful Strategic management (A. T. Kearney Inc., 1977) p. 52.
Copyright © 1977 by C. W. Hofer and M. J. Davoust. Reprinted with permission.

sector is contingent upon certain features. Such contingencies are elaborated in more detailed texts.[3]

Dimensions of Industry Attractiveness

The eleven key features of all industries and markets that are important in evaluating industry attractiveness are summarized below. The issues involved in understanding industries and markets were discussed in detail in chapter 7, and consequently only a brief discussion of their main features will be outlined here.

Size   What size is the market? Is it sufficiently large to enable objectives to be met?

Segments   Is the market segmented?

Growth rate   What is the growth rate of the market?

Position on the PLC   In what phase of the PLC is this product/market?

Product differentiation   Is the product 'commodity-like' or is it differentiable?

Profitability   What is the profitability of other companies in this industry?

Cyclicality   What is the extent of long-term or seasonal cyclicality in the industry?

Structure of the industry   What is the structure of this industry? – oligopolistic, dominant firm, or other. What is the nature and extent of concentration?

Barriers to entry   What is the nature and extent of any barriers to entry in this industry?

Level of technology   What is the level of technology in the industry? What level of R&D would be required?

Supplier characteristics   Are there special features which need to be considered of any raw material, bought out part or services?

Buyer characteristics   Are there any special features which need to be considered of the customers for the products in this market?

When seeking to establish industry attractiveness it is important to do so in respect of the entrant firm, that is, attractiveness is not an abstract issue but, as in human terms, is 'in the eye of the beholder'. An industry which may be attractive to one company will be unattractive to another. Also, the attractiveness of an industry will vary from time to time.

Another important feature in the process is the actual means of selection. There is a considerable danger of developing analysis paralysis at this stage and there is a need to focus on the key issues, both positive and negative, when deciding on the relative merit of different product or market options.

Finally, a point which links with the next section. No situation is static and this makes description difficult. It is important therefore to monitor current and to forecast likely future changes taking place in the market in order to reach the best calculated conclusion.

Dimensions of Business Strengths

The evaluation of the business strengths of the company was the subject of the internal analysis in chapter 8. Therefore, it is not intended to reiterate the issues in detail at this point.

The key areas in which the company will have core skills and key resources are:

- management;
- finance;
- marketing;
- people and organization;
- production;
- research and development.

As with industry attractiveness, business strengths need to be considered in the context of the industry under consideration. What might be a strength in one industry may be a weakness in another. Also, as before, an appreciation should be made of the changes likely to take place in the market and their impact on the business.

Evaluation of Business Strengths against Industry Attractiveness

At this stage of the choice process, strategic fit (see figure 19.2), some possible future products have been 'screened out' in the critical criteria phase. For instance, a company which was too dependent on the UK economy would remove from the list of potential future products or markets any which provided opportunities only in the UK.

The process of seeking new opportunities was discussed briefly in chapter 8. What appears in this section is the detailed analysis which is necessary to investigate all opportunities thoroughly. There are basically two approaches to the analysis, quantitative and qualitative. Each requires the preparation of a list of the key features of all products or markets to be investigated under four functional headings: markets and marketing, finance, production and personnel, as outlined in table 19.1.

The quantitative approach adopts a weighting and a rating for each feature and multiplies the two figures to result in a score. The scores for all features are then aggregated to produce a total score for that particular product or market opportunity. This can then be compared with other potential future product or market opportunities. As with most rigid systems, the outcome needs to be treated with caution as both the weighting and the rating are subjective figures. The overall total for each opportunity should, therefore, be used not as an absolute mechanism to decide between alternatives, but rather as a starting point for discussion. For purposes of calculation the weighting is the level of importance to the company of a given feature and the rating is the extent to which the product or market being investigated satisfies that feature.

A similar but qualitative approach would list the same criteria on the left-hand side and have two columns headed strengths and weaknesses. Thus, for each criterion a qualitative assessment is made of its relative position in the given situation. Deciding between alternatives, this technique is based on the relative strengths and weaknesses of each project.

These two attempts at measurement are merely formalizing the thought processes which will be necessary in seeking to select among future portfolio options.

Strategic Fit and the Product Life-cycle (PLC)

Although the PLC is either implicit or explicit in the BCG and GE models, it is not the major focus of either. There is now considerable evidence to suggest that the life-cycle has an influence, not only on the functional activities of the company but

TABLE 19.1 Evaluating alternatives

	Weighting	Rating	Score
Markets and Marketing			
Size	3		
Growth	2		
Position on product life-cycle	3		
Concentration	2		
Cyclicality	2		
Export potential	1		
Relationship to existing markets	2		
Financial factors			
DCF/rate of return/payback estimates	3		
Cash required	2		
Increase to overall profitability	3		
Value added (per man, per £1 capital)	1		
Production factors			
Knowledge of production process	2		
Utilization of surplus facilities	2		
Availability of raw materials and supplies	1		
Personnel			
Availability of factory workers	1		
Availability of management and technical staff	1		
Strength and militancy of union	2		

The weighting for each variable will remain the same for each product assessment. The rating however will change as shown in the example for instance with respect to market growth.

Variable	Measure		Weighting	Rating	Score
Market growth			2		
	Over	10% per annum		5	
	7½%	to 10%		4	
	5%	to 7½%		3	
	2½%	to 5%		2	
	0	to 2½%		1	
		Below 0		0	

also on its corporate strategy. Specifically, even if a company is a market leader throughout the cycle, different strategies will be necessary. The implications of the position of the product on the PLC are discussed in chapters 7 and 8.

The two dimensions to the matrix shown in figure 19.6 are business strengths and stages in the PLC. At the development stage, usually few companies are able to gain substantial market share and the advent of new competitors with improved products often results in a large number of suppliers with very varied product offerings. In this situation the company which is high in business strengths must concentrate on increasing market share which can usually be achieved through marketing alone. Those with lower advantages must also seek to increase market share, but may choose to do so not only through marketing but also by the more risky means of acquisition. The risk at this stage is because the future direction of

Business strengths

Stage in the PLC	High	Average	Low
Development	Share increasing primarily through marketing	Share increasing through marketing or merging	Share increasing Turnaround Quit
Growth	Maintain or increase share primarily through marketing	Increase share through marketing or merging	Increase share Turnaround Quit
Maturity	Maintain or increase share primarily through marketing or some acquisitions Efficiency strategies	Increase share through merging Shrink selectively	Quit
Decline	Maintain or increase share Selective acquistions	Shrink selectively Quit	Quit

FIGURE 19.6   Typical strategies throughout the life-cycle

the market – in terms of product features and so on – may render redundant the products of the acquired companies. For very low strengths the strategies are either to seek to turn the company round or to leave the industry.

During the growth stage the focus for the companies with high business strengths should be to maintain and, if possible, increase market share – again, this is likely to be achieved primarily through marketing. For those in the 'average' category, increasing share now becomes imperative if the company is going to gain maximum benefits in subsequent stages of the PLC. Marketing will still be the main means to reach this goal, but mergers become an increasing possibility. For those with low business strengths, this is most likely to be the last chance to gain future benefits. Therefore, since the strategies of maintaining share and concentration on efficiency are likely to be expensive, the three most likely strategies remain increasing share, turnaround, and leaving the industry.

In the maturity stage the market gets more concentrated and product differ-entiation reduces significantly. For the high business strength companies it is important at this stage to maintain market share and reap the benefits of the experience curve, thus focusing on cost reduction. For those with average strengths the only way to increase share is through merger; or as an alternative strategy it can seek to withdraw from the market gradually by blocking new invesment and generally 'running down' the business. It is thus said to shrink selectively. Those who find themselves in the low strengths category should quit the industry, seeking to minimize losses.

Once demand starts to fall the cohesive state of the oligopolistic market gets disturbed. Maintaining market share means lower sales and profit, excess capacity and redundancy. In these circumstances, it is likely that competitive action, often a price-war, will follow in order to maintain sales levels which means, in a declining market, gaining market share. What follows will depend on a large number of factors and is well documented by Harrigan.[4] However, in this situation the most likely steps are for the stronger companies to increase market share, probably through a series of acquisitions which will require partial or total asset reductions. For those with average strengths, profitability is likely to be low and so shrinking selectively or quitting are the most appropriate options.

If the market is segmented and the major companies do not operate successfully in some of the small segments, then this will afford specific opportunities for smaller manufacturers at several stages and positions in the process.

In summary, strategic fit is concerned to evaluate the appropriateness of possible future strategic options with the current and projected strengths of the company.

19.4   DECIDING AMONG STRATEGIC OPTIONS

From the strategic fit analysis a final list of acceptable projects will emerge and action will be taken to implement the strategies. However, several factors may result in a further stage in the process. For example, there may not be sufficient cash available to proceed with them all, or, if the effect would be to double the size of the company in a short period, this may put unacceptable strains on top management.

Also, it is important to review what are the likely reactions to a given course of action. All those who have a stake in the company are likely to be affected by strategic decisions. Such groups may include:

- national government;
- local government;
- customers;
- competitors;
- employees and trade unions;
- shareholders and money lenders;
- suppliers.

If any of these groups perceive themselves to be significantly affected in an adverse way, it is probable that in time they will take action to counteract the unsatisfactory aspects of the policy, and this in turn may wholly or partially frustrate the strategy so that the desired goals can no longer be achieved.

A final and often neglected feature of selecting a strategy is that of timing. There are two aspects of time which are relevant: first, the point in time in which a strategy will be initiated and, secondly, the time that it will take for the full cash outflows and revenues to be realized. The importance of timing is perhaps more fully appreciated by referring back to the military analogy, although many examples exist in the field of business strategy. In a military campaign, the plans are co-ordinated in such a way that if an action occurs too early or too late, the whole plan can fail. Good timing can be attributed to luck, but good planning emphasizes the importance of doing the right thing (strategy) at the right time. The size of the project, the risk and the timing are closely interwoven.

19.5   MANAGEMENT SUMMARY AND CHECKLIST

1   Initial screening consists of reducing the list of possible new opportunities on the basis of some critical criteria:

- the range of alternative strategies developed from the SWOT analysis;
- key features of the SWOT analysis with respect to future products and markets;
- financial objectives of the company;

- risk profile of the company;
- ethical and other non-quantitative policies.

2   The suitability of any particular product market option is determined by using either or both of the following:

- BCG matrix;
- GE matrix.

3   Key dimensions of industry attractiveness are:

- market size;
- market growth;
- position on the product life-cycle;
- product differentiation;
- profitability;
- cyclicality of profits;
- structure of the industry;
- barriers to entry;
- level of technology;
- supplier characteristics;
- buyer characteristics.

4   Dimensions of business strength in these areas:

- management;
- finance;
- marketing;
- people and organization;
- production;
- R&D.

5   Effect of the product life-cycle in determining strategy.

- Strategic choice – the analysis has been completed and it only remains to choose among the options, considering both the timing and the likely reactions of competitors or other parties affected by the decision.

NOTES

1   C. W. Hofer and D. Schendel, *Strategy Formulation: Analytical Concepts* (West Publishing Co, St Paul, Minnesota, 1978).
2   Douglas Brownlie, 'Strategic Marketing Concepts and Models', *Journal of Marketing Management*, 1, no. 2 (1985).
3   M. E. Porter, *Competitive Strategy and Competitive Advantage* (Free Press, Glencoe, 1980 and 1985); K. R. Harrigan, *Strategies for Declining Businesses* (Lexington Books, Lexington, Mass., 1980).
4   Harrigan, *Strategies for Declining Businesses*, chapter 2.

PART 6

Implementing Strategies

Introduction – Behaviour and Politics – Leadership –
Organizational Design – Strategic Planning – Programming –
Controlling Strategy – Management Summary and Checklist

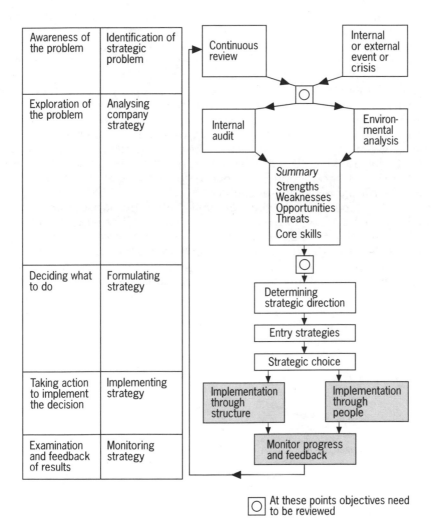

FIGURE 20.1 The strategic decision-making process

20.1   INTRODUCTION

The key features of the implementation process and its role and position in the overall planning process are outlined in figure 20.2.

The strategy is determined by the process described in previous chapters and this now has to be implemented by specified personnel in the company. Two separate features of implementation through people will be discussed, first behaviour and politics, and then leadership style and roles. Also certain features of the structure and systems of the firm can facilitate or detract from the successful implementation of policy. These features are the organizational structure, the planning function, and the control systems adopted, and are discussed in turn.

20.2   BEHAVIOUR AND POLITICS

In order to implement the chosen strategy successfully it is important to understand the behaviour and political features which result from the actions of personnel in the framework within which they work. As corporate decisions concern the business as a whole, they are likely to affect the life and job prospects of large numbers of employees and as such, most strategic actions are likely to provoke a reaction (which may be favourable or not) among employees.

In order to examine the internal behaviour of the company, it is useful to think of the political process running in parallel with the planning system. While there might be some short-term misalignment, the two processes must operate in harmony over the longer term. If 'politics' in this context describes how people interact in a given system, it cannot, as is sometimes the case, be regarded as something to be avoided. It exists and is the means by which decisions are implemented. In essence, politics is concerned with power and its use, and consequently with the resolution of conflict.

The power developed by a person in an organization may arise from a variety of sources. The formal position in the company structure will provide power in terms of superiors, subordinates and peers. The access to and control over information or a particular skill or knowledge may afford opportunities for the acquisition and use of power. Finally, power may be gained by rapid and direct access to persons with power together with the ability to influence their decisions.

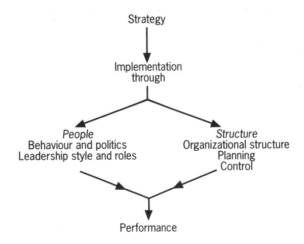

FIGURE 20.2   The role of implementation in strategic decisions

The successful implementation of strategy will require cooperation across a variety of personnel and departments within the company. In most organizations this informal interdepartmental co-operation reduces the need for formal procedures, and hastens implementation as well as improving morale. However, there can be some debilitating effects of political action, as when personal or departmental goals deflect the organization from its long-term objectives.

Resistance to change was discussed by Schon.[1] He stated that organizations are conservative, that is, they do not readily accept change. The argument went further in stating that organizations exhibit *dynamic* conservatism and that that is not only a desire to stay as they are. In addition, they fight to maintain the status quo, and to do this five different strategies could be adopted.

- Ignore and take no action to implement the change.
- Launch a counter-attack to get the decision reversed or modified.
- Contain the change within a specified area.
- Isolate the change by not integrating it into the organization.
- Respond by the least change capable of neutralizing or meeting the undesirable intrusion.

The result of any of these actions will be a failure fully to implement the strategic decision or a failure to do so in the desired time. Such actions are a major source of conflict in the implementation process.

A means for resolving conflict is critical in the implementation of *strategic* decisions, as delay or failure to meet objectives may have serious consequences because either is likely to affect the business as a whole rather than one department, product or division. The first step is to accept that conflict *will* occur and that consequently some process is necessary to resolve the conflict.

Conflict can arise from a variety of sources: competition for scarce resources, conflict as a result of some feature of the organizational structure, or a difference in personal values, aims or management style. Conflict is often regarded as destructive and to be avoided because of the emotional stress and tendency to deflect attention from the ultimate goals. However, some conflict situations can have constructive outcomes in those circumstances where it challenges complacency or stimulates alternative ideas and actions.

It is not possible to provide a process for resolving conflict which would be applicable in a wide range of situations and thus it is appropriate, having done the analysis, to encourage the implementer to develop appropriate resolution mechanisms.

20.3 LEADERSHIP

The successful implementation of any strategy will be dependent on the quality of the leadership. In this section the job of the leader will be examined, together with leadership styles and roles appropriate for different circumstances.

The work done by managers can be considered under three main activities: planning, organizing and leadership. Within each, there is a subset of tasks which go to make up the whole. While these are shown separately in table 20.1, the inter-relationships are extensive.

The planning role requires investigating skills such as problem definition and information-gathering, processing and presentation. For evaluating a situation it is necessary to be in possession of relevant knowledge and theory. However comprehensive the analysis of a problem, there are always unknown factors; and thus decision-making is the balancing of all the known facts against the risks associated with alternative courses of action. The final step in the planning process is the need

TABLE 20.1 Managerial tasks

Planning	Organizing	Leading
Investigating	Organizing the structure	Supervising
Evaluating	Staffing	Giving orders
Decision-making	Communicating	Motivating
Controlling	Co-ordinating	
	Negotiating	
	Representing	

to set up procedures to monitor and feed back information relating the progress achieved towards the given objectives. This needs to be done with the realization that the procedures introduced will affect the way people behave.

The output from the planning function will be decisions to take action. To ensure that desired goals are achieved, it is necessary to organize the resources of the institutions to meet these ends. The first step in organizing is to develop an appropriate structure. Once achieved, there is a need to provide staff to fulfil the structure. Once in post, there is then a need to ensure that the structure is operating efficiently which will require communication, co-ordination and negotiation skills. From time to time it will be necessary for the leader to represent the interests of the company on some outside body.

The actual task of leading involves the supervision of activities, the giving of orders and the ability to motivate subordinates in such a manner as to meet the objectives outlined by the planning function.

The management style of the senior management of an organization is essentially concerned with the degree of participation and the role of planning. Some companies are led by autocrats who make all the major policy decisions, while in others there is greater participation at senior management level and a desire to reach a consensus on major issues. The extent of the effect of planning on major issues would again vary widely. Some companies would only make major decisions as a result of the planning process, others would use the information as part of the decision-making process. Finally, many companies, including some with departments which have titles such as 'corporate planning', make major strategic decisions with little or no reference to the planning function. The style adopted by senior management will have a fundamental effect on subordinates and how they manage, and consequently on the success of the organization as a whole.

An alternative way of looking at leadership is to study the roles required of the CEO or senior management. Much research, particularly by Mintzberg, has been concentrated in this field.[2] In essence, there are considered to be two major managerial roles: informational and decision-making. Shapira and Dunbar consider the informational element to include such roles as figurehead, liaison, disseminator and spokesman, and the decision-making element to include leader, monitor, entrepreneur, negotiator and allocator.[3]

20.4   ORGANIZATIONAL DESIGN

Organizational design has a key role in the implementation of strategic plans. Generally, the design of an organization should be a function of the chosen strategy; indeed, failure to adjust the organization to new strategic tasks can seriously undermine the chosen strategy. It could be argued that the success of any strategy depends upon organizational effectiveness.

Organizational structure can contribute to the achievement of strategic objectives in a number of respects:

Structure	In terms of implementation by defining tasks and roles and allocating people and resources to them
Operating system	By indicating what is expected of people in roles via operating procedures and reward systems
Decision mechanisms	By facilitating communication, decision-making and reporting systems
Organizational health	The effect upon morale and motivation, the elimination of conflict and the nature of responsiveness to external threats and opportunities.

In reality, organizations are rarely designed; they grow and acquire a structure, but there is a constant responsibility for senior managers to question the appropriateness of the structure of their organization. Basically, senior managers have to reconcile or balance two conflicting pressures:

1 Pressures of standardization, control, predictability, efficiency and uniformity.
2 Pressures of uniqueness, diversity, segmentation, new technologies, flexibility and responsiveness.

While there is no best organizational form, managers have to take into account a number of factors when adapting the organization, as can be seen in figure 20.3.

The environment is a key factor in organizational design. Chandler showed that structure was determined by strategy and that significant environmental change led in turn to changes in strategy.

Mintzberg[5] has proposed a classification of organizational structures based upon a set of attributes as below

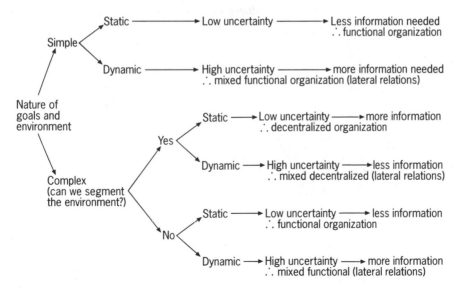

FIGURE 20.3 Organizational design decision tree
Source: R. Duncan, 'Characteristics of Organizational Environments and Perceived Environmental Uncertainty', *Administrative Science Quarterly*, 17 (1972), p. 313.

Co-ordinating mechanisms	Which allow organizations to co-ordinate work, these include informal communication, direct supervision, standardization of processes, outputs, skills and beliefs
Design parameters	The design of the structure and roles, this in turn requires the manipulation of job specifications, work standardization, training, indoctrination, the basis for unit determination (product, customer, location, and so on.), size including span of control, planning and control systems, liaison devices, decentralization of power and decision making
Situational factors	Age and size (older companies tend to be more formalized and have more elaborate structures, the effect of the industry on structure). Technical system (the effect of the production technology on organizational design and behaviour) Environmental effects such as complexity and change The extent of external power on the organization, for example, the effect of a holding company.

These attributes allowed Mintzberg to propose a generic organizational design as is shown in figure 20.4.

He then shows how the basic parts of the organization can be combined with the environment to produce different forms of organization, some of which are shown in figure 20.4 and table 20.2.

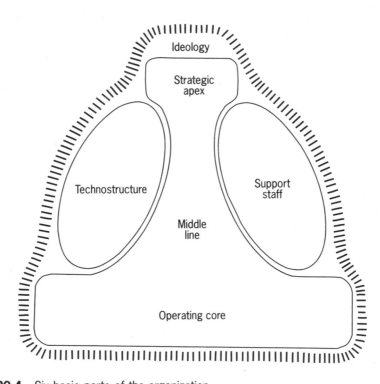

FIGURE 20.4 Six basic parts of the organization

TABLE 20.2

Configuration or type of organization	Prime co-ordinating mechanism	Key part of organization	Type of decentralization	Structure	Context	Strategy
Entrepreneurial	Direct supervision	Strategic apex	Vertical and horizontal centralization	Simple informal flexible strong leadership	Simple dynamic environment	Visionary, flexible, responsive. Often driven by crisis. Responsive but fragile
Machine organization	Standardization of processes	Technostructure	Limited horizontal decentralization	Bureaucratic formal technocratic	Simple environment bigger more mature	Planned, stable, often interrupted by crisis. Can overlook human issues. Strong control
Professional organization	Standardization of skills	Operating core	Horizontal decentralization	Bureaucratic decentralized personal autonomy little middle management	Complex stable environment May be service oriented	Fragmented, collective, stable. Often lots of detail. Democratic, difficult to control and co-ordinate
Diversified organization	Standardization of outputs	Middle line	Limited vertical decentralization	Central core division with degrees of autonomy	Diverse environment Large mature organizations	Headquarters propose corporate divisions implement business strategies
Innovative organizations	Mutual adjustment informal interaction	Support staff	Selected decentralization	Fluid, organic multidisciplinary	Complex Dynamic young industries and companies	Learning by doing, emergent strong 'bottom up' pressures effective rather than efficient. Innovative thus difficult to formalize and control
Missionary organization	Standardization of norms	Ideology	Decentralization	Follows a growth from entrepreneurial to more formal	Client focused	Strong core strategy with small operating units based on ideology as a culture. Strong in Japanese companies

Adapted from Mintzberg, *Mintzberg on Management* (Free Press, New York, 1989).

20.5 STRATEGIC PLANNING

As the complexity and competitiveness of the global business environment in which companies operate has increased, and as the amount of information available as input to decision-making has increased, more and more companies have moved towards a more deliberate plotting of their corporate future through a systematic, integrated approach to strategic planning.

Strategic planning is a process that comprises a part of the strategic management process – it provides a crucial link between strategic management and an organization's external environment. Successful strategic planning requires the precise definition of goals and objectives for strategies and for the programmes that will be derived from them. Strategic planning essentially involves the identification and analysis of internal strengths (including available resources) and weaknesses, and an assessment of these relative to the external opportunities and threats or risks present in the business environment of the organization (SWOT analysis), with a view to developing appropriate strategies that are consistent with the defined goals and objectives. Fundamentally, therefore, strategic planning is a rational process designed to formulate intended strategies that effectively align internal organizational strengths and weaknesses with the present and expected external environmental opportunities and threats.

This seemingly rational process is primarily influenced by the information assembled, by the values of the managers participating in the process and by the inherent limitations of human decision makers. Strategic planning is very much an art – the art of dealing with ambiguity; of obtaining and using information about the present and making predictions about the future in such a fashion as to optimize the long – term performance of the organization. This process invariably involves tradeoffs, and different managers will typically make different tradeoffs depending on a variety of factors: their personal values (risk averseness, and so on); the availability of information, their ability to analyse and synthesize available information, their assessment of the available information, their predictions for the future, and their general ability as managers. This is why different managers will often come up with seemingly disparate strategic plans if left alone to devise them, and it is why it is helpful to involve managers from across the organization in the strategic planning process in order to ensure that all relevant internal and external information is incorporated in the deliberations. It is also why formal strategic planning has its detractors: strategic planning is not a process of black or white or right or wrong; and good strategic planning is not easy.

If strategic planning is such an art, and if there is variation between the plans that different managers will formulate, does formal strategic planning actually result in stronger performance? Empirical evidence suggests that on the average, companies that plan their strategies do outperform those that do not. In addition, it has been identified that 'firms with strategic planning systems more closely resembling strategic management theory were found to exhibit superior long-term financial performance both relative to their industry and in absolute terms.'[6]

However, formal strategic planning has come under fire in recent years. In their book *In Search of Excellence*, Peters and Waterman express doubts about the usefulness of formal planning systems.[7] Mintzberg's *Rise and Fall of Strategic Planning* presents a direct attack on traditional perspectives of strategic planning; suggesting that *emergent* strategies may be just as successful as the *intended* strategies that are the output of a formal planning process, and that formulation and implementation of strategy are not separate elements of strategic management.[8] Mintzberg has also suggested that *crafting strategy* is a more appropriate concept than merely planning strategy. The word crafting suggesting that strategists develop a feeling of intimacy and harmony with the strategic process; the firm's strengths, weaknesses, opportunities and threats; and the other elements of strategic management.[9] The business press is also full of examples of organizations that have pursued deliberate, well-reasoned strategies – the output of formal planning process – with disastrous consequences.[10]

Numerous reasons exist for the less-than-stellar reputation of strategic planning. When corporate planning became a subject for study in the 1960s and 1970s, many books and articles failed to discuss implementation, somehow believing that, having gone through the rational decision making process, the recommendations would in some mysterious way become reality. Other reasons include:

- the misuse or lack of use of available information;
- a misplaced belief that it is possible to forecast the future accurately, resulting in: a lack of preparedness for a dynamic marketplace and changing business conditions, with no iterative process or plans to deal with contingencies;
- a strategic planning process that is strictly a corporate-level exercise and does not draw on the knowledge and expertise of business-level managers; and,
- simply poor tradeoffs/decision-making by the managers involved.

Steiner cited ten reasons which caused planning systems to fail:[11]

1   Failure to develop throughout the company an understanding of what strategic planning really is, how it is done in the company and the degree of commitment of top management to doing it well.
2   Failure to accept and balance inter-relationships among intuition, judgement, managerial values and the formality of the planning system.
3   Failure to encourage managers to do effective strategic planning by basing performance appraisal and rewards solely on short-range performance measures.
4   Failure to tailor the strategic planning system to the unique characteristics of the company and its management.
5   Failure of top management to spend sufficient time on the strategic planning process, with the result that the process becomes discredited among other managers and staff members.
6   Failure to modify the strategic planning system as conditions within the company change.
7   Failure properly to mesh the process of management and strategic planning from the highest levels of management and planning through tactical planning and its complete implementation.
8   Failure to keep the planning system simple and to monitor constantly the cost-benefit balance.
9   Failure to secure within the company a climate for strategic planning that is necessary for its success.
10 Failure to balance and appropriately link the major elements of the strategic planning and implementation process.

Which each of the causes of failure is important, the role, commitment and time allocated by the chief executive officer (CEO) is critical to the successful implementation of corporate planning. All that follows in this chapter, indeed the complete contents of this book, are an irrelevance unless the CEO is committed to planning as the way by which the company is to be managed. Bad planning becomes bureaucratic and restrictive, and can slow decision-making. A strategy that is not implemented, or not implemented well, is no strategy at all. Although planning may be the style chosen for managing company affairs, it needs to be flexible and alert to changes in the assumptions on which it is based. A rigid adherence to plans written on tablets of stone and handed down from generation to generation is not likely to lead to the best future for a company.

The major value in planning is in the resulting thinking through of the business/ environment interface. As such, it needs to be based on real dialogue between the board and planners on the one hand, and the operating managers on the other.

20.6   PROGRAMMING

An important, but often overlooked stage of the implementation of strategy is the formulation of *programmes*. Programming provides the link between strategic plans and the tactics used to implement strategies. Strategies represent the means toward an end – strategic plans set the direction and goals, and strategies provide the broad outlines of how the organization intends to pursue that direction and how the goals will be accomplished. But programmes translate these outlines into operating plans and specific actions, including the allocation of physical resources.

In many organizations programming is an annual process, but it still should be congruent with the long – term plan. Given that the overall annual plan will be created to achieve predetermined targets, for example EPS, ROCE, the plan needs to be broken down such that specific responsibilities can be assigned. Such a dis-aggregation process will result in specific programme areas which may reflect, say, differing functions in an organization, or specific SBUs, but the end result is a series of specific programmes designed to achieve corporate objectives.

Programmes specify products, services, markets, productive facilities, staffing and other fundamental decisions necessary to translate strategies into action. For example, a new programme might be: 'We will deploy a sales force of ten sales people in each of our three geographic regions to focus exclusively on product line X and develop those markets.' Budget figures will then have to be developed, but which will flow from the programming decisions: 'The ten sales people will cost us an estimated £40,000 each, which means a cost of £400,000 to pursue this new strategy in the coming fiscal year.' Programmes can vary significantly in their nature, extent and timing, and often successive 'sub-programmes' will need to be defined to translate strategy into operations.

20.7   CONTROLLING STRATEGY

A base assumption of strategic management is that selected corporate and business strategies will achieve the organization's goals and objectives. As can be seen from chapter 19, implementation involves key questions about who is going to imple-ment the plan, what they are going to do, and how they are going to do what is required. Closely allied to any implementation strategy is the notion of control. In essence, control represents the ongoing implementation, monitoring and main-tenance of the strategies of the company. It is the need to focus the attention and efforts of the managers and employees in the organization on the selected strategies on an ongoing basis, then, that actually gives rise to the need for strategic control.

Planning and Control

More and more, the control system is being viewed as a key part of the strategic management process, rather than as simply an accounting-based, performance-monitoring tool. Implementation and management control are intertwined; control being an extension of the implementation effort.

Goold and Quinn found that: 'Research that we have carried out with over 50 companies in the UK, the USA, Europe and Japan has convinced us that, for strategic planning to be worthwhile, companies must establish some form of strategic control process.'[12]

Robert Anthony has defined management control as 'the process by which managers influence other members of the organization to implement the organization's strategies'.[13] It has been argued by Anthony that planning and control are a single process.[14] A typical classification put forth by Anthony in 1965 and later by Daft and Macintosh[15] suggests that top managers are concerned with strategic planning and institutional control, middle managers are concerned with managerial control, and lower level managers and supervisors are concerned with operational control:

Strategic planning	Management control	Operational control
Choosing company objectives	Formulating budgets	
Planning the organization	Planning staff levels	Controlling hiring
Setting personnel policies	Formulating personnel practices	Implementing policies
Setting financial policies	Working capital planning	Controlling credit extension
Setting marketing policies	Formulating advertising programmes	Controlling placement of advertisements
Setting research policies	Deciding on research projects	
Choosing new product lines	Choosing product improvements	
Acquiring a new division	Deciding on plant rearrangement	Scheduling production
Deciding on non-routine capital expenditures	Deciding on routine capital expenditures	
	Formulating decision rules for operational control	Controlling inventory
	Measuring, appraising and improving management performance	Measuring, appraising and improving workers' efficiency

FIGURE 20.5   Planning and control classifications
Source: R. Anthony, *Planning and Control Systems: A Framework for Analysis* (Harvard University Press, 1965).
'Note that the activities listed under strategic planning are almost entirely planning activities, that those listed under management control are a mixture of both planning and controlling, and that those listed under operational control are almost entirely control activities' (Anthony[16]). Under the management control category, this early classification of planning and control does not incorporate a number of elements which are discussed below.

Strategic Control

Where management controls are aligned with the goals, strategies and critical success factors of the organization, management control becomes strategic control. Strategic control is the use of a variety of controls at the corporate, business, and functional levels in a company to guide, direct, motivate and support managers and employees in the pursuit of organizational goals. Strategic control also allows managers to evaluate whether the company's strategy is achieving the organization's goals.

Under the traditional cybernetic paradigm of control, also referred to as feedback or diagnostic control, managers are considered to be in control of the organization when they know when and why performance becomes 'off-track'. Diagnostic control systems measure performance relative to objectives and provide information to support corrective action. This necessitates the creation of systems and procedures which ensure that managers know what is required of them in a given time frame and which give them appropriate feedback on their action and the general state of the areas they are responsible for. Examples of elements of a diagnostic control system include responsibility centres, management reporting, and performance evaluation. Clearly, different managers in a hierarchy are responsible for differing parts of the chosen strategy, as illustrated in figure 20.6.

Although traditional diagnostic control systems of goals, measurement, feedback and corrective action are a critical component of strategic control, there are also other control mechanisms that make up a comprehensive, strategic management control system. Figure 20.7 presents a modern, integrated view of the principal elements of strategic control. This figure illustrates that the strategic hierarchy of the organization, as represented by the mission, goals, objectives and strategies of the organization, is in turn translated into programmes for implementation. This strategic hierarchy is then controlled and supported by the people, information technology and processes put in place to guide, direct, motivate and support managers and employees in working in a manner consistent with that strategic plan. These are the elements of the overall management system of an organization

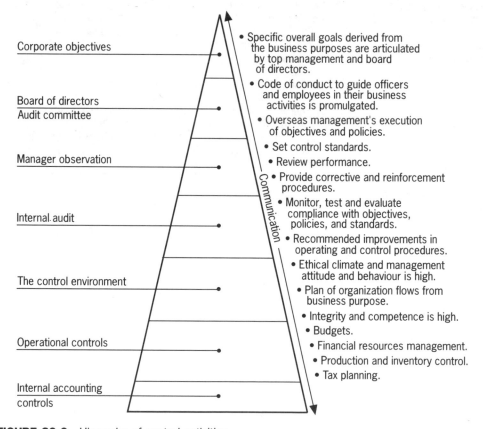

FIGURE 20.6 Hierarchy of control activities
Source: Adapted from A. L. MacKay, 'Management Control in a Changing Environment', *Financial Executive*, March 1979, p. 25.

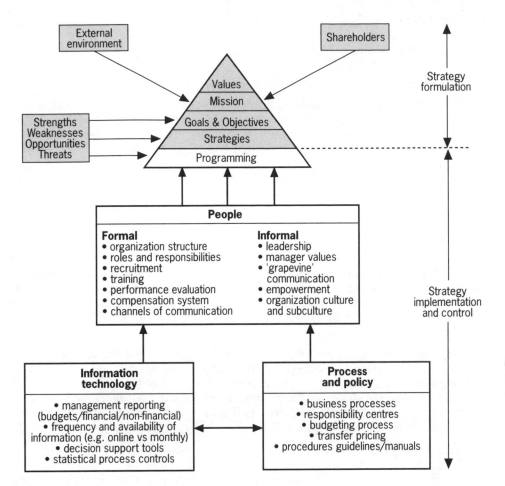

FIGURE 20.7 Overview model of strategic control
© J. P. Christy, Lakehead University, Thunder Bay, Ontario, 1995.

that are most relevant to controlling strategy: the strategic management control system.

All of these elements: people, information technology and processes are critical to controlling strategy in an organization. If the board and senior management want managers and employees to behave in a manner consistent with the goals and strategies of the organization, then these elements must be appropriately aligned with those goals and strategies. If strategic plans call for a renewed focus on the customer through product quality and customer service, yet all of the elements of the management system are focused on motivating attention to short-term, 'bottom line' financial performance, then dysfunctional behaviour – behaviour which is inconsistent with the strategy of the organization – will result. As Anthony puts it: 'Any organization – however well-aligned its structure is to the chosen strategy – cannot effectively implement its strategy without a consistent management control system.'

In a recent work, *Levers of Control*, Robert Simons[16] presents a model (figure 20.8) for the successful implementation and control of business strategy. This model is contingent on analysing and understanding four key variables:

- core values;
- risks to be avoided;
- strategic uncertainties;
- critical performance variables.

These four variables, in turn, are controlled by a different system, or lever:

- beliefs systems, used to inspire and direct the search for new opportunities (new to the traditional conceptualization of management control systems);
- boundary systems, used to set limits on opportunity-seeking behaviour (part of the traditional definition of management control systems);
- diagnostic control systems, used to motivate, monitor and reward achievement of specified goals (the traditional definition of management control systems); and,
- interactive control systems, used to stimulate organizational learning and the emergence of new ideas and strategies (a new concept related to Mintzberg's emergent strategies).

Both intended and emergent strategies, although different in the way they are developed, are an important part of modern business: 'All real-world strategies need to mix these in some way – to attempt to control without stopping the learning process' (Mintzberg 1994, p. 25). As a result: 'a theory for controlling strategy must accommodate both hierarchical and emergent models' (Simons 1995, p. 21).

As Simons puts it:

'Strategic control is not achieved through new and unique systems but through beliefs systems, boundary systems, diagnostic control systems, and interactive control systems working in concert to control both the implementation of intended strategies and the formation of emergent strategies. These systems provide the motivation, measurement, learning and control that allow efficient goal achievement, creative adaptation, and profitable growth.' (Simons 1995, p 156)

Styles of Control

Considerable interest has been shown in how companies plan and control their strategies, particularly in diversified companies. Goold and Campbell identified three types of companies:[18]

Strategic planning companies	Head office actively involved. Long-term planning at the top.
Financial control companies	Strong financial control. Targets for subsidiaries tend to have a short-term profit orientation.
Strategic control companies	A mixture of the above. Head office assists. Delegation and ownership of targets to subsidiaries.

No one style is considered 'best' and all have been successful, but the style chosen is often a function of diversity, management values and chosen strategic directions.

More recently, attention has also been placed in both academic and professional circles on the type of control philosophy prevalent in organizations[19] A continuum of control philosophy runs from a more traditional, mechanistic, hierarchical, and bottom line orientation on the one end, to a paradigm that reflects a more organic, support and empowerment-oriented, critical success factor based approach to control on the other (see table 20.3). Most organizations fall somewhere between the

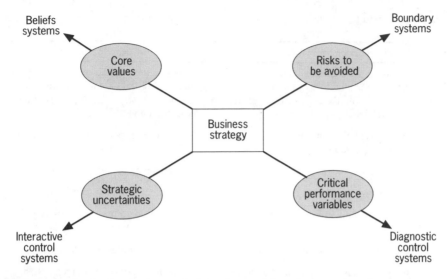

FIGURE 20.8 Controlling business strategy: key variables to be analysed
Source: R. Simons, *Levers of Control*, p. 7 (Boston: Harvard Business School Press, 1995).

two extremes, with a shift generally towards the organizational support paradigm as a result of complex change, increased competitiveness and initiatives in business such as total quality management (TQM) and business process re-engineering.

Programming and Budgeting

Many organizations do not undertake an explicit programming phase in their implementation of strategy. Many move immediately into the development of a budget, often referring primarily to past years' budgets and actual financial performance. In cases where the business environment and the strategies of the organization are rather stable, this may be appropriate. But in most cases it is important to go through a deliberate programme planning phase before developing the budget. As Ray Grisold puts it: 'Budgets are the detailed quantification of targets for near-term choices of actions. Budgeting is not planning it is the quantification of planning.'[20]

Strategy plots the future course of the business. Implicit in new strategies is new information, a revised assessment of the marketplace and modified predictions for the future. New strategic plans, therefore, typically call for new actions and a modified deployment of resources. If this is the case, then, it is highly inappropriate to develop budgets, the deployment of financial resources, based principally on old information.

Many governments and organizations around the world fall into exactly this trap. They build this year's budget based on last year's results. The problem with this is that funds are not likely to be deployed to those areas that are of new strategic importance. For example, in the case of government, if last year's budget is the primary reference for this year's budget, new policy initiatives might not take form if no provision is made for them in the budget because their resource implications were not explicitly considered. This approach tends to reinforce the status quo. In a changing business environment, this can be disastrous. This single oversight can present a significant barrier to successful implementation of strategy; that is, if implementation is not explicitly well thought out and scarce resources not appropriately deployed, the chances of the strategy being successfully turned into action is low.

TABLE 20.3 Comparison of a traditional perspective of management control and an organizational support paradigm

Elements	Traditional Perspective of Management Control	Organizational Support Paradigm
People	Managers need direction and control and cannot be trusted to act in a manner consistent with the goals of the organization i.e., CONTROL	Managers need guidance and support more than control and should be trusted to act in a manner consistent with the goals of the organization i.e., SUPPORT
	Formal, typically functional or geographic-based, organization structure	More use of cross-functional project teams and matrix structures
	Detailed, formal job descriptions	General job guidelines
	Recruitment not viewed as strategic	Recruitment considered strategic
	Centralised authority – hierarchical	Decentralized authority – employee empowerment and participation
	Content-oriented training	Content and process skill trianing
	If a performance compensation system is used, compensation should be based on the evaluation above, tied to profitability and ROI	If a performance compensation system is used, compensation should be based on the evaluation above, tied to a composite index of performance. Often the performance of a group of individuals is so integrated that a group compensation system is appropriate
	Performance evaluation of individual managers should emphasize short term profit performance and ROI, normally by profit or investment centre, as measured and reported through the financial accounting system	Performance evaluation of individual managers should reflect critical success factors (CSFs) and therefore consider financial and non-financial, and short- and long-term aspects. These are measured through the reporting system and through an evaluation of performance, often relative to stated objectives and using a composite index, such as the balanced scorecard approach. Controllability is also important and sometimes individual performance cannot be measured separately from that of others in the team, except by the team itself
	Leadership is directing subordinates	Leadership involves vision and providing guidance, support and motivation to colleagues
	Organization culture exists independently of control system and tends to be neutralized by control system	Organization culture is driven by many other aspects of control system and becomes a powerful element of control system
Information technology	Information is power and its distribution should be limited	Information is crucial to successful management and should be provided to managers and employees as needed
	Emphasis on the use of historical financial data for decision making and control	Emphasis on the use of financial and non-financial and internal and external information for decision making and control, often provided on a 'real time' basis with an increasing use of future-oriented decision support systems

TABLE 20.3 (cont.)

Elements	Traditional Perspective of Management Control	Organizational Support Paradigm
	The financial accounting system produces the primary management reports, including the key reports of actual versus budgeted financial performance. Since shareholders' needs are key, the financial accounting reports are key too	Management reporting must be designed to meet the disparate needs of different managers and must report financial and non-financial information, so traditional financial accounting systems are inadequate. Managers must have the right information to support decisions consistent with CSFs, in order to adequately serve the needs of shareholders and other stakeholders
	Monthly reports to managers linking management information to the financial reporting periods are appropriate	The frequency and timeliness of reports should be geared to the needs of managers, and include real time information, monthly reports and others in between
	Executive information is imbedded in monthly financial reports	Executive information provided by systems that provide customized summary information and the ability to 'drill down'
	Financial information will direct attention to quality problems	Statistical process control provides useful information to manage quality on a real time basis
Processes and policies	Mechanistic: emphasis on rules, policies, procedures manuals, hierarchy; rigidity	Organic: emphasis on providing a framework of mission, goals, CSFs, and strategies to employees to guide their decisions and actions day-to-day; flexibility
	Business processes are mundane	Business processes can be aligned with strategies for efficiency/effectiveness
	It is normal policy to define the scope of authority and responsibility of individual managers by responsibility centres, such as profit or investment centres, which tie into traditional financial accounting reports	Individual authority and responsibility rarely correspond with organizational or traditional reporting boundaries, and any scope of control and reporting, particularly if linked to performance evaluation, should be defined by the scope of the individual's control
	The budgeting process is essentially a senior management planning process that takes input from lower levels	The budgeting process is both a planning, communicating and commitment-seeking process that requires the input and participation of lower and higher levels of management in an iterative process
	Transfer prices can be market-based, cost based, or negotiated and relate primarily to the allocation of profit among divisions	Transfer prices should be market-based to promote decision making that is sensitive to external competitive pressures, resulting in continuous improvement and efficiency
	The actions of managers are best controlled through formal, detailed, documented rules and procedures	The actions of managers are best guided and supported by clear, simple general policy guidelines which provide a decision framework consistent with the CSFs of the organization

From a practical perspective, programming and budgeting are iterative. The identification of the budget figures that relate to defined programmes will normally require a subsequent re-examination and modification of the programmes to meet financial goals and constraints. The fundamental concept behind programming, then, is an *explicit* evaluation of the implications of new strategies on the operating plans, actions and physical resources of an organization as a prelude to the allocation of financial resources through the budgeting process. Programmes provide the context necessary to the development of good budgets.

Control Through Measurement: Budgets and Performance

The budgetary control process is a very common and important part of a strategic management control system. Budgets are essentially the result of the disaggregation process described above, where revenues are predicted and programme areas are costed, resulting in specific financial targets for individual managers. Organizations might produce budgets for divisions, functions and individuals, and often for product lines, service lines and regions. Typical budgets can include:

- sales budget;
- production or operating budget;
- general and administrative budget;
- capital budget;
- cash budget.

Budgets are commonly tied to defined responsibility centres for managers. A comparison of budget-to-actual financial and operating statistics, which triggers corrective action based on the results, is one of the most typical forms of diagnostic control. The involvement of managers in the budget creation process often forms part of the resolution of the top-down and bottom-up processes of planning.

Clearly, the design of the budgetary control system is an important consideration since it affects important concepts of authority, responsibility, accountability, co-ordination, communication and consistency. Further, while not part of this chapter, there is a strong relationship between budgeting and the behaviour of managers. For example, managers who decide to save money by cutting services in one part of the organization can have a detrimental effect on other areas, and can have longer range detrimental consequences as well.

The establishment of a control system using budgets necessitates a number of steps which follow the classic concepts of a feedback control process:

- decide what to measure;
- create performance standards;
- collect data and measure actual performance;
- compare standards against actual;
- take corrective action regarding the exceptions.

While the above may appear somewhat obvious, considerable care needs to be taken when making decisions about the implementation of these steps.

In addition to financial measures of performance, deciding what to measure requires a manager to come to important conclusions about the critical success factors in his or her part of the business. Managers have to decide what key factors should be reported in the management information system. The creation of performance standards often leads to the need to co-ordinate with other functions in the organization, as well as providing the opportunity to motivate managers as budget-holders. The collection and transmission of data concerning corporate and departmental performance is expensive, but has the potential to offer real advantage to a company. The use of such data for evaluation purposes is important, for it allows managers the opportunity to assess the degree of control they have over elements of their budgets and elements of their performance. In many instances, organizations have to set parameters around what constitutes off-track performance and the amount of discretion managers have to change the strategy or tactics as a consequence. Too many changes can destroy the system's integrity and it could be argued that a policy of no changes can be sustained as long as it is within agreed tolerances and further, that the reasons for disparate performance are well known.

Problems in Strategic Control

There are three primary problems which occur quite commonly in strategic control:

Short term orientation   A distinct danger with budget systems is that they can turn managers into short-term thinkers because of the perceived necessity to get it right every month. Organizations must be careful so as not to turn the budget itself into the goal that receives primary focus. Managers are often driven into a short-term focus to meet the budget, sometimes to the detriment of longer-term performance, or performance of the organization as a whole. Managers should be managing people and activities which relate to critical success factors, not budgets and numbers. There has to be a clear distinction created within the organization between the long and the short term. This often results in organizations developing sets of long and short term measures as in table 20.4.

Inflexibility   Changes in the environment might also require changes in strategies and programmes. Sticking to deliberate strategies, when conditions dictate otherwise, can be detrimental to corporate performance. Strategy involves more than just a planned course of action. It also recognizes that successful strategies can emerge from within the organization. In times of changes to base assumptions, if inflexibility is a characteristic of budgets within an organization, this too can lead management to make suboptimal decisions. This is true for all elements of the management control system. Change is constant, and flexibility in systems is an important part of managing that change.

TABLE 20.4 Long- and short-term measures

	Short term	*Long term*
Markets and customers	Sales volume Sales value New customers	Growth in sales Loyalty of customers Ability to sustain prices
Factor market	Cost of supplies Stock levels Delivery/availability	Relationships with suppliers Growth rates in short-term measures
Production	Produced cost Reject and scrap rates	Cost savings Plant layout Facilities plan
Finance	EPS Market value ROCE	Stock-market image ROCE

Goal incongruence   The objective of a well-defined management control system is to align the goals of the individual managers and employees with the goals of the organization as a whole to drive behaviour which is consistent with the goals and strategies of the organization. Where this is not the case, due to the existence of elements of the control system which are inconsistent with the strategy or which drive dysfunctional behaviour, corporate performance suffers. A related concept, goal displacement, occurs when strategies become goals. For example, when a sales team erects a goal of sales maximization which may be pursued at all costs: ultimately at the expense of profits.

20.9   MANAGEMENT SUMMARY AND CHECKLIST

A number of useful questions can be asked in relation to implementation and implementation efforts:

1   Behaviour and politics

- Are there political factors which are deflecting attention and effort from strategic goals?
- Is the conflict constructive or destructive?
- Are organizational problems causing the conflict and can these be changed?

2   Leadership

- Who are the actual leaders in this company?
- Is there evidence that they have the right characteristics to achieve the strategic objectives?

3   Organizational structure

- What is the nature of the environment with respect to the rate of change?
- What is the level of complexity of the operational activities of the business?
- Is the organizational structure appropriate for these key dimensions?

4   Planning

- What is the commitment of the CEO to corporate planning?
- Does the head of corporate planning report to the CEO?
- Is the long-term future of the company the result of work done by the corporate planning department alone?
- Is the planning system comprehensive, flexible and capable of rapid adaptation to incorporate the results of an unforeseen threat or opportunity? or is it partial, bureaucratic, inflexible and incapable of responding to new information?
- Does the company go through a deliberate, but iterative, programming phase rather than jumping right into budgeting?

5   Control

- Are the standards defined those which will monitor progress towards the given goals and objectives?
- Are all of the elements of the management control system aligned with the goals, strategies and critical success factors of the organization: is the business practising strategic control rather than just financial control?
- Are there features of the control system which have undesirable consequences?

NOTES

1   D. Schon, *Beyond the Stable State* (Penguin, Harmondsworth, 1969).
2   Henry Mintzberg, *The Nature of Managerial Work* (Harper & Row, New York, 1973).
3   Zur Shapira and Roger L. M. Dunbar. 'Testing Mintzberg's Managerial Roles Classification using an In Basket Simulation'. *Journal of Applied Psychology* (Feb. 1980)
4   A. D. Chandler, *Strategy and Structure* (MIT Press, 1962)
5   Henry Mintzberg, *Mintzberg on Management* (Free Press, New York, 1989).
6   L. C. Rhyne, 'The Relationship of Strategic Planning to Financial Performance'. *Strategic Management Journal* (7, 1986, pp. 423–36).
7   T. J. Peters and R. H. Waterman, *In Search of Excellence* (Harper & Row, 1982).
8   H. Mintzberg, *The Rise and Fall of Strategic Planning*, (Maxwell Macmillan Canada, 1994).
9   H. Mintzberg, 'Crafting Strategy', *Harvard Business Review* (July–August 1987, pp. 66–75).
10 The New Breed of Strategic Planner', *Business Week* (17 September 1984, pp. 62–68).
11 G. A. Steiner, *Pitfalls in Comprehensive Long Range Planning* (The Planning Executives Institute, Oxford, Ohio, 1972).
12 M. Goold and J. Quinn, *Strategic Control: Milestones for Long-term Performance* (London: Pitman Publishing, 1993, p. 7).
13 R. Anthony, *The Management Control Function* (Boston: Harvard Business School Press, p. 10).
14 R. Anthony, *Planning and Control Systems: A Framework for Analysis* (Harvard University Press, 1965).
15 R. Daft and N. MacIntosh, 'The Nature and Use of Formal Control Systems for Management Control and Strategy Implementation', *Journal of Management* (Spring, 1984 pp. 43–66).
16 R. Anthony, J. Dearden, and V. Govindarajan, *Management Control Systems* (7th edition, Homewood, Illinois: Richard D. Irwin., 1992).
17 R. Simons, *Levers of Control* (Boston: Harvard Business School Press, 1995).
18 M. Goold and A. Campbell, *Strategies and Styles* (Blackwell, Oxford, 1988).
19 A. Atkinson, 'Organization Control Systems For The Nineties', *CMA Magazine* (June 1992, pp. 16–18).
20 R. Grisold, 'How to Link Strategic Planning With Budgeting', *CMA Magazine* (July–August 1995, pp. 21–23).

Cases in Business Policy

CONTENTS

PART 1

Business Policy Framework

INTRODUCTION

International Civil Aviation has developed dramatically in the years since the start of the world's first international air transport service in 1919. Worldwide it now employs approximately 3 million people directly and another 17 million indirectly and contributes about US$700 billion a year to the world economy by transporting 1.25 billion passengers and 22 million tonnes of freight.

Air travel is becoming commonplace and there has been a steady rise in penetration since 1982, both in frequency of travel and in numbers of individuals (see figure 1). Frequent travel to nearby destinations is more common among business people than among leisure travellers. Half the market for airline services is in the US. The size of the UK market for airline services was estimated to be around £7.5 billion in 1991, with 65 per cent of the market served by UK based airlines, the rest supplied by the foreign airlines flying on international routes between the UK and the rest of the world.

Air traffic is expected to grow by 6.6 per cent between 1993 and 1997 and to continue at this level for a decade with larger than average increases coming from Eastern Europe, South East Asia including Japan, and South America.

In the short term demand has picked up in 1992 through the use of discounted tickets and buying economy class. However, as companies cut back on expenses

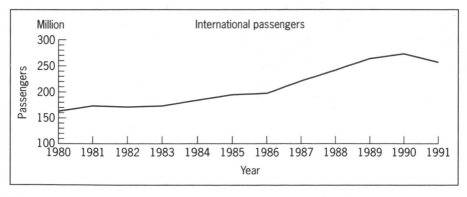

FIGURE 1 Worldwide passenger growth

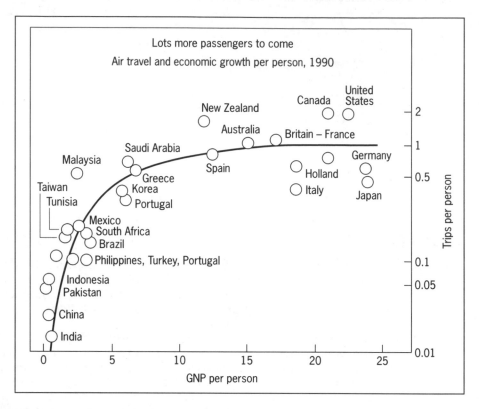

FIGURE 2   Air travel and growth per person 1990
Source: International Monetary Fund.

and travel, their profits are not returning to previous levels. In 1989 airline load factors (percentage of aircraft seats occupied by passengers) were at 64 per cent, these fell to 59 per cent in 1992 – two percentage points below the breakeven level required.

In Europe it is estimated that some 30 per cent of all passenger kilometre miles are flown by charter airlines whose destination nowadays has stretched beyond Europe to America, Africa and Asia. Charter airlines are in general more productive in terms of aircraft usage, flight crew and booking facilities.

Early next century it is estimated that holiday makers and visitors to relatives will constitute 80 per cent of air travellers as opposed to approximately 50 per cent at present. Also, in the long term air travel is likely to grow very significantly, particularly in South East Asia, figure 2 gives some indication of the potential.

However, there is a dilemma as price and profits fall, where is the money to finance growth going to come from? Boeing estimates that between 1993 and 2000 a total of 5,500 new jet aircraft will be delivered, which means that £45 billion per annum will need to be found. For this to be funded from company revenues it would require a 6 per cent profit margin which historically looks unlikely.

In terms of competition from other technologies, Airbus Industry has made some estimates recently of 'The fastest way to travel' (see figure 3). Additionally, video-conferencing, linking organizations – either permanently (for different parts of one organization) or temporarily – has reduced the need to travel. But the likely impact of this on air travel is difficult to calculate.

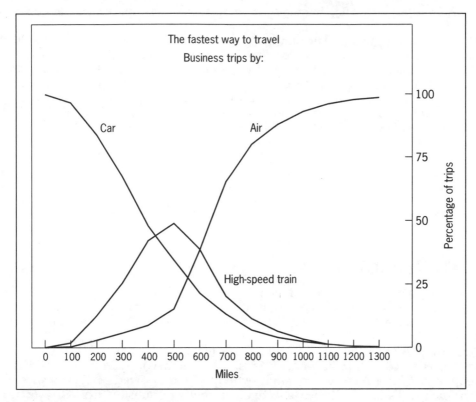

FIGURE 3   The fastest way to travel
Source: Airbus Industries.

DEREGULATION

The international Airline industry is subject to a high degree of government regulation covering most aspects of airline operations, including route allocations, runway slots, capacities, frequency and ticket pricing. For example the right to carry traffic between countries and the regulation of fares are agreed on a bilateral basis between governments. Normally each state designates only one airline on each route and thus access by new competition is restricted. Also, it is usual for the national flag carrier to obtain the best runway slots in its own country.

More recently the British Government has sought to designate more than one carrier on appropriate routes, thereby opening up competition. In recent years multilateral liberalization has already been implemented within the European Community, effectively allowing airlines to fly whatever capacity they wish within a bilateral agreement. On the 1 January 1993 the EC declared that specific route licences were no longer required. Thus any EC airline which passes financial and technical fitness tests is entitled to an operating licence in any EC state where it is based and is free to fly where it wants. Under the third airline liberalization package agreed in the summer of 1992 fares can be changed without prior consultation with the respective governments at either end of the route. Only if governments at both ends dispute the new fare must it be withdrawn. By 1997 any EC airline will be allowed to operate in the home market of any other country. However, the prospect of the EC and America allowing the freedom of each others' markets could be years away.

The aim of deregulation is to improve services and reduce fares as a result of greater competition. A major factor that is likely to restrain this impetus is the limited availability of take-off and landing slots at the major European airports. This problem has caused Virgin Airways to postpone the start of services to South Africa. BA is in a particularly strong position given that it already has access to approximately 40 per cent of Heathrow's capacity and 21 per cent of Gatwick's. A major threat will be the allocation of slots in the future, as the method will be held up for review as deregulation progresses.

As examples of the impact on prices and costs, it costs twice as much to fly from London to Paris as from New York to Washington DC (a journey of similar distance). Also the respective costs for turning round a Boeing 767 in London, Paris and Frankfurt are $1,650, $3,950 and $7,069 according to one American airline[1]. Overall the labour productivity of the US industry is 28 per cent higher than the European industry.

THE AIRLINE INDUSTRY

The top 12 world airlines are shown in table 1. However when the domestic customers of each country are removed from the statistics a different picture emerges (see table 2) and when profitability is considered we see yet another league table (table 3).

According to IATA the losses for all airlines for the years 1990–1992 were greater than the cumulative profits of the 1980s. Also all major EC airlines, with the exception of British Airways, are either wholly or partly owed by their respective governments. Thus Air France effectively receives a subsidy from the French government of nearly $½ billion. Indeed, this subsidization became an issue in the final discussions of the GATT negotiations with the Americans demanding that they be removed. However, banrupt American airlines can file for Chapter 11 protection against bankruptcy which in recent years has protected as much as a third of the US industry including several of the biggest companies. The large losses of some of the major American airlines in 1992 can be accounted for by the purchase of international route rights and take-off and landing slots as shown in table 4. Another

TABLE 1 Travel worlds top airlines 1992

	Passenger Kilometres* (bn)	*Passenger (m)*	*Fleet size*
American	156.7	86.0	672
United	149.1	66.7	536
Delta	129.5	83.1	551
Aeroflot	117.4	62.6	437
Northwest	93.7	43.0	359
Continental	70.0	38.8	319
British Airways	69.7	25.4	229
US Air	56.5	54.7	445
Air France	55.5	32.7	220
Japan Airlines	55.1	24.0	103
Lufthansa	48.1	27.9	219
TWA	46.9	22.4	172

* Revenue passenger kilometres (see appendix 10)
Source: Air Transport World.

TABLE 2 Output of the world's top ten airlines international routes (scheduled passengers only) 1991

Airline	Million
British Airways	17.927
Lufthansa	13.393
American Airlines	12.193
Air France	11.107
SAS	7.931
Japan Airline	7.820
Singapore Airlines	7.745
United Airlines	7.167
KLM	7.108

Source: International Air Transport Association (IATA).

TABLE 3 Top ten profit and loss makers 1991

Top ten loss makers	Loss ($m)	Rank by sales	Top ten profit makers	Profit ($m)	Rank by sales
US Air	1,229	11	Singapore Airlines	591	19
Northwest Airlines	1,064	9	British Airways	284	6
United Airlines	957	2	Cathay Pacific	250	21
American	935	1	KLM	177	15
Delta	565	4	China Airlines	154	34
Air France	500	3	Thai Airways	118	29
Japan Airlines	400	7	Garuda Indonesia	82	32
Iberia	292	17	Air China	76	60
Lufthansa	268	5	Swissair	75	16
America West	132	38	Quantas	72	20

Source: Sunday Times 23.5.93.

TABLE 4 Top ten profit and loss makers 1991

Buyer	Seller	Price* Route	m
American	Eastern	Latin Amercican system	471
American	TWA	Three US–London routes	445
Delta	Pan Am	European routes	526
Delta	Pan Am	NY–Mexico city	25
Northwest	America West	Honolulu–Nagoya	15
Northwest	Hawaiian	Pacific routes	9
US Air	TWA	Two US–London routes	50
United	Pan Am	Pacific routes	716
United	Pan Am	US–London routes	716
United	Pan Am	Latin American system. LA–Mexico city	148

* In some cases prices include related facilities.
Source: US General Accounting Office.

reason for the losses of some of the US companies stems from the funding of an increase in capacity of 35 per cent over a period in which demand rose by only 10 per cent.

In the last ten years a considerable number of operating alliances and cross-holdings have been established. The relationship between Delta, Singapore Airlines and Swissair is exemplary. Alliances offer the carriers the opportunity to direct traffic to their respective services and to market their combined services as an integrated product.

Cross holdings and part equity holdings have become increasingly important in establishing stability into the operating alliance. This would discourage situations like that which developed between BA and United Airlines, in which the latter dissolved the agreement as United sought to establish its own long-haul routes to Europe. Alliances and cross holdings point to increasing polarization within the industry and support the widely held belief that there will ultimately be only four or five major operators in each region of the world.

In December 1992 the Australian government announced that it had accepted BA's bid for a 25 per cent stake in Quantas. Whilst Quantas has attractive routes into and through the strong South East Asian markets, benefits to BA are also likely to accrue through similarity of fleet producing savings on maintenance and purchasing.

Currently BA are having discussions with US Air, the fifth largest US domestic air carrier. US Air has a total of 204 north American destinations – 18 of which are common to British Airways. In the year to December 1991 US Air made an operating loss of US$1.23 billion. The deal is to invest US$300 for 19.9 percent of the voting rights in US Air, which will give BA a greater link with the US domestic market bringing travellers from Boston, Pittsburgh and other points into BA's US gateways. There is an agreement between the airlines that BA may invest a further US$650 in two phases to reach an overall stake of 43.7 per cent in US Air. This moves towards the fulfilment of part of BA's longer term global strategy and also puts it on a more equal footing with the three major US carriers being able to market through ticketing to/from the majority of US cities and business centres.

BA has also taken a 49 per cent stake costing £17.25 million in TAT – a small but dynamic French carrier – which although technically a separate company has had it's planes repainted in BA's colours. However such projected arrangements do not always come to fruition, for instance BA's prolonged negotiations with KLM and the KLM, Swissair, SAS and Austrian airlines merger, which if successful would have created the largest European airline in existence.

RESERVATION SYSTEMS

Computer reservation systems (CRS) have resulted in a revolution in the airline industry; allowing travel agents to book; complex itineraries, check late seat availability on different airlines and print out tickets from a personal desktop computer. This has led to such systems becoming the largest non-government owned facilities in the world. The CRS is the way into controlling passenger flows and will become more important with passenger growth; according to Richard Allen, airline analyst with UBS Phillips and Drew.

By 1987 BA was playing a leading role, in a consortium of eight airlines, in the development of such a system: Galileo. The expected cost of which was to be £75 million. BA in the following year invested US$113 million in the Covia Partnership, which operates the Apollo Reservation system in the USA. Subsequently Apollo and Galileo agreed to merge forming a US$1.5 billion company.

The benefit of such a system for BA lies not only in its value as a marketing tool, but also in allowing BA to control its 'inventory' – that is the number of available seats at a specific price on an aircraft (there can be as many as 30 different fares on a transatlantic Boeing 747 flight). American Airlines says that one extra passenger

TABLE 5 CRS for major airlines

System	Owners	Approx value $
Worldspan	TWA/Delta	500 m
System One	Continental	500 m
Sabre	American Airlines	1.5 bn–2.0 bn
Galileo	11 US/European Airlines	400 m
Apollo	11 US/European Airlines	1.1 bn+
Amadeus	Lufthansa/Air France	600 m
Axess	Japan Airlines	500 m
Infini	All Nippon Airlines	500 m
Abacus	5 Asian Airlines	650 m

Source: Financial Times 9 March 1992 Daniel Green.

on every flight would add US$114 million to its annual turnover and nearly that to its profits.

The rewards of such a system can be high, the turnover of Sabre, the largest CRS, was US$550 million in 1991. CRSs have a reputation for being money making machines for the owners and will continue to be so as more consolidation takes place and the passenger market grows.

In the deregulated American market where operators are free to charge what they like, carriers have developed revenue management systems (RMS), not shared with a competitor, which do regular checks on the CRS with respect to prices (own and competitors'), loadings, and so on.

BRITISH AIRWAYS

In 1974 BA was formed by the merger of BOAC and BEA, this merger led to substantial financial losses and industrial strife. The state-owned airline provided an air service with scant regard for the needs of the marketplace and little desire to right its financial position.

In July 1979, the government announced its intention to sell shares in BA. In 1981 Lord King was appointed as Chairman and charged with the responsibility of restoring the group to profitability and preparing it for privatization. This heralded changes in the attitudes of BA's management and policies. Lord King could use wide powers of 'strategic' discretion to shape the future of BA as he saw fit (see appendix 2).

In February 1987 British Airways was floated on the stock exchange, at a price of 125p per share. In advance of this occasion Lord King had concentrated on rationalizing the business, through selling assets (College of Air Training, Hamble, British Airways Helicopters and Victoria Air Terminal), cutting costs via staff cuts and suspending unprofitable routes. BA announced pre-tax profits of £185 million for 1983–4 and unveiled a new corporate identity.

In 1987 a merger between BA and British Caledonian was announced and a worldwide marketing partnership between BA and United Airlines also came into effect. Lord King said of the merger:

> We acquired with BCal some very valuable assets which included a route network that meshes well with that of BA. It is in the long-term potential of that network that BCal's greatest value to us lies. It had not been exploited to its full extent, and we intend to develop these new opportunities with vigour.

Sir Colin Marshall (Chief Executive Officer) commented in that same year on the growing importance to BA of the regional network, greatly enhanced now with the purchase of BCal.

In January of 1988 BA launched two new brands, Club World and Club Europe, this was the start of airline branding as a response to the realization that competition for the European business travel market was intense. BA opened the £1 million Gatwick London Terminal at Victoria Station to offer baggage checks, reservations and ticketing facilities outside the terminal for the first time, as an aid to the weary business traveller and as a means of further differentiating the BA service.

A new First Class service as an addition to the Club World and Club Europe services was introduced in 1989. In December of that year BA continued its expansion with an agreement to acquire a 20 per cent shareholding in Sabena World Airlines, thus giving it further access to airport slots in European airports. However after an objection from the EC the partners involved decided not to proceed with the plan.

February 1990 saw the signing of a partnership agreement with Air New Zealand as one step in achieving the stated aim of: 'seeking to expand from our traditional markets, by increasing our activities at UK regional airports and outside Britain, in partnership with other airlines where appropriate' (Sir Colin Marshall).

Independent forecasts predicted airline industry growth at around 6 per cent through the 1990s. This growth rate will result in an expansion of 100 per cent early in the next century. As the market matures and the effects of increased competition through deregulation make themselves felt it is expected that two types of carrier will be created, multinational concerns and much smaller carriers serving niche markets. As a further continuation of its policy BA entered into negotiations with the USSR Ministry of Civil Aviation and Aeroflot to set up an airline, nominally Air Russia, to service Europe from Moscow's Domodedovo airport.

Later in 1990 two more BA brands were launched, World Traveller and Euro Traveller, for the Economy cabin. The year 1991 saw more divestment as BA sold British Airways Enterprises Limited to Thomas Cook Group Limited and its property maintenance branch to Drake and Scull Technical Services. Discussions continued in the USSR with Aeroflot on future collaboration.

In 1992 BA continued with disposals (British Airways Engine Overhaul and British Caledonian Flight Training Limited) and purchases (40 per cent equity stake in Delta Air and the scheduled services of Dan-Air from Gatwick). A further advertising campaign was launched aimed worldwide at the frequent flyer.

FINANCE

Group profit and loss accounts, balance sheets, turnover breakdowns and financial performance are presented in appendices 3 to 6.

Group profitability

British Airways is the only major carrier to have returned an operating surplus consistently since the early 1980s. Currently BA is one of only two major airlines in profit, the other being Singapore Airways. Significantly only these two carriers were able to bid for a stake in the Australian flag carrier Quantas in 1992. BA's profitability currently affords it a strategic discretion not yet available to its major competitors, as evidenced by the recent acquisitions of stakes in Quantas and US Air. Thus BA has been able to steal a lead on the competition in its globalization efforts.

The 1980s saw an unprecedented growth in the volume of air transport. The rate of growth has fluctuated from year to year reflecting levels of economic activity, oil prices and changing political conditions. The world economic recession and the Gulf War have temporarily stemmed this growth. BA's revenue has risen broadly in

TABLE 6 Revenue growth and profits

		1986	1987	1988	1989	1990	1991	1992
Revenue growth	BA %	7	4	15	13	14	2	6
	Industry %	11	19	13	16	13	−ve(Est)	−ve(Est)
Profits	BA (£m)	195	162	278	268	345	1340	285
	Industry (US$ bn)	(0.3)	0.9	1.6	0.3	(2.7)	−ve(Est)	−ve(Est)

Source: International Air Transport Association (IATA).

line with the industry, however profits have consistently out-performed the industry. There are two main reasons for this, BA's considerable brand strength commanding a premium price and BA's relatively low cost base.

Cost performance

A cost analysis for BA is presented in appendix 9. In real terms BA's cost base when expressed as expenditure per RTK[2] has fallen by 20 per cent since privatization. This performance is vital in a market where scheduled RPK[2] growth is currently exceeding passenger growth (7 per cent compared to 4 per cent for 1990 – source ICAO[2]). Pressure upon its cost base remains a BA priority as evidenced by the current rationalization of its European, domestic operations and the industrial relations problems this is causing.

NOTES

1   Economist.
2   See appendix 10 for definition.

APPENDIX 1   THE MAJOR AIRLINES

Air France

The company is France's foremost airline and as a freight carrier one of the country's biggest exporters. In January 1990 the company acquired approximately 70 per cent of Union de Transports Aeriens (UTA) thus taking control of Air Inter which had a near monopoly of the French domestic air transport market.

In 1991 Air France carried 13.2 million passengers worldwide achieving a market share of 13 per cent in Europe compared to 21 per cent of BA. In 1990 the company reported a turnover of FFr56.8 billion and the first loss (of FFr465 million) for a long time, due to unfavourable economic climate. According to the Chairman's statement in 1990 the group was committed to an ambitious investment programme with purchases of new aircraft and an increase in the number of long-haul flights.

The major shareholder in the company is the French Government with 99 per cent of the shares. A recent statement by the French government, however, has indicated their intention to privatize the state-owned airline.

Lufthansa

In 1990 the German company reported turnover of DM14.5 billion and profits of DM15 million, having a fleet of 161 aircraft.

Its subsidiaries include hotel companies and cargo services throughout the world. In 1989 a non-equity agreement was signed with Air France, partly aimed at BA's plans to expand, including cooperation in marketing and sales activities, a new computer system for cargo operation, joint scheduling of European services and joint operation of some long-haul routes. In 1991 the above group achieved a 33.8 per cent market share in Europe and this arrangement further reinforced the possibility of a strategic alliance with American Airlines and Quantas. Joint ventures with the airline groups Alitalia and Canadian Pacific were finally established in 1991.

The major shareholder of the company is the German Government with a 59 per cent stake.

Japan Airlines Company Ltd (JAL)

With over 100 aircraft in service, JAL flies the largest and one of the youngest fleet of Boeing 747s introducing more planes to meet growing demand.

JAL has diverse interests in resorts, hotels, catering, information and communication, travel services and other sectors. Its affiliated airline companies serve over 70 international and domestic destinations extending their global coverage of passenger and cargo operations. In 1991 the company reported operating revenues of US$10 billion and an operating loss of US$57.8 million reflecting the acute problems that the international civil aviation industry still faces.

Revenue passenger-load factor for 1992 for the domestic and international markets was 71.9 per cent and 72.6 per cent respectively. According to the company's annual report for 1991–2 the future strategies will include the introduction of more non-stop flights on main routes and promotion of lease and other cooperative tie-ups with other leading airlines to give customers a greater choice.

American Airlines (AA)

In 1990, AA's fleet comprised 500 aircraft compared with 211 of BA, and it managed to grow independently to become a global mega carrier. AA can be regarded as one of the most successful competitors in the deregulated US market and is the largest Western airline in total passenger traffic. In 1991 it was the second largest airline company in the world, carrying 76 million passengers worldwide.

In 1990 AA bought the Chicago–London route from TWA and the Miami–London route from Eastern Airlines. One year later it took over TWA's remaining London routes to Boston, Los Angeles and New York and now offers more flights over the North Atlantic than any other airline. The US airline's domestic market share in 1990 is shown in table 7.

KLM-Royal Dutch Airlines

The company operates through three main divisions. KLM Passenger Sales and Service; KLM Cargo; and KLM Operations. Its network of routes is one of the largest of all international carriers, serving 77 countries from the Netherlands.

In 1989 KLM acquired interests in Northwest Airlines (USA) and in Avio Transit Inc. (Canada). In 1991 the airline reported traffic revenue of F15.4 billion and retained losses of F1630 million accounting for 7.1 million passengers carried worldwide. The passenger load factor for 1990 and 1991 was 70.6 per cent and 69.6 per cent respectively while in 1991 the company had assets of F12.7 million. According to the annual report in 1991 capital expenditure of NLG7 billion was planned for the next five years.

TABLE 7 US airlines' domestic market shares

Airline	Market Share (%)
1. American Airlines	18.8
2. United Airlines	16.4
3. Delta Airlines	15.2
4. Texas Air	13.1
5. US Air	10.5
6. Northwest Airlines	8.7
7. TWA	6.1
8. America West	3.2
9. Others	7.8

APPENDIX 2   SUMMARY OF KEY EVENTS

Date	Event
February 1987	British Airways flotation. Shares offered at 125p payable in two instalments (65p on application and 60p in August 1987)
December 1987	Establishment of worldwide marketing partnership with United Airlines
January 1988	Acquisition of British Caledonian for approximately £200m
September 1988	BA bid for minority stake in Air New Zealand rejected
March 1989	BA fleet and properties revalued at March 1989 year end
June 1989	BA enters discussions with SABENA with the intention of acquiring a 20% stake
September 1989	BA announce intention to invest US$750m in United airlines buy-out and rights issue of £320m 9.75% convertible capital bonds announced to fund the investment
October 1989	BA pulls out of UAL investment after revision of the original transaction
December 1989	BA and KLM both acquire 20% stakes in SABENA to develop new hub at Brussels
March 1990	BA announce change in aircraft depreciation policy producing a saving of c£30m and actuarial revaluation of pension fund producing an ongoing saving of some £50m p.a.
December 1990	BA withdraws its minority shareholding in SABENA
January 1991	Outbreak of the Gulf War
April 1991	The 'World's Biggest Offer' – a marketing campaign to revive traffic levels in the wake of the Gulf War
July 1991	BA agrees to take 31% stake in new international airline venture to be known as Air Russia. BA level of investment estimated to be £20m
September 1991	BA agrees to sell its engine overhaul business to General Electric for £272m
October 1991	BA announce talks with KLM over a possible merger
February 1992	KLM merger discussions end on failure to agree percentage split of the proposed joint venture
March 1992	Deutsch BA (BA 49.0% shareholding) acquires German regional airline Delta Air
July 1992	BA announces conditional agreement to invest in US Air
July 1992	Deutsch BA launches services to 19 destinations in Germany and Europe
September 1992	BA announces conditional agreement to acquire 49.9% of French Independent carrier TAT European Airlines for £17.25m
October 1992	BA announces conditional agreement to acquire all the assets of Davies and Newman Holdings Plc for nominal £1 plus the outstanding liabilities (estimated at £35m)
December 1992	BA agrees to pay A$665 for 25% stake in Quantas
December 1992	Conditional agreement to invest in US Air is terminated following indications of likely concessions required by US Government
January 1993	BA announces revised proposals for investment in US Air
April 1993	BA avoids court case with Virgin over 'dirty tricks' campaign
May 1993	Rights issue £454m to pay for recent acquisitions
June 1993	BA hit by industrial unrest linked to cost cutting initiatives

APPENDIX 3   BRITISH AIRWAYS PLC – GROUP BALANCE SHEETS

£ million	1982	1983	1984	1985	1986	1987	1988	1989	1990	1991	1992
Fixed assets											
Tangible (NBV)											
Fleet			1,008.6	995.8	1,043	1,016	1,763	2,012	1,917	2,513	2,829
Property			168.8	158.2	166	168	236	271	339	392	420
Equipment			85.2	92.9	106	116	166	184	208	229	223
	1,033.5	1,079.2	1,262.6	1,246.9	1,315	1,300	2,165	2,467	2,464	3,134	3,472
Investments	22.2	20.4	20.1	4.2	5	5	40	111	108	108	93
Current assets											
Stocks				17	18	23	28	32	40	37	34
Debtors				608	518	582	706	796	923	795	920
Short-term loans				64	24	153	117	64	300	203	706
Cash at bank				21	33	19	50	24	32	22	27
	576.6	573.3	511	710	593	777	901	916	1295	1057	1687
Current liabilities											
Creditors			(409)	(497)	(500)	(594)	(839)	(1,048)	(1,046)	(904)	(973)
Accruals/deferred income			(360)	(524)	(488)	(546)	(632)	(700)	(770)	(696)	(733)
	(751)	(717)	(768)	(1,021)	(988)	(1,140)	(1,471)	(1,748)	(1,816)	(1,600)	(1,706)
Net current liabilities	(174)	(144)	(257)	(311)	(395)	(363)	(570)	(832)	(521)	(543)	(19)

(continued)

£ million	1982	1983	1984	1985	1986	1987	1988	1989	1990	1991	1992
Total assets less current liabilities	882	956	1,026	940	925	942	1,635	1,746	2,051	2,699	3,546
Creditors											
Due after one year			(853)	(584)	(340)	(270)	(851)	(896)	(755)	(1,366)	(1,888)
Liabilities			(46)	(69)	(103)	(66)	(150)	(100)	(64)	(55)	(54)
Provision											
	(1,074)	(1,074)	(899)	(653)	(443)	(336)	(1,001)	(996)	(819)	(1,421)	(1,942)
	(192)	(117)	127	287	482	606	634	750	1,232	1,278	1,604
Capital and reserves											
Share Capital	180	180	180	180	180	180	180	180	180	180	182
Reserves											
Revolution			30	23	19	16	212	167	121	82	60
Other			15	2	3	(4)	(7)	(9)	302	309	319
P&L account			(100)	81	278	413	248	411	629	707	1,043
Shareholders' Equity	(195)	(117)	126	286	480	605	633	749	1,232	1,278	1,604
	3	0	1	1	2	1	1	1			
	(192)	(117)	127	287	482	606	634	750	1,232	1,278	1,604

APPENDIX 4   BRITISH AIRWAYS PLC – GROUP PROFIT AND LOSS ACCOUNTS

£ million	1982	1983	1984	1985	1986	1987	1988	1989	1990	1991	1992
Turnover											
Airline	2,010.0	2,172.0	2,382.1	2,796.7	2,981	3,054	3,523	4,132	4,715	4,834	
Helicopter	38.3	40.8	43	37.6	38						
Tour holidays	87.1	100.6	79	99	120	178	217	102	98	79	
Other	8.1	8.6	9.6	9.2	10	13	16	23	25	24	
Discontinued	97.8	174.5				18					
	2,241.3	2,496.5	2,513.7	2,942.5	3,149	3,263	3,756	4,257	4,838	4,937	5,224
Operating expenditure											
Cost of sales	(2,230)	(2,311)	(2,176)	(2,581)	(2,870)	(2,993)	(3,413)	(3,816)	(4,339)	(4,653)	(4,777)
Administration			(70)	(70)	(81)	(97)	(107)	(105)	(115)	(117)	(103)
			(2,246)	(2,650)	(2,951)	(3,090)	(3,520)	(3,921)	(4,454)	(4,770)	(4,880)
Operating surplus	11.8	185.1	267.7	292.1	198.0	173.0	236.0	336.0	384.0	167.0	344.0
Exceptional item				(33.0)						(120.0)	
Other income	(2.3)	18.5	26.0	22.0	36.0	19.0	12.0	18.0	49.0	176.0	86.0
PBIT	9.5	203.6	293.7	281.1	234.0	192.0	248.0	354.0	433.0	223.0	430.0
Interest payable	(120.1)	(130.2)	(108.7)	(113.0)	(39.0)	(30.0)	(20.0)	(86.0)	(88.0)	(93.0)	(145.0)
PBT	(110.6)	73.4	185.0	168.1	195.0	162.0	228.0	268.0	345.0	130.0	285.0
Taxation	(5.4)	(9.5)	(3.2)	(2.2)	(2.0)	(14.0)	(77.0)	(93.0)	(100.0)	(35.0)	(30.0)
PAT	(116.0)	63.9	181.8	165.9	193.0	148.0	151.0	175.0	245.0	95.0	255.0
Extraordinary item	(428.2)	24.7	32.7	10.2	(12.0)	4.0			1.0		140.0
Profit	(544.2)	88.6	214.5	176.1	181.0	152.0	151.0	175.0	246.0	95.0	395.0
Dividend						(30.0)	(50.0)	(56.0)	(64.0)	(64.0)	(74.0)
Retained	(544.2)	88.6	214.5	176.1	181.0	122.0	101.0	119.0	182.0	31.0	321.0

APPENDIX 5   BRITISH AIRWAYS PLC – GEOGRAPHICAL ANALYSIS

Group turnover geographical analysis (By area of destination)

£ million	1984	1985	1986	1987	1988	1989	1990	1991	1992
UK	381.6	388	285	331	378	453	539	576	536
Cont' Europe	753.3	868	979	1,085	1,231	1,169	1,286	1,374	1,528
Europe	1,134.9	1,256	1,264	1,416	1,609	1,622	1,825	1,950	2,064
The Americas	669.9	862	1,008	982	1,175	1,374	1,619	1,615	1,645
Africa	153.8	178	179	185	237	323	356	590	665
Australasia	555.1	647	660	662	735	938	1,038	782	850
	2,513.7	2,943	3,111	3,245	3,756	4,257	4,838	4,937	5,224

Group operating surplus geographical analysis

£ million	1984	1985	1986	1987	1988	1989	1990	1991	1992
Europe	103.9	83.4	55	56	36	16	3	(10)	20
The Americas	129.6	129.6	84	65	131	181	249	123	119
Africa	26.2	26.2	14	20	37	49	52	13	119
Australasia	52.9	52.9	45	33	32	90	80	41	86
	312.6	292.1	198	174	236	336	384	167	344

APPENDIX 6   COMPARATIVE OPERATIONAL PERFORMANCE OF AIRLINES – 1991

Airline	Return on equity %	Gross margin %	Passenger load factor %	% passenger revenue of total	% international passenger km	Available ton km ATR (m)	Revenue passenger km RPK (m)	IOTA input efficiency
Air Canada	2.4	2.1	71.4	79.4	57.2	5,723	26,677	0.817
All Nippon Airways Co.	5.6	3.5	72.5	89.4	21.5	5,895	33,081	0.758
American Airlines Inc.	6.1	3.2	62.3	88.5	19.5	24,099	124,055	0.896
British Airways Plc	**14.4**	**4.7**	**70.1**	**82.2**	**94.1**	**13,565**	**64,734**	**0.907**
Delta Air Lines Inc.	6.9	3.6	61.2	93.6	13.7	19,080	95,011	0.893
IBERIA Lineas Aereas	(0.7)	(1.5)	69.3	73.7	70.4	4,603	22,112	0.793
Japan Airlines	4.2	3.5	73.2	74.1	76.7	12,097	52,363	0.724
KLM Airlines	(2.7)	(1.3)	69.6	64.0	99.6	6,587	26,504	0.734
Korean Air	2.2	1.2	72.8	59.0	87.0	5,654	19,277	0.847
Lufthansa	2.1	1.5	64.8	62.1	92.5	12,559	41,925	0.878
Quantas	8.7	2.8	68.2	66.3	100.0	5,728	27,754	0.917

Note: International performance assessments of airlines from published financial information are difficult, because (1) most airlines lease a substantial part of their fleets, and (2) different accounting and taxation rules in various countries result in different impacts upon profit and balance-sheet information. Non-financial data suffers from difficulties due to differing units of measure. The above table uses published data adjusted as far as is possible to give a common basis for comparison. Consequently some of the above figures will differ from published data, this table should be used for inter-airline comparison only.
(Source: Schefczyk, M., Operational Performance of Airlines, Strategic Management Journal Vol 14, 301–317 (1993)).

APPENDIX 7   COMPETITOR PERFORMANCE FIGURES

	KLM Royal Dutch Airlines (Fl million)				Lufthansa AG (DM million)			
	1988	1989	1990	1991	1988	1989	1990	1991
Turnover Fl m	4,601.1	5,017.1	5,356.7	5,414.0	11,065.2	11,845.4	13,055.3	14,447.1
PBT	313.7	433.7	235.7	(504.8)	148.3	184.4	217.8	60.8
PAT	313.7	373.7	155.7	(353.2)	89.4	81.6	109.7	15.2
Dividend	94.5	105.1	105.1		84.0	96.5	121.6	6.7
Retained	219.2	268.6	234.5	(630.3)	4.1	19.1	14.7	4.4
Fixed assets	5,982.6	6,936.4	9,064.8	9,516.5	6,532.6	7,845.7	9,038.0	11,013.9
Current assets	3,722.8	3,525.0	3,157.9	3,686.7	2,282.4	2,565.8	3,243.4	3,525.8
Current liabilities	2,204.7	2,194.9	2,174.2	2,323.1	996.0	1,318.9	1,710.2	1,980.9
Debt	3,423.9	4,126.3	5,856.1	7,155.7	1,344.2	2,147.7	2,183.1	3,815.9
Net assets	3,030.4	3,176.7	3,328.8	2,747.1	3,941.9	4,234.5	5,524.4	5,300.1
Current ratio	1.69	1.61	1.45	1.59	2.29	1.95	1.90	1.78
Gearing %	53.0	56.5	63.8	72.3	25.4	33.7	28.3	41.9
Operating profit margin %	6.8	8.6	4.4	(9.3)	1.34	1.56	1.67	0.42
ROCE %	10.4	13.7	7.1	(18.4)	3.76	4.35	3.94	1.15
Passengers (000)	6,632	6,880	7,168	7,484	21,427	22,546	23,400	26,600
Aircraft km flown (million)	134	145	151	163	354.2	390.0		
RPK (million)	22,810	24,019	25,366	26,504	39,658	42,468		
Load factor %	70.2	70.6	71.4	71.0	69.5	68.8	68.9	66.9
Break-even load factor %	65.8	66.4	68.9	76.9	68.7	68.6		

(continued)

	US Air Group Inc (US$ million)				Air France (FFR million)			
	1988	1989	1990	1991	1988	1989	1990	1991
Turnover	5,707	6,251	6,558	6,514	32,788.1	35,454.4	39,627.5	56,839.0
PBT	433.6	21.5	(501.1)	(173.5)	(1,604.1)	1,568.2	1,359.6	(668.0)
PAT	165.0	(63.2)	(454.4)	(305.3)	1,093.8	1,064.0	737.1	(465.5)
Dividend		13.2	33.1	44.3	194.7	288.3	199.9	
Retained	165.0	(76.4)	(487.5)	(349.6)	1,026.7	863.9	641.4	(717.2)
Fixed assets	3,569	4,227	4,442	4,371	14,335.6	15,305.2	21,874.2	39,279.3
Current assets	822	936	1,029	1,238	10,081.2	11,210.3	12,615.1	15,870.7
Total liabilities					19,268.8	20,556.4	22,687.1	41,891.0
Current liabilities	1,209	1,578	1,828	1,943				
Debt	1,333	1,468	2,263	2,115	9,885.3	10,709.6	11,488.0	21,492.5
Net assets	5,349	6,069	6,574	6,454	5,148.0	6,159.1	11,802.2	13,259.0
Current ratio	0.68	0.59	0.56	0.64	1.07	1.14	1.13	0.78
Gearing %	19.9	19.5	25.6	24.7	65.8	63.5	49.3	61.8
Operating profit margin %	7.6	0.3	(7.6)	(2.7)	4.9	4.4	3.4	(1.2)
ROCE %	8.1	0.4	(7.6)	(2.7)	31.2	25.5	11.5	-5.0
Passengers (000)	61,900	61,200	60,100	55,600				
Aircraft km flown (million)								
RPK (million)	50,342	54,229	57,212	54,909				
Load Factor %	60	60.6	59.8	58.6				
Break-even load factor %	56	60.6	64.5	62.7				

APPENDIX 8   BRITISH AIRWAYS PLC – OPERATING STATISTICS

£ million	1982	1983	1984	1985	1986	1987	1988	1989	1990	1991	1992
Employee numbers											
United Kingdom						35,389	37,969	43,617	45,224	47,221	43,744
Overseas						5,370	6,000	6,587	6,830	7,206	6,665
	53,148	45,927	37,247	38,137	40,271	40,759	43,969	50,204	52,054	54,427	50,409
Scheduled services											
RPK (million)	38,521	36,394	34,206	38,386	41,334	41,356	49,123	57,795	61,915	64,734	65,896
Load factor %	66.7	66.5	64.1	68.5	68.0	67.0	70.2	69.6	71.5	70.1	70.2
CTK (million)	1,035	986	1,122	1,292	1,356	1,444	1,793	2,249	2,400	2,463	
RTK (million)	4,503	4,307	4,244	4,810	5,155	5,267	6,345	7,636	8,290	8,641	
Overall load factor %	63	63.4	63.4	66.1	64.8	64.7	67.3	67	68.9	66.8	65.6
Group operations											
RTK (million)	4,788	4,461	4,650	5,267	5,673	5,784	6,895	8,002	8,627	8,979	
Load factor %	63.6	61.9	64.6	67.2	66.0	66.1	67.3	67.0	68.9	66.8	65.6
Passengers carried (000)	16,695	16,344	16,241	18,397	19,681	20,041	23,230	24,603	25,238	25,587	
Revenue per RTK (p)	39.08	46.00	47.85	50.07	49.27	48.88	48.01	48.73	51.36	50.54	
Net expenditure per RTK (p)	38.63	41.55	41.91	44.52	45.77	45.89	45.30	44.83	47.21	48.99	
Break-even load factor %	62.9	55.9	56.6	59.8	61.3	62.1	63.5	61.6	63.3	64.8	61.2
Aircraft and routes											
Fleet size (year end)	162	148	150	158	158	164	197	211	224	230	230
Utilisation (hrs/aircraft p.a.)	2,283	2,532	2,465	2,653	2,720	2,801	2,891	2,886	2,787	2,663	2,708
Unduplicated route km (000)	574	567	516	521	555	555	692	677	685	665	
Aircraft km flown (million)			211	229	248	257	312	364	375	389	390

APPENDIX 9   BRITISH AIRWAYS PLC – COSTS ANALYSIS (ADJUSTED TO 1991 PRICES)

£ million	1983	1984	1985	1986	1987	1988	1989	1990	1991
Average staff employed	45,927	37,247	38,137	40,271	40,759	43,969	50,204	52,054	54,427
Total RTKs (m)	4,461	4,650	5,267	5,673	5,784	6,895	8,002	8,627	8,979
RTKs per employee (000)	97.1	124.8	138.1	140.9	141.9	156.8	159.4	165.7	165.0
Total staff costs £m	754	730	765	816	897	1022	1108	1087	1074
Cost per employee £	16,412	19,609	20,071	20,255	22,009	23,240	22,080	20,891	19,733
Engineering costs £m	187	161	163	225	240	261	277	280	285
Engineering costs per RTK (p)	4.19	3.47	3.09	3.97	4.15	3.78	3.46	3.24	3.17
Landing & route costs £m	240	241	262	266	289	317	334	347	376
Landing & route costs per RTK (p)	5.38	5.19	4.97	4.69	5.01	4.60	4.17	4.02	4.19
Handling & catering costs £m	249	273	342	381	389	406	485	592	559
Handling & catering costs per RTK (p)	5.58	5.88	6.50	6.72	6.72	5.89	6.06	6.86	6.23
Selling costs £m	302	334	402	413	435	495	566	598	566
Selling costs per RTK (p)	6.77	7.18	7.63	7.28	7.52	7.17	7.07	6.94	6.30
Fuel and oil costs £m	782	714	806	729	461	473	474	572	598
Fuel and oil costs per RTK (p)	17.5	15.3	15.3	12.8	8.0	6.9	5.9	6.6	6.7
Total group expenditure £m	3404	3174	3505	3773	3839	4227	4453	4684	4770
per RTK (p)	76.3	68.3	66.5	66.5	66.4	61.3	55.7	54.3	53.1

APPENDIX 10   GLOSSARY OF TERMS

Capacity measurements

ASKs Available seat kilometres: The number of seats made available for sale multiplied by the distance flown.
ATKs Available tonne kilometres: The number of tonnes of capacity available for revenue load (passengers and cargo) multiplied by the distance flown.

Volume measurements

RPKs Revenue passenger kilometres: The number of revenue passengers carried multiplied by the distance flown.
CTKs Cargo tonne kilometres: The number of revenue tonnes of cargo (freight plus mail) carried multiplied by the distance flown.
RTKs Revenue tonne kilometres: The revenue load (passengers and cargo) in tonnes multiplied by the distance flown.

Load factors

Load factor: RPKs expressed as a percentage of ASKs.
Overall load factor: RTKs expressed as a percentage of ATKs.
Break-even load factor: The load factor required to equate total traffic revenue with operating costs.

Freedoms of the air

First freedom: The privilege to fly across the territory of another state without landing.
Second freedom: The privilege to land in another state for non-traffic purposes (ie for re-fuelling or mechanical reasons but not for the uplift or discharge of traffic).
Third freedom: The privilege to put down in another state revenue passengers, mail and freight destined for the state of airline registration.
Fourth freedom: The privilege to take on in another state revenue passengers, mail and freight destined for the state of airline registration.
Fifth freedom: The privilege for an airline registered in one state to and en-route to or from that state to take on revenue passengers, mail and freight in a second state and put them down in a third state.
Sixth freedom: The privilege for an airline registered in one state to take on revenue passengers, mail and freight in a second state, *transport them via the state of registration,* and put them down in a third state.

Case 2 **National & Provincial Building Societ**

In 1995 the building society world was startled when Abbey National launched a hostile bid for the National & Provincial Building Society. Because building societies were mutual organizations which were 'owned' by their members rather than by shareholders it had been thought that any takeover of a building society had to be by agreement. Indeed this had been the case until the Abbey National bid. The bid was not an offer for the shares of the society but rather an offer to the members (savers and borrowers) of shares in the Abbey National itself which was suggested to be approximately £650 per member. This was for a member with an account which had at least £100 in it prior to the bid. This was estimated from the statement made by the Abbey National which said it planned to offer N & P members a 'substantial premium' to the N & P's net asset value of £732 million. The Abbey National offer was estimated at approximately £1.2 million.

It was not the case that the National & Provincial was not profitable. Indeed its profits had been rising (see figure 1). In 1995 the N & P was the ninth largest building society in the UK. Until 1989 Abbey National had been the second largest building society in the country but in that year had converted to a bank by floating on the stock exchange. Since then the value of its shares had arisen consistently over the years (see figure 2).

It was not entirely clear how the offer by the Abbey National fitted its stated strategy of diversifying such that 40 per cent of its pre-tax profits came from non-traditional businesses by 1997.

Once the Abbey National had made its intentions clear then a number of other offers were made to the board of directors of the N & P. Such was the interest that the latter had to close its accounts as people rushed to get a stake in the organization. Having received several offers the board had to consider what to do.

The Abbey National was based largely in the south of the country whereas N & P was a northern based society. It was much smaller than the Abbey National as figures 3, 4 and 5 show.

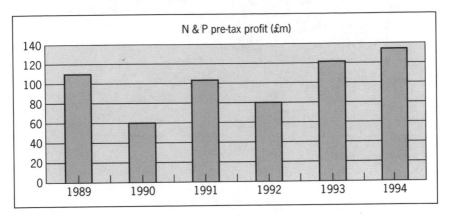

FIGURE 1   National & Provincial Building Society pre-tax profits 1989 to 1994

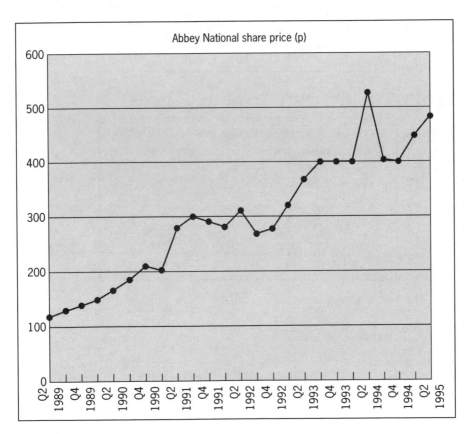

FIGURE 2   Abbey National share price (pence) 1989 to 1995

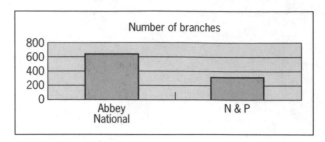

FIGURE 3   Number of branches in 1995

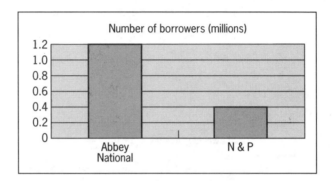

FIGURE 4   Numbers of borrowers (mortgages)

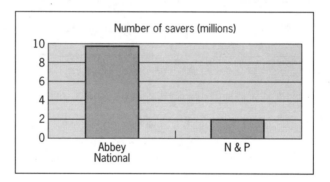

FIGURE 5   Numbers of savers in millions

FINANCIAL SERVICES

Building societies are part of the financial services sector which meets the financial needs of both the general public and industry. In the 1980s government legislation created fundamental changes in the industry leading to significant changes in the competitive environment. This meant that whereas building societies and banks had for over 50 years operated almost entirely in their own sector, they were now free to compete more broadly. In 1993 the total assets of the personal sector were £1,575 billion, as outlined in table 1.

It can be seen that pensions and life assurance accounted for 54.1 per cent of the total for 1993 with building society deposits next with 12.4 per cent. Banks (10.7 per

TABLE 1 Assets of the personal sector, 1987–1993

£ Billion	1987	1988	1989	1990	1991	1992	1993
Cash	11.5	12.5	13.3	13.2	13.6	14.6	15.5
British Govt securities	19.0	12.5	9.6	8.6	10.4	18.0	25.3
National savings	34.9	36.3	34.8	35.6	37.7	43.5	46.6
Tax instruments	0.3	0.3	0.3	0.3	0.3	0.3	0.3
N.I. Govt debt	0.2	0.2	0.2	0.2	0.2	0.1	0.1
Local auth. debt	0.6	0.6	0.4	0.2	0.2	0.3	0.3
Bank deposits	79.9	94.3	141.6	156.6	162.0	167.1	168.7
B. Soc. deps	129.3	149.6	140.6	158.5	175.8	186.3	195.2
Unit trusts	16.6	17.8	25.5	18.2	20.0	23.7	42.2
UK securities	113.6	119.1	146.0	123.4	138.1	153.8	196.7
Overseas securities	9.9	11.4	12.4	9.0	10.5	12.4	14.5
Life ass./pensions	390.2	453.8	565.4	528.0	610.9	694.8	850.6
Other instruments	9.2	11.0	13.5	15.4	16.3	18.7	18.4
Invest abroad	0.5	0.5	0.6	0.5	0.7	0.8	0.8
Total	815.7	919.9	1,104.2	1,067.7	1,196.7	1,334.4	1,575.2

Note: Data exclude trade credit and accruals adjustments.
Source: Central Statistical Office Financial Statistics, HMSO, table 9.1J, latest available Q2.

FIGURE 6 Financial needs of the personal sector

cent) and UK securities (12.5 per cent) were the only other categories above 10 per cent.

The financial needs of the personal sector are outlined in figure 6.

Borrowing

Money can be borrowed in a variety of different ways. Firstly, borrowing money to purchase a house: building societies are the main providers of mortgages. Secondly, personal loans for home improvements, car purchase etc: these can be obtained directly from a bank or from a range of companies that are often subsidiaries of

TABLE 2   Personal sector borrowing and saving

	Personal sector borrowing £ billion				New UK personal sector savings £ billion			
	House purchase	Personal loans	Credit cards	Total	Banks	Building societies	National savings	Total
1986	154.2	23.0	8.0	185.2	8.4	12.7	2.6	23.7
1987	183.4	27.8	9.6	220.8	8.4	14.1	2.5	25.0
1988	221.9	33.1	10.9	265.9	16.9	20.4	1.5	38.8
1989	255.5	38.2	11.7	305.4	22.2	17.6	−1.5	38.3
1990	287.8	40.6	13.3	341.7	16.2	18.2	0.9	35.3
1991	321.5	40.7	14.0	376.2	5.0	17.3	2.1	24.4
1992	339.9	39.9	14.1	393.9	4.4	10.5	4.0	18.9
1993	354.3	35.6	16.8	406.6	1.7	8.9	3.9	14.5

Source: CSO Financial Statistics, HMSO.

other financial institutions. Thirdly, credit can be obtained through credit cards. Details of the relative use of each means of borrowing are shown in table 2. Also shown in this table are the figures for new savings through banks, building societies and the government.

Insurance

The size of some parts of the insurance industry are shown in table 3. The majority of insurance is supplied by insurance companies, but banks and building societies have also entered the market. Also, it has been estimated that 20 per cent of building society profits come from acting as agents for insurance companies. The industry is dominated by a few large companies, but there are many smaller companies, some of which are owned by a foreign parent.

House purchase

Perhaps the largest purchase made by most people is a house. In 1975 the number of owner occupiers was 53.4 per cent of all dwellings, rising to 67.5 per cent by 1991. As can be seen from table 4, at the beginning of the 1980s building societies had an 80 per cent market share which had not varied much over many decades. However, with changes in legislation, their share dipped dramatically to approximately 50 percent in 1987 as the banks entered the market before returning to nearly 90 per cent in 1991 and subsequently falling back to 50 per cent in 1993. The reason for the change was that in periods of low inflation more borrowers move to fixed rate

TABLE 3   Life Assurance

	New business		Existing business		Property insurance new premiums
	Policies (million)	Premiums (£b)	Policies (million)	Premiums (£b)	£ million
1986	9.54	5.84	95.1	6.8	3189
1987	10.29	7.09	94.4	7.7	3589
1988	8.14	5.04	93.3	8.8	4088
1989	7.53	5.43	91.8	9.6	4660
1990	7.37	5.92	91.5	10.5	4443

Source: Association of British Insurers, *Insurance Directory and Yearbook* Vol. III 1992.

TABLE 4 UK net mortgage advances 1980–1991

	United Kingdom net mortgage advances £m							Halifax BS house price index	Building society loan to house value ratios
	Bid. Socs	Las	Ins	Banks	Misc	Other PS	Total		
1980	5,722	456	263	500		341	7,368	–	56.7
1981	6,331	271	88	2,265		353	9,483	–	61.9
1982	8,147	555	6	5,078		356	14,128	–	67.9
1983	10,928	(306)	126	3,531		40	14,520	100.0	67.5
1984	14,572	(195)	254	2,043		(42)	16,632	107.2	68.6
1985	14,711	(502)	201	4,223		60	18,573	117.0	69.2
1986	19,548	(506)	508	5,197		54	24,804	129.9	69.5
1987	15,076	(433)	988	10,104	3,952	49	29,736	149.9	67.2
1988	23,720	(329)	483	10,894	5,234	144	40,146	184.8	66.1
1989	24,002	(230)	(144)	7,108	2,952	134	33,823	223.1	66.4
1990	24,140	(322)	203	6,394	2,916	(102)	33,232	223.2	68.3
1991	20,927	(446)	(1,055)	4,775	2,172	(436)	25,939	220.5	69.0
1992	13,612	(358)	(39)	6,302	(1,394)	(102)	18,020	208.1	70.4
1993	9,271	(357)	(382)	9,712	(2,319)	(70)	15,851	202.1	69.6

Bid. Socs: Building societies excluding Abbey National plc from 1989 Q3
Las: Local authorities
Ins: Insurance companies
Misc: Other specialist mortgage lenders
Other PS: other public sector.

mortgages and the borrowing power of the banks enables them to raise capital at lower rates than building societies.

Savings and investments

Savings are usually referred to as those investments which earn interest but where the capital invested is at no risk and can be withdrawn in full. The products to meet this part of the market are largely supplied by the banks and building societies with savings accounts and Tessas. Investments are those instruments where the capital is at risk and take the form of bonds or equity which may be sold directly or by means of unit or investment trusts. Companies in this industry are often owned by other major financial institutions but some of the large companies are still independent. The size of the various sectors can be seen by referring back to table 1.

Money storage and transmission

This sector of the market was once the province of the banks, who provided facilities for keeping and withdrawing money by means of cash and cheques. Technological change has enabled customers to have immediate access to cash or cash equivalents through the introduction of credit cards and cash dispensers (ATMs). The result of this has been that building societies have moved into both these fields, and some also now offer banking facilities.

Pensions

Non-company based pensions are provided by the large financial institutions; mainly the big life insurance companies. This sector of the financial services industries has increased in importance as the government sought to extend the concept of individual provision for old age. However, the policies of some of these companies, together with the high pressure sales techniques used, has caused a cloud, which is not likely to disperse for some time, to settle over the industry.

Overview

The 1980s have been a decade of unprecedented change for the previously fairly static environment of the financial services industry. An outline of the areas in which the institutions in the various sectors operate is given in table 5 below. The largest operators in each of the different types of financial institutions are shown in appendix 2.

One result of the financial services legislation of the 1980s is that many companies felt that they needed to offer products across the whole spectrum of customers' needs, so that whilst some companies acquired businesses in other sectors, others diversified by means of a strategic alliance before, in some case, owning a facility either through acquisition or a start-up changing rapidly to wholly owned subsidiary life companies.

Table 6 outlines some of the alliances made between banks and building societies on one hand and insurance companies on the other.

BUILDING SOCIETIES

Introduction

The ideology of building societies draws on the Victorian virtues of thrift and mutual self-help. An account of the societies' origins and evolution is thus an

TABLE 5 Financial institutions market coverage

	Clearing banks	Building societies	Insurance companies	Finance houses	Retailers	Specialist mortgage companies
Standard savings accounts	•	•				
High interest accounts	•	•				
Current accounts	•	*				
Mortgages	•	•	*	*		•
Personal loans	•	*	*	•	*	
Credit cards	•	*		*	•	
Unit trusts	•	•	•		*	
Life assurance	•	•	•			
General insurance	•	*	•			
Estate insurance	*	•	•			
Commercial loans	•	*		*		
Commercial banking	•					

• Major player
* Minor player
Source: Datamonitor, Building Societies Report 1991.

TABLE 6 Strategic alliances in UK financial services

Building society	Insurance company tie	Bank	Insurance company tie
Halifax	Halifax Life	Abbey National	Abbey Life & Scottish Mutual
Nationwide	Guardian Royal Exchange	Bank of Scotland	Standard Life
Woolwich	Woolwich Life	Barclays	Barclay Life
Alliance & Leicester	Scottish Amicable	Lloyds	Lloyds Abbey Life/ Black Horse Life
Leeds Permanent	Leeds Life	Midland	Midland Personal Financial Services
Cheltenham & Gloucester	–	National Westminster	Nat West Life
Bradford & Bingley	Independent	Royal Bank of Scotland	Royal Scottish Assurance
National & Provincial	N & P Life	TSB Group	TSB
Britannia	Britannia Life		
Bristol & West	Eagle Star		

essential element in understanding their function and practice today. In the postwar period to 1986 building societies continued to expand rapidly in conjunction with growth in owner occupation. This was boosted by both the Conservative and Labour parties.

The customer's choice between building societies was limited in as much as the societies operated a cartel on interest rates, there was limited difference in the product ranges, societies had a shortage of funds to lend which meant that the consumer was given priority if he or she was already an existing saver with the society. Also the number of distribution outlets were geographically restricted. The one area where the consumer did have choice was in the number of competing building societies.

Building societies had virtually monopolistic control over the mortgage market until the late 1970s. However, the deregulation of the financial markets in 1980, particularly the lifting of balance sheet constraints on banks, and the reintroduction of a policy of rationing credit by price led to a revolution in the mortgage market.

As at the end of December 1993 there were 98 building societies in the UK, a reduction from 819 in 1950 (see appendix 3). However 88.3 per cent of total building society assets are controlled by the top 13 societies and of these only five building societies can be considered to have a truly national distribution network.

The Building Societies Association classifies building societies into four groups, A, B, C and D. Table 7 shows the summary statistics for each of these groups. More detailed information can be found in appendix 4.

TABLE 7 Summary statistics of UK building societies

	As at December 1992				
	Group A	*Group B*	*Group C*	*Group D*	*Total*
Number of societies	13	12	18	55	98
Total assets £m	245,390	22,607	6,871	3,026	277,894
% of total assets	88.3%	8.1%	2.5%	1.1%	100.0%

The 1986 Act established the Building Societies Commission and gave it wide powers of control over societies' affairs. The Act also provided for all building societies to become members of an Ombudsman scheme and introduced a statutory investors' protection scheme.

The other major features of the 1986 Act were as follows:

- Provision was made to convert to company status with the agreement of its members.
- Building societies could raise 20 per cent of their funds from non-retail sources (increased to 40 per cent in 1987).
- Societies can provide a range of house buying and financial services including money transmission, estate agency, mortgage management, credit broking, foreign exchange, conveyancing, underwriting life insurance and so on.
- Societies can hold 5 per cent of their commercial assets for new asset holding powers of unsecured lending, ownership of land and residential property, and investment in subsidiaries and other associates.

Thus the 1986 Building Societies Act has allowed the societies to diversify their activities away from pure mortgage lending and savings into other areas, so allowing them to compete on a wider scale with other financial institutions.

Marketing

Price is the major platform for competition although some branding takes place through advertising and promotion. Table 8 outlines the advertising expenditure of banks and building societies.

TABLE 8 Advertising in the personal financial sector at rate card cost 1980–1992

	Banks £m	Building societies £m	Sector total £m
1980	16.3	19.3	63.7
1986	57.7	61.5	258.5
1987	66.7	76.4	313.3
1988	92.6	93.6	380.0
1989	111.1	105.9	398.7
1990	102.7	121.8	411.6
1991	75.1	106.4	427.8
1992	55.0	112.2	373.3
1993	74.1	100.7	461.8
1994 (until 30 Sept.)	90.3	112.6	576.0

Source: Meal.

There are many building societies which are geographically focused (Scarborough Building Society for instance) but very few are focused on a particular customer segment (for example Ecology Building Society).

In the savings and current account markets, however, brand identification has been achieved mainly through advertising, for example Leeds Permanent Liquid Gold account and Halifax Card Cash and Maxim accounts. Probably the strongest brand identification for building societies is the actual building society name itself.

For savings, estate agency and current accounts, the brand identification is developed with the customer through the society's network of branches and agents. However building societies struggle to achieve complete brand identification with the customers in the lending market due to a large proportion (30–80 per cent depending on the society) of mortgage business being generated by intermediaries. The choice of channel is therefore important to develop the brand identification with the customer.

Strategic groupings for building societies are shown in Figure 7. The key factors used are the breadth of products offered by the society and the geographic scope of the society's activities within the UK.

This grouping has divided societies into five main categories. The nationally diversified societies such as Halifax and Alliance & Leicester represent the strongest challenge to the clearing banks. All these societies have diversified through organic growth into current accounts with the exception of the Alliance & Leicester which acquired Girobank. A number of large societies have, however, elected to remain focused within the personal finance markets and as a result they have been able to focus their capital and management resources on the development of their relative positions.

The majority of building societies, both large and medium sized, have developed into an array of other financial services, including insurance, life insurance and estate agency (see appendix 5). The development of tied insurance arrangements provides a means of gaining access to new financial markets without incurring heavy capital and other large scale start up costs. As a result, the smaller societies have elected to diversify out of the core housing finance market. The societies categorized as a diversified regional societies have all taken the opportunity to build a presence in the insurance sector. A number of diversified regional societies have also developed into the estate agency sector. The level of their involvement has naturally been smaller but the more limited capital base of these societies may result in some societies pulling out of the estate agency sector.

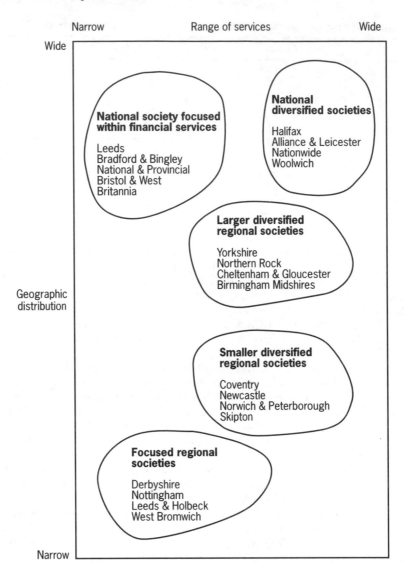

FIGURE 7   Strategic groupings of UK building societies

The smallest players in the building society sector, classified as focused regional societies, remain focused within the housing finance and savings markets. These societies are generally focused in one of two ways; by customer or geography. The geographic societies are likely to come under pressure as they are unable to raise funds as cost effectively as larger societies while they are unable to charge premium rates or satisfy the needs of a niche segment of customers whom the larger societies do not cater for.

Market channels

Historically the only major distribution channel was the full service branch. It still is the major distribution channel but its role in the distribution portfolio is changing. The number of branches increased year on year to 1987 but has subsequently fallen year on year, although the large fall in 1989 was largely due to Abbey National converting to a bank. (See appendix 6 for details of channels.) The introduction of electronic payment systems and ATMs has led to a decline in the use of branches for simple transactions. There has been an increase in the use of branches for more complex transactions such as mortgage and loan applications or financial advice.

Consequently building societies are placing increasing importance on redesigning their branches to make them more attractive and conducive to the selling of financial services. This redesigning incorporates giving over more space to the customers.

In comparison to the banks, building society branch networks appear small. However building societies supplement their branch networks with agency networks (see Appendix 6).

Building society agencies consist of professional offices of estate agencies, mortgage brokers, financial advisers or accountants. They do not offer a full branch service but corporate image is becoming increasingly important in the financial retailing market and this is difficult to control in the agency situation. The cost of agencies is increasing, which has reduced the level of profitability and the expansion into the estate agency sector means that the agency agreements are frequently with competitors.

The types of distribution channel used by building societies are as follows:

- Full service branch
- ATMs
- Offshore branches
- Telephone banking
- Intermediaries
- Mail services
- Estate agencies
- Direct sales force
- Telemarketing
- Agents

The intermediary distribution channel accounts for an estimated 50 per cent of all mortgage originations and is particularly strong in the south of the UK. This is an important distribution channel to all lenders except the banks. Centralized lenders are totally dependent on intermediaries, small building societies are heavily dependent on them (some 80–95 per cent of their mortgage business is originated by intermediaries) and larger building societies use intermediaries for asset growth. The intermediary channel is fragmented. Smaller brokers dominate the market. Life company mortgage firms place around 10 per cent of intermediary mortgage business and influence a similar amount. 'Corporates', such as large estate agency chains, originate around 25 per cent of intermediate mortgage business. The importance of intermediaries in the mortgage market is unlikely to diminish in the future.

Operating costs

The cost income ratios for some banks and building societies are shown in appendix 4. The average of building societies at 43 per cent places them in a better cost position than the banks average of 58 per cent. However these averages hide wide variations from the Cheltenham & Gloucester's 26 per cent to the Alliance & Leicester's 64 per cent (largely due to their acquisition of Girobank). Similarly

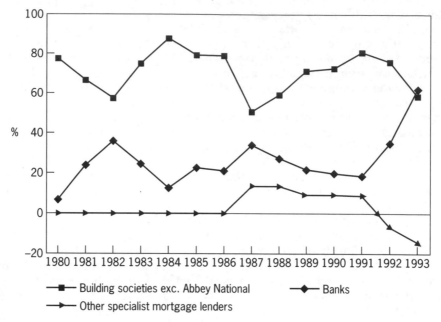

FIGURE 8   UK net mortgage advances – market shares 1980–1993

Abbey National still appears to retain the cost structure of a building society at 45 per cent.

MORTGAGE DEMAND

Mortgages are still the biggest product for building societies and the demand for mortgages and market share figures are outlined in table 9.

A recent survey for the Henley Centre for forecasting has provided some information about the future of the housing market and answers to two questions in particular.

- Do you expect to be a renter or owner in the year 2000?
- Will mortgage lending move downmarket?

The results of the survey are outlined below in figures 9 and 10.

MONEY TRANSMISSION

A key area in which many building societies are trying to increase their penetration in the transfer of money is by the opening of ATMs and by the marketing, resources and facilities being put into their banking activities.

The data in table 10 shows that the percentage of UK residents who have a bank account is apparently 74 per cent ('penetration' figures for the three categories).

ESTATE AGENTS

The market for estate agency services is dependent upon the velocity of the housing market as a whole. Estate agents receive a commission from the vendor for selling the house based on the price of the house. Therefore, if the market declines and property becomes difficult to sell, the estate agent's income is reduced.

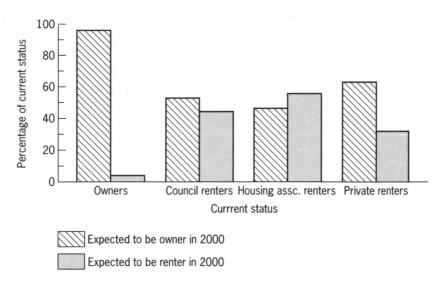

FIGURE 9   Expected housing tenure
Source: Henley Centre for Forecasting, *Household Formation to the Year 2000*

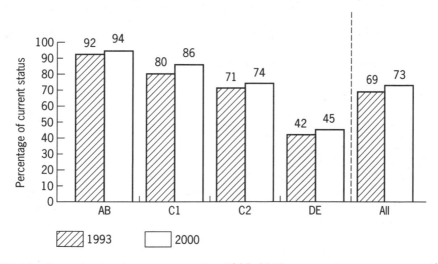

FIGURE 10   Future levels of owner occupation 1993–2000 – percentage owner occupation by social grade
(Note) Data from the BSA puts the current ownership level at 69%, which is slightly higher than the FIGURE produced by other sources.
Source: Building Societies Association 1993/The Henley Centre, *Planning for Social Change 1994/95*.

TABLE 9 The housing market in Great Britain 1975–1992

	Total dwelling 000's A	Great Britain Owner occupied 000's B	Owner occupied Stock % B/A	England & Wales Housing transactions 000's	Owner occupied moves %	England & Wales Average house price £
1975	19,871	10,610	53.4%	1,174	12	11,945
1976	20,118	10,818	53.8%	1,190	12	12,759
1977	20,367	11,026	54.1%	1,239	12	13,712
1978	20,542	11,120	54.1%	1,365	13	15,674
1979	20,739	11,348	54.7%	1,306	13	20,143
1980	20,903	11,618	55.6%	1,268	11	23,514
1981	21,085	11,898	56.4%	1,350	12	24,503
1982	21,251	12,270	57.7%	1,540	13	24,577
1983	21,448	12,605	58.8%	1,669	14	27,192
1984	21,654	12,914	59.6%	1,760	14	29,648
1985	21,851	13,225	60.5%	1,742	13	31,876
1986	22,062	13,576	61.5%	1,800	13	36,869
1987	22,284	13,964	62.7%	1,938	14	42,546
1988	22,518	14,419	64.0%	2,149	15	52,632
1989	22,734	14,828	65.2%	1,580	11	57,365
1990	22,928	15,094	65.8%	1,398	9	62,820
1991	23,136	15,259	66.0%	1,305	9	65,050
1992	23,300	15,404	66.1%	1,138	6	63,633

Source: Housing Finance, Tables 1, 16, 19, Building Societies Association 1993.

Banks, building societies, insurance companies and financial conglomerates were attracted to estate agency in the late 1980s for a number of reasons:

- the commission that could be earned from the sale of property in a booming market;
- the opportunity for cross-selling other financial products and services;
- as a defensive measure due to their competitors entering the market;
- as a way of acquiring a distribution channel on the high street.

In the period 1986 to 1988 it was estimated that some 3,500 outlets, out of a total of some 16,000, came under institutional control. See appendix 7.) By January 1989 the top 14 estate agency chains owned 5,167 estate agency branches, approximately one third of the total market. It was also estimated 'that those chains handled approximately 45 per cent of the value of the UK's estate agency business'.

Lloyds bank was the first institution to enter the market in 1982. However the upsurge in institutional buying did not start until 1986. Even retailers such as Asda have experimented with estate agency. The subsequent economic and property market recession saw all the major estate agency chains making substantial losses. Also the realization of the incremental business that the estate agency was providing (one society, Databank 1991, calculated that the ownership of an estate agency chain contributes only 3 per cent of total new mortgage business each year) was not a significant justification to keep sustaining heavy losses.

Therefore the majority of large estate agency chains are being rationalized, sold off or both. There is no reason to suggest why this should not be the case in the

TABLE 10 Penetration and profile of main account – current, 1991

	Bank account without interest		Bank account with interest		Building society with interest	
	Penetration %	Profile %	Penetration %	Profile %	Penetration %	Profile %
Total	27	100	35	100	12	100
Men	30	53	36	50	11	46
Women	25	47	34	50	12	54
15–19	8	3	44	12	14	11
20–24	28	10	33	9	15	12
25–34	33	22	34	18	12	19
35–44	35	22	39	19	10	14
45–54	34	17	33	13	13	15
55–64	24	11	35	13	13	15
65+	23	16	30	16	9	16
AB	28	16	47	21	8	10
C1	31	27	42	28	10	14
C2	31	33	33	28	13	33
D	20	14	27	14	16	24
E	20	10	27	9	11	13

Base 1695 adults
Source: British Market Research Bureau (BRMB)/Mintel Special Report, *Banks and Building Societies*, 1991.

future with the remaining chains waiting for an upturn in the property market so they can sell when the capital losses are not as great.

APPENDIX 1   ECONOMIC STATISTICS

	Unemployed ('000s)	PSBR £bn	House price inflation % p.a.	Real personal disposable income % p.a.	Saving ratio %
1986	3,107	2.5	11.7	4.1	8.6
1987	2,822	–1.4	14.9	3.5	6.8
1988	2,295	–11.9	26.3	6.0	5.6
1989	1,795	–9.3	18.3	4.5	6.6
1990	1,661	–2.1	–0.3	2.5	8.3
1991	2,287	7.7	–1.2	–0.5	9.8
1992	2,771	30.4	–6.4	0.7	10.9

Sources: Henley Centre, UK Economic Forecasts July 1993, Halifax House Price Index.

APPENDIX 2   *CONCENTRATION IN THE UK FINANCIAL SERVICES SECTOR*

Industry concentration: the size of the 15 largest operators in UK financial services industries 1992

Rank	Banks	Total Assets £m	Index by size
1	Barclays Bank	138,108	100
2	National Westminster	122,569	89
3	HSB Holdings	86,011	62
4	Midland Bank	65,632	48
5	Abbey National	57,405	42
6	Lloyds Bank	55,433	40
7	Royal Bank of Scotland	32,180	23
8	Bank of Scotland	25,987	19
9	TSB Group	25,810	19
10	Standard Charter	23,470	17
11	Warburg Group	14,292	10
12	Kleinwort Benson	9,947	7
13	Carter Allen Holdings	5,677	4
14	Bank of England	5,492	4
15	Hambros	5,345	4

Rank	Life insurance	Total Assets £m	Index by size
1	Prudential Corp	38,801	100
2	Standard Life	19,680	51
3	Norwich Union	17,775	46
4	Legal & General	17,739	46
5	Scottish Widows	11,580	30
6	Commercial Union	9,625	25
7	Sun Life Corp	8,957	23
8	Sun Alliance	8,459	22
9	Friends Provident	7,616	20
10	Allied Dunbar	7,468	19
11	Equitable Life	7,096	18
12	Royal Insurance	6,975	18
13	Scottish Amicable	6,636	17
14	Eagle Star	6,126	16
15	Lloyds Abbey Life	4,935	13

Rank	General insurance	Total Assets £m	Index by size
1	Royal Insurance	3,464	100
2	General Accident	3,219	93
3	Commerical Union	2,746	79
4	Sun Alliance	2,678	77
5	Guardian Royal Exchange	2,201	64
6	Eagle Star	1,625	47
7	Norwich Union	1,252	36
8	Prudential Corp	1,049	30
9	Cornhill Insurance	595	17
10	Co-operative Insurance	412	12
11	Legal & General	345	10
12	Provincial Group	331	10
13	Nat Farmers Union	315	9
14	Nat Ins & Guarantee Corp	183	5
15	Gan Minister Insurance	149	4

Rank	Estate agents	Total Assets £m	Index by size
1	Halifax	580	100
2	Royal Life	573	99
3	Hambros	480	83
4	Black Horse	397	68
5	Abbey National	394	68
6	Nationwide	372	64
7	General Accident	370	64
8	Legal & General	290	50
9	Woolwich	281	48
10	Scottish Widows	175	30
11	National & Provincial	144	25
12	Bristol & West	128	22
13	Arun Estates	127	22
14	Reeds Rain	97	17
15	Alliance & Leicester	86	15

Rank	Building societies	Total Assets £m	Index by size
1	Halifax	58,710	100
2	Nationwide	34,119	58
3	Alliance & Leicester	20,479	35
4	Woolwich	20,165	34
5	Leeds Provincial	16,631	28
6	Cheltenham & Gloucester	14,789	25
7	Bradford & Bingley	11,910	20
8	National & Provincial	10,708	18
9	Britannia	8,524	15
10	Bristol & West	7,141	12
11	Northern Rock	4,415	8
12	Yorkshire	4,185	7
13	Birmingham Midshires	3,745	6
14	Skipton	2,717	5
15	Portman	2,594	4
16	Others	57,058	
		277,894	

Source: *The Times 100* 1992/93.

APPENDIX 3   NUMBER OF BUILDING SOCIETIES 1910–1990

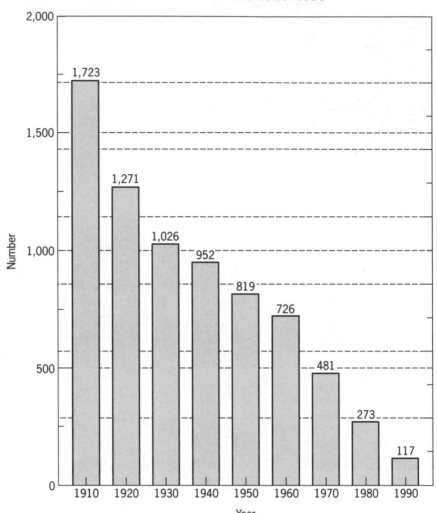

Source: Building Societies Association *Housing Finance*, May 1993, Table 24.

APPENDIX 4   *UK BUILDING SOCIETIES BACKGROUND INFORMATION, 1989–1993*

Market Shares of Total UK Net Mortgage Advances

	1989	*1990*	*1991*	*1992*	*1993*
Abbey National	12.08	13.99	13.87	13.69	18.74
Halifax	18.28	16.17	14.94	17.65	18.77
Nationwide	6.86	10.79	10.41	2.97	0.17
Woolwich	3.04	6.85	5.87	4.97	5.68
Alliance & Leicester	5.20	6.01	4.98	(2.19)	(0.96)
Leeds Permanent	6.38	4.10	5.17	4.83	4.20
Cheltenham and Gloucester	3.63	6.76	8.48	5.55	3.42
Bradford and Bingley	3.44	4.67	4.29	5.35	3.68
Britannia	2.38	2.42	3.06	2.63	3.62
National and Provincial	2.38	1.84	5.10	5.79	2.36
Bristol and West	3.35	2.23	3.32	2.91	1.81
Northern Rock	1.25	1.56	3.24	5.73	6.11
Yorkshire	0.93	1.38	2.11	2.54	2.42
Birmingham Midshires	1.47	1.21	0.28	0.47	2.33
Portman	0.19	0.17	0.41	1.13	0.57
Coventry	0.94	0.85	1.24	1.50	1.03

Source: UBS Philips and Drew, Building Society Research (August 1994).

Management expenses/total income ratios (%)

	1989	*1990*	*1991*	*1992*	*1993*
Abbey National	45.21	44.06	43.70	41.85	41.83
Halifax	51.41	47.05	41.00	38.11	39.02
Nationwide	60.98	54.10	51.43	50.11	47.48
Woolwich	46.61	52.38	57.49	49.81	47.84
Alliance & Leicester	48.57	58.34	61.98	60.41	61.74
Leeds Permanent	53.47	46.26	41.79	39.50	37.44
Cheltenham & Gloucester	30.52	27.56	25.90	22.10	25.07
Bradford and Bingley	47.35	45.90	44.20	39.16	42.77
Britannia	44.05	49.00	44.52	42.19	42.31
National and Provincial	48.81	53.24	41.91	38.89	44.10
Bristol and West	51.13	51.12	53.00	57.15	55.72
Northern Rock	54.44	53.55	47.45	37.03	33.75
Yorkshire	45.38	43.18	40.07	37.56	37.30
Birmingham Midshires	58.24	67.15	55.59	48.52	47.86
Portman	43.14	57.41	47.22	42.93	48.41
Coventry	41.65	41.33	40.75	38.43	38.99

Source: UBS Philips and Drew, Building Society Research (August 1994).

GLOSSARY OF TERMS for APPENDIX 4

Total Income	is the net interest margin plus other income
Net Interest Margin	is the difference between interest received *from* borrowers and interest paid to savers.
Total Income	is management expenses plus provisions plus profits
Mean Capital	is reserves (retained profits) plus subscribed capital (shares quoted on the exchange)
Mean Assets	is liquid assets plus mortgage assets plus commercial assets (loans) plus fixed assets (premises) plus other assets
Weighted Assets	The assets are weighted according to risk based on nationally agreed weighting figures.

APPENDIX 4 continued

Extract of financial performance from annual financial statements

	1992			1993		
	Estate agency £m	Provisions £m	Attrib. profits £m	Estate agency £m	Provisions £m	Attrib. profits £m
Abbey National	(20.0)	(274.0)	317.0	(2.0)	(218.0)	390.0
Halifax	(18.0)	(373.0)	458.0	(4.0)	(271.0)	574.0
Nationwide	(15.4)	(329.0)	117.0	(9.8)	(282.0)	168.0
Woolwich	(11.0)	(145.0)	95.0	(3.4)	(123.0)	136.0
Alliance & Leicester	(8.0)	(204.0)	88.0	(5.0)	(126.0)	133.0
Leeds Permanent	0.3	(105.0)	101.0	0.1	(131.0)	127.0
Cheltenham & Gloucester	–	(211.0)	86.0	–	(76.0)	132.0

Source: UBS Philips & Drew, Building Society Research (August 1994).

Building societies financial performance top 20 building societies ratios (%)

	1989	1990	1991	1992	1993	Average
Profitability						
Pre-tax profit/mean capital	30.06	26.37	19.83	15.52	19.51	22.26
Post-tax profit/mean capital	19.39	17.40	13.50	11.24	12.92	14.89
Pre-tax profit/mean assets	1.36	1.17	0.90	0.76	0.93	1.02
Post-tax profit mean assets	0.88	0.77	0.61	0.51	0.61	0.68
Capital strength						
Total capital/risk						
Weighted assets	11.65	11.67	11.72	12.63	13.14	12.16
Tier 1 capital/risk						
Weighted assets	9.73	9.34	9.37	10.08	10.75	9.85
Revenue, cost & growth						
Net interest receivable/Mean assets	2.17	2.09	2.08	2.18	2.25	2.15
Management expenses/mean assets	1.28	1.33	1.37	1.28	1.25	1.30
Management expenses/total income	47.65	49.53	48.89	44.44	43.30	46.76
Growth in assets	22.72	29.09	17.25	10.45	7.29	17.36
Other key ratios						
Other income & charge/total income	18.93	21.30	23.79	22.43	22.53	21.80
Provisions/mean assets	0.04	0.17	0.49	0.77	0.78	0.45
Non retail funds/Total funds	16.94	19.30	21.12	21.49	22.59	20.29

APPENDIX 5   BUILDING SOCIETIES MARKET COVERAGE

	Estate agents	Personal loans	Current account	Credit cards	Unit trusts	Life/General insurance
Halifax	599	Yes	Yes	Yes	Yes	Own
Nationwide	300	Yes	Yes	No	Yes	Tied
Woolwich	258	Yes	Yes	No	Yes	Own
Alliance and Leicester	72	Yes	Yes	Yes	Yes	Tied
Leeds Permanent	89	Yes	No	Yes	Yes	Own
Cheltenham & Gloucester	0	Yes	No	No	No	–
Bradford & Bingley	0	Yes	No	No	Yes	Independent
Britannia	25	Yes	Yes	No	Yes	Own
National & Provincial	14	Yes	No	Yes	Yes	Own
Bristol & West	93	Yes	Yes	No	Yes	Tied
Northern Rock	0	Yes	Yes	No	Yes	Tied
Yorkshire	0	Yes	No	No	Yes	Indendent
Birmingham Midshires	22	Under negotiation	No	No	Yes	Tied

APPENDIX 6   DISTRIBUTION NETWORKS AND STRATEGIC ALLIANCES IN FINANCIAL SERVICES

Table 1   Distribution networks of the largest UK building societies 1987 and 1993

	1987				1993			
	Branches	Estate agencies	ATMs	Agencies	Branches	Estate agencies	ATMs	Agencies
Halifax	745	306	1,200	2,277	688	600	1,600	1,153
Nationwide	910	446	323	2,722	719	303	756	261
Woolwich	417	0	198	1,454	497	257	375	570
Alliance & Leicester	413	0	107	1,832	406	78	553	612
Leeds Permanent	481	36	101	2,609	453	89	103	127
Cheltenham & Gloucester	173	0	0	28	236	0	0	0
Bradford & Bingley	252	0	56	728	257	0	61	433
Britannia	248	0	27	723	201	25	44	71
National & Provincial	324	0	52	655	319	14	78	180
Bristol & West	171	0	54	382	175	135	69	0
Total	4,134	788	2,118	13,410	3,951	1,501	3,639	3,407

Source: Building Societies Yearbooks 1988 and 1994/95, Building Societies Association.

Table 2   Distribution networks of the largest UK retail banks 1987 and 1992

	1987				1993			
	Branches	Estate agencies	ATMs	Agencies	Branches	Estate agencies	ATMs	Agencies
Bank of Scotland	545		302	N/a	490		391	N/a
Barclays	2,767		1,384	N/a	2,281		2,683	N/a
Lloyds	2,162	454	1,918	N/a	1,884	393	2,446	N/a
Midland	2,127		1,397	N/a	1,716		1,945	N/a
National Westminster	3,101		2,342	N/a	2,541		3,042	N/a
Royal Bank of Scotland	835		575	N/a	633		751	N/a
TSB Group	1,574	47	1,672	N/a	1,369	130	1,912	N/a
Total	13,111	501	9,590	N/a	10,914	523	13,170	N/a

APPENDIX 7   UK ESTATE AGENCY PRINCIPAL NETWORKS

	1987	1988	1989	1990	1991	1992	1993
Abbey National	88	388	406	427	373	350	344
Alliance & Leicester	–	31	110	100	92	81	80
Birmingham Midshires	–	13	96	72	71	26	22
Bradford & Bingley	–	–	–	–	–	–	–
Bristol & West	–	71	70	173	158	154	151
Britannia	–	33	44	40	34	29	25
Cheltenham & Gloucester	–	13	16	20	–	–	–
Halifax	306	575	688	622	565	550	531
Leeds Permanent	36	127	110	112	108	91	88
Nationwide	446	520	430	400	378	361	303
National Provincial	–	–	–	–	–	14	14
Northern Rock	–	57	63	87	79	–	–
Norwich & Peterborough	–	6	8	9	12	10	11
Nottingham	–	15	15	16	18	18	17
Portman	–	–	7	7	8	12	13
Principality	18	22	20	19	19	20	20
Wolwich	–	13	72	130	314	257	257
Yorkshire	–	3	18	43	49	31	–
Other building societies	–	–	–	–	–	–	–
General Accident	427	612	550	500	434	390	368
Hambros	460	510	494	473	486	453	444
Black Horse	451	551	476	450	397	388	383
Legal & General	–	–	108	238	270	264	238
Prudential	618	805	734	238	–	–	–
Royal Life	250	650	732	618	584	517	487
Scottish Widows	–	–	–	103	171	172	172
Sun Alliance	–	–	–	75	88	80	67
TSB	47	144	150	186	144	130	121
Building societies	849	1889	2197	2344	2349	2004	1876
Insurance companies	1289	2067	2124	1867	1640	1876	1776
Banks	501	695	626	636	541	518	504
Other major networks	795	937	730	573	700	704	– n/a
Total corporate estate agents	3479	5588	5677	5420	5230	4847	– n/a
Independent agents	13,021	12,912	12,323	10,580	8,770	7,153	n/a
Total	16,500	18,500	18,000	16,000	14,000	12,000	

Sources: Various – *Building Societies Year Book*, Building Societies Association, *Estate Agency News*.

APPENDIX 8   RATIO OF HOUSE PRICES TO AVERAGE EARNINGS

Year	Ratio
1952	3.7
1953	3.5
1954	3.4
1955	3
1956	2.8
1957	2.7
1958	2.7
1959	2.7
1960	2.6
1961	2.8
1962	2.8
1963	2.9
1964	2.9
1965	3
1966	3.1
1967	3
1968	2.9
1969	2.8
1970	2.8
1971	3
1972	3.6
1973	4
1974	4.2
1975	3.6
1976	3.5
1977	3.3
1978	3.2
1979	3.6
1980	3.5
1981	3.3
1982	3
1983	3.1
1984	3.3
1985	3.5
1986	3.6
1987	3.7
1988	4
1989	4.3
1990	3.6
1991	3.3
1992	2.8
1993	2.7
1994	2.7
1995	2.6

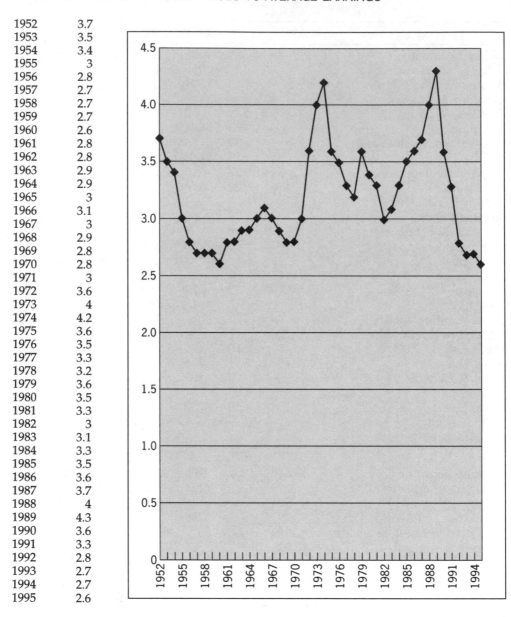

THE PHARMACEUTICAL INDUSTRY

The pharmaceutical industry is one of the world's largest and most heavily regulated industries and is defined as being concerned with the manufacture and marketing of products for the prevention, diagnosis and treatment of diseases of humans and animals. There are three main medicine categories:

- Prescription Only Medicines (POM): these are not advertised to the general public and are available only on a doctor's or dentist's prescription or through a hospital. They comprise ethical and generic drugs.
- 'Semi Ethicals' or Pharmacy Only (P): these cannot be advertised to the general public, are available on a doctor's or dentist's prescription, but can also be bought without a prescription by the general public in the presence of a pharmacist.
- General Sales List Products (GSLs) are products which can be advertised and bought over the counter freely (OTC).

Since 1985 the industry has grown by 10 per cent per annum compound or 4 per cent in real terms. Almost 50 per cent of the value of the worldwide pharmaceuticals industry in 1991 was accounted for by the United States of America and Japan, as illustrated in figure 1.

The US pharmaceuticals industry, with a total value of $26.8 billion in 1992, prospered mightily in the 1980s. Profit margins widened substantially and revenue growth marched steadily upwards. The steep price increases which could be afforded by major corporations contributed to hefty double digit profit gains of 17–20 per cent. But because of the pressure exerted by the Food and Drugs Administration to limit price increases, most analysts agree that annual profit gains will slow to 13–15 per cent by 1995 (*Financial Times*, 23 July 1992). Some analysts even predict that overall industry earnings growth could dip below 10 per cent.

The Japanese market, the second largest in the world with a total value of $17.4 billion in 1992, holds substantial potential for further growth as the population ages rapidly and consumers become increasingly health conscious. However, price pressures are evident in the UK as well. The prices of some medicines have been reduced nine times in the past 14 years and the Ministry of Health cut drugs prices by 9 per cent on average in 1992 (*Financial Times*, 27 October 1992). Smaller companies, unable to survive through the industry's consolidation due to the lack of financial and R&D resources, are receptive to cross-border mergers and acquisitions.

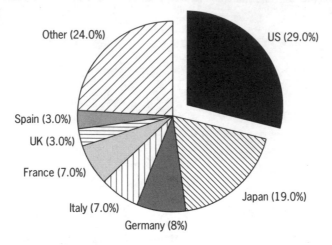

FIGURE 1   World pharmaceuticals industry geographical split 1991
Source: Glaxo Report and Accounts 1992.

The same picture is apparent in most European countries. In Germany, which is the third largest market in the world, the health insurance organizations (which provide cover for everyone in work) slashed the amount they were willing to pay for drugs, cutting prices on average by 5 per cent and imposing a two-year price freeze. In Italy, the Treasury, which sets drugs prices, has refused to allow any further increases. At present the less developed economies account for 76 per cent of world population but less than 15 per cent of pharmaceutical consumption.

The OTC and generics sectors had annual worldwide sales of around $20 billion in 1989. The move towards greater health awareness, health education and preventive measures have fuelled growth in OTC products. The fastest growing sector of OTC sales is dietary supplements and vitamins. The market for vitamins has grown dramatically in the UK from £20 million in 1981 to £81 million in 1991. Vitamin usage tends to be less reactionary and more preventative and for this reason this sector is set to expand further as health awareness grows and preventative measures are perceived as 'health insurance' for the future. The generics industry contains a large number of relatively small companies, geared especially to this end of the industry. Several companies are owned by the large research-based multinationals which have been anxious to get a foothold in the generic industry.

Demand for pharmaceuticals is determined by illness, social and demographic factors. A pattern likely to be prevalent in most developed countries of the world is the increase in the age of the population. As chronic disease tends to become more prevalent with longevity, this means a corresponding rise in the use of all types of medical care. For example, UK drug expenditure per head in the over-65 age group is more than four times the level for the rest of population. Companies which will benefit most from the changing demographic pattern will be those that provide for the chronic disease of old age: arthritis, coronary disease, hypertension and central nervous system illness. Pollution and allergy-related diseases are also increasing due to the increase in industrial development. The growth in the respiratory related diseases is greater than the overall diagnostic growth in the UK.

The industry is very susceptible to government regulations. Currently, regulations deal with every facet of a pharmaceutical company's activities: innovation, manufacturing, licensing, marketing, pricing and profits, distribution and international markets. There is increasing pressure for cost containment from public

TABLE 1 Leading pharmaceuticals companies by nominal pharmaceutical R&D spending 1992

Company	R&D spend ($m)	Sales ($m)	R&D as % of sales
Glaxo	1052.7	7247.0	14.5
Merck	987.8	8019.5	12.3
Roche	953.3	4119.9	23.1
BMS	845.0	5908.0	14.3
Hoechst	785.8	6263.9	12.5
Bayer	688.8	5306.4	13.0
Ciba-Geigy	677.8	4052.3	16.7
Sandoz	675.0	4440.7	15.2
SmithKline	654.6	4370.1	15.0
Johnson	569.0	3795.0	15.0

Source: The Financial Times, 22 April 1993.

authorities through aggressive price controls, due to the growth of expenditure on health care facilities generally as a result of the ageing population and the growing cost of health technology.

Technology, and more specifically the rapidly increasing cost of research and development (R&D), is a crucial characteristic of the industry. Worldwide spending on pharmaceutical based R&D increased by an average of 16 per cent per annum during the 1980s. The global total for R&D has risen from $15.3 billion in 1988 to $24 billion in 1990 which represented 15 per cent of overall pharmaceuticals sales revenue. The reason for this increase is that successful R&D has become critical to success in the pharmaceutical industry. The development process has become riskier and much more expensive in the past few years and a steady flow of new product development is the main competitive weapon of a drug company. The cost of developing a 'blockbuster' drug can be as much as $250 million. Expenditure by the large drug companies is shown in table 1.

Patents

The protection of proprietary information in the pharmaceutical industry is a critical issue. The original compound developed by the manufacturer is patented, establishing a legal monopoly which gives the innovator the opportunity to recoup its R&D and marketing costs. The patent is usually given for a period of 15 to 20 years from the time the compound is registered, that is, before the compound is actually developed – a process which often takes considerable time. In the UK, for example, product development takes up to 12 years and an investment of $100 million to $150 million. This leaves just a few years, before the patent expires, for the company to recoup its costs and generate a profit.

However, as from 1 January 1993 the EC has granted an extra five years of patent protection to drug companies (*The Times*, 26 January 1993) which might help reduce some of the risks facing the industry.

It is estimated that every day a drug is held back from the market due to ongoing clinical trials it is costing the company £1 million. Nevertheless, it is still of vital importance that such drugs are launched simultaneously into all the major world-wide markets and that critical mass is achieved quickly.

The approval and registration procedure in each market varies, so the company needs to apply for separate licences in each individual country, incurring additional costs in the process. Furthermore, lead times for the approval of new drugs differ markedly across countries. The single European market will alleviate a large proportion of these problems as rules within the EC will be harmonized.

Generic drugs are copies of off-patent branded products which have usually been invented by the mainstream, research-based section of the industry. Generics are much cheaper than their branded counterparts (by up to 50 per cent and are attractive to the state-owned health agencies, the most important buyers of pharmaceuticals. In Europe generics account for about 10 per cent of the total prescribed drugs sales whereas this figure is much higher, at 20–25 per cent in the US and Japan. Since 1983 the number of prescriptions issued in generic form in the UK has grown considerably to 36 per cent of the total in 1989 as drug buyers have become increasingly price conscious, and this trend is expected to continue. Moreover, nearly 80 per cent of existing drugs will come off-patent over the next five years. Therefore, the recent trend is for major companies to supply their own generic versions of their patented products when the patent comes close to expiry, in an attempt to pre-empt generic drug manufacturers and maximize their return on the R&D investment. This will encourage more consolidation in the industry as large ethical based companies buy out small generic producers.

The OTC business, though not a substitute for ethical drugs, is another area in which drug companies can focus their attention. The growing importance of the OTC business to traditional pharmaceuticals companies is illustrated by recent joint ventures: for example, Procter & Gamble with Syntex, and Johnson & Johnson with Merck. A critical characteristic in the OTC business is the importance of size. A large stable of OTC products helps companies gain access to supermarket chain buying departments. ICI sold its US OTC business in 1989 on the grounds that it did not have 'critical mass'.

Parallel importing constitutes another threat to drug manufacturers with products costing less in overseas countries being imported back to the source country, undercutting the manufacturer's price and resulting in a reduction of profits.

The industry is organized on an international scale since R&D costs are so high they can only be recovered by worldwide sales. The industry has come to be dominated by a very small number of very large companies. However, the industry leader Merck has only a 4.5 per cent market share, emphasizing that the industry leaders have concentrated power in therapeutic segments, rather than throughout the whole market. For example, Glaxo has around 35 per cent share of the respiratory drug market, but an overall market share of less than 4 per cent (see appendix 3 for the main competitors).

The risk that a new drug will fail its clinical trials means continuing success is only assured with a flow of new products. This has led to a spate of recent mergers, both as a means of combating increasing R&D costs by achieving economies of scale and as a defence against the cost-cutting moves by governments.

This sector is believed to be on the threshold of a significant shake-out with mergers and acquisitions continuing and small companies being squeezed out. In 1989 half of world sales were in the hands of 25 companies. It is believed that by the end of the decade that figure will be nearer 15!

The market is now driven by large buyers, that is, managed health care programmes, government agencies, even mail order companies, all seeking drugs at the lowest possible cost. In the UK, for example, the National Health Service accounts for over three-quarters of pharmaceuticals sales. SmithKline Beecham, for example, one of the world's largest pharmaceuticals companies, depends on these healthcare providers for 50 per cent of its US sales and expects this proportion to rise to 80 per cent by the end of the decade.

THE SCIENTIFIC INSTRUMENT INDUSTRY

The market for scientific and industrial instruments embraces a wide range of products and equipment for measuring, monitoring, testing, recording and controlling physical phenomena and material characteristics in R&D or in industrial and other processes. The range of products in this sector is somewhat diverse. Consequently, the types of companies engaged in supplying these different products vary considerably both in the range of their operations and in size.

The UK market for scientific and industrial instruments is estimated to have had a value of £3.1 billion in 1991; this represents a fall of 4.1 per cent on the previous year or a 10.2 per cent fall in real terms. The trend indicates that the industry is highly dependent on economic conditions. During the 1980s, the scientific instruments market benefited from the upturn in the UK economy and in Europe generally, but has now entered a slow growth period due to the recession which has affected most countries worldwide.

Although applications for scientific and industrial equipment have end users spread widely through all sectors of the economy, the overall levels of business are primarily dominated by the fortunes of the energy, manufacturing and utility companies. These are either in relation to their expenditures on plant and machinery, R&D or the incorporation of instruments into the products they make. In the chemical and petrochemical sector, decisions on new and updated plant and equipment are frequently taken on a global or at least regional basis, so sales to these end-users are dependent on the world/regional economy.

The industry is international with many companies operating on a global basis. This has become inevitable due to the high cost of product development and the way in which end-user markets may be dominated by international customers operating in world markets.

Companies involved in this industry often have other activities outside this business sector, so that the instrument products may be only part of a much wider manufacturing or distribution operation. These activities may be related in the sense that they cover other types of electronic and computer equipment, additionally other companies with very diverse operations are also involved in the industry (see table 2 for the main competitors).

Despite the number of major international companies there is also a large number of fairly small, local companies with sales turnover of £5 million or less. These companies are often highly specialized. The industry is, therefore, fragmented with

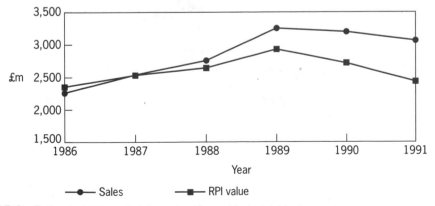

FIGURE 2 Estimated UK market for scientific and industrial instruments
Source: Keynote Report 1992, Scientific Instruments.

TABLE 2 Leading pharmaceuticals companies by nominal pharmaceutical R&D spending 1992

Company	Other business
ABB (Sed/Swiss)	Electrical, mechanical engineering
Ciba-Geigy (Swiss)	Chemicals, pharmaceuticals
Emerson Elect. (USA)	Electrical, electronics
Fisons (UK)	Pharmaceuticals
GEC (UK)	Defence equipment, electrical, electronics, telecommunications
Hewlett Packard (USA)	Computers, defence equipment
Honeywell (US)	Defence equipment, electrical
Philips (Neth)	Electronics, computers, consumer products
Siemens (Ger)	Electrical, electronics, consumer products, computers, telecommunications
Tektronix (USA)	Electronics, computers

Source: Scientific Instruments Keynote Report 1992.

no one company or group of companies dominating the whole spectrum of activities encompassed by the sector. The market is segmented into numerous product markets with individual suppliers as specialists in particular sub-sectors. Therefore the segments within the industry are more concentrated. Within each segment, obtaining critical mass, that is volume sales, is crucial to cover the high costs of R&D, production and marketing. Overall the effect of these high costs is to lower margins in what should be a high margin, high technology market.

The fragmented market allows entry into the industry on a small scale if the entrant is a highly specialized company or on a larger scale by companies which have the backing of big chemical, engineering, electrical or electronics groups.

The products of the industry are found in all sectors of manufacturing, research, health, public and private services and education (see figure 3). Major end-users include companies engaged in the oil, gas, chemical, metal processing and engineering industries, as well as utilities. Therefore buyer power is not very strong given the diverse range of products and client base.

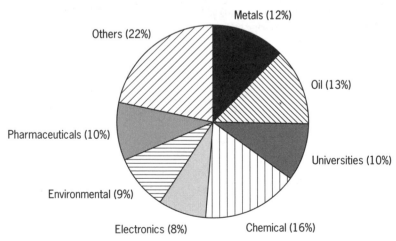

FIGURE 3   Instruments sales by industry – 1989
Source: Smith New Court Research, investment analyst report.

FISONS

Fisons up to 1982

In the 15 years prior to 1982 the stated aims of the company were as follows:

- Reduce Fisons' dependence on fertilizer sales which then accounted for 80 per cent of the group's total business.
- Expand into businesses Fisons had identified as strong growth areas, notably drugs.
- To divest from some of the ill-assorted acquisitions that the company had made over the years and use the finance to build up the high growth areas.

The aim was to be large, perhaps in a fairly small pond, but the objective was to be first or second in a particular market. At this time Fisons was considered the leader in the narrow field of anti-asthma drugs, and it ranked second in the UK fertilizer market. However, despite the leading positions in all of its markets, the fortunes of its major businesses had begun to decline, with a loss of £13.3 million in 1980.

1983–1993

In 1983 a new structure of Fisons emerged with the core businesses of horticulture, pharmaceuticals and scientific equipment. In 1984 John Kerridge took over as Chairman and Chief Executive, directing the strategy which the company was to follow for the rest of the decade. In the annual report he restated the aims and strategy (initially stated in 1983) as follows:

- to achieve growth in terms of both volume and quality of earnings;
- to operate in attractive industries which had growth potential and a record of profitability for successful participants and were therefore exit low margin industries;
- to operate in areas where Fisons could aspire to be an effective competitor by virtue of size and financial and managerial resources.

Kerridge believed the three markets in which Fisons operated had these inherent qualities and that they could be exploited by organic and acquisitive growth. This would broaden the product and geographical scope within these clearly defined markets. Kerridge also emphasized the need for tight cost control, and to generate positive cash flow in order to finance capital expenditure and R&D to sustain organic growth. This was to be augmented by selected acquisitions. The emphasis was to be on higher productivity and a competitive cost base to allow a more aggressive marketing strategy. The management approach was one of strong central control, clear strategic goals, tight financial control, and maximum delegation of authority. All the divisions operated autonomously.

The worldwide recession in 1983 and subsequent cuts in public expenditure created an unfavourable operating environment. Fisons' strategy to counter these adverse conditions was to achieve growth via new product launches, new market penetration, and by increasing productivity and efficiency in all divisions by tight cost control. A rights issue raised £27.7 million and the sale of FBC, the agrochemicals business, to Schering for £60 million left nil borrowings, enabling the company to finance further acquisitions. The economic environment improved from 1984, allowing the company to expand.

In 1991 two drugs, Optricom (eye treatment) and Imferon (used to treat anaemia), were withdrawn from the US market, due to the failure of the processing facilities to meet Federal Drugs Agency (FDA) requirements. This was compounded by sales in the other divisions suffering from the intensifying world recession, despite Fisons' global market and product portfolio. The prime concern of Egan, who replaced Kerridge in 1991, was to restore investor confidence in the company and restructure the management team to address the main problems. Cedric Scroggs was appointed Chief Executive in 1992, and Fothergill, the Chairman of the Pharmaceutical Division left the company.

Egan needed to implement a strategy to turn the company around and refocus the management on its core skills. He instigated a strategic review of the long-term prospects of the businesses. This review led to the subsequent divestment of horticulture and consumer health businesses. Although profitable and with a high market share, consumer health needed a high advertising budget to ensure growth. It was felt that Fisons did not have critical mass to achieve growth. Additionally, the three distinct geographical businesses could easily be sold to raise much needed cash to reduce borrowings. With many large players looking to get into the OTC market, there was no difficulty in realizing a good price and the UK division was sold to Roche for £90 million and the US division to Ciba Geigy for £93 million. The strategic reason was to allow the concentration of management and financial resources on the core businesses of ethical pharmaceuticals and scientific equipment.

Egan left the original organic growth strategy in place, but an increase in costs to bring the production facilities up to approved status resulted in lower margins. Capital expenditure in 1992 amounted to £112 million as the company upgraded technical facilities and invested in improved production facilities. Investment in R&D in both the pharmaceutical and scientific equipment markets was also increased, emphasizing the need for product development despite the problems facing the company.

The review acknowledged that Fisons' distinctive competence was in science-based activities. It also highlighted the need for strategic alliances in research, selling, marketing and manufacturing, in order to provide growth for Fisons within these markets. Therefore, the strategy under Egan altered, emphasizing divestments in the short term, and alliances not acquisitions to foster growth in the long term. Acquisitions could no longer be financed by cash flow or by the disillusioned shareholders in the short term, and the new strategy also underlined the long-term commitment to R&D.

Horticulture division

Fertilizers were Fisons' traditional business but in the 1960s fertilizers ceased to be a growth industry in the UK. New competitors had entered the market, new capacity came on stream in the late 1960s and early 1970s with the effect of driving down prices, squeezing the margin available on this high volume, commodity type business. In straight nitrogen fertilizer, Fisons' main competitor ICI held a market share of 60 per cent, four times that of Fisons. In compound fertilizers, ICI was thought to have 35 per cent of the market, with Fisons accounting for approximately 25 per cent.

By 1979 profits from the group's fertilizer division were only £2.9m, 51 per cent lower than the previous year, although sales rose by 22 per cent to £196.2m. In 1982 it was decided to exit fertilizers by selling the operations to Norsk Hydro, realizing that even rationalization of the operations could not restore profitability to previous levels.

The disposal of the fertilizer division enabled the group to concentrate on the development of its growth horticulture and agrochemical businesses, through both organic growth and by acquisitions. Agrochemicals was another of Fisons' traditional businesses. Fisons had started to accelerate its agrochemicals research programme. Nevertheless, by 1980, realizing that agrochemicals were vastly different from fertilizer and required cost intensive research, which Fisons could not sustain, Fisons formed a joint venture with Boots agronomical division. The new company, called FBC, was officially launched in January 1981, and was expected to be Britain's dominant producer of pesticides and herbicides. However the venture was not a success and was sold in early 1983 to Schering.

The focus of the Horticulture Division was to increase competitiveness via cost control and higher productivity. The reliance on the commodity peat business in the USA was to be lessened through the development of value added products for professional and amateur gardeners. The division was strengthened through the purchase of Bees Seeds from Shell as they had strong established brand names, which would be used to launch Fisons into the seeds market. This was to be combined with the aggressive promotion of existing brands such as Levingtons. However, sales of these products were not sufficient to offset the volatility of peat prices. The commodity peat market was weak following oversupply from good harvests which led to lower margins, or when the harvest was poor such as in 1986, increased production and distribution costs eroded margins. The company responded to the growing environmental pressures on peat and fertilizers by introducing an organic range of fertilisers. To avoid growing environmental pressures concerning peat conservation, Fisons gave ownership of its peatlands to English Nature.

Despite being badly affected by the recession, acquisitions were made in 1991 to increase market share in Canada and Belgium. However, following the strategic review instigated by Egan, Fisons were to divest themselves of this business. The North American operations which contained the bulk of the peat commodity business was sold to Macluan Capital Corp. for £39 million in May 1993, with the higher margin European businesses still to be divested.

Scientific Equipment Division

Fisons had two main operating areas:

- clinical laboratory supplies, which was generally low margin, high volume business;
- analytical instrumentation, which was lower volume, higher margin, high technology business.

The strategy of the Scientific Equipment Division was to invest in high-growth segments of the industry and divest or curtail investment in mature or declining markets. The acquisition of Curtin Matheson Scientific (CMS), the third largest distributor of high technology bio-medical products in the US in 1983, altered the focus of the Division. It took Fisons into new areas of diagnostic equipment and more importantly provided synergies by marketing UK products in the USA giving Fisons a presence in the US scientific equipment market where it had little previous exposure. The CMS strategy was developed further by the acquisition of a number of small specialist equipment manufacturers in the US. This helped strengthen the customer service and distribution systems which were critical for success.

Other acquisitions were made within the high-growth areas of this fragmented market. An Italian company, CEST, with a leading position in the high resolution gas chromatography market was acquired in 1985 for £12.5 million. In 1986 Applied

Research Laboratories, a leading manufacturer of spectrometers, was acquired for $45 million. As a result of this strategy, Fisons became one of the global leaders within the markets it operated in. In order to retain competitiveness, especially with fluctuations in the exchange rates, the emphasis remained on cost control and improving efficiency.

Fisons' scientific equipment business was yet another victim of the recession of the early 1980s. Much of the Division's sales were exported. These were adversely affected by the strong pound and American competition. Home sales had also been hit by cuts in Government expenditure, particularly in the education field. New product development was becoming increasingly important, especially in the high-technology areas where the rapid changes in technology offered the greatest growth potential. In the short term though, growth was derived from reducing costs, higher efficiency, and increasing competitiveness.

In 1989 Fisons made a large acquisition for £244 million, VG Instruments, a leading world supplier of mass spectrometers and surface analysis equipment. This acquisition made Fisons the third largest manufacturer in this segment of the market, behind Schimadu of Japan with sales of £345 million compared to £155 million for VG in 1989. Furthermore, VG was a high-technology, higher-margin operation with a diverse end client and geographic base. Lower technology laboratory equipment businesses were sold to Sanyo Electric as they were not consistent with the strategy of focusing on high technology businesses.

In 1992 profits fell for the first time since 1980, due to the recession reducing orders. The laboratory supplies business proved to be more resilient in the recession, whereas the instruments market is highly competitive with equipment prices being individually negotiated to meet the customer's requirements. The strength of sterling resulted in Fisons reducing prices in order to maintain competitiveness with dollar-based competitors. The strategy of the division in light of the recession was to protect market share at the expense of margins. The laboratory supplies business (CMS), gained market share via a strategy of aggressive marketing, improved customer service, and good relationships with both the suppliers and customers.

Fisons' instruments consists of organic instruments serving the growth industries of pharmaceuticals, environmental and novel materials, inorganic and surface science instruments serving industries such as metals, construction, electronics and petrochemicals. Higher sales growth and margins were produced by the organic businesses. Customers in these industries continued to invest in equipment to maintain their competitive advantage. The R&D at Fisons is therefore focused on the organic businesses. The trend in the industry is towards the application of advanced technologies in smaller, low cost instruments using powerful software.

Pharmaceuticals Division

Fisons operated in three main pharmaceutical markets:

- ethical medicines (patented prescription);
- over the counter medicines;
- branded consumer health products such as vitamins.

Fisons started to build up its drug business in the late 1960s as part of its new corporate strategy. The early discovery of Intal, a drug for the treatment of asthma, established Fisons' position in pharmaceutical research and was followed by the development of Proxicromil, another asthma drug, and the hope was it would be a lucrative follow-on to Intal. The incidence and mortality of asthma is increasing, due to higher levels of pollution and smoking. Asthma is a chronic illness which requires continual therapy for life and therefore is an attractive therapeutic market. There is no ideal cure so it requires a high level of R&D to improve products *vis à vis* the competition. Fisons specialises in inhaler drugs for asthma, and it is the inhaler devices that deliver the drugs that are patented, hence quality of the device is important. The growth rate of respiratory-related diseases is higher than that of all illness diagnosed in the UK.

In 1979 pharmaceuticals accounted for over 50% of Fisons' profits, although they represented only 18% of sales. However, in 1982 the patents started to run out on the company's major drug, Intal and inevitably the profits started to fall off. Furthermore, the development of Proxicromil was halted – after investing £12 million and six years of research – as it had been found to have an unsatisfactory safety profile for long-term administration during clinical trials. Such setbacks are common in the industry: the US company SmithKline and French spent almost £20 million on the development of an anti-cancer drug called Metiamide before abandoning it.

Fisons' ethical drug business was dominated by the sales of asthma and allergy-related medicines, notably Intal. The company had a wide geographical spread, which was important in the global pharmaceutical market. The focus of this division was the penetration of the two largest markets, the US and Japan, and obtaining approval for selling existing drugs in these two markets. Slowly the company began to obtain critical mass in the US, mainly through the sale of Intal.

During the 1980s the UK government enforced an across-the-board reduction in DHSS prices, and there was concern that if other governments were to follow the same strategy, there would be adverse implications for expansion opportunities and R&D levels in the industry. This policy undermined growth, and the focus was on tight cost control.

The main new product launch during the period was Tilade, an anti-inflamma-tory product, which was launched in the UK and other European markets in 1988. However, the FDA and the Japanese authorities declined to give Tilade approval at this stage. A cardio-vascular compound, Dopacard, was also registered, the only other major R&D success for Fisons at this time. Growth in the Pharmaceutical Division was primarily organic, resulting from developing patented compounds for other applications and penetrating new markets. Acquisitions were generally small. Weddel was acquired in the generics market to increase Fisons' market share in the UK. Radiol, a UK consumer health care company was acquired for £4.3 million in 1986, emphasizing the importance of the consumer health division. Radiol's brands were integrated with the successful existing brands, such as Sanatogen vitamins and Paracodol analgesic. Other acquisitions involved buying pharmaceutical com-panies in new markets such as Mexico and Italy, to gain a market presence.

In 1988 Fisons made the first of its larger acquisitions in a bid to foster growth. Pennwalt in the US was acquired for £250 million. Pennwalt had synergies with Fisons through its product areas: prescriptive drugs for coughs and colds, hyper-tension drugs, and anti-allergy and anti-fungal OTC brands. More important was the presence Pennwalt would give Fisons in the US market. The acquisition doubled the total prescription product sales force in the US, and also provided Fisons with much-needed R&D and production facilities in the US. Furthermore, a stronger US presence could help secure FDA approval more rapidly, as the approval delays were becoming longer, Tilade being a prime example. In 1990 Tilade was finally recommended for approval in Europe but not by the FDA. In the US, Imferon doubled its sales to become the third largest seller behind Intal and Rynacrom. Fisons attempted to gain a greater share of the second largest market by increasing its stake in Fujisawa-Fisons to 65 per cent.

R&D was originally focused on asthma and allergy compounds where Fisons had specialized knowledge. By the end of the decade it was slightly broader, focused in four carefully defined areas;

- inflammation and immunology, developing the Tilade and Tipredane compounds;
- cardio-vascular, based on Dopacard;
- gastro-intestinal;
- central nervous system disorders, stroke/epilepsy, based on Remacemide, a Pennwalt compound.

Fisons' sales growth was greater than the growth of the respiratory market as a whole following the eventual approval of Tilade in the US in 1992, and increased sales of Intal and Tilade in Japan. Profits, however, were hampered in 1991 and 1992 by the costs of complying with FDA standards. The withdrawal of Optricom and Imferon in the US cost £45 million of sales and £33 million of profits. Approval of Optricom was still withheld at the end of 1992, compounding Fisons' problems.

New product launches were limited as the Division concentrated on the development of existing products and markets. More importantly, a series of alliances was entered into in 1992. The US sales force of Rhone-Poulenc Rorer (RPR) agreed to market Tilade in the US, doubling the sales force available to Fisons, which was vital to maximize sales quickly. Fisons in return promoted RPR's inhaled steroid for severe asthma as a complement to Tilade, appropriate for milder asthma cases. Fisons formed a second alliance with an ophthalmic specialist, Allergan Inc. where Fisons would co-promote an Allergan product in return for future assistance in the development and marketing of Optricom and Tilavist, a Tilade derivative. The decision was taken to discontinue redevelopment work on Imferon as the cost and timescales necessary to meet regulatory approval were considered uneconomic. The Imferon production facilities were 35 years old and required capital investment of £25–30 million to meet FDA standards. Dopacard did not fit with Fisons' sales and marketing expertise and so was licensed to Porton Products for worldwide development and sales, with the patent providing protection for Fisons to license its proprietary knowledge.

Spending on R&D rose to £64.5 million in 1992, focusing on the two most promising compounds, Tipredane and Remacemide, with other new compounds being explored in different therapeutic areas. However, in 1993 failure at the clinical trials stage led to Fisons halting further development of Tipredane. Its development was so far behind that of Flixotide, the main rival from Glaxo, that it would not have produced the commercial results needed to justify future (or previous) investment. The development of Remacemide continues but it was considered that Fisons did not have the expertise needed to market a stroke/epileptic drug.

In June 1995 there were rumours in the City that Fisons were about to make an agreed bid for Medeva following the disposal of the Scientific Instruments and Laboratory Supplies Divisions for £500 million earlier in the year. It was expected that Fisons would offer 250p for each Medeva share valuing the company at £75 million Medeva's results from 1990 are shown in table 3.

TABLE 3 Medeva's results from 1990

To 31 Dec	1990	1991	1992	1993
Sales	52.62	82.4	144.2	200.4
PBT	4.01	16.7	36.0	46.1

APPENDIX 1   FISONS' SALES & PROFITS

Profit & loss account (£m)

	1982	1983	1984	1985	1986	1987	1988	1989	1990	1991	1992
Turnover	350.5	365.4	552	646.7	702.6	760.3	823.7	1019.8	1205.1	1239.9	1284.2
Costs	320.6	330.4	499.2	579.8	621.6	661.9	700	852.8	975.8	1067.1	1143.5
Profit before interest & tax	29.9	35	52.8	66.9	81	98.4	123.7	167	229.3	172.8	140.7
Interest	-8.8	-3.8	-4.5	5.4	4.1	10.7	8.4	2	0.9	-10.2	-17.1
Profit before tax	21.1	31.2	48.3	72.3	85.1	109.1	132.1	169	230.2	162.6	123.6
Taxation	-6.6	-6.1	-10.3	-15.7	-18.5	-23.9	-28.8	-37.3	-51.3	-42.8	-27.9
Profit after tax	14.5	25.1	38	56.6	66.6	85.2	103.3	131.7	178.9	119.8	95.7
Extraordinary items	-3.8	-6.6	-4.2	-3.7	-4.9	-3.9	-6.9	-11.9	-9.8	0	0
Attributable profits	10.7	18.5	33.8	52.9	61.7	81.3	96.4	119.8	169.1	119.8	95.7
Dividends	-4.7	-6.7	-9	-13.3	-15.9	-19.7	-29.4	-40.1	-51.6	-60.2	-60.2
Retained profit	6.0	11.8	24.8	39.6	45.8	61.6	67	79.7	117.5	59.6	35.5

Analysis of sales results by division (£m)

Sales (£m)	1980	1981	1982	1983	1984	1985	1986	1987	1988	1989	1990	1991	1992
Pharmaceutical Div.			126.4	158.2	198.5	220.8	249.8	281.9	327.6	473.0	478.5	484.1	427.0
Scientific Equipt Div.			85.1	101.0	291.1	358.2	380.6	410.0	419.5	467.7	603.5	644.5	676.0
Horticulture Div.			42.0	49.7	63.0	67.7	72.2	68.4	76.6	79.1	82.0	96.7	108.0
Agriculture activities			97.0	56.5									
	0	0	350.5	365.4	552.6	646.7	702.6	760.3	823.7	1019.8	1164.0	1225.3	1211.0

Appendix 1 continued

Analysis of profit contribution by division (£m)

Sales (£m)	1980	1981	1982	1983	1984	1985	1986	1987	1988	1989	1990	1991	1992
Pharmaceutical Div.			19.4	25.0	31.2	39.0	49.8	62.8	91.5	127.7	151.7	120.8	71.0
Scientific Equipt Div.			4.8	5.7	15.8	19.2	23.2	27.0	27.0	31.2	67.2	68.4	35.0
Horticulture Div.			2.7	3.0	5.8	8.7	8.0	8.6	5.2	8.1	10.4	11.5	11.0
Agriculture activities			3.0	1.3									
	0	0	29.9	35.0	52.8	66.9	81.0	98.4	123.7	167.0	229.3	200.7	117.0

Fisions' worldwide sales (%)

	1984	1985	1986	1987	1988	1989	1990	1991	1992
N. America	42.7	48.2	46.9	45.2	44.9	47.2	47.7	52.0	52.0
UK	20.6	19.1	19.3	18.6	18.7	15.4	13.9	14.0	13.0
Europe	13.6	14.3	17.2	18.7	18.6	20.0	23.1	23.0	23.0
Asia	13.2	11.4	9.7	10.7	11.0	11.0	10.3		
Africa	1.6	1.7	2.0	2.0	1.8	1.6	1.3	11.0	12.0*
Australia	7.1	4.8	3.9	3.7	4.1	3.8	2.9		
S. America	1.2	0.5	1.0	1.1	0.9	1.0	0.8		
	100.0	100.0	100.0	100.0	100.0	100.0	100.0	100.0	100.0

* Rest of world figures for 1991 and 1992.

APPENDIX 2 FISONS' BALANCE SHEETS (£M)

	1982	1983	1984	1985	1986	1987	1988	1989	1990	1991	1992
Fixed assets											
Intangibles	21.2	22	7.8	6	5.4	6.1	7.2	12	0	0	0
Tangibles	74.8	80.8	117.9	127.8	171	190.4	243.8	297.2	344.7	380.2	433.1
Investments	57.4	3.8	5.1	6.7	17	14	15.6	16.4	9	0	0
Total fixed assets	153.4	106.6	130.8	140.5	193.4	210.5	266.6	325.6	353.7	380.2	433.1
Current assets											
Stocks	62.3	66.3	112.3	116.6	139.1	135	156.6	172.9	218.9	243.7	266.4
Debtors	61.5	72.2	132.1	142.9	158.6	160.6	225.8	286.6	356.2	422.9	630.7
Investment										201.8	169
Cash	5.3	81.7	56.1	141.4	148.2	149.3	151.8	189.9	229.6	84.6	65
Total current assets	129.1	220.2	300.5	400.9	445.9	444.9	534.2	649.4	804.7	953	1131.1
Current liabilities											
Creditors due within 1 year	-64.8	-72.2	-149.2	-190.9	-245.1	-276.9	-424.7	-466.1	-664.3	-826.2	-962.1
Net current assets	64.3	148	151.3	210	200.8	168	109.5	183.3	140.4	126.8	169
Total assets less current liabilities	217.7	254.6	282.1	350.5	394.2	378.5	376.1	508.9	494.1	507	602.1
Creditors due after 1 year	-72.1	-68.2	-86.6	-46.7	-69.9	-47	-44.6	-131	-70	-51.1	-68.0
Provisions for liabilities	-8.0	-8.0	-8.0	-8.5	-8.8	-1.1	-1.9	-5.7	-6.0	-6.1	-6.1
Net assets	137.6	178.4	187.5	295.3	315.5	330.4	329.6	372.2	418.1	449.8	528.0
Capital & reserves											
Share capital	37.3	44.8	49.8	60.4	61.1	123.4	147.7	148.8	171.8	172.6	172.8
Share premium account	33.5	53.8	54.4	142.6	147.2	90.7	27.3	37.3	21.7	30.8	32.3
Revaluation reserve	19.1	18.7	18.3	14.7	23.5	22.6	22	40.2	38.2	33	14.8
P&L account	46.5	55.1	47.2	63.4	73.7	92.7	131.7	144.5	183	209.5	302.4
Other reserves			10.9	9.5							
	136.4	172.4	180.6	290.6	305.5	329.4	328.7	370.8	414.7	445.9	522.3
Minority interests	1.2	6.2	6.9	4.7	1.2	1	0.9	1.6	3.4	3.9	5.7
Shareholders' funds	137.6	178.6	187.5	295.3	306.7	330.4	329.6	372.4	418.1	449.8	528.0
Number of shares (millions)	149.2	179.2	199.2	241.6	244.4	493.6	590.8	595.2	687.2	690.4	691.2

APPENDIX 3   COMPETITOR AND INDUSTRY DATA

Key ratio analysis of competitors*

	1988	1989	1990	1991	1992
RoNA	32.2	36.5	35.3	32.6	32.6
Stockdays	59	44	43	47	45
Debtor days	83	79	80	86	97
Creditor days	55	58	53	58	62
Current ratio	1.99	1.38	1.39	1.38	1.43
Acid ratio	1.56	1.09	1.15	1.12	1.19
Interest cover	19.8	9	10	10.8	13.4
Gearing	18.9	39.5	30.8	30.6	26.7

* Figures are obtained by averaging the performance of the following companies: Unichem plc; Wellcome plc; Fisons plc; SmithKline beecham; Glaxo plc; and Proctor & Gamble.

Formula of ratios used:
  Stockdays = Stock/Cost of goods sold × 365 days
  Current ratio = Current assets/Current liabilities
  Acid ratio = (Current asssets – Stock)/Current liabilities
  Gearing = Medium-long term loan/Net assets
  Interest cover = Profit before interest and tax/Interest paid

APPENDIX 4   INDUSTRY COMPARISONS

Pharmaceutical industry margins

	1988 %	1989 %	1990 %	1991 %	1992 %
Industry	20	21	21		
Fisons*	28	27	32	25	17
Glaxo	39	37	38	35	
ICI	27	30	35	34	
Wellcome		20	21	29	
SmithKline		17	18	21	

* Pharmaceutical Division only.
Source: Keynote Report UK Pharmaceutical Industry 1992.

Industry ROCE for 1988–92

	1988 %	1989 %	1990 %	1991 %	1992 %
Industry Pharmaceuticals	32	36	35	32	32
Scientific	17	14	16		

Source: Industrial Performance Analysis, ICC Business Publications.

APPENDIX 5   PER CAPITA CONSUMPTION OF PHARMACEUTICALS*

	£ per person per annum 1989
Japan	198
US	110
France	99
Germany	95
Switzerland	89
Italy	88
Canada	83
Finland	77
Belgium	74
Sweden	73
Austria	62
UK	54
Denmark	54
Spain	52

* refers to total consumption, including prescription, hospital and OTC pharmaceuticals at manufacturers' selling prices.
Source: Association of the British Pharmaceutical Industry from EFPIA, PMA and JPMA.

APPENDIX 6   FISONS' R&D EXPENDITURE AS A PERCENTAGE OF DIVISIONAL SALES

	1990	1991	1992
Pharmaceuticals	12.1	11.5	15.2
Scientific Equipment	1.8	3.2	3.0
Overall	5.7	6.2	6.5

APPENDIX 7   SHARE PRICES

Year	FT-SE100 index	Fisons
1984 qtr3	1250	140
1984 qtr4	1250	175
1985 qtr1	1400	175
1985 qtr2	1400	210
1985 qtr3	1500	290
1985 qtr4	1750	300
1986 qtr1	1650	310
1986 qtr2	1650	250
1986 qtr3	2000	320
1986 qtr4	2350	370
1987 qtr1	2480	340
1987 qtr2	1800	260
1987 qtr3	1750	270
1987 qtr4	1700	275
1988 qtr1	1800	240
1988 qtr2	1650	235
1988 qtr3	2250	260
1988 qtr4	2150	280
1989 qtr1	2300	360
1989 qtr2	2400	370
1989 qtr3	2200	340
1989 qtr4	2350	380
1990 qtr1	2400	365
1990 qtr2	2100	370
1990 qtr3	2200	500
1990 qtr4	2600	515
1991 qtr1	2500	510
1991 qtr2	2450	305

In the early 1990s the furniture and furnishing industry was struggling to cope with the dampening effects of the recession from 1989. It faced the fourth consecutive difficult year in 1992. The industry was plagued with bankruptcies and re-dundancies, a situation far from the optimism and strong consumer demand of the mid-1980s. In 1990, Lowndes Queensway, at that time the second largest in the retail sector, collapsed due to its huge debts. In 1992 there were two further casualties: ELS ceased trading early in the year and Airedale Holdings, the holding company for kitchen specialist Magnet, was put into administrative receivership towards the end of the year.

The size of the domestic furniture industry by product type, in 1991, for each of the five segments specified earlier is given in table 1. Domestic furniture sales included domestic sales to households and contract sales to hotels, public houses, nursing homes and so on. The upholstered furniture segment had the largest share of total spending on furniture, followed by kitchen furniture. The kitchen furniture segment held the largest share of the furniture market in the mid-1980s.

CONSUMER EXPENDITURE

The UK market for household furniture recovered during the mid-1980s, after the effects of the recession of the early 1980s began to ease. The size of the furniture market grew in real terms between 1986 and 1988 but then fell back rapidly. Consumer expenditure on furniture grew strongly in 1987 and 1988, recording real gains of 7.8 per cent and 16.3 per cent respectively. In 1992, however, consumer expenditure on furniture fell to £3.12 billion, which was little different from that recorded in 1986 in real terms. The industry was also finding difficulty regaining the share of household expenditure which it had achieved prior to the last recession. Although there had been annual fluctuations in the percentage share of the consumer expenditure spent on furniture, the long-term trend has been for the share to fall. Table 2 shows consumer spending on furniture between 1986 and 1992.

INDUSTRY PERFORMANCE

During 1987 and 1988, cheap available credit stimulated housing moves and created a boom, which had the knock-on effect of boosting sales of household goods. However, by late 1988 and early 1989, annual sales started declining in real terms

TABLE 1 Industry segmentation and size – 1991

Main segment	Product type	Value £m.1991
Kitchen furniture	Built-in or fitted storage units, freestanding storage units, tables and seating	1,000
Bedroom furniture	Fitted and freestanding storage units and dressing tables	650
Bed & mattresses	Storage divans, bases for mattresses, wooden beds, bed heads, and interior sprung and foam mattresses	550
Living room/dining room furniture		
Non-upholstered	Dining tables, seating, sideboards, wall storage units, room dividers, cabinets, bookcases, occasional tables	–
Upholstered	Sofas, sofa beds, futons, armchairs, and sectional seating	1,250
Others		75

TABLE 2 Consumer spending (£ billion)

Year	Gross domestic product	Total consumer expenditure	Consumer expenditure on furniture
1983	261.2	185.6	2.68
1984	280.6	198.8	2.70
1985	307.9	217.5	2.85
1986	328.2	241.6	3.15
1987	360.7	265.3	3.52
1988	401.4	299.4	4.14
1989	441.8	327.4	4.36
1990	478.9	347.5	4.48
1991	495.9	364.9	4.54
1992	516.0	382.2	4.86

due to the high interest rates halting the housing market and curbing consumer spending. Future prospects for the furniture and furnishing industry remain uncertain, as expenditure on furniture depends to a great extent on the housing market.

ADVERTISING EXPENDITURE

The furniture market is essentially retailer driven. When making a purchase consumers tend to think about retailers, and there is little brand awareness. In addition, furniture is considered to be a major consumer purchase and thus consumers are willing to travel outside their local area to make the best purchase. Hence, advertising by the retailers is extremely important. Advertising expenditure

TABLE 3 Advertising expenditure by selected furniture and furnishing retailers, 1988–1992

Name	1988	1989	1990	1991	1992
MFI	18,332	17,029	15,162	15,810	19,144
Allied	6,334	10,522	8,192	9,180	10,484
Magnet	7,642	5,895	5,457	6,373	7,123
Courts	4,452	4,199	5,227	4,859	4,911
Kingsway Group	–	–	–	1,350	3,834
World of Leather	2,557	2,561	1,940	2,013	2,570
Northern Upholstery	884	949	1,265	1,624	2,106
Cantors	968	1,383	1,514	1,666	2,073
Texstyle World	461	545	689	1,009	1,425
ELS Superstore	2,870	2,231	2,105	2,240	1,175

Source: *Retail Business Quarterly Trade Reviews* No. 25, March 1993.

tends to be high, for example, in 1992 furniture retailers spent about £82 million on media advertising. Table 3 gives the advertising spend of selected stores. MFI was the sector's heaviest advertiser with an expenditure of over £19 million. Approximate figure for other heavy spenders are Allied (£10.5 million), Magnet (£7 million) and Courts (£5 million).

INDUSTRY SEGMENT PERFORMANCE

Industry segment performance for the living and dining room, kitchen and bedroom furniture is given below.

Living and dining room furniture

Upholstered furniture represent 65 per cent of the sector and non-upholstered wooden the remaining 35 per cent. Seating (convertibles) accounts for the bulk of the upholstered furniture, while wall storage units represent the highest proportion of retail sales of non-upholstered furniture. Upholstered furniture has a shorter life span due to its greater daily use and susceptibility to changing tastes and fashions. Seating is a more important necessity compared to the other types of living room or dining furniture.

Kitchen furniture

Sales growth in real terms for kitchen furniture was weaker compared to living/dining room furniture. The negative growth could be attributed to the low level of housing activity and depressed prices of the residential housing market. Further segmentation of the kitchen furniture market sector into built-in and non-fitted segments could be made, roughly at equal proportions.

Bedroom furniture

Sales of fitted bedroom furniture experienced considerable growth during the 1980s until 1987, after which time the sector reached a plateau, and then declined sharply in 1990 as the recession deepened. The non-fitted bedroom furniture segment has shown much better resilience to recessionary pressures. The fitted bedroom furniture is primarily an adult and luxury furniture area and therefore considered dispensable when budgets are stretched. On the whole, the bedroom furniture

TABLE 4 Factors affecting the UK furniture industry sectors

Sector	Factors
Living/dining room furniture	Economic climate and personal disposable income Design and fashion Changes in lifestyle
Kitchen furniture	Frequency of house moves Population age shifts Household structure (number of households, owner occupation) Economic climate and personal disposable income
Bedroom furniture	Economic climate and personal disposable income Population age shifts Frequency of house moves Household structure (number of households, owner (occupation) Housebuilding completions

sector has declined more than the other sectors during the early 1990s. Factors affecting the demand for the different segments are shown in Table 4.

IMPORTS

A combination of domestic recession and strong sterling in the late 1970s and early 1980s allowed imports to gain an increasing foothold in the UK market. This development was exacerbated by the lack of innovation and fashion awareness on the part of the UK manufacturers, and the low level of promotional spend.

Imported furniture accounts for about a quarter of annual domestic furniture consumption. The level of import penetration increased from 15 per cent in 1980 to 23 per cent in 1986 and fell slightly to 20 per cent in 1991. Dining and living room furniture accounted for the largest share of imports with 31 per cent of the total in 1991. The demand for dining and living room furniture has weathered the recession better than the demand for the other types of furniture.

MANUFACTURERS AND RETAILERS IN THE FURNITURE INDUSTRY

The UK furniture industry has traditionally been highly fragmented and is dominated by a large number of small privately-owned companies. Over the years successive economic recessions and booms have seen the emergence (through acquisitions and mergers) of a few large companies.

TABLE 5 Import penetration of domestic furniture by types, 1986–1991

Type	%					
	1986	1987	1988	1989	1990	1991
Chairs of all types	23	21	21	20	21	22
Bedroom	10	9	10	12	13	11
Dining/living room	21	25	29	31	30	31
Kitchen	26	23	22	19	16	16
Other wooden furniture	8	8	5	6	8	7
Parts of wooden furniture	12	14	13	12	12	13

TABLE 6 Major players in the market segments

Market segment	Major players
Kitchen	MFI, Spring Ram Corporation plc, Symphony Group plc, Bernstein plc and MKD Holdings Ltd
Bedroom	MFI, Sharps Individual Bedrooms Ltd
Beds and mattresses	Silentnight Holdings plc, Airsprung Furniture Group plc, Slumberland plc, Reylon Group plc, Hillsdown (Sleepeeze Ltd).
Dining/living room	Hillsdown (Walker & Homer Group plc and Christie-Tyler plc), Cornwell Parker plc, Ercol Furniture Ltd

There are between 5,000 and 6,000 manufacturers of furniture in the UK. Of these only a few have a turnover in excess of £15 million, confirming the fragmentation of the industry. There is also geographic fragmentation with London and the South East having the largest share of manufacturers at 25 per cent. The remaining 75 per cent are distributed across the UK.

The two largest furniture manufacturers in the UK are Hillsdown Holdings plc (mainly concerned with food) which owns Christie-Tyler plc (furniture), and MFI Furniture Group plc. The major players in the market segments are given in table 6.

Appendix 7 provides a brief profile on each of the major manufacturing companies in the furniture industry.

RETAILERS

Furniture is sold via a variety of retail channels and their approximate market shares are estimated, as shown in table 7.

Leading out-of-town furniture chains include MFI, Magnet, IKEA, Courts and Allied Stores with around a total of 700 outlets. The High Street Furniture Specialists include Maples, Perrings, Cantors, Habitat and Furnitureland. The major DIY furniture stores are B&Q, Texas, Homebase and Wickes.

There is also fragmentation on the retailing side with about 20,000 retail outlets plus mail order companies dealing with furniture in the UK. By the end of 1989 there were seven major multiple retailers which between them held 30 per cent of the furniture and floor covering market. The largest individual chain was MFI with

TABLE 7 Estimated shares of the retail furniture market

Type of outlet	% share
MFI	13
Other out-of-town chains	7
High Street	55
Department stores	10
DIY	11
Mail order	2
Others	2
Total	100

140 outlets and between 10 per cent and 11 per cent of the market by value. Until August 1990, the second largest player was Lowndes Queensway which had around 6.5 per cent of the market, achieved through 270 stores, most of which were out of town. However, the firm collapsed with huge debts of around £200 million, including £120 million owed to 20 banks. With the collapse of Lowndes Queensway, MFI became the largest specialist furniture retailer in the UK and claimed 13 per cent of the retail furniture market in 1991. MFI currently has 175 furniture outlets. Table 8 lists the leading furniture retailers and the number of outlets.

The trend towards out-of-town sites has dramatically altered the face of retailing in the UK during recent years, and drawn consumers' attention away from the traditional High Street stores. The out-of-town market was pioneered by MFI and Queensway, MFI is particularly strong in self-assembly kitchen and bedroom furniture. Since a management buy-out in 1987 and the purchase of Hygena Ltd and Schreiber, MFI has begun trading up to higher quality ranges of furniture which sell at higher prices. The out-of-town trend has also been followed by familiar High Street stores such as Habitat.

A major new entrant to this sector of retailing in recent years has been the Swedish furniture group IKEA which opened its first store in late 1987 and has since continued to expand its operations. In October 1992, IKEA bought over the Habitat operations in UK and France from Storehouse. IKEA is the largest furniture retailer in the world, with stores of up to 130,000 sq. ft in area, often holding as many as 15,000 product lines.

ENVIRONMENTAL ANALYSIS

The economic climate is vital with interest rates being particularly important. An active market for furniture depends on an active housing market which in turn is influenced by the level of mortgage rates. Interest rates also influence credit rates. Given that furniture often involves a substantial financial outlay, credit sales will form an important element in total sales.

UK furniture producers have seen domestic demand for their output fall much more than overall consumer spending. Sharply reduced housing demand has led to the diminished demand for furniture. With high interest rates and high unemployment, consumers have also reduced their discretionary spending. The strong pound of the late 1980s and early 1990s allowed imports to retain their persistent grip on the UK furniture market, while the interest rate cuts and devaluation of sterling in 1992 did little to stimulate demand for furniture.

TABLE 8 Leading Furniture Retailers, February 1993

Name	Number of Outlets
Allied Maples	140
Cantors	105
MFI	175
Courts	95
IKEA	5
Habitat	39
Perrings	40
Saxon Hawk	35
Magnet	208
Sharps	115

Demographic trends are an important social factor that have implications for the furniture industry. The prime market for the furniture industry is the 25–34 age group. This population segment incorporates the highest percentage of adults marrying or cohabiting for the first time and buying or renting their first home and the contents that go with it.

MFI BACKGROUND

Chronology of events

1960s   Mullard Furniture Industries Limited (MFI) pioneered self-assembly furniture
Started as a mail order business
1970s   Began 'cash and carry' retailing through edge-of-town chain stores
1971   Went public
1981   Acquired Status Discount Limited, major competitor
1982   Acquired Hygena brand name
1985   MFI was acquired by Associated Dairies Group plc (Asda)
1987   Buy-out of MFI from Asda by group of directors, managers and institutional investors
Acquired Hygena
1988   Acquired Schreiber
1992   Refloat on the London stock exchange

Pre-1987

Mullard Furniture Industries Limited (MFI) was set up by two friends, Noel Lister and Donald Searle, in the early 1960s. It started as a mail order company with a variety of merchandise including furniture. MFI's merchandise was cheap and of poor quality. As fully-assembled furniture does not travel well by mail order, the development of flatpack articles for assembly by the customer made excellent sense. MFI flourished as the demand for such merchandise grew. In 1971, MFI went public and was the darling of the stock exchange in 1972.

Even in 1972/3 when mail order houses were booming, the Board of MFI recognized that credit mail-order was a difficult business to be in and began to develop retail operations. As anticipated, problems did start to occur on the mail-order side of the business in 1974 due to increases in postal and distribution costs, a fall in response to advertisements and an increasing number of bad debts. Margins began to decline, and MFI responded to this squeeze by reducing prices and extending credit, but this only exacerbated the situation. Profits dropped from their peak of £2.2 million in 1973 to £800,000 in 1974. In May 1975, profits declined further to £78,000.

However, at the same time, the retail operation was flourishing. Many of the new shops were profitable from the opening day and reached payback on their initial investment within three or four months. In May 1973, the company had 16 shops but within a year the number of outlets increased to 24. It was a race to open stores fast enough to generate the cash flow which was needed to keep a very sick mail-order operation going.

In an attempt to turn around the company's worsening financial position, the board decided to concentrate on retailing. A number of retailers from supermarkets and successful High Street chains were hired and J. Seabright was brought as a new Joint Managing Director.

At the beginning of September 1974, the board agreed to 'wind down' the mail-order operation, cut back on credit and make a major effort to recover the debt which was standing at £3.5 million. Nearly half the workforce was made redundant, an organizational restructuring took place and financial controls were tightened. In order to make the firm more competitive, initiatives were also introduced on training, merchandise selection, pricing, quality and consumer service.

Between 1974 and 1980, 95 shops were opened and 20 less profitable stores were closed. Pre-tax profits rose from £78,000 in 1975 to £44 million in 1985. In 1981, MFI acquired Status Discount Limited who were at that time their major competitor. The acquisition enabled MFI to increase market share and expand its retail distribution network.

Also, MFI introduced carpets and electrical appliances into its product range, thus promoting the one-stop shop approach to house furnishing. The sale of related products through existing distribution outlets can lead to increased turnover and margins without adding excessively to operating costs.

The strategies adopted in the 1970s enabled MFI to become a major market player in 1986. They had a market share of 7 per cent in a highly fragmented market. In April 1985, Associated Dairies, the Asda superstores group, launched a successful £605.8 million takeover bid for MFI and created the fourth largest retailing group in Britain after Marks and Spencer, J. Sainsbury and Great Universal Stores. The terms of the offer were 15 Asda shares for eight MFI shares with a cash alternative of 270p per ordinary share. The board of MFI agreed to the bid because at the time they felt the company was being stalked by a number of other companies and were keen to move into what they perceived as a 'friendly marriage'. They felt Asda and MFI were companies with like minds about retailing and with similar experience. It was also felt that the combination of the two companies would provide a solid platform for further expansion and would allow both to benefit from economies of scale. However, the marriage was not a happy one and in July 1987, Asda announced that it was to sell its furniture and carpet stores.

The management buy-out took MFI out of the merged company in October 1987. The entire deal came to a staggering £705 million, a UK record for a buy-out and was financed by debt of £515 million and £190 million of equity. Asda, which was to retain a 25 per cent stake in MFI, accepted the management buy-out since the cash proceeds enabled it to finance its investment programmes and reduce its borrowings. The buy-out team was led by Derek Hunt who had had substantial experience in the furniture industry and overall the team commanded considerable respect in the City.

As an integral part of the management buy-out, MFI bought Hygena Limited, its major supplier, for £200 million. The MFI management had not originally planned to purchase Hygena, but the decision to take over was made when MFI found that Hygena, which was selling 95 per cent of its goods to MFI, was considering supplying to other retailers. MFI depended on Hygena for nearly half of its supplies, and felt that enormous consequences could arise should Hygena supply to other retailers. MFI planned to increase Hygena's capacity utilization and reap the benefits of economies of scale.

In November 1988, MFI purchased Schreiber Furniture, a leading manufacturer and retailer of more upmarket bathroom and kitchen furniture, for £35 million. MFI funded the Schreiber purchase through cashflow and proceeds of sale and leaseback deals. Derek Hunt, the leader of the buy-out team considered the purchase of Schreiber as a vital move in introducing new Schreiber ranges to the MFI stores. He maintained that the Schreiber acquisition fitted perfectly with MFI's business plan since Schreiber's customers were the 35–55 age range while Hygena appealed to younger customers. Both the Schreiber and Hygena names gave MFI some upmarket options within its established trading format. At about the same time, MFI entered into a joint venture with Sir Phil Harris's Carpetright London, to retail carpets. MFI later reduced its holdings in Carpetright to 33 per cent.

MFI was performing well at the time of the Schreiber acquisition but from the beginning of 1989 it was hit by a downturn in expenditure on furniture. Restraints on consumer expenditure and high interest rates discouraged people from moving house. MFI found that rather than trading down, people were simply not buying furniture.

MFI took measures to counter the difficult financial conditions. There were small cuts in the number of staff and temporary workers were not re-employed when their contract expired, especially in the Hygena and Schreiber manufacturing units. Stock control was also tightened, and capital expenditure was cut. MFI anticipated cost savings of more than £10 million. The cut in capital expenditure involved a review of longer-term expansion plans leading to cutbacks of approximately £15 million to £20 million. Cashflow difficulties led MFI to negotiate a refinancing package, announced in August 1989. Despite these difficulties, MFI's position in the furniture market was assisted by the serious problem faced by Lowndes Queensway.

Lowndes Queensway, with an estimated 6.5 per cent market share, eventually went into liquidation in 1990. While MFI consolidated its position as the leading furniture retailer and manufacturer in the UK, it too suffered losses of £3.5 million in 1990 and £24.2 million in 1991 as a result of falling market demand. Its operating profits were not able to cover the interest payments of its huge debt bill arising from the management buy-out. Its plans to refloat on the stock exchange had to be delayed as more pressing problems of profitability and debt repayment had to be resolved. In April 1991, MFI's bankers rescheduled the loan, for the second time, giving MFI a one-year breather. MFI also reduced its workforce by 5 per cent during 1991.

In 1992, MFI estimated its market share to be 11.4 per cent of the value of the UK household furniture market (excluding wall coverings), which was substantially higher than the market share of 8.3 per cent calculated from its 1992 turnover and total industry sales value. MFI's Hygena and Schreiber product brands are the best recognized brands in the UK in their sectors. It commands the market for self-assembly kitchens and bedrooms. MFI is also the clear market leader by volume in rigid kitchens.

MFI operates 174 retail superstores, mainly edge-of-town locations. Of the 174, 129 stores have gross floor areas of over 30,000 square feet each. Total gross floor area in use is 5.8 million square feet, including 2.3 million square feet of superstore warehouse space. Its new superstore formats incorporate new features which show higher sales per outlet or per square foot compared to the rest of the network. Greater asset utilization and efficiencies are being pursued with the objective of maximizing sales per square foot and total sales. Forty-two locations have been identified for new superstores, of which 20 would be relocations. In addition, 107 superstores would be suitable for refurbishment in the new format, which could release 700,000 square feet for subletting or other uses.

Overseas, MFI has a retail business of some 15 stores in France through Hygena. Although its French operation is profitable, it accounts only for a small proportion of the total business. Its US operations were also on a small scale.

MFI owns one of the largest furniture manufacturing operations in Europe and manufactures 60 per cent of the goods it sells. It manufactures products in-house only where the production process is capable of significant automation, where there are likely to be high volume sales and a rapid return on the new investment. Group sales of internally-sourced goods have risen from 48 per cent to 60 per cent. The Hygena Group produces cabinets, drawer fronts, doors and worktops using highly automated manufacturing techniques and flexible working arrangements and committed to quality. All its factories conform to BS 5750/ISO 9002 quality standards. MFI's manufacturing strategy consists of being able to meet customer quality standards and shorter delivery leadtimes.

MFI was refloated on 18 July 1992 at 117p a share, a premium of 2p above issue price. The flotation which valued the company at £669 million saw applications for only 44 per cent of its public offer of 137 million shares. The other 410 million shares were placed with institutions. Asda also sold off its 25 per cent interest in MFI.

Currently, MFI has three operating divisions: retail, manufacturing and group merchandise. Each division has its own board, chaired by the Group Chairman, and includes at least three other Group Board members.

MFI had been a byword for cheap, flat-pack, self-assembly furniture sold in warehouse-style stores. However, it changed the strategy at the time of the buy-out. MFI attempted to improve its image by making periodic advances on the higher quality and more expensive end of the furniture market under the slogan 'Take a Look at Us Now'. this appeared to be a sensible move as it responded aptly to the rising consumer aspirations of the 1980s. Led by Derek Hunt, MFI began expanding its product range, improving quality and customer service, and introducing new superstore formats.

Since quality is becoming an important factor in the purchase decision for furniture products, MFI launched its new 'Customer Promise' code of practice to emphasise customer service and product quality. MFI increased advertising expenditure to generate greater public awareness of its new upmarket image. However, its advances upmarket has been retarded by its strategy to continue selling value-for-money products in the same premises as its quality ranges.

From a study done by Manchester Business School in 1985, the concepts identified with the ideal furniture retailer were found to be 'fast delivery', 'good customer service', 'quality' and 'good value for money'. For the High Street retailers (Waring & Gillow, Wades and Cavendish Woodhouse), 'well-trained staff' was the only concept that appeared firmly in that sector. MFI and Queensway had 'wide product range' but did not have 'well laid out' stores and 'good displays'. They were thus perceived by the shoppers as far away from being the ideal retailer. Habitat, now owned by IKEA, was rated first against four concepts and was highly differentiated in the 'fashionable', 'co-ordinated ranges' and 'good product design' sectors. It was also closest to being the ideal retailer.

MFI has been moving closer to and is striving towards the ideal retailer position through its upmarket promotion effort of offering well-laid-out merchandise and good displays in its new superstore formats. Its product design is, however, still not thought to be satisfactory and the shopper's poor perception of its quality persists. IKEA has on the other hand moved even nearer to the ideal position.

APPENDIX 1   MFI PROFIT AND LOSS ACCOUNT (£M)

Year end Year	Oct 1983	Oct 1984	Oct 1985	Oct 1986	Oct 1987	Apr 1988	Apr 1989	Apr 1990	Apr 1991	Apr 1992	Apr 1993
Sales											
Turnover	246.33	300.90	334.10	386.00	420.50	251.00	601.70	594.90	620.70	644.40	603.9
Trading profit	31.97	39.30	44.80	45.60	45.90	47.90	119.50	62.70	54.60	78.10	41.0
Interest	(1.58)	(0.20)	(0.30)	(2.10)	(2.40)	(21.90)	(53.90)	(66.20)	(78.80)	(69.30)	(25.5)
Profit before tax	30.40	39.10	44.50	43.50	43.50	26.00	65.60	(3.50)	(24.20)	7.80	15.5
Taxation	(13.96)	(14.70)	(18.70)	(15.20)	(15.40)	(8.60)	(19.80)	(4.10)	2.60	(3.80)	(0.2)
Pref. div						(2.50)	(13.30)	(12.30)	(13.30)	(16.7)	(4.3)
Profit after tax	16.44	24.40	25.80	28.30	28.10	14.90	32.50	(19.90)	(34.90)	(12.7)	11.0
Extraordinary items		0.80	2.70					(1.60)	(2.90)		
Dividends	(6.36)	(9.06)	(9.37)							(21.8)	
Retained Profit	10.08	16.09	19.18			14.90	32.50	(21.50)	(37.80)	(12.70)	(10.8)
Number of employees	2716	3515	4254	4998	5500	6443	7610	8025	8222	7848	7579
Retail area sq. ft (million)						4.99	5.71	5.98	6.23	6.12	6.04
Capital expenditure						54.6	107.6	24.4	17.8	16.7	23.2
Number of shares											582 m
Share price: high p											183
low p											118

APPENDIX 2   MFI BALANCE SHEET (£)

Year end Year	Oct 1983	Oct 1984	Oct 1985	Oct 1986*	Oct 1987	Apr 1988	Apr 1989	Apr 1990	Apr 1991	Apr 1992	Apr 1993
Fixed assets	66.83	89.60	126.58		171.90	245.00	275.10	240.80	224.00	211.40	213.3
Current assets											
Stock	34.97	33.46	49.30		60.70	61.41	106.50	72.80	71.50	69.60	65.3
Investment	0.00	8.74	0.00								2.0
Debtors	17.07	30.05	11.70		13.30	23.60	35.20	43.20	36.00	35.30	29.8
Cash	0.14	7.87	1.45		6.10	32.80	12.20	14.60	28.80	32.10	23.5
Total current assets	52.18	80.12	62.45		80.10	117.80	153.90	130.60	136.30	137.00	120.6
Current liabilities	-41.65	-55.17	-61.10		-79.30	-165.40	-221.00	-136.00	-152.70	-655.70	-116.8
Net current assets	10.53	24.95	1.35		0.80	-47.60	-67.10	-5.40	-16.40	-518.70	3.8
Total assets less current liabilities	77.36	114.55	127.93	0.00	172.70	197.40	208.00	235.40	207.60	-307.30	217.1
Long term loan	14.3	13.41	0.00		6.40	482.00	475.00	503.30	502.80	0.00	70.7
Short term loan											27.8
Provisions	5.71	8.34	2.08		2.30	0.00	11.00	23.80	26.00	11.10	
Total assets less liabilities	57.35	102.79	125.85		164.40	-284.60	-278.00	-291.70	-321.20	-318.40	118.6
Capital and reserves:											
Share capital	20.85	50.20	54.08			156.10	171.00	174.30	174.30	122.70	563.6
Goodwill reserve	0.00	0.00	0.00			-455.40	-497.00	-490.50	-487.90	-485.20	-455.0
Other reserve	0.08	0.08	0.08				4.20	4.20	4.20	55.70	–
P&L A/c	36.42	52.51	71.69			14.70	43.80	20.30	-11.80	-11.60	–
Total	57.35	102.79	125.85			-284.60	-278.00	-291.70	-321.40	-318.40	118.6

*Consolidated in ASDA accounts in 1986

APPENDIX 3   FURNITURE RETAILERS – INDUSTRY RATIOS

	1990–1	*1989–90*	*1988–9*
Profitability ratios			
Return on capital	1.2	–1.6	27.7
Return on assets	0.4	–0.5	8.8
Return on shareholders funds	18.9	–10.5	105.9
Pre-tax profit margin	0.2	–0.3	4.8
Turnover ratios			
Sales/figures assets	5.4	5.0	5.3
Stock turnover	8.1	7.8	7.6
Credit period	18.0	16.0	14.0
Liquidity ratios			
Liquidity	0.9	0.9	0.9
Quick ratio	0.5	0.6	0.6
Gearing ratio			
Equity gearing*	0.0	0.0	0.1

* Equity gearing = Shareholders' funds/total liabilities
Source: Industrial Performance Analysis 1992/3 Edition, ICC Business Publications Ltd.

APPENDIX 4   HOUSEBUILDING IN GREAT BRITAIN

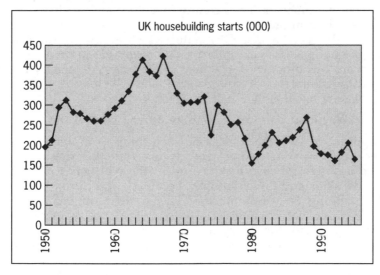

Housebuilding in Great Britain

APPENDIX 5   EXTRACTS FROM AN INTERVIEW WITH DEREK HUNT – *MANAGEMENT WEEK* SPECIAL REPORT, OCTOBER 1991

Q How many items can you walk away with now that you couldn't years ago?

A One of the difficulties we still have as a business is that adopting an aggressive discount stance in the national press and the tabloids doesn't reflect the sort of display techniques and stores that we're running today. One of the big problems we always had in display was that we didn't want to lose our roots – £9.99 coffee tables and £19.99 two-door wardrobes – but at the same time the market was progressing in kitchens and bedrooms to such an extent that the £9.99 coffee tables looked at odds with a £5,000 kitchen or a £2,000 bedroom.

So we gathered all the cheaper, portable merchandise and put it in a self service place in what we call our 'Pronto' area so, depending on the size of the store, around 7,000 square feet is now-self service and the customer helps himself. That made a difference to our operation because although it's only 15 per cent of merchandise, it's over 50 per cent of the customers. It freed up the rest of the operation in the store to get on and sell the £2,000, £3,000, £4,000, £5,000 products and made a significant difference to the business.

Q: This isn't the MFI I remember. It appears you have completely repositioned the business.

A: Yes we have. I know I'm talking merchandise to you but actually I'm talking finance, because if we can take the customer's order and give a delivery date, we can almost make it to order. Now I'm talking at the moment about the stuff we make ourselves, which accounts for about 65 per cent of our stock. Eighty-five per cent of what we sell is made in the UK. That's not because we're particularly patriotic, but it's much easier to control inventory and quality with a domestically made unit than one made in some remote factory in Italy or somewhere. We've made the merchandise flow better, which means we can carry the same quantity of goods at the centre, but we've been able to give better service as well. It means our production planning in the factory is much easier; we don't have to carry mountains of raw material, and it helps the store manager too because he now has less than half the stock he used to.

Q: From a management point of view, how do you control the two businesses?

A: We recognized in 1987 that there's no such thing as a merger, there are only takeovers, and we were taking over Hygena. But the trick of taking it over wasn't to buy five massive factories up in the North East. The trick was to preserve the skills and the philosophy, because if you didn't you'd put a lot of money to nothing. So we didn't flood Hygena with our management: we put one guy in on secondment and that was John O'Connell, who'd previously been MFI's Managing Director. Before that he'd been our Stock Controller, and he'd had a relationship with Hygena that went back ten years. He was the only MFI representative who actually went to work in Hygena. I sat on the Hygena board and so did J. R. Hart, the Finance Director, but we weren't actually involved, and we've kept it that way. So Hygena's still kept a lot of its own culture and, probably more importantly, its own way of doing things. We've allowed the relationship to evolve rather than having a revolution and here we are four years on starting to enjoy it, but it's taken four years. We have not lost any of the original Hygena managers.

Q: **So you had compatible management cultures?**

A: Yes, we are all the same. This is a hands-on business. Every Hygena director works in the business and the commonality doesn't just end there. I think we're all failed grammar school boys. I hesitate to use that phrase, but we've all got a mortgage and we come from a similar background.

Q: **If you are all from that sort of background do you have a problem recruiting people? More traditional managers might grate at some of the things you've been saying.**

A: We tested that theory a couple of years ago because our Personnel Director wanted to retire and we also needed a new Marketing Director, because we wanted to promote the existing one. MFI's traditional rule would have been to look for somebody in the business and teach them the skill. In fact we got someone from outside because we felt we should let a bit of daylight in. We hired Martin Archer from Waring & Gillows, and we hired Neil Palfreeman from Gateway. This is going back a couple of years now. They're both still with us, both very successful and they're both very happy.

Q: **You've changed the way MFI works, but what about the physical structure you had before? Are you now compromising the way you sell, or have you got more work to do?**

A: An MFI store pre-1987 was 40,000 or more square feet, split into 20,000 for warehouse and 20,000 for retail. If it was smaller than that, it was always a 50:50 split between warehouse and selling floor. The last model that we opened in Croydon last week was 35,000 square feet, with only 10,000 for the warehouse and 25,000 for the selling floor. My guess is, if we open a store this time next year, it'll be 25,000 square feet, 5,000 warehouse and 20,000 selling. In most of the stores that we opened in the Croydon mode, we've been able to sublet the balance, although in fact at Croydon we didn't. At the moment we have 150,000 square feet under negotiation to other retailers, and yet we've been able to maintain and improve the turnover on 10,000 square feet less space in those stores.

Q: **Did you work all this out yourselves? What thought process goes into making those sort of decisions?**

A: We refit ourselves every three to four years and write it off within that period, so somewhere in the organization there's always somebody who's got on the drawing board what the business is going to look like in another three years' time.

When the IRA burnt out our two Belfast stores in January, the only temporary space we could get was 6,500 square feet. I insisted that we had the biggest possible range on show and we opened within about a fortnight of burning down.

In that 6,500 square feet they took £110,000 in the first week. Throughout the whole time these two stores were shut it took £70,000 a week. So if you left it where it was, that store was going to do between £3 million and £4 million a year out of 6,000 square feet. So that obviously helps the thinking – then you say, why are we using 20,000 square feet?

APPENDIX 6

UK population 1971 to 1991 estimated and 1996 to 2001 projected

| *Thousands* | | | | | | | | | *% Change* |
Age group	*1971*	*1976*	*1981*	*1986*	*1991*	*1996*	*2001*	*1971 to 2001*	*1991 to 2001*
Under 4	4,553	3,721	3,455	3,642	3,882	4,019	3,927	-14	1
5 to 9	4,684	4,483	3,677	3,467	3,670	3,879	4,020	-14	10
10 to 14	4,232	4,693	4,470	3,690	3,498	3,677	3,888	-8	11
15 to 19	3,862	4,244	4,735	4,479	3,727	3,517	3,703	-4	-0
Under 20	17,331	17,141	16,337	15,278	14,777	15,092	15,538	-10	5
20 to 24	4,282	3,881	4,284	4,784	4,484	3,752	3,547	-17	-21
25 to 29	3,686	4,239	3,828	4,237	4,740	4,457	3,711	0	-22
30 to 34	3,284	3,629	4,182	3,787	4,225	4,698	4,414	34	4
35 to 39	3,187	3,225	3,689	4,158	3,790	4,182	4,666	46	23
20 to 39	14,439	14,974	15,983	16,966	17,239	17,089	16,338	13	-5
40 to 44	3,325	3,136	3,185	3,561	4,142	3,750	4,150	25	0
45 to 49	3,532	3,262	3,090	3,142	3,159	4,088	3,706	5	5
50 to 54	3,304	3,423	3,179	3,023	3,074	3,462	4,016	22	31
55 to 59	3,365	3,151	3,271	3,055	2,920	2,991	3,363	-0	15
40 to 59	13,526	12,972	12,725	12,781	13,655	14,291	15,235	13	12
60 to 64	3,222	3,181	2,935	3,055	2,894	2,765	2,838	-12	-2
65 to 69	2,736	2,851	2,801	2,641	2,793	2,618	2,531	-7	-9
70 to 74	2,029	2,260	2,393	2,364	2,282	2,381	2,379	17	4
75 to 79	1,956	1,499	1,708	1,837	1,864	1,818	1,925	-2	3
80 to 84	803	849	968	1,132	1,248	1,306	1,319	64	6
85+	485	538	602	709	897	1,054	1,171	141	31
Over 60	11,231	11,178	11,407	11,738	11,978	11,942	12,163	8	2
Totals	56,527	56,265	56,452	56,763	57,649	58,414	59,274		

APPENDIX 6 *continued*

Change in UK population by age structure 1991–2001

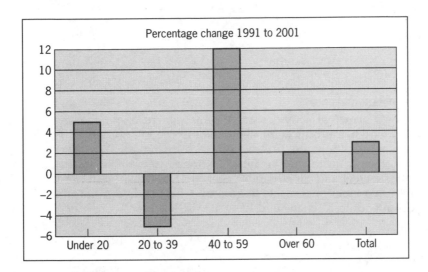

Source: Annual Abstract 1993, Table 25, HMSO.

APPENDIX 7   COMPETITOR PROFILES

IKEA Ltd

Ikea is part of an international chain with stores in 26 countries. Four stores have been opened in the UK and the company plans to open a further two stores per year.

Financial profile Year end	31/08/88	31/08/89	31/08/90	31/08/91
Sales & profits				
Sales (£000)	17,052	51,440	67,772	91,373
Profits (£000)	–2,126	4,117	3,188	1,416
Margin (%)	–12.5	8.0	4.7	1.5
Year-on-year-growth				
Sales (%)	0.0	201.7	31.7	34.8
Profits (%)	11.5	–293.6	–22.6	–55.6
Employees				
No of staff	175	514	533	688
Sales per emp (£)	97,440	100,078	127,152	132,810

Sharps Individual Bedrooms Ltd

The company's principal activities are the design, construction and supply of custom built fitted bedroom furniture. In this subsector Sharps claims the leading share. In the bedroom sector as whole it is estimated to take around 8 per cent of the market. Sharps is increasing the number of its showrooms from 85 in 1991 to 110 by the end of 1992.

Financial profile

Year end	31/12/87	31/12/88	31/12/89	31/12/90
Sales & profits				
Sales (£000)	25,422	32,364	27,821	23,631
Profits (£000)	−7,731	−1,453	−8,680	−8,907
Margin (%)	−30.4	−4.5	−31.2	−37.7
Year-on-year-growth				
Sales (%)	13.7	27.3	−14.0	−15.1
Profits (%)	920.1	−81.2	497.0	2.6
Employees				
No of staff	610	638	654	582
Sales per emp (£)	41,675	50,727	42,540	40,603

The Spring Ram Corporation plc

The company's principal activities are the manufacture and marketing of quality bathroom and kitchen products for the home improvement market. The group does not publish a breakdown of its consolidated turnover, but a very substantial proportion comes from kitchen furniture. Kitchen manufacturers in the group are Ram Kitchens (Select and Elite brands), Sterling Kitchens, Premium Kitchens, Next Dimension (own-label manufacturing) and Chippendale Contracts. The group markets Chippendale Kitchens and New World Kitchens.

Financial profile

Year end	31/12/88	05/01/90	04/01/91	03/01/92
Sales & profits				
Sales (£000)	85,173	121,017	145,285	194,173
Profits (£000)	16,561	24,116	30,065	37,569
Margin (%)	19.4	19.9	20.7	19.4
Year-on-year-growth				
Sales (%)	42.8	39.4	22.4	33.6
Profits (%)	58.3	42.9	27.1	25.0
Employees				
No of staff	1,097	1,451	1,647	2,082
Sales per emp (£)	77,642	81,829	88,212	93,263

Stag Furniture Holdings plc

The group manufactures freestanding bedroom furniture, living room furniture and dining room furniture via Stag Meredew, its larger subsidiary, and Jaycee. It is estimated to have a share in the bedroom furniture sector of around 5 per cent and around 2 per cent of the wooden and upholstered dining room/living room furniture sector.

Financial profile

Year end	31/12/88	31/12/89	31/12/90	31/11/91
Sales & profits				
Sales (£000)	39,317	40,998	28,489	26,806
Profits (£000)	2,117	2,387	1,167	2,044
Margin (%)	5.4	5.8	4.1	7.6
Year-on-year-growth				
Sales (%)	5.7	4.3	−30.5	−5.9
Profits (%)	36.4	12.8	−51.1	75.1
Employees				
No of staff	1,283	1,349	977	813
Sales per emp (£)	30,645	30,391	29,160	32,972

Source: Key Note Furniture, Edition 9 1992 and Edition 7 1990

PART 2

Strategic Direction

Case 5 **Ladbrokes**

Ladbroke's racing origins go back for more than 100 years to the Warwickshire village of Ladbroke where it commenced trading in 1887. Here a partnership was set up which, having relocated to Howard Street of London Strand at the turn of the century, soon established itself as the country's quality betting firm. Today Ladbroke Racing is the world's largest commercial off-track betting organization.

By 1989 the group employed more than 77,000 people worldwide and was one of the largest companies on the London Stock Exchange, its turnover exceeding £3.6 billion. Profits of £32 million recorded in 1980 had grown to £302 million in 1989.

In 1984 the board stated its group strategy as follows:

- All divisions should operate in growth industries and should aim to be market leaders.
- Growth should be both organic and through acquisitions.
- Costs should be managed efficiently and profitability maximized.
- Margins should be improved.

It was announced in September 1993 that Cyril Stein would step down as Executive Director. From 1983 until 1989, he held the dual responsibility of Chairman and MD. He had been connected with Ladbroke since 1956, having joined the company that his uncle had purchased in 1954, commencing work as a junior manager. The company has grown very substantially over the last ten years with a relatively unchanged board of directors. Changes in membership have been gradual and four out of the eight positions have been unchanged since 1983.

Stein's achievements include strategic acquisitions, direction and ultimate growth of the group since 1983. However, he has never erased the stigma of losing the group's casino licence. Ladbroke had acquired its interest in this lucrative market in 1971 but were forced out of the business in 1979. The authorities ruled that Ladbroke was not fit and proper to run its four West End casinos. Tactics used to gain other casinos were highlighted as improper and unfair.

In 1987 rumours about a horse racing scandal involving Ladbroke swept the country. The share price fell by 37p in one day, wiping off £200 million from the value of the company. The city found Stein intolerant and prickly, with a hatred of verbosity and a preference for a hands-on approach with both internal and external dealings. His vision of the company as his own must to some degree have determined their overall policy. Since 1986 there has been a corporate planning position on the board.

GAMBLING MARKET

Gambling covers two closely related activities:

- Betting; that is, gambling through betting offices or playing the football pools.
- Gaming; That is, playing bingo, gaming at a casino, buying lottery tickets, playing cards and playing on a with-profits slot machine.

Britain has the world's biggest, non state-controlled, bookmaking industry. It also has the second highest number of casinos of any country in Europe.

In 1990 the rate of increase in turnover of bookmakers slowed, although until then it had shown continued growth. Stakes went up from £3.1 billion in 1982–3 to a high of £4.02 billion in 1989–90. At constant 1982 values, therefore, the amount staked per bookmaker has increased. In addition to these figures which are 'off-course', there was about £500 million laid 'on the course'. Accurate figures for on course betting are hard to come by, as this money is not subject to tax. Some of this will represent 'laid off' bets by off-course bookmakers protecting their position.

The increase was partly due to the operators broadening the areas on which they would take bets. However horse racing still accounts for 70–80 per cent of turnover. The majority of the rest goes on the dogs. Since 1989–90, however, the total stakes have dropped to £3.61 billion in 1992–3 at 1982 prices. This has been due to the recession.

The major bookmakers are expanding their turnover by looking abroad for opportunities. In Europe some countries do not allow off-course betting while in some non-European states betting is state-owned. In the USA, although it varies from state to state, most-off course betting is illegal.

In the UK the main strategies used to increase stakes have been to encourage customers to stay longer, for example smarter shops, seating, televised racing and more options for ante-post betting. Bookmakers are also keen to extend credit card

TABLE 1 Expenditure on gambling (£m constant 1985 prices)

Expenditure	1986	1987	1988	1989	1990	1991	1992
Gross	9322	9945	10072	10205	10077	9468	9501
Net*	2169	2296	2318	2341	2310	2177	2184

* Stake less winning.
Source: Keynote – betting and gaming 1993.

TABLE 2 Expenditure on gambling (£m) 1991–1992 at current prices

Activities	1991/2		1990/1	
	£m	%	£m	%
Betting offices	6786	48.3	6748	48.5
Gaming machines	3807	27.1	3815	27.4
Casinos	1914	13.6	1929	13.9
Football pools	840	6.0	773	5.6
Bingo	661	4.7	618	4.4
Lottery tickets	56	0.4	28	0.2
Total sales	14063	100.0	13911	100.0

Source: HM Customs and Excise/Gaming Board.

betting in an attempt to attract the more affluent customer. This all favours the larger chains. The betting shop market is dominated by four main players; Ladbrokes (1939 offices), William Hill (1669 offices), Coral (Bass) (897 offices) and Stanley Leisure (250 offices).

Football pools

The first pool was established in 1922 by the founder of Littlewoods and football pools are now the most popular form of gambling in the UK. In the year to July 1991 around £770 million was staked on the pools by almost 14 million people, of which around £21 million was returned as winnings. Stake money grew slowly over 1990–1 after a sharp increase in 1989–90. Growth in stake money is often related to changes in the first dividend offered by the companies. In August 1989, Littlewoods increased its first dividend to £1.5 million, which resulted in a series of jackpot winnings in the 89–90 season.

Football pools generate large sums from small stakes (the average stake with Littlewoods is only £1.80). Turnover is little affected by boom or recession, with most punters betting on a regular weekly basis. The spectacular rises seen in some years (including that forecast for 1991–2) reflect increases in the minimum stakes. The pools market is very concentrated, with just three major companies in the market. These are Littlewoods (77 per cent), Vernons (20 per cent) and Zetters (3 per cent).

Most factors affecting the gambling industry are legislative. Most gambling is explicitly excluded from the normal behaviour of the marketplace by a legal requirement that it should satisfy 'unstimulated demand'. This means that gambling can grow only slowly.

There are three regulating bodies:

- The Gaming Board of Great Britain, which licenses casinos, bingo halls, lotteries, football pools and gaming machines. It also polices the operation of these sectors.
- The Horse-Race Betting Levy Board, which oversees bookmakers, collects the levy, and runs the Totaliser Board and the National Stud.
- Her Majesty's Customs and Excise, which covers the legal sectors of the betting and gaming market, that is, bookmakers, casinos, bingo halls, lotteries (council and societies), football pools and gaming machines.

THE DIY MARKET

The DIY market covers materials and tools purchased for home repairs and other improvements made by householders. There is a spectrum from hard to soft products in the DIY market, with home furnishings and displays of co-ordinated styles at the soft end, for example, and timber, cement and building materials at the hard end.

The DIY market (in terms of turnover) grew at annual compound growth rate of around 14 per cent per amount between 1984 and 1988 (see table 3). Reasons for this growth are linked to prosperity in the housing market which in turn was influenced by the availability and price of mortgages. In 1989, growth slowed as a result of the decline in the housing market and the recession. The recovery is expected to continue, especially now that the UK economy is emerging from the recession. The major companies in the market are shown in table 4.

Over the past 20 years there has been a process of concentration in the DIY market. The number of large-scale superstores increased to 1,000 by mid-1991 while

TABLE 3 Estimated value of sales by DIY retailers and percentage of total retail sales (£billion at current prices), 1985–91

	1985	1986	1987	1988	1989	1990	1991	1992
DIY	2.36	2.88	3.23	3.79	4.29	4.67	5.19	5.49
All retailers	87.9	95.8	102.8	113.4	120.4	128.3	135.4	139.9
DIY sales as % of total	2.68	3.00	3.14	3.34	3.56	3.64	3.83	3.93

Source: Keynote report on DIY 1993.

the number of small outlets declined by 5,000 in the face of competition from superstores. The saturation level is estimated by the trade to be 1,300 superstores.

DIY retailers spent £56 million on TV and press adds in 1991. The top seven accounted for 94 per cent of this. B&Q and Texas were the largest spenders, with £20.8 million and £16.6 million respectively. Each of them spent more than twice as much as the third leading advertiser, Do-It-All, who spent £8.2 million on advertising in 1991. This may give Texas a competitive advantage over its competitors in positioning itself where it wants to be (the soft end of the market). Currently Texas is 'keeping its powder dry' on promotions in the coming season while Do-It-All is launching a series of aggressive tele-advertising campaigns in an attempt to regain lost market share.

There is also a trend towards differentiation with major superstore chains concentrating on different segments of the market. B&Q, Homebase and Do-It-All are moving towards the hard end, with Texas moving towards the softer end. Sales of DIY goods are seasonal, traditionally sales slump in January (after the Christmas spending spree) and recover to a peak in April, especially the Easter week.

In 1991, B&Q and Texas initiated a price war in an attempt to gain market share. The Payless and Do-It-All union lost market share while B&Q and Texas managed

TABLE 4 Estimated value of sales by DIY retailers and percentage of total retail sales (£billion at current prices), 1985–91

Chain and ownership	Number of stores	Market share	Turnover in UK (£m)	Pre-tax profit (£m)	Date of latest accounts
B&Q plc (Kingfisher plc)	280	14.0	1,018	67.1	01.02.92
Texas Homecare Ltd (Ladbroke Group plc)	224	8.8	651.3	25.4	31.12.91
Do-It-All Ltd (WH Smith plc and Boots plc)	225	5.6	415.2	–3.4	28.02.92
Homebase Ltd (J. Sainsbury plc)	70	3.0	219.8	4.9	14.03.92
Wickes Building Supplies	67	2.5	185.8	17.1	31.12.91
Great Mills (Retail) Ltd (RMC Group plc)	92	2.5	187	9.3	31.12.91
A.G. Stanley Ltd	410	1.5	110.8	6.7	31.03.92
FADS (The Boots Co plc)	–	1.5	110.0	–	–
Focus DIY Ltd (Focus Retail Group plc)	28	0.6	46.3	2.2	31.10.92
Other DIY	–	28.4	–	–	–
Other retailers	–	22.4	–	–	–
Builders merchants	–	9.2	–	–	–

Number of UK stores at the end of 1992 (Texas and Wickes also have stores in other countries)
Source: Company Accounts/Press and Keynote Report on DIY 1992.

to increase theirs. There was a price to pay for gaining market share, however. This was reflected in the lower profit margin in its 1991 and 1992 results. Nevertheless, the higher sales achieved gave rise to higher overall profits.

The major superstores have been able to negotiate rebates from suppliers on their purchases in the past to help fund discounts, hence protecting their own margin. Major manufacturers are beginning to react to this by building stronger brand images, through advertising, in order to balance this power. For example, ICI is spending heavily on promoting its Dulux and Crown paints. In the 1992 B&Q – Texas price war, most suppliers were unwilling to participate with B&Q's request for rebates, and ICI withdrew its supplies of paints from B&Q because of this loss-leading practice.

Data from the British Market Research Bureau indicates that DIY is a very widespread activity, undertaken to some extent by all adult age groups, by both sexes and by all socio-economic groups. The most active sector of the population is that between 25 and 44 years old (81 per cent of population participating) with 45–65 year olds next (71 per cent of population participating). However, there is little differentiation between socio-economic groups although the C2s are most strongly represented.

A survey carried out in early 1992 by the adhesives manufacturer Evode suggested that the lack of 'how-to' advice in DIY stores is a major obstacle to growth in the DIY market. It also estimated that the widespread availability of detailed instruction leaflets could encourage more extensive DIY activity and generate an increase in sales of £1.5 billion per year.

The opening of the single European market may present an opportunity for growth. On average, the British spend $65 per head per year, while the Germans spend $133, the French $99, those in Belgium $84, the Dutch $75, the Italians $47 and the Spanish $35. Some UK companies already had a strong presence in Europe, for example Texas is already established in Spain.

Self-assembly furniture and home security are expected to continue to be the fastest growing sectors. In the longer term, more ambitious jobs such as plumbing and double glazing are likely to be tackled by a large number of households and therefore provide a growth area.

THE HOTEL INDUSTRY

The hotel industry has become competitive and concentrated. The operating environment of today's hotel industry is becoming increasingly volatile, uncertain and complex. International travel is predicted to double by the year 2000, and hotels are making preparations to increase their share.

Entry to the industry is becoming more difficult. The single European market imposes tougher standards for safety, consumer protection and the standardization of VAT. The availability of city centre sites is becoming scarce, with planning permission and building regulations getting tougher in order to protect the environment. However, there are still opportunities for potential hotels in certain market segments such as the one star market, for example the segments which are focused of volume instead of service.

Large multinational corporations and travel agencies have substantial buying power. Due to the intensification and oversupply of rooms in certain markets, hotels now offer corporate rates to smaller companies. An important factor in the hotel industry is the satisfaction of the transient needs and wants of the business traveller. Therefore, a hotel has to keep a close eye on changes in the market environment, otherwise it may well lose its competitive advantage, and consequently its guests.

There is strong competition in the hotel industry. Hotels are poaching each others' best employees and trying to entice each others' guests with corporate discounts. Frequent guest programmes and international hotel chains are expanding into other market segments where the competition is based on gaining a share of that particular market segment and, last but not least, hotels buy each others' properties, rename them and market them under the new corporate flag. This all happens despite the growth in business travel all over the world.

The hotel industry is differently concentrated in the various markets with the smaller family-run hotels particularly important in some areas. However, in the UK and USA the larger hotel chains have a major share of the market. In the USA, over 60 per cent of all hotels are affiliated to hotel chains of some sort (corporate, independent or management). The ten largest chains in the US have a 30 per cent share of all hotels in the US. In France, the largest hotel market in Europe, the majority of the 45,000 hotels are small and about 50 per cent are ungraded. The 20 largest UK hotel groups own 77.1 per cent of the industry. The largest, Trusthouse Forte, has a share of 19.8 per cent of all bedrooms of the 50 largest hotels in the UK. In addition to this, approximately 2 per cent of all hotels are part of the ten largest UK hotel companies.

THE UK PROPERTY INDUSTRY

Historically, good quality commercial property was an equity-type investment that, by and large, provided a hedge against inflation, and over the long term produced both rising income and capital value. Banks were the natural providers of construction finance with life assurance companies and pension funds the natural long-term financiers or owners. This order of things came about in the postwar period where a shortage of many types of property meant that tenants were obliged (and prepared) to pay ever-rising rents to secure their space needs. Britain's common law has led to a pattern of long occupational leases (usually 25 years), linked with agreement to an ever-upwards review of rentable values. The original tenant would often be responsible under English law for the rent under a lease even when it were subsequently assigned to a third party. The relative security of income provided in this system of operation led to British investors being prepared to buy property on low starting yields, with those of top quality newly let buildings sometimes as low as 4 per cent.

During the 1980s banks became much more involved in commercial property finance. Loans increased from £5 billion to a peak of over £40 billion in 1991. Coupled with a more relaxed attitude to planning permission this led to the creation of property traders – 'merchant developers'. Ultimately landlords were chasing tenants, with the oversupply leading to a fall in rental values. This in turn prompted investors to demand much higher yields to compensate for the disappearance in growth. In 1991 the only mechanism by which the market could adjust to these new expectations was by a sharp fall in capital values.

The new era has seen the development of shorter leases and leases without break clauses. Power is increasingly transferring to the tenant and incentives to lease are more frequently offered. Rents continued to fall throughout 1992 and showed little signs of stopping, indeed in the last quarter of 1992 they fell at a rate faster than in either of the two preceding quarters. Over 27 million square feet of floor space is available in central London alone with occupier demand remaining weak. The problem continues to be exacerbated by a reluctance on the part of potential sellers to place buildings on the market at reduced capital values.

The death of new construction in the early 1990s will ultimately result in bringing the property market back into balance. Not all segments have suffered from oversupply, for example rents have consistently risen in Scotland and there continues to be a shortfall in high-quality large units. Regional development is the most likely to show recovery first due to only a limited oversupply at present. Evidence over the past 20 years suggests a clear link between changes in the inflation trend from downwards to upwards and the rate of property rent growth. Cost savings from relocations may act as a stimulus to the growth in regional office and industrial units, but this is still dependent upon disposal of unwanted existing leases. Government policy, however, has seen a determined effort to relocate civil service departments into areas of reduced rental value and lower salary costs.

LADBROKE DIVISIONS

Ladbroke Gambling Division

Ladbroke is the biggest bookmaking firm in the world with operations in Britain, Eire, Belgium and the US. Ladbroke plc is the largest bookmaking chain in the UK with 1960 shops and it accounts for around 25 of all off-course betting in the UK. Its spread of shops throughout the country has protected it against the worst impact of the recession with increased turnover in the North and Scotland helping to offset the fall in London and the South East. Ladbroke claims to have increased its turnover in 1991, boosting its share of a static market although its betting operations have shown a fall in profitability. The organization is continually upgrading its shops, installing cafe bars and satellite TV (it owns 15 per cent of Satellite Information Services).

Ladbroke had been waiting to acquire a pools operator for some time and an unsuccessful bid for Vernons had been made to the Sangster Family in 1974. However Vernons was acquired by T-Line for £90 million.

In 1989 Ladbroke bid for T-Line Vernons, the strategy was to value the assets realistically but to remain ambivalent to the possibility of other offers. It also intended to sell the Industrial Division for £55 million. Final value was £185 million, provisional profit forecasts indicated £15 million giving an approximate multiple of 13. Ladbroke proposed strategy after the purchase was to take the name of Vernons Offshore and to establish the pools business in Europe and the United States. The motives for the acquisition appear to have been synergy, entry into new markets and acquisition of market power, as organic growth was not easily possible.

Ladbroke DIY Division

Currently, Texas Homecare stores offer around 30,000 product lines, over 60 per cent of which are own labels. The advantages of using own labels are two-fold. First, it enables Texas to differentiate itself from other superstores. Secondly, it reduces the number of different brands that need to be held in stock. By limiting stocks to one or two of the leading brands and own label for each line of product, stockholding costs can be reduced significantly. In 1991, the company embarked on a major product range review based on EPOS data. The result was the shedding of approximately 1,000 lines which also helped to reduce costs of stockholding.

Traditionally, Texas has been positioned near the hard end for example, building material, of the market. The softer end of the DIY market includes items such as home furnishings and displays of co-ordinated styles, and in recent years there has been a move in this direction. This move has probably been initiated by the growing proportion of older people in the UK population since the soft-end DIY product would appeal to the growing number of DIY'ers aged over 40. It is also likely to attract more female customers whose earnings level has increased dramatically over the last decade.

Perhaps more important is the potential for product differentiation of the soft-end DIY products for which Texas would be able to charge a premium price. Other areas in the DIY market are either dominated by strong brands and severe competition from own labels (such as paints) or are facing the profitability 'nut-cracker', namely overcapacity and low margins (such as wallpapers).

Ladbroke's immediate strategy for Texas is to increase its market share. The DIY market is a growing and profitable industry to be in. The more attractive option for Texas is to choose to focus on the soft end of the market and build volume in that market segment by differentiating its products from those of its competitors, as this will gain them market share and allow them to increase margins. This they have done with some success with their Pretty Chic department. However, this strategy will require a high level of investment, both in building awareness (that is branding, advertising and promotion) and product development.

Ladbroke Hotel Division

Hilton International, one of the two Hilton groups, is owned by Ladbroke and operates outside the US. Hilton hotels in the US are operated by an entirely different company, Hilton Hotels Corporation. In order to get into the US market Hilton International has had to adopt a different name for its hotels, Vista. Meanwhile, the Hilton Hotel Corporation has gone international under a new name, Conrad.

Ladbroke's hotels have grown from a base of just three hotels in the 1970s to be number two in the UK in the 1980s and catapulted to the level of world brand leader through acquisition of the Hilton International chain.

In the early 1980s objectives were to increase bedroom capacity through extension of existing properties and the building of new hotels in areas of high demand, with particular emphasis on the London sector of the market. Tourist and business demand for hotel beds in the UK was very strong, with the total number of bedrooms increasing to 3,764 and operating profit up by 70 per cent. Ladbrokes grew through acquisition during the early 1980s. A 50 per cent interest in BFT travel Inc. was purchased and Comfort International was taken over.

In 1987 Ladbroke bought the Hilton chain outside America for (£645 million) in cash and landed a prestigious brand name with 91 hotels and 35,000 bedrooms. They believed that they could cure Hilton's over-reliance on a customer base of US tourists and business travellers. Hilton's profits dropped from $60 million to $47 million in 1986, mostly because of the effects of Chernobyl and the bombing of Libya. However, even with profits at 1985 levels, Ladbroke still paid an exit multiple of around 30. Ladbroke paid such a high figure believing it could improve Hilton's overall margin on sales which was then at a level of 6 per cent. This was little more than a quarter of Ladbrokes' existing hotel division.

The take-over of the Hilton group boosted the profit performance of Ladbroke group substantially. In the first year after the take-over the hotel division contributed 45 per cent of the operating profits. The new team at Hilton International sharpened its sales and marketing forces to meet objectives and targets in a highly competitive market. For example, fine dining restaurants were closed where customers did not patronize the dining rooms and $600,000 was spent to determine

Hilton International's image in the minds of current and potential customers. Ladbroke cashed in on the name it had acquired, opening a further 12 hotels under the name Hilton, and turning its others into Hilton National. They built new hotels as far a field as Nagoya in Japan and Nova Scotia in Canada.

During 1990 Ladbroke was honoured by the award of the Queen's Award for Export Achievement, relating to its Hilton International Hotels Division. The profit levels of the hotel group showed steady improvement until 1991 during which time trade was lost due to the Gulf War. Bedroom capacity exceeded 50,000 beds.

Hilton has also expanded globally by a mixture of acquisition and organic growth and now operates 152 hotels in 47 countries. The expansion was financed by a stock issue of 216 million shares carried out by Ladbroke in order to raise $789 million. In particular Hilton International is concentrating expansion in the Far East because Japanese travellers recently eclipsed Americans as the leading group of Hilton guests. Hilton added ten hotels in 1992 with eight due to follow in 1993. Expansion is centred on the UK. There is little opportunity to reduce fixed costs as they have been targeted in the past. Variability of the world economics means that the volume of trade is patchy and unpredictable.

The spend on new units in 1992 was £113 million and the proceeds from two sales and two sale and lease-backs was £70.1 million. This intention is to continue to raise funds by further sales, it was therefore implied that no equity will be invested in the eight units planned for 1993.

Profitability fell in 1992, due partly to decreased performance but to unfavourable movements in the value of the pound against other major currencies.

Hilton's main market segment is the business traveller (70 per cent of Hilton's customers). This is a good market to be in: firstly the average expenditure per night is £38 as against £14 for all other tourists; secondly, business travellers are not influenced by seasonality; thirdly, in a recession, tourists will spend less money on their holidays – especially on the more expensive holidays. Although the recession definitely has its impact on the business traveller, companies tend to downgrade on flightclass rather than on their hotels.

Belonging to an international hotel chain, like Hilton, definitely has advantages for the business traveller. These are the expectations of a similar standard of service in all properties, corporate discounts and use of a central reservation system.

The market in 1986 was worth $300 billion (600 million trips) and expectations are that 800 million trips will be made in 1995, worth $400 billion.

Ladbroke Property Division

The Ladbroke Property Division is split up into seven groups:

1   Ladbroke Group Properties Limited – UK Prime Office
2   London and Leeds Corporation – USA, Eastern Seaboard
3   London and Bardco Investment
4   Ladbroke City and County Land Companies Limited – Shopping Centres
5   Gable House Properties – Specialist Schemes
6   Ladbroke Group Homes
7   Gable Retirement Homes Limited

The size of the Division is very small at less than 5 per cent of group turnover and employing only 100 staff. The relatively small nature of the operation in the USA enables it to act as a local developer, with an extensive knowledge of the market and the opportunities available. The main areas of operation, both in the UK and the US, are offices, shopping, retail parks and industrial.

During 1986 there was an expansion of the portfolio of properties on the Eastern Seaboard of the USA. The Property Division continued to prosper in 1987 with all of its businesses in an expansion phase. Each main business operates in a different market or specialist sector of the industry. In practice they dovetailed sensibly all making good use of a centralized service. Out of town retailing was very much a growth area in 1987 and Ladbroke expanded its operation rapidly. In just two years the company had become one of the leading UK developers in this area.

In general the market is currently over supplied in the UK and the recession has seen the introduction of turnover-related rents. Investment yields in this area have fallen from 11 per cent to 8 per cent.

It was Ladbroke's opinion that it enjoyed the best of both worlds by having seven individual property businesses operating in seven countries, rather than one vast empire. It could move swiftly and decisively, yet enjoy Ladbroke group's financial backing. By 1989 Ladbroke applied the policy of concentrating upon prime development even more rigorously. It also believed that the strength of the balance sheet provided a facility to ride out the depressed periods.

APPENDIX 1

Acquisitions 1979 onwards

Year	Value £m
1979	
Laskys Hifi	3.2
Myddleton Hotels	3.9
Westmoreland Hotel London	11.25
1981	
Wallis Holday Group	1.9
Beeson Holiday Centre	1.2
Machine Hire Business	4.0
Turf Accountants	4.0
Central TV 10%	2.5
1982	
London & Leeds Property	4.9
Demming Leisure (Betting)	4.1
Town & Country Lesiure	5.5
1983	
BFT Travel Inc USA	
Lanton Leisure snooker clubs	
Central TV further 10% stake	
United Trade Press Holdings Ltd 75%	
MW Publishers	
Home & Law Magazines 80%	
1984	
Comfort Hotels	71.0
Le Tierce off-track racing Belgium	
Detroit Race Course	
Olivers (UK) Ltd Coffee & Bread Shops	1.1
Wootten Publications	
1985	
Home Charm Group plc (Texas & Multicolour wallpapers)	196
Rodeway Inns Inc USA	10.0
Senews 75% (local newspapers)	9.0

1986
   Gable House Properties   34.0
   Fellbridge Hotel & Health Club   26
   Architectural Press Holdings   7.0
   John Nelson & Ganton House

1987
   Hilton Hotels   645.0
   Hampden Homecare Northern Ireland

1988
   Thomas T-Line (Vernon Pools)   165.0
   Sandfords DIY   35.0

1990
   Canterbury Downs Race Track 50%
   Meeus Investments Ltd

Divestments 1979 onwards

Year	Value £ m
1979	
Cashcade Lotteries	1.0
1981	
RV Goodham, Linfield Park Casinos	
1983	
Social Clubs	
1986	
Laskys	30.25
1987	
Rodeway Inns	12.0
Olivres Breadshops	4.7
Holiday Villages	54.0
Home and Law Magazines	34.8
1988	
Thomas T-Lines Industrial	15.0
Cable TV	
Retirement Homes	
Lanton Leisure	8.7
1989	
Satellite Information Systems 18%	
1991	
Platanoff & Harris	1.4

Comparison of buy and sell in period

Company	Acquired	Sold	Value in	Value out
Laskys	1979	1986	3.2	30.25
Olivers	1984	1987	1.1	4.7
Rodeway Inns	1985	1987	10.0	12.0

APPENDIX 2   PROFIT AND LOSS ACCOUNT (£M)

Year	1974	1975	1976	1977	1978	1979	1980	1981	1982	1983
Turnover	254.7	268.8	319.1	387.7	469.1		665.1	705.2	762.0	846.9
Cost of sales	243.2	255.5	303.4	363.3	427.4		625.8	665.6	699.1	777.0
Gross profit	11.5	13.3	15.7	24.4	41.7	0.0	39.3	39.6	62.9	69.9
Administration expenses									19.8	23.2
Income from other companies									-0.3	1.3
Operating profit	11.5	13.3	15.7	24.4	41.7	0.0	39.3	39.6	42.8	48.0
Interest	1.4	0.9	0.4	0.3	0.8		7.2	7.1	7.4	6.2
Exceptional property item										
Profit after interest	10.1	12.4	15.3	24.1	40.9	0.0	32.1	32.5	35.4	41.8
Tax	5.1	6.4	6.9	9.2	17.6		4.3	4.2	7.2	13.7
Profit after tax	5.0	6.0	8.4	14.9	23.3	0.0	27.8	28.3	28.2	28.1
Minority interests	0.0	0.2	0.4	0.6	0.5		1.0	0.2	0.9	1.7
Profit attributable to shareholders	5.0	5.8	8.0	14.3	22.8	0.0	26.8	28.1	27.3	26.4
before extraordinary items										
Extraordinary items	0.1						7.8			
Profit attributable to shareholders	5.1	5.8	8.0	14.3	22.8	0.0	34.6	28.1	27.3	26.4
Dividends	0.9	1.5	2.1	3.6	4.5		7.9	9.8	11.5	13.2
Retained profit for year	4.2	4.3	5.9	10.7	18.3	0.0	26.7	18.3	15.8	13.2

APPENDIX 2 continued

Year	1984	1985	1986	1987	1988	1989	1990	1991	1992
Turnover	1115.9	1342.6	1765.6	2135.4	2848.0	3659.5	3800.5	3785.7	4166.5
Cost of sales	1035.6	1227.6	1605.0	1913.9	2518.6	3250.9	3382.1	3418.7	3816.0
Gross profit	80.3	115.0	160.6	221.5	329.4	408.6	418.4	367.0	350.5
Administration expenses	25.2	28.2	33.3	42.5	53.4	60.3	59.4	61.4	61.6
Income from other companies	2.5	2.5	3.4	0.3	0.5	5.2	6.9	6.6	3.5
Operating profit	57.6	89.3	130.7	179.3	276.5	353.5	365.9	312.2	292.4
Interest	7.4	14.2	29.4	19.1	24.2	51.3	60.3	101.8	105.6
Exceptional property item									146.7
Profit after interest	50.2	75.1	101.3	160.2	252.3	302.2	305.6	210.4	40.1
Tax	17.4	29.2	36.8	56.1	78.7	88.4	76.2	52.8	38.5
Profit after tax	32.8	45.9	64.5	104.1	173.6	213.8	229.4	157.6	1.6
Minority interests	3.5	2.7	2.1	0.5	4.0	6.7	0.4	4.0	0.4
Profit attributable to shareholders before extraordinary items	29.3	43.2	62.4	103.6	169.6	207.1	229.0	153.6	1.2
Extraordinary items		0.0	22.0	36.7	26.0	4.9	−13.5	0.0	0.0
Profit attributable to shareholders	29.3	43.2	84.4	140.3	195.6	212.0	215.5	153.6	1.2
Dividends	19.1	23.1	33.7	54.5	69.6	83.8	91.5	109.9	121.0
Retained profit for year	10.2	20.1	50.7	85.8	126.0	128.2	124.0	43.7	−119.8

APPENDIX 3   BALANCE SHEET (£M)

Year		1982	1983	1984	1985	1986	1987	1988	1999	1990	1991	1992
Fixed assets												
Intangible assets		41.60	45.90	76.70	187.20	267.60	293.40	600.10	792.50	830.50	831.30	832.60
Tangible assets												
Operating assets		168.60	174.20	244.40	380.80	563.40	1188.50	1563.30	2155.10	2290.30	2265.80	2165.00
Investment properties		103.70	118.50	166.20	294.20	363.60	364.20	514.50	757.70	712.50	717.70	666.00
Investments		5.70	9.10	10.50	16.50	19.40	25.80	42.10	55.60	65.10	83.00	104.80
	Total	319.60	347.70	497.80	878.70	1214.00	1871.90	2720.00	3760.90	3898.40	3897.80	3768.40
Current assets												
Dealing properties		75.10	90.00	113.40	92.80	175.60	135.60	181.90	258.80	263.80	281.50	228.00
Stocks		15.20	23.00	21.00	29.00	58.90	93.60	110.70	152.40	186.00	194.20	215.30
Films		6.50	5.90	3.10	1.00	0.90						
Debtors		52.50	46.60	80.70	96.80	154.40	246.50	227.10	322.80	248.60	299.40	313.00
Investments		2.70	2.80	4.90	2.30	11.10	19.80	16.40	64.10	12.40	10.30	9.20
Cash at the bank		9.70	12.60	48.90	20.70	25.60	68.60	84.00	112.60	83.00	309.30	100.80
	Total	161.70	180.90	272.00	242.60	426.50	564.10	620.10	910.70	793.80	1094.70	866.30
Current liabilities												
Amount falling due within 1 year		76.50	95.10	163.20	173.70	340.60	446.00	480.00	636.50	557.60	614.70	599.30
Net current assets		85.20	85.80	108.80	68.90	85.90	118.10	140.10	274.20	236.20	480.00	267.00
Total assets less current liabilities		404.80	433.50	606.60	947.60	1299.90	1990.00	2860.10	4035.10	4134.60	4377.80	4035.40
Long term creditors												
Amount falling due after 1 year		167.60	187.70	241.10	354.50	542.30	717.50	823.90	1541.50	1522.00	1392.60	1485.70
Provisions												
Deferred taxation		16.30	14.20	16.70	19.50	21.90	18.50	18.10	27.90	27.80	28.00	16.70
	Total	220.90	231.60	348.80	573.60	735.70	1254.00	2018.10	2465.70	2584.80	2957.20	2533.00
Capital and reserves												
Called up share capital		14.50	14.60	17.70	20.50	27.00	42.30	42.40	85.60	86.00	108.10	108.70
Share premium account		43.00	44.20	96.30	108.80	151.60	338.10	342.20	312.90	321.00	770.50	771.30
Merger reserve					17.40							
Revaluation reserve		31.50	35.10	90.10	255.60	329.20				1242.50	1118.20	914.20
Capital reserve										229.7	213.3	210.8
Profit and loss account		119.00	124.60	125.80	143.30	191.00	858.10	1607.40	2035.40	613.70	642.80	507.80
Shareholder's fund		208.00	218.50	329.90	545.60	698.80	1238.50	1992.00	2433.90	2492.90	2852.90	2512.80
Convertible capital bonds										83.00	83.00	
Minority interests		12.90	13.10	18.90	28.00	36.90	15.50	26.10	31.80	8.90	21.30	20.20
	Total	220.90	231.60	348.80	573.60	735.70	1254.00	2018.10	2465.70	2584.80	2957.20	2533.00
Percentage of intangibles to fixed assets		13.0	13.2	15.4	21.3	22.0	15.7	22.1	21.1	21.3	21.3	22.1

Capital and reserves – profit and loss account figures for 1987–9 inclusive incorporate the revaluation reserve figure.

APPENDIX 4 TURNOVER & PROFIT – GEOGRAPHICAL AND SBU (£M)

Geographical diversification – turnover

	1982	1983	1984	1985	1986	1987	1988	1999	1990	1991	1992
UK	729.2	788.1	950.3	1066.3	1328.1	1680.7	2057.3	2325.7	2604.9	2583.5	2700.9
USA	0.0	18.7	114.2	153.3	175.0	148.0	257.0	586.3	590.7	573.1	705.7
Europe	26.8	35.0	47.9	120.0	150.4	200.2	334.7	498.9	390.6	408.0	502.8
Asia & Australia						20.4	120.7	138.3	117.9	110.9	114.3
Rest of World						11.6	78.3	110.3	96.4	110.2	142.8
Interest/asset leases	6.0	5.1	3.5	3.0	1.8	1.8	0.0	0.0	0.0	0.0	0.0
Discont'd activities	0.0	0.0	0.0	0.0	110.3	72.7	0.0	0.0	0.0	0.0	0.0
Totals	762.0	846.9	1115.9	1342.6	1765.6	2135.4	2848.0	3659.5	3800.5	3785.7	4166.5

Capital and reserves – profit and loss account figures for 1987–9 inclusive incorporate the revaluation reserve figure.

Geographical diversification – profit

	1990	1991	1992
UK	230.3	172.7	61.3
USA	17.9	16.8	-46.1
Europe	56.7	33.7	20.4
Asia & Australia	33.7	26.8	26.4
Rest of Wcrld	12.3	13.4	16.2
Interest/asset leases	-54.4	-53.0	-38.1
Discont'd activities	0.0	0.0	0.0
Totals	296.5	210.4	40.1

Geographical diversification – profit margin %

	1990	1991	1992
UK	8.8	6.7	2.3
USA	3.0	2.9	-6.5
Europe	14.5	8.3	4.1
Asia & Australia	28.6	24.2	23.1
Rest of world	12.8	12.2	11.3

Turnover by SBU

	1982	1983	1984	1985	1986	1987	1988	1989	1990	1991	1992
Hotels	56.5	36.8	42.9	86.5	87.2	223.4	688.8	830.1	780.1	758.1	901.8
Racing	597.2	637.4	787.3	984.4	1190.5	1322.7	1608.8	2170.3	2304.5	2252.9	2410.7
Property	16.3	33.3	148.0	111.1	121.6	152.6	110.1	130.1	155.2	121.8	160.2
Retail				132.2	213.2	351.6	440.3	529.0	560.7	652.9	693.8
Media					7.2	10.6					
Holidays	86.0	134.3	134.2	25.4	33.8						
Interest/asset leases	6.0	5.1	3.5	3.0	1.8	1.8					
Discont'd activities					110.3	72.7					
Totals	762.0	846.9	1115.9	1342.6	1765.6	2135.4	2848.0	3659.5	3800.5	3785.7	4166.5

1982 – Hotels includes holiday turnover/profit.
1982–1984 – Holidays includes retail turnover/profit.
1982–1985 – Holidays includes media and other entertainments turnover/profit.

Profit by SBU

	1982	1983	1984	1985	1986	1987	1988	1989	1990	1991	1992
Hotels	10.0	7.4	12.6	20.1	21.8	47.2	118.9	167.8	174.3	163.8	151.7
Racing	17.3	20.6	21.7	35.2	49.5	62.0	77.5	91.1	91.7	64.5	64.8
Property	3.5	8.4	17.2	18.0	21.4	22.3	32.2	35.9	45.2	-12.4	-35.4
Retail				7.8	13.8	26.0	34.5	40.1	39.7	47.5	43.8
Media					0.6	0.9					
Holidays	11.3	11.8	9.1	4.5	5.4						
Exceptional property item											-146.7
Interest/asset leases	-6.7	-6.4	-10.4	-10.5	-18.7	-9.1	-10.8	-32.7	-54.4	-53.0	-38.1
Discont'd activities					7.5	10.9					
Totals	35.4	41.8	50.2	75.1	101.3	160.2	252.3	302.2	296.5	210.4	40.1

Profit by SBU – profit margin %

	1982	1983	1984	1985	1986	1987	1988	1989	1990	1991	1992
Hotels	17.7	20.1	29.4	23.2	25.0	21.1	17.3	20.2	22.3	21.6	16.8
Racing	2.9	3.2	2.8	3.6	4.2	4.7	4.8	4.2	4.0	2.9	2.7
Property	21.5	25.2	11.6	16.2	17.6	14.6	29.2	27.6	29.1	-10.2	-22.1
Retail				5.9	6.5	7.4	7.8	7.6	7.1	7.3	6.3
Media					8.3	8.5					
Holidays	13.1	8.8	6.8	17.7	16.0						
Interest/asset leases	-111.7	-125.5	-297.1	-350.0	-1038.9	-505.6					
Discont'd activities					6.8	15.0					

APPENDIX 5   LADBROKE – COMPANY DATA

Year	1979	1980	1981	1982	1983	1984	1985	1986	1987	1988	1989	1990	1991	1992
Number of employees total														
Hotels				15792	17211	18479	21182	25003	32167	48070	51015	52039	53429	52894
Property				3596	2940	2697	4382	4116	8909	26295	26988	26968	27283	27083
Racing				34	41	53	59	161	539	924	146	145	129	101
Entertainments & retail				9029	9122	9859	10688	11318	12165	12234	14470	14453	14693	14254
Media				3011	5002	5762	4582	4015	6948	8125	9251	10304	11324	11456
Holidays							1352	94	113					
Group services				122	106	108	119	141	151	156	160	169		
Discontinued business								5158	3342	336				
Number of shares (millions)					146.17	176.60	205.43	269.78	422.86	424.50	855.74	859.97	1081.37	1087.24
Average share price (pence)	197	160	209	149	197	215	262	347	423	399	471	294	260	209
Average P/E ratio	5	3	6	8	13	14	16	18	18	14	15	12	10	13

APPENDIX 6　MARKET INFORMATION

	Real consumer expenditure % change	Permanent dwellings completed UK % change	Overseas travel and tourism visits to the UK by overseas residents 000's	Do-it yourself goods £m	Household major appliances £m	Radio, TV and other durable goods £m
1975	-0.40	15.15				
1976	0.44	0.88				
1977	-0.45	-3.29				
1978	5.65	-8.12	12646			
1979	4.35	-12.75	12486			
1980	0.08	0.07	12421			
1981	0.09	-18.00	11451	1800	2128	1769
1982	1.00	-11.51	11635	1927	2356	2061
1983	4.52	14.31	12464	2230	2778	2477
1984	1.95	5.52	13644	2459	2947	2742
1985	3.79	-5.86	14449	2822	3180	2940
1986	6.42	4.04	13897	3363	3584	3253
1987	5.51	4.68	15566	3626	4000	3750
1988	7.43	6.93	15800	4109	4380	4232
1989	3.34	-8.46	17338	4371	4687	4296
1990	0.67	-10.50	18021	4303	4907	4257
1991	-2.08	-6.5	16665	4598	5135	4347

Sources: Central Statistical Office, Dept; of the Environment, *Employment Gazette* March 1993.

APPENDIX 7 THE GAMBLING ENVIRONMENT

Off course betting was first licensed in 1960. Offices were first allowed to provide carpets and televised racing in 1986.

The number of bookmakers is limited by the Horse-Race Betting Levy Board. Licences for new premises are hard to obtain as they will not issue licences to areas that are already catered for. The main route to expansion therefore is by acquisition and take-over.

At present bookmakers would like to increase the potential for betting by allowing evening opening for greyhound racing as well as for horse race meetings in the summer, along with Sunday racing. In order to improve turnover book-makers are working closely with the racing bodies. There are also helpful signs from the government that some legislative restrictions, such as the ban on evening opening, may be eased. The European Commission is about to produce a report on gambling across Europe which might have substantial repercussions throughout the industry. At this stage, though, surmises about its content are pure speculation.

The pressure to increase the amount of money that the levy generates for horse racing has concentrated minds wonderfully in the racing community. The major bookmakers report that since late 1990 there has been a marked change in attitude towards the need to move the horse racing industry onto a more business-like basis. This is reflected by the setting up of the British Horse Racing Authority by the Jockey Club. The Jockey Club now seems to recognize that if the levy is to increase, then the racing industry must co-operate with the betting industry to optimize betting turnover. Moves such as ensuring that races at different meetings start at different times are starting to take place as this encourages people to bet on more than one meeting.

Although the short-term impact of the changes in the Levy and the Associated changes in betting tax have been difficult in the short term for the industry, the implications for the long-term are positive. Essentially the government is com-mitted to putting more money into racing and this is likely to benefit bookies.

The industry is also hopeful that 1993 will see legislation allowing evening opening. One major obstacle to this in the past has been the opposition of the Greyhound Racing Lobby, as they claim it would damage their industry. The possibility of bookmakers supporting greyhound racing through a voluntary levy along the same lines as horse racing is now being discussed and this is likely to soften the Greyhound Racing Lobby's objections.

Evening opening is likely to have significant impact on turnover. The chances of Sunday opening for bookmakers are more remote and, in any case, this may not increase turnover but simply spread Saturday's business across the whole weekend. However, the Jockey Club is likely to force the issue to the fore this year as it plans to stage Sunday meetings with on-course betting in defiance of the law. In the current chaotic state of Sunday trading legislation this is a high risk strategy but one which could encourage moves towards legislation.

The Government announced in the Queen's speech that it intends to introduce legislation to set up a national lottery. This will revolutionize the sector. The National Lottery is forecast to generate £1bn a year.

APPENDIX 8   ROCE INDUSTRY AVERAGES

Industry averages ROCE %

Industry	1987–8	1988–9	1989–90	1990–1
Retail–DIY	32.4	16.9	−1.2	−3.2
Property	6.9	5.2	3.5	0.5
Racing	7.7	9.2	7.5	n.a.
Hotels	6.5	9.6	9.5	8.0

Source: Industry Performance Analysis, 1993, ICC Publications Ltd.

APPENDIX 9   THE HOTEL INDUSTRY

Hotels in the UK

	Number of hotels	Number of bedrooms
England	22,547	764,005
Scotland	3,285	49,601
Wales	1,758	26,226
Northern Ireland	122	3,111
Total	27,712	842,943

Source: National Tourist Boards.

Selected UK hotel groups by turnover 1990–1991

Group	Turnover (£m)	Gross profit (£$)	Financial year end	No. of hotels	No. of bedrooms
Forte	2,662.0	73.0	31.1.1990	338	29,530
Hilton International	78.8	22.4	31.12.1990	35	7,199
Bass Hotels	570.0	n.a.	30.9.1991	76	7,728
Queen's Moat Houses	543.3	90.4	31.12.1991	102	10,624
Rank Hotels	57.0	6.8	31.10.1990	50	6,581
Mount Charlotte Hotels	190.9	32.8	30.12.1990	109	14,263
De Vere Hotels*	75.6	6.7	27.9.1991		
Savoy Hotel*	79.2	2.3	31.12.1991		
Stakis Hotels	83.4	27.6	30.9.1990	30	3,718
Swallow Hotels*	70.4	n.a.	28.9.1991		
Ladbroke Hotels*	60.9	9.5	31.12.1991		
Holiday Inns UK*	108.5	34.1	28.9.1990		
Jarvis Hotel*	46.1	8.0	30.3.1991		

*Not available (the hotel divisions of these companies are part of a much larger group and do not publish these figures separately).
Source: Keynote: Hotel Industry 1992.

Occupancy rates

	Average occupancy		Average achieved room rate (per room)		Income before fixed charges**	
	1991 %	% change 1990/91	1991 £	% change 1990/91	1991 £	% change 1990/91
All UK	61.4	−11.5	60.58	−2.5	8,340	−22.6
England*	58.0	−12.4	47.54	−1.2	6,358	−24.4
Scotland	63.5	−4.2	48.54	1.5	6,944	−7.8
Wales	54.8	−7.4	44.84	0.0	6,072	−16.3
London	66.4	−13.0	83.69	−3.7	12,168	−23.9

* Excluding London.
** Per available room per year.
Source: Pannell Kerr Forster Associates.

THE CONSTRUCTION INDUSTRY

The performance of the construction industry in the UK has been notoriously cyclical, and as in most countries is significantly influenced by government decisions. Firstly government is a customer providing infrastructure for national needs such as roads, hospitals, schools, and so on. The second major government influence on the construction industry is in the management of the economy through the use of interest rates. In inflationary situations government expenditure is tightened and interest rates rise thus exerting a double downward pressure on demand for construction industry products.

Output for the industry is shown in table 1 and in the longer term in figure 1.

THE HOUSING MARKET

The main social trends affecting the housing market in the past decade are:

- the rise in the divorce rate;
- a tendency towards smaller families;

TABLE 1 Output of the construction industry (£m at current prices), 1986–1990

	1986	1987	1988	1989	1990
New housing					
Public sector	842	933	922	979	968
Private sector	4,697	5,812	7,547	7,088	5,901
Total	5,539	6,745	8,469	8,067	6,869
Other new works					
Public sector	3,888	3,870	4,318	5,095	5,845
Private sector					
Industrial	2,632	3,204	4,023	4,936	5,265
Commercial	4,226	5,247	6,610	9,217	10,441
Total	10,746	12,321	14,951	19,248	21,551
Repairs and maintenance					
Housing	7,427	8,360	9,327	10,210	10,694
Other works					
Public sector	3,768	4,024	4,251	4,635	5,030
Private sector	2,642	3,112	3,547	4,014	4,331
Total	13,837	15,496	17,125	18,859	20,055
Total all works	30,122	34,562	40,545	46,174	48,475

Source: Monthly Digest of Statistics, HMSO, May 1991.

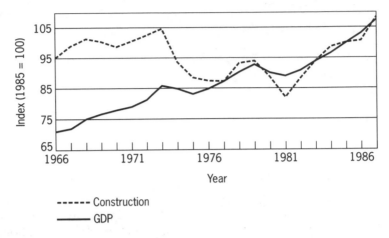

FIGURE 1   Trends in construction and GDP (output based), 1966–87
Source: Blue Book, Central Statistical Office, HMSO.

- increased affluence which generally allowed young couples to set up home earlier;
- the growth in the number of pensioners within the population requiring smaller dwellings.

The number of households in Great Britain, 1961–87 is shown in table 2. As can be seen the number of household units rise from 16.2 million in 1961 to 21.4 million in 1987. At the same time the average number of occupants drops from 3.09 to 2.55 persons.

Recently, the Bank of England concluded that more than half of the increases in demand for houses in the 15 years to 1985 was due to demographic, rather than to economic, factors such as income and interest rates. Baby-boomers born in the 1960s have created increased demand forcing up house prices. But in the mid-1970s the birth rate dropped by a third. So over the next two decades the number of potential first-time buyers (who have the biggest impact on the balance between demand and supply in the housing market) will drop sharply.

The Department of the Environment forecasts that much of the extra demand for dwellings will come from single-person households, which will grow from 5.3 million in 1987 to 7.1 million by 2001. A declining proportion of single-person households will be of pensionable age, as more pensioners will be surviving as part of a couple, which indicates that there will be increased demand for small dwellings (mainly flats) in urban areas.

Another factor which is having a depressing effect on the demand for houses is the rapid escalation of land prices in the late 1980s (see table 3). Most companies have a land bank of at least two years and are now finding that houses built on land purchased at those prices cannot be sold even at cost.

TABLE 2 Number of households and average size – UK 1961–87

	Households	*Average size (persons)*
1961	16,189	3.09
1971	18,317	2.89
1981	19,493	2.71
1987	21,373	2.55

Source: OPCS.

TABLE 3 Housing land prices in England and Wales (£000 per hectare) 1981/1988

	1981	1988
North	92.2	101.0
North West	94.7	115.3
Yorkshire/Humberside	66.9	111.4
West Midlands	122.6	311.0
East Midlands	79.2	251.6
East Anglia	41.4	419.9
South East	186.0	896.3
Greater London	327.5	2437.7
Wales	32.0	115.3

Source: Department of the Environment.

The economic issues affecting house purchase are the mortgage rate (see appendix 1) and earnings. It can be seen from appendix 2 that the house-price to earnings ratio rose rapidly in 1989 and as earnings have risen only slowly a substantial fall in prices was predictable if the ratio was to continue broadly at its historic level. The result of this is that many householders who purchased a house in 1989/90 are in a negative equity position, thus further dampening the demand for housing.

THE BUILDING MATERIALS INDUSTRY

This industry includes a wide range of products from bricks and tiles to glass, refractory goods and structural steel work. The nature of the items, bulky and low cost, requires local sites so that in production terms the manufacturing units are often small (see table 4).

However the production is often capital-intensive and distribution and marketing are on a national scale, so that large groups have formed for most of the product groups. For instance brick and roof tile production is heavily concentrated among a few large firms operating highly automated plant. Over the past 70 years many small brickworks have closed and firms remaining in the industry have merged or been absorbed by larger concerns. In the 1920s there were around 2,400 firms manufacturing bricks in England and Scotland, nowadays there are around 90.

Brick and roof tile production is a capital-intensive industry and manufacturers can earn very high profit margins when operating at or near full capacity, with the average pretax profit margin for leading companies being around 22 percent in 1988–9.

Brick and roof tiles are used for all types of new private and public sector building work, but housebuilding is the major market for them. It is estimated that

TABLE 4 Number of local units of selected building materials manufacturers (1991)

	Employment range						
	1–9	10–19	20–49	50–99	100–499	500+	Total
Sand, Gravel, Clay	252	118	49	4	4	–	427
Clay products	93	24	48	54	55	4	278
Cement	171	10	12	6	23	2	224
Ready mix concrete	1,060	81	30	5	4	–	1,180
Other concrete prods	460	158	177	115	23	–	990
All building mats	2,806	467	499	251	256	72	4,351

Source: Business Monitor PA 1003 1992.

up to 60 percent of UK brick output and a similarly high proportion of roof tile production are taken up by housebuilding.

Most brick and tile manufacturers serve all sectors of the construction industry, but some tend to specialize in particular markets. The London Brick Co. Ltd, owned by Hanson plc, is the monopoly producer of fletton bricks and the company's customers are predominantly housebuilders. Butterley Brick Ltd, also owned by Hanson, is a non-fletton producer, making a wide range of special architectural and engineering bricks aimed at the commercial and industrial sectors of the construction industry. With house building currently in recession, companies such as Baggeridge Brick Plc and Salvesen Brick Ltd have stated that their aim is to gain an increasing share of the architectural specification market. (See appendix 3 for details of companies in the brick and tile industry.)

Details of demand for some products within the industry are shown in appendix 4, both by volume and value, and some international comparisons are available in appendix 5.

An outline of the market share held by some of the major companies are shown in table 5.

Imports and exports constitute only a small proportion (5 per cent approximately) of total UK demand but in boom periods this may rise slightly. This is especially of the case with cement where it takes a longer time period to bring in new capacity such that in 1989–90 cement imports rose to 12–15 per cent of UK demand. As the recession bites stocks of bricks are said to equal some six months of demand and many companies are either moth-balling or closing plants.

The distribution channels are either to sell direct to construction companies or through builders' merchants, and for some products through DIY stores and garden centres. Builders' merchants carry relatively small stocks of brick and roof tiles and distribution mainly takes place direct between manufacturer and customer or contractor. Builders' merchants and brick factors play a role, however, by arranging bulk deliveries from manufacturer to customer. Some of the largest brick and tile manufacturers have their own distribution companies: for example Marley Transport Ltd distributes Marley roof tiles, paving and concrete building products on a nationwide basis.

TABLE 5 Estimated market shares for brick and concrete products

%	Bricks	Concrete roof tiles	Concrete blocks
Hanson	32		
Ibstock Johnston	12		
Redland	9	39	
Streetley	6		
Tarmac	6		14
Baggeridge brick	5		
Marley	4	49	14
George armitage	4		
Salvesen brick	3		
Blockleys	3		
ARC			10
RMC			5
ECC			5
Boral			5
Forticrete			5
Others	16	22	42

Concrete blocks and paving blocks and bricks are widely available through builders' merchants. Garden centres are important in the retail sale of paving blocks and bricks for garden paths and patios.

MARLEY PLC

Marley was founded in 1924 by Owen Aisher as Marley Joinery Works, later to be renamed Marley Tile (Holding) Company Ltd, and now Marley Plc. The main business of the company is the manufacture of structural clay products in which it has built up production facilities in the UK, Europe, North and South America, Southern Africa and New Zealand. The main products include roof tiles, concrete blocks, flooring and bricks.

The company has not however restricted itself to these core areas and has moved into plastic products, retailing (divested), automotive components, insurance, vehicle leasing, and some others. As of 1992 Marley has four business divisions: plastics; roofing; bricks, blocks and pavers; and automotive components.

Description of the company

In 1978 and 1979 Marley undertook a major reorganization and restructuring of its business. It invested heavily in a number of areas, particularly in vehicle leasing, DIY and a manufacturer of cups and saucers in the USA. The cost of financing these investments left Marley exposed in the short term to the effects of the severe and long-lasting downturn during the early 1980s. The financial consequence was that the trading profits were not high enough to absorb fully the cost of financing the investment programme of the late 1970s and, as a result, performance suffered.

The reorganization, while expensive in the short term was vital to the continuing health of Marley, and was dramatic. The UK roofing, flooring, distribution and transport businesses were reorganized; the German subsidiary was successfully transformed from a flooring to a plumbing business, while the UK merchanting operations became specialist plumbing merchants. The major reorganization during this period was the metamorphosis of the old Marley Homecare outlets, which were small, city centre shops, into Payless DIY, a modern, out-of-town DIY business comprising 59 stores together covering some 1,200,000 square feet.

These reorganizations, according to Mr Aisher in the 1983 Chairman's Report, enabled Marley

> to employ fewer people than in 1980 and to have increased sales by 70 per cent, and to have plants with the most modern machinery in each industry. By weeding out the underperformers from the portfolio, Marley has been able to concentrate on its mainstream activities, which make Marley a coherent group of related companies providing a wide range of materials and services for the construction industry.

The long awaited improvement in the UK economy towards the end of 1982 enabled Marley to reap benefits from its investments, although overseas businesses were still affected by both economic and managerial difficulties.

In 1985, Jack Aisher stepped down as Chairman and was replaced by Robert Clark, with George Russell as Chief Executive. The board was fully reconstructed. The Aisher family, the founders, did not totally disappear but were represented in a newly-established board of non-executive directors.

The new board set new objectives and a new strategy. The strategy was pointed out in the 1985 annual report:

- elimination of loss-makers;
- reorganization of the capital structure; and
- new management.

The US business, which had lost money since its acquisition in 1979 was sold for £11 million. All the Plumb Centres were sold, Marley Floors' Leighton Buzzard factory closed. Marley also decided to sell Payless to Ward White for £94 million. This showed a profit over book value of £8.8 million. At the time it was the third largest DIY retailer in the UK with 65 stores, situated mainly in the South and making profits of £10 million on sales of £215 million.

The loss of Payless' profits was balanced by interest savings. The cash virtually eliminated Marley's borrowings and, following sales of its Plumb Centres and US plastic housewares interest, the new management explained that it could now concentrate on what the group knew best: building materials, while also retaliating against new entrants like Polypipe in plastic piping. Overseas it was hoping to develop a materials business in the US to help finance its exposure to problem-ridden South Africa (weakening Rand); by far its most important market abroad at that time.

A year of acquisitions for Marley was 1986, the aeriated concrete blockmaker Thermalite was bought for £52 million and US facing brick manufacturer General Shale for $93.9 million. General Shale was one of the top three brickmakers in the US with interests in concrete blocks, ready-made concrete and lightweight aggregates. Marley also acquired Nottingham Brick, together these purchases added up to £74 million, for which the company issued 65 million shares.

In 1988 a new £20 million Thermalite plant was opened. This replaced old and fully written down capacity. Marley purchased Webster Brick (USA) for £9.3 million and Errol Brick in Scotland. The following year Clarke retired as Chairman, Russell assumed the dual roles of Chairman and CEO and the board was strengthened by the appointment of three new executive directors. Further businesses were acquired in 1989–90 with the purchase of a plastics product company in Australia and two companies involved in plastic mouldings for the building industry in the USA and Germany. Further details of Marley can be seen in appendix 6.

REDLAND PLC

The company comprises three main divisions of bricks, tiles and aggregates. It is, however, also involved in the distribution of fuel oils. Products include concrete and clay rooftiles, interlocking slates, plastic and metal roofing systems and wall and floor tiles. Within the company's aggregate business the portfolio consists of ready-mixed concrete, sand and gravel, stone products and cement. The company has also moved to consolidate its position in the plasterboard and fuel oil industry both within the home market and internationally.

Redland has asserted as its strategy growth through acquisition. Targeted industries are extensions of its core businesses: brickmaking, aggregates, and tilemaking. An exerpt from Redland's 1978–79 company report states the company's main consideration in acquisition, 'to assemble a group of complementary businesses capable of sustaining future profitable growth through their own cash flows'.

While the company has shown in the past decade a great propensity to acquire businesses, it has also demonstrated that it is not reluctant to divest itself of those enterprises that prove to be unprofitable. Redland plc's strategy was reiterated in both the 1983–84 and the 1986–87 accounts. This reaffirmed the direction the company took in the early 1980s with its concentration upon the core businesses. The concentration of resources in areas where the company has a competitive advantage and to reduce the debt burden in times of economic boom has allowed the company to follow its predatory acquisition policy during times of recession. This has involved the acquisition of complementary companies to the core business to create a more integrated building materials company with greater market dominance. Worldwide this has resulted in the creation of one of the most powerful groups in this industry. Further details of Redland are shown in appendix 7.

TARMAC PLC

By 1990 Tarmac consisted of seven divisions: Quarrying Products, Construction, Properties, Housing, Building Materials, Industrial, and Tarmac USA.

The Board consists of the Chairman and the Group Financial Director, chief executives in each division, and three non-executive directors.

Between 1980 and 1982 Tarmac pursued a policy of backward vertical integration through the development of the company's Quarrying Division. This was carried out through a process of selective acquisitions primarily in the UK. Indeed this policy was actively pursued throughout the following ten years resulting in over 100 acquisitions. This acquisitions policy gave the company quarry locations throughout the country.

During the period 1983–6 Tarmac, while maintaining its focus on the construction industry in the UK changed its strategic focus. Having established itself as a primary player in the quarrying products sector the company then moved up the value-added chain developing its position in the building materials sector. The aim, being to develop a fully integrated company from raw materials through to construction projects. By developing building materials the company was able to maximize the potential of its Quarrying Division by offering better access to potential markets and ensuring quality and continuity of supply to its Construction Divisions.

The £10 million deal for the purchase of Hemelite in 1983 indicates Tarmac's strategic development into the value-added building materials sector. Hemelite, with its 10 per cent market share in the UK and 12 manufacturing plants scattered throughout the UK, illustrates a continuation of Tarmac's strategy of attaining high market share leading to economies of scale.

At the same time, Westbrick and RBS Brooklyns, the fifth biggest brick maker, was bought for £20.6 million in 1984. Westbrick produced high-quality facing bricks from its six brick works and RBS Brooklyns manufactures and markets a wide range of concrete products including building blocks for interior and exterior use.

A significant move was made during this period, in geographic terms, with the acquisition of Lone Star Industrial in the USA for £6.5 million. The firm was the biggest American cement manufacturer, involved in quarrying, ready-mixed concrete and concrete block-making activities. At the same time operations in Texas, which had previously been limited, were also expanded by the acquisition of a readymix concrete business in Dallas.

The growth of the company and changing environment led to a change in company structure in 1986. A significant feature of this change was that Tarmac USA was split from the Quarrying Divisions and developed as an independent profit-generating centre based on the potential USA market. This new division adopted similar strategic methods to those used in other parts of the company, in essence growth through acquisition and integration to develop a dominant market share.

Continuing its policy of developing a fully integrated construction organization Tarmac moved further up the value chain in its selection of target acquisitions in the late 1980s. In particular Tarmac acquired Crown House engineering who specialized in lighting, heating and air conditioning systems. The price was £26.4 million.

As stated in the 1985 company report this process fulfilled the Tarmac board's desire to offer a full set of services or products, from sand to brick, and from brick to housebuilding, and from housebuilding to interior settings.

Moves were also made during this period to diversify geographically into Europe. The acquisition of Ruberoid (for £10.6 million) which makes bricks indicates the beginning of this move while projects such as the Channel Tunnel facilitated the process. Primarily acquisitions in this period were focused on France and included companies such as the Sablieres dela Neste Group, Establissement Barriand S. A. and Establissements Hecquet, S. A. Further information concerning Tarmac can be obtained from appendix 8.

APPENDIX 1   MORTGAGE INTEREST RATE

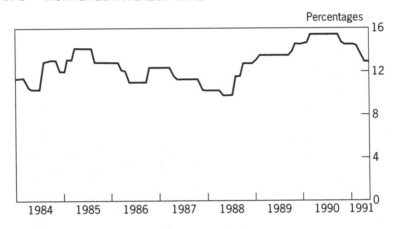

Mortgage interest rate
Source: Central Statistical Office.

APPENDIX 2   HOUSING PRICE TO EARNINGS RATIO

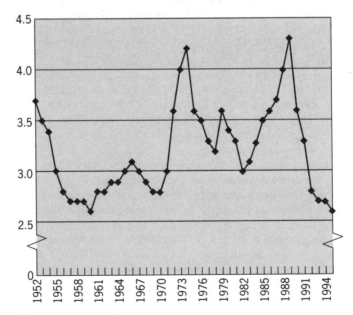

Ratio of house prices to average earnings

APPENDIX 3   LEADING UK MANUFACTURERS OF BRICK AND ROOF TILES

UHC	Operating subsidiaries	Products
Hanson plc	London Brick Co Ltd Butterley Brick Ltd ARC Ltd	Fletton bricks Non-fletton bricks Concrete blocks
Marley plc	Marley Roof Tile Co.Ltd Thermalite Ltd Thermalite Scot. Ltd Marley Paving Co Ltd Nottingham Brick plc Errol Brick Co. Ltd	Concrete and clay roof tiles Concrete blocks Concrete blocks Concrete block paving Facing bricks Facing bricks
Redland plc	Redland Roof Tiles Ltd Redland Bricks Ltd	Concrete & clay roof tiles & Cambrian interlocking slates Clay bricks, paving bricks
Ibstock Johnsen plc	Ibstock Building Products Ltd	Clay bricks and paving bricks
Tarmac plc	Tarmac Building Materials Ltd	Clay bricks and roof tiles; concrete blocks; brick paviours
Steetley plc	Steetley Building Products Ltd	Clay bricks and roof tiles concrete products, clay pavers
Baggeridge Brick plc		Clay bricks and paving bricks
Marshalls plc	Armitage Brick Ltd	Clay bricks and paving bricks
Christian Salvesen plc	Salvesen Brick Ltd W.H. Colliers Ltd	Clay bricks Clay bricks
Blockleys plc		Clay bricks and paviours

APPENDIX 4   DEMAND FOR BUILDING MATERIALS

Title	Source	Units	1985	1986	1987	1988	1989	1990	1991
Sand & gravel	1	Tonnes (m)		103.3	110.3	128.1	126.1	112.9	
Cement	1	Tonnes (m)		13.3	14.4	16.6	16.8	15.1	
Ready mix concrete (RMC)	1	metres^3(m)		21.5	24.3	28.8	29.6	26.8	
Bricks	1	millions		3971	4222	4682	4654	3804	
Clay roofing tiles	1	(1000 metre)^2	2143	2587	3019	3459	3756	3381	
Concrete roofing tiles	2	Dlrs. '000s	28.4	31.2	33.9	38.3	33.7		
Concrete building blocks	2	(1000 metre)^2	6204	7263	8083	9169	9000		

Source: Monthly statistics of *Building Materials and Components Business Monitor PAS 2410*, HMSO.

Title	Source	Units	1981	1982	1983	1984	1985	1986	1987	1988	1989	1990	1991
Bricks	1	£m	247.1	273.9	348.3	404.2	414.2	470.3	552.3	691.5	676.1	529.6	416.2
Clay roof tiles	1	£m	9.4	12.1	16.3	16.3	17.0	22.3	26.6	32.4	37.6	30.4	29.9
Cement/concrete blocks	1	£m	542.0	601.3	611.1	660.3	642.7	665.5	718.2	847.3	927.6	861.9	738.8

Source: Monthly statistics of Dept of Environment.

New dwellings completed 1977–90

1977	1977	1980	1983	1984	1985	1986	1987	1988	1989	1990
France		450900	502600	371800	343500	349800	356200	380600	414800	
Germany: East	106826	120209	122636	121657	99000	101000	91000	93500	83400	
Germany: West		409012	363094	312217	366816	252248	251940	217343	208334	268100
Spain		126101	130485	170147	176333	178190	193410	202600	222300	
United Kingdom	313500	251814	180065	203172	212172	208555	212448	225400	244939	212232

(000's)

	1977	1980	1982	1983	1984	1985	1986	1987	1988	1989	1990
Australia	45	78	80	97	117	111	141	121	135	160	155
New Zealand	24	14	16	18	20	22	23	20	19	22	
United States	1602	1137	1005	1390	1652	1703	1756	1668	1530	1422	1308

Building materials and components: production (GB)

	Unit	1977	1978	1979	1980	1981	1982	1983	1984	1985	1986	1987	1988	1989
Building bricks (excluding refractory and glaze)	Millions	5067	4842	4887	4562	3725	3517	3806	4012	4100	3971	4222	4682	4654
Crushed rock aggregates:														
Used as roadstone (coated)	Thousand tonnes	14374	13910	14413	14366	13179	17739	18562	17424	18188	19239	22599	28860	
Roadstone (uncoated)	"	35756	37807	41765	42896	35949	35259	38522	36660	41168	44185	50784	54187	
Fill and ballast	"	29227	31131	31722	31619	31049	37129	40416	42234	42426	45227	53411	59989	
Concrete aggregate	"	15259	15872	15588	13653	11205	12721	14582	14360	13214	13715	15443	17978	
Clay-roofing tiles	Thousand metres squared	1192	1207	2265	1698	1635	1632	2206	2051	2143	2587	3019	3459	

APPENDIX 6   MARLEY – BUILDING MATERIALS

Profit margins

Profit margin by activity (%)

	1983	1984	1985	1986	1987	1988	1989	1990	1991
Manufac. & distr. of building materials	11	11	6	9					
Other manufacturer	0	1	5	7					
Retailing & merchanting of building materials & home improvement products	4	5	5						
Other activities	59	25	21	4					
Roof tiles					8	9	7	4	6
Bricks, blocks & pavers					17	19	11	1	(4)
Plumbing, moulding & flooring	Company restructuring				10	11	11	10	12
Automotive components					10	6	3	2	2
Property					53	54	64	100	98
Other activities					5	3			

Profit margin by geographical area (%)

	1983	1984	1985	1986	1987	1988	1989	1990	1991
UK	8.0	9.2	8.4	8.3	11.4	13.9	10.3	3.3	3.1
Western Europe	2.8	6.3	2.8	4.9	8.4	10.7	11.1	17.7	16.8
Africa	8.3	13.1	8.3	10.6	10.1	9.9	11.3	7.8	15.5
North America	-0.7	-1.1	-0.7	6.8	10.9	10.4	10.2	2.9	4.0
Other markets	0.0	0.0	0.0	0.0	0.0	7.5	10.3	12.5	11.2

Sectoral/geographic breakdown (%)

Turnover by activity (%)

	1983	1984	1985	1986	1987	1988	1989	1990	1991
Manufac. & distr. of building materials	–	48	43	68					
Other manufacturer	10	12	14	9					
Retailing & merchanting of building materials & home improvement products	38	38	39	0					
Other activities	2	3	3	23					
Roof tiles					26	28	31	31	28
Bricks, blocks & pavers					25	28	29	25	21
Plumbing, moulding & flooring					21	23	25	30	38
Automative components					10	11	12	14	13
Property					1	3	3	1	1
Other activities					17	7	0	0	0

Company restructuring

Profit by activity (%)

	1983	1984	1985	1986	1987	1988	1989	1990	1991
Manufac. & distr. of building materials	(1)	66	40	80					
Other manufacturer		1	10	8					
Retailing & merchanting of building materials & home improvement products	20	25	26	0					
Other activities	16	8	10	12					
Roof tiles					18	19	21	21	25
Bricks, blocks & pavers					41	41	31	4	(13)
Plumbing, moulding & flooring					19	20	26	55	73
Automative components					9	5	3	5	3
Property					5	13	16	14	12
Other activities					8	2	3	0	0

Company restructuring

Turnover by geographical area (%)	1983	1984	1985	1986	1987	1988	1989	1990	1991
UK	63	63	66	57	60	67	65	61	57
Western Europe	15	14	14	19	14	9	9	10	13
Africa	8	10	7	9	8	8	8	9	9
North America	13	12	12	15	18	14	15	16	17
Other markets	1	1	1	1	1	2	4	5	4

Profit by geographical area (%)	1983	1984	1985	1986	1987	1988	1989	1990	1991
UK	84	74	86	62	64	74	64	36	28
Western Europe	7	11	6	12	11	7	9	33	33
Africa	11	17	9	12	8	6	9	13	22
North America	(2)	(2)	(1)	13	18	11	14	8	10
Other markets	0	0	0	0	0	1	4	11	7

Segmental information

	Turnover by origin		Operating profit		Net operating assets	
	1991 £m	1990 £m	1991 £m	1990 £m	1991 £m	1990 £m
Business activity						
Building components						
Roofing	158.1	195.6	9.4	7.5	78.4	93.3
Bricks, blocks and Pavers	119.0	157.5	(5.0)	1.5	120.2	124.1
Plumbing, Moulding and Flooring	219.5	193.8	27.0	19.3	85.0	86.1
Automative components	73.0	87.5	1.2	1.8	31.4	28.6
Property	4.7	5.1	4.6	5.1	8.7	7.1
	574.3	639.5	37.2	35.2	323.7	339.2
Unallocated non-operating assets and liabilities, net					(9.9)	(8.7)
Capital employed					313.8	330.5
Geographical areas						
United Kingdom	329.3	397.2	10.3	14.7	187.9	195.5
Western Europe	73.8	61.6	12.4	10.8	31.6	27.8
South Africa	52.2	55.4	8.1	3.9	18.8	16.1
North America	96.6	100.4	3.9	2.3	75.4	88.5
Other markets	22.4	24.9	2.5	3.5	10.0	11.3
	574.3	639.5	37.2	35.2	323.7	339.2

The figures for each geographical area show the net operating assets, turnover and operating profits of the companies located in that area; export sales and related profits are included in the area from which those sales were made.
Turnover by destination is not materially different from that shown above. Intra-group turnover between business segments and geographical areas is not significant.
The geographical analysis for 1990 has been restated on a comparable basis.

APPENDIX 6   MARLEY – ACQUISITIONS AND DISPOSALS

1979	Ingrid (USA) – houseware manufacturer (A)
1981	British Moulded Fibre Ltd – manufacturer of components for the automative industry (A)
1982	Klein Plastic Products (USA) – plastic hardware manufacturer (A)
1982	Furlong Bros – roofing manufacturers (A)
1983	Soltron (USA) – manufacturer and distributor of high quality small home appliances (A)
1983	Cochrane & Co. Pty (SA) – valve distributor (A)
1985	Plastic Consumer Products (Ingrid) (USA) – (D)
1985	Plumb Centre – leading supplier of plumbing products (D)
1985	Floorstyle–fixing service for contract flooring (D)
1985	Marleymix – supplier of dry bag concrete
1985	Payless – DIY chain (D)
1986	Thermalite – aerated concrete block manufacturer (A)
1986	General Shale – brick manufacturer (USA) (A)
1986	Nottingham Brick – (A)
1988	Webster Brick – (USA) (A)
1988	Errol Brick – (A)
1988	British Mouldings (NZ) – PVC cladding products (A)
1989	Carter Holt Harvet – plastic products (NZ) (A)
1990	DG Mouldings – plastic buildings materials (USA) (D)
1990	KKF Karl Fels – automotive components manufacturer (Germany) (A)
1991	Marley Roofing – (USA) (D)

A - acquisition   D - disposal

APPENDIX 7   REDLAND – BUILDING MATERIALS

Geographic performance

Results by region %	82–3	83–4	84–5	85–6	86–7	87–8	1988	1989	1990	1991
Sales										
UK	54.1	51.9	46.5	50.5	46.2	49.4	50.7	31.3	25.5	
Continental Europe	23.0	22.0	22.8	22.3	27.5	24.8	25.6	35.3	44.3	
USA	12.0	15.0	17.0	16.2	17.3	18.6	16.3	23.8	22.7	
Australia/Far East	9.0	9.0	11.4	9.3	7.8	6.4	6.5	8.7	7.0	
Other	2.0	2.0	2.3	1.7	1.2	0.8	0.8	1.0	0.5	
Profit (PBIT)										
UK			44.4	48.8	48.3	50.5	46.1	41.8	28.4	18.3
Continental Europe			31.6	24.8	30.8	27.8	29.7	31.0	46.3	61.3
USA			12.0	16.0	15.4	15.2	17.2	17.6	17.5	12.4
Australia/Far East			9.4	8.8	4.9	5.6	6.0	8.8	7.4	7.5
Other			2.6	1.6	0.7	1.0	0.9	0.8	0.4	0.5

Regional performance – margins

Results by region %	82–3	83–4	84–5	85–6	86–7	87–8	1988	1989	1990
UK	7.34	8.77	8.97	9.35	11.50	11.25	11.12	*22.52	17.42
Europe	8.23	11.49	13.02	10.76	12.29	12.30	14.16	14.80	16.39
USA	11.02	6.18	6.60	9.57	9.78	8.98	12.90	12.50	12.09
Australia/Far East	13.68	7.48	7.75	9.17	6.93	9.57	11.29	17.16	16.52
Other	19.04	20.80	10.34	9.09	6.25	14.20	12.50	13.33	12.50

*

APPENDIX 7 continued

Product performance

Results by product %	85–6	86–7	87–8	1988	1989	1990	1991
Sales							
Roofings				35.2	45.2	51.0	69.4
Aggregates				27.1	38.1	35.4	24.2
Bricks and other				37.7	16.7	13.6	6.5
Profit (PBIT)							
Roofings		42.0	39.8	41.6	41.5	54.1	
Aggregates		31.5	31.9	36.8	38.5	29.2	
Bricks and other		26.6	28.3	21.6	20.0	16.7	

Product performance – margins

Results by product %	1988	1989	1990
Roofing	14.3	15.5	16.6
Aggregates	16.5	17.0	12.9
Bricks & other	7.00	20.1	19.3

Redland changed accounting year in 1988 such that figures for 1988 are for nine months.

Segment information

	Year ended 31.12.91			Year ended 31.12.90		
	Turnover £ million	Operating profit £ million	Net assets £ million	Turnover £ million	Operating profit £ million	Net assets £ million
Roofing	868.7	128.9	546.6	836.1	139.1	493.2
Aggregates	507.1	45.0	766.5	581.3	75.0	750.0
Bricks and other	127.8	12.4	209.1	222.5	42.9	197.8
	1,503.6	186.3	1,522.2	1,639.9	257.0	1,441.0

APPENDIX 7 continued

Geographical analysis of turnover, operating profit and net assets

	Year ended 31.12.91			Year ended 31.12.90		
	Turnover £ million	Operating profit £ million	Net assets £ million	Turnover £ million	Operating profit £ million	Net assets £ million
United Kingdom	326.6	34.1	435.2	419.0	72.8	418.1
Germany	437.0	85.8	204.9	373.2	71.5	168.4
Other continental European countries	300.8	28.5	262.3	352.7	47.6	257.5
United States of America	318.0	23.8	517.1	371.6	45.2	495.8
Australasia and the Far East	112.3	13.6	100.8	115.1	19.3	99.2
Other	8.9	0.5	1.9	8.3	0.6	2.0
	1,503.6	186.3	1,522.2	1,639.9	257.0	1,441.0

Net assets are defined as total assets less current liabilities excluding short term investments and bank loans and overdrafts.

Acquisitions and divestments since 1978

Date	Acq./div.	Country	Company	Products
1979	A	UK	Automated Building Components	Fastenings; timber roof, wall and floor trusses; mobile home structures
1979	A	USA	Season – All Industries	Aluminium replacement windows and storm doors
1980–1	D	UK	Redland Industrial Services	Waste disposal; industrial cleaning business
1981–2	D	SA	Ghaist Redland	
	D	UK	Redland Automation	
	A	UK	Hafad Gritstone	Quarry
	A	Aust.	Rocla Industries	Quarry; RMC
1982–3	A	UK	Cawoods Holdings	Coal and oil distribution
	D	UK	Cawoods Refractories	
	D	UK	Cawoods Concrete Products	
	A	UK	Stourbridge Brick	Brick
	A	USA	McDonough Bros	Quarry
	A	USA	Manco Prestress	Prestressed concrete
	A	NL	Delta Brick	Brick
	A	NL	Ruga Beheer	Bricks

Year	A/D	Country	Company	Product
1983–4	A	UK	Shaws Fuels	Oil distribution
	A	USA	Waco RMC	RMC
1984–5	D	USA	Season All Industries	Window systems
	D	UK	Redland Reinforced Plastics	Pipe Mftrs
	D	UK	Redland Claddings	Slate sheeting
	A	UK	Birtley Brick	Clay bricks
	A	UK	Rosemary Brick and Tile	Bricks and tiles
	A	NL	Mosa	Wall and floor tiles
	A	NL	Teewen Poviso	Bricks
	A	NL	Decostone	Kitchen linos
1985–6	A	UK	Tilbury Roadstone	Quarry
	A	USA	Downy Bros	Quarry
	D	UK	Redland Prismo	Road surfacing
1986–7	A	UK	Lone Star Petroleum	Fuel distribution
	A	France	La Sabliers d'Igoville	Quarry
	A	US	Genstar Stone	Aggregate
	A	US	Bernath Concrete	Concrete
1987–8	A	UK	Astbury Quarries	Quarry
	A	Italy	Asfath Bretner	Flatroof products
	A (45%)	Norway	Norgips A/S	Plasterboard
	A	Aust/NZ	Monnier	Roof tiles
	A	Ireland	Iberian Trading	Plasterboard
	A	Aust.	Synkoloid	Plasterboard
	D	UK	D.H. Jones	Fuel distribution
	D	US	Gang-Nail Systems	Fastenings
1988–9	A	SWE	Orebro Kartongbruk	Plasterboard
	A	US	Malaney Concrete	Concrete
	A	UK	ARC Roof Tiles	Roof tiles
	A	US	Albuquerque Materials	Coatings
	A	US	Arundel Asphalt	Asphalt
	A	France	Escogypse	Plasterboard
	D (5%)	Ger.	Braas	
	D (55%)	UK	British Fuels	Fuel distribution

APPENDIX 8   TARMAC – BUILDING MATERIALS

Divisional sales and profits

Turnover	1979	1980	1981	1982	1983	1984	1985	1986	1987	1988	1989	1990
Divisions												
Quarry	28.7%	28.0%	28.8%	35.0%	35.7%	37.1%	38.4%	22.1%	19.0%	17.1%	16.6%	17.1%
Building	14.6%	14.7%	18.2%	19.4%	17.0%	15.0%	13.4%	4.7%	4.6%	4.8%	4.1%	3.4%
Construction	35.2%	35.6%	29.2%	23.4%	26.0%	23.6%	23.2%	23.7%	24.2%	24.1%	26.1%	32.0%
International	8.5%	7.4%	8.0%	5.0%								
Housing	10.1%	11.9%	12.7%	13.5%	15.0%	16.1%	19.2%	24.5%	25.4%	27.7%	26.1%	23.0%
Properties	1.0%	0.5%	0.8%	1.6%	1.7%	2.8%	1.6%	1.2%	1.6%	2.5%	2.1%	1.4%
Industrial & oil	1.8%	1.9%	2.3%	2.0%	4.6%	5.3%	4.2%	14.7%	13.4%	13.0%	14.0%	13.9%
Tarmac USA								9.1%	11.7%	10.7%	11.1%	9.1%
Total (%)	100.0%	100.0%	100.0%	100.0%	100.0%	100.0%	100.0%	100.0%	100.0%	100.0%	100.0%	100.0%
Total (1990 £m)	1900.7	1700.0	1555.9	1634.4	1732.1	1887.4	2122.4	2238.6	2714.5	3241.6	3721.8	3606.9

Profit	1979	1980	1981	1982	1983	1984	1985	1986	1987	1988	1989	1990
Divisions												
Quarry	46.2%	41.9%	41.1%	52.3%	51.8%	52.8%	53.8%	32.3%	24.9%	20.0%	22.1%	29.0%
Building	21.0%	25.0%	23.1%	17.4%	9.4%	9.9%	9.6%	5.3%	5.6%	5.9%	6.5%	6.2%
Construction	2.1%	7.5%	6.9%	6.4%	8.6%	7.3%	6.0%	6.5%	6.6%	5.4%	6.8%	14.5%
International	2.1%	-1.6%	2.7%	3.5%								
Housing	20.4%	18.5%	16.9%	13.5%	16.4%	19.0%	21.6%	31.6%	35.5%	48.6%	40.4%	24.4%
Properties	4.2%	2.4%	3.2%	1.9%	1.7%	2.1%	1.8%	2.3%	2.3%	3.5%	4.7%	4.6%
Industrial & oil	4.0%	6.3%	6.1%	4.9%	12.1%	8.9%	7.2%	10.8%	8.8%	6.8%	9.9%	13.8%
Tarmac USA								11.3%	16.2%	9.7%	9.6%	7.5%
Total (%)	100.0%	100.0%	100.0%	100.0%	100.0%	100.0%	100.0%	100.0%	100.0%	100.0%	100.0%	100.0%
Total (1990 £M)	102.3	104.8	102.4	120.2	142.7	176.9	211.8	242.8	340.3	481.0	471.5	259.0

Segment analysis 1990–1991

	Turnover					
	1991			1990		
	Total £m	Intersegment £m	External £m	Total £m	Intersegment £m	External £m
Business segment						
Quarry products	572.8	(25.6)	547.2	619.7	(31.0)	588.7
Housing	744.6	-	744.6	851.9	-	851.9
Construction	1,123.1	(38.5)	1,084.6	1,198.6	(19.1)	1,179.5
Building materials	120.0	(4.0)	116.0	131.9	(5.6)	126.3
Industrial products	460.1	(21.8)	438.3	504.7	(22.7)	482.0
Properties	21.0	-	21.0	43.4	-	43.4
Tarmac America	273.4	-	273.4	334.8	-	334.8
	3,315.0	(89.9)	3,225.1	2,685.0	(78.4)	3,606.6
Country of origin						
UK			2,751.3			3,101.4
USA			305.9			357.1
Europe			156.6			139.1
Other			11.3			9.0
			3,225.1			3,606.6

The analysis of turnover by geographical market is not materially different from that by geographical origin.

	Profit before interest and exceptional items		Net assets	
	1991 £m	1990 £m	1991 £m	1990 £m
Business segment				
Quarry products	52.9	80.0	729.2	790.2
Housing	37.3	67.3	449.6	580.5
Construction	40.8	40.0	(72.7)	(68.6)
Building materials	1.5	17.0	164.1	155.7
Industrial products	13.8	38.0	136.9	146.0
Properties	(11.0)	12.7	74.0	70.4
Tarmac America	(10.2)	20.8	481.1	566.6
Central costs and liabilities	(8.1)	(8.7)	(40.5)	(20.6)
	117.0	267.1	1,921.7	2,220.2
Unallocated net liabilities			(538.1)	(606.8)
			1,383.6	1,613.4
Country of origin				
UK	132.4	248.5	1,342.6	1,560.0
USA	(14.4)	17.5	515.2	600.7
Europe	4.7	9.5	108.6	80.8
Other	2.4	0.3	(4.2)	(0.7)
Central costs and liabilities	(8.1)	(8.7)	(40.5)	(20.6)
	117.0	267.1	1,921.7	2,220.2
Unallocated net liabilities			(538.1)	(606.8)
			1,383.6	1,613.4

Sales by region

Year	1979	1980	1981	1982	1983	1984	1985	1986	1987	1988	1989	1990
Area												
UK	81.76%	85.67%	82.77%	84.31%	85.95%	85.94%	83.18%	83.17%	80.93%	84.26%	83.58%	84.92%
USA						5.44%	9.53%	9.33%	11.97%	11.51%	11.84%	9.79%
Europe	7.64%	4.70%	5.58%			4.41%	4.12%	4.82%	4.01%	3.31%	4.14%	4.75%
Others	10.60%	9.63%	11.65%	15.69%	14.05%	4.22%	3.17%	2.68%	3.10%	0.93%	0.44%	0.54%
Total	100%	100%	100%	100%	100%	100%	100%	100%	100%	100%	100%	100%

APPENDIX 9 BUILDING MATERIALS

Marley plc

FT group: Building materials
Market capitalization (£000): 270,011
Price at B/S date (pence): 96.0
Nominal value: 25p

Year ended	Dec 31 1987	Dec 31 1988	Dec 31 1989	Dec 31 1990	Dec 31 1991
Profit & loss account (£000)					
Turnover	565,686	600,322	638,400	639,500	574,300
Prof bef int & tax	64,046	80,018	69,700	39,400	42,100
Profit before tax	55,241	70,222	56,200	22,000	27,000
Attrib to members	37,834	46,818	41,800	13,100	15,200
Preference dividends	17	17	0	0	0
Ordinary dividends	12,749	16,452	17,400	17,600	17,600
Av no of employees	10,876	10,681	11,041	11,077	10,119
Wages & salaries	121,634	125,447	140,000	142,700	132,600
Balance sheet (£000)					
Ordinary capital	68,981	69,162	69,300	69,800	70,200
Shareholders' funds	213,867	234,706	263,800	218,600	219,600
Net capital employed	308,052	347,072	375,100	354,700	366,900
Current assets	166,882	210,008	212,000	205,000	229,000
Current liabilities	128,904	163,023	161,100	141,800	172,500
Total assets	415,025	476,272	495,800	475,200	488,400
Total loans	78,296	91,715	97,800	125,700	139,200
Intangibles	0	430	400	1,600	2,500
Performance ratios					
ROCE %	20.0	26.0	20.1	10.5	11.9
Profit margin %	11.3	13.3	10.9	6.2	7.3
Gearing ratio	26.9	28.2	27.1	36.6	38.9
Earnings yield %	11.10	13.14	13.20	4.07	4.22
Dividend yield %	4.43	5.20	6.42	7.00	6.09
P/E ratio	10.84	9.62	8.74	43.21	37.07
Growth % per annum					
Total assets	1.19	14.76	4.10	(4.15)	2.78
Turnover	1.63	6.12	6.34	0.17	(10.20)
Profit before tax	61.72	27.12	(19.97)	(60.85)	22.73
Ordinary share record (pence)					
Net asset value	77.4	84.7	95.0	78.1	78.0
EPS (gross max)	16.88	21.41	17.43	4.93	5.86
Gross dividends	6.73	8.47	8.47	8.47	8.47
Dividend cover	2.5	2.5	2.1	0.6	0.7
Net cash flow	17.7	19.7	19.0	9.2	9.8
Share price range (pence) – year ended December 31					
	1987	1988	1989	1990	1991
High	196.0	185.5	192.0	150.0	137.0
Low	110.0	127.0	113.0	82.0	87.0

Redland plc

FT group: Building materials
Market capitalization (£000): 1,486,826
Price at B/S date (pence): 437.5
Nominal value: 25p ord

Year ended	Mar 26 1988	Dec 31 1988ᵃ	Dec 31 1989	Dec 31 1990	Dec 31 1991
Profit & loss account (£000)					
Turnover	1,4250	1,502.3	1,309.8	1,411.5	1,299.2
Prof bef int & tax	206.9	220.6	276.2	291.7	236.6
Profit before tax	184.5	197.5	245.1	244.4	186.0
Attrib to members	116.2	127.1	162.9	143.2	97.0
Preference dividends	0.0	0.0	0.0	0.0	0.0
Ordinary dividends	43.3	54.3	64.3	69.8	84.9
Av no of employees	17,027	20,029	18,025	17,853	16,060
Wages & salaries	215.3	243.3	274.7	295.3	279.0
Balance sheet (£000)					
Ordinary capital	68.0	68.4	68.8	69.0	85.0
Shareholders' funds	512.4	615.5	723.6	763.0	1,032.3
Net capital employed	1,123.1	1,383.0	1,829.3	1,652.2	1,887.9
Current assets	520.4	479.2	709.0	682.6	976.8
Current liabilities	356.7	388.2	428.0	392.3	488.2
Total assets	1,463.7	1,747.6	2,236.0	2,016.6	2,347.0
Total loans	446.5	623.0	801.5	578.1	576.9
Intangibles	0.0	0.0	8.2	14.3	20.9
Performance ratios					
ROCE %	19.9	19.6	20.0	15.9	14.3
Profit margin %	14.5	14.7	21.1	20.7	18.2
Gearing ratio	41.8	46.6	45.3	36.3	30.9
Earnings yield %	10.90	10.15	11.58	10.13	5.70
Dividiend yield %	4.68	4.55	5.53	5.70	5.93
P/E ratio	10.60	12.91	9.82	11.53	24.16
Growth % per annum					
Total assets	14.49	19.40	27.95	(9.81)	16.38
Turnover	45.54	5.42	(12.81)	7.76	(7.96)
Profit before tax	41.27	7.05	24.10	(0.29)	(23.90)
Ordinary share record (pence)					
Net asset value	182.8	218.8	255.5	268.4	303.8
EPS (gross max)	48.18	57.21ᵇ	63.38	57.55	32.01
Gross dividends	20.72	25.66ᵇ	30.25	32.39	33.33
Dividend cover	2.3	2.2	2.1	1.8	1.0
Net cash flow	42.8	43.9	55.3	47.8	24.7

Share price range (pence) – year ended December 31

	1987	1988	1989	1990	1991
High	559.8	438.3	621.0	623.0	658.0
Low	338.2	373.2	403.3	525.8	416.0

ᵃ 9 months
ᵇ Based on 12 months to December 31.

Tarmac plc

FT group: Building materials
Market capitalization (£000): 845,142
Price at B/S date (pence): 116.0
Nominal value: 50p ord

Year ended	Dec 31 1987	Dec 31 1988	Dec 31 1989	Dec 31 1990	Dec 31 1991
Profit & loss account (£000)					
Turnover	2,163	2,754	3,409	3,607	3,225
Prof bef int & tax	281	424	445	263	94
Profit before tax	258	391	371	183	31
Attrib to members	161	243	229	117	14
Preference dividends	a	a	0	3	11
Ordinary dividends	52	72	81	82	40
Av no of employees	28,031	28,928	32,073	34,876	31,734
Wages & salaries	287	329	419	485	475
Balance sheet (£000)					
Ordinary capital	356	359	361	364	364
Shareholders' funds	711	794	1,419	1,600	1,374
Net capital employed	1,159	1,448	2,191	2,194	2,054
Current assets	950	1,396	1,647	1,583	1,427
Current liabilities	601	858	1,042	968	818
Total assets	1,720	2,297	3,214	3,146	2,845
Total loans	261	403	504	481	543
Intangibles	0	0	0	0	0
Performance ratios					
ROCE %	37.0	36.6	30.8	12.0	4.3
Profit margin %	13.0	15.4	13.1	7.3	2.9
Gearing ratio	24.7	30.9	24.6	23.0	28.3
Earnings yield %	12.15	12.72	17.51	8.42	0.30
Dividiend yield %	3.92	3.73	6.22	6.15	4.95
P/E ratio	10.91	10.48	7.59	15.51	14800.00
Growth % per annum					
Total assets	42.84	33.54	39.90	(2.12)	(9.58)
Turnover	25.89	27.32	23.79	5.79	(10.58)
Profit before tax	53.72	51.41	(5.02)	(50.75)	(83.04)
Ordinary share record (pence)					
Net asset value	99.9	110.6	196.8	219.9	188.3
EPS (gross max)	30.23	45.40	42.20	20.55	0.44
Gross dividends	9.74	13.33	15.00	15.00	7.33
Dividend cover	3.1	3.4	2.8	1.4	0.1
Net cash flow	22.2	31.7	29.3	13.8	4.5

Share price range (pence) – year ended December 31	1987	1988	1989	1990	1991
High	350.0	267.0	378.0	289.0	283.0
Low	187.0	204.0	208.8	186.0	95.0

Source: Extel Handbook of Market Leaders.

INTRODUCTION

Redland's results for 1993 turned out to be ahead of expectations, largely due to growth in Germany, the strength of the recovery in the United States and the upturn in new housing in the United Kingdom. This followed several years of recession and depression in the construction industry. During 1993 the company strengthened its position in the roofing markets of the Far East and had opened its first factory in China. In March 1991 Redland announced the formation of a joint venture with Stresnik Industria Gradbenega Materials of Yugoslavia. Through its German partner Braas Co GmbH, Redland acquired a 50.69 per cent stake in the venture while Stresnik took 39.62 per cent and SGP Kograd Dravograd Prodjetje, another Yugoslavian company, acquired a 9.69 per cent holding. This venture followed closely on the heels of the acquisition of West Germany's leading prefabricated chimney manufacturer, Schiedel, for £30 million.

Such moves were typical of Redland. From 1949 the firm had grown largely through the formation of alliances, in no less than 35 different countries, spanning Australia and the Far East, the United States, Europe and the Middle East. On the question of this approach to international expansion Redland's chairman, Sir Colin Corness, stressed the importance of evaluating and planning such ventures through consultation with potential partners. He stated that it would be difficult 'trying to manage all our joint ventures from the UK – there would not be time to sleep'.[1] Implicit in his feelings was the recognition of the necessity to work with people from different countries, where there would be different norms of behaviour and different business practices.

The nature of the products of the construction and building materials industry is such that exporting is not a viable option. This is due to the weight/value ratio of the products and also because of the local and regional traditions in using certain kinds of materials. In this sense the industry is not a global industry as is often the case with multinational companies.

GROWTH AND DEVELOPMENT

During the 1930s Redland had pioneered a process of extruding concrete roof tiles through a continuously moving machine. This replaced the previous system, whereby the cement and sand mixture was simply pressed into shape using

Case study prepared at the University of Huddersfield by Brian Kenny and Edward Lea.
© 1995 B Kenny and E C Lea.

TABLE 1 Redland Performance 1961–1970 (rounded figures)

Year	Turnover (£mn)	Pre-tax profit (£mn)	Return on capital employed (%)
1961	11.5	2.5	25
1962	15.0	2.8	32
1963	25.0	3.0	18
1964	32.0	4.8	26
1965	38.0	5.1	27
1966	44.0	5.0	20
1967	45.1	5.1	15
1968	45.6	6.5	19
1969	46.8	6.0	14
1970	51.3	5.2	12

wooden moulds. Following the end of World War 2, when the demand for building materials was very heavy, the company embarked upon an expansion strategy which involved joint ventures in the Far East and South Africa and, in the early 1950s, West Germany. Redland technology, based on the original extrusion process, was central to these and subsequent similar joint ventures, even into the 1990s. Appendix 1 provides some information on the process.

Between 1960 and 1965 the expansion and diversification programme had proved very successful. Pre-tax profits had more than doubled and return on capital employed remained healthy. Between 1966 and 1970 however, performance deteriorated, exacerbated by the effects of recession in the late 1960s (See table 1 and appendix 3 provides further financial information on Redland.)

In 1971 Lord Beeching, formerly head of British Railways, the UK's state-owned railway system, became Chairman of Redland for just one year. He took over from Alex Young who had headed the company for 40 years and who then became a non-executive director. In the previous three years the two other main architects of Redland, Tony White and Harold Carter, had stepped down. In his first statement to shareholders Lord Beeching summed up his new strategy for the group by pointing to the limitations of the domestic market and the opportunities for overseas growth. He referred to the scope for development and that the 'necessity to finance their growth by loans and retained profits prevents them from making the same cash contribution as successful development at home'.[2]

At the end of 1971 Redland's pre-tax profit had risen to over £7 million on a turnover of over £65 million and a return on assets of over 19 per cent. During this year turnover and profits from the group's overseas subsidiaries were £23.5 million and £3.6 million respectively.

Although Redland's profits continued to rise in 1973 the group's waste treatment and disposal offshoot Redland-Purle (acquired at the end of 1971 for £16.8 million), made no contribution following extensive write-offs. At 100p on a price-earnings ratio of 9.25, the market appeared to take little account of Redland's strength in overseas earnings. For example, profits from Germany were up by two-thirds over 1972 and dwelling completions for 1973 in that country were forecast to rise to 725,000 from 660,000 in 1972.

By 1980 Redland was firmly established as a major company in the international building materials market. Indeed in 1980 the UK contribution to pre-tax profits (26 per cent) was considered the weakest area in its broadly based geographical spread of markets. Total pre-tax profits amounted to £57.3 million on a turnover of £397 million and net debt to shareholders' funds stood at 20.5 per cent. During the 1979–80 recession the drastic cuts in UK public expenditure coupled with sustained high interest rates depressed capital investment in buildings of all types. Chairman Colin Corness referred to the British Government's preference for sacrificing long-term investment in the infrastructure of the country by noting the 'drastic cuts in public expenditure at both central and local levels coinciding with exceptional and sustained high interest rates'.[3]

At the end of 1980 Redland sold off its waste disposal business, Redland-Purle, which was at that time the largest private sector waste operator in the United Kingdom. The contribution from Purle during 1980 was estimated to be £3.25 million in pre-tax profit on a turnover of £28 million, with a net book value of £15 million. Following the £20 million cash sale, Colin Corness commented that he had never been completely comfortable with a business which was prone to throwing unpleasant surprises.

By 1981 continental Europe accounted for 51 per cent of Redland's profits and 39 per cent of sales. The North American profit contribution had fallen from 6 to 2 per cent and Monier (Australia) provided 13 per cent. Overall, pre-tax profit had declined to £45.6 million from £57.3 million in 1980 and the UK market had continued its decline. However, in spite of the poor prospects in the UK, the company saw the need for further acquisitions in Britain; particularly in view of a tax system which discriminated against overseas earnings by not allowing tax paid to be set against advanced corporation tax (ACT) liability. Colin Corness commented that this meant there was 'a strong case for supplementing our flat UK earnings with acquired profits, attracting mainstream UK Corporation Tax as an offset to ACT'.[4]

In 1982 Redland made a £138 million offer for Cawoods, a quarry owner and fuel distributor with interests in offshore oil. It was agreed that the oil interests would be offered back to the Cawood shareholders for £21 million. This took Redland into the unfamiliar area of fuel (coal) distribution, although the concrete and aggregates operations made a geographic fit. The combined market shares did not exceed the monopoly barriers in either industry and thus there were no obvious monopolies and merger competition problems. At the end of 1986 Cawoods was merged with the British Fuel Company (which was jointly owned by British Coal and AAH Holdings). The resulting venture, named British Fuels, was managed by Redland with a 55 per cent share, AAH with 25 per cent and British Coal with 20 per cent. Redland's Financial Director indicated that the new group would enjoy a broader geographical spread, a better product mix and that there would be benefits from being a larger force in the market.

Within 18 months Redland had sold its holding in British Fuels to a management buy-out in which British Coal retained a significant stake. An exceptionally mild winter in the UK during 1987 caused British Fuel profits to fall by some 9 per cent. By 1989 Redland's exposure to the UK housing construction market represented only 10 per cent of group profits. The company had grown to be the world's biggest manufacturer of roof tiles and the fourth biggest brick maker; it had also become number two in the manufacture of plasterboard. In tiles it had captured 60 per cent of the UK market while Braas, its West German associate, had a 56 per cent market share in West Germany. The company was also the biggest producer of roof tiles in the United States, where it had 11 plants. Table 2 shows Redland's principal activities as at the end of 1990.

During the period 1990 to 1993 further acquisitions and disposals were made, although there were largely confined to Europe.

TABLE 2 Redland principal activities at the end of 1990

Company	Partner	Product(s)	Stake	Year
Vereeniging Tile (South Africa)	Vereeniging Brick & Tile	Roof tiles and bricks	Initially 49%	1949 Sold in 1989
Braas (Germany)*	Various	Roofing products	12% rising to 50.8%	1954
Redland-Braas-Vadero (Netherlands)	Bredero (until 1986)	Roof tiles	55% rising to 100%	1963
Societe Francaise Redland (France)	St Gobain	Roof tiles	42.7%	1966
Redland Iberica (Spain & Portugal)	Uralita	Roof tiles	47%	1972
Zanda (Sweden & Norway)	Euroc	Roof tiles	49%	1974
Several in the Middle East	Various	Ready mixed concrete	40/49%	1976–80
Western-Mobile (USA)	Koppers (until 1988)	Aggregates	505 rising to 100%	1986
Redland Plasterboard (Europe)	CSR	Plasterboard	51% falling to 20%	1987
Monier PGH	CSR	Roof tiles, bricks and pavers	49%	1988

* Since 1954 Redland had obtained, through Braas, a presence in Austria, Italy, Denmark, Hungary and East Germany.

- In March 1992 Redland acquired Steetley, the UK-based construction materials group, for £62 million.
- At the end of the same year, the company sold off the assets of Steetley's refactory (bricks) business and its clay roof tile business (the latter as a result of an undertaking given to the UK Secretary of State for Trade and Industry).
- In March 1993 Redland sold the whole of the issued share capital of Steetley Iberia, the Spanish-based aggregates and ready-mixed concrete business, for cash.

By the end of 1993 the group's various interests had extended to China where it had installed a concrete plant in Guangzhou. Redland had an 80 per cent shareholding in partnership with the local authority and had contributed US$4 million worth of equipment and services. Plans for a second plant near Shanghai were also well in hand. (See appendix 2 for further details of subsidiary companies as at 1993.)

REDLAND AND BRAAS (GERMANY)

Redland's entry into the German market had begun in 1954 when a joint venture was established with entrepreneur Rudolph Braas. The latter had built up a substantial business repairing and rebuilding war-damaged homes and Redland had provided the machinery and the technical expertise during the early days of Braas' operations.

As far back as 1971 the European contribution to Redland's profits under Braas amounted to some 40 per cent of the total. Despite the usual cyclical fluctuations suffered by the construction sector, Braas continued to be a major success story for Redland and the importance of this early entry into western Europe proved to be instrumental in the group's expansion into eastern Europe. This growth was helped by acquisitions and joint ventures managed through Braas and involved some level of diversification away from Redland's core business of roof tiles. For example, in 1971 Braas acquired a German company which produced plastic sheet and film for the cladding of flat and low-pitch roofs. The rationale behind this was the tendency for high-rise accommodation developments in Germany and eastern Europe, which precluded the need for roof-tiles.

The chairman of Braas, Erich Gerlach, helped lead the Yugoslavian deal among other notable ventures. In 1990 he was instrumental in the acquisition of four out of five former state-owned East German tile plants for a price of DM25 million. Braas planned to produce up to 100 million tiles a year with just 320 workers working 39 hours a week in two shifts a day. Previously, the plants had employed a total of 690 workers working 42 hours a week three shifts a day producing 60 million tiles a year.

Of the original workforce about 150 workers were considered to be bureaucrats and not managers in the western sense. Cash-flow and other financial controls were virtually non-existent and output was determined by how many houses the state had decided to build or repair and 'upon the ability of raw material producers to keep the company supplied and the availability of transport to deliver the finished product'.[5] Braas was also quick to change the way these plants were run. Outdated British and German equipment, some of it more than 20 years old, was replaced. Bonus schemes linked to achievement of targets were introduced and computers were installed at the east German headquarters in a move to improve efficiency in order processing and accounting.

A major problem in eastern Germany was the recruitment of salesmen. Because plants had never had to sell their produce, there was no concept of marketing or indeed, the need to market. Other West German companies were already exporting roofing materials to eastern Germany and over half of all roofing sales in 1990 were supplied by these companies. Sales from east German plants were some 20 per cent only of their 1980 figure. It was considered by Redland that East Germany could eventually contribute about 30 per cent of Braas' sales and profits.

REDLAND AND LAFARGE COPPEE

Lafarge Coppee, France's largest cement producer (second largest in the world), and one of the world's leading producers of construction materials, first approached Redland in the middle of 1990. The French group was keen to expand its plaster-board activities and to challenge British Gypsum (part of BPB Industries), one of only three plasterboard manufacturers active in the UK. Plasterboard is a dry, easily-handled material generally used for internal house walls but increasingly being adapted to use in the construction of commercial property.

Redland's existing stake in the plasterboard industry was via a 51 per cent 49 per cent joint venture with CSR of Australia. CSR subsequently withdrew from the scene on payment of £16 million and a LaFarge (80 per cent)/Redland (20 per cent) joint venture was formed. For its 80 per cent holding, Lafarge paid £39 million and with Redland's £16 million payment, the £55 million total accounted for CSR's original 49 per cent holding in the plasterboard operation.

This venture significantly changed the balance of power in one of Europe's building materials market segments. Lafarge became Europe's second largest producer of plasterboard, reducing the gap between itself and BPB. Production capacity of plasterboard was distributed between BPB (44 per cent), Lafarge/Redland (30 per cent), Knauf of West Germany (20 per cent) and other producers (6 per cent).

Lafarge had four plasterboard plants in France and also had operations in Spain in partnership with Uralita. BPB also had interests in Spain with a 65 per cent interest in Inveryeso, the country's biggest plaster company. The two companies were also competing fiercely in Italy, where Lafarge had a 20 million square metre plant near Pescara and where BPB was also building a new plant. Redland was considered a good geographical fit by Lafarge. The former had a 45 per cent shareholding in Norgrips covering Scandinavia and had plants in the Netherlands.

The Joint Managing Director of Lafarge expected the European plasterboard market to grow by an average of 5 per cent a year over the period 1990–5. Scandinavia, like the US, had by 1990, already switched from traditional plastering techniques and in the major markets of France, West Germany and the UK, plasterboard had displaced traditional plaster. In southern Europe, however, the substitution had hardly begun.

With UK demand at little more than half the total production capacity of 315 million square metres, it was expected that 1991 would be a difficult year. However, the group was planning to make its presence known by reducing costs and improving service to customers served by the Redland plant at Bristol. In December 1992, Redland sold its 20 per cent holding to Lafarge for cash, although the 1992 company report showed a net loss as a result of the transaction.

REDLAND AND AUSTRALIA

In April 1987 Redland bid for the balance of the shares it did not already hold in the Australian-based roof, tile and building materials group, Monier Ltd. At the time Redland held 49.9 per cent of the shares in Monier and the bid for the remaining 50.1 per cent was initially estimated to cost in the region of AUS$250.5 million (£112.3 million), at a price of AUS$3.14 per share.

CSR, the Australian building products, resources and sugar group, then offered AUS$3.50 per share for the balance of 50.1 per cent of Monier and at the end of April 1987, Monier agreed to accept an increased offer from CSR of AUS$3.80 per share. The increased offer had largely resulted from Redland's rejection (as a major Monier shareholder) of CSR's original offer. It was subsequently agreed between the two companies to run Monier as a joint venture.

Redland's Finance Director had said that the agreement was based on genuine compatability of the two companies' aims in the building materials industry but that it was the intention to keep Monier as an independent jointly-owned company. The decision to retain an interest in Monier was an indication that Redland believed that Australia was an attractive market and that with Monier's 100 per cent ownership of activities in the US this would give scope for further expansion in the latter.

During this period of bid, counter-bid and negotiation, Equiticorp Tasman, an acquisitive, diversified New Zealand group, had taken a 4 per cent stake in CSR and announced its intention of bidding for Monier. Subsequently, Redland increased its stake in Monier to 50.1 per cent, making Monier a subsidiary of Redland. Nevertheless Equiticorp Tasman succeeded in securing an initial 33.8 per cent shareholding in Monier rising by the end of 1987 to 48 per cent. Following negotiations Redland and Equiticorp agreed to split Monier in such a way that Equiticorp bought Redland's stake for AUS$320 million and Redland paid AUS$298 million to buy back the tile business. At the end of June 1987 Monier had a turnover of AUS$727 million and pre-tax profit of AUS$45 million. Roofing tiles contributed AUS$295 million of sales and AUS$45 million of pre-tax profit.

At the end of 1988, CSR, which had been overtaken by Equiticorp in its bid for Monier, entered into a joint venture with Redland. CSR bought the bricks and pipe businesses of BTR Nylex and this was merged with Monier Redland roofing operations. The benefits of the merger included common administration and accounting systems, pooled management and the ability to push two important products through one distribution channel.

In addition, CSR took over management of the brick and tile business and had access to technologies developed by Redland for fixing up old brick kilns by increasing their output or enhancing them to make premium (or higher-value-added) bricks.

Together Redland and CSR had in 1987 set up a joint venture in Bristol, UK, to manufacture plasterboard and a new plant, producing some 35 million square metres of plasterboard a year. Redland had moved into plasterboard because of the long-term growth pattern in the market. In only a year of operation Redland/CSR gained some 15 per cent of the UK market which was previously dominated by BPB and to a lesser extent by West Germany's Knauf Group.

In spite of growth predictions the plasterboard market was not an easy one. As the lowest cost producer, BPB responded to the new entrants by price cutting which caused losses for the Redland/CSR joint venture.

REDLAND AND THE UNITED STATES

Redland interests in the United States were added to indirectly, through its venture with Monier of Australia in the early 1970s. Monier had already invested in the US market by the time of the joint venture, on the basis that concrete roof tiles had yet to achieve wide-scale adoption in that market. In 1968 Redland acquired US Prismo Universal Corporation's highway-making business and successive losses from that company were turned into a £130,000 profit in 1973.

During the period 1980 to 1981 recession had hit the US construction industry and profit contribution from this area dropped from 6 per cent to 2 per cent, while the strength of sterling and the impact of high interest rates further diminished performance. Redland increased its US interests at the end of 1982 through the acquisition of 80 per cent of the Texas quarry group Boston Industries for $70.4 million (nearly £44 million). Boston operated two limestone deposits; one with 100 million tons of reserves similar to Redland's Leicester-based quarry in the UK, and the other with 500 million tons. Total annual sales of the quarries amounted to $40 million and output was estimated to double by the late 1980s. Besides limestone aggregate for use with cement, the Boston operation also produced and marketed lime, ready-mixed concrete and other products.

Redland at this time also controlled seven other American companies involved in road making, traffic control and roofing products. However it was considered that no integration with Boston was planned as none of the three companies was Texas-based and many had suffered severely from the effects of recession.

In January 1985, faced with construction cuts and sluggish demand for its sand, gravel and stone at home, Redland again turned to the US for further growth through acquisition. David Taylor, who was Redland's Director of the company's aggregate activities, pointed to the 30 per cent decline in UK demand for aggregates over the past decade and the need to develop other markets. During this period other UK companies were actively involved in developing US interests. Tarmac had purchased the Florida quarries of US cement company Lone Star for $79.3 million and both RMC and ARC cement companies were actively seeking aggregate companies.

A year after David Taylor's signalled intentions, Redland entered into a partnership with US insurance company USSA, to develop 800 acres of land in San Antonio, Texas. The residential and commercial project was estimated to take several years on land which was originally earmarked for quarrying stone. Ownership was split 49.3 per cent to Redland, 34.5 per cent to USSA and the remainder to a third party.

In September 1986, Redland formed a joint venture with Pittsburgh-based construction materials company, Koppers. The company paid £24 million for a 50 per cent holding in the new jointly-owned company Western-Mobile. This resulted in the acquisition of aggregate company MPM – operating in Colorado and New Mexico – and Western Paving, which shipped construction aggregates in Colorado, Kansas and Wyoming and was also a road surfacer. The acquisition gave quarries, gravel pits and readymix plants a complete, backed-up road surfacing operation. Redland's management pointed out that 'Koppers management of Western Paving is now going to be the management of the Western-Mobile joint venture, so we are confident there is scope for improving the performance of MPM where we will be able to cut back the loss-making operation'.[6]

Within a week of sealing the Koppers venture, Redland had acquired Maryland-based quarrying company Genstar Stone for US$317.5 million (£220 million), from the Imasco Corporation of Canada. Genstar was described by Redland as a 'high quality aggregates business with all the characteristics we now know to look for of a large proven reserve economically located to serve a buoyant market'. Genstar's operating profits had grown from $11 million in 1981 to US$30 million in 1985 and

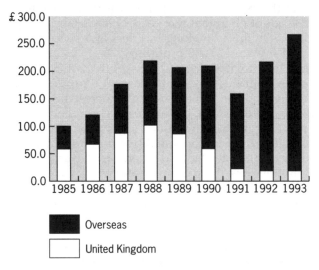

FIGURE 1   Redland plc operating profits 1985 to 1993

in the seven months to July 1986, it was US$1 million ahead of the comparative period.

The acquisition gave Redland nine aggregates production sites with total estimated reserves of more than 1.5 billion tons – enough for more than 40 years production. (The main market for aggregates in the US was in road construction valued at US$3.96 billion a year and spending on roads in Maryland alone was running at US$500 million a year.)

As a consequence of its developments overseas, by 1993 the major proportion of Redland's profits came from its overseas investments as shown in figure 1.

MANAGEMENT, ORGANIZATION AND PLANNING

The senior management at Redland paid very close attention to the detail of their various activities around the world and concentrated their effort upon the identification of growth markets based on both geography and product. They considered that the two main driving forces of interest to their businesses were economic welfare, expressed through Gross Domestic Product growth, and people, expressed through demographic change. Such information was considered to be vital to the company. Appendix 4 shows information on geographic, demographic and economic comparative indicators.

In terms of objectives, the company was concerned to maintain real growth in earnings per share and continually compared their performance against competitors in the construction and building materials industry. They understood the value and the role of the financial institutions and maintained very close contact with them. To assist in this they monitored very closely the performance of their competitors in the sector of building materials as they saw them not only as industrial competitors but also competitors in the financial markets. Tables 3 and 4 show share price information from the building materials sector on two dates.

Since the mid 1970s Redland's joint venture strategy had been based on a perceived need to reduce the risks associated with going into a foreign country, untried and uninformed. When setting up a venture Redland would agree with its partner to make particular key decisions jointly and such decisions would generally include:

TABLE 3 *Financial Times*, 26 April 1991 when the FT-SE 100 = 2488

High	Low	Name	Price	Yield gross	P/E
286	198	Blue Circle	246	6.3	9.7
749	594	RMC	644	4.0	11.5
658	503	Redland	569	5.9	11.3
190	135	Rugby Group	155	5.5	10.4
283	216	Tarmac	242	6.4	14.0

TABLE 4 *Financial Times*, early 1994 when the FT-SE 100 = 3234

High	Low	Name	Price	Yield gross	P/E
391	262	Blue Circle	307	4.6	25.8
1079	805	RMC	960	2.7	27.1
640	466	Redland	537	5.8	28.1
185	125	Rugby Group	145	2.9	19.6
206	135	Tarmac	153	4.5	13.6

- the investment of capital above a pre-defined limit;
- entry into new product areas or territories;
- approval of the annual accounts;
- agreement on the distribution of dividends; and
- the appointment of senior management.

These were considered in essence to be the basis of an 'equal' partnership, irrespective of Redland's majority shareholding. The arrangements on dividend payments were normally that, unless otherwise agreed, 50 per cent of the annual net-of-tax profits would be distributed to the partners, pro rata their share in the company. This 'investor orientation' is also reflected in the group's obligation to protect shareholders' income against the effects of inflation by increasing the payments accordingly. Although the use of equity funding for acquisitions was not barred, it would not be used if it affected the planned dividend growth. Generally, the group would look for a company 'where we can apply executive skills which will exploit our high liquidity and low gearing'.[7]

Certain city observers had come to describe Redland as a 'nice' company with regard to its preference for joint ventures rather than aggressive takeovers. Colin (by then Sir Colin) Corness, however, was quick to point out the rationale behind the strategy by asserting that Redland's niceness didn't stem from an antipathy in principle towards hostile takeovers 'but rather from the force of circumstance . . . we don't depend on growth through acquisition . . . because we would be liable to regulatory constraints . . . we are looking for a large number of small acquisitions (worldwide)'.[8]

Prior to Lord Beeching taking over as Chairman of Redland in 1970 the management organization had evolved as a kind of pear-shaped structure. At the top (thin) end were three influential directors, Tony White, Alex Young and Harold Curter, whose style of management was both autocratic and entrepreneurial. Each of seven UK operating divisions had its own board of directors and these were visited every so often by the 'powerful triumvirate'. In essence, Redland was little more than a federation of companies which had been acquired over a decade or more. Typically, the managers of these companies had built up their businesses to the size which suited their managerial talents.

By the middle of 1971 there were two boards at the UK head office in Reigate, Surrey. The main board dealt with the statutory formalities such as dividend policy and the appointment of directors, and there was also the management board or group management committee. The management board had two tiers, the top level comprising the Chairman Lord Beeching, Managing Director Colin Corness and Finance Director, Terry Dawson. The rest of the management board comprised the heads of the operating divisions, which replaced the previous subsidiary board structures. However, it was considered by the management that further structure changes would be necessary in a move towards establishing a board with a greater concentration of people whose interests were company wide.

In June 1990 Redland appointed three chairmen to head its core businesses. Kevin Abbott, aged 36, at 'Roof tiles', George Phillipson, 51, at 'Aggregates' and Peter Johnson, 42, at 'Bricks'. All three had been board directors since April 1988. George Phillipson and Peter Johnson were previously managing directors of their businesses and Kevin Abbott was Chief Executive of Roof tiles. These three were not young by Redland standards; for example, Colin Corness had taken over as Managing Director of Redland in 1967 at the age of 35 and had masterminded the group's overseas growth success. His attention to detail was well known and it was said he would put as much effort into correct phrasing of a paragraph in the annual report as to a multi-million pound deal. He was considered a part of the 'establishment' on doing things in their proper manner. This included ensuring that fellow directors were smartly turned out at company occasions, including board meetings. Nonetheless, he was respected by most who knew him and just as important, liked by them also. In the words of an adviser 'he is the model of what a British industrialist should be'.[9]

In 1991, Robert Napier aged 46, Managing Director since 1987, was appointed Chief Executive. He was also a director of United Biscuits (Holdings) plc. Planning had always been an important function at Redland and this was handled by a small group in the planning team of up to five people out of the headquarters staff of 48. The planning process involved all of the Redland companies worldwide, the chief executives of these companies following agreement of the plan with the local board, presented their annual plans to the group management committee. Following agreement with the group management committee the plans were approved by the board of Redland in order that the budget preparations for the next financial year could take place.

The planners were responsible for preparing scenarios which would help the company take a view of how and why developments might take place which would affect the company. Part of this process included use of sophisticated forecasting methods which drew upon available national models and Redland's own in-house expertise. In addition the planning team were responsible for a monthly economic progress report which could cover as many as 30 countries.

ORGANIZATION FOR CORPORATE GOVERNANCE

The Redland board usually met nine times a year to review trading and key business decisions. Substantial executive authority was delegated by the board to a committee of the board called the group committee, consisting of the executive directors, the Chairman of the Board of Management, Braas, and D. R. W. Young, Group Director of Human Resources. The board had reserved the power to approve all main issues, including the approval of group strategic plans and budgets.

The audit committee was formally constituted with written terms of reference and was chaired by a non-executive director. It comprised five non-executive directors. This committee met with the Chief Executive, the Financial Director and the external and internal auditors. The external auditors attended part of each audit committee meeting without the executive directors for independent discussions. The audit committee reviewed the annual accounts and the interim and preliminary announcements prior to submission to the board, compliance with accounting standards, the scope and extent of the external audit programme, reports from the internal audit function and the appointment and remuneration of the auditors. The Chairman of the audit committee reported to the board on matters discussed at the audit committee meeting.

The senior appointments and compensation committee approved the terms of employment of executive directors and determined their remuneration, including share options. The committee also monitored the performance of the Chief Executive and, together with the Chief Executive, of the other executive directors. The appointment of all directors of the company was made by the board through a formal process after considering the proposals of the senior appointments and compensation committee.

NOTES

1   *Acquisition Monthly*, December 1990, p. 56.
2   *Times Business News*, 24 May 1971.
3   *Financial Weekly*, 22 August 1980.
4   *Yorkshire Post*, 28 August 1981.
5   *Financial Times*, 16 January 1991.
6   *Financial Times*, 25 September 1986.
7   *Financial Weekly*, 3 July 1981.
8   *Financial Weekly*, 10 August 1989.
9   *The Independent*, 6 August 1990.

APPENDIX 1

Growth of Tile Manufacture Based on Extrusion Process

Although concrete tiles of a sort had existed since the 1840s the process was really pioneered by Redland after the first world war. Marley started production at about the same time and also very close geographically to Redland.

Concrete tiles were initially made by hand, in plain tile form, and there was no patent cover available to either company at this stage. Even so, the handmade product was very competitive against slate and clay. From the outset the handmade concrete tile possessed its characteristic benefits over other materials:

- dimensional accuracy;
- wider colour range;
- price advantage;
- better technical performance through higher strength, lower weight and much better frost resistance; and
- geographic scope, due to more widely available raw materials, to make concrete tiles anywhere justified by the market.

Concrete tile making started in south east England where the clays are technically inferior to the Staffordshire (Etruria) clays. To this advantage was added the extrusion process, developed for plain tile making prior to the second world war. There was still no patent cover at this stage.

With its considerable production cost advantage, concrete started to gain share strongly against slate and clay, both of which remained manual processes before the second world war. The moulding of clay tile was notably less efficient than the extrusion process used for concrete. After the second world war came the first development of an interlocking concrete tile in the form of Redland's '49' tile (in 1949). This was a major step, although the concept of an interlocking design was already established in the clay tile market. Moreover, the concrete tile enjoyed the protection afforded by registration of the design. Marley followed with its own interlocking ranges, modified in shape and detail to avoid infringement of Redland's rights.

By this stage, the interlocking concrete tile had become a very efficient way of covering a roof through the use of a single layer of accurate and low cost tiles.

International Growth

The concrete tile market expanded rapidly from this point. In 1950, Redland introduced *Double Roman*, still the most popular model in the UK and elsewhere. This was followed in the early 1950s by *Renown, Regent* and other models. The expansion was based on offering wide choice of colour, shape and profile. It therefore provided a new concept of roof design to architects.

Throughout, Redland combined a strong business strategy with the developing technology. The success of the early 1950s therefore led to new UK plants and to overseas licensing of the process. This was highly opportune timing given the need to rebuild postwar Europe. The alliance with Braas (1954) was a key building block in Redland's international growth and a precursor to others in France (Saint Gobain) and elsewhere.

Technology, Competitive Advantage and Ease of Copying

Technical process details are only available to joint venture licensees. These benefit from technology in which:

- product design is optimized both for processing and end performance;
- extrusion provides speed and accuracy of tile forming;
- effectively a continuous process is used. It is the tile forming which is the 'clever' aspect;
- highly developed expertise in formulation again balances processing characteristics and end performance.

It is true to say that the process is relatively easy to copy. It is fairly straightforward and is patented only as to specific areas of the plant. However, design protection always exists and it is difficult for competitors to achieve Redland's high levels of efficiency. Redland has always managed to maintain its innovative and marketing edge. It has also stayed more closely focused on concrete tile as opposed to derivative businesses.

APPENDIX 2

Principal operating companies (1993)

	Principal activities	% beneficial interest in equity
United Kingdom		
Redland Aggregates Limited, Leicester	Sand and gravel, stone quarrying, road surfacing materials, road surfacing, burnt products and concrete products	100
Redland Bricks Limited, Staffordshire	Clay bricks	100
Redland Distribution Limited, Nottinghamshire	Road transportation services	100
Redland of Northern Ireland, Limited, Co. Antrim	Concrete roof tiles, pipes and bricks, and sand and lime mortar	100
Redland Properties Limited*, Surrey	Property management	100
Redland Readymix Limited, Leicester	Ready-mixed concrete	100
Redland Roof Tiles Limited, Surrey	Concrete and clay roof tiles and Cambrian interlocking slates	100
Redland Technologies Limited, West Sussex	Research and development and engineering services	100
Ready Mixed Concrete (Eastern Counties), Essex	Ready-mixed concrete	50
Redland Magnesia Limited, Cleveland	Magnesia products	100
Redland Minerals Limited, Nottinghamshire	Industrial minerals	100
Continental Europe		
Austria		
Bramac Dachsteinwek GmbH, Pöchlarn	Concrete and clay roof tiles	25.4
Schiedel Kaminwerke GmbH, Wartburg	Prefabricated chimney systems	50.8
Belgium		
RBB NV, tessenderlo	Concrete roof tiles	50
Redland Koramic Bricks, NV, Westmalle	Clay bricks	50
Denmark		
BC Danmark A/S, Middelrup	Concrete roof tiles	50.8
Dan Tegl Tag A/S, Aalborg	Clay roof tiles	50.8
France		
Redland Granulats SA, Rungis Cedex	Sand and gravel, stone quarrying, ready-mixed concrete, road surfacing and road surfacing materials	100
Coverland SA, Malmaison Cedex	Concrete and clay roof tiles	66.7

APPENDIX 2 *continued*

	Principal activities	% beneficial interest in equity
Germany		
Braas GmbH, Oberursel	Concrete roof tiles, flat roofing membranes and plastic products for the construction industry	50.8
RuppKeramik GmbH, Buchen-Hainstadt	Clay roof tiles	50.8
Schiedel GmbH Co, Murich	Prefabricated chimney systems	50.8
Hungary		
Bramac Kft., Veszprém	Concrete roof tiles	14.5
Italy		
Braas Italia S.p.A., Chieres	Concrete and clay roof tiles and flat roofing products	50.8
Netherlands		
Redland Dakprodukten 3V	Concrete and clay roof tiles	100
Norway		
Zanda A/S, Slemmestad	Concrete roof tiles	50.8
Portugal		
Lusoceram-Empreendimentos Ceramicos SA, Lisbon	Clay roof tiles and clay blocks	4
Spain		
Redland Ibérica SA, Madrid	Concrete roof tiles	47
Industrias Transformadoras del Cemento Eternit SA, Madrid	Concrete and clay roof tiles	47
Sweden		
Zanda AB, Sennan	Concrete roof tiles	50.8
Vittinge Tegel AB, Morgongäva	Clay roof tiles	50.8
Switzerland		
Braas Schweiz AG, Villmergen	Concrete roof tiles	50.8
North America		
Canada		
Redland Quarries Inc., Ontario	Stone quarrying, road surfacing materials and calcined dolomite	100
United States of America		
Genstar Stone Products Company, Maryland	Stone quarrying, sand and gravel, road surfacing materials, road surfacing, ready-mixed concrete and calcium carbonate products	100
Monier Inc., California	Concrete and clay roof tiles	100
Redland Brick Inc., Maryland	Clay bricks	100

APPENDIX 2 *continued*

	Principal activities	*% beneficial interest in equity*
Redland Stone Products Company, Texas	Stone quarrying, sand and gravel, road surfacing materials, ready-mixed concrete and burnt lime	100
Western Mobile Inc., Colorado	Stone quarrying, sand and gravel, road surfacing materials, road surfacing and ready-mixed concrete	100
Australasia and the Far East		
Australia and New Zeland		
Monier PGH Limited, NSW	Concrete and clay roof tiles, clay bricks, pavers and pipes	49
China		
Sanshui Redland Building Materials Co. Ltd, Guangzhou, Indonesia	Concrete roof tiles	80
PT Monier Indonesia, Jakarta	Concrete roof tiles	60
Japan		
Nippon Monier Co. Ltd, Osaka	Concrete roof tiles	60
Malaysia and Singapore		
CI Holdings Berhad, Kuala Lumpur	Concrete roof tiles, concrete paving, taps and road surfacing materials	25.7
Thailand		
CPAC Roof Tile Co. Limited, Bangkok	Concrete roof tiles	24.8
Middle East		
Bahrain		
Delmon Ready Mixed Concrete Products Co. WLL and Delmon Precast Co. WLL, Manama	Ready-mixed concrete and precast concrete	49
Oman		
Readymix Muscat LLC and Premix LLC, Ruwi	Ready-mixed concrete	40
Qatar		
Readymix Qatar WLL and The Qatar Quarry Co. Ltd, Doha	Ready-mixed concrete and stone quarrying	49 and 25 (respectively)
Saudi Arabia		
Qanbar Steetley (Saudi) Limited, Dammam	Ready-mixed concrete	50
United Arab Emirates		
Readymix Gulf Limited, Sharjah	Ready-mixed concrete	40

* Shares of these undertakings are held directly by the parent company. Otherwise shares are held by subsidiary undertakings. Beneficial interest is identical to voting rights.

APPENDIX 3

Redland plc profit & loss account

Year ending 31 December	1992 (£ million)	1993 (£ million)
Turnover (including share of associates)	2,089.9	2,473.7
Group share of sales of associates	(199.7)	(257.4)
Turnover	1,890.2	2,216.3
Cost of sales	(1,300.6)	(1,543.9)
Distribution costs	(230.1)	(255.1)
Gross profit	359.5	417.3
Administration expenses	(140.1)	(147.2)
Group share of profits of associates	14.8	34.0
Operating profit	234.2	304.1
Profit on disposals of properties	13.7	8.9
Profit on disposal of businesses		2.7
Loss on disposal of an investment in an associate	(22.5)	
Interest payable net	(26.4)	(36.8)
Profit on ordinary activities before tax	199.0	278.9
Tax on profit of ordinary activities	(62.4)	(85.0)
Profit on ordinary activities after tax	136.6	193.9
Minority interests	(48.4)	(59.3)
Preferred stock dividends	(5.7)	(5.9)
Attributable profit	82.5	128.7
Dividends	(111.2)	(128.1)
Retained profit (loss)	(28.7)	0.6
Earnings per share (p)	18.6	26.1
Adjustment for the loss on the disposal of an investment (p)	5.1	
Adjusted earnings per share (p)	23.7	26.1
Dividends per share (p)	25.0	25.0

APPENDIX 3 *continued*

Redland plc balance sheet

As at 31 December 1993	Group	
	1992 (£ million)	1993 (£ million)
Fixed assets		
Tangible assets	2,103.9	2,043.4
Investments	157.5	156.0
	2,261.4	2,199.4
Current assets		
Stocks	293.5	259.2
Debtors–due within one year	518.3	503.0
Debtors–due after more than one year	79.2	52.9
Short term investments	271.5	284.3
	1,162.5	1,099.4
Creditors–due within one year		
Short term borrowing	(340.5)	(176.8)
Trade and other creditors	(531.3)	(540.8)
Corporate taxation	(51.3)	(98.7)
Dividends	(80.3)	(86.5)
	(1,003.4)	(902.8)
Net current assets	159.1	196.6
Total assets less current liabilities	2,420.5	2,396.0
Creditors – due after more than one year		
Loans	(557.7)	(456.7)
Convertible bonds - subordinated	(34.5)	(34.5)
Other creditors	(74.9)	(91.0)
Provisions for liabilities and charges	(161.0)	(135.5)
	1,592.4	1,678.3
Shareholders funds		
Capital & reserves		
Called up ordinary share capital	119.8	128.8
Share premium account	556.8	555.0
Revaluation reserve	176.3	176.5
Other reserve	169.1	169.1
Profit and loss account	220.4	258.5
Ordinary shareholders funds	1,242.4	1,287.9
Minority equity interests	184.5	221.4
Preferred stock	165.5	168.9
	1,592.4	1,678.2

APPENDIX 3 *continued*

Redland plc Segment information

Turnover, operating profit and net assets by class of business (£ million)

	Year ended 1992			Year ended 1993		
	Turnover	Operating profit	Net assets	Turnover	Operating profit	Net assets
Roofing	1,011.5	161.1	716.7	1,247.1	213.7	762.6
Aggregates	824.0	50.9	1,419.0	975.1	65.1	1,320.5
Bricks and other	254.4	22.2	353.8	251.5	25.3	205.4
Total*	2,089.9	234.2	2,489.5	2,473.7	304.1	2,288.5

Geographical analysis

	Year ended 1992			Year ended 1993		
	Turnover	Operating profit	Net assets	Turnover	Operating profit	Net assets
United Kingdom	498.1	24.8	710.6	497.7	22.8	581.8
France	262.1	7.2	352.3	374.2	8.2	364.7
Germany	522.6	114.5	281.9	625.0	150.3	291.7
Other European	305.5	46.7	248.4	309.6	47.1	166.5
North America	371.1	26.7	773.6	498.0	54.5	743.0
Australasia & Far East	117.3	13.2	119.9	148.2	17.7	135.2
Other	13.2	1.1	2.8	21.0	3.5	5.6
Total*	2,089.9	234.2	2,489.5	2,473.7	304.1	2,288.5

* The slight discrepancy in total assets compared with the balance sheet is due to minority interests.

APPENDIX 3 continued

Redland plc nine year financial review

£ millions	Year ending								
	1985	1986	1987	1988	1989	1990	1991	1992	1993
Sales									
United Kingdom	285.8	328.2	358.6	456.0	470.1	409.2	318.1	488.0	485.6
Overseas	355.3	417.1	623.4	809.2	839.7	1,002.3	981.1	1,402.2	1,730.7
Group share of associates	291.2	288.6	290.6	128.3	237.7	228.4	204.4	199.7	257.4
Fuel distribution (sold in 1988)	359.3	266.1	527.4	505.6					
Total sales	1,291.6	1,300.0	1,800.0	1,899.1	1,547.5	1,639.9	1,503.6	2,089.9	2,473.7
Profit									
United Kingdom	60.6	68.7	88.8	104.8	88.8	61.1	27.9	24.6	22.9
Overseas	40.3	51.7	89.1	115.6	119.8	150.6	136.0	194.8	247.2
Group share of associates	23.8	23.4	18.3	10.7	32.7	28.7	14.7	14.8	34.0
Operating profit	124.7	143.8	196.2	231.1	241.3	240.4	178.6	234.2	304.1
Profit on disposal of properties					18.6	16.6	7.7	13.7	8.9
Profit/(losses) on disposal of businesses						(10.6)			2.7
(Losses) on the disposal of an investment in an associate								(22.5)	
Net interest payable	(11.9)	(13.1)	(11.1)	(9.6)	(9.7)	(12.0)	(0.3)	(26.4)	(36.8)
Profit before tax	112.8	130.7	185.1	221.5	250.2	234.4	186.0	199.0	278.9
Tax and minorities	(44.6)	(50.1)	(68.3)	(79.2)	(82.2)	(90.6)	(80.9)	(110.8)	(144.3)
Profit after tax	68.2	80.6	116.8	142.3	168.0	143.8	105.1	88.2	134.6
Preferred stock dividends						(9.9)	(8.1)	(5.7)	(5.9)
Attributable profit	68.2	80.6	116.8	142.3	168.0	133.9	97.0	82.5	128.7
Fixed assets	na	na	na	na	1,184.9	1,286.6	1,317.0	2,261.4	2,199.4
Current assets	na	na	na	na	760.0	744.3	1,050.9	1,162.5	1,099.4
Creditors (less than 1 year)	na	na	na	na	(482.0)	(392.3)	(488.2)	(1,003.4)	(902.8)
Net current assets	na	na	na	na	332.0	352.0	562.7	159.1	196.6
Total assets minus current liabilities	554.5	888.7	902.5	1,000.8	1,516.9	1,638.6	1,879.7	2,420.5	2,396.0
Creditors (more than 1 year)	na	na	na	na	541.0	611.4	566.1	828.1	717.7
Shareholders' funds	na	na	na	na	975.9	1,027.2	1,313.6	1,592.4	1,678.3
Ordinary shares (million)	na	na	na	na	274.5	251.7	323.3	443.5	493.1

APPENDIX 4

Note on the European Construction Industry

(Extracted from *Review of Construction Markets in Europe*, EIC 1994, by kind permission of the publishers).

- The total value of construction output in 1992 was about 820 billion ECUs. About 70 per cent is in the European union, 14 per cent in western Europe excluding the union and 16 per cent in eastern and central Europe.
- Within the union the united Germany is the largest construction market, being 80 per cent larger than that of France and nearly three times that of the UK.
- In eastern and central Europe Russia dominates the area in terms of population, land area, GNP and construction output. The Ukraine and Poland are the next most important countries.
- Most countries with construction output per capita below 1,000 ECUs have growth potential.
- Average construction output as a percentage of GNP is similar in the three broad areas considered at between 11 and 14 per cent. In 1989 in eastern and central Europe it was much higher. Within areas there is considerable variation.
- GNP per capita in the European union is about five times that in eastern and central Europe. Construction output per capita is about four times as high.
- Cement consumption per volume of construction work in eastern and central Europe is at least double that in western Europe, Portugal and Turkey also have very high usage.

Comparative indicators (geographic, demographic and economic) in 1992

Countries	Population (million)	Land area (thousand sq km)	Population density (people per sq km)	GNP (billion ECU)
European Union				
Belgium	10.0	31.0	322.6	172.2
Denmark	5.2	43.0	120.9	110.1
France	57.4	552.0	104.0	1,020.0
Germany	80.6	357.0	225.8	1,359.9
Greece	10.3	132.0	78.0	60.2
Ireland	3.6	70.0	51.4	34.6
Italy	56.9	301.0	189.0	946.7
Luxembourg	0.4	3.0	133.3	8.2
Netherlands	15.2	37.0	410.8	248.1
Portugal	10.6	92.0	115.2	65.1
Spain	39.0	505.0	77.2	443.3
UK	57.7	245.0	235.5	806.3
Total	346.9	2,368.0	2,063.7	5,274.7

APPENDIX 4 *continued*

Western Europe excluding European Union

Austria	7.9	84.0	94.0	106.7
Cyprus	0.7	9.0	77.8	5.2
Finland	5.1	338.0	15.1	79.3
Norway	4.3	324.0	13.3	72.7
Sweden	8.7	450.0	19.3	190.8
Switzerland	6.8	41.0	165.9	194.1
Turkey	58.6	779.0	76.2	201.7
Total	92.1	2,025.0	461.6	850.5
All Western Europe				
	439.0	4,393.0	99.9	6,125.2

Construction Output 1989 to 1992

Countries	Total value of output at 1992 prices (billion ECU)			
	1989	1990	1991	1992
European Union				
Belgium	18.4	19.6	20.1	20.9
Denmark	14.0	13.4	12.2	12.1
France	97.0	99.4	99.7	96.7
Germany	127.3	133.7	138.4	146.0
Ireland	3.9	4.6	4.5	4.5
Italy	96.7	99.2	100.6	101.9
Netherlands	26.2	26.4	25.9	26.7
Portugal	7.7	8.2	8.5	8.7
Spain	53.6	58.4	60.8	57.1
UK	71.4	72.9	67.7	64.7
Total	516.2	535.8	538.4	539.3
Western Europe excluding European Union				
Austria	21.5	22.8	24.1	25.2
Finland	15.1	15.1	13.0	10.8
Norway	11.2	10.1	9.6	9.5
Sweden	28.2	29.0	27.8	25.8
Switzerland	28.9	29.0	27.4	26.8
Total	104.9	106.0	101.9	98.1
All Western Europe				
	621.1	641.8	640.3	637.4

APPENDIX 4 continued

Comparative indicators (construction industry) in 1992.

Countries	Construction output as % of GNP	Construction output per capita (ECU)	Construction output per sq km (thousand ECU)	Number of dwellings built (thousands)	Number of dwellings built per 1,000 population	Cement consumption (thousand tonnes)	Cement consumption per million ECU's of output (tonnes)
European Union							
Belgium	12.1	2,090	674	46.0	4.6	5,070	243
Denmark	11.0	2,327	281	16.0	3.1	1,280	106
France	9.5	1,685	175	299.0	5.2	21,634	224
Germany	12.9	2,180	492	na	na	43,800	249
Greece	13.1	767	60	na	na	7,700	975
Ireland	13.0	1,250	64	22.5	6.3	1,448	322
Italy	10.8	1,791	339	277.6	4.9	44,520	437
Luxembourg	12.2	2,500	333	2.7	6.8	688	688
Netherlands	10.8	1,757	722	86.2	5.7	5,000	187
Portugal	13.4	821	95	65.0	6.1	7,538	872
Spain	12.9	1,464	113	222.9	5.6	26,051	456
UK	8.0	1,121	264	169.6	2.9	10,940	169
Total	11.0	1,666	244	1,207.5	3.5	175,669	304
Western Europe excluding European Union							
Austria	23.6	3,190	300	41.0	5.2	4,916	195
Cyprus	17.5	1,286	100	7.8	11.1	950	1,056
Finland	13.6	2,118	32	37.0	7.3	1,200	111
Norway	13.1	2,209	29	17.8	4.1	1,151	121
Sweden	13.5	2,966	57	57.3	6.6	2,100	81
Switzerland	13.8	3,941	654	35.4	5.2	4,234	158
Turkey	9.0	311	23	232.0	4.0	22,870	1,257
Total	13.8	1,273	58	428.3	4.6	37,421	319
All Western Europe	11.3	1,583	158.0	1,635.8	3.7	213,135	307

In early 1995 Ann Iverson became the Chief Executive of Laura Ashley. She had recently completed a period of four years with the Storehouse group and was generally credited with turning around the performance of Mothercare, one of the retail chains in the group. Her immediate aim at Laura Ashley was to instill what she called 'basic retail focus and discipline ... I am a specialist at identifying strategy and preparing a diagnosis for a company – anything from a major reposition to just putting a company back on track'. The previous Chief Executive (Dr Jim Maxmin) left in May 1994 following policy disagreements with the board.

There was a big task facing Ann Iverson, for the company had suffered from five years of restructuring and management upheavals. Even in the early 1990s Laura Ashley – in common with other retailers of clothing in the UK – had felt the effects of the long recession which had begun in 1989. Unlike many other retailers, however, Laura Ashley had created a significant international base. In 1992 over 60 per cent of its shops were outside the UK.

In terms of competition Laura Ashley was unusually positioned in that it was, exceptionally for a clothing retailer, vertically integrated in manufacturing, and still unusual but less so, involved in furnishings. In the UK Next and Principles were probably the closest competitors. In global terms it was difficult to identify a competitor, though there was national competition wherever Laura Ashley operated. Vertically integrated retailers were not unknown in international markets and examples included Benetton, BATA, IKEA and Stefanel. In such retailers the supply chain ran from raw material procurement to production of the finished products to retailing while control was retained throughout.

For the financial year ending January 1995 Laura Ashley reported its largest ever loss before tax. (See appendix 1 for financial and other information. This was not the first loss and it inevitably affected its share price. In 1987, two years after the company was floated on the Stock Exchange, the share price had reached a peak of 213 pence but subsequently fell to a low of 44 pence. In the early part of 1995 the share price hovered around 80 pence (See figure 1). Appendix 2 provides information on the Laura Ashley share price and the performance of the FT-Se 100 index.

BACKGROUND

The business had been started by Bernard and Laura Ashley in Pimlico, London in 1953 when they had begun by designing and printing tea-towels and scarves which

Case study written by Professor Edward Lea at the University of Huddersfield for the purposes of class discussion. Copyright © 1995, E C Lea.

they sold to department stores. They expanded their product range to include furnishing and dress fabrics based on their own designs and the success of these led them to establish production facilities in Wales in 1967.

They believed they could expand faster by opening their own retail outlets and the first of these was in South Kensington, London, supported by poster advertising in the London Underground showing the distinctive Laura Ashley designs. The success of this enabled them within two years to withdraw from the department store channels and concentrate on their own retail outlets. In this way the basic structure of Laura Ashley as a vertically-integrated design, production and retail organization was established.

By the mid 1980s Laura Ashley was already operating across four continents with production facilities in both Wales and Holland, and it was decided to launch the company publicly by selling 25 per cent of the shares. This was undertaken in November 1985 raising £23 million of new capital for the company with 70 per cent of the employers worldwide participating to become shareholders.

Company objectives up to 1985, while the company was owned virtually 100 per cent by the Ashley family and Ashley family trusts, were related to steady, stable growth in size and profits to ensure a background record for a successful flotation. Following flotation in December 1985 at a price of 140 pence the objectives were related more towards successful financial performance as expressed in earnings per share. This was encouraged by the introduction of performance-related share option

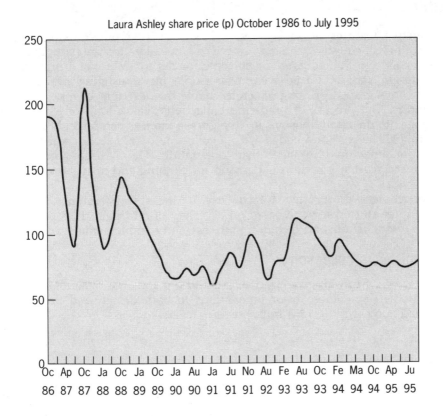

FIGURE 1   Laura Ashley share price

schemes for senior executives. This meant that the share price became more important. Information on this is shown in figure 1, the Laura Ashley share price for the period October 1986 to July 1995. Following flotation the share price had risen rapidly but soon fell and remained consistently low. Companies with publicly quoted share prices are always reluctant to see their share price fall relative to others. It can be monitored by logging the company share price along with those it considers to be its competitors, or with one of the stock exchange indices. Appendix 2 shows the Laura Ashley share price and the performance of the FT-SE 100 index over the period.

In terms of product range strategy Laura Ashley had become best known for its prints in feminine designs targeted on the under-30s woman, but as well as expanding to furnishings, ceramics and wallpaper it had also considered other clothing ranges, for example by test marketing a range of baby clothes, and had considered men's shirts. Childrenswear (up to age 12) accounted for less than 10 per cent of Ashley clothing sales in the UK and were said by a company director to be 'those that grandparents like to dress their grandchildren in. We are definitely not in the Benetton area of the market.'

In fact the retailing strategy was under constant review, addressing the basic question of whether the company should remain committed to selling a little of everything in all its stores or adopt the Next approach of separate stores selling different product ranges.

DESIGN

The distinctive features of Laura Ashley design were reputed to be based on traditional English country values evocative of a nostalgia for the past. The staff at the design centre in Fulham were responsible for design, fabric and print research and the design staff at Carno were responsible for translating design from a drawing to an engraved printing screen to enable the design to be reproduced as a printed fabric. The process of preparing collections was a long one based upon discussions with the retail divisions up to eighteen months beforehand. They began with up to 400 sketches and ended with a collection of 125 styles, some of which would be manufactured in more than one fabric. These discussions included forecasting and regularly reviewing demand for clothing and furnishing 18 months ahead.

Two collections were produced each year for the spring/summer season and autumn/winter and these were based on a variety of fabrics such as linen, tweed and cotton/wool blends and included knitwear and complementary accessories.

Home furnishings collection

Each year a new furnishings collection, including a separate decorator collection, was prepared. It contained major innovations in both design and products and incorporated successful designs from previous years.

Production

During the 1980s production of over 80 per cent of the products took place largely at two centres: Carno in Wales and Helmond in Holland. The balance of the products which were bought in were mainly knitwear, ceramic tiles, paint, lighting and also about one-fifth of wallpaper needs produced to Ashley designs or specifications.

The role of the product division, which processed more than 12 million metres of fabric into over 2 million garments per year, was to respond to changes in demand from the retail divisions at prices competitive with those which outside suppliers would charge. A manufacturing base meant that Laura Ashley had a higher cost base than other retailers and expansion had to take place in both retailing and manufacturing at the same time, while designs and prices available to the retail divisions were inevitably limited and did not offer the flexibility gained by pure retail chains.

Cotton cloth was imported from Europe, China and South America and other fabrics supplied from the UK and Europe. These fabrics went through a series of processes which included washing, bleaching, dyeing, printing and finishing. Making up incorporated computer facilities which enabled optimal use of the fabric in cutting up to 150 layers at a time. The cut fabric was then supplied to a garment making up plant on the 'make-through process' which, although more expensive, enabled flexibility of response to orders from the retail divisions. The make-through process had lower productivity than those processes where one person specialized for a part of the garment. Of Laura Ashley's 5,000 employees 1,300 of them were employed in making up. Most of these were employed in small clothing factories of about 100 women which was viewed as the optimum size, that is large enough to reap the economies of scale but small enough to maintain managerial control. Each factory would produce about 3,500 garments weekly, covering a wide range of styles with pay based on piecework rates. Quality control was the responsibility of the individual machinist as any returns were identified with that person and deducted from the performance rate and hence affected pay. Wallpaper production was based at both Carno and Helmond with an annual output of about 17 million metres.

In the year following the flotation Laura Ashley had unveiled a number of plans:

- To continue the development of its retail outlets worldwide supported by additional production capacity in Wales.
- To diversify into areas where its brand name would be of value.
- To diversify into newly targeted areas of opportunity.

The first objective would be achieved by researching international markets and determining the best way of entering them.

To achieve the second objective Laura Ashley engaged in a number of small takeovers:

- Willis and Geiger was a US safari outfitter with sales of £1.8 million per annum and just breaking even, was bought for £1.8 million. The company was founded in 1902 and produced clothing for exploration with sales through six franchised outlets.
- Penhaligons was a 117-year-old London perfume house with five shops in London and sales of £1.5 million per annum. It was just breaking even when Laura Ashley bought it for £1 million.
- In Australia, the company offered £4.2 million for a menswear retailer with nine shops which sold moleskins and other 'bushranger' clothing and had reported profits of £600,000 before tax in its last accounts.
- Sandringhams was a leather goods manufacturer in Wales.
- Bryant of Scotland was a high-quality lambswool and cashmere knitwear company with annual sales of £4 million.

TABLE 1 Employees in Laura Ashley 1988 and 1992

	1988	*1992*
Manufacturing	2,384	987
Retailing	3,435	3,963
Administration	1,132	1,218
Total	6,951	6,168

For the third objective Laura Ashley allocated £150,000 for the opening of five leased shops in the USA called Mother and Child with plans to open a further 26 in the USA and four in continental Europe. In these shops it was planned that approximately 45 per cent of the sales would be babywear and 30 per cent childrenswear.

As time went by the company became less committed to manufacturing its own products and by the end of the 1980s more than half were sourced from outside the United Kingdom. Table 1 shows the employees in the company at the end of financial years ending 1988 and 1992.

Retail Divisions

There were four retail divisions: UK, North America, Continental Europe and Pacific Basin. A major feature of the Laura Ashley chain was the policy which attempted to ensure that all the shops were designed to create the same look and produce the same atmosphere wherever they were situated throughout the world. The Paris Green shopfronts were instantly recognizable and the interiors presented high-quality wooden fitments while in-shop and window displays were extensively planned and co-ordinated. In principle the shops were located in prime retail positions, although a number were associated with other retail developments.

The product range varied from country to country according to customer demand, and promotion for the shops was largely by magazine advertising with the primary objective of informing customers of new product ranges. This was supported by catalogues (which also varied from country to country) to support mail order sales which accounted for 5 per cent of UK and USA turnover and 9 per cent of continental European turnover. Stock control and associated product planning was helped by the use of electronic point-of-sales (EPOS) tills which recorded daily sales figures by product lines and informed head office as quickly from San Francisco as from London.

Laura Ashley in the UK

By 1991 the company had 191 shops in the UK of which ten were located in London, and they accounted for 30 per cent of UK sales. UK sales were fairly evenly divided between clothing and furnishings through shops which averaged about 2,500 square feet of sales area.

Laura Ashley had concession stores in Sainsbury Homebase centres selling only furnishing products. The association with the Sainsbury Homebase centres which were located on edge-of-town sites with large car parking areas had begun in 1981 and by 1989 47 of Laura Ashley's UK stores were in Homebase. In 1988 the company introduced its Mother and Child shops into the UK having pioneered the idea in the USA. These were followed in 1989 by three Laura Ashley Home shops which averaged 7,000 square feet of sales area.

Towards the end of the decade one of the problems faced by the company was a fall off in sales of furnishings which was associated with the general rise in interest rates which in turn had affected mortgages and hence house sales.

International Divisions

The major international markets for Laura Ashley were continental Europe and the USA, though recent developments had begun to build a significant company presence in the Pacific Basin. In each of these markets the company had adopted different market entry methods. There had been a limited number of franchise arrangements in Europe, leasing of property in the USA combined with manufacturing franchises, and in the Pacific there had initially been a joint venture in Australia which had subsequently been bought back and more recently a new joint venture in Japan.

Laura Ashley in the USA

Laura Ashley was promoted in the USA as a very high quality, exclusive designer label. In the USA 10 per cent of Laura Ashley's customers were in the very highest socio-demographic category and the general customer base was further upmarket than in the UK. Another difference was that a much higher proportion of the staff were graduates and the company had a deliberate policy of employing mature staff to serve on the home furnishings side. One consequence of these differences was in the prices Laura Ashley could charge in the which were approximately 150 per cent more for clothing and 100 per cent more for furnishings than in the UK.

In the American retail division 70 per cent of sales were in clothing. The interior design and decoration side of the USA division was approached in a different way as designers from Laura Ashley shops would visit the homes of customers to give advice. Organizationally Laura Ashley Inc., the Laura Ashley subsidiary in North America, was allowed extensive autonomy with respect to product policy and store location. It operated on a nationwide basis and had located stores in 40 states in the USA and four provinces in Canada.

It was relatively easy to open new stores in the USA, as they were located in shopping malls on leases and some of the existing outlets had very large catchment areas, for example up to 150 miles for the Palm Springs store. In general, it was believed that Laura Ashley could trade profitably in the USA with a catchment area as small as 350,000 people.

Laura Ashley had negotiated a number of licensing agreements in the USA for furnishings, printing and for the manufacture of bedlinen. Although national advertising was not undertaken in the USA the licensees promoted their Ashley products actively. The Mother and Child operation was first established in the USA in 1987 and expanded to over 80 boutiques which were located inside Laura Ashley shops.

Towards the end of the decade there were problems with sales of clothing where delays had been experienced in getting deliveries from the UK factories. In addition merchandising problems dogged the US operations for the whole of the period under review.

Laura Ashley in Scandinavia

Laura Ashley operated 15 franchises in Sweden. Iceland, Finland, Norway and Denmark.

Laura Ashley in continental Europe

Until 1986 the company operated through concessions in departmental stores following which it expanded by relocating into free standing shops and in 1989 introduced the Mother and Child shops to Paris and Brussels. In the 1990s the company planned to expand into Spain by the 'shop in shop' method with a major departmental store.

Laura Ashley in the Pacific

At first Laura Ashley had formed a joint venture with an Australian company. The Pacific division was formed when Laura Ashley bought out its Australian partner and gained full ownership of eight shops in 1985 and then proceeded to establish a further 22 shops there. This was followed by the formation of a new 50/50 joint venture with Japan United Stores Company (JUSCO) a subsidiary of the AEON group.

INTERNATIONAL MARKETS

In early 1989 Laura Ashley acquired Revman Industries, an American company which designed and manufactured fashion bedroom furnishings for sale to large American department stores and other appropriate retail outlets. This was a separate operation to its USA retail division. Revman required additional financing and Laura Ashley was faced with the problem of raising additional equity at a time when its gearing was already high. It resolved this, to some extent, through the Japanese company the AEON group with which Laura Ashley had formed a joint venture. AEON subscribed for Laura Ashley shares at a price of 85 pence when the market price of the shares fell as low as 49 in 1990. In doing so AEON expanded its ownership of the joint venture from 50 to 60 per cent and also purchased a share of Revman Industries such that Laura Ashley's share of ownership fell to 47.5 per cent and Revman became an associate company rather than a subsidiary. AEON agreed that they would not buy (other than through a rights issue) or sell any further shares in Laura Ashley for the next ten years without the approval of the Laura Ashley board.

Determining in which countries to operate was extremely complicated. The wealth of the people was one factor but Laura Ashley had also to pay attention to exchange rates. A profit made in one country could be wiped out by an adverse movement in the exchange rates. International operations required the company to maintain a close watch on all international developments. Laura Ashley were operating in 27 countries so changes in exchange rates were of great importance. It was the policy of the company to translate the trading results of overseas subsidiaries into sterling at an average rate for the accounting period. In the latter part of the 1980s and early 1990s clothing and textile markets were strongly affected by the shifting relationships between international currencies. The over-valuation of sterling made exports to Europe difficult and while a weaker pound could have offered opportunities for clothing exports, the falling dollar worsened markets in the USA and other dollar-based markets. Similarly, imported fabrics were affected adversely by a weaker pound.

Towards the end of the decade the American economy had deteriorated with respect to both its balance of trade and government budget deficit, and the stockmarket crash of October 1987 had precipitated a plunge in the value of the dollar worldwide which was taking the USA a long time to recover from.

In November 1990 the UK government had joined the exchange rate mechanism (ERM) of the European Monetary System as part of its economic policy to control inflation. The £ sterling entered the wide band of the ERM pegged to the German mark at 2.95 marks to the pound. In September 1992 intense currency speculation caused problems in the ERM and sterling (along with the Italian lira) was forced to leave the system and floated downwards. The UK government was then able to reduce interest rates. In early 1995 city forecasts were that sterling would continue to weaken against the American dollar and the German deutschmark over the following twelve months.

Laura Ashley dealt with currency translation by using average rates of exchange for the accounting period for the profit and loss accounts of its companies operating overseas. For the balance sheets the net assets of those companies were translated to sterling at the time of the balance sheet date. This was not an unusual way to deal with the uncertainty over exchange rates. ICI, like many multinational companies, hedges against currency movements on all major transactions by buying or selling on the forward currency market to lock in any profits immediately. The key currency for ICI was the deutschmarke and it was estimated that every 10 pfennigs which the pound sterling fell increased ICI's profits by £10 million. Companies which have relatively large overseas earnings and do not hedge tend to be more sensitive to changes in currency exchange rates. (Appendix 3 provides further detail on exchange rates.)

Different countries had different inflation rates and also had different variations around those inflation rates. Table 2 shows the average inflation rate over the period 1960 to 1990 and the standard deviation of that rate for a selection of countries. Figure 2 shows inflation rates for the industrialised countries.

The years of losses led Laura Ashley to review its position and resulted in a rationalization of its manufacturing base and the sale of non-core businesses such as Penhaligons, Sandringham and Bryant of Scotland leading to a shift in focus from in-house to external supply of goods.

Market research in the early 1990's determined that the typical Laura Ashley customer was a working female between the ages of 25 and 45 with an income of over £17,000 pa. In late 1991 Dr Jim Maxmin joined Laura Ashley as Chief Executive from his previous post as Chief Executive of Thorn EMI's worldwide rental activities. He introduced what he called the 'Simplify, Focus and Act' programme where the priorities were to 'simplify' the business and make it more efficient, to redouble focus on the brand, the customer and the business, to understand what was needed to improve products and systems and to encourage staff to act by using their intelligence and knowledge to improve the quality of service and operation.

TABLE 2 Inflation and its variability 1960 to 1990 for selected countries

	Annual average inflation	*Standard deviation*
Spain	10	8
Ireland	9	8.5
UK	8	7.4
Denmark	7.5	5.7
Australia	7	6.8
France	6.8	6.2
Japan	5.7	7.1
USA	5.2	5.2
Austria	4.4	2
West Germany	4	1.7

Source: The Economist 19 November 1992.

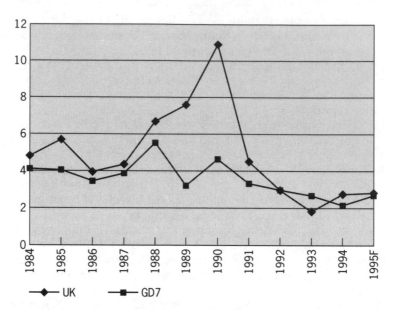

FIGURE 2 Inflation in UK and GD7 countries 1984 to 1994 and forecast 1995

Simplifying the business had begun by abolishing a variety of divisional boards which resulted in the departure of 100 senior managers. To guide the business staff prepared a new mission statement (reproduced below).

> Our mission is to establish an enduring relationship with those who share a love of the special lifestyle that is Laura Ashley. We will act so as to protect the integrity of that relationship and to ensure its long term prosperity.

APPENDIX 1

Laura Ashley – profit and loss account year ending 28 January

£ millions	1995	1994
Turnover	322.6	300.4
Cost of sales	(164.4)	(142.0)
Gross profit	158.2	158.4
Other operating expenses	(187.5)	(156.1)
Operating profit/(loss)	(29.3)	2.3
Income/(loss) from associates and discontinued activities	0.5	1.8
Profit/(loss) before interest	(28.8)	4.1
Interest payable	(1.8)	(1.1)
Profit/(loss) before tax	(30.6)	3.0
Tax	(0.9)	(1.9)
Profit/(loss) after tax	(31.5)	1.1
Dividend	0	(0.2)
Retained profit/(loss)	(31.5)	0.9
Earnings/(loss) per share (pence)	(13.41)	0.45

APPENDIX 1 *continued*

Laura Ashley – balance sheets as at 28 January

	1995	*1994*
Fixed assets		
Tangible fixed assets	47.4	60.9
Investments	0.9	10.8
	48.3	71.7
Current assets		
Stocks	64.1	70.8
Debtors	21.0	17.1
Cash	13.9	16.7
	99	104.6
Creditors due within 1 year		
Borrowings	(0)	(0.3)
Creditors	(55.3)	(53.9)
Dividend	(0)	(0.2)
	(55.3)	(54.4)
Net current assets/(liabilities)	43.7	50.2
Total assets less current liabilities	92.0	121.9
Creditors due after 1 year		
Borrowings	(13.5)	(32.8)
Creditors	(1.5)	(2.3)
Provisions for liabilities	(21.3)	(0.7)
	(36.3)	(35.8)
Net assets	55.7	86.1
Capital & reserves		
Share capital	11.7	11.7
Share premium account	48.8	48.8
Profit & loss account	(4.8)	25.6
Shareholders' funds	55.7	86.1

APPENDIX 1 *continued*

Laura Ashley ten year record

£ million	1986	1987	1988	1989	1990	1991	1992	1993	1994	1995
Turnover	131.5	170.9	201.5	252.4	296.6	328.1	262.8	247.8	300.4	322.6
Operating profit/(loss) before exceptional operating costs	16.7	21.4	23.8	23.6	6.1	3.4	(0.6)	1.1	2.3	4.1
Exceptional operating costs										(33.4)
Operating profit/(loss)	16.7	21.4	23.8	23.6	6.1	3.4	(0.6)	1.1	2.3	(29.3)
Income/(loss) from associates	2.1	0	0	0	(0.2)	0.1	1.9	1.5	1.8	1.5
Exceptional items	0	0	0	0	(6.7)	(2.6)	(8.1)	0	0	(1.0)
Net interest payable	(0.9)	(0.5)	(2.4)	(4.9)	(8.6)	(12.4)	(2.3)	(0.8)	(1.1)	(1.8)
Profit/(loss) before tax	17.9	20.9	21.4	18.7	9.4	(11.5)	(9.1)	1.8	3.0	(30.6)
Tax	(6.4)	(6.4)	(6.8)	(5.6)	0.3	2.5	0	(1.0)	(1.9)	(0.9)
Profit/(loss) after tax	11.5	14.5	14.6	13.1	(9.1)	(9.0)	(9.1)	0.8	1.1	(31.5)
Dividends	(1.83)	(4.49)	(4.69)	(4.69)	(1.7)	(0.1)	(0.1)	(0.1)	(0.2)	0
Retained profit/(loss)	9.7	10.0	9.9	8.4	(10.8)	(9.1)	(9.2)	0.7	0.9	(31.5)
Fixed assets	42.0	60.4	76.3	81.2	82.5	67.1	60.5	66.3	71.7	48.3
Net current assets	27.8	22.1	11.0	46.4	(2.2)	66.9	52.8	53.9	50.2	43.7
Long term creditors	(8.4)	(9.7)	(8.6)	(43.7)	(3.5)	(41.4)	(28.0)	(34.4)	(35.1)	(15.0)
Provisions for liabilities	(4.2)	(4.4)	(4.9)	(4.1)	(3.9)	(0.4)	(0.5)	(0.3)	(0.7)	(21.3)
Net assets	57.2	66.4	73.8	79.8	72.9	92.2	84.8	85.5	86.1	55.7
Total assets less current liabilities	69.8	82.5	87.3	127.6	80.3	134.0	113.3	120.2	121.9	92.0
Shareholders' funds	57.2	68.4	73.8	79.8	72.9	92.2	84.8	85.5	86.1	55.7
Earnings/(loss) per share (pence)	6.3	7.2	7.3	6.6	(4.7)	(4.39)	(3.86)	0.34	0.45	(13.41)
Dividend per share (pence)	1.0	2.25	2.35	2.35	0.85	0.1	0.1	0.1	0.1	0
Number of shares (millions)	183.0	199.6	199.6	199.6	199.6	199.6	234.8	234.8	234.8	234.8

APPENDIX 1 *continued*

Laura Ashley – shareholder profile subsequent to the 1985 flotation and to the 1992 and the 1995 financial accounts

Shares (thousands)	1986	1992	1995
Jusco (Europe) BV		35,221	35,221
Ashley family	143,437	125,021	80,021
Individuals	17,522	12,223	10,114
Banks & nominee companies	25,296	53,832	94,296
Others	13,345	8,507	15,254
Total shares (000)	199,600	234,804	234,906

Source: Company Annual Reports.

APPENDIX 2

Date	Laura Ashley share price (p)	FTSE 100 index	Date	Laura Ashley share price (p)	FTSE 100 index
Oct–86	191	1632	Aug–91	74	2500
Jan–87	182	1741	Nov–91	98	2541
Apr–87	126	1973	Dec–91	91	2392
Aug–87	95	1809	Aug–92	64	2366
Oct–87	212	1749	Dec–92	78	2771
Dec–87	139	1758	Feb–93	80	2878
Jan–88	90	1723	May–93	110	2838
Apr–88	105	1737	Aug–93	108	3101
Oct–88	143	1852	Sep–93	104	3164
Nov–88	128	1900	Oct–93	91	3078
Jan–89	119	1967	Dec–93	82	3412
Apr–89	100	2079	Feb–94	94	3267
Oct–89	85	2112	Apr–94	85	3149
Nov–89	70	2350	May–94	77	3123
Jan–90	65	2400	Aug–94	74	3142
Apr–90	73	2221	Oct–94	77	2999
Aug–90	69	2050	Dec–94	74	3083
Nov–90	75	2600	Apr–95	78	3130
Jan–91	61	2400	May–95	74	3260
Apr–91	74	2488	Jun–95	76	3412
Jun–91	85	2566	Jul–95	81	3315

APPENDIX 3

Sterling index (exchange rates)
(1985 = 100)

End 1986	91.5
End 1987	90.1
End 1988	95.5
End 1989	92.6
April 1990	87.1
April 1991	91.7
April 1992	91.3
April 1993	80.5
April 1994	80.0
April 1995	78.1

Source: *Economic Trends*, (CSO).

Case 9 Compass

In November 1993, Francis Mackay, Chief Executive of Compass Group, announced an innovative agreement with Burger King, the restaurant chain owned by Grand Metropolitan plc. This gave Compass exclusive rights to market the Burger King brand in workplaces, hospitals, schools, colleges and railway stations throughout Europe.

According to the Chairman, Dr Lenton, Compass's insistence on quality of product and service allied to a long-established policy of being second to none in value for money, placed considerable pressure on the company's margins. Nonetheless, the group recorded a 30.5 per cent profit increase for 1993. This, according to the Chairman, was achieved in part by continued improvement in the efficiency of food preparation and service operations.

BACKGROUND

The Compass Group was incorporated on 16 January 1987 as Chiefrule Limited and changed its name to Compass Group Limited following a management buy out by the owners, Grand Metropolitan plc, in the following July. The purchase included the companies and business comprising the contract services division of Grand Metropolitan.

The company was re-registered as a public limited company under the Companies Act 1985 on 15 November 1988. Compass Services originated from the contract catering business of Midland Counties Industrial Catering Company Limited, which commenced business in 1941 and was purchased by Grand Metropolitan in 1968. In 1983, as part of diversification programme, Compass acquired Rosser & Russell, whose business comprising the provision of heating and ventilating services to the building industry had been in existence for over 100 years. In 1981 Compass Healthcare purchased the first of the 15 hospitals which it owned and operated by 1993.

In July 1987 a consortium led by the senior management of Compass and supported by 3i plc, CIN Venture Managers Limited and Prudential Venture Managers Limited acquired Compass from Grand Metropolitan at a price of approximately £163 million in what was the largest UK-funded management buy-out at that time. In the four years to 1988 Compass had achieved a turnaround in its profitability, realizing in the year to 25 September 1988, an operating profit of £24.7 million against break-even for the year to September 1984. While a number of small acquisitions had been made by Compass since 1984, most of this growth had been internally generated.

The management of Compass believed that, against the background of the expanding services industry, the key to growth was the provision of high-quality services to an expanding customer base. Accordingly over the years, increasing emphasis had been placed on enhancing the skills of management and staff through appropriate training and on implementing quality assurance programmes. At the same time, the business had been reorganized and internal controls improved to achieve more effective management. This dated back to the appointment of Gerry Robinson in July 1984 as Managing Director of Compass Services' International activities. He was appointed Managing Director of Compass in 1985, established the existing Compass management team and led the management buy-out.

In December 1988 the Group went public. Referring to the flotation, a leading leisure analyst remarked on the 'healthy outlook' for the industry and the lack of 'operational gearing' within the company, the latter being substantiated in view of the contractual, cost-plus nature of most of the Group's business. The directors of the Group had considered that a listing on the Stock Exchange was appropriate at this stage of development. The resulting increase in the company's equity and reduction in borrowings would provide an excellent base for the further expansion of the Group.

Existing development plans were concentrated on the then current areas of operation where the Group had a proven track record, but as and when suitable acquisition opportunities emerged, the listing would provide the Group with the greater financial flexibility to respond. Additionally, the directors believed that obtaining a listing would enable a greater degree of employee participation in the Group.

CONTRACT CATERING

The principal business of Compass at the time of the buy-out was the provision of a comprehensive range of catering services to the industrial and commercial business sectors. Compass Services was one of the UK's two largest contract caterers (the other being Gardner Merchant Limited, a subsidiary of Trusthouse Forte plc) with over 2,200 catering outlets and around 19,000 employees. Initially, the business concentrated on providing factory canteen services to the manufacturing sector, in line with shifts in employment trends and the demand for improved services.

Compass expanded into the provision of cafeterias, canteens and higher quality restaurants over a range of commercial sectors (including banking, insurance and retail) as well as in schools, hospitals and leisure centres and to local authorities. As explained below, most contracts are agreed on a cost-plus pricing basis and their average life is greater than six years.

Compass operated in both sectors of the Social Catering market, namely employee catering and institutional catering, and was also engaged in specialist retail catering in the commercial catering market. Employee catering accounted for 22 per cent of the social catering market and was the market in which Compass principally operated in 1988. Institutional catering was an area where expansion was planned while specialist retail catering in the commercial catering market was being approached on a selective basis. Compass's client portfolio for employee catering was extensive and included major concerns such as BP Oil Limited, Shell UK Limited, The Rover Group plc, IBM United Kingdom Limited, Rank Xerox (UK) Limited, and The Royal Bank of Scotland plc.

TABLE 1 Services Outlets (1987)

	Compass Services' outlets as at 25 September 1988
Education	124
NHS and private health care	60
MOD	17

Table 1 shows the number of Compass Services' outlets in the institutional catering market, as of December 1988.

The size of Compass's operation enabled it to benefit significantly from economies of scale, including its purchasing power with suppliers. The company had had certain minor activities overseas consisting of catering and accommodation services. However, it had substantially decreased these in the years prior to the buyout, in the course of a managed reduction.

Compass had identified the key to growth as the provision of higher quality services and accordingly had combined the implementation of a quality assurance programme with a 'Healthy Eating' programme and other catering standards controls aimed at attracting new clients. The company was also engaged in specialist retail catering in the commercial catering market. At the end of 1988 Compass operated 79 specialist contracts in areas such as leisure centres, sports grounds, the London Zoo, the Natural History Exhibition Centre and within department stores.

Contracts

Compass Services operated three main types of contract to suit varying client requirements: cost-plus, fixed price and concession. Cost-plus contracts, which were by far the most significant, represented approximately 75 per cent of Compass's total contracts at the time. These contracts effectively operated on a cost recovery basis, in addition to which Compass Services received a predetermined management fee, which was reviewed annually. The client provided the on-site facilities and equipment, keeping Compass's capital requirements low, whilst Compass supplied the management and trained staff required to provide the services. Although the initial period of these contracts was normally agreed for 12 months with six months' notice on either side thereafter, Compass's experience showed that the average life of such contracts is greater than six years. The cost-plus structure of these contracts and wide customer base meant that these contracts provided Compass Services with strong cashflows and a steady profit performance. The majority of employee catering contracts were operated on a cost-plus basis.

Fixed contracts gave the client a predetermined total price based upon a specific schedule of services to be provided. Where the client requested a fixed price contract Compass Services would endeavour to run the first year of the contract on a cost-plus basis to establish a pattern of costs and requirements in order to determine an appropriate fixed price, subject to annual reviews, for the remainder of the contract. Compass's experience showed that fixed price contracts had an average life of approximately four years.

Concession contracts, which all fall within specialist retail catering, were entered into when Compass paid a concession fee or rental for the opportunities to provide catering facilities to the general public. In concession contracts, Compass Services determined tariffs.

Related Catering Activities

Other activities of the division included a design and planning service for the installation of kitchen and restaurant facilities and a manned security business. The design and planning function was originally a customer support service ancillary to the mainstream catering operation. Over a number of years this had developed to embrace a range of activities on a national basis including the supply of utensils and crockery, the supply of industrial cooking and refrigeration equipment and the design, planning and installation of kitchen and restaurant facilities.

The manned security service was originally provided to clients looking for a combined services contractor. Due to the rapid growth of Compass's security operation, it was managed and marketed independently of the catering service. The directors believed it to be an area with considerable scope for growth. In August 1988, Compass acquired Security Arrangements Limited, a manned security business with around 600 contracts, at a cost of £8.6 million.

HEALTHCARE

Compass Healthcare, which was at the time of the buy-out, the sixth largest commercial UK private hospital operator on the basis of the number of registered beds, owned and managed six modern hospitals in locations selected for their private patient potential. The hospitals were opened or acquired as shown in table 2.

The West Sussex and Esperance hospitals were acquired, while the other four were developed as new hospitals. All of the units provided acute hospital services, contained operating theatres, and typically offered radiology, pathology, physiotherapy, pharmacy and consulting room facilities. Five of the hospitals provided a health screening service to the general public which was marketed as 'Bodycheck'. In addition, facilities were provided for day care surgery, and specialist services available at certain hospitals included colposcopy for examination of the cervix, surgical laser treatment of cancerous and pre-cancerous tissue and computer-assisted equipment for the assessment of knee-disorders. The Droitwich hospital's brine pool offered facilities for hydrotherapy and spa bathing.

TABLE 2 Compass Hospitals 1981–1987

Hospital	Location	Date opened/acquired	Number of registered beds
West Sussex Clinic	Worthing	May 1981	28
Bath Clinic	Bath	November 1982	55
Hampshire Clinic	Basingstoke	December 1984	52
Droitwich Private Hospital	Droitwich	April 1985	36
Saxon Clinic	Milton Keynes	May 1986	24
Esperance Private Hospital	Eastbourne	January 1987	50

Compass Healthcare's position in the market

In the ten years to 1988 the independent acute medical-surgical sector had undergone radical change. Following the period of pay-bed closures implemented between 1976 and 1979, there was a rapid growth in the number of private hospitals, accompanied by a rapid expansion in medical insurance coverage. Medical insurance, which is the principal source of revenue for the sector, can be taken as a good indicator of trends. Between 1977 and 1986 the number of people covered by medical insurance more than doubled and since 1986 the number of people covered has continued to rise. The directors believed that this sector had strong growth prospects.

Compass Healthcare's revenue was drawn largely from the major provident associations and medical insurance companies. The market penetration of medical insurance was at the time, approximately 10 per cent nationally, providing a substantial untapped market among the uninsured population. Along with this growth, the sector had been transformed from one served principally by voluntary and religious organizations to a more commercially oriented sector, generally offering a wider range of services.

Compass Healthcare's relationships with consultants and with the general practitioners who refer the majority of patients to them were extremely important to the continued development of the hospitals. A consultant's choice of private hospital was dependent upon two prime factors, namely hospital standards and proximity to the hospital where he or she was based. As a result the senior management and staff carried out regular reviews with consultants with the aim of ensuring the provision of the required facilities and services to the consultants' standards.

The directors believed that, with the exception of Droitwich, none of Compass Healthcare's hospitals faced significant direct competition from other private hospitals within the Area Health Authority in which they were situated, which the directors considered to be their normal catchment areas.

Occupancy

A major measure of the utilization of hospital facilities was the bed occupancy rate, although it should be recognized that this did not include services provided to day patients and out-patients. Overall, in 1988, Compass Healthcare's hospitals operated at an annual level of over 58 per cent occupancy, an improvement of over 5 per cent on the previous year. West Sussex, Bath and Hampshire were operating at an average occupancy rate of approximately 70 per cent. These different levels of occupancy reflected the various stages of maturity of Compass Healthcare's hospitals. The management considered an occupancy rate in the mid to high 70s to be a reasonable target. As a large proportion of operating costs are of a fixed nature, an increase in occupancy rate has a significant positive impact on operating profits.

ROSSER & RUSSELL BUILDING SERVICES

The core business of Rosser & Russell was the provision of mechanical and electrical engineering services to the non-residential sector of the construction industry, mainly in the South East of England. The division typically acted as a sub-contractor on a building project and, after winning a tender, might itself subcontract certain parts of the work. Examples of projects in which Rosser & Russell had been involved included the National Westminster Bank Tower and the Broadgate development in the City of London, and the new passenger terminal at Stansted airport.

In addition, Rosser & Russell's services and maintenance division had seen substantial growth in the two years prior to the buy-out. The division operated services contracts using skilled staff either based on site or on call. The services offered included planned maintanance and management of mechanical and electrical services on premises and plant room maintenance. The range of services was extensive and was tailored to the customer's specific requirements.

Rosser & Russell concentrated mainly in the South East of England, which in 1987, accounted for some 47 per cent of all private non-residential new building services output. Although market shares in this industry could not be determined with confidence, Compass believed that the division was among the ten leading operators on a national basis, and among these was one of the most profitable. In the year to 25 September 1988 the division won orders to the value of £65 million, a significant increase over the previous year.

Competitive tendering was a vital area of Rosser & Russell's business. The division had invested in recruiting skilled estimators and had a substantial database for component costing. After a contract was handed over to the project team, a detailed operational programme was produced and, during the life of a contract, extensive operational and financial reviews were carried out regularly with the aim of ensuring that both installation and financial targets were met.

The size of contracts in which Rosser & Russell was normally involved varied significantly, the company had tended to be involved in contracts up to £6 million, generally having an installation period of up to 18 months.

ORGANIZATION AND PERSONNEL

The management of the catering operation in the UK was divided into six geographical regions. Each region was headed by a regional managing director who reported to the board of Compass Services. The regional managing director was supported by regional directors to whom operating managers reported. Each operating manager was responsible for controlling the quality and profitability of the contracts under his or her direct supervision. As well as operating existing contracts, each regional management team was responsible for sales and marketing, personnel and training and restaurant design functions. Data processing, finance, corporate advertising and purchasing support were provided centrally.

Compass recognized that the skills of its management and staff were essential for its future success, and accordingly continued emphasis was placed on the ongoing training and motivation of personnel throughout its operations. The Group placed considerable value on the participation of and communication with management and staff within the organization.

The directors considered that Compass had a good industrial relations record, with no significant industrial dispute in recent years. Most employees participated in an executive share option scheme introduced following the management buy-out. In order to improve further the degree of employee participation the company approved the establishment of an additional executive share option scheme and of a savings-related share option scheme, both of which became effective following listing on the UK Stock Exchange.

FINANCIAL RECORD 1984–1988

Up-to-date, detailed results are given in appendix 1. The four financial periods ended 25 September 1988 saw a turnaround in financial performance from break-even to an operating profit of £24.7 million. The principal reasons for this transition were given as:

- the appointment of a number of key senior executives who identified both the potential opportunities and the more profitable areas in each business;

TABLE 3 Financial results 1984–1988

Year ended September	1984 (£m)	1985 (£m)	1986 (£m)	1987 (£m)	1988 (£m)
By turnover					
Compass Services	179.4	184.9	198.9	216.3	227.4
Compass Healthcare	2.8	5.3	7.8	11.0	14.8
Rosser & Russell	15.4	18.4	15.9	27.1	34.7
	197.6	208.6	222.6	254.4	276.9
By operating profit					
Compass Services	0.7	7.7	9.6	13.8	18.5
Compass Healthcare	0.5	0.6	0.7	1.5	3.7
Rosser & Russell	(1.2)	(2.4)	(1.6)	1.5	2.5
	0.0	5.9	8.7	16.8	24.7

- improved operational disciplines and efficiencies which generated tighter financial control and higher margins;
- the development of the manned security and kitchen planning services into significant profitable businesses in their own rights;
- improved procedures and controls within Rosser & Russell, including greater selectivity in contract tendering; and
- the development and expansion of Compass Healthcare's business including the acquisition and development of two further hospitals.

Since the buy-out, Compass had taken further action to improve profitability including:

- the disposal of Compass vending business and the withdrawal from a number of overseas activities from which the directors did not expect satisfactory contributions.
- the introduction of innovative pricing and payment policies for Compass Healthcare, in addition to a number of advanced medical techniques and procedures;
- the introduction of quality assurance projects; and
- the development of in-house cash management procedures which ensured optimal use of the Group's cash resources.

The combination of growth in profits and reduction in working capital requirements in the 60-week period from the buy-out until 25 September, 1988 had generated an operating cash flow of £22.9 million, of which £8.5 million had been invested in captial expenditure and £8.6 million in acquisitions.

Table 3provides a breakdown of the Group's turnover and operating profit by division for the five financial periods ended 25th September, 1988:

GROWTH AND DEVELOPMENT

During 1989, both Rosser & Russell and Compass Security were disposed of, leading to an addition of £14 million in extraordinary profits. By the end of 1993 Compass had expanded into retail catering and had established a strong presence in Europe and Scandinavia, particularly in contract, hospital and airport terminal catering services.

This was a period of significant change for Compass and was under Chairman Francis Mackay's 'right direction' market-led strategy of investing in the establishment of independent operating companies. The latter were encouraged to grow organically in the workplace, healthcare and the stores and leisure markets. Many acquisitions were made in 1993 including on-station caterers Travellers Fare (£28.2 million), Scandinavian Service Partner (£82.9 million), the largest airport restaurant operator in Europe, and Letheby & Christopher (£7.0 million), the premier sports and event catering organization in the UK.

New Famous Foods was established as a portfolio of brands which was considered by Compass to be unparalleled in Europe. The range included franchised international brands and the company's own brands through acquisition. These included Uppercrust, Dixie's Donuts, Le Croissant Shop and Franks Deli.

In healthcare, Compass expanded into medical insurance, health assessment services and a plastic surgery scheme. By the end of 1993 the company had no less than 15 private hospitals in the UK. The effect of reforms in the National Health Service were becoming clear and the UK government's drive to extract value for money offered Compass a valuable opportunity to participate in this expanding market.

The Bid for Gardner Merchant

In mid-1992 Compass made a bid for its main rival in contract catering, Gardner Merchant. More than half the canteens in the business sector were run by contractors and the opening of the door to the public sector had set up substantial prospects. The growth of the contractors' role in providing the 3 billion-plus meals a year that Britons consume at work, in schools, hospitals and prisons partly explained why Compass Group outbid some serious competition, including a management buy-out team, to set up the acquisition of its rival.

In June 1992, Compass shares were suspended while details were worked out of the £500 million to £550 million purchase from Forte, the hotels and restaurants group. Compass planned to buy the bulk of Forte's contract catering division for £450 million with ARA Services of the US taking the rest. Compass would have become the market leader with as much as 37 per cent of the corporate contract catering market. ARA would have also leap from fourth to second with an estimated 20 per cent, ahead of Sutcliffe, part of P&O, with about 18 per cent. The acquisition of Gardner would have meant the top four became the top three.

Rocco Forte, Chief Executive of the Forte group, called off the talks with Compass and ARA when it became clear agreement could not be reached on price. He stated that he had received 'approaches for Gardner' which indicated a better price than Compass' valuation. One reason Compass may not have been prepared to pay the premium was fear that it would lose some of Gardner's biggest customers. A source close to the talks had indicated that there was a good deal of opposition from some of the big contractors, such as British Aerospace and Midland Bank, who had already done business with Compass.

At the end of 1992, speculation arose that Compass was preparing an offer for Gardner's non-UK parts of the business. After the collapse of negotiations in the summer of that year, Forte had ruled out Compass as a possible future buyer of Gardner Merchant. It was considered likely, however, that Forte would examine any approach to buy Gardner Merchant's foreign business with an open mind.

Forte was believed to be negotiating to sell the business to the Gardner Merchant management, although it had rejected reports that it would sell it for less than the

£400 million it had laid down as the minimum price. Reliable sources had indicated that a management buy-out would be backed by CinVen, the UK's second largest venture capital investor.

Forte stated that Gardner Merchant would not be sold unless three conditions were satisfied. Firstly, that the minimum price would have to be achieved; secondly, that Gardner Merchant would not be broken up and thirdly, that the Gardner Merchant senior management team would remain in place. Clearly, if the subsidiary's management could raise the £400 million it would have little difficulty in satisfying the remaining two conditions and a bid from Compass to buy Gardner Merchant's foreign business could make it easier for the management to buy the UK operation.

Gardner Merchant was particularly strong in the Netherlands, where it was the market leader. It also had operations in France and Germany, which were believed to be of particular interest to Compass. Compass was thought to be less interested in Gardner Merchant's US operation but it was thought possible that this could be sold to ARA Services, the US company which joined Compass in its original bid for Gardner Merchant.

As it happened, in December 1992, Gardner Merchant was bought out by its management for £402 million in a deal led by CinVen.

CONTRACT CATERING MARKET

The value of of the UK market in 1993 amounted to £2 billion (an increase of 27 per cent over 1992), with an additional £458 million coming from overseas earnings. From 1990 to 1993 the total number of outlets increased from 9,388 to 13,355 while the number of meals served grew from 608 million to 940 million. Compass, Gardner Merchant and Sutcliffe Catering held the major share of the value of the market, having 20 per cent, 36 per cent and 14 per cent, respectively. The top 132 companies (including the latter), accounted for almost 90 per cent of total market turnover in 1993. In this year, there were some 2,457 contract catering businesses of which only 5 per cent had an annual turnover of more than £1 million.

Institutional catering involves the provision of food services for both public and private sector establishments such as schools and colleges, hospitals and the Ministry of Defence. Until the late 1980s much of the institutional catering market was not open to outside contract caterers.

Although contract caterers tendering for public sector contracts had generally met strong competition from the tenders of existing in-house catering teams, a number of significant contracts were awarded to Compass and other contract caterers. The change in local authority legislation effective from April, 1989 required local authorities to seek tenders for new contracts for catering and other services.

In 1990, Gardner and Compass had more than half the business sector that was contracted out, but that in turn was only half the £1.5 billion whole and in-house caterers were also part of the competition. The contractors' penetration came down to only 15 per cent if public sector canteens were included. In business catering, the contractors' share had nearly doubled in ten years, enabling Gardner, Compass and Sutcliffe to keep profits moving ahead. However, growth had started to flag, according to a report at the time, from a city analyst.

Clients under financial pressure tended to strike a harder bargain with the outside caterer, for instance by asking for more of the savings to be passed on. The traditional cost-plus contract in the UK had enabled groups like Compass to retain

much of the discount achieved in buying materials, as well as taking the management fee represented by the 'plus'.

Europe

In continental Europe, payment was more likely to be based on agreed prices for the
meals, leaving the contractor with less predictability. Foreign competition, particularly from France, was becoming more of a threat. According to analysts Hoare
Govett the UK was the only major European country in which foreign operators
had not taken a significant market share.

There are basically two differences; one, the cost-plus versus the fixed-price
approach and the other, British eating habits. In the more snack-orientated UK, staff
canteens are used by less than 40 per cent of employees, while on the continent the
take-up is at least 55 per cent. In the early 1990s the presence in the UK of the
French groups – Sodexho, Eurest and the contract catering division of Accor –
remained tiny, but most commentators believed that this would change.

Compass's catering business was far more dependent on the UK corporate sector
than Gardner Merchant's. About £230 million of Gardner's £800 million turnover in
1991 was attributable to overseas activities. It was market leader in the Netherlands
and had significant shares in France, Belgium and Germany. After several years of
investment, Gardner had critical mass in these markets and thus each new contract
gained tended to be much more profitable than those signed in the start-up
years.

CONSUMER CATERING MARKET

While the consumer catering industry is characterized by single outlet businesses,
large companies are significant in some areas of the trade, notably fast food systems
catering, travel-related catering, hotels and, of course, public houses. Prominent
among the big operators are the brewers, which typically own hotels, fast food
chains and branded restaurant chains, as well as public houses.

Consumption patterns

In 1991 expenditure on the purchase of food away from home (excluding institutional canteen sales) represented 3.8 per cent of the total household budget. Table 4
shows the relationship between spending on eating out and total consumer
expenditure over the the period 1987–91 in 1991 price terms.

The increase in retail prices is given to provide a broad indication of inflation. The
coverage of consumer expenditure and the retail index is different, so the latter
cannot be used to deflate the former to give consumer expenditure at constant
prices.

Table 5 shows the trends in expenditure by segment over the period 1986 to 1991.
Burger bars, pizza houses, fish and chip shops, and other fast food and takeaway

TABLE 4 Increases in the consumer catering market and consumer expenditure,
1987–91 (percentage increase on previous year)

	1987	1988	1989	1990	1991
Consumer catering market	15.8	10.6	9.8	10.0	5.0
Total consumer expenditure	9.8	12.8	9.3	6.9	5.1
Retail prices	4.2	4.9	7.8	9.5	5.9

Source: EIU Special Report 2169, 1993.

TABLE 5 Household catering expenditure by segment, 1986–1991 (£ per household per week)

Food	1986	1987	1988	1989	1990	1991
Consumer catering	7.14	7.45	8.25	8.96	9.88	9.83
Not takeaway food	0.70	0.78	0.88	1.07	1.20	1.35
Meals eaten out, on premises	4.37	4.70	5.13	5.?1	6.11	6.01
Meals eaten out, off premises	1.20	1.30	1.52	1.64	1.70	1.75
Sandwiches & similar	0.49	0.31	0.30	0.30	0.30	0.29
Fish & chips	0.38	0.36	0.42	0.44	0.47	0.43

Source: EIU Special Report 2169, 1993.

outlets in total accounted for £4.35 billion of the eating out market in 1993 with fish and chip shops and ethnic takeaways together accounting for up to half this total. The two latter categories had suffered competition from burger bars, pizza houses and other non-traditional fast food concepts in recent years. Burger and especially pizza establishments enjoyed considerable growth during the 1980's, continuing into the 1990s. Travel-related catering, and in particular roadside diners, motorway service areas and rail-related catering, was another growth area of the eating out market as was 'destination' catering at museums, theme parks, stately homes, zoos and other such attractions.

The Burger Market

The burger market was, in 1992, the largest sector in the fast food business. With estimated sales of £1 billion in 1992 it had enjoyed substantial real growth over the period 1982 to 1992. The Economist Intelligence Unit (EIU) estimated that in 1992 the total number of burger outlets in the UK was in excess of 4,000, and the sector had probably approached saturation. National burger chains controlled around one quarter of burger outlets and by far the largest was McDonald's, which by late 1992 had around 470 outlets in the UK (or more than one in ten of the total). In late 1992 Burger King had around 200 outlets. Both these groups had developed the counter service business and one was in effect, the only genuine competitor for the other.

The second chain by size was Wimpy, which rediscovered its origins by concentrating upon the waitress service end of the burger bar business. As such Wimpy outlets were arguably, closer to a low-priced restaurant in format than McDonald's or Burger King counter service outlets. In January 1993 Wimpy had 235 outlets.

There were a number of (much smaller) burger chains in the UK, apart from the 'big three'. These included the Casey Jones chain, part of Travellers Fare, and Granada's Burger Express – although among national burger chains such minor groups were together estimated to account for less than one fifth of the sector.

In order to develop further their business opportunities, margins and long-term security, burger outlets (or, at least major nationally organized chains) had been active in upgrading their facilities, in developing new market niches – such as drive-in establishments, and broadening their menus. The latter trait was much in evidence with the advent not only of salads, but also of vegetarian products (such as the Spicy Beanburger from Burger King) and of chicken and fish products to provide an alternative diet to hamburgers. Low fat products, such as the low calorie burger developed in the USA by McDonald's, and which the company intended to launch in the UK in the medium term, had also started to make their presence known.

National burger chains by number of outlets in late 1992 were as follows: McDonald's 470; Wimpy 232; Burger King 197; and Casey Jones 18.

Pizza Outlets

In 1992 it was estimated that the value of the UK pizza catering market amounted to £650 million and that there were around 4,300 pizza outlets. Broadly one quarter (or a little over 1,000) were organized as national chains. The largest operator Pizza Hut, had some 286 outlets. Perfect Pizza was second with 224 and third was Pizzaland, which controlled over 130 restaurants.

Market Shares (percentage of value) in 1991 stood at: Pizza Hut 30; Pizzaland 11; Perfect Pizza 5; Deep pan Pizza 6; Pizza Express 6; and others 42.

The pizza catering market included one of the most dynamic food service sectors over the past few years – home delivery service. By late 1991, an estimated 65 per cent of all pizza outlets operated such a service, either as an adjunct to their eat-in or takeaway operations, or as a stand alone business. Apart from the convenience of home delivery to customers, the concept allowed entry to the fast food market for a relatively modest financial outlay on the part of operators. Rapid ordering systems, commonplace in the USA, were being introduced, while improved insulation in packaging allowed the targeting of wider catchment areas for motorcycle delivery.

One other area of the pizza catering market which was likely to become of considerable importance in the 1990s was the pizza slice. This concept involves the selling from kiosks or at cafe-style eat-in establishments of slices of pizza which are continuously cooked and served to waiting customers. The potential for pizza slice sales was considerable, given the ease with which outlets could be set up in busy locations such as railway stations, food courts, airports, shopping centres, tourist attractions, museums, and even schools, offices and factories.

The sector had been hit by the recession since 1991 which led to a fall in the number of meals eaten in pizza restaurants and a dip in the home delivery sector. As the major chains had been adding outlets through this period, competition had intensified. From mid-1991 price promotions became common in both the restaurant and delivery sectors. Delivery companies offered cheap or free pizzas when another pizza was ordered, free soft drinks with orders and often they offered to accept the special offer coupons of rival companies. The restaurant chains offered cheap buffets, fixed price meals, special offer booklets and deals in conjunction with other traders (soft drinks companies, cinemas and petrol stations).

Prospects for the 1990s

Two of the factors which have had the greatest influence on the food market in recent years are convenience and health. In the consumer catering market the most important recent manifestation of convenience has been in the home delivery of meals. This type of service was pioneered in the pizza sector, although it has spread to some other takeaway oriented outlets – some Indian and Chinese restaurants, for example. Independent chains, often franchised, were first into this area, although the majors had followed suit.

In 1993 home delivery was the fastest growing part of the consumer catering market and rapid growth was likely during the rest of the 1990s. However, the pizza sector was already beginning to become saturated. In some areas consumers had a choice of four or five operators, some of them with special offers (for example, buy one large pizza, get a second for only £2.99). As competition intensified, however, there would be some casualties and inevitably, rationalization in the sector with some large national chains emerging. The spread of home delivery to other cuisines could provide the impetus for the development of regional chains.

Increased health consciousness had made an impact on many types of restaurant in a variety of ways. The ultimate effect had been an increase on the menu of the amount of foods which are perceived as healthy, and cooked (if at all) in 'healthy' ways. Self-service salad bars were a standard fixture in many pizza restaurants and American-style restaurants (the modern salad bar is basically an import from the USA). Most restaurants offered some vegetarian options, which could appeal to meat eaters seeking a healthy or new option, as well as to vegetarians. In particular, pubs tended to soften their steakhouse and carvery themes and offered a number of 'healthier' options (as well as becoming more child-friendly, with highchairs, children's menus and, perhaps, a children's club).

Even fast food outlets had been affected. Some offered grilled burgers as well as fried food, and the situation was similar for chicken outlets. A chain such as Kentucky Fried Chicken faced a dilemma because the word 'fried' is associated with an unhealthy type of cooking but at the same time it is part of a well established name.

One approach which has not yet taken off but which could do so in the future is that of stressing the freshness and quality of the ingredients used. This could take a number of forms. The food ingredients used could be organic, fresh, high quality (free range eggs, extra virgin olive oil, free range chicken and so on); they could be prepared and cooked on the premises, cooked fresh each day. As well as simply appealing to people who like this kind of thing, the point was to contrast this approach with establishments which microwaved or baked bought-in frozen food and which selected ingredients for their cheapness more than anything else. This in turn might have had a wider effect, if parents in a pub restaurant were concerned whether their children's cod nuggets were made up of prime fillet or, on the other hand, minced fish.

The following figures show projections of percentage consumer spending growth (year on year), together with actual figures for the period 1986 to 1991.

TABLE 6 Percentage consumer spending

Actual figures						Projected figures				
1986	1987	1988	1999	1990	1991	1992	1993	1994	1995	1996
6.2	5.2	7.4	3.5	0.8	−2.1	–	2.0	1.8	2.2	2.9

Source: Economist Intelligence Unit, 1993.

APPENDIX 1

Consolidated profit and losss accounts 1989–1993

	1989 (£m)	1990 (£m)	1991 (£m)	1992 (£m)	1993 (£m)
Turnover	343.0	352.7	320.9	345.1	497.0
Operating costs	(311.1)	(315.0)	(282.8)	(308.2)	(450.2)
Income from shares in associated companies	–	0.7	–	–	–
Operating profit	31.9	38.4	38.1	36.9	46.8
Interest receivable and similar income	0.4	0.4	0.8	0.3	1.2
Interest payable and similar charges	(9.0)	(9.3)	(6.9)	(5.4)	(6.5)
Profit on ordinary activities before taxation	23.3	29.5	32.0	31.8	41.5
Tax on profit on ordinary activities	(8.0)	(10.2)	(10.5)	(10.6)	(13.6)
Profit on ordinary activities after taxation	15.3	19.3	21.5	21.2	27.9
Minority interests	(0.1)	(0.1)	(0.1)	–	–
Profit on ordinary activities attributable to the members of Compass Group plc	15.2	19.2	21.4	21.2	27.9
Extraordinary profit	–	14.0	3.0	–	–
Profit for the financial period	15.2	33.2	24.4	21.2	27.9
Dividends	(6.8)	(6.9)	(7.7)	(8.4)	(10.8)
Profit for the period retained	8.4	26.3	16.7	12.8	17.1
Earnings per share (p)	25.2	28.8	31.9	33.1	35.9

APPENDIX 1 *continued*

Consolidated balance sheets 1989–1993

	1989 (£m)	1990 (£m)	1991 (£m)	1992 (£m)	1993 (£m)
Fixed assets					
Tangible assets	70.9	75.6	118.4	122.1	160.3
Investments	0.1	–	–	–	–
	71.0	75.6	118.4	122.1	160.3
Current assets					
Stocks	2.8	2.9	3.8	4.4	10.9
Debtors	45.5	37.5	36.2	38.3	72.3
Cash at bank and in hand	2.5	6.0	5.2	4.7	24.2
	50.8	46.4	45.2	47.4	107.4
Creditors: amounts falling due within one year	(86.1)	(68.3)	(75.6)	(77.2)	(149.8)
Net current liabilities	(35.3)	(21.9)	(30.4)	(29.8)	(42.4)
Total assets less current liabilities	35.7	53.7	88.0	92.3	117.9
Creditors: amounts falling due after more than one year	(45.3)	(38.6)	(50.3)	(43.0)	(68.1)
Provisions for liabilities and charges	(6.8)	(7.1)	(6.3)	(4.5)	(9.1)
Minority interests	(0.2)	(0.3)	(0.4)	(0.4)	(0.4)
Net assets	(16.6)	7.7	31.0	44.4	40.3
Capital and reserves					
Called up share capital	3.3	3.3	3.4	3.4	4.5
Share premium account	111.4	111.4	111.4	112.1	200.9
Other reserves: goodwill	(151.9)	(146.9)	(155.0)	(155.0)	(266.5)
revaluation	6.1	6.1	21.3	21.1	20.9
Profit and loss account	14.5	33.8	49.9	62.9	80.5
	16.6	7.7	31.0	44.4	40.3

APPENDIX 1 *continued*

Asset analysis 1989–1993

	1989 (£m)	1990 (£m)	1991 (£m)	1992 (£m)	1993 (£m)
Net assets					
Catering					
United Kingdom	(8.2)	(9.7)	(13.4)	(15.4)	(18.7)
Overseas	1.7	1.1	(0.4)	0.2	(12.2)
Healthcare					
United Kingdom	50.8	55.9	85.1	97.6	105.5
	44.3	47.3	72.1	82.4	74.6
Interest bearing liabilities, being loans less cash at bank	(60.9)	(39.6)	(41.1)	(38.0)	(34.3)
Net assets	(16.6)	7.7	31.0	44.4	40.3
Geographical analysis					
United Kingdom	42.6	46.2	71.7	82.2	86.8
Other European countries	–	–	–	–	(12.8)
North America	1.7	1.1	0.4	0.2	0.6
	44.3	47.3	72.1	82.4	74.6

APPENDIX 1 *continued*

Sales analysis 1989–1993

	1989 (£m)	1990 (£m)	1991 (£m)	1992 (£m)	1993 (£m)
Turnover					
Catering					
United Kingdom •	234.9	250.8	261.0	285.8	382.2
Overseas	8.6	7.2	3.9	2.1	53.9
Healthcare					
United Kingdom	26.8	40.3	56.0	57.2	60.9
Turnover	270.3	298.3	320.9	345.1	497.0
Geographical analysis of turnover					
United Kingdom	261.7	291.1	317.0	343.0	443.1
Other European countries	–	–	–	–	50.2
North America	8.6	7.2	3.9	2.1	3.7
	270.3	298.3	320.9	345.1	497.0
Operating profit					
Catering					
United Kingdom		24.0	26.4	24.5	30.6
Overseas		1.3	0.2	0.1	3.1
Healthcare					
United Kingdom		9.7	11.5	12.3	13.1
Operating profit		35.0	38.1	36.9	46.8
Geographical analysis of operating profit					
United Kingdom		33.7	37.9	36.8	43.7
Other European countries		–	–	–	2.9
North America		1.3	0.2	0.1	0.2
		35.0	38.1	36.9	46.8

PART 3

Growth and Decline

Case 10 Queens Moat Houses

John Bairstow was on his way to becoming a millionaire through his estate agency business in 1969 when he started his first hotel. He converted his house near Brentwood into an hotel to offer accommodation for Ford executives visiting the nearby plant. This was a success and so he copied the idea at Harpenden for General Motors executives visiting the plants around Luton. In 1982 he purchased 26 hotels from Grand Metropolitan a transaction which may have been helped by his close friendship with Maxwell Joseph, the Grand Metropolitan boss.

Queens Moat concentrated on the commercial sector, benefiting from the increase in business travel both within the UK and from overseas. The hotels were in provincial, attractive locations which also benefited from the tourist market.

HISTORY FROM 1984

1984

The directors stated that the increased first half profitability (to £2.75 million) was due to the company's expansion programme. This had added more than 900 bedrooms in 12 months and included the first contribution from Grand Metropolitan hotels. The management considered that the benefits of recent purchases would increase further in 1985. The group remained keen to expand by further acquisition and extending existing hotels.

1985

The group added 622 bedrooms through acquisition and construction. Further contacts were exchanged to buy the long lease of Telford Golf and Country Club in Shropshire. Mr John Bairstow, Chairman, said that the 1984 £26 million rights issue had reduced gearing and facilitated expansion by acquisition and organic growth without the need for further shareholder finance.

1986

Queens Moat purchased Dean Park Hotels for 5.58 million shares, the Holiday Inn, Liverpool and the Royal Hotel, Nottingham for £21.2 million in cash. In April, John Bairstow announced an intention to raise £35 million by the placing of first mortgage debenture stock 2020. This was an unusual move considering the economic climate but analysts considered borrowings were well matched by assets. The group also began expansion plans for western continental Europe, operating on the same business traveller/local community priorities as in the UK. August and November saw the group expand into property by the purchase of 72 per cent of the Bedford (Ford End) Property Company (£511,000) and the Dutch hotel group, Rilderberg for £15.5 million.

1987

Queens Moat continued their European expansion programme by the purchase of hotels in West Germany and Belgium for £8 million and a further hotel in Shrewsbury. They announced improved results, of which the main contributors were the longer held hotels. The results showed the business traveller market was booming with average occupancy rates at 60 per cent, this was in contrast to an uneven tourist market. The acquisitions had cost £100 million, but provided the group with a European base complete with local management. Expansion continued throughout the year, funding coming from further rights issues and payment by shares. Queens spent a further £19 million on expansion and committed to a building programme for £15 million financed through the Business Expansion Scheme.

1988

Chairman John Bairstow stated the group was considering purchasing a further hotel in London due to the demand from provincial customers for rooms in the capital. This was accompanied by a statement that Queens Moat were not shifting away from the business traveller or shunning the tourism-sensitive London market. The Chairman said that property prices in London were too high. QMH's acquisition programme slowed down during 1988 with the purchase of only two hotels, bringing the hotels owned to 117 of which 77 were in the UK. Occupancy rates continued to rise to 65 per cent in the UK, in contrast to 53 per cent for West Germany. The property revaluations were regarded as conservative. In October the group announced an agreement to purchase seven more German hotels, making the group the largest owner-operator in West Germany.

1989

The year began positively for the group as it announced pre-tax profits up by 70 per cent. The UK accounted for £32.7 million, West Germany and Switzerland for £13.3 million and Belgium and the Netherlands £9.8 million. The group also announced property revaluations which placed the total value at £1.03 billion which showed a surplus of £170 million. QMH also took a 9 per cent stake in the Vaux Group described by John Bairstow as an 'hotel company with a brewery attached'. The group also announced their third rights issue in two years, this time a call for £141 million. They also hoped to have £75 million of this remaining in 1990 to take advantage of forced sales due to the high interest rates.

Further expansion had taken place with the purchase of individual properties, however the scarcity of medium-sized European chains and the high prices demanded by the provincial UK market had reduced the speed of expansion. The rights issue ran into trouble when some 700 shareholders had cheques returned due to postal delays and a printing error. Queens Moat provided a chance for those shareholders to re-apply. However, the take-up was less than 17 per cent of the 1.16 million shares on offer. This can be attributed to the fall in the share price, reducing the premium available on the market. The group also increased its stake in the Vaux brewing group by 9.15 per cent.

1990

In January Queens Moat put forward a £176 million paper bid for the Norfolk Capital group, it was expected to be bolstered by a cash alternative. Queens Moat were interested in the quality hotel assets of Norfolk which had under-performed. Norfolk was under attack by Balmoral, its largest shareholder, with an approximately 13 per cent equity stake. Queens Moat continued to build up a stake of 6 per cent in Norfolk but refused to offer cash; as well as reducing the offer period to 21 days in comparison to the normal 60. The group also announced a property revaluation of £1.4 billion, a surplus of £125 million on the 1988 figure.

At the same time as the bid Queens Moat purchased two German hotels for £13.2 million. On 26 February the company announced it had gained control of Norfolk Capital, declaring its 2 for 5 bid unconditional. John Bairstow said the company would benefit from the new hotels. However, with regard to the other parts of the business, he said 'we do not understand the clubs business and will have to get to know them very quickly'. One month later 50 per cent of the clubs business was on sale, Norfolk's defence document had valued the business at £58 million. The group also announced a 64 per cent rise in pre-tax profits for the first six months of 1990.

1991

The company announced a sale and lease back deal for £66 million which would reduce gearing from 61 per cent to 57 per cent as well as being a step towards restructuring the group's finances to provide more stability. The share price stood at 82p compared to 125p in May 1989. The deal was considered good news for the hotel industry as the London price per room equated to £100,000, at a time when hotel values were considered to be weakening.

The group also announced a rise in pre-tax profits of 51 per cent. This was regarded as a good performance in view of the recession and the Gulf War. The stability of the group was derived from its geographical diversity, with 177 hotels spread across six European countries. In May, Queens Moat announced a further rights issue for £184 million; however the share price stood at 30 per cent discount to the net asset value, suggesting any shareholder taking up the offer would lose 30 per cent of their capital immediately. Some £45 million of the proceeds were already earmarked for further European expansion into Austria and eastern Europe.

The question being asked was whether the phenomenal earnings growth of the 1980s could be continued; if not, the company would be unable to rely on shareholders to fund further growth. In August the company announced pre-tax profits of £36.2 million for the first six months in comparison to £39.5 million for the same period in 1990. The downturn was limited by the spread of hotels; 90 of the 193 hotels are on the continent providing 48 per cent of pre-tax profits.

John Bairstow said 'the Gulf War affected all our markets quite sharply, but while the continental markets picked up straight away, the UK recession meant that recovery in the UK was much slower' . . . 'We can't identify why some hotels are doing better or worse than others; there seems no pattern to it.'

The company ruled out any further acquisitions in the short term but felt that the UK's economic recovery would be accompanied by attractive opportunities to acquire assets and businesses.

1992–1993

The group was the third largest hotel owner/operator in the UK in terms of number of rooms. It had over 22,000 rooms, around half of which were located in continental Europe and the USA. There were 103 hotels in Great Britain, rated mostly with three or four stars and located in major towns and cities throughout England, Scotland and Wales. A feature of many of the hotels was the larger than average conference and banqueting facilities.

MANAGEMENT

Management had been decentralized to the individual hotels through, in many cases, an incentive scheme which involved managers setting up private companies to run the hotels. In early 1992 those involved in this scheme in the UK had peaked at 62. Similar management incentive schemes were operated in the European businesses whose hotel numbers were as follows: Germany 37; Holland 28; France 7; Belgium 5; and Austria 5. The company also had leisure and property divisions which in 1992 generated incomes of £7.4 million and £1.6 million.

The incentive scheme was intended to motivate managers to keep costs low and take a keen interest in local marketing, by giving them freedom to operate their hotels autonomously. At its height, over half of the hotels were involved in the scheme.

Within the incentive scheme, managers negotiated an annual rent with Queens Moat based on the hotels' past performance, profit forecasts and capital investments. They then formed limited liability companies in which the managers owned a minimum of 75 per cent of the equity. Queens Moat was responsible for the structure of the hotels, exteriors and heavy equipment. Hotel managers handled interior repairs and refurbishment (an internal repairing lease). If the manager failed to reach his or her target, this was usually written off or carried forward.

Bairstow professed a hands-off management style such that neither monthly accounting reports nor treasury information were required either from wholly-owned hotels or from those run through the incentive scheme. At board meetings papers were given to directors as they arrived and they were taken away as they left, because confidentiality was of the essence in a company growing rapidly through acquisitions.

In 1989 the company was valued at £1 billion on the Stock Exchange and in 1992 boasted £2 billion assets. Bairstow was assiduous in keeping the city informed of company plans and aspirations.

In keeping with a company of this size Queens Moat Houses had its own jet and a £5 million villa on the French Riviera. It was suggested that head office costs could be defrayed by letting the villa.

FINANCE

On 29 October 1993 Queens Moat Houses published a 34-page catalogue of mistakes and mismanagement with respect to its results for the year 1992. This resulted in outsiders getting an insight for the first time, into the problems which could not have been deduced from any of the previous published accounts. The revaluations included alleged breaches of company law, including the unlawful payment of more than £20 million in dividends (which were financed by rights issues); the earlier overstatement of profits; and losses of more than £1 billion largely attributable to a £803.9 million property write down.

The Finance Director's report in the revised 1992 accounts, which were dated October 1993, highlighted a number of areas for revision. These were of such a serious nature that the original accounts were effectively 'over-ruled' and replaced by the revised accounts. The matters highlighted in these accounts were a symptom of the difficulties of QMH, rather than the cause.

The main changes to the accounts are listed below.

- The group had set up 'incentive fees' with hoteliers. These took the form of a licence fee paid by the hotelier to the group. The fee continued to be payable for a period beyond the accounting year. However, the group had present valued or capitalized future payments and brought them back to the 1992 year. The amended accounts apportioned only that part of the fee relative to the current accounting year. Consequently the net assets in 1991 were reduced by £48.6 million and pre-tax profits reduced by £13.5 million.
- QMH had entered into a number of sale and lease back transactions which were in effect financial leases. A sale and leaseback is a means of raising money, by selling the freehold interest in a property which you occupy, and then taking a lease on the premises from the purchasers at an agreed rental. The sale and leaseback used by QMH were, however, very different. The rental included an amortization of the loan, that is to say the 'rental' was in fact an interest payment together with partial repayment of capital, like a traditional house mortgage (interest and capital repayment). Secondly, QMH could repurchase the asset during the term of the lease (this would be done by paying off the outstanding balance, excluding any increase in the value of the property; again like a house mortgage) therefore, QMH would retain any increase in value of the freehold property. Thirdly, these deals were in some instances structured to pay low initial rents, like a low start interest rate mortgage. They were in essence closer to a mortgage or financial lease than to a traditional lease. Altering the status to a financial lease meant that the 1991 net assets were reduced by £41.2 million (due to a fall in the value of the property) and pre-tax profits by £18.3 million. This form of transaction had the same effect as increasing the gearing of QMH. The company issued shares to buy one property and then refinanced that property to buy another.
- Previously the board had not depreciated fixtures and fittings, or plant and equipment. Certain repairs and maintenance procedures had also been capitalized. The change in this accounting policy reduced net assets by £2.5 million and 1991 pre-tax profits by £50.9 million. Additionally pre-opening marketing expenses and professional fees which should have been written off had been capitalized. Writing off these assets reduced 1991 pre-tax profits by £21.9 million.
- Incorrect accounting procedure on the disposal of assets led to a further reduction in 1991 pre-tax profits by £24.2 million.

The net effect of the total adjustments was to reduce the group's net assets in 1991 by £105.3 million to £1,192.6 million.

The write down in property valuations was the main reason for the group's losses. Wootton (the largest firm of chartered surveyors in Europe) valued the group's property for the new board of directors at £861 million as at December 1992. Only five months earlier, the group's former valuers, Weatherall, Green & Smith (one of the top five UK firms), had produced a draft valuation of £1.35 billion for the same assets. Weatherall, Green & Smith valued the group's property portfolio for the accounts for the year to December 31 1991 at £2 billion. Both the valuations followed the guidelines as laid down by the Royal Institution of Chartered Surveyors. A figure was eventually agreed at £1.2 billion.

The Royal Institution of Chartered Surveyors has since prepared the 'Mallinson Report' which made specific reference to QMH and the valuations. The report states that increased emphasis should be placed upon disclosure of the comparable evidence used to arrive at the valuation of a property. Also the valuations should state the economic assumptions upon which the valuations are based. The British Association of Hotel Accountants made its own contribution to the debate with a statement of recommended practice on valuations; which strongly advises the use of a discounted cash flow method based on future income.

Shares suspended

On 30 March 1993 a non-executive director approached the major banks with the bad news and the shares were suspended the next day. Andrew Coppel was approached by one of the banks to join the QMH board and the old board, including Bairstow, were replaced. Andrew Le Poidevin was appointed to sort out the finances and Michael Cairns, who had taken early retirement from Inter-Continental Hotels, was appointed to sort out the strategy and operations.

There was £1.5 billion of debt owed to 74 banks led by Barclays. The survival of QMH depended therefore on a financial restructuring package involving a huge debt for equity swap.

THE UK HOTEL INDUSTRY

In 1992 the UK hotel industry was suffering from a continued downturn in business. The domestic tourism sector had been reduced, mainly due to the effects of the recession in the UK. The overseas tourism market, which was severely affected by the Gulf War, had slightly improved but could not compensate for the decrease in domestic tourism. As a result, the occupancy level of most hotels fell. Between 1987 and 1991 the business traveller's occupancy rate fell by nearly 20%, overnight accommodation is one of the first expenses to be cut when a business begins to 'tighten its belt'. The major hotel groups are shown in table 1.

TABLE 1 Major UK Groups, 1992

Parent Company	Hotels	Bedrooms
Forte	361	29,350
Mount Charlotte	109	14,263
Queens Moat Houses	102	10,624
Holiday Inn	34	6,379
Stakis	30	3,718

Hotel classification: Hotels are classified by the AA in a one to five star system

Group	5 Star	4 Star	3 Star	2 Star	Others
Forte	4	38	163	23	133
Mount Charlotte	0	20	45	1	43
Queens Moat Houses	1	19	65	1	16
Holiday Inn	0	16	5	0	13

Source: Keynote, Hotel Report 1992, p. 18.

TABLE 2 Charge-out rates and revenue
Average occupancy and charges in 1991

	Average % 1991	Occupancy % 1990	Average £ 1991	Rate % 1990
All UK	61.4	69.4	60.58	62.1
England	58.0	66.2	47.54	48.1
Scotland	63.5	66.3	48.54	49.3
Wales	54.8	59.2	44.84	44.8
London	66.4	86.2	83.69	90.2

Income before fixed charges per available room per year

	£ 1991	£ 1990
All UK	8,340	6,455
England	6,358	4,806
Scotland	6,944	6,402
Wales	6,072	7,254
London	12,168	15,989

Occupancy Rates

Average achieved room rates fell by approximately 25 per cent after mid-1991. In London, however, discounts on published tariffs of 50 per cent were not uncommon. Rates at three star hotels outside London were worst hit by the downturn in domestic demand. Their rates dropped by 7 per cent to an average room rate of £69 in 1992. London five star hotels bucked the trend by increasing rates by 3 per cent. Hotels attempted to brand themselves, but only with very limited success. Details of occupancy rates and changes in prices are shown in table 2.

In addition to the major chains there are a further 128 with a turnover in excess of £5 million annually and 658 have a turnover of £1–5 million.

Horwath Consulting and the English Board of Tourism reported in their annual survey that room occupancy levels in English hotels fell in 1991 to its lowest level since 1982. London suffered particularly badly as occupancy levels in luxury hotels fell by 17 per cent.

Hotel Operations

After a 44 per cent increase in turnover between 1986 (£4.3 billion) and 1990 (£6.2 billion), turnover finally fell in 1991 to £5.8 billion. Turnover is derived from a number of revenue generating areas. According to Horwath Consulting, hotels generated around 48 per cent of their revenue from rooms in 1991; 45 per cent came from food and beverages with other operating departments accounting for the remainder.

Due to the overcapacity of hotel rooms, major hotel projects were on hold at this time. Expansions, other than by acquisition and management contracts, were unlikely in this climate.

Where hotels suffer due to the UK and worldwide recession, the advertisement budgets do not appear to be influenced. In fact, the opposite is true and hotels attempt to increase their business. As such, advertising expenditure by the major hotel groups increased by 30 per cent in 1991. During the recession hoteliers appear to concentrate on refurbishment rather than on new buildings. British hotels are the highest spenders in Europe in terms of refurbishing hotels.

Technology looks to play an increasingly important role in the distribution process, despite the recession. A MORI poll for IBM concluded that while two thirds of the hotels were linked to computer reservations systems, 46 per cent of managers intended to invest in technology in the coming years.

Hotels operating under management contracts are increasing in number. Such an operating system can retain and even improve the trading position of an hotel, helping to ensure the future operation and protecting the creditor's asset. Management contacts provide an attractive method for hotel groups to bring in a steady income stream without adding heavily to their debt.

UK Hotel Demand

UK residents account for 60 per cent of the demand for UK hotels. The recession and economic uncertainty in the UK led to a fall in demand of 4 per cent between 1990 and 1991. The number of visitors from the US and Canada fell by nearly 5 per cent over the same period. Visitors from continental Europe increased their share from 11.1 per cent to 13.3 per cent over the period.

The number of overseas visitors had increased steadily throughout the 1980s from 12.4 million in 1978 to a peak of 18.0 million in 1990. However, in 1991 the number of visitors decreased due to the world recession and the weakness of the dollar. The number of overseas visitors fell from 18.01 million in 1990 to 16.31 million in 1991. Whereas the level of holiday visitors remained quite constant from 1987 to 1991. The business visitor level shows a decrease in 1991, which was mainly a result of the recession in Europe and elsewhere.

Tables 3 and 4 illustrate sources of hotel income and guests by country of origin.

TABLE 3 Sources of Hotel Income

	1987 %	1988 %	1989 %	1990 %	1991 %
Segments					
Business	49.2	49.1	39.9	42.0	41.6
Conference	5.1	5.0	13.0	15.0	17.9
Holidays	32.8	31.7	28.3	28.2	19.0
Others	12.9	14.2	18.8	14.9	20.3
Total	100.0	100.0	100.0	100.0	100.0

Source: Keynote, Hotel Report 1992, p. 6. Figures rounded.

TABLE 4 Hotel Guests by Country of Origin

	1987 %	1988 %	1989 %	1990 %	1991 %
UK	61.8	62.2	57	63.9	59.9
US & Canada	19.1	15	17.1	15.8	15.5
Europe	11.1	12.6	13.9	10.9	13.3
Japan	2.4	3.5	3.4	4.6	4.1
Others	5.6	6.7	8.6	4.8	7.2
Total	100.0	100.0	100.0	100.0	100.0

Source: Keynote, Hotel Report 1992.

APPENDIX 1   COMPETITOR TURNOVER AND PROFIT

Group	Turnover (£m)	Profit before interest and tax (£m)	Financial year end
Forte	2662	72	31.1.92
Mount Charlotte	191	33	30.12.90
Stakis	83	28	31.9.90
Holiday Inns	108	34	28.9.90

APPENDIX 2   FACTORS CONSIDERED IMPORTANT WHEN CHOOSING A HOTEL

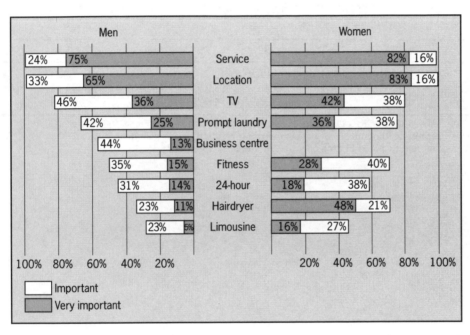

Source: Visa International Corporate Travel Survey, September 1994

APPENDIX 3 COMPANY HISTORY

1968	John Bairstow begins hotel career
April 1982	Buys 26 hotels from Grand Metropolitan for £30m
Nov. 1986	Buys Dutch Bilderberg Hotels for £15.5m
Aug. 1988	Buys 7 Crest Hotels for £96m
Feb. 1990	Wins control of Norfolk Capital for £157m
Aug. 1990	Buys 49% of HI Management of France for £30m
March 1991	£184m rights issue; paid £45m for 15 Continental European Hotels
June 1991	Issues £180m of convertible cumulative redeemable preferred shares
Aug. 1992	Net debts of £790m revealed with interim results
March 1993	Shares suspended
May 1993	Martin Marcus, Deputy Chairman and David Hershey, Finance Director, resign
July 1993	Bairstow to quit as Chairman, eight other directors resign

APPENDIX 4   QMH SALES GENERATED (%) BY REGION

Country/year	1991	1992	1993
UK	48	38	41
Germany	27	29	28
Netherlands	16	15	16
France	4	9	7
Belgium	4	6	5
Other	1	3	3

APPENDIX 5   THE EFFECT OF ECONOMIC CHANGE ON THE HOTEL INDUSTRY

Year	1986	1987	1988	1989	1990	1991	1992
GDP	88.6	92.8	97.5	99.6	100	97.8	97.3
Hotel	12,855	12,960	13,648	13,934	14,410	14,382	n/a
TT(£m)	4,279	4,781	5,514	5,862	6,212	5,790	n/a

1. GDP is an index of Gross Domestic Product for the UK with 1990 being 100.
2. Hotel represents the number of hotels and other residential establishments in the UK.
3. TT is the total turnover in £m generated by the businesses in 2.

APPENDIX 6   QUEENS MOAT HOUSES PLC

Balance sheet

	1988 (£m)	1989 (£m)	1990 (£m)	1991 (£m)	1992 (£m)	1993 (£m)
Property	963.9	1353.1	1739.6	1943	735.6	927
Tangible fixed assets	71.5	93.9	128.5	179.8	155.5	
Other fixed assets	18.6	41.8	101.5	22.8	3.3	0.6
Total fixed assets	1054	1488.8	1969.6	2145.6	894.4	927.6
Stock	24.6	42.8	41.6	37.8	40.3	32.2
Debtors	32.8	67.7	121.5	58	125	66.3
Cash	42.9	136.7	76.5	381.6	179	209.7
Other c/a	3.7	9.8	14.4	12.9	6.3	0.1
Current assets	104.1	256.9	254	490.3	350.6	308.3
Total assets	1,158.1	1,745.7	2,223.6	2,635.9	1,245	1,235.9
Shareholders' equity	669.4	989.7	1168.9	1192.6	−388.9	−377
Non-current liabilities	6.6	−0.1	0.8	36.5	73.1	
Medium/long loans	400.7	599.4	751.2	1093.3	744	
Short term loans	8.5	41.3	151.6	148.6	600.6	1433.8
Net assets	1,085.2	1,630.3	2,072.5	2,471	1,028.8	1,056.8
Creditors	47.3	68.4	90.3	101.4	180.7	127.7
Tax	19.1	35.5	47.6	45.5	35.5	
Proposed dividend	6.3	11.6	13.2	18		
Provisions for liabilities						51.4
Liabilities and equity	1,157.9	1,745.8	2,223.6	2,635.9	1,245	1,235.9

Profit and loss account

	1988 (£m)	1989 (£m)	1990 (£m)	1991 (£m)	1992 (£m)	1993 (£m)
Sales	234.4	409.4	484.5	314.7	387.4	381.3
Operating profit	54.4	92.2	135.5	22.4	−923	49.8
Other income	2.7	7.1	9.8	10.8	11.8	13.9
Profit before interest	57.1	99.3	145.3	33.2	−911.2	63.7
Interest	15	36.9	51.2	89.5	129.3	110.1
Profit before tax	42.2	62.4	94.1	−56.3	−1040.5	−46.4
Tax	7.3	9.7	15.9	12.5	7	2
Profit after tax	34.9	52.7	78.2	−68.8	−1047.5	−48.4
Attributable profit	34.9	52.7	78.2	−68.8	−1047.5	−48.4
Dividend	11.2	18.4	24.7	33.7	23.7	14.7
Retained profit	23.7	34.3	53.55	−102.5	−1071.2	−63.1

The origin of the BBA group lies in the chance meeting of two men in Sweden. William Fenton, a Scot, was employed as weaving manager in a textile mill at Jonsered. The other was Walter Wilson Cobbett, a merchant of industrial supplies, who was on holiday.

Fenton had invented a solid twill woven cotton belting. This, he thought, would improve on the current plain woven beltings that were beginning to supersede leather and canvas belts for driving machinery. Fenton was to have sole responsibility for manufacturing, Cobbett sole responsibility for selling.

Fenton left Sweden in 1879 and started up in a small factory in Dundee, calling himself a 'belt and hosepipe maker' and manufacturing the belting under the brand name 'Scandura'. In 1897 the business became a joint stock company, incorporating the separate business of two sons who had started manufacturing separately in 1888. The new company required new premises, and in 1901 the business moved to Cleckheaton in Yorkshire.

In the inter-war years, the growing friction materials business necessitated the acquisition of the British Asbestos Company. The Second World War provided a significant impetus to BBA products and growth. For instance, every RAF aircraft which fought in the Battle of Britain was fitted with BBA (Mintex) brakes. BBA looms were manufacturing materials for tanks, other army vehicles, parachutes and gas masks. The plant was working 24 hours a day, seven days a week, and the number of employees rose from 400 to 1,400.

In 1960, BBA obtained a quotation on the Stock Exchange, but the Fenton and Pearson (Cobbett's descendants) families retained dominant positions on the board until 1985.

PRODUCTS, MARKETS AND PERFORMANCE 1984

Industrial

In 1945, experiments were started with PVC as a coating material in an attempt to produce a fire-resistant belt. After a disastrous fire at Cresswell Colliery in 1950, a directive was issued by the Ministry of Fuel to the effect that all belts used in collieries were to be flame-proof. The Scandura product was, and became the first coal conveyor belting to be officially recognized as such. Scandura belts carried coal, clay, copper, phosphates, potash, quarry stone and lumber, as well as products from the food industry and the packaging industry.

Other Scandura products included asbestos yarns for packing and sealing purposes, asbestos cloth for thermal insulation, as well as jointings and packings, tapes, laggings, linings and tubings. Scandura screen mats were available for the grading of aggregates, and Scandura compensating seals were fitted to ducting and pipework. Endless belts manufactured by the company were widely used on rolling machines in the cigarette industry. Scandura also produced glass cloth, webbings and tubings for heat insulation and general industrial applications.

BBA's other industrial activities included Sovex Marshall, the conveyor makers and system-handling engineers. Their document systems were installed in many government buildings, banks and insurance houses; Postube in a pneumatic tube system for handling documents and small parts.

Marshall Mechanisation formed the other main branch of the company's activities and produced a large range of standard conveyor products. The automotive division supplied machinery for inter-process handling of large and small automotive components.

Automotive

The company had a long history of successful innovation in the brake-lining business, Jaguar being the first major user to fix Mintex (BBA) disc brakes in 1959. With its worldwide production facilities BBA supplied more disc brake pads as original equipment than any other manufacturing group in the world. In addition, licensing agreements were in operation for the manufacture of BBA friction materials in several overseas countries.

Also prominent in the list of BBA automotive companies was plastic bearings manufacturer, Railko. In the 1930s Railko developed a new centre-pivot bearing material – requiring no lubrication – for use in railway bogies. BBA obtained a 50 per cent stake in the company in 1962, and it became a wholly-owned subsidiary in 1970.

Railko developed a wide range of bearing and controlled-friction materials which were used extensively throughout the marine, railway, automotive, mechanical handling and other industries.

Geographical

From the very first meeting of its founders in Sweden, the company had developed international connections. Export ledgers for the latter part of the nineteenth century show that the company was represented by agents in France, Germany, Spain, Australia, India, Russia, Holland, Sweden, and even in the Sudan, Brazil and Trinidad.

After the Second World War, BBA's overseas activities continued to expand. By 1984, the company had manufacturing plants in Australia, Canada, South Africa, the USA and Germany. Of the group's 7,000 employees, some 2,500 worked overseas.

BBA Performance to 1984

In 1980, as BBA took the brunt of savage destocking by both car and component manufacturers; the automotive proportion of profits fell from 83 per cent to an overall loss, with Mintex moving into loss and Textar (a German friction material manufacturing subsidiary) generating a much lower overall contribution and second half losses. Regina Fibreglass and Sovex Marshall continued in loss, but Scandura Ltd put up a good performance. The German company was quick to recover in 1981 but UK losses were a persistent feature of group profits between 1979 and 1984.

Within the UK, Mintex remained in loss between 1980 and 1984, Sovex Marshall returned a small operating profit in 1984, and Regina Fibreglass (in which BBA had a 49 per cent stake) was sold to Pilkington Brothers for £1.5 million cash in 1981, after a trading loss of some £1 million in 1980. The remaining UK companies generally were reasonably successful over this period, with Scandura Ltd making good progress until it was badly affected by the miners' dispute in 1984; however, even in that year the company continued to generate profits. One major problem was that new friction materials have a longer life (the life expectancy of clutches, for example, is now at least as long as the life of a car). Imports, although not of great significance in terms of volume penetration, have had an adverse effect on margins, which were already being affected by a price war between the three major manufacturers within the UK – Mintex, Don (Cape Industries) and Ferodo (Turner & Newall). After years of rationalization and restructuring at Mintex, the company seemed no nearer to achieving a position of profitable trading.

Table 1 and 2 illustrate BBA performance and profit before tax for the years 1979 to 1984.

CHANGES IN 1985

Following the arrival of Dr John White as Group Managing Director at BBA, the automotive interests of Cape Industries were acquired in March 1985 for £15.75 million of which £10.5 million was paid in cash and the remainder (which attracted no interest) was payable after five years. The acquisition was accompanied by a one-for-four rights issue (14,473,316 shares) at 60p which raised £8.1 million net. The Cape deal involved the acquisition of three UK companies, Don International, Trist Draper and TBL (which collectively lost £544,000 at the operating level on turnover of £24.6 million in 1983).

TABLE 1 BBA performance 1979–1984

	Turnover (£000)	Profit before tax (£000)	Earnings per share	Tax rate	Net dividend
1979	137,316	8,168	9.30p	31%	2.63p
1980	135,423	850	(0.90p)	215%	1.74p
1981	130,607	3,559	1.50p	75%	1.74p
1982	150,904	4,547	2.10p	73%	1.74p
1983	156,112	5,513	3.57p	56%	1.74p
1984	176,110	5,409	0.92p	77%	1.74p

TABLE 2 Profit before tax, 1979–1984

	UK £000	Overseas £000	Total
1979	3,647	4,521	8,168
1980	(948)	1,798	850
1981	(754)	4,313	3,559
1982	(279)	4,826	4,547
1983	708	4,805	5,513
1984	(154)	5,563	5,409

Trist Draper was a wholesaler distributor to the replacement market of commercial vehicle parts. It had 16 branches, about 140 employees and a turnover of £5.8 million in 1983, which resulted in £141,000 of trading losses.

TBL was a specialist manufacturer of friction materials for railways and industrial applications; the company also manufacturers a range of automatic transmission components. It was based at Bristol, sharing a site with Don and has some 70 employees.

Also included in the purchase were two overseas companies, Don International SA (Don SA) of Belgium, and Svenska, Bromsbandsfabriken AB (SBC) of Sweden, which together made an operating profit of £812,000) on turnover of £12.14 million in 1983, together with interests in associated companies in India, Spain, Malaysia and New Zealand. Cape's share of profits before tax for these associates in 1983 was £263,000. The UK companies improved their operating performance during 1985, but remained in loss. Net assets of the companies acquired at 31 December 1985 were approximately £20.7 million.

Overseas, progress was generally satisfactory, with Textar in Germany and Bendix Mintex, the Australian associate, being particularly strong performers. Scandura Inc. in the United States has been consistently in profit, although profitability dipped sharply in 1982 as a result of a weakening of demand for industrial belting and a severe drop in demand for mining belting. The company registered a good improvement in sales and profits in 1983 and 1984.

On 13 August 1985, BBA announced the acquisition of the rubber belting business of Uniroyal Inc. in the US and Canada for about $US13.5 million (£9.3 million). Uniroyal was merged with Scandura Inc. in the United States to form the second biggest materials handling company in that country.

SECTOR ANALYSIS PERFORMANCE 1984–1985

Automotive

In the UK Mintex-Don, the largest UK company within the BBA group, manufacturers friction materials, mostly for the motor industry, including brake linings, clutch linings and disc pads. The original equipment (OE) market for friction materials was supplied via the brake and clutch manufacturers – Lucas Girling, Automotive Products and Laycock – while the replacement market was served via 23 service depots, through factors and garages. Mintex enjoys a 20–25 per cent share of the UK market, with about 25 per cent of export from the UK and a turnover of about £30 million. In the UK, competition comes from Ferodo, Antela (automotive products) and imports.

The problems experienced at Mintex during the first half of the 1980s have been outlined above, and despite five separate series of redundancies, the last of which were made during 1984 and were estimated to have removed some £2 million of the operating costs, there was no sign of a return to profitable trading: the company lost almost £2 million at the operating level in 1983, and more than £2 million in 1984. Prior to the acquisition of Cape's automotive businesses it was hoped that Mintex would achieve break-even by 1985.

Don International formerly competed directly with Mintex in the manufacture of brake and clutch linings and their distribution via a network of depots. Turnover at Don and TBL in 1983 was £18.8 million and together the two companies lost £403,000 at the trading level.

At the time of the acquisition it was stated that Mintex and Don would be rationalized into one strong and profitable UK manufacturing operation. This process was quickly completed, with the two companies merged to form Mintex-Don. In terms of manufacturing capability the companies fitted together very neatly: respective strengths were in different sectors of the market, with BBA stronger in passenger cars and Cape stronger in commercial vehicles.

Rationalization and restructuring along the following lines took place over the next 18 months or so:

1 Mintex ceased production of commercial vehicle linings and concentrated on the passenger car market, while Don concentrated on the manufacture of commercial vehicle (CV) linings. Don were undoubtedly the UK market leader at the 'heavy' end of the market, and enjoyed a good technical reputation in Europe. Mintex operated from two manufacturing sites and Don from four. The combined group operated from two CV and two passenger car sites.
2 The distribution networks were significantly rationalized; both Don and Mintex operated from 22 depots (including Trist Draper), some of which were in direct competition within the same city. The rationalization to 16 depots removed approximately £1.5 million from overhead costs.
3 A material and product strategy was formulated which co-ordinated, much more closely than in the past, R&D and production on a group-wide scale. For example, Mintex and Textar operated more or less as autonomous units within the group; subsequently production was better co-ordinated with spare capacity in the UK being utilized to take pressure off the Textar factories in Germany; some 15 per cent of Mintex's output was exported directly to Textar where it was packaged in Textar 'colours'. Significant cost savings accrued as a result of these developments, and increased collaboration and discussion led to improvements in the operating efficiencies of the UK companies.
4 The merger of Don and Mintex resulted in considerable savings in both fixed and operating costs including administration, sales, finance, computing and R&D.

At the time of the Don acquisition BBA estimated that the reduction of expense would be between £2.5 million and £3 million per annum. It had been expected that some £1.5 million of sales would be lost as a result of the merger, but this figure proved far too high with relatively few sales being lost, and the profit impact in a full year was some £4 million to £4.5 million. In addition, there was an increase in the gross margin. Arising from the increased market share of the merged Mintex-Don (40 per cent to 45 per cent), the company was able to be far more aggressive in terms of pricing, and significant price increases were pushed through (for some lines by up to 40 per cent); Ferodo, which had also been in loss in the UK and enjoyed a similar percentage share of the market, was happy to follow suit. These price increases gave BBA scope to trim unprofitable volume. The overall cost of the merger to BBA was £2.5 million to £3.5 million.

At the time, Cape, because of problems elsewhere within the group, was a forced sale. Furthermore, Don was in considerably better shape than BBA had anticipated, particularly with regard to the quality of its management and to the technological competence of the company. BBA was also impressed with the general condition of Don's manufacturing plant and fixed assets. It should also be noted that the workforce at Mintex and Don reacted positively to the measures taken towards rationalizing the two companies, realizing the dreadful state that the industry was in.

Railko manufactures reinforced plastics, bearings and components. The company made pre-tax profits of £546,000 in 1984 after net interest receipts of £64,000, on turnover up 22 per cent to £3.7 million. Some 33 per cent of turnover was for export.

Overseas   Textar had been a major success story in recent years, and the company managed to increase turnover and profits in 1984, despite the impact both of lower car and commercial vehicle registrations in Germany, and the strike by the IG Metall workers. Textar, like Mintex-Don, manufactured brake and clutch linings, enjoying a 33 per cent share of the German market and some 40 per cent of exports from Germany, in competition with Jurid, Pagid and Beral.

The notably better performance of Textar compared with Mintex stems from a number of factors, including the much stronger showing of German car manu-facturers compared with their UK counterparts, better manufacturing facilities and practices, and the different structure of the UK and German markets. The latter factor is important: in Germany the original equipment (OE) market for brake linings and disc brake pads is serviced by sale direct to the brake manufacturers as in the UK, but in Germany the car manufacturers specify the components to be used in the manufacture of the brakes. Of greater significance, the replacement market was supplied by the motor manufacturers so the vehicle manufacturers had been able to control and hold prices in Germany much better than the brake and clutch manufacturers in the UK, and this had a very significant effect upon margins in the replacement market.

Industrial

UK   Scandura Limited is the largest company within the industrial division, having in an average year a turnover of some £15 million per annum. During 1984 Scandura was badly affected by the miners' dispute, and in September that year moved into monthly losses of about £100,000. Nevertheless, the impact of the strike was mitigated to some extent by sales of belting to other outlets, both in the UK and overseas.

Scandura's activities can be subdivided into two main categories; belting, and industrial textiles and seals. The larger of these two subdivisions was belting; both heavy and lighter beltings being manufactured. The largest single user of heavy belting was the NCB (which accounted for 40 per cent of Scandura's total turnover), to whom Scandura was one of four technically-approved suppliers, the others being Fenner, TBA and Dunlop. Scandura's sales to the NCB doubled in the previous ten years and the company supplied 30 per cent of the NCB requirements, although NCB orders fell by some 40 per cent in 1984 as a result of the strike. Exports of heavy duty belting were significant, particularly to Canada, India, Spain, New Zealand and Scandinavia.

Within industrial textiles and seals, a high proportion of turnover was made up of inter-group sales of dry asbestos yarn which was used in the manufacture of automotive friction materials, although nevertheless some 45 per cent of Scandura's yarn-based products were exported. The only significant competitor in the UK for asbestos yarns and fabrics was Turner & Newall. Asbestos cloth was also made for use in the manufacture of laminates and for protective clothing. In addition Scandura manufactured sheet rubber and asbestos jointing for automotive gaskets and for flanged joints in petrochemical installations. Scandura had an estimated 12 per cent of the UK market for these products.

Sovex Marshall supplied standardized mechanical handling systems and equip-ment for unit handling. Principal customers include the Post Office, the printing trade, document handling, baggage and freight at airports and seaports. There are a large number of competitors in this area, including GEC-Elliot, Fenamec, Lamson,

Crabtree-Vickers, Denag and Desicon. Sovex Marshall was at one time a persistent loss-maker, but measures to improve the performance were taken in 1984 and these resulted in a return to trading profits (after losses of some £200,000 on turnover of about £3 million in 1983).

Overseas In the United States, Scandura Inc. manufacturers heavy-duty solid woven PVC belting for coal conveying and for the conveying of grain and feed. A somewhat thinner version was used for the conveying of citrus fruits in California, Florida and Texas. The company had successfully introduced belting into the food processing industries and for use in warehouses, supermarkets and department stores. Scandura Inc. had a good trading record and had remained consistently profitable; profits of up to £2 million were being earned a few years previously, although they then fell to below £1 million as a result in the fall-off in demand from the mining industries. The move out of solid-woven and onto plastic belting for the food processing industries, combined with a management shake-up, led to a recovery in profits over the next couple of years.

The Uniroyal companies, acquired in August 1985, were to be merged with Scandura Inc. Uniroyal's businesses returned to profit after a number of years of losses, but BBA saw further scope for cost reduction and margin improvement. Turnover of the combined grouping was anticipated to total about £55 million in 1985, of which the Uniroyal business would contribute the greater proportion. This would place the combined company in a strong position as number two in the US market, behind Goodyear. Prospects for gains in market share were thought to be good, particularly following the withdrawal of Goodrich from the market. Given the potential for cost-saving and improvements in volume for the enlarged company, good progress was anticipated in the US market. Early inspection of the Uniroyal manufacturing plants encouraged BBA in the belief that it had made a good purchase.

AUTOMOTIVE PRODUCTS (AP) 1985

On 27 January 1986 BBA offered 56.25 million BBA shares, valuing automotive products at approximately £113.6 million. This was declared unconditional on 17 March 1986.

Automotive Division

This division accounted for approximately one-third of AP group turnover and manufactured a range of products for the original equipment (OE) manufacturers. For example, AP clutches had a high (possibly 90 per cent) market share in the UK, and a growing share in Europe. The division included brakes and steering and suspension systems, and some other products in which sales were relatively small in comparison with aforementioned products.

Automotive replacement parts

Replacement parts were sold both through the OE manufacturer and also through AP's own distributor network, Antela. Antela had 89 depots through which it distributed spares to the garage trade. It had a turnover of £25 million and a market share of under 2 per cent. Approximately 30 per cent of Antela's turnover was accounted for by AP products. In a weak, over-supplied market AP had moved to franchising, and over 50 per cent of the depots were franchised. Profits had been on an improving trend over the previous two years.

Precision hydraulics

The division manufactured flying control and landing gear for civil and military aircraft, and hydraulics for military and defence applications. Turnover in 1985 was about £14 million. An industrial relations problem was resolved, and turnover was expected to reach £19 million with good margins.

GUTHRIE 1988

After 1985 there were significant improvements in EPS achieved without a major acquisition. However, in 1988 BBA acquired Guthrie, which was approximately one-third the size of BBA in terms of sales and assets.

In April 1988, Permodalan Nasional Barhad accepted BBA's £135 million cash for its 61 per cent stake in Guthrie. BBA were offering 2.7 cumulative convertible preference shares (at 6.75 per cent) for each Guthrie share which, with BBA shares at 154p, valued the cumulative preference shares at 292p, against a pre-bid price for Guthrie of 198p and a cash alternative of 270p.

Reasons for the offer

In the automotive components business, Guthrie's concentration in North America complemented BBA's activity in Europe and Australia. Guthrie's activity in structural plastics for the automotive industry in the USA would facilitate BBA's further growth in this area in Europe.

BBA had sought for some time to extend its activity in niche markets in industrial textiles for a wide range of end-users. Guthrie's hose and floor-covering business would provide a major step forward in this regard.

It was argued that the spread of businesses of the two groups in North America, Europe and Australia offered an excellent geographical fit, protecting the enlarged group from exposure to any one economy. The sector spread of the new group would markedly improve the industrial balance of the two companies' activities.

The Business of Guthrie

The activities of Guthrie are structured under six operating divisions: Automotive Components, Aviation Services, Electrical Equipment, Fire Protection Equipment, Textiles and Floor Coverings, and Trading.

Automotive Components   This division consisted principally of Butler Metal, based in Ontario, and Butler Polymet, which had plants in Toronto and North Carolina and a research centre in Detroit. Butler Metal was a major supplier to General Motors and had contracts for the supply of important motor components for the GM-10 series of intermediate cars. Butler Polymet manufactured and assembled structural plastic mouldings and had major contracts with Ford for the load floor for the Taurus and Sable estate cars and for bumper assemblies. Both companies had been awarded high quality ratings from General Motors, and Butler Polymet had gained Ford's prestigious Q.1 rating.

Aviation Services   This business was conducted through Page Avjet Corporation, an aircraft sales and service business which provided a range of products and services to general and commercial aviation in the USA. The principal base was at Dulles, and there were other significant operations at Orlando, Miami, Detroit and Minnea-polis. Page had one of the largest independent aircraft modification and main-tenance centres in the world and had an established reputation for the design and installation of high-quality interiors. It also undertook specialized engineering projects, including supplemented fuel tanks for Boeing 727 and 737 aircraft, engine noise reduction kits for DC-8 aircraft, and cargo doors. Page also operated a Jet Sales Division which bought and sold executive jet and airline passenger and cargo aircraft, and had a franchise with the Beech Aircraft Corporation.

Electrical Equipment   This division consisted of Ajax Magnethermic Corporation and Trench Electric. Ajax was one of the world's leading manufacturers of induction heating and melting equipment and its products were widely used in steel mills, foundries and the metal processing industries. Its headquarters and research and development centre were in Ohio and it had manufacturing facilities in Kentucky, North Carolina, Canada and the UK. Trench Electric, based in Toronto and with a marketing subsidiary in Germany, designed and manufactured specialized high voltage electrical transmission equipment for public utilities and major electrical contractors throughout the world.

Angus Fire Armour was one of the world's leading suppliers of fire-fighting and fire-protection equipment. Its principal customers were fire brigades, industries with high value installations, and government and military departments, but its products had widespread applications and were widely used in most countries in the world. Its principal products included Angus Duraline, the best selling fire hose in the UK, fire-fighting foam, fixed fire protection systems, extinguishers and sprinklers.

Textiles and Floor Coverings   The principal UK company in this division was Duralay, which was the largest manufacturer of carpet underlay in Europe. 'Super Duralay' was the UK market leader, and Duralay also supplied retailers such as Harris Queensway, Allied Carpets and John Lewis with own-brand underlays. Duralay had developed a new range of floor-covering accessories, and further growth resulted from the acquisition of P. C. Cox (Newbury) Limited, a manu-facturer of adhesive and mastic applicators.

In Australia, Tascot Templeton manufactured Wilton, Axminster and bonded carpets for the Australian market and also had an active export trade. Palm Beach Towel was the second largest towel manufacturer in Australia and supplied a broad range of high-quality towels and towelling products.

Trading   This division consisted largely of the group's wholesaling, retailing and packaging interests in Malawi, which were sold in March 1988. Guthrie Export Services provided export and buying services for government and private cus-tomers.

In the year ended 31 December 1987, the Guthrie Group had turnover of £319.8million (1986: £321.0million), profit before taxation of £22.6million (1986: £17.6million), and earnings per share of 21.8p (1986: 19.1p). Net tangible assets attributable to shareholders at that date amounted to £106.9 million, and net cash balances were £13million.

BBA PRODUCTS 1993

After 1988 there were some minor acquisitions and divestments, but the product market portfolio did not change significantly. In 1993 the group operated in three divisions as shown below.

Automotive

This division has three principle activities; friction materials which are mostly brake and clutch linings and the manufacture of brakes and transmission systems.

Industrial

There are two activities within this division.

High Performance Textiles   This sector produces conveyor belting, yarns and high temperature textiles, Duralay, which is Europe's leading carpet cushion underlay and accessories manufacturer, hose and foam products for fire extinguishers and high performance textiles. Products for this latter group include packaging materials, a fabric softener for detergents and a root control system for the construction industry.

Heavy Electric   This sector's main products are high voltage instrument transformers and power reactors.

Aviation

Aviation Services provide ground support facilities (fuelling, cleaning and baggage handling). The industry is fragmented and further acquisition opportunities will occur as the industry becomes more concentrated. Signature, as the BBA business is now called, is a significant player in this market. Aviation Engineering services and refurbishes aircraft. Component Manufacturing makes landing and steering gear.

In the autumn of 1993 Dr White, the Managing Director, retired on the grounds of ill health and his place was taken by Roberto Quarto.

APPENDIX 1   BBA – FINANCIAL RECORD 1979–1993

	1979 (£m)	1980 (£m)	1981 (£m)	1982 (£m)	1983 (£m)	1984 (£m)	1985 (£m)	1986 (£m)	1987 (£m)	1988 (£m)	1989 (£m)	1990 (£m)	1991 (£m)	1992 (£m)	1993 (£m)
Turnover	137	135	131	151	156	176	230	553	673	1,012	1,244	1,229	1,252	1,322	1,417
Profit after int.	8.0	0.4	3.6	4.5	5.5	5.4	13.1	26.6	41.2	64.0	71.0	59.3	30.9	47.4	(12.8)
Exceptional items			1.3	0.7	0.6	1.5	(3.9)			(1.6)	(11.1)	(22.5)	(26.2)	(22.6)	(80.0)
Profit to ord. shdrs			(3.5)	5.7	14.7	(9.0)	2.5	15.0	28.7	37.2	35.3	22.6	(0.5)	11.4	(35.3)
Fixed assets			40	43	45	50	72	165	180	301	372	377	393	484	461
Net current assets			21	23	28	28	51	90	145	195	214	204	182	82	227
Capital employed	54	73	62	67	73	78	123	256	326	497	586	581	575	566	689
Creds. after 1 year			2	3	3	4	8	10	13	22	22	22	21	23	96
Provisions			46	47	59	59	84	204	233	267	351	319	374	373	374
Share capital			14	14	14	14	23	46	51	142	148	150	168	168	191
Reserves			30	31	32	32	49	142	166	107	155	131	163	153	157
Shareholders' funds			45	46	46	47	72	188	217	249	303	281	331	321	348
Minority interests			1	1	13	12	12	16	16	18	48	38	43	52	26
			46	47	59	59	84	204	233	267	351	319	374	373	374
Capital expenditure			5	6	7	7	11	33	40	62	71	69	56	64	64
No. of employees			5980	5425	5726	5610	7366	17234	18294	24828	23485	23468	22025	23086	20705
Earnings/share (p)	10.5	0.0	2.6	3.4	4.6	2.2	8.2	10.2	15.0	18.3	20.2	15.7	7.2	8.1	(5.1)
Share price: high (p)	55	48	39	39	40	59	147	288	248	188					
low (p)	35	21	19	21	23	25	50	114	102	139					
	1979	1980	1981	1982	1983	1984	1985	1986	1987	1988	1989	1990	1991	1992	1993
Inflation	59.9	70.7	79	85.9	89.8	94.3	100	103.4	107.7	113	121.8	133.3	141.1	146.2	148.5
Margin %	5.84	0.30	2.75	2.98	3.53	3.07	5.70	4.81	6.12	6.32	5.71	4.83	2.47	3.59	(0.90)
ROCE %	14.81	0.55	5.81	6.72	7.53	6.92	10.65	10.39	12.64	12.88	12.12	10.21	5.37	8.37	(1.86)
ROSF %			(7.78)	12.39	31.96	(19.15)	3.47	7.98	13.23	14.94	11.65	8.04	(0.15)	3.55	(10.14)
Gearing %			30.4	36.2	18.6	25.4	36.9	20.6	34.3	77.9	60.7	75.2	48.1	45.6	58.6
Sales/employee £			21,906	27,834	27,244	31,373	31,225	32,088	36,788	40,760	52,970	52,369	56,844	57,264	68,438
Sales/emp adjusted £			41,178	48,118	45,053	49,404	46,368	46,083	50,724	53,566	64,582	58,341	59,826	58,165	68,438

APPENDIX 2   BBA – DATA BY INDUSTRY AND GEOGRAPHIC REGION

£ million

	1981	1982	1983	1984	1985	1986	1987	1988	1989	1990	1991	1992	1993
Industrial													
Sales													
Industrial	37	42	42	46	55	94	107	227	396	445	459	486	556
Automotive	94	109	114	130	174	460	566	694	713	632	596	621	574
Aviation								91	135	152	198	215	286
Profit													
Industrial	1.18	2.04	1.89	2.57	4.41	12.4	10.4	20.6	39.6	46.2	35.3	39	55.3
Automotive	7.55	6.35	6.48	12.69	26.4	41.4	52.9	52.4	34.6	34.6	19.8	37.6	21.5
Aviation								10.4	17.7	16.1	14.1	10.7	12.2
Assets emp.													
Industrial	15.5	16.1	20.2	22.6	31.9	63.1	n/a	n/a	230.5	198.1	199.4	217.5	213.2
Automotive	30.1	30.6	38.1	36	52	140.6	n/a	n/a	267.1	246.8	244.1	267.6	235.3
Aviation									44.7	69.7	85.5	115.1	124.7
Geographic													
Sales													
UK				48	66	173	214	287	287	270	244	252	259
Europe				91	120	241	277	319	350	388	389	404	434
N America				24	29	67	66	232	372	379	439	469	584
Rest of world				13	15	73	116	174	235	192	180	197	140
Profit													
UK				0.71	3.41	5.93	18.1	26.8	22.8	16.9	8.5	18.81	15.2
Europe				5.36	8.21	15.1	15	20.3	25.6	22.5	16.9	26.3	25.5
N America				1.33	2.86	8.2	7.7	19.6	36.5	38.5	31.3	25.3	37.9
Rest of world				-0.31	0.93	8.17	8.9	13.3	20.5	15.4	9.4	13.8	9.4
Net assets emp.													
UK									173	175	173	167	159
Europe									120	114	123	144	181
N America									165	159	162	204	230
Rest of world									72	56	60	73	1

APPENDIX 3   BBA – SECTOR AND GEOGRAPHIC DATA 1993

Automotive division	*Total sales £574m*		*Total profit £21.5m*	
	Friction material	Brakes	Clutches	Other
% total sales	52	15	24	9
	UK	Europe	N. America	Rest of world
% total sales	33	57	6	4
% total profit	31	62	5	2
Industrial division	*Total sales £556m*		*Total profit £55.3m*	
	Industrial textiles	Heavy electrical		Engineering plastics
% total sales	56	32		12
	UK	Europe	N. America	Rest of world
% total sales	24	19	56	1
% total profit	21	19	60	–
Aviation division	*Total sales £286m*		*Total profit £12.2m*	
	Aviation services	Aviation engineering		Component manufacturer
% total sales	22	17		61
	UK	N. America		
% total sales	11	89		
% total profit	13	87		

APPENDIX 4   AUTOMOTIVE PRODUCTS (£ MILLION)

	1981	1982	1983	1984	1985
Turnover	202	230	223	242	260
Operating profit	7.3	1.3	14.3	13.2	17.2
Profit after interest and tax	(2.2)	(14.1)	4.0	3.9	7.5
Fixed assets	73.5	78.6	73.3	77.8	79.2
Working capital	74.2	73.3	.75	80.6	65.9
	147.7	151.9	148.3	158.4	155.1
Capital and reserves	100.3	87.8	87.4	86.9	88.2
Net borrowings	47.4	64.1	60.9	71.5	66.9
	147.7	151.9	148.3	158.4	155.1
Earnings/share	−7.54	−27.7	4.18	3.72	9.92
ROCE %	4.9	0.9	9.6	8.3	11.1
No. of employees	10,493	9,285	9,186	85,522	8,172
Turnover					
UK				187.7	189
Europe				28.5	46
Rest of world				19.4	25.2
Profit					
UK				10.5	14.6
Europe				0.9	1
Rest of world				1.6	2.1

APPENDIX 5   GUTHRIE CORPORATION (£ MILLION)

Turnover	1983	1984	1985	1986	1987
Turnover	280.5	359.5	332.1	321	319.8
Operating profit	11.1	16.8	18.2	19.7	22.3
Profit after interest and tax	5.3	9.1	11.7	14.7	17.8
Fixed assets					55.8
Working capital					75.8
					131.6
Capital and reserves					107.2
Net borrowings					24.4
					131.6
Earnings/share (p)	7.5	12.8	16.5	19.1	21.8

1987

	Profit	Turnover
Sector analysis		
Auto Components	5.61	65.0
Aviation Services	5.97	78.7
Electric Equipment	2.72	51.4
Fire Protection Equip.	3.68	56.7
Textiles, Flooring	3.48	56.5
Trading	0.83	11.5
	22.29	319.8
Geographical analysis		
Africa	1.05	11.3
Australia	1.69	14.2
Canada	4.28	63.7
UK and Europe	3.22	92.0
USA	12.05	138.6
	22.29	319.8

APPENDIX 6   TURNER & NEWALL ACCOUNTS

		1989	1989	1989	1989	1989
Turnover	£M	1,188	1,294	1,359	1,390	1,662
Profit before tax	£M	84	70.5	40.4	63	48.4
Prof. to shdrs	£M	62.6	47.9	11.1	26.2	19.2
Extraord. items	£M	5.9	3.5			
Fixed assets	£M	446.8	555.7	552.8	618.5	797
Working capital	£M	307.3	323.4	316.5	302	449.2
Total cap. emp.	£M	754.1	879.1	869.3	920.5	1246.2
Sharehldrs' equity	£M	477.4	487.4	524.1	516.3	559.3
Long term cap.	£M	681.4	801.3	789.9	847.3	1148.7
Short term loans	£M	72.7	77.8	79.4	73.2	97.5
Total cap. emp.	£M	754.1	879.1	869.3	920.5	1246.2
No. of shares	M	27.05	358.6	436.9	438.1	438.1
No. of employees	000's	39.8	42.1	39.1	38.1	41
Inflation		121.8	133.3	141.1	146.2	148.5
Margin %		7.07	5.45	2.97	4.53	2.91
ROCE %		12.33	8.80	5.11	7.44	4.21
ROSF %		17.60	14.46	7.71	12.20	8.65
Gearing %		42.73	64.40	50.72	64.11	105.38
Sales/emp	£'000	29.85	30.74	34.76	36.48	40.54
Sales/emp adj.	£'000	36.39	34.24	36.58	37.06	40.54

APPENDIX 7   SHARE PRICES (PENCE)

	1984	1985	1986	1987	1988	1989	1990	1991	1992	1993	1994
BBA H	57.5	148.1	290.0	250.0	189.0	180	178	160.2	157.3	1990.0	230.0
BBA L	24.5	49.9	115	103	140	140	98.9	100.0	105.8	147.0	174.0
Nominal value 25p											
T&N H	107.5	114.1	239.8	321.0	200.0	220	213.1	193	174	223	260
L	60.3	73.5	80.1	139.0	154.0	160	135.1	103	99	167	157
Nominal value 100p											
Index H	1510	1490	1750	2450	1880	2460	2460	2720	2830	3490	3500
L	1290	1270	1390	1600	1590	1800	2000	2120	2290	2750	2870

H = High
L = Low
T&N = Turner & Newall.

APPENDIX 8   WORLD PRODUCTION OF CARS AND COMMERCIAL VEHICLES

Vehicles (millions)

| | Cars and commercial vehicles | | | | | | All cars and light commercial vehicles |
	UK	France	West Germany	Italy	Japan	North America	World
1950	0.78	0.36	0.31	0.13	0.32	6.67	
1960	1.81	1.37	2.06	.64	0.48	8.26	
1970	2.10	2.75	3.84	1.85	5.29	9.48	
1975	1.65	2.86	3.19	1.46	6.94	10.41	
1978	1.61	3.51	4.19	1.66	9.04	14.71	
1980	1.31	3.38	3.88	1.61	11.04	9.38	
1982	1.16	3.15	4.06	1.45	10.73	8.25	
1983	1.29	3.34	4.15	1.57	11.11	10.72	
1984	1.13	3.06	4.04	1.60	11.46	12.75	
1985	1.31	3.02	4.45	1.57	12.27	13.60	
1986	1.25	3.19	4.60	1.83	12.26	13.22	
1987	1.39	3.49	4.63	1.91	12.25	12.61	
1988	1.54	3.70	4.63	2.11	12.70	13.19	
1989	1.56	3.92	4.85	2.22	13.03	13.05	44.45
1990	1.57	3.77	4.98	2.12	13.49	11.63	45.12
1991	1.45	3.61	5.01	1.87	13.25	10.48	43.24
1992							44.40
1993							42.63

APPENDIX 9 *ACQUISITIONS MONTHLY* PROFILE OF DR JOHN WHITE

If Dr John White makes running a public company sound and look perfectly simple, it must be due to his clear-sighted, highly organized, tough, no-nonsense approach to business. This self-confessed workaholic was appointed Group Managing Director of BBA group at the beginning of 1985. Since his appointment as a director of BBA in October 1984, the company's share price has risen from 32p to 149p. Impressive enough.

The Yorkshire-based component manufacturer has had its share of problems. In recent years, although BBA's overseas subsidiaries made good return, the UK businesses produced losses. It is for this reason that White was chosen to steer the company on a more profitable course.

A key element in his strategy is making acquisitions. In 1985 alone, BBA made eight acquisitions in the UK and overseas worth a total of around £44 million.

White, himself, has vast experience of making acquisitions. He says he handled his first take-over at the age of 26 and, now aged 43, has completed 23 acquisitions, only one of which proved unsuccessful. These purchases were all part of the 'corporate turnarounds' which seem to be White's trademark in his career to date.

He feels his first big break came in 1967 when Professor Roland Smith offered him a senior research fellowship at the Institute of Science & Technology at Manchester, drafting him on permanent secondment to Stavely Industries. For Stavely, he investigated the problems and necessity of applying modern marketing to the machine tool industry.

Armed with this experience and a well-earned doctorate, White went to Bullough Limited where he was first of all a member of a team running a holding company which comprised eight engineering and two chemical companies. A man with a keen eye for a good acquisition, he identified recovery possibilities at Newton Derby, a small public company. On behalf of Bullough, White was involved in acquiring Newton Derby and then restructuring and running the company as Managing Director.

From 1975 to 1978, White used his expertise to good advantage for the Hepworth Iron Company and its parent Hepworth Ceramic Holdings Ltd. As Assistant Managing Director of Hepworth Iron, his executive workload was the formation of a European group in the clay pipe industry. An organization of four companies in West Germany, Holland, Belgium and France was built up by acquisition and rapidly formed into a successful cohesive group.

Tarmac plc recruited White in October 1978. To appreciate White's contribution to Tarmac over a period of six years, one has only to look at the figures. He was first in charge of Permanite, a building materials subsidiary, just breaking even on a £20 million turnover. Over the next years, he was responsible for creating the 20-company strong Tarmac Building Products Ltd with sales of £210 million and profits of £12.2 million.

The Pearson and Fenton families who ran BBA for three generations must have felt themselves fortunate to head-hunt White. BBA is a small (£176 million sales and profits of £5.4 million in 1984) multinational engaged in the manufacture of friction materials for the automotive industry and industrial textiles, principally for conveyor belting. White says that BBA will remain as a furnisher of components and expansion will be made within its core businesses.

BBA's first major acquisition since White's arrival was that of a major UK competitor to BBA's friction materials subsidiary, Mintex. It acquired Don, Cape

Industries' subsidiary, for £15.8 million in April of this year and both companies are to be reorganized to achieve lower costs all round. Other major purchases have been the acquisition of the US rubber belting subsidiary of Uniroyal Inc. for £13.5 million and the take-over of a high-tech USM company, Synterials, which is involved in the design and manufacture of complex precision moulds.

Target companies for BBA are those within its own core businesses where there is a high cost of market entry and the company is producing a good cash flow within a dying industry. The price should reflect a hefty discount to net assets.

White says that BBA's small board – the Chairman, himself as group MD, Finance Director and one non-executive director – can quickly respond to proposals or decisions and this is of great importance on the acquisition front. White goes after acquisitions himself, doing the necessary research, identification and negotiations without the assistance of intermediaries. 'If someone brought a company to me that I did not already know about, I would worry that I am losing my touch.'

When considering a take-over in a particular sector, he normally has a list of ten potential companies and then chooses just one to go for. When it comes to the actual purchase, he says that it the Chairman of the target company leaves, as is often the case, he likes 'the original executives to have the first option on filling the top management position in the new subsidiary'.

White has produced a fascinating corporate philosophy checklist for BBA's own management. In it, he talks of 'grit and gumption as preferable to inertia and intellect' and says that long-term growth requires 'resources – notably men and money' as well as 'sustained performance rather than superficial genius'.

In many ways, this philosophy draws on his deep religious faith. White is a member of the Central Board of Finance of the Methodist Church, and has just completed 24 years as a local lay preacher.

He says he will always finish every task he has set himself before he goes to bed at night. This tenacity is presumably the quality which helps him to engage in his favourite hobby of dry-stone walling in his Leicestershire smallholding. He says he sees an analogy between this hobby and his business life – 'taking small pieces and fitting them together to make a solid object.' (*Acquisitions Monthly*, December 1985).

APPENDIX 10

BBA Corporate Philosophy

The inertia of history is a powerful influence on corporate philosophy. BBA in its 103 years of existence has strayed little from:
1   Yorkshire paternalism;
2   weaving of heavy textiles; and
3   friction technology via woven or pressed resin media.

The philosophy of BBA for the next few years will be to adapt rather than abandon the inertia.

Management

1   Grit and gumption are preferable to inertia and intellect.
2   The Victorian work ethic is not an antique.
3   The man can only serve one master to whom he is responsible for a minimum number of succinctly defined tasks.
4   Most companies owned or yet to be acquired posses adequate people waiting to be transformed by dedicated leadership.

5   The effectiveness of an organization is in inverse proportion to the number of hierarchical layers.

Markets

We shall concentrate markets where:

1   The products are in a state of maturity or decline – 'Sunset Industries'.
2   The scale of our presence in a market segment will allow price leadership.
3   The capital cost of market entry is high.
4   Fragmentation of ownership on the supply side facilitates rapid earnings growth by acquisition of contribution flows.

Money

1   The longer run belongs to Oscar Wilde, who is dead.
2   The key macro and micro variables of our business are so dynamic that poker becomes more predictable than planning and reactivity than rumination.
3   Budgets are personal commitments made by management to their superiors, subordinates, shareholders and their self-respect.
4   The cheapest producer will win.
5   The investment of money on average return of less than three points above market should be restricted to Ascot.
6   Gearing should not exceed 40 per cent. The location from which funds emanate should be matched to the location from which the profit stream permits their service.
7   We are not currency speculators, even when we win.
8   Tax is a direct cost to the business and, accordingly, should be eschewed.
9   Victorian thrift is not an antique.
10 Nothing comes free, cheap assets are often expensive utilities.

Monday
Our tactic is to:

1   Increase the metabolic rate of BBA through directed endeavour;
2   Increase profit margins by drastic cost reduction;
3   Massage and thereby extend the life cycle of the products in which we are engaged;
4   Become market dominant in our market niches by:
    (a) outproducing the competition;
    (b) Transforming general markets where we are nobody to market niches where we are somebody.
    (c) Buying competitors;
5   Use less money in total and keep more money away from the tax man and the usurer;
6   Avoid the belief that dealing is preferable to working;
7   Go home tired.

Maybe
1   The replication of our day-to-day tactic provides long-term growth.
2   We need to address 'Monday' this week and what our reaction will be to what may be on 'Monday' for the next three years.
3   Three years is, in the current environment, the limit of man's comprehension of what may be.
4   Long-term growth necessitates:
    (a) Resource – notably men and money.
    (b) Sustained performance rather than superficial genius.

COMPANY BACKGROUND – GKN

GKN was founded in 1902 under the name Guest, Keen and Nettlefolds Ltd by the merger of Guest, an iron and steel manufacturer, Keen, which manufactured nuts and bolts and Nettlefolds, which manufactured wood screws. Guest was based in South Wales, with the two manufacturing companies being based in the Midlands. In 1919 the group acquired Joseph Sankey, which was involved in the automotive industry. This set the pattern for their business activities through to the end of the second world war, with a balance between iron and steel production and steel-using activities.

Following the second world war GKN developed its interests in both steel making and the manufacture of steel-based products such as forgings, pressings and fabrications. Much of this expansion supported the rapidly growing British motor industry, and GKN also entered the defence industry with the FV432 armoured personnel carrier, which it both designed and built for the British Army.

From the early 1960s GKN went into the manufacture of more technically sophisticated products. Through the acquisition of Birfield in 1966 it became involved in the manufacture of the constant velocity joint (CVJs) used in front-wheel drive cars, and gained a shareholding in Uni-Cardan, a European transmissions group. In 1967 the production and steel-using activities were separated, prior to the nationalization of steel-making operations.

GKN's involvement in CVJs and front-wheel drive transmissions was to its advantage in the 1970s when the British motor industry started to weaken. Continental manufacturers thrived and were increasingly using the front-wheel drive configuration for small to medium sized cars. GKN was also able to exploit its experience in this technology in America, where it would later build two CVJ factories at the start of the 1980s. In 1974 it entered the pallet hire business by establishing the Chep national pallet pool in the UK, in partnership with Brambles Industries of Australia. Chep expanded into continental Europe in 1978.

Growth into the automotive industry had largely been achieved through a series of acquisitions. This was halted by the intervention by the Monopolies Commission in 1983 which thwarted GKN's bid for Automotive Engineering (AE).

By 1984 GKN had grown to be the biggest engineering group in the UK. It comprised 216 subsidiaries and employed 34,000 people which was less than half the number employed ten years previously.

At that time the company was organized into four divisions as follows:

Automotive components and products

This sector of GKN produced transmission equipment for the car, truck, tractor and other vehicle manufacturers, together with axles, bearings, pistons, military vehicles and a whole range of automotive components from cabs and chassis to couplings and disc brakes. The principal area of production was the UK, but the company also owned plant in West Germany, Italy, USA, France and Denmark.

Industrial supplies and services

This business was varied, having interests in pallet hire, scaffolding, vending machines, threaded metal fasteners, tools, piling, soil improvement and specialist foundation services. Its principal areas of operation were the UK, South Africa, USA, West Germany, Holland, France and Belgium. The group further included home improvement systems, aluminium and plastic extrusion, safety footwear and clothing, water treatment, locks, hinges, steel reinforcement, brewery kegs and racking and storage systems.

Wholesale and industrial division

This division was concerned with replacement parts for vehicles, steel stockholding and processing, together with distribution of hardware, gardening equipment and tools, DIY and leisure goods to supermarkets. Its activities were based in the UK, France, USA and Ireland.

Special steels and forgings

Based in the UK, this division was responsible for electrically-melted alloy and special carbon steels as well as forged steel products for the automotive, agricultural, aerospace, mining and railway industries. Its products included camshafts, crankshafts, gas turbine discs, steering and suspension joint assemblies.

Trevor Holdsworth took over GKN at a low point in 1980. His successor described his term in office as taking GKN from 'Midlands metal basher to world leader in innovation and development of sophisticated new engineering products, and in the use of the most advanced technology in design and production'.

Holdsworth stated an aim to rebuild and expand GKN through the 1980s and beyond via new technology, new products and services, new markets and new facilities. He saw a need to make GKN a global player. On the international front GKN gained markets and joint ventures in Europe, Japan and North America.

During the period 1984–8 GKN followed a programme of rationalization, divesting or transferring to related company status business seen as non-strategic. This included industries such as steel fasteners, which had been part of the original company offerings, and steel production. At the same time new ventures such as waste management were started.

Prior to announcing his retirement Holdsworth 'prepared for succession', announcing in 1986 that David Lees would be taking over, and that the MD and remaining deputy MD would stand down to allow a new team to move in. The team consisted of the then executive directors, who were given more focused responsibilities in the 1987 reorganization. The members of this team were around ten years younger than those retiring.

In David Lees' first statement as Chairman he said: GKN had a clear strategy in place, a management team well capable of executing it, and an international spread of manufacturing and service businesses that gives us a sound base for further growth.[4] He stated his aim to continue expanding the service businesses through acquisition, investment and organic growth. The strategy for automotive was to continue to develop the business internationally, with new product development seen as a key issue, and he declared the expansion of defence interests as a strategic aim.

In 1990 there was some board reorganization. Defence was no longer a main division of the business, and automotive was split into GKN automotive drive line systems and engineered and agritechnical products. The Defence MD became MD of engineered and agritechnical products. The new division names were not directly reflected in the operational review. The Business Development Director left, and was not replaced. The company also made other changes to address the weakened demand in many markets, which Lees saw as not being reversed in the short term. These included actions to improve performance and reduce costs and involved shortening of management reporting lines. Training and management development were seen as areas where investment must continue, even if investments in plant and machinery had to be delayed. Quality was also emphasized, with GKN obtaining 16 new quality awards.

Strategically eastern Europe was seen as offering opportunities to the automotive businesses, with an immediate prospect for acquisition in East Germany. This would be used to supply the Eastern European automotive market with driveline components. Defence is still seen as strategically important. The year of 1990 also saw the launch of the Chep pallet pool in the USA. This was to be aggregated with the European business, and this is seen as a business with development potential in the 1990s.

In the 1993 annual report, the prospects for the divisions of GKN were as follows:

Automotive driveline products

Accounting for some 57 per cent of group sales in 1993, this division is responsible for the production of constant velocity joints (CVJs), the most important single product in the GKN portfolio. The CVJ was developed over 35 years ago to make front-wheel drive possible in motor vehicles and is now incorporated in 84 per cent of light commercial vehicles and passenger cars. GKN is the world's largest producer of CVJs and driveshafts with approximately 30 per cent of world output. (The next largest producer, NTN of Japan provides 15 per cent, most of the remainder being accounted for by in-house manufacture by the vehicle constructors.) In 1993 GKN manufactured almost 48 million CVJs in the UK, Germany, France, Spain, Italy and the USA as well as in the plants of ten associated companies throughout the world.

This division also contains a joint venture (48.5 per cent) with Siemens in Germany, Emitec, which produces metal substrates for catalytic converters. Sales volumes in this company increased by 31 per cent in 1993.

Engineered and agritechnical products

This segment includes GKN defence, the axles division and the powder metallurgy division. The agritechnical products division is based in Germany and markets agricultural driveline systems and tractor attachment systems.

GKN Sankey comprises the engineering products and industrial products divisions; GKN Wheels based in the UK and Denmark and GKN Sheepbridge Stokes for automotive, commercial and industrial diesel engines. The Powder Metallurgy division provides a wide range of powder metal parts for the industrial and automotive markets.

Sales by the defence business exceeded £100 million and a government-to-government agreement with Kuwait to export the Warrior fighting vehicle will secure jobs through to 1997.

Industrial services

The principal businesses in this segment are the Chep pallet hire business (joint venture with Brambles of Australia), the Cleanaway waste management concern and a variety of other businesses including scaffolding hire and vending machines.

The divestment of businesses accounted for a £24 million reduction in sales in 1993. Chep now has over 30 million pallets in Europe with a 50 per cent growth in cross-border shipments. All national operations showed an increase in activity in 1993.

In August Chep launched a European autocrates pool. The first contract is for components deliveries for General Motors making over eight million deliveries a year between 11 vehicle manufacturing centres and approximately 600 suppliers.

Chep has six million pallets and a national network of 150 depots. It doubled in size in 1993. A wide range of pilot operations in the grocery and allied and other industries will provide continued growth opportunities.

INDUSTRY TRENDS

The automotive components industry

The world's car and commercial vehicle makers in North America, Europe and Japan are facing a financial squeeze in the face of weak demand and the intensifying pressures of a global market. Some 50 to 70 per cent of the production cost of a car is accounted for by components and materials from outside suppliers. The leading vehicle makers are creating global operations, forcing the component producers to match this international expansion if they wish to maintain their central supplier roles. The vehicle makers are seeking to spread more of the research and development burden for new products onto the component makers. The leading suppliers are taking on the role of being systems producers, rather than suppliers of individual components. They are working closely with the car makers through simultaneous engineering, so that they are integrated into both the design and manufacturing engineering processes.

The pressures from the vehicle makers are forcing a restructuring of the components industry. Component manufacturers are cutting the number of their own suppliers drastically and are moving to a global sourcing under pressure for rationalization. The industry, traditionally fragmented, is starting to become more concentrated. The biggest groups are growing through acquisition – as witnessed most recently by the UK group T&N's purchase of Goetze, the German piston ring maker. At the same time large corporations for which the auto industry has previously been peripheral, such as Siemens and Mannesmann, are moving into specialist areas of the automotive components sector, where they can bring their technological and financial strengths to bear.

Industrial services industry

In the grocery industry pallet problems are costing $2 billion annually as a result of product damage, lost productivity, high freight rates and increased handling caused by the use of substandard pallets. The problem stems from the industry's pallet exchange system, which involves shippers and receivers voluntary exchanging pallets of supposedly like quality on a unit-by-unit basis. However this rarely occurs. This has caused an increased interest in third party pallet exchange. The major advantage of pallet pooling is that all participants use standard high quality pallets.

The concept of pallet pooling has been widely accepted in the UK but has yet to gain attention in the USA, where it faces the challenge of demonstrating that it is universally cost-effective.

The aerospace and defence industry

The world market used to be dominated by military requirements but this is no longer the case – in the early 1980s this segment took up 70 per cent of demand, in 1990 the split was even, but in 1994 the civil segment dominates with 70 per cent of the market.

Competition takes place on a worldwide scale with more than half of global production being exported. The US is the leader with four major players producing more than twice as much as the whole of the European aerospace industry. The European aerospace industry is second in the world with growth in civil production over the last ten years and an increasing rate of both exports and imports in this segment during the 1980s.

This high degree of concentration is due to the levels of investment required in order to be a player in the aerospace industry. For example, since 80 per cent of a modern helicopter consists of computer systems, emphasis is now placed upon the role of computer technology in development programmes. Therefore research and development (R&D) is an extremely important factor which is underlined by an unusually high percentage of highly-skilled personnel employed in that function. In 1990, 24 per cent of all industry employees were assigned to R&D activity.

There are major differences in corporate cultures between the civil and defence subsidiaries of large companies. For example, Boeing considered that this was leading to suboptimal performance and therefore separated its civil and defence arms, with a subsequent increase in performance in both units. The implications of this are that any company with interests in both segments, such as Westland, can face difficulties if it attempts to increase its civil-related business by scaling down its commitment to defence.

In UK defence procurement, competitive tendering for contracts and fixed price contracts were introduced from 1985 onwards. This was highly significant because it exposed some UK firms to competition from abroad for the first time and this led to rising imports.

The impact of the UK government's change in policy for the defence industry was further accentuated by the end of the Cold War in the late 1980s, and a further drop of world exports by a third due to the weak oil prices and the Third World debt crisis. The impact upon the UK defence industry has been a reduction in domestic sales by 20 per cent and an increase in imports by 10 per cent.

A further problem, which has had an even greater impact under the influence of fixed contracts, has been the explosion of development costs in recent programmes. Financing these increasing costs is a major challenge facing the industry in the future.

Companies which have remained in defence have consolidated their competitive position with divestments of non-core businesses, acquisitions of competitors and joint ventures. This has further increased market concentration, with weak firms unable to establish strong market share thereby being vulnerable to take-over.

Government procurement practices remain a critical factor, with many governments still protective of their national defence industries – for example, of the 1993 UK defence budget 75 per cent was committed to UK firms, with 16 per cent available for collaborative arrangements and only 9 per cent for imports.

Success in export markets will become increasingly important as real UK defence spending reduces. The UK is the second highest exporter of defence equipment after the US with 20 per cent of the world market. Figure 1 illustrates the major customers of UK companies, and the leading importers over recent years.

In 1990, the MOD published *Options for Change* – its plan for defence expenditure over the next decade – which identified reductions in tanks, guns, infantry battalions, ground attack aircraft and naval surface escorts. More emphasis will be placed on increased mobility and flexibility for scaled-down armed forces, giving rise to the concept of air cavalry. As such, it is envisaged that there will be a greater requirement for helicopters which Westland are well placed to take advantage of with the development of their new EH101 helicopter.

Furthermore, the fortunes of the civil aerospace industry in the UK are expected to improve after 1995, with demand forecast to increase steadily in line with the growth of travel and leisure industries.

The government may also play a crucial role in supporting Britain's aerospace industry given its strategic importance. Britain is one of only four countries to retain a complete aerospace capability, and the industry is the biggest contributor to Britain's exports.

Despite the differences between the defence and civil segments, there are synergies which are particularly clear in the helicopter industry, whereby all helicopter manufacturers to a large extent depend upon military orders, with nearly all the civil helicopters being derived from military variants.

Within this global market there are eight major helicopter manufacturers – four in western Europe:

- Aerospatiale of France;
- Augusta of Italy;
- Messerschmitt-Bolkow-Blohm of Germany; and
- Westland of the UK;

and four US-based companies:

- Bell;
- Boeing-Vertol;
- Hughes (subsidiary of McDonnell-Douglas); and
- Sikorsky (subsidiary of United Technologies Inc.).

These companies compete across a wide spectrum of aircraft types, from light utility to large tactical transport and anti-submarine warfare aircraft. Forecasts of the world market to the end of this decade suggest civil and military sales of some 35,000 helicopters, of which half will be for military use with the US demanding the majority of the medium to large aircraft. Most of the civil market will be dominated by smaller aircraft in which the above European manufacturers concentrate.

Although European manufacturers traditionally grew through the reliance on licensed production of US helicopters, in recent years they have branched out extensively on their own, with many indigenous civil and military designs keenly

UK defence equipment expenditure

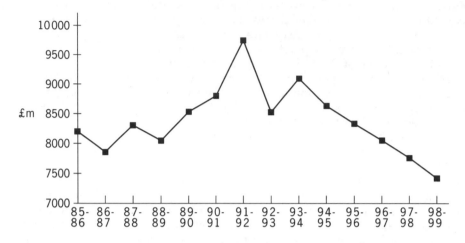

UK defence exports 1985–1989

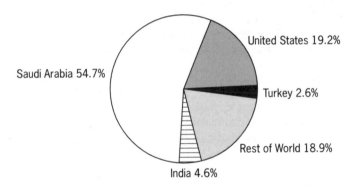

World's leading importers of defence equipment 1988–1992

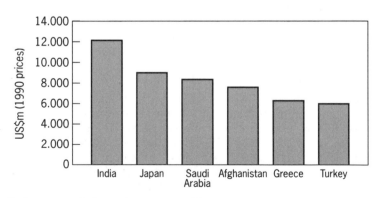

FIGURE 1　Defence, expenditure, exporters and importers
Source: Keynote, Market Review, Industry Trends and Forecasts UK Defence Industry, 1993.

competing with US versions. At the same time, the increasing R&D costs of new helicopters have resulted in vigorous efforts to establish international collaboration on a wide range of ventures, with the development of specialist European companies for these purposes. These strategic alliances are a key feature of the helicopter industry.

For example, the Eurocopter consortium – jointly owned by Aerospatiale and Messerschmitt-Bolkow-Blohm – is developing anti-tank helicopters for the armies of both countries for the 1990s. A second group is the Anglo-Italian EH Industries – owned by Westland and Augusta – which was set up to develop the EH101 helicopter for the Royal Navy (as a replacement for the Sea King anti-submarine helicopter) and the Italian Navy, as well as civil variants.

Among the four European companies, Aerospatiale is the largest competitor with a range of interests encompassing aircraft, helicopters, tactical missiles, space and strategic systems. Helicopters account for approximately 23 per cent of product sales (on turnover of FF435 billion), with a programme that concentrates predominantly on the civil helicopters with the Ecureuil, but also produces the Super Puma, Dauphin and Tiger military models.

Augusta – part of a large Italian conglomerate with diverse interests – has a range of helicopters, including the A-109 general purpose helicopter and A-129 Mungusta. Augusta has also, under license, built versions of some Sikorsky, Bell and Boeing-Vertol helicopters. Furthermore, the company is working with Westland on the EH101 helicopter.

The German company Messerschmitt-Bolkow-Blohm is concentrating on smaller light helicopters, primarily the BO-105 utility aircraft built in several military and civil versions including the PAH-1 anti-tank model.

Of the US companies, Sikorsky – part of the US$18 billion turnover United Technologies Corporation with sales balanced among the aerospace, defence, building and automotive businesses – is the major competitor. With its significant helicopter portfolio – encompassing the successful Black Hawk, Apache and the Sea Hawk – it is the largest supplier to the US Navy and Army.

WESTLAND

The principal activities of the corporation are the manufacture and supply of helicopters and hovercraft for both civil and military uses and a wide range of sophisticated manufactured components and support services for customers in different sectors of the aerospace industry. These activities are organized into three divisions: helicopters, aerospace and technology. However, helicopters contribute approximately two-thirds of sales and profits.

By the mid-1980s the company did not have a viable product to promote, given the commercial failure of the W30. As such, there was a significant gap in the order book which was not helped by the ongoing development (in conjunction with Augusta) of the new EH101 model, which would not realize any sales revenues until the mid-1990s.

With concern over its immediate corporate survival, the company sought firm commitments from the UK government on their intentions to place orders. Subsequently, in 1987 the government placed an order for £300 million, also underwriting the R&D costs of the EH101. This highlights the significance of continuing government support, but more importantly the need to develop products with complementary life cycles. The failure of the W30 created a void that was not filled.

In the period following the restructuring, Westland actively sought to develop and strengthen its aerospace and technology divisions by acquiring companies and thus widening its product portfolio. In 1987 Westland acquired a 60 per cent stake in Hermetic aircraft – a US aerospace service company – for £2.5 million, to act as a customer support base for the aircraft air-conditioning business which dominated its technology division. The same year Westland also bought a 65 per cent stake in Marex Technologies – a UK company involved in making controlling and data-acquisition systems for the offshore and industrial process control industry. Although small acquisitions, they augmented the company's goals of broadening its product base to encompass support services to the civil aircraft industry and providing leadership in high-tech areas of aerospace R&D. In addition to the favourable features of the EH101, and having learnt a lesson from previous projects, several military and civil versions were developed simultaneously.

An indication of the EH101's potential were the sizeable orders won. In 1991, an order for 44 anti-submarine helicopters was placed by the UK Navy and another 50 ordered by the Canadian government, which together were worth £1.2 billion. By 1994, the order books stood at £1.9 billion but the deliveries do not start until 1996 and in the interim the company will benefit from upgrading work and trickle of Sea King and Lynx deliveries.

GKN/WESTLAND

In 1988, GKN acquired a 22 per cent share in Westland at a cost of £48 million (112p per share) from Fiat and Hanson. With conversion of preferred and preference shares GKN would control 26.6 per cent of Westland. They also secured a first refusal deal with United Technologies Corporation (UTC). The rationale behind the deal was meant to be an 'extension of GKN's defence business' (1988 annual report) with a focus on mobile forces. It was, and still is, suggested that there is a synergy between the armoured cars GKN makes which are used for quick response and a similar capability given by helicopters. The two were used as platforms for similar weapons systems and from a marketing view the buyers were often the same people.

In the early months of 1994 GKN purchased UTC's 17.9 per cent interest in Westland at 290p per share taking the GKN share to 45 per cent. In March 1994 GKN made a bid, at 290p, for the rest of Westland shares. The bid was complicated by some ongoing litigation with the Arab Organization for Industrialization (AOI).

In 1993, the company was awarded £385 million damages for cancellation of a 1979 contract. This had significant implications for the financial resources available for future product developments, acquisitions and so on.

At the time of the GKN bid (see below), no money had been received. There was considerable doubt that the whole sum would be exchanged and also whether it would come in the form of cash. In the offer document GKN commented:

> Before announcing its Offers, GKN fully evaluated Westland on the basis of public information about its prospects. GKN believes that before the speculation about the possibility of a GKN bid began in November last year, the market view of Westland's value fairly reflected Westland's prospects and the uncertainties. Little new information about Westland has been published since then. The fact is that, after the market digested the implications of the AOI announcement at the beginning of July last year, until bid speculation started at the end of November, the Westland share price traded in a range of between 210p and 250p. This trading range is consistent with GKN's own view of Westland's underlying value as a stand-alone business, given the large uncertainties surrounding its products.

In April the offer was raised to 335p or 290p for each Westland (2.5p nominal value) share to be worth 44p per share. The alternative was 165.6p in cash and 0.3096p of a new GKN share. GKN shares were standing at 538p plus a pro rata payment for the AOI settlement which was not yet finalized, but was reckoned to be worth 44p per share.

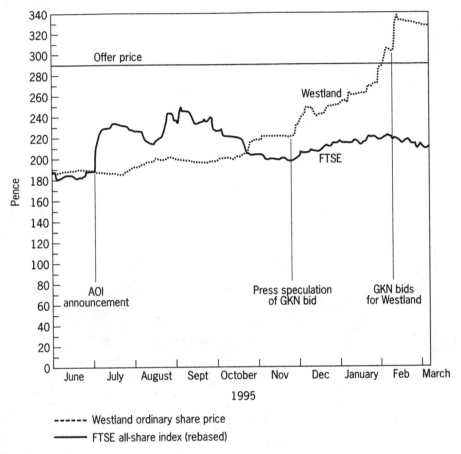

FIGURE 2   Share price reflecting speculation since November
Source: Datastream.

APPENDIX 1 ACQUISITIONS, DIVESTMENTS AND JOINT VENTURES

Date		Country	Company	Activity
Acquisitions				
Aug.	1984	US	Godfrey Holmes	Automotive distribution
	1984	USA	Beck/Arnley	Automotive parts
	1984	USA	Hayward Baker	Ground engineering
	1985	USA	Kwikform America Inc	Scaffolding and formwork business
	1985	USA	Automotive Parts	Automotive components
Nov.	1985	Australia	Quinton Hazell Automotive Div.	Wholesale vehicle parts distributor/retailer
	1985		Manchester Steel	Steel
	1986		British Vending	Vending services
Jun.	1987	Italy	Saini SpA	Power metallurgy
Jul.	1987	Australia	Macbro Rental Pty	
Sep.	1987	UK	Adapt Vending	Vending services
Sep.	1987	UK	Compass Vending	Vending services
Dec.	1987	UK	General Plumbing & Roofing Services	Property maintenance
Jun.	1987	Holland		Bicycle accessories
Apr.	1987	USA	Sparks Tune Up Centers	Car tune up & lubrication
Feb.	1988	UK	Cory Coffee Service	Vending services
Feb.	1988		Triplex/Lloyd	Engineering steels
Oct.	1988		22% of Westland	Helicopter producer
	1988	USA	Woodbine Corporation	Specialist ground modification
Aug.	1988	USA	Mid-American Industries Inc	Automotive parts distribution
	1988		F.H. Lloyd	Steel plant/rolling mill
	1988		Woodstone, via United Engineering Steels	Rolling mill
	1988		British Bright Bar	
	1988	USA	National Automotive Superstores	
Jan.	1989		Hollicell	uPVC windows, cladding
Feb.	1989	Italy	Comaxle Srl	Leading supplier axles for 4 wheel drive tractors
	1989	USA	Daves Auto Stop	
	1989	USA	Roberts Automotive	
	1989	USA	Save Auto Stores	
	1989		Midland Bright Drawn Steel	
	1990	USA	H&H Rentals	Equipment rental
	1991	UK	Caird Group	Dry waste collection
	1993	East Germany	GKN Walterscerd Getrrebe	Gearboxes

APPENDIX 1 continued

Date	Country	Company	Activity
Divestments			
Jan. 1984	Australia		Tractors and truck wheels
1984	UK		Pistons and truck wheels
Sep. 1985		Hardware Distrib.	Fasteners, safety footwear
1985		Industrial Services and Suppliers	
1986		Firth Cleveland	
1986		Granville Chemical	
1986	Ireland	GKN Autoparts	Steel stockholding
1986		GKN Steelstock	
1986	France	Uni-Cardan Service	
1986 & 1988	Germany	GKN Stenman	
1987		GKN Birwelco	Petrochemical plant, refuse incinerators
Jan. 1987		Scandinavian Security Systems	Security Systems
Oct. 1987		Laycock	Clutch business
1987		Chep	Third party pallet manufacturing
Sep. 1987		South London Pistons	Specialist engine parts distribution
Oct. 1987		Allied Steel & Wire	
1988		GKN Sankey	Brewery keg & equipment
1988			Builders hardware
1988	USA		Security locks
Acquisitions			
Sep. 1988	USA	GKN Aftermarket	Import parts
Sep. 1988	USA	Worldparts	
Sep. 1988	USA	Beck/Arnley	
1989		GKN Kwikform	
Aug. 1989	UK	GKN Autoparts	Industrial Services Div.
Oct. 1990	Australia	GKN Autoparts	Distribution
1991		Small peripheral businesses	Industrial Services & Distribution
1991	UK	ACS Coffee Service	Vending services
1991		GKN Stenman	
1991	Holland	GKN Property Maintenance	
1992		Dudley Plating	Engineering products
Aug. 1993		Automatic Catering Supplies Company	Vending services

Joint ventures (inc minority interests)

Date		Country	Company	Activity
	1983	Spain	Carraro SpA	Manufacture of axles and associated components
Jul.	1983		GKN Kwikform 60%	Scaffolding & buildng services
Jan.	1983		British Bright Bar 40%	
	1984	Germany	Viscodrive GmbH, 50%	Development & sale viscous control units
Mar.	1986	Spain	Increased % holding in Ayra Surex SA	Driveline components
	1986	Spain	Industrias Mecanicas de Galicia SA 66%	C.V. drive shafts
Apr.	1985	Australia	GKN Kwikform Industries 66%	Scaffolding & building services
	1985	Japan	Viscodrive Japan KK 51%	Viscous control units
	1985	Mexico	Sintermex SA 17.65%	
	1986	Japan	Translite KK 60% Manufacturing Co. Ltd	Composite leaf springs
	1985		United Engineering Steels	
Mar.	1987	Germany	Increased holding in ViscodriveGmbH to 75%	
Jan.	1989		Hollicell	uPVC windows, cladding
Aug.	1986	Germany	Emitec GmbH	Metal substrates for catalytic converters
Dec.	1986	USA	GKN Dyno-Rod Inc 60%	
Jan.	1988		Increased holding in Uni-Cardan to 96.7%	
Feb.	1988	Australia	Unidrive Pty Ltd 30%	
	1988		Venture Pressings Ltd	Body pressing for Jaguar cars
Mar.	1988	China	Shanghai GKN Drive Shaft Company 25%	
Feb.	1989		GKN-Brambles Enterprises	
	1988		Acquired remainder of GKN Kwikform Industries	
	1989	Germany	United Engineering Steels	Automotive suspension and steering components
Sep.	1990	USA	Chep Pallet Pool	

APPENDIX 2   GKN FINANCIAL RECORD (£ MILLION)

GKN group financial record *(adjusted to 1993 prices)*

	1993	1992	1991	1990	1989	1988	1987	1986	1985	1984	1983	1982	1981	1980	1979
Sales															
Subsidiaries	2022	2034	2028	2286	2594	2626	2636	2975	3286	3303	3280	3181			
Associated companies	617	543	534	623	700	505	706	666	451	425	315	284			
	2639	2577	2563	2909	3295	3131	3342	3641	3737	3728	3595	3465	3451	4068	4896
Operating profit	107	129	100	167	236	209	191	211	236	217	200	148	153	78	345
Share of net profit before tax of associated companies before exceptional items	27	24	31	65	70	54	53	35	22	19	15	5	9	15	50
Profit before interest and tax (as reported pre–92)							244	246	258	236					
Interest payable less receivable	-25	-23	-31	-39	-42	-28	-40	-55	-60	-54	-67	-89	-98	-95	-80
Profit before exceptional items and taxation	109	130	100	193	264	235									
Profits before losses on sale or closure of businesses (as reported post–91)	-1	-4	-23	-29	-10	-46									
Exceptional costs charged by associated companies (as reported post–91)	-10	-1	-4	-37	-1	0									
Profit on ordinary activities before taxation	98	124	73	127	253	189	204	191	199	182	148	64	64	-2	315
Taxation	-41	-58	-43	-63	-86	-73	-69	-74	-88	-94	-80	-57	-51	-68	-110
Minority interests	-18	-17	-18	-20	-20	-16	-18	-19	-16	-16	-10	-9	-13	-15	-17
Earnings of the year	39	49	12	44	147	100	116	98	94	73	58	-2	0	-85	187
Extraordinary items (as reported pre–92)							-31	-52	-30	-32	-38	-92	-47	-106	
Dividends	-52	-51	-55	-57	-61	-56	-47	-45	-43	-38	-33	-23	-25	-27	
Transfer to reserves	-13	-2	-43	-13	86	45	39	1	21	3	-13	-117	-72	-218	

APPENDIX 2 continued

GKN group financial record (adjusted to 1993 prices)	1993	1992	1991	1990	1989	1988	1987	1986	1985	1984	1983	1982	1981	1980	1979
Balance sheet															
Tangible fixed assets	672	707	707	778	803	711	734	790	884	996	950	1051	1128	1256	1445
Stocks	265	313	307	368	470	457	523	611	678	779	671	748	850	986	1293
Debtors less creditors (excluding leases)	−227	−100	−92	−95	−110	−114	−101	−104	−125	−130	−87	−75	−128	−40	70
Net operating assets	710	920	922	1050	1163	1055	1155	1297	1437	1645	1534	1724	1849	2202	2809
Investments	321	300	294	297	342	338	293	403	194	228	221	176	195	70	110
Taxation and dividend payable	−59	−78	−59	−66	−91	−89	−69	−56	−64	−62	−78	−49	−38	−44	−155
Net borrowings (as reported pre-88)											−399	−637	−621	−696	−652
Provisions for liabilities and charges	−149	−151	−121	−119	−131	−108	−116	−120	−93	−94	−70	−71	−66	−63	−67
Assets employed	823	992	1036	1162	1283	1196	1262	1524	1474	1717	1208	1143	1319	1468	2045
Equity interest	656	668	699	762	816	817	850	932	947	1059	1082	1028	1228	1381	1942
Minority interests	157	163	149	154	103	89	90	118	87	163	126	115	91	87	102
Net borrowings	10	160	189	247	364	291	322	474	441	495					
Assets employed	823	992	1036	1162	1283	1196	1262	1524	1474	1717	1208	1143	1319	1468	2045
Statistics															
Earnings per share	14.7	19.0	4.3	17.1	57.5	41.0	48.1	41.2	39.7	32.2	29.0	0.0	0.0	0.0	115.3
Earnings per share before exceptional items	18.7	21.0	15.0	40.5	61.3	58.2									
Dividends per share	20.5	20.9	21.6	23.0	24.5	22.5	20.1	18.8	17.9	16.7	15.0	13.9	15.1	16.9	48.4
Operating profit to sales of subsidiaries	5.3%	6.3%	5.0%	7.3%	9.1%	7.9%	7.3%	7.1%	7.2%	6.6%	6.1%	4.6%	4.4%	1.9%	
Operating profit to net operating assets	15.0%	14.0%	10.9%	15.9%	20.2%	19.7%	16.6%	16.2%	16.4%	13.2%	13.0%	8.6%	8.3%	3.6%	12.3%
PBIT to assets employed							19.3%	16.1%	17.5%	13.8%					
Earnings of the year to equity interest							13.8%	10.6%	10.0%	6.9%	5.4%	0.0%	0.0%	0.0%	9.6%

APPENDIX 3   GKN FINANCIAL DATA BY SBU

Ratio analysis for GKN by business (£ million)

	1985	1986	1987	1988	1989	1990	1991	1992	1993
Automotive and engineering									
Operating profit	108	101	92	100	117	90	60	95	96
Net operating assets	536	640	618	562	671	671	644	675	496
Sales	1001	1143	1208	1282	1373	1436	1413	1523	1559
ROCE	20.15	15.78	14.89	17.79	17.44	13.41	9.32	14.07	15.32
Gross profit to sales	10.79	8.84	7.62	7.80	8.52	6.27	4.25	6.24	4.87
Sales to fixed assets	1.87	1.79	1.95	2.28	2.05	2.14	2.19	2.26	3.14
Industrial services and distribution									
Operating profit	32	36	46	58	75	59	35	31	31
Net operating assets	260	258	215	236	277	266	231	227	214
Sales	823	723	693	705	742	604	512	471	463
ROCE	12.31	13.95	21.40	24.58	27.08	22.18	15.15	13.66	14.49
Gross profit to sales	3.89	4.98	6.64	8.23	10.11	9.77	6.84	6.58	6.70
Sales to fixed assets	3.17	2.80	3.22	2.99	2.68	2.27	2.22	2.07	2.16

	1985	1986
Steel and forgings		
Operating profit	18	9
Net operating assets	166	193
Sales	376	
ROCE	10.84	
Gross profit to sales	4.79	4.66
Sales to fixed assets	2	

APPENDIX 4   FINANCIAL DATA – GEOGRAPHIC

Ratio analysis for GKN by region (£ million)

	1985	1986	1987	1988	1989	1990	1991	1992	1993
UK									
Operating profit	29	25	48	58	62	52	29	38	37
Net operating assets	287	286	270	243	274	339	325	300	170
Sales	689	621	714	824	772	728	649	661	659
ROCE	10.10	8.74	17.78	23.87	22.63	15.34	8.92	12.67	21.76
Gross profit to sales	4.21	4.03	6.72	7.04	8.03	7.14	4.47	5.75	5.61
Sales to fixed assets	2.40	2.17	2.64	3.39	2.82	2.15	2.00	2.20	3.88
Continental Europe									
Operating profit	56	77	69	69	91	77	62	67	38
Net operating assets	309	405	398	379	458	422	393	429	372
Sales	580	721	707	695	796	824	815	834	779
ROCE	18.12	19.01	17.34	18.21	19.87	18.25	15.78	15.62	10.22
Gross profit to sales	9.66	10.68	9.76	9.93	11.43	9.34	7.61	8.03	4.88
Sales to fixed assets	1.88	1.78	1.78	1.83	1.74	1.95	2.07	1.94	2.09
America									
Operating profit	51	28	13	21	24	12	3	14	22
Net operating assets	168	176	131	133	152	126	114	138	136
Sales	484	451	398	368	411	374	354	403	481
ROCE	30.36	15.91	9.92	15.79	15.79	9.52	2.63	10.14	16.18
Gross profit to sales	10.54	6.21	3.27	5.71	5.84	3.21	0.85	3.47	4.57
Sales to fixed assets	2.88	2.56	3.04	2.77	2.70	2.97	3.11	2.92	3.54
Rest of the world									
Operating profit	4	7	8	10	15	8	1	7	10
Net operating assets	32	31	34	43	64	50	43	35	32
Sales	71	73	82	100	136	114	107	96	103
ROCE	12.50	22.58	23.53	23.26	23.44	16.00	2.33	20.00	31.25
Gross profit to sales	5.63	9.59	9.76	10.00	11.03	7.02	0.93	7.29	9.71
Sales to fixed assets	2.22	2.35	2.41	2.33	2.13	2.28	2.49	2.74	3.22

APPENDIX 5   GKN CHEP LIMITED FINANCIAL ANALYSIS 1988–92

Consolidated profit and loss accounts

	1988 £'000	1989 £'000	1990 £'000	1991 £'000	1992 £'000
Turnover	49,983	60,771	73,687	79,342	80,342
Operating profit	20,323	22,349	26,690	30,087	27,314
Interest	−4,088	−7,204	−10,171	−9,677	−8,444
Profit before taxation	16,235	15,145	16,519	20,410	18,870
Taxation	−4,423	−3,580	−2,515	−4,912	−2,574
Profit after taxation	11,812	11,565	14,004	15,498	16,296

Consolidated balance sheet

	1988 £'000	1989 £'000	1990 £'000	1991 £'000	1992 £'000
Fixed assets					
Tangible assets	60,034	73,165	88,909	91,146	100,613
Intangible assets					
	60,034	73,165	88,909	91,146	100,613
Current assets					
Stocks	1,284	672	2,604	1,064	2,265
Debtors	9,787	12,781	14,461	13,477	13,817
Investments					
Bank and deposits	1,396	790	1,354	1,199	
Other	111	370	276	638	3,018
	12,578	14,613	18,695	16,378	19,100
Current liabilities					
Creditors	−6,678	−8,368	−8,154	−11,463	−12,890
Loans/overdraft	−1,832	−2,360	−2,724	−2,721	−2,129
Other	−14,437	−11,988	−16,794	−13,108	−15,996
	−22,947	−22,716	−27,672	−27,293	−31,015
Net current assets	−10,369	−8,103	−8,977	−10,914	−11,915
Total assets less current liabilities	49,665	65,062	77,932	80,232	88,698
Long term debt	−36,792	−52,202	−63,970	−66,177	−74,598
Creditors due after more than one year	−13		−58	−62	
Net assets	12,860	12,860	13,904	13,993	14,100
Shareholders' funds					
Called-up share capital	6,129	6,129	6,129	6,129	6,129
Reserves	6,731	6,731	7,775	7,864	7,971
	12,860	12,860	13,904	13,993	14,100
Authorised capital	10,000	10,000	10,000	10,000	

		1988	1989	1990	1991	1992
Turnover		49,983	60,771	73,687	79,342	80,342
Profit before tax		16,235	15,145	16,519	20,410	18,870
Net tangible assets		49,665	65,062	77,932	80,232	88,698
Shareholders' funds		12,860	12,860	13,904	13,993	14,100
Profit margin	%	32.48	24.92	22.42	25.72	23.49
Return on shareholders' funds	%	126.24	117.77	118.81	145.86	133.83
Return on capital employed	%	40.92	34.35	34.25	37.50	30.79
Liquidity ratio		0.49	0.61	0.58	0.56	0.54
Long term debt		38,637	54,562	66,752	68,960	76,727
Gearing	%	0.75	0.81	0.83	0.83	0.84
Number of employees		742	822	938	924	1,042

APPENDIX 6 WESTLAND BALANCE SHEET AND PROFIT & LOSS ACCOUNT

Consolidated balance sheet

£m	1984	1985	1986	1987	1988	1989	1990	1991	1992	1993
Fixed assets										
Intangible assets			4.70	4.30	4.00	3.70	3.30	3.00	2.70	2.30
Tangible assets	105.80	95.70	93.10	108.90	105.40	109.70	112.10	133.70	133.90	133.10
Investments	1.10	1.40	1.50	1.50	1.60	1.80	1.10	1.10	1.50	1.70
	106.90	97.10	99.30	114.70	111.00	115.20	116.50	137.80	138.10	137.10
Current assets										
Stocks	138.20	114.80	109.70	160.20	169.90	128.90	127.00	133.20	145.80	146.30
Debtors	78.10	72.50	69.30	71.80	81.90	92.70	85.70	101.90	102.90	111.10
Cash in hand & at bank	2.40	1.90	70.70	25.90	3.20	13.60	14.20	12.80	7.70	33.00
	218.70	189.20	249.70	257.90	255.00	235.20	226.90	247.90	256.40	290.40
Total assets	325.60	286.30	349.00	372.60	366.00	350.40	343.40	385.70	394.50	427.50
Creditors: due within 1 year	127.30	132.10	104.20	121.40	145.80	128.60	125.50	136.70	134.10	153.60
Net current assets	91.40	57.10	145.50	136.50	109.20	106.60	101.40	111.20	122.30	136.80
Total assets – current liabilities	198.30	154.20	244.80	251.20	220.20	221.80	217.90	249.00	260.40	273.90
Creditors: due after > 1 year	46.20	49.60	65.40	40.40	37.20	42.50	43.30	44.30	40.40	39.60
Provisions for liabilities & charges	15.90	68.40	67.30	65.40	39.90	27.40	11.80	12.30	14.90	14.30
Net assets	136.20	36.20	112.10	145.40	143.10	151.90	162.80	192.40	205.10	220.00
Capital & reserves										
Called-up share capital	14.80	14.80	50.70	44.10	44.10	44.20	44.20	44.20	44.20	44.30
Share premium account	1.10	1.10	21.60	3.80	3.90	4.70	5.30	5.60	6.80	7.80
Revaluation reserve	24.00	23.10	22.60	31.70	25.90	24.50	23.50	41.80	39.40	38.20
Other reserves	5.00	3.30	14.80	34.40	34.40	34.20	35.00	34.60	34.70	34.00
P&L account	79.60	-20.00	-13.80	12.30	14.00	24.10	33.10	46.20	59.10	73.80
Shareholders' funds	124.50	22.30	95.90	126.30	122.30	131.70	141.10	172.40	184.20	198.10
Minority interests	11.70	13.90	16.20	19.10	20.80	20.20	21.70	20.00	20.90	21.90
Equity	136.20	36.20	112.10	145.40	143.10	151.90	162.80	192.40	205.10	220.00

APPENDIX 6 continued
Consolidated profit & loss account

£m	1984	1985	1986	1987	1988	1989	1990	1991	1992	1993
Turnover	296.30	308.40	344.40	381.60	358.10	431.90	411.00	467.40	422.10	448.00
Cost of sales	-253.60	-270.00	-306.50	-338.50	-315.00	-393.30	-368.70	-417.40	-373.60	-391.70
Trading profit	42.70	38.40	37.90	43.10	43.10	38.60	42.30	50.00	48.50	56.30
Net R&D and launching costs	-19.40	-15.60	-5.70	-7.50	-4.70	-8.30	-10.60	-12.50	-10.80	-14.70
Profit bef. redun. & restruc. costs	23.30	22.80	32.20	35.60	38.40	30.30	31.70	37.50	37.70	41.60
Redun. & restruc. costs in cont. op.									-5.20	-6.10
Operating profit	23.30	22.80	32.20	35.60	38.40	30.30	31.70	37.50	32.50	35.50
Disposal of surplus fixed assets										-0.50
PBIT	23.30	22.80	32.20	35.60	38.40	30.30	31.70	37.50	32.50	35.00
Net interest payable	-6.50	-11.50	-5.90	-1.20	-7.80	-6.40	-5.50	-6.80	-7.60	-4.50
Profit bef. except. items & taxation	16.80	11.30	26.30	34.40	30.60	23.90	26.20	30.70	24.90	30.50
Exceptional items	-14.00	-106.60	0.10	-16.00	-13.20	-3.20		-7.00		
Pre-tax profit	2.80	-95.30	26.40	18.40	17.40	20.70	26.20	23.70	24.90	30.50
Taxation	0.70	-0.30	-6.00	-5.50	-3.00	-2.60	-5.30	-4.70	-5.10	-7.90
Net profit	3.50	-95.60	20.40	12.90	14.40	18.10	20.90	19.00	19.80	22.60
Minority interests	-2.40	-3.10	-3.30	-3.80	-2.60	-1.00	-1.70	1.10	-0.80	-1.30
Profit attrib. to shareholders	1.10	-98.70	17.10	9.10	11.80	17.10	19.20	20.10	19.00	21.30
Extraordinary item after taxation	-5.70					-0.20				
Dividends	-4.90	-1.80	0.00	-8.20	-7.90	-8.00	-8.30	-8.60	-9.00	-9.40
Net movement shareholders funds	-9.50	-100.50	17.10	0.90	3.90	8.90	10.90	11.50	10.00	11.90

APPENDIX 7 WESTLAND FINANCIAL DATA BY SBU & GEOGRAPHY

Sales analysis – geographical

£m	1984	1985	1986	1987	1988	1989	1990	1991	1992	1993
Destination of total turnover										
North America	43.10	27.10	29.50	41.70	40.90	50.40	62.90	61.30	66.80	56.50
India			22.50	66.20	49.70	115.60	40.50	19.60		
Asia							25.00	68.60	6.30	7.60
Middle East	20.10	12.00	18.60	4.90	5.20	1.90				
Countries in European Union/Comm.	43.30	35.80	38.40	44.70	45.50	37.70	37.80	52.50	45.60	95.50
Other European countries									27.70	15.80
Other	30.60	19.20	17.40	19.70	15.60	21.20	22.40	25.80	14.30	16.80
UK	180.70	247.50	244.70	229.40	240.50	244.70	258.60	274.60	292.60	294.90
- intragroup transactions	−21.50	−33.20	−26.70	−25.00	−39.30	−39.60	−36.20	−35.00	−31.20	−39.10
Consolidated turnover	296.30	308.40	344.40	381.60	358.10	431.90	411.00	467.40	422.10	448.00

Sales & profit analysis – by activity

£m	1984	1985	1986	1987	1988	1989	1990	1991	1992	1993
Sales										
Aerospace			46.70	42.10	42.90	47.60	58.80	81.60	81.00	74.10
Helicopters			219.90	255.50	235.00	297.00	263.30	311.00	262.50	295.10
Helicopter & Aerospace	216.90	219.70								
Technology	81.70	92.50	89.40	97.80	94.00	103.30	105.40	87.60	90.90	91.70
HQ & consolidation adjustments	−2.30	−3.80	−11.60	−13.80	−13.80	−16.00	−16.50	−12.80	−12.30	−12.90
	296.30	308.40	344.40	381.60	358.10	431.90	411.00	467.40	422.10	448.00
PBIT										
Aerospace			4.90	4.33	0.90	3.50	5.80	7.40	4.50	7.60
Helicopters			12.67	18.10	28.60	19.70	19.20	25.90	26.20	26.70
Helicopter & Aerospace	12.06	9.79								
Technology	11.99	14.55	13.03	12.41	9.10	8.00	9.60	5.60	5.30	6.30
HQ & consolidation adjustments	−0.75	−1.54	1.60	0.76	−0.20	−0.90	−2.90	−1.40	−3.50	−5.10
	23.30	22.80	32.20	35.60	38.40	30.30	31.70	37.50	32.50	35.50

APPENDIX 8   WORLD PRODUCTION OF CARS AND COMMERCIAL VEHICLES

Vehicles (millions)

| | Cars and commercial vehicles | | | | | | All cars and light commercial vehicles |
	UK	France	West Germany	Italy	Japan	North America	World
1950	0.78	0.36	0.31	0.13	0.32	6.67	
1960	1.81	1.37	2.06	.64	0.48	8.26	
1970	2.10	2.75	3.84	1.85	5.29	9.48	
1975	1.65	2.86	3.19	1.46	6.94	10.41	
1978	1.61	3.51	4.19	1.66	9.04	14.71	
1980	1.31	3.38	3.88	1.61	11.04	9.38	
1982	1.16	3.15	4.06	1.45	10.73	8.25	
1983	1.29	3.34	4.15	1.57	11.11	10.72	
1984	1.13	3.06	4.04	1.60	11.46	12.75	
1985	1.31	3.02	4.45	1.57	12.27	13.60	
1986	1.25	3.19	4.60	1.83	12.26	13.22	
1987	1.39	3.49	4.63	1.91	12.25	12.61	
1988	1.54	3.70	4.63	2.11	12.70	13.19	
1989	1.56	3.92	4.85	2.22	13.03	13.05	44.45
1990	1.57	3.77	4.98	2.12	13.49	11.63	45.12
1991	1.45	3.61	5.01	1.87	13.25	10.48	43.24
1992							44.40
1993							42.63

THE CHEMICAL INDUSTRY

At the end of 1991 the chemical industry was described as a $1,230 billion a year industry. Typically the chemical industry sells approximately half its turnover to other manufacturing businesses (including other sectors of the chemical industry itself), rather than to consumers directly. Other important customer industries include electrical appliances, factory equipment, defence, cars, packaging and construction. Western Europe, Japan and North America account for about 70 per cent of the world's chemical production and consumption. Nevertheless, substantial opportunities exist for less developed nations, particularly at the lower-technology end of the industry.

The chemicals industry is composed of five main sectors:

1 *Petrochemicals* Mostly produced at high volume and low prices. Used as building block chemicals to make other synthetic materials. The sector is characterized by a relatively small number of high volume producers. Products are generally commodity-like, or closely related. Low margins are made up by high volumes required to make returns in this capital-intensive industry. Recently it has been characterized by excess capacity and in particular is closely tied to economic cycles.

2 *Plastics* A $120 billion-a-year industry. Sales in 1989 were 90 million tonnes, 75 per cent of which were accounted for by polyethylene, polystyrene, polypropylene and PVC. These plastics are also commodity-like. The speciality sector involves engineering plastics.

3 *Inorganic bulk materials* These are high-volume substances that do not contain carbon. The biggest-selling products in this area include chlorine, sodium hydroxide, sodium carbonate, titanium dioxide and hydrogen peroxide. The industry is very similar in structure, margins and fortunes to the petrochemical industry.

4 *Fine chemicals or specialities* These are sold in small volumes at high prices and use relatively sophisticated manufacturing routes. Chemicals are usually highly specific, but can be low or high technology in nature (see also separate section).

5 *Pharmaceuticals* A $130 billion-a-year industry with 75 per cent sales within the developed countries of western Europe, North America and eastern Asia. Two distinct subsectors are the leaders and the generics. The latter usually follow on

with mass production of popular drugs once the patent protection of the leader has expired. Note that there is increasing pressure for price regulation of pharmaceuticals. Although high margins can be won at present during periods of patent protection, intensifying regulation and high R&D costs increase uncertainty in this sector.

Analysts predict that the industry faces a long slow decline in petrochemicals and plastics prices. Speciality chemicals companies should do better than the industry average. Overall industry growth predictions for 1990 were 2.5 per cent, the lowest for many years.

SPECIALITY CHEMICALS

Demand patterns for many chemicals are splintering. Bulk chemicals may mean high turnover, but they sell into strongly cyclical demand and with strong competition, prices are set commodity-style in the open market. Fragmentation is forcing the industry to do far more to tailor specific types of materials to meet customer needs. Implications are that chemical companies have to hone their marketing and technical skills to meet specialized subsegments, rather than aim their products across the board.

As part of the changes in the direction of more fragmented markets, chemical companies are trying to move upmarket. Hence movement out of basic commodity materials like polyethylene and polystyrene. Specialities offer high margins (40 per cent is not uncommon against single digits on the bulk side), possibility of dominating a niche, customer loyalty and relative immunity from boom/bust fluctuations. Furthermore the growing pressure to adopt more stringent pollution controls is more easily accommodated in smaller production plants. As an illustration of the fragmentation in speciality chemicals 15 product categories are sold by more than 1,000 end producers in Europe alone. Contributing to those consumer products are 20 ingredient product categories.

The past success of speciality chemicals led the larger chemical companies to acquire and develop speciality businesses in the mid-1980s. The idea was to get off the economic ups and downs by switching into stable but fast-growing specialities. Both ICI and Rhone-Poulenc spent heavily to acquire speciality businesses, yet neither have been particularly successful; R-P has seen its specialities operating margins around the 5 per cent mark, against 15 per cent for more conventional speciality chemical companies.

ENVIRONMENTAL FACTORS

Environmental protection is becoming increasingly arduous for chemical companies. Spending on environmental measures is cutting into ordinary capital expenditure worldwide. Europe is estimated to be five years behind the US in its implementation of measures, but is having to invest during a recession rather than the good times. In the UK environmental spending is running at 20 to 25 per cent of all capital investment, according to the Chemical Industries Association. This was forecast to double from £20 million in 1990 to £400 million in 1992. In Germany both BASF and Bayer (estimated to spend £300 million a year on environmental costs) warned that the German government's increasing environmental legislation was making Germany a more unattractive location for the industry. Potential annual costs for the chemical industry, according to Bayer, could be DM1.3 billion. It claims this measure would force the company to close its basic inorganic chemicals business and titanium dioxide operations. Levies could add costs equivalent to 15 per cent to turnover. In the UK the 1993 environmental protection act was expected to cost £1.5 billion in capital investment and £300 million in additional running costs, according to the Chemical Industry Association.

In Europe environmental legislative pressure is coming from two directions. Firstly national government involvement is increasing, although at different local rates. Secondly, the European Commission is looking at measures to standardize environmental regulations. The most important measure being considered is the carbon dioxide tax, aimed to encourage use of alternative energy sources. Broader interpretation of environmental liability is also making acquisitions and disposals increasingly difficult.

A dampener on merger and acquisition activity is growing uncertainty about many companies' environmental credentials. Substantial hidden costs may be incurred if products or processes are affected by environmental legislation in the pipeline. Environmental difficulties of the former communist countries are rapidly coming to the fore. Industry leaders are concerned that the increasing environmental legislation threatens to take away Europe's competitive edge. There is continued criticism, particularly in Germany, that rising costs could drive the chemical industry out of that country. Integrated Pollution Control (IPC) legislation was phased into Britain in 1994 and gives Britain one of the strictest environmental control systems in Europe. ICI reports that the proportion of its capital spending on environmental costs will rise from 10 to 15 per cent, and perhaps to 20 per cent by 2000.

LAPORTE

The company was founded in 1888 by Bernard Frederick Laporte, born in Hanover, Germany in 1862. Although his family originated in France, they had emigrated to Germany, but finally settled in Belgium where Bernard was brought up. He began his career with a German chemicals company but after only a few years set up his own chemicals trading business in Yorkshire. Among the first products he sold was barium peroxide, which he imported, but he saw the potential of hydrogen peroxide as a high-class bleaching agent and in 1888 set about making it, finally establishing a works at Shipley. Within a year Bernard had opened a branch in Booth Street, Bradford. In 1898, attracted by Luton's straw hat industry, then at the height of its fame and a large user of bleaching agents, he built a peroxide plant at Ray's Yard, Vicarage Street. The link between Laporte and Luton had begun.

Early 1970 saw three major events, each of exceptional long-term significance to the company. First the Burmah Oil Company Limited bid for the group, an offer which Laporte strongly resisted and which was eventually withdrawn. Second, shortly after this, Laporte and Solvay et Cie SA, Belgium's leading chemical company, announced a plant to combine their international interests in active oxygen-based products. Together they formed the equally owned Interox Group. Third, Laporte commissioned Europe's first large-scale titanium dioxide plant by the 'chloride' route. This was a very big step which put significant financial strains on the company.

The Interox venture marked the start of an association that lasted until May 1992. It is probable that this venture was established to ward off further unwanted takeover bids. Table 1 indicates the proportion of Laporte's recent group turnover attributable to Interox.

The delayed profitability of the plant, the 1973 energy crisis and general world recession caused the company to question its dependence on capital-intensive

TABLE 1 Interox share of Laporte turnover (£m)

	1992	1991	1990	1989	1988
Laporte companies	£534	£431	£463	£449	£364
Interox operation	£74	£185	£187	£168	£153
Total	£608	£616	£649	£617	£516
Laporte companies	88%	70%	71%	73%	70%
Interox operation	12%	30%	29%	27%	30%

businesses, where high volumes of production had to be maintained if assets were to earn a reasonable return. Emphasis moved from size to added value in selected products and services. Nevertheless, following the formation of Interox, much was achieved from the combination of technical and commercial strengths of Laporte and Solvay in the peroxygen field. In 1978 Interox America was formed and was now entering the biggest and most competitive market in the world.

1980s

The beginning of the 1980s was a time of world recession, exacerbated by the continuing heavy expenditure in consolidating Interox America. On January 1 1980, Ken Minton was appointed Group Managing Director, with Richard Ringwald CBE as Chairman and Chief Executive. Profit responsibility was pushed downwards, businesses were redefined in terms of their ROCE and other financial targets and a fundamental decision was made to take Laporte into expanding speciality areas.

In 1984 the entire titanium dioxide business was sold off to SCM (now owned by Hanson). This accounted for 28 per cent of total group assets. The sale released more than £80 million for compensating investments. In the USA between 1984 and September 1987 12 companies were acquired, taking the business there into timber treatment (by 1987 it was one of the three largest in North America), building chemicals, pool and spa chemicals and chemicals for the paper and water treatment industries. Between 1980 and the end of 1987 the company had invested £134 million in new acquisitions. By 1985 Laporte had changed from a business heavily dependent upon a small number of bulk chemicals to one making specialities. In 1986 Richard Ringwald was succeeded by Ken Minton as Chief Executive with Roger Bexon (former deputy chairman of British Petroleum) becoming Chairman.

Innovations and new product development are meant to provide competitive advantage and greater added value. Sub-strategies (divisional strategic plans) are set by the individual divisions where R&D is sharply focused, divisions control their own product and process development programmes and technical centres to carry them out. The company is raising expenditure on R&D both in absolute terms and as a percentage of sales, as well as accomplishing technology transfer between areas.

The principal event of 1992 was the reorganization of the Interox joint venture with Solvay (a joint venture that lasted 21 years) whereby Solvay kept the hydrogen peroxide, persalts and related businesses, while Laporte kept the organic peroxides and persulphates businesses. This separating of the operations of Interox was directly in line with the long-term strategies of the two companies Solvay – capital-intensive bulk chemicals and Laporte – speciality chemicals. The profits from the Interox joint venture had been on a plateau for four years, much of this due to the weakness of the demand for washing liquids as opposed to the powders which use perborates. Laporte dissolved the peroxygen products division that comprised the

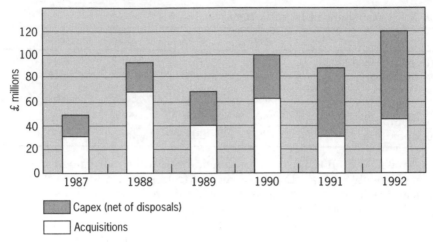

FIGURE 1 Capital expenditure and investments

operations from Interox and injected the speciality peroxy chemicals business (organic peroxides and persulphates) into its existing organic speciality chemicals division which nearly tripled in size from a turnover of £34 million in 1991 to £90 million in 1992.

From 1983 to 1990 the company spent £275 million on 60-odd purchases which it financed through property sales and retained profits. Between 1987 and 1992 the company spent in the range of £33 and £72 million each year (see figure 1). In April 1992 Rockwood, a major supplier of iron oxide pigments in the USA, was acquired for £33 million; and later in 1992 Silo in Italy, another supplier of iron oxide pigments was acquired for £23 million. These resulted in further additions to the colouring products subdivision within the construction chemicals division. The combination of Silo and Rockwood should benefit each other in terms of information transfer and global marketing efforts. A further £12 million was spent on other acquisitions in 1992. In the first two months of 1993, Laporte acquired Evode which brought over 20 new businesses into the Laporte group. Laporte's high gearing level at the time of purchase necessitated a cash call of £84.4 million to finance the deal. The last rights offering prior to this was in 1990. Laporte had been in contact with directors of Evode Group plc for some time about the benefits of Evode becoming part of an enlarged Laporte. It finally did in February 1993.

EVODE ACQUISITION

Evode is a third the size of Laporte and the acquisition involved over 2,000 employees and 20 companies. 'Evode is a major compounder and converter operating in worldwide markets. The group is an international producer of adhesives, sealants, powder coating, thermoplastic compounds and footwear components. Evode is a leader in chosen markets.' This is how Evode Group plc described itself in its 1991 annual report. By late 1992 Evode was the target of a hostile takeover bid by Wassall, a mini conglomerate. Evode was acquired by Laporte plc in early 1993 in a white knight deal.

Evode had acquired Chamberlain Phipps, a shoe components group, in 1989 for £89 million. The acquisition of Chamberlain Phipps brought with it a number of problems which Evode had to spend a lot of time and expense sorting out just as business was hit by the recession. This exercise left Evode with an uncomfortably high level of gearing, approximately 200 per cent if preference shares are considered as debt.

In early 1992 Evode cut its final dividend by 60 per cent as UK profits fell by two-thirds. Despite the cut the company had to transfer £1.8 million from reserves to fund the payment. The fall in UK profits reflected the effect of the recession on the key industries which it supplied, that is construction, automotive, and electrical consumer goods. This fall in profits occurred despite the group shedding 25 per cent of its workforce (600 people, since 1990) and the implementation of a strict rationalization and cost reduction programme.

By mid-1992 Evode's interim pre-tax profits showed an increase of 28 per cent on the 1992 figure (£3.8 million in 1992 compared with £3.0 million in 1991). This increase in profits was mainly due to a strong performance from Evode's North American and Italian subsidiaries. Earlier in the year the shoe component business, acquired as part of the Chamberlain Phipps group, was sold for £11.9 million. The proceeds of the sale were put towards the group debt of £46 million.

The hostile takeover bid by Wassall in November 1992 valued Evode at £98 million. Evode strongly rejected the offer stating that it failed to reflect the company's value. It continued to reject further 'inadequate' offers from Wassall and initiated discussions with Laporte. In January 1993 Laporte, acting as a white knight, acquired Evode with an offer worth £134 million, including debt. At that time, Evode's net assets were valued at £112 million and had a market capitalization of £100.3 million.

The basic Evode business was sound but had been hampered by some bad acquisitions in the 1980s which had left it too weak financially to grow. It operated in a number of market segments, had market leadership in some of these segments, and had a number of strong brands. The adhesives and sealants division had achieved market leadership in the UK DIY and building industry sectors, trading under the Evo-Stik brand. The footwear adhesive and commission coating sector were also brand leaders. The industrial coatings division was the dominant supplier of sound-deadening materials to the UK automotive industry. Evode was the largest non-integrated compounder of PVC in North America. The plastics division was the leading independent compounder of thermoplastic elastomers in Europe.

CAPITAL EXPENDITURE

Laporte focused its efforts on speciality chemicals that were supposed to require less capital expenditure than capital-intensive bulk chemicals. However, when analysing the trend in capital expenditure (see figure 1), it is obvious that the company was investing more each year over the years 1987–92 in capital projects. The year 1992, was particularly heavy in terms of capital expenditure as £74million was deployed. This was mainly in the absorbents, metals and electronic chemicals and organics divisions which amounted to £58 million. In the absorbents division, Organo Bentonites invested heavily in new clay processing plants in the United States, expanding capacity by 40 per cent (Southern Clays Inc.) The metals and electronic chemicals division invested in an ultra high purity chemicals plant in France. Organics invested in capital projects to extend its product range of both organic and peroxy specialities. The year 1992 saw some major projects introduced, and capital expenditure in 1993 was forecast to be substantially lower. Investment was mainly in the divisions with more mature products in order to create economies that would lower costs. Therefore, because of the heavy investment in 1992, expenditure in 1993 was expected to be around £50 million.

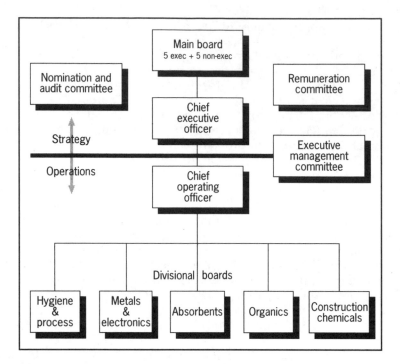

FIGURE 2   Laporte organizational structure
Source: Company reports.

STRUCTURE

The traditional role of the Chief Executive Officer (CEO) has been divided into separate strategic and operational functions. The CEO, Ken Minton (who has been on the board since 1976) is in charge of strategic development alone, while the Chief Operating Officer (COO), Dr David Wilbraham is responsible for day-to-day operations. This split in responsibilities of the CEO occurred in early 1992, allowing Minton to take a broader view of company direction and reporting to the board while the monitoring of divisional performance could be ensured by Wilbraham.

There is an executive management committee of 11 senior managers, constituting five executive directors (CEO, COO, finance, operations, personnel and administration), five central managers (manufacturing services, deputy finance director, strategic planning director, chairman North American region and group legal advisor) and one divisional manager (organics). This executive management committee derives the strategic proposals that are submitted to the board of directors.

The breakdown of operations by country are shown in table 2.

PERSONNEL

Appointments to the new divisional boards are largely made from within, reflecting the strength and depth of management that has been developed. At the very top of the organization, the present CEO, Ken Minton at 58 years of age has been with the company for his full career. Working his way up through operations he was elected to the board in 1976 when he was 41 years of age and operations director.

TABLE 2 Breakdown of operations by country

Country	Number of companies	Region	Total number	Sales%	Profit%
England	16	UK	16	27.0%	31.0%
United States	22	North America	24	34.0%	19.0%
Canada	2	"			
France	8	Europe	25	21.0%	10.0%
Germany	3	"			
Italy	2	"			
Netherlands	1	"			
Belgium	1	"			
Spain	2	"			
Austria	1	"			
Switzerland	4	"			
Finland	1	"			
Norway	1	"			
Sweden	1	"			
Australia	4	Australasia	11	12.0%	3.0%
New Zealand	1	"			
Singapore	2	"			
Malaysia	1	"			
Taiwan	1	"			
Thailand	2	"			
Brazil	3	South America	6	na	na
Peru	1	"			
Eire	2	"			
South Africa	1	South Africa	1	na	na
Total	83		83		

Source: Company Reports.

RESEARCH AND DEVELOPMENT

Sub-strategies (divisional strategic plans) are set by the individual divisions. As a result, R&D is sharply focused since divisions control their own product and process development programmes and technical centres to carry them out. Company reports state that Laporte is raising expenditure on R&D both in absolute terms and as a percentage of sales, as well as accomplishing technology transfer between areas in improving competitiveness.

The following details explain the business of each division:

Organics

This division manufactures fine chemicals for the pharmaceutical, agrochemical and polymers industries. Until 1991 the division was by far the smallest, contributing only 5 per cent of all profits. However, since the reorganization of the Interox joint venture with Solvay in 1992, the product range has been expanded to include organic peroxides and persulphates used in the polymer industry and other industrial markets. The division comprises two main product sectors: speciality organics products and speciality peroxy products.

Absorbents

This division manufactures products used as absorbents and rheological aids. They are produced from natural clays and are used in the food, petrochemical, paper and paint industries. Absorbent granules are supplied for pet litter and industrial applications. The principal sectors in this division are: (1) Activated bentonite and (2) Organo bentonites: These are used in the refining of vegetable oils that are used to make processed foods, cooking aids and personal hygiene products. (3) Fulacolor and (4) Laponite: These provide essential thickening properties to a wide range of domestic products such as concentrated soaps, toothpaste, and paints. (5) Pet Hygiene Products: For example pet litter. (6) Aluminium sulphate and sulphuric acid.

Metals and Electronic Chemicals

The three product sectors comprising this division are:

1 Semiconductor chemicals and services: This subdivision produces ultra-pure chemicals for the manufacture of silicon chips. Related products include photomasks which photoprint microcircuits onto silicon wafers and pellicles which are protection membranes. There is also a silicon wafer recycling business and a cleanroom clothing business.
2 Printed circuit board chemicals: These involve the production of chemicals and the provision of supporting technical services for the manufacture of printed circuit boards.
3 Metal processing chemicals: This sub-division supplies a range of inorganic chemicals for the steel, aluminium and foundry industries, and some special applications.

Hygiene and Process Chemicals

This division combines speciality chemical products with associated applications technology and technical support in four distinct product groups:

1 Paper and industrial process chemicals: These provide applications in the pulp and paper, water treatment, mineral processing, pigments and catalyst industries.
2 Water technologies and biochemical products: These are used for maintenance of swimming pool and spa waters.
3 Hygiene chemicals: These are high grade sanitizers and cleansers for the food processing, beverage, dairy, farm and institutional catering industries.
4 Surface treatment chemicals: These are products used for the cleaning, protection and modification of metal surfaces in the steel and metal-working industries, and the automotive, industrial paints and coatings markets.

Construction Chemicals

This division comprises three main product related subdivisions:

1 Building chemicals: These including adhesives and sealants, concrete repair materials, waterproofing products, membranes and structured coatings.
2 Timber treatment chemicals: These include preservatives, waterproofers, flame retardents, anti-sapstain formulations and mould inhibitors.

3   Colouring Products: For example synthetic iron oxide pigments.

Each of these divisions comprises a number of businesses that operate independently from each other. Each business is an autonomous piece of the Laporte portfolio of speciality companies which acts as an independent profit centre. The divisions share a central administration and personnel function.

APPENDIX 1   COMPETITIVE INFORMATION

Allied Colloids

Turnover is 35 per cent in Europe, 30 per cent in America and 18 per cent in the UK. It is a manufacturer of chemicals for the mining, paper, textile, sewage and water treatment industries. Environmental legislation in developed countries is forcing change towards 'cleaner chemicals' and some of the company's products are expected to benefit.

Harcross Chemicals Group

The holding company, Harrisons & Crossfield plc, is heavily committed to the UK: turnover 63 per cent and net assets 57 per cent. Next largest market in terms of turnover is the US with 19 per cent. Harcross Chemicals Group, the chemical and industrial division, returned margins of only 5 per cent. It operates in five main sectors; chrome chemicals, iron oxide pigments, zinc oxide and aluminium chloride, organic chemicals and chemicals distribution. The organics division is one of the largest producers of polymer additives in Europe ant its speciality businesses include surficants, adhesives, elastomers, sealants and radiation cure chemicals. The building and automotive industries are among the major customers for the company's chemical products.

Foseco

Described as 'the ultimate holding company of an international group whose principle business is speciality chemicals', with 100 operating companies in 36 countries. Foseco has recently been acquired by Burmah Castrol to strengthen the expansion of Burmah Castrol Chemicals. Over 55 per cent turnover and operating profits from the metallurgical Chemicals division; foundries, wrought aluminium, refactories and ceramics and ceramic welding. Next largest division is construction and mining chemicals (26 per cent turnover and operating profit). Specially formulated products in this business are based on Foseco's resin cement technologies. Foseco's timber treatment operations have been merged with Burmah Castrol's chemicals coatings business.

Croda

Principle activities are the manufacture of oleochemicals, lanolins, adhesives, gelatine, speciality proteins, technical oils, fire-fighting chemicals, food specialities, resins, rust prevention chemicals, paints and water-based inks. Lanolin derivatives are used in cosmetics and Croda supplies cosmetics manufacturers as well as undertaking some of its own production. Some 38 per cent sales, 79 per cent profits and 90 per cent of net assets are in the UK.

Hicksons

Hicksons 'specialises in the provision of high quality chemical products' and is organised into three strategic business divisions; fine chemicals, performance chemicals and applied chemicals. Hicksons have interests in flooring distributors, timber treatments and distribution.

Cookson Group

Cookson has three major product areas, ceramics, plastics and metals. It has disposed of its shareholding in Tioxide Group to ICI. Cookson is a leading supplier of ceramic raw materials in Europe and manufactures specialist high temperature, corrosion resistant ceramic products. The plastics sector supplies polypropylene for the horticultural packaging market, epoxy laminates for printed circuit boards and specialist materials for fibre optics. In metals, lead-free solders have been developed and are marketed internationally. Cadmium free materials are now being produced for the multilayer capacitor industry.

By the very nature of the specialities sector in which Laporte operates, it is difficult to identify specific competitors. For example, Laporte states that it is both a competitor and a customer of ICI in specific areas. In 1991 Laporte's sales were less than a seventh of the world's 25th largest chemical company (Norsk Hydro, with sales of $4,924 million).

Table 3 summarizes the main activities of the top 20 UK chemical companies in term of turnover, and indicates where Laporte falls in comparison.

TABLE 3 Leading UK chemical companies by turnover, 1991–1992

Company	Sales (£m)	Rank	Main activity in chemicals
ICI	12,906	1	All sectors
Unilever	7,517	2	Cosmetics, soaps, detergents, toiletries
Glaxo holdings	3,397	3	Pharmaceuticals
BP Chemicals	3,164	4	Petrochemicals & bulk organics
BOC Group	2,731	5	Bulk inorganics
Reckitt & Colman	1,987	6	Consumer chemicals
Courtaulds	1,943	7	Fibres, coatings, films, marine paints
Wellcome	1,762	8	Pharmaceuticals
Fisons	1,284	9	Pharmaceuticals & agrochemicals
Cookson Group	1,164	10	Ceramics, specialised plastics & metals
Shell Chemicals (UK)	717	11	Petrochemicals & plastics
Albright & Wilson	663	12	Bulk inorganics, specialised bleaches
Laporte	608	13	Specialities
Foseco	573	14	Metallurgical, construction & mining
Harcros Chemical Grp	516	15	Specialities (additives & surficants)
Ellis & Everard	383	16	Commodity distribt'n & retail pharmacy
Croda International	363	17	Cosmetics, resins, water based inks
Hicksons	343	18	Speciality chemicals
Evode Group	279	19	Adhesives & sealants
Allied Colloids	255	20	Specialities (water treatment, textile)

Source: Annual Reports and Accounts.

APPENDIX 2   ALLIED COLLOIDS ACCOUNTS

Consolidated balance sheets (£000)

	Apr 2 1988	Apr 1 1989	Mar 31 1990	Mar 30 1991	Mar 28 1992
Fixed assets					
Tangibles	50,695	65,643	80,411	86,854	94,826
Investments	–	–	–	–	5
	50,695	65,643	80,411	86,854	94,831
Current assets					
Stocks	30,214	34,445	37,387	42,896	47,117
Trade debtors	33,038	38,306	45,044	52,978	52,990
Other debtors	8,284	8,313	10,599	9,109	7,387
Prepayments &c	1,549	1,236	1,925	3,803	804
Cash	11,761	23,360	21,830	10,806	16,015
	84,846	105,660	116,785	119,592	124,313
Creditors (due within one year)					
Bankers	1,457	2,795	3,590	7,216	15,297
Secured term loans	766	79	846	745	30
Trade creditors	9,152	12,961	18,668	19,962	21,397
Current taxation	16,556	21,401	26,043	15,797	12,817
Tax & social security	654	896	1,119	1,234	1,947
Other creditors	1,387	2,809	2,418	2,049	1,089
Accruals &c	5,893	6,166	6,515	8,649	6,464
Dividend	4,180	5,122	6,321	6,998	7,869
	40,045	52,229	65,520	62,650	66,910
Net current assets	44,801	53,431	51,265	56,942	57,403
Total assets less current liabilities	95,496	119,074	131,676	143,796	152,234
Creditors (due after one year)					
Taxation	10,168	9,755	–	–	–
Other creditors	–	17	18	9	1
Secured term loans	1,968	6,217	8,640	7,797	7,178
Provisions for liabilities & charges					
Deferred taxation	6,620	6,988	6,424	5,500	183
Other provisions	-	72	79	74	66
	18,756	23,049	15,161	13,380	7,428

Consolidated profit and loss account (£000)

	Apr 2 1988	Apr 1 1989	Mar 31 1990	Mar 30 1991	Mar 28 1992
Turnover	162,964	182,254	220,216	232,910	254,481
Cost of sales	94,069	108,154	129,635	138,030	149,347
Gross profit	68,895	74,100	90,581	94,880	105,134
Distribution costs	10,538	11,307	14,793	16,505	16,804
Admin expenses	23,508	27,996	36,261	40,536	46,874
Interest received	–	–	–	(1,887)	(1,412)
Interest	(575)	(1,399)	(1,741)	873	783
Profit (loss) bef tax	35,414	36,196	41,268	38,853	42,085
Corporation tax	10,205	9,711	11,801	10,319	10,200
Overseas tax					
Current	2,293	3,273	2,627	3,914	5,235
Deferred	380	368	563	(924)	(292)
Exceptional def'd tax	–	–	–	–	(5,025)
Total Taxation	12,878	13,352	14,991	13,309	10,118
Profit (loss) aft tax	22,546	22,844	26,277	25,544	31,967
Ordinary dividends	5,827	6,783	8,255	9,071	10,167
Retained profit (loss)	16,719	16,061	18,022	16,473	21,800
Parent company	217	(44)	46	(393)	204
Subsidiaries	16,502	16,105	17,976	16,866	21,596
Retained profit (loss)	16,719	16,061	18,022	16,473	21,800

Geographical analysis (£000)

	Apr 2 1988	Apr 1 1989	Mar 31 1990	Mar 30 1991	Mar 28 1992
Turnover by origin					
United Kingdom				103,886	102,393
North America				65,445	74,750
Europe				40,660	47,017
Asia				8,520	13,432
Australasia				14,399	16,889
				232,910	254,481
Profit (loss) before tax by origin					
United Kingdom				29,285	29,208
North America				1,194	3,128
Europe				3,600	4,040
Asia				1,342	2,238
Australasia				2,418	2,842
Net interest				1,014	629
				38,853	42,085
Net assets by origin					
United Kingdom				58,965	71,373
North America				49,467	52,588
Europe				14,665	13,759
Asia				5,746	6,289
Australasia				6,550	7,298
Net borrowings				(4,977)	(6,501)
				130,416	144,806
Turnover					
United Kingdom	30,830	34,417	37,543	40,801	40,851
North America	52,509	57,790	70,194	70,463	79,480
Europe	50,077	57,534	72,210	82,174	88,710
Asia	13,899	12,678	16,965	20,768	23,321
Africa	5,463	5,578	6,112	4,270	5,375
Australasia	10,186	14,257	17,192	14,434	16,744
	162,964	182,254	220,216	232,912	254,481

APPENDIX 3   LAPORTE FINANCIAL DATA, 1980–1992 (£ MILLION)

	1980	1981	1982	1983	1984	1985	1986	1987	1988	1989	1990	1991	1992
Turnover													
Laporte	196	214	240	290	355	371	422	463	516	617	649	615	608
Interox	129	137	156	192	242	240	271	299	357	438	455	424	522
Assoc. cos	67	77	84	98	113	131	151	164	153	168	187	184	74
									6	11	7	7	12
Profit													
Operating	5.5	9.8	12.6	17.9	25.4	23.3	29.0	38.5	51.9	61.8	66.0	60.0	77.5
Interox	8	8.6	10.6	13.9	21.3	27.6	32.5	35.0	30.6	29.5	34.1	30.8	9.6
Assoc. cos									1.8	2.1	1.0	0.1	1.6
Except items									1.5	11.8	(1.7)		
Interest	(1.8)	(3.2)	(3.1)	(1.6)	0.8	4.9	2.7	1.7	(1.4)	(3.1)	0.9	5.5	(2.1)
PBT	11.7	15.2	20.1	30.2	47.5	55.8	64.2	75.2	84.4	102.1	100.3	96.4	86.6
Taxation	8.5	8.9	9.1	12.0	18.7	19.8	21.7	25.5	31.2	34.5	28.7	26.8	22.6
PAIT	3.2	6.3	11.0	18.2	28.8	36.0	42.5	49.7	53.2	67.6	71.6	69.6	64.0
Dividend/share pence	4.7	4.7	5.8	7.0	8.8	8.3	10.3	12.0	13.1	15.7	17.8	18.9	19.5
Assets employed													
Fixed assets	47.5	49.4	53.1	54.2	44.8	71.4	87.1	94.1	115.4	140.2	160.0	205.0	325.9
Investments	39.9	44.2	46.0	40.7	57.0	58.9	69.5	71.2	73.8	86.3	77.5	87.2	11.2
Stocks	33	33.4	35.8	30.0	27.5	34.0	39.9	38.4	51.8	58.5	58.2	64.2	93.2
Debtors	37.2	43.8	47.1	54.0	59.3	72.6	78.4	89.2	109.7	128.7	143.3	148.4	160.8
Creditors	31.8	32.1	37.4	44.3	68.7	73.6	81.0	86.9	133.5	159.2	154.2	155.0	207.6
Deferred tax	2.8	3.5	3.4	4.1	3.3	1.9	3.7	5.7	7.5	4.4	8.0	10.9	24.8
Net (borrow)/cash	(27.8)	(33.4)	(35.4)	(6.9)	40.9	9.5	18.8	2.5	(46.2)	(74.1)	24.4	(24.6)	(125.6)
Minor. int./other					11.9	(0.2)	(0.9)						
Net tangible assets	95.2	101.8	105.8	123.6	169.4	170.7	208.1	202.8	163.5	176.0	302.1	314.3	233.1
Total assets less current liabilities									259.0	301.6	453.8	456.6	506.3
Capital expenditure									25.3	31.0	41.2	54.5	74.1
No. of employees	4,702	3,874	3,501	3,515	3,597	3,581	4,061	4,249	4,600	5,349	5,568	5,498	5,360
No. of shares (50p) ML									139.6	140.2	175.4	176	154.2
Share price – high									419	492	582	628	657
– low									329	338	428	433	432

APPENDIX 4   DETAILED ACCOUNTS

Consolidated balance sheets (£m)

	Jan 1 ª1989	Dec 31 ª1989	Dec 30 ª1990	Dec 29 1991	Jan 3 1993
Fixed assets					
Tangible	115.4	140.2	160.0	205.0	325.9
Investments	73.8	86.3	77.5	87.2	11.2
	189.2	226.5	237.5	292.2	337.1
Current assets					
Stocks	51.8	58.5	58.2	64.2	93.2
Trade debtors	60.4	75.4	77.7	80.3	107.9
Due by associated cos	25.1	28.5	26.5	21.7	1.6
Other debtors	17.5	16.4	15.5	17.5	21.9
Pension prepayments	–	1.4	4.7	6.4	8.7
Prepayments &c	6.7	7.0	8.1	22.5	20.7
Sterling deposit int	–	–	10.8	–	–
Cash	72.9	75.6	176.9	142.0	144.8
	234.4	262.8	378.4	354.6	398.8
Creditors (due within one year)					
Bank & other loans	–	–	–	51.5	62.1
Bankers	18.2	25.0	10.0	–	–
Bank overdrafts	–	–	–	1.6	1.7
Euro-commercial paper	19.9	9.3	7.8	–	–
Debenture loans	–	–	–	–	0.9
Other loans	0.2	0.5	0.3	–	–
Finance leases	–	–	–	0.1	0.2
Trade creditors	37.1	43.6	47.5	44.8	62.5
Due to associated cos	3.3	7.5	5.6	2.5	1.2
Taxation	25.8	29.9	28.4	26.2	27.9
Social security	1.9	1.9	1.9	1.9	2.2
Other creditors	18.2	17.7	12.7	16.5	15.3
Accruals &c	28.0	37.5	28.0	23.1	31.7
Dividends	12.0	14.8	19.9	22.0	23.9
	164.6	187.7	162.1	190.2	229.6
Net current assets	69.8	75.1	216.3	164.4	169.2
Total assets less current liabilities	259.0	301.6	453.8	456.6	506.3
Creditors (due after one year)					
Bank loans	65.6	95.9	119.0	100.0	194.2
Debenture loans	11.7	11.6	11.5	11.5	10.5
Other loans	1.3	0.8	0.4	–	–
Finance leases	–	–	–	1.5	1.8
Due to associated cos	–	–	0.8	0.4	–
Taxation	0.9	1.3	1.8	4.9	8.6
Pension schemes	0.8	1.1	1.4	1.5	15.8
Other creditors	3.3	6.8	6.5	8.8	14.9
Government grants	4.4	3.7	3.2	2.8	2.6
Provisions for liabilities & charges					
Deferred taxation	7.5	4.4	8.0	10.9	24.8
	95.5	125.6	152.6	142.3	273.2
Net assets	163.5	176.0	301.2	314.3	233.1
Capital	69.8	70.1	87.7	88.0	77.1
Share premium account	3.8	5.3	134.0	136.3	149.0
Revaluation reserve	11.8	12.7	11.5	10.9	–
Other reserves	10.9	22.0	11.4	19.8	5.9
Goodwill reserve	b	(195.9)	(226.9)	(257.3)	(336.4)
Profit & loss account	39.7	233.1	261.8	293.7	335.8
Associated cos	27.5	28.7	21.7	22.9	1.7
Shareholders' funds	163.5	176.0	301.2	314.3	233.1

ª Figures for Laporte PLC prior to reorganization. ᵇ Not shown separately.

Geographical analysis (£m)

	Jan 1 ª1989	Dec 31 ª1989	Dec 30 ª1990	Dec 29 1991	Jan 3 1993
Turnover – by origin					
United Kingdom	172.8	177.2	181.4	150.3	167.0
North America	98.4	125.4	132.1	140.6	184.5
Europe	29.0	61.9	76.4	71.2	105.3
Australasia	55.5	67.2	56.3	52.8	53.2
Rest of the world	1.9	6.4	9.1	9.3	11.8
	357.6	438.1	455.3	424.2	521.8
Profit (loss) before tax					
United Kingdom	32.6	36.6	38.8	29.5	28.6
North America	11.6	14.1	15.8	17.9	25.3
Europe	4.5	11.5	13.2	9.4	17.6
Australasia	5.2	5.7	3.6	3.1	4.3
Rest of the world	(0.3)	0.4	0.7	0.1	1.7
Associated companies	33.4	35.1	36.2	30.9	11.2
Exceptional items	9.7	6.7	(6.2)	–	–
Net interest	(1.4)	(3.1)	0.9	5.5	(2.1)
	95.3	107.0	103.0	96.4	86.6
Net assets					
United Kingdom			120.4	157.2	170.2
North America			39.7	52.0	84.7
Europe			31.3	33.5	88.2
Australasia			17.4	18.7	22.7
Rest of the world			3.3	8.7	16.5
Non-operating assets			11.7	(42.9)	(160.3)
Associated companies			77.4	87.1	11.1
			301.2	314.3	233.1
Profit (loss) before tax					
Peroxygen products		33.0	35.2	–	–
Construction chemicals		13.0	10.5	10.6	17.9
Absorbents		24.1	25.1	11.7	12.1
Metals & electronic chemicals		12.7	16.7	15.2	14.2
Hygiene & process chemicals		10.4	12.9	14.1	16.1
Organic speciality chemicals		6.0	3.7	4.9	15.8
Miscellaneous		4.2	4.2	3.6	3.0
Discontinued business		–	–	30.8	9.6
Exceptional items		6.7	(6.2)	–	–
Net interest		(3.1)	0.9	5.5	(2.1)
		107.0	103.0	96.4	86.6
Net assets					
Peroxygen products			73.8	–	–
Construction chemicals			38.8	49.2	60.4
Absorbents			54.5	77.0	107.3
Metals & electronic chemicals			37.9	52.2	70.8
Hygiene & process chemicals			25.6	27.7	36.5
Organic speciality chemicals			51.8	60.6	111.4
Miscellaneous			7.1	7.3	7.0
Discontinued business			–	83.2	–
Non-operating assets			11.7	(42.9)	(160.3)
			301.2	314.3	233.1

ª Figures for Laporte PLC prior to reorganization.

APPENDIX 5   APPARENT UK DEMAND FOR CHEMICALS

	1985 £m	1986 £m	1987 £m	1988 £m	1989 £m	1990 £m
Inorganic	1,692	1,571	1,612	1,790	1,849	1,755
Organic		2,262	2,747	3,069	3,266	2,900
Fertiliser	957	825	753	713	798	842
Formulated pesticides	270	278	296	399	469	484
Resins & plastics	2,534	2,673	3,276	4,097	4,353	4,336
Synthetic rubber	205	192	196	205	207	225
Dyestuffs	394	460	565	638	729	698
Paints	1,079	1,173	1,256	1,419	1,458	1,521
Printing ink	197	223	243	280	284	327
Pharmaceuticals	2,642	3,057	3,418	3,912	4,226	4,313
Soap & detergent	849	900	954	1,029	1,176	1,319
Perfume & cosmetics	1,090	1,156	1,235	1,287	1,356	1,621
Photographic	530	535	562	560	602	540
Fats & flavouring	269	241	259	314	354	405
Adhesives	468	509	544	592	636	680
Polishes & miscellaneous	1,949	2,201	2,470	2,587	2,897	2,967

APPENDIX 6   EVODE GROUP PLC

Chairman: A.H. Simon BSc MBA
Secretary: E.J. Pratt FCA FBIM
Registrars: Barclays Registrars
Reg Office: Common Road, Stafford ST16 3EH
Tel: 0785 57755   Fax: 0785 214403

FT Group: Chemicals
Market capitalization (£000): 79,012
Price at B/S date (pence) 73.0
Nominal value: 20p Ord

	Sep 30 a1987	Sep 30 1988	Sep 30 a1989	Sep 29 1990	Sep 3 1991
Profit & loss account (£000)					
Turnover	95,848	122,399	197,398	271,431	279,000
Prof bef int & tax	7,421	10,818	16,075	22,381	14,100
Profit before tax	6,118	9,106	11,466	14,769	6,400
Attrib to members	3,744	5,842	7,703	9,541	5,100
Preference dividends	40	40	305	2,877	5,100
Ordinary dividends	1,606	2,277	4,243	4,589	2,600
Av no of employees	1,659	1,942	2,593	3,650	3,675
Wages & salaries	16,728	19,842	30,427	43,434	47,900
Balance sheet (£000)					
Ordinary capital	7,692	8,618	14,025	14,297	14,500
Shareholders' funds	32,432	36,080	45,967	59,373	59,200
Net capital employed	44,704	56,545	101,754	114,273	112,100
Current assets	43,031	53,418	100,152	104,321	96,500
Current liabilities	28,274	46,333	94,648	103,188	78,400
Total assets	69,022	89,536	162,941	174,392	166,600
Total loans	8,234	17,413	42,031	46,932	48,300
Intangibles	130	435	376	323	200

	Sep 30 ª1987	Sep 30 1988	Sep 30 ª1989	Sep 29 1990	Sep 3 1991
Performance ratios					
ROCE %	18.2	24.2	28.4	22.0	12.3
Profit margin %	7.7	8.8	8.1	8.2	5.1
Gearing ratio	21.4	33.4	52.2	54.2	55.7
Earnings yield %	9.65	9.50	10.04	10.38	0.00
Dividend yield %	3.55	3.48	5.30	9.01	0.00
P/E ratio	14.21	14.04	12.03	12.34	0.00
Growth % per annum					
Total assets	47.65	29.72	81.98	7.03	(4.47)
Turnover	36.84	27.70	61.27	37.50	2.79
Profit before tax	63.89	48.84	25.92	28.81	(56.67)
Ordinary share record (pence)					
Net asset value	83.0	82.6	6.9	16.3	15.0
EPS (gross max)	16.39	19.09	15.27	9.86	0.00
Gross dividends	6.05	7.00	8.05	8.56	4.77
Dividend cover	2.7	2.7	1.9	1.2	0.00
Net cash flow	13.2	15.9	11.9	12.3	6.3

Latest gross dividends (pence)					
Years ended	Actual	Adjusted	Ex Date	Payable	Tax %
Sep 30 1989	Int 2.16	8.05	31.7.89	22.9.89	25
	Fin 5.893		12.2.90	2.4.90	25
Sep 29 1990	Int 2.373	8.56	23.7.90	21.9.90	25
	Fin 6.187		28.1.91	2.4.91	25
Sep 29 1991	Int 2.373	4.77	29.7.91	27.9.91	25
	Fin 2.4		27.1.92	1.4.92	25

[a] Assuming merger with Supra Group PLC had been effective throughout year.

Activity analysis

Turnover (1991): Adhesives 26.4%, coatings 20%, plastics 34.8%, footwear 18.8%. Geographical: United Kingdom 46.7%; Other EEC 15.9%; Americas 26.5%; Rest of world 10.9%.

Earning and dividends

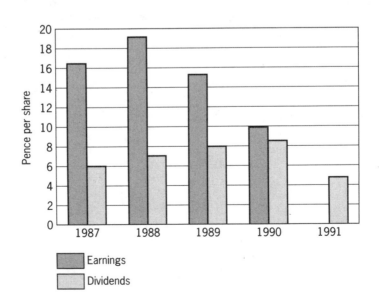

Share price

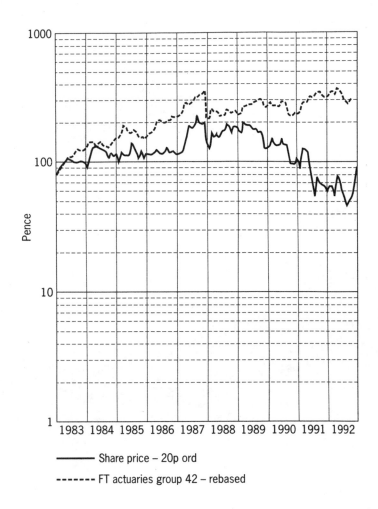

Source: Extel Handbook of Market Leaders.

Share price range (pence) – years ended December 31

	1987	1988	1989	1990	1991
High	229.0	192.0	213.0	158.0	124.0
Low	112.0	147.0	120.0	90.0	43.0

PART 4

Strategy Implementation

'TOPFLIGHT'

The downsizing of BA in the early 1980s resulted in a shortage of managers. This situation was made worse by a boom in air travel in the late 1980s. Furthermore, the business was now more technology-driven and technology had become an important strategic variable.

As a response BA decided to develop an in-company management identification and education programme. Three levels of manager were identified:

- top executives – potential directors;
- senior managers – potential senior general managers; and
- middle managers – potential senior managers.

The top executives were placed in senior executive programmes at Harvard and INSEAD. The senior managers were put through an MBA programme with Lancaster University, and the middle managers attended a diploma programme at Lancaster.

For senior managers, the process began with the establishment of a profile for a senior BA leader. Drawing upon several sources, including BA's future strategic needs, a list of 'surface' competences was established (see table 1). 'Surface' means competences which are easily understood by the organization. Source competences (see table 2) are more casual and need to be established by means of psychological testing. Another way of describing the difference would be to say that source competences are individual and enduring, whereas surface competences can be developed with experience. Clearly, the establishment of such a profile is not without problems. For example:

- Is the profile future orientated?
- Is it accurate?
- If the organization is subject to rapid environmental change, of what value is the profile?
- Short versus long term perspective?
- Corporate needs versus departmental?
- Specialism versus generalism?
- What about successful managers who do not conform to the profile of competence?

TABLE 1 British Airways' senior management surface competences

Vision	The ability to develop innovative, well-formed, coherent and future-orientated scenarios.
Direction	The ability to generate strategies, plans and tactics based on a good assessment of priorities, facts, risks and possibilities.
Business Orientation	A business attitude and business sense that permeates every decision and action.
Results Orientation	The drive to be in command, to have responsibility and achieve results and to champion worthy causes.
Managing Relations	The personal qualities and interpersonal skills that promote open and constructive relations with superiors, subordinates, peers and people outside the department.
Resource Management	The ability and skill to determine needs and manage the acquisition and deployment of resources, both human and physical, in a businesslike way.
Large Organisation Perspective	An appreciation of and sensitivity to the complex interdependencies in a large national airline.

Source: The Photofit Manager, ed. Marion Devine, Unwin Hyman 1990, reproduced with permission.

TABLE 2 British Airways' senior managers source competences

Intellectual effectiveness
- Critical analytical thinking
- Synthesis
- Conceptual thinking
- Original and divergent thinking
- Flexibility of thinking
- Balanced thinking

Relationship with others
- Social impact
- Interdependence
- Managing upward relations
- Managing downward relations
- Managing other relations

Work approach
- Judgement
- Decisiveness
- Effectiveness, drive
- Energy and stamina

Source: The Photofit Manager, ed. Marion Devine, Unwin Hyman 1990, reproduced with permission.

The above represent some key questions which you should address after reading the BA (A) case.

STRATEGY, STYLE AND COMPETENCE

Dynamic environments necessitate strategic change. This in turn leads to organizational development activities such as reorganizing, new definitions of roles, jobs and so on. Hence the need to ensure that management development is in line with strategic and organizational development.

The tasks, therefore, for top management, are to create long-term objectives and strategies giving the organization a sense of direction; to create an organizational structure which allows the strategy to be implemented and to ensure that the knowledge and skills in the organization are appropriate both currently and in the future.

Much of the above will be accomplished by means of small decisions taken over time. Often, however, the changes are more dramatic and larger. This latter form can result in wholesale changes to accepted practices and beliefs. Clearly the greater the pace of change and the larger the resulting quantum of change the more difficult it becomes to know where the target is both in terms of strategy and establishing the dimension of managerial competence.

No one generic managerial style is recommended, senior managers differ. There is a strong relationship between strategy implementation and dimensions of style such as autocracy versus democracy, risk taking versus conservatism. The appropriateness of a particular managerial style will depend upon circumstances. The key task is to match style with strategic tasks.

In his annual report for 1993–4, Burnley Health Care Trust Chairman James Rawson said it was a 'people organisation' that had had a year of substantial achievement. He praised the efforts of staff and voluntary organizations for their support and stated that:

> We have completed new recognition agreements with our staff organisations which will improve communication in the future, and the reorganisation into clinical directorates is beginning to show the benefits which we expected from this change.[1]

During the year more patients than ever before had been treated in both in-patients and out-patients and the quality of service had improved, according to the annual report. However, in early September angry health service staff attending the annual meeting of the Trust Board accused Burnley Health Care National Health Service (NHS) Trust management of putting cash before care, when workers and members of the public turned out in force to attend the annual meeting of the Trust Board. The 2½-hour long meeting at Burnley's Friendly Hotel was attended by about 100 members of the public and staff.

One NHS worker accused the Trust of having one of the most demotivated workforces in the whole of the country, and stated that the board kept staff oppressed, ill-informed and with no reassurance about their jobs. It was also described as an elite two-tier system geared up to privatization and said that the board had pushed over and passed off the questions that staff had put to its members during the meeting. Various members of staff had indicated that they were unsure about their futures with the wholesale changes, ward closures and reorganizations taking place at the hospital.

Ian Mahady's Dismissal

In the middle of September 1994, senior obstetrics and gynaecology consultant Ian Mahady's compulsory redundancy from his post at Burnley General Hospital caused a major row. A consultant in Burnley for 14 years, Mr Mahady alledgedly received his dismissal letter as clinical director of the department and was given three hours to clear his desk. Other consultants, the local council, the patients' watchdog Community Health Council, general practioners (GPs) and patients all became involved and a public meeting was called for November at which Mr Mahady was invited to put his case. In addition:

- The British Medical Association (BMA) asked for the case to be taken to Health Secretary, Virginia Bottomley;
- patients called for Mr Mahady's reinstatement; and
- some consultants expressed concern about the implications of the dismissal, which they said was not ethical.

More than 20 consultants signed an open letter to the Chairman of the Trust Board, James Rawson, deploring and condemning the manner and speed with which Mr Mahady was removed from the hospital for purely financial reasons, while he still had post-operative patients under his care. In the open letter, consultants condemned the board's interference in the management of Mr Mahady's patients and pointed out that it was difficult, ethically, to continue to admit and treat patients when they could not be certain they would be allowed to provide continuing care. Burnley Health Care NHS Trust announced that it had decided on the redundancy because the department was overstaffed while the number of patients was dropping, and said it was doing everything possible to minimize any concerns and upset. Trust Chief Executive Maggie Aikman stated that Mr Mahady was given time and confidentiality to accept a redundancy package, including a large sum in excess of his entitlement which, if accepted, would give him the opportunity to pursue his career elsewhere. She said that all Mr Mahady's patients had been contacted and were being seen by other consultants.

On 20 September 1994 The Royal College of Obstetricians and Gynaecologists in London expressed concern about the issues surrounding the dismissal, the staffing ratios at the hospital and the continuing training of junior staff, with the departure of Mr Mahady. The college was to ask the country's Chief Medical Officer, Kenneth Calman, to raise the matter with Health Secretary Virginia Bottomley and also to write to the North-West Regional Health Authority Chairman Sir Donald Wilson, the Trust Board and the Community Health Council. Mr Mahady also confirmed that the BMA was to take legal action on his behalf for constructive dismissal, appealing to Virginia Bottomley about the nature of his dismissal and its implications for other consultants.

THE PUBLIC CAMPAIGN

Members of the public, campaigning against the redundancy of Mr Mahady, pledged to support him all the way and said the hospital needed more staff; not job cuts. More than 5,000 people had signed a petition calling for the reinstatement of Mr Mahady and the resignation of members of the Burnley Health Care NHS Trust who had dismissed him.

At a public meeting in Burnley Town Hall on 12 October 1994, Peter Pike, Burnley's Labour Member of Parliament, said he had spoken to Trust Chairman James Rawson and Chief Executive Maggie Aikman earlier that day and they had stressed there was no question of Mr Mahady being reinstated. Mr Pike said he was still awaiting a reply from Health Secretary Virginia Bottomley to whom he had written on 30 September calling for her to look into the way the Trust was run and how staffing matters were dealt with. He pledged that hospital trusts would be abolished under a Labour Government.

Burnley Borough Council leader, Councillor Kath Reade said she had received letters and calls from patients who no longer knew who they were supposed to see. She described Mr Mahady's dismissal as a symptom of the 'disease' of managers and accountants running the health service like a private business. Burnley Council fully supported the campaign she said, and called for the inquiry set up by the Trust into the redundancy to be completely objective, fair and independent.

One of the campaign organizers, Steve O'Donnell, said they had been contacted by nurses and staff who wanted to attend and offer support, but feared for their jobs if they spoke out. Mr O'Donnell suggested that if Burnley Trust were allowed to get away with this, they would think they could get away with anything.

Mr Mahady told the meeting that at the time of his dismissal all the gynaeco-logists had waiting lists and some patients said that they now had to wait more than an hour for appointments with other doctors. He also indicated that his dismissal was an example of the very low morale of staff and the lack of respect management had for medical staff. He pointed out:

> I'm not the only one who's had problems. Whether I'm being made an example of, I'm not sure. But my legal advisers assure me they've made a big mistake in sacking me the way they did and we're going to fight them. If this can be allowed to happen to me it can happen to anyone.[2]

CALL FOR A GOVERNMENT INQUIRY

The dismissal of Mr Mahady and the call for Mrs Aikman's resignation was subsequently raised at Westminster by Peter Pike. He asked junior health secretary Gerald Malone if he was aware of the concern of health staff in Burnley about the dismissal of Mr Mahady and also that the Chief Executive had been asked to resign. Mr Pike said that if the Trust was not living up to the guidelines set down for such matters, then it needed to be looked into. He commented:.

> The guidelines are precise. They state that fair procedures should be set out which allow openness and that a climate should be established between those who manage the institutions and those who are employed in them so that such matters can be properly investigated. This has underlined what I have said from the outset. The whole thing is mystifying and extremely worrying and the people of Burnley, Pendle and Rossendale must be thinking the same thing. Everything that has happened has underlined my call for an independent inquiry into this whole issue, and I will continue to press for it. The Secretary of State Virginia Bottomley must accept that the Government has some responsibility for what's happening here in Burnley.[3]

THE CHIEF EXECUTIVE'S RESIGNATION

Mrs Aikman's resignation had in fact been called for by James Rawson, Chairman of the BHC Trust. Mr Rawson had raised a vote of no confidence in Mrs Aikman and asked her to resign, but the Chief Executive hit back claiming she was being used as a scapegoat.

Councillor Frank Clifford, of the Burnley Community Health Council, the local health watchdog, likened the dispute to a 'ship on a rough sea' and indicated that the conflict had come as a great surprise to him. He had constantly been briefed by both Mrs Aikman and Mr Rawson over the Ian Mahady issue and they had always appeared at one. The Chairman said he was unaware as to whether or not Mr Rawson had the full backing of the board in his decision, but did feel the emergency trust meeting held on 24 October was too late, some five days after the conflict.

On 25 October Mrs Aikman resigned from her position and an acting Chief Executive, David Meakin, was appointed. When questioned the Trust board refused to name the cash figure offered to Mrs Aikman; who dramatically resigned during a lengthy and tense meeting at the hospital. After the meeting a brief statement said simply that from 28 October, Mrs J. M. Aikman had resigned as Chief Executive and that no further comment or statement would be made by either party.

Trust board Chairman James Rawson refused to comment and had instructed staff and members not to reveal the amount to be paid in a 'golden handshake' to the Chief Executive, who had been the main instigator in Burnley becoming a self-governing Trust in 1992.

Burnley MP Peter Pike had demanded to know more. He pointed out that the public had a right to know what was going on and how much public money was being paid to Mrs Aikman to get her to leave. He said it was very worrying that the Trust was now offering money to Mrs Aikman to go so soon after offering a large sum to consultant Mr Ian Mahady to resign. He stated that:

> Before all this controversy, the general manager who Mrs Aikman succeeded, before the Trust came into being, was also given a cash settlement. You can't keep spending health care money like this. Where's it all going to end?[4]

Mr Pike further stated that all the money would have to come from the Trust's own funds.

THE CONSULTANTS' RESPONSE

On 31 October 1994 consultants and senior medical staff at Burnley General Hospital held what was considered to be the most important meeting in their history. Members of their official body, the 70-strong Medical Advisory Committee (MAC), met with the Trust board chairman James Rawson and other members to discuss the whole issue of staff morale, the involvement of medical staff in the running of the hospital and the resignation of Mrs Aikman.

Consultants called on the board to be 'open and accountable' instead of taking vital decisions behind closed doors and then refusing to comment on them. They were ready to take a vote of no-confidence in the Chairman or the whole board, if they were not happy with what the board had to say. Their Chairman Dr Peter Ehrhardt was angry that the Trust Board refused to give any further comments on Mrs Aikman's resignation or make public the amount involved. He insinuated that the resignation of one key person was the tip of the iceberg and commented:

> The Trust Board has to be open and accountable if it is to learn from its past mistakes. The Board's refusal to comment on this issue begs too many questions. This is public money, taxpayers' money, and the public have a right to know what's going on. Mistakes have obviously been made, but how is this Trust, the staff and people of Burnley, or any other Trust going to learn from them if the facts aren't made public? It's not like a private business where people are only responsible to themselves or their shareholders, this is a hospital, the NHS is very special and what happens here affects people's health, people's lives and people's happiness. The Trust members are not entitled to try to shove their problems under the carpet and leave them.[5]

In September, the MAC passed a vote of no confidence in the medical director, Dr Sam Pickens, who had written a letter of apology to every member and said he hoped to improve communications with them.

PUBLIC BALLOT

A public ballot run by campaigners calling for the reinstatement of Mr Mahady asked: 'Do you have confidence in the senior management of Burnley Health Care

Trust?' The count revealed that more than 450 people had voted in the space of 1½ hours with 417 people voting NO and 40 people voting YES. Campaigners said they had heard a catalogue of complaints from members of the public and former patients of Mr Mahady, who claimed that they had gone to the bottom of other consultants' waiting lists.

EXIT OF THE MEDICAL DIRECTOR

On 3 November 1994, consultants at Burnley General Hospital called for the resignation of their colleague Dr Sam Pickens as Medical Director. The resignation – with Dr Pickens relinquishing his place on the board but continuing as a full-time physician at the hospital – resolved the immediate dispute between managers and medical staff which had thrown the Health Trust into turmoil. Consultants' spokesman Dr Peter Ehrhardt said no one had won in the bitter dispute but he now hoped that both sides could go forward and work together.

A statement issued by the board said that Dr Pickens, who had been made Medical Director the previous year, had decided to resign because the 'divisive dispute' was having a detrimental effect on the smooth running of the Trust and the morale of staff and patients. He hoped his resignation would enable it to be resolved.

The Trust board had refused to confirm or deny claims that more than £1,250,000 had been discussed in 'golden handshakes' despite calls from all quarters that the public had a right to know how its money was being spent. Since the dismissal of Ian Mahady – who allegedly turned down an offer of £100,000 – the Trust also refused to comment on claims that more than £250,000 was paid for the resignation of Chief Executive Maggie Aikman, and that Dr Pickens asked for £1 million to give up his job. This followed from the consultants' body, the Medical Advisory Committee, giving the Trust a 48-hour ultimatum for the resignation of Dr Pickens or they would reportedly 'make the hospital unworkable'.

THE COMMUNITY HEALTH COUNCIL'S POSITION

In early November 1994, the patients' watchdog, the Community Health Council (CHC), backed calls by three local MPs for an urgent independent inquiry into the crisis raging at Burnley Health Care Trust. Burnley MP Peter Pike made his fourth demand of Health Secretary Virginia Bottomley to step into the dispute and hold a full inquiry. In this he was joined by Pendle MP Gordon Prentice and Rossendale and Darwen MP Janet Anderson. The MPs and the CHC were also united in condemning the undisclosed settlement – said to be in excess of £250,000 – to former Chief Executive Maggie Aikman.

At a specially-called meeting of the Burnley, Pendle and Rossendale CHC, members unanimously backed the inquiry call. The Chairman, Councillor Frank Clifford, indicated that public confidence in the Trust was evaporating at an alarming rate. It was considered vital that the doors were thrown open wider to allow closer public scrutiny of the running and structure of the Trust if that confidence was to be rebuilt.

The CHC's Chief Officer, Paul Etherington, suggested that the last few weeks had seen chaos built upon chaos and that people were rapidly losing confidence in the ability of the Trust to manage health services.

THE TRADE UNION'S STAND

In the last days of October 1991 the Joint Trade Unions Committee at the hospital met to discuss the dispute and afterwards the secretary, Mrs Andrea Jackson, said that the events of recent weeks were not isolated incidents, but symptomatic of the way in which the Trust had treated staff for a long time. The unions had been complaining about the way staff were being treated for a long time, this issue had just brought it all out into the open.

Asked if disillusioned staff had totally lost confidence in the Burnley Trust and were looking around for other jobs, Mrs Jackson commented it was known that people had withdrawn applications for jobs because of the dispute, and if the situation didn't improve then people would leave. The hospital unions were seeking an early meeting with the Trust board to discuss the general climate and conditions for staff at the hospital. In recent months staff had also been upset by the introduction of car parking charges at the hospital, the Trust's policy of temporary contracts for staff, enforced shift changes, and what they said was the Trust's refusal to recognize all the trade unions.

THE GENERAL PRACTIONERS' VIEW

Concerned GPs met with consultants at Burnley General Hospital early in November 1994 to discuss the crisis. Family doctors wanted to see an early end to the dispute before it began to have an effect on their patients. However, a spokesperson for the GP's official body, the Lancashire Medical Committee, denied that the dispute was affecting the number of referrals by GPs to Burnley Health Care. David Noblett, the Secretary of the committee, said some patients from Burnley were being referred by their GPs out of the district but this had always been the case and there were no figures to suggest that GPs had begun cutting down their referrals to Burnley General in recent weeks. He indicated that GPs were obviously concerned at the effect the dispute was going to have on the Burnley General Hospital and were looking for an early resolution in the long term interest of health care in Burnley.

STEP-DOWN OF THE TRUST CHAIRMAN

In mid-November 1994 rumours swept the town that James Rawson, the Chairman of the Burnley Health Care Trust, had resigned. Mr Rawson, speaking from his home in the Ribble Valley, said that he had absolutely no comment to make and a Trust spokesperson said he knew nothing about a resignation. However, Burnley councillors on the General Purposes and External Affairs Sub-Committee reported that the whole issue at the Trust had become a 'public scandal' and they believed Mr Rawson had now resigned.

Burnley and Pendle MPs had earlier called for Mr Rawson to resign, and a councillor had recently commented that it was 'the eighth wonder of the world' that Mr Rawson was still in office. Councillors also called for the Trust's Human Resources Director Ken Huchinson to resign.

One councillor indicated that the sweeteners being paid to the individuals involved were a matter of public concern and that he had it 'from a very good source' that payments to Mrs Aikman and Dr Pickens were around £250,000. He called for the position of Mr Hutchinson, the BHC Trust's Human Resources Director, to be looked into by a public inquiry and added:

It's perfectly obvious that the totally unfair dismissal of Mr Mahady could not have gone on without his involvement, and he's been a prime source of a long running dispute over the issue of union recognition.[6]

Councillor Harry Brooks said the whole issue was a public scandal and stated that the situation was absolutely absurd and unacceptable in that which two of the principal players had gone, but the head man, James Rawson, was still there and showed no inclination at all to go and no embarrassment about being there.

On 21 November 1994, James Rawson was purported to have been 'taken ill' among rumours that he had been told to resign by Health Minister Virginia Bottomley. Spokespeople for both the Trust and the Regional Health Authority stated that Mr Rawson was still Trust Chairman and that they could not comment on any private correspondence between the Secretary of State – who appoints all NHS Trust chairmen – and Mr Rawson.

Mr Rawson's letter of resignation arrived at the Department of Health in London on 24 November and was accepted by the Secretary of State, Virginia Bottomley. The Minister was reported to have written to Mr Rawson calling on him to consider his position in the wake of weeks of turmoil at the Burnley Trust since the dismissal of Mr Mahady.

Mr Rawson had held the £20,000 post since the Trust was formed and before that was Chairman of Burnley, Pendle and Rossendale Health Authority. A former industrialist, he headed textile firms in Burnley and Rossendale before joining the government's Small Firms Service. A long-serving member of the Conservative Association, he was awarded the OBE in 1985.

REINSTATEMENT OF IAN MAHADY

On 12 December 1994 it was announced that Ian Mahady was to be reinstated. The news came as the findings of an inquiry panel into the crisis were released in full. Inquiry members, Dr David Warrell and Mr Robert Atlay were heavily critical of the management processes at the Trust and described the three hours' notice given to Mr Mahady as totally unacceptable.

Their report indicated that there were insufficient grounds to justify dismissing Mr Mahady because of redundancy and called for his reinstatement. Furthermore, the Trust's new Chairman Dr Fred Archer said the board would now meet Mr Mahady to work out how to manage his reinstatement as an NHS consultant. The report also stated that decisions about a likely candidate for redundancy had been taken by the Trust board before the British Medical Association had been contacted and that the redundancy decision was based on figures which were inconsistent.

The report was critical over the handling of the redundancy as neither the Finance Director nor the Medical Director had been given an appropriate brief on how it should be carried out. The three hours' notice decision was at the insistence of the Chairman James Rawson who had since resigned. The panel investigated claims that Mr Mahady was said to be authoritarian, could be old fashioned and held back progress, but they emphasized that at no time were questions were raised about Mr Mahady's medical competence.

Mr Mahady's redundancy was declared because of an alleged failure to meet contract requirements, but the panel said the arrangements to appoint a fourth consultant was inadequately prepared and the business proposal was badly managed. However, the overall performance of the obstetric and gynaecology directorate was in fact increasing and no other solutions to redundancy were properly investigated.

In its summary the panel suggested that the Trust board review its scheme of delegation and clarify the roles of senior executives and some managers. The relationship between the management and the medical profession within the Trust needed to be addressed and personnel policies and procedures should be more fully documented. The board was also advised by the panel to examine in detail its human resource function.

The panel proposed three options to the Trust: the reinstatement of Mr Mahady as consultant in the obstetrics and gynaecology department; his reinstatement into another post within the Trust; or his appointment to another post, other than at Burnley.

However, the dispute was to continue well into January 1995 when a survey of local GPs, carried out by the Burnley, Pendle and Rossendale Community Health Council, suggested that Mr Mahady's return would result in many GPs refusing to refer patients to the Women's Health Unit. Of 138 questionnaires sent out a response rate of nearly 42 per cent had been received; 22 per cent of those responding had indicated that they would reduce their referrals to Burnley's maternity and paediatric services if Mr Mahady returned. Mr Mahady replied that the CHC was scaremongering and that he was appalled by the survey which was mischievous, unhelpful and had not been carried out correctly.

The Trust had agreed to reinstate Mr Mahady following the results of the independent inquiry in early December 1994 but it was not until the middle of January 1995 that the board announced he would be returning to Burnley General Hospital. Ian Mahady officially resumed active duty on Monday, 6 February 1995.

BHC TRUST CORPORATE OBJECTIVES AND PLANS[7]

In early 1994 the Trust Board recommended the following four proposals and formally agreed to adopt them as their aims and objectives for 1994–5.

1 Patient Activity

The Trust set the following activity levels:

- 45,297 finished consultant episodes of care/treatment;
- 40,407 new out-patient appointments; and
- 57,000 accident and emergency department appointments.

Each of these figures represented a 6 per cent increase on 1993–4. In addition, waiting times and waiting lists for non-urgent appointments would each be reduced to a maximum of three months (this would result in an overall total waiting experience of six months maximum) and *Patient's Charter* standards concerning patient activity would be met or exceeded (see appendix 3).

2 Pattern of Service

Particular service developments would be effected in the following specialties:

- ENT (ear, nose and throat);
- ophthalmology; and
- orthopaedics.

Further work would also be undertaken to ensure that the Mental Health Service is patient-sensitive and based on a community model of care. This would involve collaboration with statutory and voluntary agencies.

An option appraisal would be undertaken on the possibility of creating a community-based challenging behaviour service within Mental Health.

The current operational policy of the Younger Disabled Unit would be reviewed in the light of the appointment of a new consultant and the request from East Lancashire Health Authority for less priority to be given to respite care.

Planning work would be finalized on the fourth phase of major development at Burnley General Hospital.

3 Quality Issues

Patient's Charter standards concerning quality issues would be met or exceeded and there would be a greater emphasis on clinical audit and collaborative care planning. There would also be greater consultation and involvement with the public and closer relations established with the Community Health Council.

Increased emphasis would be placed on 'front line' staff through redeployment and training and on the techniques of quality and work developed on:

- customer survey reports being fed back into the organization of the Trust;
- benchmarking;
- accreditation;
- training in customer awareness;
- improvement of internal and external communications;
- celebrating and communicating success – especially by applying for meritorious awards; and
- encouragement of complaints and reviews of the system.

4 Management Issues

In relation to aspects of management, objectives were set including the following points:

- Improvement in the use of capital assets to achieve greater value for money.
- Improvement in the relationships between the primary and secondary elements of the service and especially the communications between general practitioners and consultants.
- Further development of the Human Resources strategy to include extension of the process of local pay bargaining and support for restructuring re-rostering and re-profiling the service.

BUSINESS PLANNING

Previous planning reflected the fact that Burnley Health Care was one of the early Trusts and had the right to believe that it was organizationally ahead of nearby provider units. The range of services and patient activity had increased significantly and the Trust had so far met the vast majority of its objectives.

Risk analysis indicated that there were a number of issues which could deflect the Trust from meeting its strategic aims. Basically these were aggregated under three headings:

- more competition;
- more demands on the Trust to demonstrate not only the quality of care provided but also the effectiveness of treatment; and
- less financial certainty as a result of the reduction in longer-term block contracts.

There was more competition as there were more Trusts emerging and many of these were looking to expand. Likewise, there were the private, voluntary and other statutory sectors. As a whole BHC Trust had to be aware that some of its traditional community services could be undertaken by general practitioners themselves if they so chose.

Trust were facing increasing demands to demonstrate not only the quality of care but also the effectiveness of treatment. The year of 1994–5 saw the start of league tables and a possible further extension of the *Patient's Charter* (see appendix 3). Central direction assisted by the distinction between purchasing and providing, was insisting more and more on a demonstration that the vast amount spent on the NHS each year was providing effective care. Purchaser patterns and priorities over the following few years were likely to demand contracts based on 'outcomes' or detailed care protocols rather than just on a simple quantitive contract.

A further challenge to the Trust in 1994–5 was to deal with the higher levels of instability. These were caused by:

- more general practitioner fundholders;
- much more specific contracts;
- new management arrangements in the NHS; and
- possible changes in local government.

In the recent past the NHS had been somewhat cushioned from market realities by the political imperative for a 'smooth take-off'. The stability ensuing from long-term block contracts – provided largely by a single purchaser – would no longer be generally available. Furthermore the growth of general practitioner fundholders added a further element of volatility into the system.

The business plan developed by the Trust reflected the need for change and there were three constant strands running through the whole plan. These are summarized as follows:

- The need to have services which are competitively priced. This in turn meant that costs would need to be reduced by eliminating all wasteful practices throughout the organization.
- The need to provide a service which had the highest possible quality in terms of customer service and care and the need to recognize the growing demands for objective measures of the effectiveness of the service.
- The need to build flexibility into the Trusts services in order to deal with the constant change and volatility which it would encounter in future years.

In turn these imperatives had led the Trust to review their human resources, estates and quality strategies and the latest planning was incorporated in the business plan.

Quality

The Trust believed that quality had at least three applications.

Professional quality This involves the professional competence with which the clinical elements of our service provide and include:

- the diagnosis of the patient's condition;
- matching that diagnosis with an appropriate treatment of the care regime or protocol; and
- delivery of that care protocol to a technically excellent standard.

Many clients were not able to appreciate whether their care was delivered with technical excellence. Traditionally the authority had judged its own professional quality in-house via medical audit, the standard-setting processes and peer and professional review. Purchasers of health care wanted more and more to be able to judge professional quality based on objective data and outcomes.

Quality perceived by the clients   In the absence of clients being able to appreciate professional quality, they perceived the quality from a range of other indicators. These included issues such as comfort and cleanliness of buildings and the attitudes of staff as addressed by the *Patient's Charter* and local charters.

Quality of systems   Like many Trusts, Burnley Health Care used the clinical and para-clinical directorate operational model. As a whole district Trust it followed that there were a large number of individual directorates and the board expected each directorate to be responsible for improving the quality of its own service.

There was a five-year strategy for the introduction of a comprehensive quality improvement plan. It relied initially on minimizing what can be regarded as inhibitors to quality issues such as organizational instability, staff contracts which are non-motivating, lack of training opportunities and so on.

The Trust had created firm foundations for quality; especially professional quality. Clinical audit and standard-setting processes were well established in the clinical professions.

The Trust had in place a small group headed by the Chief Executive Officer to give structure, leadership and support to quality. It reported regularly to the full board in public open meetings.

Marketing

In order to ensure organizational survival the Trust needed to respond to the changes in the NHS, introduced by the new internal market which was both new and unique.

The most powerful customer was the general practitioner (GP), who was primarily interested in issues of quality and especially issues such as waiting lists and waiting times for treatment. GP fundholders were beginning to be interested in price alongside the issues of quality.

Product   In order to ensure that the 'product' met customer requirements the following issues had to be addressed:

- Waiting lists and waiting times for out-patient appointments were a critical factor in choice of provider and had to be kept as short as possible.
- Patients wished to see a consultant more often than junior medical staff and required longer out-patient consultation times.
- GPs were beginning to want to change the pattern of care with more shared care and joint protocols between consultants and themselves.
- The ratio of day cases in some specialties was low and needed to be increased. Many people would prefer to have procedures without having to stay overnight in the hospital.
- Some new techniques were being established which reduced length of stay in hospitals and also benefited the patient by reducing recovery time. Keyhole surgery fell into this category.

Place   The location of service provision was an important factor for both GPs and patients. While patients were prepared to travel to receive good prompt service, it had been observed by customer analysis that they would prefer a local service.

There was a considerable outflow of patients from the north of the Trust. This could probably be significantly reversed if there were a more convenient out-patient service. A strategy group would be established during 1994–5 with the local GPs to look at their requirements.

NOTES

1   BHC NHS Trust Annual Report 1993–4.
2   *Burnley Express* 14 October 1994.
3   *Burnley Express* 23 October 1994.
4   *Burnley Express* 1 November 1994.
5   Ibid.
6   *Burnley Express* 11 November 1994.
7   BHC NHS Trust Annual Report 1994–5.

APPENDIX 1

Role of local authorities

Local government has had a long history of involvement in health service provision. In 1993 local authorities retained two important health responsibilities: personal social services and environmental health services. The former cover a range of caring, protective and support services for children, the family, the elderly, the mentally ill, and the mentally and physically handicapped. Local authorities provide residential and community-based care and support services in collaboration with the NHS and the independent sector and they have a particularly important role to play in the development of community care.

Local authority environmental health services are responsible for a variety of matters which affect health, ranging from pest control and noise pollution to the inspection and registration of food premises. Local authorities are also responsible for other services including housing, education, cleansing, waste disposal, and the provision of sport and leisure facilities.

APPENDIX 2

The National Health Service

The founding of the National Health Service in 1948 was probably one of the most challenging initiatives of its time. Some 40 years on, a radical Conservative government decided that the NHS needed reform. The basic problem was cost. The founders of the NHS had believed that, when medicine became freely available, the population would become healthier and demand for treatment would fall away. In fact, the opposite appeared to be the case. The advances of medical science meant that more and more conditions, once incurable, could be relieved and new technology had brought new standards of care. However, because everyone has the right to be treated, demand for these costly services soared.

Britain's spending on the NHS was about £500 per year per head of population in 1990, a total budget of about £28 billion. To some extent, costs could be kept down by paying doctors and nurses less than they would earn elsewhere. (With a total staff of nearly a million people in 1990, the NHS was Europe's biggest employer.) The other way of keeping costs down was by rationing care and waiting lists for operations increased as a result.

The most radical change was to create what was called an 'internal market' by splitting the service into 'purchasers' and 'providers'. The internal market was a way of making the NHS work more like private industry, where competition is supposed to keep prices low and quality high. In this marketplace of medical care, purchasers were those who bought treatments for patients; providers were those who provided them. District health authorities were the main purchasers, while hospitals and GPs were the principal providers. The notion was that purchasers should buy, and providers should provide, the best quality care at the most competitive prices.

Until 1991, health authorities had been responsible for running the hospitals in their districts. Later, the authorities were slimmed down, and hospitals took on their own day-to-day management. Health authorities still had a broad responsibility to ensure that hospitals in their district could provide the range of care needed by the local population as a whole but their main job was to make annual contracts with hospitals.

Organization

The NHS is organized on several levels (see figure 1). The Secretary of State for Health heads a department of several thousand civil servants. The Department of Health's Policy Board, which is chaired by the Secretary of State, decides the strategy of the health service.

Regional health authorities (RHAs) distribute funds to district health authorities, family health services authorities and fundholding general practitioners. Their main functions are to decide how resources should be allocated and to mediate in any disputes between 'purchasers' and 'providers'.

District health authorities purchase services for their local population and manage hospitals, apart from those which have become NHS trusts.

NHS trusts report directly to the Department of Health; they earn their income principally from contracts with district health authorities and fundholding GPs.

Family health services authorities (FHSAs) usually serve the same community as the local district health authority. Their main function is to ensure that GPs, dentists, pharmacists and opticians do their work and are paid for it.

Secretary of State for Health

Department of Health
Policy Board
NHS Management Executive

Special Health   Regional Health   NHS Trusts
Authorities   Authorities

District Health   Family Health
Authorities   Services Authorities

Community Health
Councils

Figure 1   Organization of the NHS

Community health councils (CHCs) are statutory bodies which represent consumer interests and provide advice and information to the public. Their members are authorities, voluntary organizations and RHAs.

APPENDIX 3   THE *PATIENT'S CHARTER*

The *Patient's Charter* lays down patients' rights and a number of standards which are expected of the health services.

- To receive health care on the basis of clinical need, regardless of ability to pay.
- To be registered with a GP.
- To receive emergency medical care at any time, through your GP or the emergency ambulance service and hospital accident and emergency departments.
- To be referred to a consultant acceptable to you, when your GP thinks it necessary, and to be referred for a second opinion if you and your GP agree this is desirable.
- To be given a clear explanation of any treatment proposed, including any risks and any alternatives, before you decide whether you will agree to the treatment.
- To have access to your health records, and to know that those working for the NHS are under a legal duty to keep their contents confidential.
- To choose whether or not you wish to take part in medical research or medical student training.
- To be given detailed information on local health services, including quality standards and maximum waiting times.
- To be guaranteed admission for treatment by a specific date no later than two years from the day when your consultant places you on a waiting list.
- To have any complaint about NHS services – whoever provides them – investigated and to receive a full and prompt written reply from the Chief Executive or General Manager.
- To change doctors easily and quickly.
- To have appropriate drugs and medicines prescribed.
- To be offered a health check on joining a doctor's list for the first time.
- If between 16 and 74 and have not seen your doctor in the previous three years: to have the health check to which you are entitled under the existing health promotion arrangements; and to be offered a yearly home visit and health check if 75 years old or over.
- To be given detailed information about local family doctor services through your family health services authority's local directory.
- To receive a copy of your doctor's practice leaflet, setting out the services he or she provides.

Charter standards
The *Charter Patient's* set a number of national Charter Standards and suggested that health authorities, FHSAs and GPs should also publicise their own local standards. Some of the standards concern themselves with the way people should be treated and the standards of behaviour they should expect from NHS staff, while others are more quantitive measures. These are:

- Respect for privacy, dignity and religious and cultural beliefs. Patients' dietary requirements should be met, and private rooms should be available for confidential discussions with relatives.

- Arrangements to ensure that everyone, including people with special needs, can use services. This includes ensuring that buildings are accessible to people in wheelchairs.
- Information to relatives and friends. Health authorities should ensure that, if you wish it, friends and relatives are informed about the progress of your treatment.
- Waiting times for the ambulance service: 14 minutes if you live in an urban area, 19 minutes in a rural area.
- Waiting time for initial assessment in accident and emergency departments: you should be seen immediately and your need for treatment assessed.
- Waiting time in out-patient clinics: you should be given a specific appointment time and be seen within 30 minutes of that time.
- Cancellation of operations: Your operation should not be cancelled on the day you are due to arrive in hospital, though this could happen due to emergencies or staff sickness. If your operation has to be postponed twice, you will be admitted to hospital within one month of the date of the second cancelled operation.
- A named qualified nurse, midwife or health visitor to be responsible for each patient.
- Discharge of patients from hospital. Before you are discharged, a decision should be made about any continuing health or social care you may need, and if necessary, any arrangements for this should be made.

Index